MW00736669

ZAGAT®

Movie
Guide
2008

EDITOR
Curt Gathje
COORDINATOR
Larry Cohn

Published and distributed by
Zagat Survey, LLC
4 Columbus Circle
New York, NY 10019
T: 212.977.6000
E: movies@zagat.com
www.zagat.com

ACKNOWLEDGMENTS

We thank the Arizona Film Society, DC Independent Film Festival, MSC Film Society, Olympia Film Society, Peachtree Film Society, University Film Society, Yale Film Society, Carol Bialkowski, Jason Briker, Kimberly Butler, Ed Dwyer, Gwen Hyman, Marilyn Laurie, David Margolick, Joshua Mooney, Pia Nordlinger, Maura O'Connell, Bernard Onken, Jane Rosenthal, Arthur Schlesinger Jr. and Bill Wolf, as well as the following members of our staff: Josh Rogers (assistant editor), Reni Chin, Jeff Freier, Michelle Golden, Roy Jacob, Natalie Lebert, Mike Liao, Dave Makulec, Andre Pilette, Becky Ruthenburg, Sharon Yates and Kyle Zolner.

The reviews published in this guide are based on public opinion surveys, with numerical ratings reflecting the average scores given by all survey participants who voted on each establishment and text based on direct quotes from, or fair paraphrasings of, participants' comments. Phone numbers, addresses and other factual information were correct to the best of our knowledge when published in this guide; any subsequent changes may not be reflected.

Contents

Ratings & Symbols

Zagat | Name | Symbols | | | | | Zagat Ratings
Top Movie

Title,
Director,
Cast,
Running
Time

| | | | OVERALL | ACTING | STORY | PROD. |

Ⓩ Tim & Nina Uncut ◖

2001 | Directed by Quentin Tarantino | With Brad Pitt, Angelina Jolie | 90 minutes | Rated PG

▽ 25 | 19 | 25 | 12

Review,
surveyor
comments
in quotes

Tim and Nina's "courtship in Paris" is the "ooh-la-la" subject of this chop-socky/docudrama hybrid (think *Breathless* meets *Rush Hour*) that "inspires" the insipid but is "boring as heck" for everyone else; all applaud Pitt's "butch but tender" take on Tim as a "young buck", while Jolie is "so adorable" as "Nina in love" that many "want to adopt *her*"; P.S. the interminable cinéma-vérité "dinner scenes in bed" aren't for the squeamish.

Ratings

Overall Excellence, Acting, Story and **Production Values** are rated on a scale of 0 to 30.

0	–	9	poor to fair
10	–	15	fair to good
16	–	19	good to very good
20	–	25	very good to excellent
26	–	30	extraordinary to perfection
	▽		low response	less reliable

Symbols

Ⓩ Zagat Top Movie (highest ratings, popularity and importance)

✉ Oscar winner for Best Picture, Actor, Actress, Director, Screenplay, Foreign Language Film

◖ filmed in black & white

Ⓕ foreign language film

∅ not yet on DVD

About This Survey

Here are the results of our 2008 Movie Survey, our sixth edition of the ultimate moviegoer's guide, covering 1,950 outstanding films. We've added 40 films from the last year as well as 310 earlier titles for a total of 350 new entries since our last edition. Like all our guides, it's based on the collective opinions of thousands of savvy consumers.

WHO PARTICIPATED: Input from 17,643 avid moviegoers forms the basis for the ratings and reviews in this guide (their comments are shown in quotation marks within the reviews). Viewing an average 2.2 movies per week, these surveyors collectively see roughly 2 million films annually. We sincerely thank each of them – this book is really "theirs."

HELPFUL LISTS: Whether you're looking for an action-packed blockbuster, a thought-provoking documentary or a slice of old Hollywood, our lists should help you find exactly the right film. See Top New Releases (page 7), Favorite Films of All Time (page 8), Top Ratings (pages 9–19) and Top Foreign Language Films (page 20). We've also provided 67 handy indexes. Though the vast majority of films in this book are currently available on DVD, we have flagged those that are not with the following icon - ∅.

ABOUT ZAGAT: This marks our 28th year reporting on the shared experiences of consumers like you. What started in 1979 as a hobby involving 200 of our friends has come a long way. Today we have over 300,000 surveyors and now cover dining, entertaining, golf, hotels, movies, music, nightlife, resorts, shopping, spas, theater and tourist attractions worldwide.

SHARE YOUR OPINION: We invite you to join any of our upcoming surveys – just register at **zagat.com,** where you can rate and review establishments year-round. Each participant will receive a free copy of the resulting guide when published.

AVAILABILITY: Zagat guides are available in all major bookstores, by subscription at **zagat.com** and for use on a wide range of mobile devices via **Zagat To Go** or **zagat.mobi.**

FEEDBACK: There is always room for improvement, thus we invite your comments and suggestions about any aspect of our performance. Just contact us at **movies@zagat.com.**

New York, NY
September 5, 2007

Nina and Tim

Nina and Tim Zagat

What's New

For this sixth edition of our Movie Guide, we asked surveyors where they preferred to see movies. While 52% named the traditional theater, a surprising 48% opt to do their moviegoing "at home." We attribute that to the rising popularity of high-tech home theater systems – and see it as a harbinger of where we'll enjoy first-run entertainment in the future.

 THE ENVELOPE, PLEASE: Equally interesting were surveyors' choices of the best new releases of the last 12 months. It was a *fantástico* year for **foreign language features,** with Germany's *The Lives of Others* voted Top Film Overall in a list that also included *Letters from Iwo Jima* (in Japanese), *Pan's Labyrinth* (Spanish), *Volver* (Spanish) and the polyglot *Babel*. Professionwise, **teachers** were the subjects of *Freedom Writers*, *The History Boys* and *Notes on a Scandal*, **world leaders** were depicted in *The Last King of Scotland* and *The Queen,* and **Victorian magicians** took center stage in *The Illusionist* and *The Prestige.* **Documentaries** like *An Inconvenient Truth* and *Who Killed the Electric Car?* echoed the current fascination with all things green. **Animation** was as popular as ever (*Cars, Happy Feet* and *Meet the Robinsons*) but surprisingly enough, only one sequel made the list: *Pirates of the Caribbean: At World's End.* See facing page for a full list of the year's winners.

DOUBLE FEATURES: As for the season's hottest players, nine actors garnered double berths in the Top 40: **Cate Blanchett** (*Babel, Notes on a Scandal*), **Jennifer Connelly** (*Blood Diamond, Little Children*), **Michael Caine** (*Children of Men, The Prestige*), **Judi Dench** (*Casino Royale, Notes on a Scandal*), **Leonardo DiCaprio** (*Blood* *Diamond, The Departed*), **Greg Kinnear** (*Invincible, Little Miss Sunshine*), **Edward Norton** (*The Illusionist, The Painted Veil*), **Ryan Phillippe** (*Breach, Flags of Our Fathers*) and **Mark Wahlberg** (*The Departed, Invincible*). In the director's chair, **Clint Eastwood** scored twice with *Flags of Our Fathers* and *Letters from Iwo Jima.*

DVD WANNABES: We annually ask voters to name their favorite films not available on DVD that should be. This year's mentions included *The African Queen, Becket, El Cid, Enchanted April, I'm No Angel, Isadora, Kiss of the Spider Woman, Let It Be, Looking for Mr. Goodbar, The Magnificent Ambersons, O Lucky Man!, Personal Best, Shoot the Moon, Song of the South, That Man From Rio, The Wrong Box, Yentl* and "anything with John Garfield."

NEW TO THIS EDITION: Though we're trying to age gracefully, we will admit to a slight face-lift this year with a revamped design including new fonts and easier-to-use indexes. We hope you like the improvements and thank everyone who shared their opinions with us. Here's looking at you, kids!

New York, NY
September 5, 2007

Curt Gathje

Top New Releases

Overall Quality ratings are to the left of names. Lists exclude places with low votes, unless indicated by a ▽.

<u>28</u> Lives of Others

<u>27</u> Letters from Iwo Jima
Pan's Labyrinth

<u>26</u> Departed, The
Queen, The

<u>25</u> Last King of Scotland
Blood Diamond

<u>24</u> Waitress
Little Miss Sunshine
Cars
Hot Fuzz
Inconvenient Truth
Notes on a Scandal
Volver
Little Children

<u>23</u> Wordplay
Flags of Our Fathers
Illusionist, The
Breach
Dreamgirls

Painted Veil
Casino Royale
Who Killed the Electric Car?
Charlotte's Web
Pursuit of Happyness

<u>22</u> 300
We Are Marshall
Fracture
Prestige, The
Bridge to Terabithia
Devil Wears Prada
Freedom Writers
History Boys
Babel
Meet the Robinsons
Children of Men

<u>21</u> Zodiac
Invincible
Happy Feet
Pirates Caribbean/World's End

Favorite Films of All Time

Based on surveyors' choices of their five favorite films.

1. Godfather, The
2. Casablanca
3. Star Wars
4. Gone with the Wind
5. Shawshank Redemption
6. Braveheart
7. Lord of the Rings/Fellowship
8. Citizen Kane
9. Godfather Part II
10. Raiders of the Lost Ark
11. American Beauty
12. When Harry Met Sally...
13. Beautiful Mind
14. It's a Wonderful Life
15. African Queen
16. Schindler's List
17. Matrix, The
18. Princess Bride
19. Wizard of Oz
20. Annie Hall
21. Usual Suspects*
22. Pretty Woman
23. Sound of Music
24. Moulin Rouge!
25. Pulp Fiction
26. 2001: A Space Odyssey
27. Gladiator
28. Affair to Remember
29. Breakfast at Tiffany's
30. Goodfellas*
31. Almost Famous
32. Saving Private Ryan
33. Singin' in the Rain*
34. Apocalypse Now
35. Lawrence of Arabia
36. Bridget Jones's Diary
37. Star Wars V/Empire Strikes*
38. Shrek
39. Silence of the Lambs*
40. Animal House
41. Forrest Gump
42. All About Eve
43. Top Gun
44. Blade Runner
45. Memento*
46. E.T. The Extra-Terrestrial
47. Chocolat
48. Graduate, The
49. Dr. Strangelove
50. To Kill a Mockingbird*
51. Dirty Dancing
52. Airplane!
53. Blazing Saddles*
54. Shakespeare in Love*
55. Die Hard
56. Doctor Zhivago*
57. Harry Potter/Sorcerer's Stone
58. American Pie
59. American President
60. Willy Wonka/Choc. Factory
61. 12 Angry Men
62. As Good As It Gets
63. English Patient*
64. Ferris Bueller's Day Off
65. Rear Window
66. Amadeus
67. Caddyshack
68. Chinatown*
69. Fargo
70. Good Will Hunting*
71. Maltese Falcon
72. Sixth Sense
73. Dead Poets Society
74. Grease*
75. Great Escape

* Indicates a tie with film above

subscribe to zagat.com

Top Overall Quality Ratings

Ratings are to the left of names. (See page 20 for Top Foreign Language Films.)

CLASSIC (PRE-1960)

29 Casablanca

28 Wizard of Oz
Lady Eve
Singin' in the Rain
Rear Window
It Happened One Night
Citizen Kane
All About Eve
African Queen
Third Man
Best Years of Our Lives
Grapes of Wrath
On the Waterfront
Paths of Glory
Fantasia
Bridge on the River Kwai
Some Like It Hot
Sunset Boulevard
All Quiet on Western Front
Gone with the Wind
North by Northwest
High Noon
12 Angry Men
Double Indemnity
Maltese Falcon

27 Sweet Smell of Success
Snow White
Philadelphia Story
Woman of the Year
Treasure of the Sierra Madre
Heiress, The
Notorious
Searchers, The*
Ox-Bow Incident
Brief Encounter
Duck Soup
Holiday
It's a Wonderful Life
Christmas Carol
Great Expectations
Witness for the Prosecution
Big Sleep
Night of the Hunter
Hamlet
Sullivan's Travels
Streetcar Named Desire
Stalag 17
How Green Was My Valley
Quiet Man
Top Hat

MODERN (1960 TO DATE)

29 Godfather, The
Godfather Part II
Schindler's List
Lawrence of Arabia
To Kill a Mockingbird

28 Star Wars
Shawshank Redemption
Pianist, The
Finding Nemo
Dr. Strangelove
Lord of the Rings/Return
Spellbound
Man for All Seasons
Lion in Winter
Hotel Rwanda
Sound of Music
Psycho
Raiders of the Lost Ark

27 One Flew Over Cuckoo's...

My Fair Lady
I Never Sang for My Father
Usual Suspects
West Side Story
Taxi Driver
Young Frankenstein
Silence of the Lambs
Manchurian Candidate | 1962
Chinatown
Apocalypse Now
Lord of the Rings/Fellowship
Patton
Annie Hall
Sting, The
Chicago
Lord of the Rings/Two Towers
Gandhi
Great Escape
Million Dollar Baby
Advise & Consent

Wild Bunch
Princess Bride
Graduate, The
Goodfellas
Toy Story
Days of Wine and Roses

Doctor Zhivago
Breaker Morant
Fitzcarraldo
Mary Poppins
[26] March of the Penguins

BY GENRE

ACTION/ADVENTURE

CLASSIC

[27] Treasure of the Sierra Madre
[25] Adventures of Robin Hood
Mutiny on the Bounty
King Kong
Captains Courageous
[23] Captain Blood
[22] Mark of Zorro
Around the World in 80 Days
[21] Tarzan and His Mate
Tarzan the Ape Man

MODERN

[29] Lawrence of Arabia
[28] Star Wars
Lord of the Rings/Return
Raiders of the Lost Ark
[27] Lord of the Rings/Fellowship
Lord of the Rings/Two Towers
Great Escape
[26] Star Wars V/Empire Strikes
Papillon
Magnificent Seven

AMERICANA

CLASSIC

[28] Best Years of Our Lives
Grapes of Wrath
[27] It's a Wonderful Life
[26] Shadow of a Doubt
Meet Me in St. Louis
Mr. Smith Goes to Washington
[25] Yankee Doodle Dandy
Member of the Wedding
Mr. Deeds Goes to Town
All the King's Men

MODERN

[29] To Kill a Mockingbird
[26] Christmas Story
[25] Music Man
Badlands
Seabiscuit
[24] Stand by Me
American Graffiti
Far From Heaven
Forrest Gump
Straight Story

ANIMATED

CLASSIC

[28] Fantasia
[27] Snow White
[26] Pinocchio
Cinderella
Bambi
Lady and the Tramp
[25] Peter Pan
Sleeping Beauty
[24] Dumbo
Alice in Wonderland

MODERN

[28] Finding Nemo
[27] Toy Story
[26] Shrek
Beauty/Beast
Shrek 2
Incredibles, The
Monsters, Inc.
Toy Story 2
[25] Lion King
[24] Iron Giant

BIOGRAPHY

CLASSIC
- 25 Yankee Doodle Dandy
- Sergeant York
- 24 Scarlet Empress∇
- 23 Diary of Anne Frank
- Viva Zapata!
- Lust for Life
- Anastasia
- 22 Song of Bernadette
- Pride of the Yankees

MODERN
- 29 Lawrence of Arabia
- 28 Man for All Seasons
- 27 Patton
- Gandhi
- 26 Raging Bull
- Amadeus
- Becket
- Ray
- Anne of the Thousand Days
- Last Emperor

CHILDREN/FAMILY

CLASSIC
- 28 Wizard of Oz
- 27 It's a Wonderful Life
- Christmas Carol
- 24 Lili
- Bells of St. Mary's
- National Velvet
- Old Yeller
- Jungle Book
- 23 Father of the Bride
- 22 20,000 Leagues Under Sea

MODERN
- 28 Sound of Music
- 27 Princess Bride
- Mary Poppins
- 26 E.T. The Extra-Terrestrial
- Christmas Story
- Sounder
- Willy Wonka
- 25 Babe
- Whale Rider
- 24 Harry Potter/Goblet of Fire

COMEDY

CLASSIC
- 28 Some Like It Hot
- 27 Woman of the Year
- Mister Roberts
- 26 Adam's Rib
- Great Dictator
- Man Who Came to Dinner*
- Monkey Business
- Harvey
- 25 Auntie Mame
- Lavender Hill Mob

MODERN
- 27 Young Frankenstein
- Annie Hall
- Graduate, The
- 26 This Is Spinal Tap
- When Harry Met Sally...
- Manhattan
- Local Hero
- 25 Waiting for Guffman
- Blazing Saddles
- Tootsie

CRIME

CLASSIC
- 28 Rear Window
- On the Waterfront
- 26 Arsenic and Old Lace
- Anatomy of a Murder
- 25 Public Enemy
- Lavender Hill Mob
- High Sierra
- Dial M for Murder
- To Catch a Thief
- 24 Little Caesar

MODERN
- 29 Godfather, The
- Godfather Part II
- 27 Usual Suspects
- Sting, The
- Chicago
- Goodfellas
- 26 Departed, The
- Pulp Fiction
- Capote
- Mystic River

CULT

CLASSIC

29	Casablanca
28	Wizard of Oz
	All About Eve
	Fantasia
27	It's a Wonderful Life
	Gun Crazy
26	Red Shoes
25	Forbidden Planet
23	Freaks
20	7th Voyage of Sinbad

MODERN

28	Star Wars
	Shawshank Redemption
	Dr. Strangelove
	Sound of Music
27	Manchurian Candidate	1962
	Princess Bride
26	Monty Python/Holy Grail
	Breakfast at Tiffany's
	Blade Runner
	Willy Wonka

DRAMA

CLASSIC

28	Citizen Kane
	Best Years of Our Lives
	Grapes of Wrath
	On the Waterfront
	Paths of Glory
	High Noon
	12 Angry Men
27	Heiress, The
	Ox-Bow Incident
	Great Expectations

MODERN

29	Godfather, The
	Godfather Part II
	Schindler's List
	To Kill a Mockingbird
28	Shawshank Redemption
	Pianist, The
	Lion in Winter
	Hotel Rwanda
27	I Never Sang for My Father
	Taxi Driver

DRAMEDY

CLASSIC

28	All About Eve
	African Queen
27	It's a Wonderful Life
	Sullivan's Travels
	Stalag 17
	Dinner at Eight
26	Women, The
	Mr. Smith Goes to Washington
25	Sabrina
	Lady Vanishes

MODERN

27	One Flew Over Cuckoo's...
	Sting, The
26	Breakfast at Tiffany's
	Crimes and Misdemeanors
	Sense and Sensibility
	Charade
	Bend It Like Beckham
	Cool Hand Luke
25	Apartment, The
	Fargo

EPIC

CLASSIC

28	Bridge on the River Kwai
	Gone with the Wind
26	Ben-Hur
25	Mutiny on the Bounty
	Gunga Din
24	Ten Commandments
	Giant
23	Duel in the Sun
22	Around the World in 80 Days
	Robe, The

MODERN

29	Lawrence of Arabia
27	Gandhi
	Doctor Zhivago
26	Last Emperor
	2001: A Space Odyssey
	Braveheart
	Spartacus
25	Empire of the Sun
	Once Upon a Time/West
	Passage to India

FANTASY

CLASSIC
28 Wizard of Oz
27 Christmas Carol
26 Harvey
25 Miracle on 34th Street
 King Kong
 Lost Horizon
24 Ghost and Mrs. Muir
 Brigadoon
20 Topper
 7th Voyage of Sinbad

MODERN
28 Lord of the Rings/Return
 Raiders of the Lost Ark
27 Lord of the Rings/Fellowship
 Lord of the Rings/Two Towers
 Princess Bride
 Toy Story
 Mary Poppins
26 Willy Wonka
24 Indiana Jones/Last Crusade
 Harry Potter/Goblet of Fire

FILM NOIR

CLASSIC
28 Third Man
 Sunset Boulevard
 Double Indemnity
 Maltese Falcon
27 Sweet Smell of Success
 Big Sleep
 Night of the Hunter
 Gun Crazy
 Laura
26 Out of the Past

MODERN
27 Chinatown
26 Blade Runner
 L.A. Confidential
 Memento
25 Fargo
 Cape Fear | 1962
24 Body Heat
 Blood Simple
23 Seven
22 Last Seduction

HORROR

CLASSIC
25 Frankenstein
 Bride of Frankenstein
24 Dracula
 Invasion/Body Snatchers
 Mummy, The
23 Freaks
 Cat People
 Thing, The
22 Invisible Man
21 House of Wax

MODERN
27 Young Frankenstein
25 Exorcist, The
 Shining, The
24 Rosemary's Baby
 Hush... Hush, Sweet Charlotte
23 Thing, The
22 Poltergeist
 Halloween
 Carrie
 Pit and the Pendulum

MUSICAL

CLASSIC
28 Wizard of Oz
 Singin' in the Rain
27 Top Hat
 King and I
26 American in Paris
 Band Wagon
 Meet Me in St. Louis
 Swing Time
25 Yankee Doodle Dandy
 Shall We Dance

MODERN
28 Sound of Music
27 My Fair Lady
 West Side Story
 Chicago
 Mary Poppins
26 Fiddler on the Roof
 Cabaret
 Funny Girl
25 Music Man
 That's Entertainment!

ROMANCE

CLASSIC

- <u>29</u> Casablanca
- <u>28</u> Lady Eve
- It Happened One Night
- African Queen
- Gone with the Wind
- <u>27</u> Philadelphia Story
- Notorious
- Brief Encounter
- Holiday
- How Green Was My Valley

MODERN

- <u>27</u> My Fair Lady
- West Side Story
- Annie Hall
- Graduate, The
- Doctor Zhivago
- <u>26</u> Room with a View
- Charade
- Manhattan
- Romeo and Juliet
- <u>25</u> Harold and Maude

SCI-FI

CLASSIC

- <u>26</u> On the Beach
- <u>25</u> Forbidden Planet
- Day the Earth Stood Still
- <u>24</u> Invasion/Body Snatchers
- <u>23</u> War of the Worlds
- Thing, The
- <u>22</u> 20,000 Leagues Under Sea
- <u>20</u> Fly, The
- <u>19</u> Journey to Center of Earth
- <u>16</u> Godzilla

MODERN

- <u>28</u> Star Wars
- <u>26</u> E.T. The Extra-Terrestrial
- Star Wars V/Empire Strikes
- Blade Runner
- 2001: A Space Odyssey
- <u>25</u> Matrix, The
- Alien
- <u>24</u> Star Wars VI/Return of Jedi
- Close Encounters
- Terminator, The

THRILLER

CLASSIC

- <u>28</u> Rear Window
- Third Man
- North by Northwest
- <u>27</u> Notorious
- Night of the Hunter
- Vertigo
- 39 Steps
- <u>26</u> Shadow of a Doubt
- Gaslight
- Strangers on a Train

MODERN

- <u>28</u> Psycho
- <u>27</u> Taxi Driver
- Silence of the Lambs
- Manchurian Candidate | 1962
- <u>26</u> Jaws
- Pulp Fiction
- Memento
- Seven Days in May
- Sixth Sense
- <u>25</u> Counterfeit Traitor

WAR

CLASSIC

- <u>29</u> Casablanca
- <u>28</u> Paths of Glory
- Bridge on the River Kwai
- All Quiet on Western Front
- Gone with the Wind
- <u>27</u> Stalag 17
- Caine Mutiny
- Mister Roberts
- <u>26</u> Twelve O'Clock High
- <u>25</u> Mrs. Miniver

MODERN

- <u>29</u> Schindler's List
- <u>28</u> Pianist, The
- Hotel Rwanda
- <u>27</u> Apocalypse Now
- Patton
- Great Escape
- <u>26</u> MASH
- Saving Private Ryan
- Henry V
- Fog of War

WESTERN

CLASSIC

28 High Noon
27 Searchers, The
Ox-Bow Incident
Stagecoach
26 Red River
Shane
25 My Darling Clementine
Destry Rides Again
24 Oklahoma!
She Wore a Yellow Ribbon

MODERN

27 Wild Bunch
26 Butch Cassidy/Sundance Kid
Hud
Unforgiven
Magnificent Seven
25 Outlaw Josey Wales
Once Upon a Time/West
Man Who Shot Liberty Valance
24 Good, the Bad and the Ugly
Little Big Man

BY DECADE

1910s/1920s

29 Napoléon▽
28 Greed▽
General, The
Gold Rush
27 Intolerance▽
Potemkin
Metropolis
26 Cabinet of Dr. Caligari
Nosferatu
25 Birth of a Nation

1930s

28 Wizard of Oz
It Happened One Night
All Quiet on Western Front
Gone with the Wind
27 Snow White
Duck Soup
Holiday
Top Hat
Dinner at Eight
Wuthering Heights

1940s

29 Casablanca
28 Lady Eve
Citizen Kane
Third Man
Best Years of Our Lives
Grapes of Wrath
Fantasia
Double Indemnity
Maltese Falcon
27 Philadelphia Story

1950s

28 Singin' in the Rain
Rear Window
All About Eve
African Queen
On the Waterfront
Paths of Glory
Bridge on the River Kwai
Some Like It Hot
Sunset Boulevard
North by Northwest

1960s

29 Lawrence of Arabia
To Kill a Mockingbird
28 Dr. Strangelove
Man for All Seasons
Lion in Winter
Sound of Music
Psycho
27 My Fair Lady
West Side Story
Manchurian Candidate

1970s

29 Godfather, The
Godfather Part II
28 Star Wars
27 One Flew Over Cuckoo's...
I Never Sang for My Father
Taxi Driver
Young Frankenstein
Chinatown
Apocalypse Now
Patton

1980s

28 Raiders of the Lost Ark
27 Gandhi
Princess Bride
Breaker Morant
Fitzcarraldo
26 E.T. The Extra-Terrestrial
Raging Bull

Amadeus
Star Wars V/Empire Strikes
Soldier's Story

1990s

29 Schindler's List
28 Shawshank Redemption
27 Usual Suspects
Silence of the Lambs
Goodfellas
Toy Story
26 Saving Private Ryan
Beauty/Beast
Hoop Dreams
Pulp Fiction

2000s

28 Pianist, The
Finding Nemo

Lord of the Rings/Return
Spellbound
Hotel Rwanda
27 Lord of the Rings/Fellowship
Chicago
Lord of the Rings/Two Towers
Million Dollar Baby
26 March of the Penguins
Shrek
Shrek 2
Beautiful Mind
Incredibles, The
Crash
Departed, The
Ray
Akeelah and the Bee
Rabbit-Proof Fence
Fog of War

Top Acting Ratings

Ratings are to the left of names.

CLASSIC (PRE-1960)

<u>29</u> All About Eve
Hamlet
On the Waterfront
Brief Encounter
African Queen

<u>28</u> Casablanca
Streetcar Named Desire
12 Angry Men
Lady Eve
Now, Voyager
Adam's Rib
Philadelphia Story
Sweet Smell of Success
Little Foxes
White Heat
Night of the Hunter
Born Yesterday
Kind Hearts and Coronets
Grapes of Wrath
Heiress, The
Woman of the Year*
Caine Mutiny
Sunset Boulevard

Witness for the Prosecution
Bridge on the River Kwai
It Happened One Night
Third Man
Ball of Fire
Snake Pit
His Girl Friday
Bad Day at Black Rock

<u>27</u> Treasure of the Sierra Madre
Jezebel
Citizen Kane
Some Like It Hot
Rear Window
Double Indemnity
Room at the Top
East of Eden
Bringing Up Baby
Man Who Came to Dinner
Notorious
Paths of Glory
To Have and Have Not
Desk Set

MODERN (1960 TO DATE)

<u>29</u> Godfather Part II
Godfather, The
One Flew Over Cuckoo's...
Monster
Capote
Ray
Lion in Winter
Taxi Driver
Queen, The
Becket
To Kill a Mockingbird
Schindler's List
Last King of Scotland
Pianist, The

<u>28</u> Hotel Rwanda
Beautiful Mind
Million Dollar Baby
Silence of the Lambs
Days of Wine and Roses
Gandhi
Man for All Seasons
Patton

Shawshank Redemption
Lawrence of Arabia
Raging Bull
Notes on a Scandal
Inherit the Wind
Mystic River
Sophie's Choice
Iris
Prime of Miss Jean Brodie
My Left Foot
Midnight Cowboy
TransAmerica
Chinatown
Vera Drake
Departed, The
Apartment, The
Hud
Walk the Line
Sleuth
Frances
American History X
Raisin in the Sun
My Brilliant Career

Top Story Ratings

Ratings are to the left of names.

CLASSIC (PRE-1960)

28 | Hamlet
Casablanca
All Quiet on Western Front
Paths of Glory
Witness for the Prosecution
Grapes of Wrath
Wizard of Oz
Great Expectations
Best Years of Our Lives
Double Indemnity
Rear Window
Christmas Carol

27 | All About Eve
Wuthering Heights
On the Beach
Citizen Kane
Heiress, The
12 Angry Men
Bridge on the River Kwai
39 Steps
Place in the Sun
Strangers on a Train
Dial M for Murder

Gone with the Wind
It's a Wonderful Life
Rebecca
Searchers, The
Gun Crazy
Sunset Boulevard
Third Man
Brief Encounter
Maltese Falcon
Anatomy of a Murder
Of Mice and Men
North by Northwest
Stalag 17
Laura
Gentleman's Agreement
Lady Eve
Vertigo

26 | Ox-Bow Incident
Sweet Smell of Success
Hunchback/Notre Dame
Some Like It Hot
Diary of Anne Frank

MODERN (1960 TO DATE)

29 | Godfather, The
To Kill a Mockingbird

28 | Schindler's List
Godfather Part II
Shawshank Redemption
Usual Suspects
Star Wars
Manchurian Candidate | 1962
Hotel Rwanda
Seven Days in May

27 | Man for All Seasons
Henry V
Great Escape
Dr. Strangelove
Raiders of the Lost Ark
Breaker Morant
Romeo and Juliet
Lord of the Rings/Return
Psycho
Christmas Story
Pianist, The
House of Games

Sting, The
One Flew Over Cuckoo's...
Day of the Jackal
Killing Fields
Lord of the Rings/Fellowship
Princess Bride
Lawrence of Arabia
Inherit the Wind
Spellbound*
Sixth Sense
I Never Sang for My Father
Lion in Winter
West Side Story*
Gandhi
My Fair Lady
Memento
Sound of Music
Wait Until Dark
Fiddler on the Roof
Advise & Consent
Silence of the Lambs

26 | Doctor Zhivago
Lord of the Rings/Two Towers

Top Production Values Ratings

Ratings are to the left of names.

CLASSIC (PRE-1960)

29] Fantasia
   Wizard of Oz
   Gone with the Wind
28] Singin' in the Rain
   Citizen Kane
   Ben-Hur
   Bridge on the River Kwai
   Third Man
27] North by Northwest
   Searchers, The
   King and I
   American in Paris
   Casablanca
   Quiet Man
   Sunset Boulevard
   Snow White
   Red River
   Ten Commandments
   Rear Window
26] Gold Diggers of 1933
   Band Wagon
   Paths of Glory

Top Hat
Great Expectations
Some Like It Hot
Notorious
Lady from Shanghai
Vertigo
Ziegfeld Follies
African Queen
Heiress, The
Bambi
Night of the Hunter
Touch of Evil
Sweet Smell of Success
Gigi
All About Eve
Moulin Rouge
Red Shoes
Cinderella
Star Is Born
Woman of the Year
Pinocchio
42nd Street
Laura

MODERN (1960 TO DATE)

29] Lord of the Rings/Return
   Finding Nemo
   Lord of the Rings/Two Towers
   Lawrence of Arabia
   Lord of the Rings/Fellowship
   Godfather, The
   Star Wars
   Chicago
   Godfather Part II
   Schindler's List
28] Winged Migration
   Star Wars V/Empire Strikes
   Matrix, The
   Last Emperor
   March of the Penguins
   Saving Private Ryan
   Toy Story
   Raiders of the Lost Ark
   Pianist, The
   Shrek 2
   Doctor Zhivago
   Sound of Music
   Shrek

Monsters, Inc.
Incredibles, The
Apocalypse Now
Star Wars VI/Return of Jedi
Toy Story 2
Star Wars III/Revenge of Sith
Nightmare Before Christmas
27] 2001: A Space Odyssey
   Beauty/Beast
   West Side Story
   Jurassic Park
   My Fair Lady
   Patton
   Braveheart
   Brazil
   Cars
   Gandhi
   Last Samurai
   Blade Runner
   Harry Potter/Sorcerer's Stone
   Wild Bunch
   Harry Potter/Goblet of Fire

Top Foreign Language Films

Overall Quality ratings are to the left of names.

CLASSIC (PRE-1960)

29 Seven Samurai
Rashomon

400 Blows
Wages of Fear

28 Children of Paradise
Beauty/Beast
Grand Illusion
Open City▽

26 Wild Strawberries
Black Orpheus
Rififi
Smiles of a Summer Night
Alexander Nevsky
M
Diabolique
Mon Oncle

27 Bicycle Thief
Seventh Seal
Rules of the Game▽
La Strada
Nights of Cabiria
Triumph of the Will*

25 Mr. Hulot's Holiday
Blue Angel

MODERN (1960 TO DATE)

29 Sorrow and the Pity

28 Shoah
Lives of Others
Battle of Algiers
Yojimbo
Das Boot

27 Ran
Life Is Beautiful
Persona
Au Revoir Les Enfants
Letters from Iwo Jima
Jean de Florette
Pan's Labyrinth
Spirited Away
Day for Night

26 Cinema Paradiso
Conformist, The
King of Hearts
City of God
Babette's Feast
8½
Amarcord
Fanny and Alexander
Z

Cries and Whispers
Talk to Her
Amélie
Seven Beauties

25 Two Women
Antonia's Line
Garden of the Finzi-Continis
Leopard, The
Hiroshima, Mon Amour
Aguirre: The Wrath of God
Maria Full of Grace
Scenes from a Marriage
Farewell My Concubine
La Dolce Vita
Marriage of Maria Braun
All About My Mother
Contempt
Hero
My Life As a Dog
Like Water for Chocolate
Shoot the Piano Player
Juliet of the Spirits
Breathless
Eat Drink Man Woman

MOVIE
DIRECTORY

	OVERALL	ACTING	STORY	PROD.

About a Boy
21 | 23 | 22 | 21

2002 | Directed by Chris Weitz, Paul Weitz | With Hugh Grant, Toni Collette, Nicholas Hoult, Rachel Weisz | 101 minutes | Rated PG-13

This "wonderfully funny romantic comedy" features Grant's "best work" as a "rich, self-absorbed" "skirt-chaser pretending to be a single dad" who strikes up a "sweet friendship" with a "lonely young boy" and "redeems himself in the end"; those who "expect the usual superficial" "chick-flick fluff" are "pleasantly surprised" by this "clever" adaptation of the Nick Hornby novel.

About Last Night. . .
17 | 16 | 17 | 16

1986 | Directed by Edward Zwick | With Rob Lowe, Demi Moore, James Belushi, Elizabeth Perkins | 113 minutes | Rated R

"Brat pack" fans still find this "very '80s" romantic comedy "relatable" for its interpretation of "young" lovers as they struggle "to commit or not to commit" (it's based on the David Mamet play *Sexual Perversity in Chicago* with "not much resemblance to the original"); admirers of the "pre-fame" Moore and "at-his-prime" Lowe call it a "true guilty pleasure", even if the "silly", "self-absorbed" milieu is "so 20 years ago."

About Schmidt
21 | 26 | 20 | 21

2002 | Directed by Alexander Payne | With Jack Nicholson, Kathy Bates, Hope Davis, Dermot Mulroney | 125 minutes | Rated R

It's a "change of pace for Nicholson" ("no eyebrow raising"), who plays a "lethargic" "Middle America everyman" trying "to give his life purpose before it's too late" in this "heartbreaking" yet "hilarious" dramedy "guaranteed to scare anyone approaching retirement"; though it "drags at times", the "brilliant acting overcomes any plot shortcomings" – and the "Kathy Bates hot-tub scene" "will leave your head spinning."

Absence of Malice
21 | 25 | 21 | 20

1981 | Directed by Sydney Pollack | With Paul Newman, Sally Field, Bob Balaban | 116 minutes | Rated PG

"Newman and Field ignite the screen" in this "textured" "hard-hitting" courtroom drama demonstrating how "guilt by association" causes a "newspaper to ruin a man's career"; most say that the "irresponsible press" is a topic made for the movies, but some feel this "slight" effort "should have been better" – starting with the "not-believable ending."

Absent-Minded Professor, The ◑
19 | 17 | 19 | 17

1961 | Directed by Robert Stevenson | With Fred MacMurray, Nancy Olson, Keenan Wynn | 97 minutes | Rated PG

Despite its "charming", "classic Disney" formula, this "bouncy tale" involving an invention dubbed "flubber" divides voters: flubbergasted fans claim it "stands up well over time", but deflators find it "kinda corny", adding it "may not appeal" to small fry, since its black-and-white cinematography "looks old"; although popular enough to inspire a couple of remakes, the "original is the best."

Abyss, The
20 | 19 | 19 | 25

1989 | Directed by James Cameron | With Ed Harris, Mary Elizabeth Mastrantonio | 146 minutes | Rated PG-13

"Eye-popping" F/X – notably the "breakout use of morphing" – are the raison d'être of this "underwater opus", a "fun" cocktail comprised of a "little sci-fi, a little action and a little romance"; it's also a little "long" and "sputters" at the finale, so diehards recommend the "director's cut", which "fleshes out the far-too-abrupt ending in the original version."

Accidental Tourist, The
| 20 | 24 | 21 | 19 |

1988 | Directed by Lawrence Kasdan | With William Hurt, Kathleen Turner, Geena Davis | 121 minutes | Rated PG

This "zany" romantic drama about love, loss and "alphabetizing the groceries in your cupboard" is "as good as" Anne Tyler's best-seller and might "break and mend your heart in one sitting"; its "perfect cast" includes a "terrific" Hurt and an "offbeat", "pitch-perfect" Davis (who "copped an Oscar"), though some argue the picture is "too quirky" and "inert" for mainstream audiences.

Accused, The ⊠
| 23 | 28 | 23 | 21 |

1988 | Directed by Jonathan Kaplan | With Kelly McGillis, Jodie Foster, Bernie Coulson | 108 minutes | Rated R

Not for the "faint of heart", this "white-knuckle" thriller about a gang rape and its courtroom consequences is "based on true events" and dominated by a "phenomenal" Foster, who won a "thoroughly deserved" Oscar for her "captivating" job; the "excruciating", "very graphic" re-enactment of the crime is "definitely for mature audiences" – but far from gratuitous given the picture's "socially responsible" message.

Ace Ventura: Pet Detective
| 15 | 16 | 12 | 14 |

1994 | Directed by Tom Shadyac | With Jim Carrey, Courteney Cox, Sean Young | 86 minutes | Rated PG-13

The "vulgar", "puerile humor" of this "silly, turn-your-brain-off" comedy about a pet detective tracking down a kidnapped dolphin was "Carrey's breakthrough", though some would "rather eat dirt" than sit through it; still, the "rubber-faced" star is so "over the top" that few notice this venture is "inanely short on plot."

Adam's Rib ❶
| 26 | 28 | 25 | 23 |

1949 | Directed by George Cukor | With Spencer Tracy, Katharine Hepburn, Judy Holliday | 101 minutes | Not Rated

"Chemistry abounds" in this "sparkling" matchup of Tracy and Hepburn, "probably the best pairing" of these "two pros", who are so "delightful" that many "wish they'd made even more movies together"; plotwise, this "battle-of-the-sexes" comedy concerns "married attorneys on opposing sides of a case", but fans say it's worth watching for the "effortless comedic timing" alone.

⏁ Adaptation
| 22 | 26 | 21 | 22 |

2002 | Directed by Spike Jonze | With Nicolas Cage, Meryl Streep, Chris Cooper | 114 minutes | Rated R

"You'll either love or hate" this "story within a story within a story", a "dark", "twisted" "head trip" about a screenwriter trying to adapt an unadaptable book; some find it "confusing", and even fans feel the "ending seemed to belong to a different film", but still "it's one of the most original movies ever made", bolstered by "superb acting."

Addams Family, The
| 17 | 19 | 16 | 20 |

1991 | Directed by Barry Sonnenfeld | With Anjelica Huston, Raul Julia, Christopher Lloyd | 102 minutes | Rated PG-13

That "creepy, kooky" family spawned from the *New Yorker* cartoons" and popularized by the '60s TV series makes its "ookie" screen debut with all its "madcap", ghoulish antics intact; "like MTV's *The Osbournes*", the story revolves around "misunderstood but lovable" types doing "quirky, offbeat" things.

Adventures of Priscilla, Queen of the Desert, The

23 | 24 | 22 | 22

1994 | Directed by Stephan Elliott | With Terence Stamp, Guy Pearce, Hugo Weaving | 104 minutes | Rated R

"Outlandish drag queens" and the "Australian outback" collide in this "razor-sharp" road comedy, a "flaming romp" about "boas, false eye-lashes" and a bus "ride through the desert"; highlights include Stamp's "campy" performance as a "post-op transsexual looking for love" and a "fabulous" soundtrack that will thrill "ABBA fans"; P.S. yup, "that's really Guy Pearce!"

Adventures of Robin Hood, The

25 | 22 | 24 | 24

1938 | Directed by Michael Curtiz, William Keighley | With Errol Flynn, Olivia de Havilland | 102 minutes | Not Rated

This "swashbuckliest swashbuckler of them all" is the "definitive telling" of the tale, filmed in "gorgeous Technicolor" and "acted with verve" by a "charismatic" Flynn and a "perfect" de Havilland; ok, it might be "a bit dated", but its "lightning-quick dialogue", "exciting" swordplay and those famous "green tights" are "still engaging" enough to inspire a "whole genre of films" – plus a "whole lot of parodies."

Advise & Consent ◑

27 | 27 | 27 | 24

1962 | Directed by Otto Preminger | With Henry Fonda, Charles Laughton, Walter Pidgeon, Don Murray | 139 minutes | Not Rated

A "grown-up study of Washington" (which should be "required viewing for all of Congress"), this "interesting", "behind-the-scenes" drama stars Fonda as a Cabinet candidate whose confirmation hearings inaugurate a "gutsy" exposé of hardball politics; voters consent it's a "talky chestnut", but it's still a front-runner for "one of Preminger's best."

☑ Affair to Remember, An

26 | 25 | 25 | 23

1957 | Directed by Leo McCarey | With Cary Grant, Deborah Kerr, Richard Denning | 119 minutes | Not Rated

The "ultimate chick flick", this "three-hanky tearjerker" begins with a "glamorous" "shipboard romance" that turns "tragic" after an "unexpected twist" at the "Empire State Building"; though the "inspiration for many other weepies" (notably *Sleepless in Seattle*), this one's the "standard", thanks to the "captivating banter", ultra-"suave Grant" and some "classic NY" scenery; just don't bother to see it with your boyfriend – men "don't get it."

Affliction

20 | 25 | 19 | 19

1998 | Directed by Paul Schrader | With Nick Nolte, Sissy Spacek, James Coburn | 113 minutes | Rated R

Granted, it's "grim, grim, grim", but this "disquieting" adaptation of Russell Banks' novel of "family dysfunction" in New Hampshire is still "eminently watchable" due to its "strong performances": Nolte's "wrenching" work and Coburn's "scary", Oscar-winning turn in particular; though admittedly a "great exposé on abuse", some of the afflicted find it so "mind-numbingly downbeat" that they want to "slash their wrists" afterward.

	OVERALL	ACTING	STORY	PROD.

🄩 African Queen, The ✉⊘   28 | 29 | 26 | 26

1951 | Directed by John Huston | With Humphrey Bogart, Katharine Hepburn, Robert Morley | 105 minutes | Not Rated

"Curmudgeonly riverboat captain" Bogie and "feisty missionary" Hepburn "sizzle" as they take a "trip up a hellish river" and "discover love, courage" and the "best use of leeches since the Middle Ages" in this "beautifully crafted" drama; its "legendary reputation" owes a lot to Huston's "no-nonsense direction", James Agee's "witty" screenplay, the fine "location shots" of "deepest Africa" and, of course, that "undeniable chemistry" between the two shining stars; in sum, "they don't make 'em like this anymore."

After Hours   21 | 20 | 22 | 19

1985 | Directed by Martin Scorsese | With Griffin Dunne, Rosanna Arquette, Teri Garr | 96 minutes | Rated R

From the ever-"creative" Scorsese comes this "offbeat" cult curio, a "pitch-black comedy" set in '80s SoHo recounting the after-hours adventures of a "straight-laced guy" out on the town and out of cash in a "pre-ATM" world; the "numerous subplots" (involving an "ice cream truck", a "headbanger nightclub" and a potty-mouthed sculptress) strike the straightlaced as "confusing" verging on "weird", but most tout its "razor-sharp performances" and "deft" wit.

After the Sunset   17 | 18 | 17 | 19

2004 | Directed by Brett Ratner | With Pierce Brosnan, Salma Hayek, Woody Harrelson | 97 minutes | Rated PG-13

The "non-Bond" Brosnan is "still cool" in this romance about a jewel thief on a "Caribbean jaunt" enticed into "one last heist" with the "spicy" Hayek (with a "quirky" FBI guy in hot pursuit); the "banter", "lush scenery" and "gratuitous bikini" shots make for some good "eye candy", but even with a last-reel "twist", it's a "no-brainer caper" and non-takers "yawn good night."

Against All Odds   18 | 19 | 18 | 18

1984 | Directed by Taylor Hackford | With Rachel Ward, Jeff Bridges, James Woods, Jane Greer | 128 minutes | Rated R

A "decent remake" of *Out of the Past*, this "twisted", "oversexed" romance finds a "hot, hot, hot" Bridges as a "washed-up quarterback" (with "remarkable abs") entwined in a "tense love triangle" with a "knockout" Ward and the "sinister" Woods; "steamy" love scenes and a "cool" car chase make for a "good rainy-day flick", but what really stays with viewers is that prime example of "'80s cheese", "Phil Collins' theme song."

Age of Innocence, The   22 | 24 | 22 | 26

1993 | Directed by Martin Scorsese | With Daniel Day-Lewis, Michelle Pfeiffer, Winona Ryder | 139 minutes | Rated PG

"Scorsese does Edith Wharton justice" in this "exquisite period drama" concerning "forbidden love" among "upper-class NYers" in the "opulent" "Gilded Age"; Day-Lewis gives a "subtle, understated" performance as the "tortured" lover, while the "gorgeous production" supplies a "sumptuous feast for the eyes" that "captures the smallest details in a languorous way" – maybe that's why the pace is a little on the "slow" side.

Agnes of God

21 | 25 | 22 | 19

1985 | Directed by Norman Jewison | With Jane Fonda, Anne Bancroft, Meg Tilly | 98 minutes | Rated PG-13

Make sure to "be in a serious mood" for this "powerful" drama about a "hysterical nun who may or may not be pregnant"; while there's some mighty "serious acting by some great women", voters split on the story ("compelling" vs. "convoluted") and the quality ("thought-provoking" vs. "underbaked"); either way, it's "worth sitting through for the ending."

Agony and the Ecstasy, The

23 | 23 | 22 | 24

1965 | Directed by Carol Reed | With Charlton Heston, Rex Harrison, Diane Cilento | 138 minutes | Not Rated

"All who love art" can get a "romanticized history lesson" via this "well-made epic" featuring Heston as Renaissance man Michelangelo, commissioned to limn the ceiling of the Sistine Chapel while "sparring" with "foil" Pope Julius (the "excellent" Harrison); "good storytelling" makes for an "unparalleled study of the artistic process", even if a few philistines agonize "could this movie be any longer?"

Aguirre: The Wrath of God 🄵

25 | 25 | 23 | 25

1977 | Directed by Werner Herzog | With Klaus Kinski, Helena Rojo | 100 minutes | Not Rated

"Shot on a small budget under unbelievable conditions", this "staggering" saga of 16th-century Spaniards seeking El Dorado by crossing the Andes and then descending the Amazon stars Kinski as a "hopelessly mad" "megalomaniac conquistador"; the film's "hauntingly beautiful" but "static" pacewise , and it's "hard to tell who's more obsessed – the characters in the movie or the director and actors who made it."

A.I.: Artificial Intelligence

16 | 20 | 15 | 23

2001 | Directed by Steven Spielberg | With Haley Joel Osment, Jude Law, Frances O'Connor | 146 minutes | Rated PG-13

"*Pinocchio*" meets "*Blade Runner*" in this tale of a "robot boy who wants to be loved" in a devastated, tech-sprawled future, but the scenario is a "strange mélange", one part Stanley Kubrick's "brooding" vision (he first optioned the story), one part Spielberg's "sugar"-coated "sentimentalism"; biggest "downer": that "Amazingly Inept ending."

Air Force One

18 | 19 | 18 | 21

1997 | Directed by Wolfgang Petersen | With Harrison Ford, Gary Oldman, Glenn Close | 124 minutes | Rated R

The "furrowed-browed" Ford plays a "butt-kicking" American president whose plane is hijacked by a "Russian madman" in this "escapist" thriller, a gripping mix of "edge-of-your-recliner suspense" and multi-"million-dollar stunts"; granted, cynics nix its "far-fetched" plot but admit that this piece of "harmless fun" "works best with popcorn" nearby.

☑ Airplane!

24 | 19 | 20 | 19

1980 | Directed by Jim Abrahams, David Zucker, Jerry Zucker | With Robert Hays, Julie Hagerty, Lloyd Bridges, Leslie Nielsen, Peter Graves, Robert Stack | 88 minutes | Rated PG

"Funny as heck", this "laugh-a-second spoof" mocks "'70s-era disaster films" with a "scatter-gag" barrage of "relentless slapstick", "constant plays on words" and the "best appearance by Ethel Merman in decades"; granted, it's "infantile" and some of the humor might be perceived as "politically incorrect" today, but there are so many "one-liners you'll remember years later" – 'don't call me Shirley!' – that it's no surprise this flick "launched a thousand imitators."

Airport
	OVERALL	ACTING	STORY	PROD.
	17	15	18	18

1970 | Directed by George Seaton | With Burt Lancaster, Helen Hayes, Dean Martin, George Kennedy | 137 minutes | Rated G
The "first" and arguably the "best" of the "disaster flick" genre, this "gripping", "old-fashioned" drama unfolds on one particular night when nothing's going right at a major airport; given the "big, lumbering production" with a bevy of nearly "out-of-work actors" spouting "soap opera–city" dialogue, it's become a "guilty pleasure", though in its heyday it inspired "myriad sequels and spoofs."

Akeelah and the Bee
	26	26	25	24

2006 | Directed by Doug Atchison | With Laurence Fishburne, Angela Bassett, Keke Palmer | 112 minutes | Rated PG
"All ages" are "pleasantly surprised" by this "entirely uplifting" drama featuring Palmer's "phenomenal debut" as a single-parent schoolgirl vying for a national spelling-bee title; she "holds her own" in a "feel-good" tale that "makes you want to break out the dictionary", and even if it "pulls your heartstrings blatantly" right up to the "triumphant ending", it's still "compelling" viewing – like *Rocky* for intelligent people."

Akira 🄵
	23	-	21	26

1988 | Directed by Katsuhiro Otomo | Animated | 124 minutes | Rated R
"Defining the anime genre", this "groundbreaking" "classic" "based on the Japanese comic book" is "more violent than it needs to be" and thus "not for younger viewers"; the "confusing" sci-fi plot (something to do with "how power corrupts") might "make you wonder if something was lost in translation", but it's so "visually stunning" you won't care.

Aladdin
	24	-	22	25

1992 | Directed by Ron Clements, John Musker | Animated | 90 minutes | Rated G
Disney's "fast-moving" animated version of the Aladdin story is "stolen" by Robin Williams' "infectiously manic" vocal performance as a "genius" genie; overall, its "likable characters" and "humorous storyline" appeal to both "adults and kids alike", while the "enchanting" Oscar-winning soundtrack will leave you "singing for days."

Alamo, The
	18	18	20	21

1960 | Directed by John Wayne | With John Wayne, Richard Widmark, Laurence Harvey | 167 minutes | Not Rated
A "big-as-Texas" slice of "Americana", this "entertaining" rendition of the Battle of the Alamo still "appeals as a period film", although it strikes some as "overblown", "hokum history" with a "surprisingly boring" Wayne as Davy Crockett; even so, that "slam-bang, operatic finale" "mostly justifies" the "dreary opening hour."

Alexander Nevsky ◐🄵
	26	22	25	26

1938 | Directed by Sergei Eisenstein | With Nikolai Cherkassov | 107 minutes | Not Rated
"Propaganda" was never better than this "exceptional" war epic, made to rally Soviet support for Stalin; shot in "haunting" black-and-

white and set to a "superb Prokofiev score", it recounts the trials and tribulations of a 13th-century Russian prince, and even if the "clanky" script "ultimately collapses under the weight of all the ideological baggage", it's still a "triumph of expressionism" from "genius" director Eisenstein.

Alfie

22 | 26 | 22 | 20

1966 | Directed by Lewis Gilbert | With Michael Caine, Shelley Winters, Vivien Merchant | 114 minutes | Not Rated

This "little charmer" of a drama stars the "phenomenal" Caine in the career-making role of a "philandering playboy who gets his comeuppance" after dalliances with a flock of '60s birds; although it seems "a bit dated" and might be "politically incorrect" today, its "brutally honest" script still "asks the important questions" – and there's an "excellent" Sonny Rollins score as a bonus.

Alice

20 | 23 | 21 | 21

1990 | Directed by Woody Allen | With Mia Farrow, William Hurt, Judy Davis, Joe Mantegna | 102 minutes | Rated PG-13

As usual, the "Manhattan locations play a starring role" in Woody Allen's "modern-day New York version of *Alice in Wonderland*", wherein an uptight Upper East Side matron undergoes a spiritual (and sexual) awakening after ingesting herbal potions; it's among the "least stereotypical" of the director's films, both "funny and touching", if rather "underappreciated."

Alice Doesn't Live Here Anymore ✉

24 | 26 | 23 | 21

1974 | Directed by Martin Scorsese | With Ellen Burstyn, Kris Kristofferson, Jodie Foster | 112 minutes | Rated PG

In this "early Scorsese" drama, Burstyn won an Oscar for her role as a "blue-collar" gal "trying to find herself" after a marriage breakup, and the "poignant", very "real" outcome marked a "watershed" for "feminists" in a "time when men and women were changing their roles."

Alice in Wonderland

24 | - | 25 | 25

1951 | Directed by Clyde Geronimi, Wilfred Jackson, Hamilton Luske | Animated | 75 minutes | Rated G

Disney's wonderfully "wacky" animation transforms Lewis Carroll's children's book into an "intelligent cartoon" rife with "hidden messages" and a slightly "schizophrenic" edge to boot; indeed, "family entertainment" mavens say this "imaginative" production is such a "terrific adaptation" that it "almost makes you forget the classic Tenniel illustrations."

Alien

25 | 22 | 25 | 26

1979 | Directed by Ridley Scott | With Sigourney Weaver, Tom Skerritt, Veronica Cartwright | 117 minutes | Rated R

"Often imitated but never equaled", this "fierce" sci-fi "horror classic" could pass as a "Hitchcock-in-space" thriller thanks to its "jaw-dropping visuals" and "heart-pounding" plot about an outer space "survey team" that inadvertently brings a "new guest" home to dinner; "Weaver rocks" in "macho-man" mode and is only upstaged by the "slimy", "really gross" title character, the "best movie monster this side of Frankenstein."

Aliens
OVERALL 23 **ACTING** 21 **STORY** 22 **PROD.** 26

1986 | Directed by James Cameron | With Sigourney Weaver, Michael Biehn, Bill Paxton | 137 minutes | Rated R

This "second installment" in the *Alien* franchise is just as "scream-out-loud scary" as its predecessor, with a "*Rambo*-esque" emphasis; expect the "same high-quality production values" and "edge-of-your-seat tension", and if there's debate as to whether it "trumps" or "just lives up to" the original, one thing's certain: Weaver is still one "bad-ass" chick.

☑ All About Eve ⊠◑
28 29 27 26

1950 | Directed by Joseph L. Mankiewicz | With Bette Davis, Anne Baxter, Gary Merrill | 138 minutes | Not Rated

"Fasten your seatbelts" – the "ladies lunch on each other" in this "scalding", "wickedly funny" look at the "vicious world of showbiz"; a "boffo" Davis is "electrifying" as the "fading star" (opposite a "strong" Baxter as the rising one), but both are indebted to Mankiewicz's "perfect script", a "catty" catalog of "sharp-tongued dialogue" that "puts today's scenarios to shame"; in sum, this is one of the "best backstage bitchfests of all time."

All About My Mother ⊠🇫
25 26 25 23

1999 | Directed by Pedro Almodóvar | With Cecilia Roth, Penélope Cruz, Marisa Paredes | 101 minutes | Rated R

Though "all the major characters are women", this "captivating story" via Spanish director Almodóvar is definitely "not a chick flick": rather, this "unusual", Oscar-winning drama about a mother searching for her dead son's transsexual dad provides a very "modern definition of what makes a family"; fans single out Roth's "stunning" work and Cruz's "breakout performance" – that is, when they're not "crying their hearts out" or "laughing their heads off."

All Dogs Go to Heaven
17 - 17 18

1989 | Directed by Don Bluth, Gary Goldman, Dan Kuenster | Animated | 89 minutes | Rated G

"Great for toddlers and young children", this "cute" animated flick about a "ghostly canine" sent from heaven to do good on earth might be a "non-Disney film" but still boasts "Disney quality"; surveyors split on the end result: a "listless, uninspired cartoon" vs. a "wonderfully sweet tearjerker."

☑ All Quiet on the Western Front ⊠◑
28 26 28 25

1930 | Directed by Lewis Milestone | With Lew Ayres, Louis Wolheim, Raymond Griffith | 131 minutes | Not Rated

"One of the first anti-war films" (and the "last word" on the subject for many), this "devastating" WWI saga is a "harrowing" glimpse at the "unglorious nature" of battle; over 75 years later, it "still packs a wallop", and though a bit "slow" by modern standards, this "faithful adaptation of the novel" will "stay with you."

All That Jazz
24 23 22 26

1979 | Directed by Bob Fosse | With Roy Scheider, Jessica Lange, Ann Reinking, John Lithgow | 123 minutes | Rated R

A "brilliantly original" "autobiopic" from Bob Fosse about Bob Fosse, this "prescient" drama might be "self-indulgent" and plainly "inspired by 8½", but it's also a "warts-and-all" "character sketch" with, no surprise, "imaginative choreography"; look for a "great star turn" by Scheider and lots of "sardonic" dialogue.

All the King's Men ✉◑

25 | 26 | 25 | 22

1949 | Directed by Robert Rossen | With Broderick Crawford, John Ireland, Mercedes McCambridge | 109 minutes | Not Rated

The "American dream goes sour" in this "classic political drama" adapted from the Pulitzer Prize–winning novel about the rise and fall of a Huey Long–esque politician "corrupted by power"; this Best Picture winner is memorable for its "strong story" – and "even stronger acting by Crawford" (who also won a statuette).

All the President's Men

25 | 26 | 26 | 23

1976 | Directed by Alan J. Pakula | With Robert Redford, Dustin Hoffman, Jason Robards | 138 minutes | Rated PG

"History comes alive" in this "truth-is-stranger-than-fiction" account of the "Watergate" scandal, a "riveting", torn-"from-the-headlines thriller" that "captures you every time" "even though you know the outcome"; as reporters Woodward and Bernstein, Redford and Hoffman are truly "memorable" (ditto those "ties and sideburns"), and in the end this "gripping" effort brings "clarity to the events of that confusing time."

All the Right Moves

16 | 15 | 16 | 15

1983 | Directed by Michael Chapman | With Tom Cruise, Craig T. Nelson, Lea Thompson | 91 minutes | Rated R

"Rookie" Cruise shows his youthful "promise" tackling this "teen drama" about a "rebel football hero" who's determined to escape "small-town life", facing off with "unlikable coach" Nelson and love interest Thompson as he "learns to play by his own rules"; the "predictable formula" leaves many unmoved, but as a flashback to the star's "pre-couch hopping days", it's "ok escapist fare."

Almost Famous ✉

23 | 24 | 24 | 22

2000 | Directed by Cameron Crowe | With Billy Crudup, Frances McDormand, Kate Hudson | 122 minutes | Rated R

"Almost perfect" filmmaking, director Crowe's "feel-good" "semi-autobiographical story" about his work as a "teenage *Rolling Stone* reporter" "on the road with a rock band" is half "coming-of-age" romance, half unadulterated "love song" to the '70s; while Crudup's "underrated" portrayal of a rocker and McDormand's "outstanding" mom earn kudos, "Hudson steals the show" as the "vulnerable groupie."

Along Came a Spider

16 | 20 | 18 | 18

2001 | Directed by Lee Tamahori | With Morgan Freeman, Monica Potter, Michael Wincott | 104 minutes | Rated R

Playing a forensic psychologist trying to rescue a senator's daughter from a psychopathic kidnapper, "Freeman carries" this "better-than-average" thriller adapted from the James Patterson book; but even though this "prequel of sorts to *Kiss the Girls*" is "competent" enough, foes fret it's "pretty predictable", except for that "nice twist at the end."

Altered States

19 | 20 | 20 | 20

1980 | Directed by Ken Russell | With William Hurt, Blair Brown, Bob Balaban | 102 minutes | Rated R

"Sometimes you don't know which end is up" in this "mind-bending" sci-fi "journey" starring Hurt as a scientist experimenting with sensory

	OVERALL	ACTING	STORY	PROD.

deprivation via an isolation chamber and select hallucinogens; although the "trippy" visuals and "convoluted" plot were considered "shocking" at the time, it may now look "like a relic from another era."

☑ Amadeus ✉   26 | 27 | 25 | 27

1984 | Directed by Milos Forman | With F. Murray Abraham, Tom Hulce, Elizabeth Berridge | 158 minutes | Rated PG

"Genius thwarted by mediocrity" is the theme of this "lively" Mozart biopic that's admittedly "not historically accurate", given its depiction of the "tortured" composer as something of a cross between a "twerp" and a "rock god"; awash in "lush period details", "timeless music" and "surprisingly nuanced performances" by Abraham and Hulce, it even manages to "make classical music seem racy" – and was quite the Oscar magnet, taking home eight of them.

Amarcord ✉🅵   26 | 25 | 25 | 26

1975 | Directed by Federico Fellini | With Magali Noël, Bruno Zanin, Pupella Maggio | 127 minutes | Rated R

"Fellini's warmhearted look back to his childhood", this Foreign Language Oscar winner is a "wonderful depiction" of "small-town life" in 1930s "fascist Italy", an "evocative" film that's simultaneously "lyric, tragic, vulgar and comic"; fans say this "beautiful reminiscence" reveals the famed director "at his most accessible" – and most "surreal."

Amélie 🅵   26 | 26 | 24 | 25

2001 | Directed by Jean-Pierre Jeunet | With Audrey Tautou, Mathieu Kassovitz | 122 minutes | Rated R

"Sweet as sucre", this "candy-coated" "picture postcard" of a romance concerns a "modern-day Pollyanna from Montmartre" "who wants to fix everyone's life" to make up for "what's missing in hers"; in the title role, a "new star has arrived" in "gamine" Tautou, a "21st-century Audrey Hepburn" whose "doe-eyed", "cute-as-a-button" looks alone will "put a huge grin on your face"; indeed, this "brimming-with-goodwill" picture is so "magical", you'll "hardly notice the subtitles."

☑ American Beauty ✉   24 | 27 | 23 | 24

1999 | Directed by Sam Mendes | With Kevin Spacey, Annette Bening, Wes Bentley, Thora Birch | 121 minutes | Rated R

The "desperation of modern suburban life" is the theme of this "engrossing" Best Picture winner that polarizes viewers: fans hail this tale of a man's "midlife awakening" and "resurrection" as a "truthful commentary on American society", but thornier types fuss it's a "pretentious", "angry" tract "disguised as existentialist philosophy"; nonetheless, there are plenty of bouquets for Spacey's "dead-on" performance and Alan Ball's "seriously meaty", "rapierlike screenplay."

American Gigolo   19 | 19 | 18 | 19

1980 | Directed by Paul Schrader | With Richard Gere, Lauren Hutton, Nina Van Pallandt | 117 minutes | Rated R

The "eye candy can't be beat" in this "stylish" (albeit "so '80s") drama about a "cool-drink-of-water" callboy – the "first true metrosexual" – who's suspected of murder; it was "Gere's breakout part", though some say he's upstaged by his "Giorgio Armani" duds and that "cool" Giorgio Moroder soundtrack.

| | OVERALL | ACTING | STORY | PROD. |

American Graffiti
24 | 23 | 23 | 23

1973 | Directed by George Lucas | With Richard Dreyfuss, Ron Howard, Cindy Williams | 110 minutes | Rated PG

"Spot future stars" (including an early Harrison Ford) in this "end-of-an-era" dramedy that "launched a dozen careers" and proves that "Lucas once directed actors, not just pixels"; "covering one night" in 1962 – "but what a night" – it "captures a time and place" in teenage, West Coast America by mixing "cool cars", "period jukebox hits" and "Wolfman Jack" into a "classic growing-up story" that really "makes nostalgia compelling."

American History X
25 | 28 | 24 | 23

1998 | Directed by Tony Kaye | With Edward Norton, Edward Furlong, Beverly D'Angelo | 119 minutes | Rated R

"Neo-Nazi violence" and "racism" lie at the heart of this "scalding" drama about "white supremacists" that's "like a punch in the gut" thanks to the "gifted" Norton's "all-too-convincing" portrait of a "scary" "skinhead"; though surely "horrifying", this "powerful" film will also "make you think."

American in Paris, An ✉
26 | 23 | 22 | 27

1951 | Directed by Vincente Minnelli | With Gene Kelly, Leslie Caron, Oscar Levant | 113 minutes | Not Rated

A "debonair" Kelly and "beautiful Caron" "dance up a storm" in this "unforgettable" Gershwin musical that might tempt you to "visit Paris"; sure, the "silly story" is a bit "hackneyed", but "who cares?" when the production's so "visually compelling" (especially that climactic ballet "integrating Impressionist art" in its settings); no surprise, it took home six Oscars, including Best Picture.

Americanization of Emily, The ◑
24 | 24 | 22 | 21

1964 | Directed by Arthur Hiller | With James Garner, Julie Andrews, James Coburn, Melvyn Douglas | 115 minutes | Not Rated

"Considered controversial in its day", this "powerful anti-war" film tells the story of a "cynical" American naval officer scheming to avoid duty in the D-day invasion while romancing a priggish English lass; Andrews is "quite good" in her "first role to depart from her sweet image", though Paddy Chayefsky's screenplay gets mixed notices: "literate" vs. "preachy."

American Pie
19 | 16 | 18 | 18

1999 | Directed by Paul Weitz | With Jason Biggs, Shannon Elizabeth, Tara Reid | 95 minutes | Rated R

"You'll never look at an apple pie the same way" after a gander at this "drop-dead funny" slice of "raunch" about some teenage dudes, "hormones a-raging", who "vow to lose their virginity on prom night"; while bluenoses berate its "toilet humor" as "moronic", "baked-goods" buyers say its "laugh-a-minute" plot is an "intelligent gross-out", the "Gen-X" version of *Porky's.*

American President, The
21 | 22 | 21 | 21

1995 | Directed by Rob Reiner | With Michael Douglas, Annette Bening, Martin Sheen | 114 minutes | Rated PG-13

"Only in Hollywood" could the "President openly date a lobbyist", but no one "believes it for a second – or cares" – since this "feel-good" romance is so darned "entertaining"; voters like Douglas' "humanized" Chief Exec and Bening's "luminous" gal pal but reject the "rose-colored" script and its "telegraphed happy ending", sighing "pass the popcorn."

American Psycho | 19 | 22 | 18 | 19 |

2000 | Directed by Mary Harron | With Christian Bale, Chloë Sevigny, Willem Dafoe, Reese Witherspoon | 101 minutes | Rated R
Dark comedies don't get much more "pitch black" than this stylishly "freaky" look at a "yuppie psychopath" whose "decadent '80s lifestyle", "status worship" and "serial killing" is alternately "sick, disturbing and hilarious"; Bale is "to die for", the soundtrack's "killer" and the "witty" script still manages to conjure up the "heebie-jeebies" – even if the violence is "rather bland compared to the book."

American Splendor | 23 | 25 | 22 | 22 |

2003 | Directed by Shari Springer Berman, Robert Pulcini | With Paul Giamatti, Hope Davis, Harvey Pekar | 101 minutes | Rated R
An "average slob" gets the big-screen treatment in this "subversive" biopic of underground comics scribe Harvey Pekar, a "schlubby" "anti-hero"; deftly employing "three parallel realities" – "actors, cartoons" and Harvey himself – to tell its story, this "offbeat" picture is nothing if not "original", though some feel it "falls short of its potential" and wonder "what does it amount to in the end?"

American Tail, An | 21 | - | 21 | 22 |

1986 | Directed by Don Bluth | Animated | 77 minutes | Rated G
"One of the first good non-Disney" pieces of animation, this "wonderful" "story of the immigrant experience" follows the adventures of a Russian mouse separated from his kin after arriving in America; a "family favorite", its "clever" concept with a "touch of pathos" makes "hearts melt."

American Werewolf in London, An | 20 | 17 | 21 | 21 |

1981 | Directed by John Landis | With David Naughton, Jenny Agutter, Griffin Dunne | 97 minutes | Rated R
"Filmed with style and wit", this "tragicomic gorefest" "shows some bite" as it follows the misadventures of two American "zombies" abroad; best remembered for its "transformation scene" combining "superior makeup" and "amazing special effects" – and second-best known for Agutter's "hot shower scene" – this one's so "suspenseful and creepy" that it "helped revitalize the horror genre" in the early '80s.

Amistad | 21 | 24 | 22 | 24 |

1997 | Directed by Steven Spielberg | With Morgan Freeman, Djimon Hounsou, Matthew McConaughey | 152 minutes | Rated R
Examining the "dark underside of American history", this "little-known" true story of 19th-century "Africans forced into slavery" "starts on a slave ship and culminates in court"; while some say this "gripping", "difficult" story is an "underappreciated" Spielberg opus, others find it so "heavy-handed" and "manipulative" that they're left "out to sea."

Analyze That | 14 | 17 | 12 | 15 |

2002 | Directed by Harold Ramis | With Robert De Niro, Billy Crystal, Lisa Kudrow, Joe Viterelli, Cathy Moriarty | 96 minutes | Rated R
That the "novelty" of mobsters in therapy is "worn out beyond belief" doesn't stop Billy and Bobby from reuniting for this "lame" sequel to

Analyze This, a "profanity"-fest with "few laughs" fashioned from a "one-joke concept"; in the final analysis, most shrink from recommending this "disappointment", saying they'd rather "sleep with the fishes."

Analyze This
| | 18 | 21 | 18 | 18 |

1999 | Directed by Harold Ramis | With Robert De Niro, Billy Crystal, Lisa Kudrow, Chazz Palminteri | 103 minutes | Rated R
"*Sopranos*" nuts see some familiar plot threads in this "funny Mafia movie" featuring the "hilarious pairing" of "De Niro as a mobster with anxiety attacks" and Crystal as his reluctant shrink; though some analysts shrug it off as a "flat" "trifle", supporters call it an "amusing send-up" that may be "ridiculous, but it works."

Anastasia ✉
| | 23 | 27 | 24 | 23 |

1956 | Directed by Anatole Litvak | With Ingrid Bergman, Yul Brynner, Helen Hayes | 105 minutes | Not Rated
The Oscar-winning, ever "appealing" Bergman and a "great" Brynner make quite a "combo" in this dramatic biography of Anastasia, the legendary daughter of the last Russian czar and pretender to the throne – or is she?; told with "sympathy and empathy", it's a "cuddle-up-with-your-honey" picture with acting "so good you find yourself rooting for those inept royals"; "is it true?" – c'mon, "does it matter?"

Anastasia
| | 20 | – | 19 | 22 |

1997 | Directed by Don Bluth, Gary Goldman | Animated | 94 minutes | Rated G
"Disney isn't the only one" making "amazing animation" these days: this cartoon version of a lost (and found) Russian princess is an "astonishingly good feature", although it "doesn't seem to be kid material"; still, it's a "visually appealing" extravaganza oozing "style", even if the "bat steals the show."

Anatomy of a Murder ◑
| | 26 | 27 | 27 | 24 |

1959 | Directed by Otto Preminger | With James Stewart, Lee Remick, Ben Gazzara | 160 minutes | Not Rated
Stewart "pulls out all the stops" as a "down-to-earth" lawyer in this courtroom drama that's a "spellbinding" look at a "sensational" "backwoods" revenge killing; "considered risqué" in the '50s given Remick's "sultry" turn and its use of the then-verboten word "'panties'", it remains as "riveting" as ever; P.S. "Duke Ellington and his band" lay down the cool progressive jazz soundtrack.

Andromeda Strain, The
| | 20 | 18 | 25 | 20 |

1971 | Directed by Robert Wise | With Arthur Hill, David Wayne, James Olson, Kate Reid | 131 minutes | Rated G
"Science provides the thrills" in this piece of "thinking man's sci-fi" based on the early "Michael Crichton thriller" concerning a "dangerous" virus from outer space; though it may be "low-tech" (with "out-of-date special effects" and "sprayed-on perspiration"), it supplies enough "palpable tension" to keep things "interesting."

Angels with Dirty Faces ◑
| | 24 | 24 | 22 | 20 |

1938 | Directed by Michael Curtiz | With James Cagney, Pat O'Brien, Humphrey Bogart | 97 minutes | Not Rated
Two toughs from the slums take different career paths – one becoming a "lowlife", the other a priest – in this "cautionary melodrama" from

the days when "good was good and bad was bad"; "cliché-ridden" though it may be, it was designed to "scare the bejesus out of would-be delinquents" – or at least have them "doing Cagney impersonations for weeks" afterward.

Anger Management
13 | 18 | 13 | 16

2003 | Directed by Peter Segal | With Adam Sandler, Jack Nicholson, Marisa Tomei | 106 minutes | Rated PG-13

The "unlikely" pairing of "silly" Sandler with "versatile" Nicholson as patient and therapist is a "cute idea gone awry" in this "disappointing" comedy flush with "juvenile bathroom humor"; when cooler heads prevail, primary blame goes to the "ridiculous premise", an "incoherent" affair which neither "great cameos" (Heather Graham, Woody Harrelson) nor a "surprise ending" can temper.

Animal Crackers ◑
26 | 24 | 18 | 20

1930 | Directed by Victor Heerman | With the Marx Brothers, Lillian Roth, Margaret Dumont | 97 minutes | Rated G

"Hooray for Captain Spaulding!"; this "timeless" Marx Brothers "romp" is best remembered for Groucho's "priceless entrance" and "fabulously stupid" quips ("I shot an elephant in my pajamas, but how he got in my pajamas, I'll never know"); needless to say, the "storyline isn't the point" here, but the "zany" pace doesn't leave time for logic anyway.

☑ Animal House
24 | 20 | 21 | 20

1978 | Directed by John Landis | With John Belushi, Tim Matheson, Tom Hulce, John Vernon | 109 minutes | Rated R

"Raunchy and vulgar", this much-admired "granddaddy of the frat boy gross-out comedies" features the much-"missed" Belushi "at his side-splitting best" as Bluto Blutarsky, a "seven-year college" vet; "no, it ain't Shakespeare", but rather a "textbook" study of "toga parties", "road trips", "food fights" and "anarchic libidos on parade" that's so much of a "guy's movie" that some fellas say they "thought it was a documentary."

Anna and the King
19 | 21 | 21 | 24

1999 | Directed by Andy Tennant | With Jodie Foster, Chow Yun-Fat, Tom Felton | 148 minutes | Rated PG-13

Take a "trip to Thailand" via this "touching" romance that's a "nonmusical rendition" of The King and I, based on the true story of Brit school teacher Anna Leonowens; though "slow" pacing and the "absence of chemistry" between Foster and Yun-Fat leave things "rather flat", at least this "lush" production ("magnificent scenery", "elaborate costumes") is "gorgeous to look at."

Anna Christie ◑
▽ 26 | 27 | 24 | 23

1930 | Directed by Clarence Brown | With Greta Garbo, Charles Bickford, Marie Dressler | 89 minutes | Not Rated

The "amazing Garbo" is in "fabulous voice" for her talking pictures "breakout", this adaptation of Eugene O'Neill's "deep" drama about a hard-luck Swedish lass whose connections to her father and sweetheart are haunted by her "waterfront hooker" past; it's "definitely a classic" that "leaves an impact", and just beholding Greta at her "peak" is "reason enough to watch."

Anna Karenina ☽
26 | 26 | 26 | 25

1935 | Directed by Clarence Brown | With Greta Garbo, Fredric March, Freddie Bartholomew | 95 minutes | Not Rated

"Let's hear it for Tolstoy", whose "huge novel" gets a "brilliant" celluloid spin in this romance of "choices and consequences", starring "Garbo at her best" as the restless Russian who trades mundane wedlock with husband Rathbone for notoriety with the "marvelous" March; classicists insist it's a "moving" ride "from the second it starts" to the climactic encounter between Anna and "the train."

Anne of the Thousand Days
26 | 27 | 26 | 26

1969 | Directed by Charles Jarrott | With Richard Burton, Geneviève Bujold, Irene Papas | 145 minutes | Rated PG-13

"History buffs" and "Anglophiles" like this "top-notch" period drama, a "powerful" recounting of "Henry VIII's inability to commit", featuring "brilliant" work by Burton as the "boorish" king and Bujold as the "sensuous Anne Boleyn"; the "beautiful production" is alternately "transporting" and "heart-wrenching", while the Oscar-winning "costumes alone are worth the watch."

Annie
19 | 19 | 20 | 20

1982 | Directed by John Huston | With Albert Finney, Carol Burnett, Aileen Quinn, Tim Curry | 126 minutes | Rated PG

Little Orphan Annie's "rags-to-riches" saga morphs into a "colorful" "children's musical" with a "splendid cast" in this "stylized" "adaptation of the comic strip" that first bowed on Broadway; parents say it's "perfect for kids", and even those who find it "bloated" and "boring" find themselves leaving the theater humming 'Tomorrow.'

☒ Annie Hall ✉
27 | 26 | 25 | 24

1977 | Directed by Woody Allen | With Woody Allen, Diane Keaton, Tony Roberts | 93 minutes | Rated PG

"Every neurotic's favorite comedy", this Oscar-winning Allen film about an "insecure" "Jewish nebbish" smitten with a nutty, "la-di-da"-spouting "shiksa" is "among his deftest creations"; its "pitch-perfect NY" setting, "pure-genius script" and "very funny" set pieces (the "lobster-cooking episode", the "split-screen family dinner scene") make for "essential Woody."

Anniversary Party, The
18 | 23 | 17 | 17

2001 | Directed by Alan Cumming, Jennifer Jason Leigh | With Alan Cumming, Jennifer Jason Leigh, Phoebe Cates, Kevin Kline, Jennifer Beals, Gwyneth Paltrow | 115 minutes | Rated R

"Hollywood shallowness" gets the "cinema verité" treatment in this "dark", "low-budget" tale of a "dysfunctional" writer and actress celebrating their wedding anniversary with various friends and hangers-on; party-poopers don't dig the "unsympathetic" characters and all that "talk, talk, talk", but others relish the "smart" skewering of "Southern California culture" by the "engrossing" ensemble cast.

Antonia's Line ✉🄵
25 | 26 | 25 | 24

1995 | Directed by Marleen Gorris | With Willeke van Ammelrooy, Els Dottermans | 102 minutes | Rated R

"About women and for women", this "liberating" drama recounts 50 years in one lady's life, told in "flashback" from her "death bed";

"shockingly feminist" to chauvinists, its "charming performances" and "empowering message" are so "unforgettable" that it more than "deserves the Best Foreign Film Oscar" it received.

Antwone Fisher | 23 | 26 | 24 | 22 |

2002 | Directed by Denzel Washington | With Derek Luke, Denzel Washington, Joy Bryant | 120 minutes | Rated PG-13

"Buy a box of tissues before you rent" this "inspiring true-life story about a boy from the 'hood who makes something of himself despite many obstacles"; this "emotional roller coaster" is "wonderfully acted" and represents a "terrific directorial debut by Denzel", who "manages to bring realism to what could have been a manipulative storyline."

Antz | 20 | - | 19 | 23 |

1998 | Directed by Eric Darnell, Tim Johnson | Animated | 87 minutes | Rated PG

Opinion splitz on this fully computer-animated feature about an insect's "rebellion" against conformity; fans buzz that this "highly creative" film "for all ages" tells a "well-executed" story, yet drones swat it for "ugly animation" and a "subversive socialist subtext" that's "not recommended" for "younger children"; P.S. Woody Allen's voice-over as a "neurotic ant is a must-hear."

Apartment, The ✉◐ | 25 | 28 | 25 | 23 |

1960 | Directed by Billy Wilder | With Jack Lemmon, Shirley MacLaine, Fred MacMurray | 125 minutes | Not Rated

"Sex in the big, bad city" has never been as "realistic" or "touching" as in this "sad-edged romance" set in '60s Manhattan, recounting the exploits of a "hapless" "junior executive in love with his boss' mistress"; it pits a "baby-faced" Lemmon opposite a "tender" MacLaine and "understated" MacMurray, and besides being "very amusing" (and a Best Picture Oscar winner), it's also a "powerful social comment masquerading as comedy."

⚡ Apocalypse Now | 27 | 27 | 25 | 28 |

1979 | Directed by Francis Ford Coppola | With Martin Sheen, Marlon Brando, Robert Duvall | 153 minutes | Rated R

The "Vietnam nightmare" meets Joseph "Conrad's *Heart of Darkness*" in this "landmark" Coppola opus that's one part "gut churner", one part "acid trip" as it examines the "insanity of war"; true, it's "long", the "last half hour is disappointing" and many wonder "what the heck Brando's saying", but ultimately this "sprawling" "meditation on the human mind" just plain "grabs you"; P.S. the expanded version (*Apocalypse Now Redux*) divides voters.

Apollo 13 | 24 | 24 | 25 | 26 |

1995 | Directed by Ron Howard | With Tom Hanks, Bill Paxton, Kevin Bacon, Gary Sinise | 140 minutes | Rated PG

"Even though you [presumably] know the outcome", this "space race" drama based on the "remarkable true story" of the "perilous voyage of Apollo 13" stays "suspenseful"; with a roster of "big-name actors" exuding the "right stuff", it delivers "get-up-and-cheer escapism" that might be "a tad corny" but will "make you proud to be an American" – "isn't history wonderful?"

| | OVERALL | ACTING | STORY | PROD. |

Apprenticeship of Duddy Kravitz, The — 22 | 24 | 24 | 20

1974 | Directed by Ted Kotcheff | With Richard Dreyfuss, Micheline Lanctôt, Jack Warden | 120 minutes | Rated PG

A "nice Jewish boy in Montreal comes of age" and tries to ascend the "slippery slope of success" in this "little-known comic gem" "tinged with sadness"; a "moving" adaptation of Mordecai Richler's novel, it's a "genius" "showcase for Dreyfuss" as the titular "hustling" "mensch."

Armageddon — 15 | 14 | 14 | 21

1998 | Directed by Michael Bay | With Bruce Willis, Billy Bob Thornton, Ben Affleck, Liv Tyler | 144 minutes | Rated PG-13

An "asteroid hurtles toward the earth" in this "high testosterone" "explosionfest" with a "far-fetched" "patriotic story" involving a "*Dirty Dozen*-style space mission" and "tongue-in-cheek heroics"; foes say this "blockbuster" is "all budget and no brain" with "state-of-the-art special effects as the real star of the film."

Around the World in 80 Days ✉ — 22 | 20 | 22 | 25

1956 | Directed by Michael Anderson | With David Niven, Cantinflas, Shirley MacLaine | 175 minutes | Rated G

"It's the scenery, stupid" that makes this globe-trotting "epic" "travelogue" based on "Jules Verne's classic book" "worth watching", though lots of "stars popping up in cameo roles" add to the "visual cornucopia"; however, some find it a "boring", "three-hour ride" and "can't believe" it snagged a Best Picture Oscar.

Arsenic and Old Lace ◑ — 26 | 26 | 25 | 22

1944 | Directed by Frank Capra | With Cary Grant, Priscilla Lane, Raymond Massey | 118 minutes | Not Rated

"Elderberry wine" makes for "murderous fun" in this "macabre" black comedy about two "vengeful old ladies" killing off bachelors while "chewing the scenery"; as their nephew, a "frantic" Grant "hams it up unashamedly" and delivers the "world's best double takes" in this "funny" adaptation of the Broadway hit.

Arthur — 20 | 21 | 19 | 19

1981 | Directed by Steve Gordon | With Dudley Moore, Liza Minnelli, John Gielgud | 117 minutes | Rated PG

There's "not a dull moment" in this "silly" yet "tender" romantic comedy about a "falling-down-drunk" millionaire looking for love; although top billing goes to "sexy short guy" Dudley Moore opposite "Liza Minnelli as Liza Minnelli", this "priceless" picture arguably belongs to Gielgud, who delivers its most "classic line" – "I'll alert the media" – "as if he were playing Hamlet."

☒ As Good As It Gets ✉ — 22 | 25 | 21 | 21

1997 | Directed by James L. Brooks | With Jack Nicholson, Helen Hunt, Greg Kinnear | 139 minutes | Rated PG-13

Fans feel the "title says it all": this "smart comedy" about the "unlikely pairing" of a "cantankerous" "obsessive-compulsive jerk" and a "kooky" "single-mom waitress" crackles with "sharp", "NY neurotic" dialogue; but even though both Hunt and Nicholson grabbed Oscars for their "tour-de-force" turns, some shrug they "play themselves" in this "overhyped" and "overrated" flick.

	OVERALL	ACTING	STORY	PROD.

Asphalt Jungle, The ❶ — 24 | 24 | 24 | 23

1950 | Directed by John Huston | With Sterling Hayden, Louis Calhern, Sam Jaffe | 112 minutes | Not Rated

Sure, this "prime example of juicy film noir" is one of the "original caper" pictures, about a "carefully planned" "jewel heist gone terribly wrong", but it's also appealing for an "early" turn by Marilyn Monroe in a "blow-you-away" bit part; otherwise, this "dark tale" of "greed" and "emotion" supplies enough "twists and compelling characters" to make it "one of Huston's most underrated films."

Atlantic City — 24 | 27 | 22 | 22

1980 | Directed by Louis Malle | With Burt Lancaster, Susan Sarandon, Kate Reid | 104 minutes | Rated R

This "valentine to a lost city" pairs a "stunning" Lancaster and Sarandon as unlikely lovers "trying to redeem their lives" in the "bleak atmosphere" of a "dying town"; "sad, bittersweet" and "overlooked", it boasts a "superb" John Guare script full of "characters worth caring about" but is most remembered for the scene of "our heroine bathing herself with sliced lemons."

Atlantis: The Lost Empire — 16 | - | 14 | 21

2001 | Directed by Gary Trousdale, Kirk Wise | Animated | 95 minutes | Rated PG

Centering on the search for the "legendary" sunken civilization, this "sophisticated action" flick is a Disney production featuring elements of "Jules Verne" and "Japanese anime" but no "song-and-dance numbers" or cute talking animals; though its blend of traditional and CGI animation is "visually stunning", some say the story's "subpar" and a bit "too violent for minors."

Auntie Mame — 25 | 25 | 24 | 25

1958 | Directed by Morton DaCosta | With Rosalind Russell, Forrest Tucker, Coral Browne | 143 minutes | Not Rated

"Defining diva-dom for generations", this "stylish" comedy about a wide-eyed kid's "wacky rich" auntie stars a "larger-than-life Russell" as a "great old broad"-cum-"force of nature"; it might be "overlong and underplotted", but "great one-liners" barbed with "sharp wit" ("life is a banquet and most poor suckers are starving to death") assure its rep as the "campiest of camp classics."

Au Revoir Les Enfants ⒡ — 27 | 26 | 27 | 24

1987 | Directed by Louis Malle | With Gaspard Manesse, Francine Racette | 104 minutes | Rated PG

"Powerful and haunting", this "must-see" drama explores "anti-Semitism" in WWII "occupied France" via its depiction of a "Jewish boy hidden" in a French school; though there's certainly "no happy ending" here, it "brings the events of the Holocaust to a personal level" so devastatingly that you'll "never forget" it.

Austin Powers: International Man of Mystery — 19 | 18 | 17 | 19

1997 | Directed by Jay Roach | With Mike Myers, Elizabeth Hurley, Michael York | 90 minutes | Rated PG-13

"No-brainer" alert: this "shagadelic" "spoof of James Bond movies" delivers "tons of laughs" with "dumb" jokes and overall "retro '60s silliness" – "oh, behave!" – courtesy of "comic genius" Myers in a dual role as a spy with "mossy teeth" and a villain with a pet pussycat; there's debate over its "crude" "toilet humor" but wide agreement that you needn't "bother with the sequel."

Auto Focus 16 | 22 | 17 | 18

2002 | Directed by Paul Schrader | With Greg Kinnear, Willem Dafoe, Rita Wilson, Maria Bello | 105 minutes | Rated R
The "rise and fall" of "sick puppy" sitcom star Bob Crane is charted in this "raw" look at a "mid-level actor turned sex addict" and his enabler buddy; even though Kinnear and Dafoe are "suitably creepy" as "partners in grime", straitlaced surveyors find it "hard to empathize with the characters and their obsessions" and feel the film is "devoid of any uplifting moments" – it's "like watching a train wreck."

Avalon 24 | 25 | 24 | 23

1990 | Directed by Barry Levinson | With Aidan Quinn, Elizabeth Perkins, Armin Mueller-Stahl | 126 minutes | Rated PG
"Touching" and "oh-so-true", this third installment of director Levinson's "semi-autobiographical" "homage to the immigrant experience" (and "growing up in Baltimore") follows a "bravura cast" across several generations; the "wistful humor" and "nostalgic" sense of time and place make for a "rare" dose of "heartfelt" entertainment, best summed up by its most renowned line: "why did you cut the turkey?"

Aviator, The 23 | 25 | 22 | 27

2004 | Directed by Martin Scorsese | With Leonardo DiCaprio, Cate Blanchett, Kate Beckinsale, John C. Reilly | 170 minutes | Rated PG-13
Martin Scorsese takes off with a "bottomless budget" in this "sweeping" biopic of "eccentric" gazillionaire Howard Hughes, where the lift-off is supplied by "sumptuous" production design (including one of the "most realistic plane crashes" ever filmed) and Cate Blanchett's "dead-on", Oscar-grabbing take on Kate Hepburn; more debatable is Leo's title turn ("formidable" or "hollow"), though most agree on the "too-long" running time and "soulless", "conventional" windup.

Awakenings 22 | 26 | 23 | 20

1990 | Directed by Penny Marshall | With Robert De Niro, Robin Williams, John Heard | 121 minutes | Rated PG-13
A true story about the search for a "cure for comatose patients" gets "thought-provoking" treatment in this "touching" drama, featuring Williams "playing it straight" for a change opposite a "memorable" De Niro; while some berate its "sentimental", "hanky-wringing" edge, most find it both "amusing and moving", despite the "potentially mawkish" subject matter.

Awful Truth, The ✉◐ 25 | 26 | 24 | 23

1937 | Directed by Leo McCarey | With Irene Dunne, Cary Grant, Ralph Bellamy, Alexander D'Arcy | 91 minutes | Not Rated
"Two spoiled rich people" on the verge of divorce try to "win each other back" in this "laugh-out-loud" romantic comedy top-billing the "classic combo" of Grant and Dunne; it's "one of the better screwball" pictures "from the golden age of Hollywood" with enough "crackling dialogue" and sheer "fun" to leave nostalgics sighing "they don't make 'em like this anymore."

| | OVERALL | ACTING | STORY | PROD. |

Babe
25 | 22 | 25 | 26

1995 | Directed by Chris Noonan | With James Cromwell, Magda Szubanski, Danny Mann | 89 minutes | Rated G

"Believe the hype": fans are in "hog heaven" over this "porcine" comedy about a "talking pig" who "wants to be a sheepherder so he won't get eaten"; "cute without being cutesy", it features Oscar-winning "computer effects" that allow "animals to interact" with humans so realistically that it may "turn you into a vegetarian."

Babel 🄵
22 | 25 | 21 | 24

2006 | Directed by Alejandro González Iñárritu | With Brad Pitt, Cate Blanchett, Adriana Barraza, Rinko Kikuchi | 143 minutes | Rated R

Sort of an "international version of *Crash*", this "tapestry" of "cleverly intertwined" tales makes you "ponder life" as it leaps across continents to prove "we're connected to people we don't know" and to lament the "barriers between cultures"; Pitt and crew are "uniformly excellent", but some find it too "confusing" and "not as good as critics want you to think."

Babette's Feast ✉🄵
26 | 26 | 26 | 25

1987 | Directed by Gabriel Axel | With Stéphane Audran, Bibi Andersson, Jarl Kulle | 102 minutes | Rated G

"Sumptuous enough to make vegetarians drool" (though "slow as molasses"), this "classic foodie" dramedy is an "unusual" tale based on the Isak Dinesen story about the "power of redemption" cooked up in one "magnificent meal"; "still mouthwatering after all these years", this "intriguing" Danish treat is so "delectable" and "savory" that it could be the "Zagat signature movie."

Baby Boom
19 | 20 | 20 | 18

1987 | Directed by Charles Shyer | With Diane Keaton, Sam Shepard, Harold Ramis | 103 minutes | Rated PG

"Career vs. home and family" is the theme of this "very '80s" "light comedy" starring a "sharp, understated" Keaton as a driven "woman who wants it all" – and gets it when she inherits a baby and hooks up with dreamboat Shepard; though tough guys dismiss it as a "feel-good chick flick", "warm-and-fuzzy" folk find it a "likable" tale of "triumphant romance."

Baby Doll ⓞ
20 | 23 | 19 | 20

1956 | Directed by Elia Kazan | With Carroll Baker, Karl Malden, Eli Wallach, Mildred Dunnock | 114 minutes | Not Rated

"One of the steamier movies of the '50s" (and "still racy" today), this "darkly amusing" "cult classic" via Tennessee Williams revolves around the misfortunes of a frustrated Southerner whose "19-year-old bride won't let him touch her until she turns 20"; Baker's "Lolita"-esque title turn "riled the Legion of Decency" at the time, particularly that scene of her "curled up in a crib, sucking her thumb."

Backdraft
18 | 18 | 18 | 23

1991 | Directed by Ron Howard | With Kurt Russell, William Baldwin, Scott Glenn, Robert De Niro | 132 minutes | Rated R

"Big fires and cute firemen" sum up the appeal of this disaster thriller aflame with a "stellar cast" and some mighty "eye-opening", "amazingly realistic" special effects; ok, the "melodramatic storyline's a bit soft" and the actors struggle with the "moronic dialogue", but the action sequences will "keep you hanging on until the end."

Back to the Future
23 | 20 | 25 | 24

1985 | Directed by Robert Zemeckis | With Michael J. Fox, Christopher Lloyd, Lea Thompson | 111 minutes | Rated PG

A "time-traveling DeLorean" propels the "delectably dimpled Fox" into a "fun ride to the past" (and the chance to observe his parents as "goofy teenagers") in this "perfect blend of sci-fi, fantasy and pop culture"; "irrepressibly entertaining" and very popular, it spawned an "incredible ride" at the Universal theme park as well as two "terrible sequels."

Bad and the Beautiful, The ✉️◗
24 | 25 | 24 | 24

1952 | Directed by Vincente Minnelli | With Lana Turner, Kirk Douglas, Walter Pidgeon, Dick Powell | 118 minutes | Not Rated

Douglas is at his "jaw-clenching best" playing a "manipulative producer" in this knowing, "behind-the-scenes" look at Tinseltown that could be "Hollywood's best movie about itself"; told in a series of flashbacks by a director, an actress and a screenwriter, it's "lush, hammy" stuff that's "over the top in just the right way"; P.S. "never loan Lana Turner your car."

Bad Day at Black Rock
24 | 28 | 24 | 22

1955 | Directed by John Sturges | With Spencer Tracy, Robert Ryan, Anne Francis | 81 minutes | Not Rated

This "taut little thriller" is "mean, lean" moviemaking about "bigotry and intolerance" in a "small town with a secret", starring an "excellent" Tracy in "one of his more unusual roles"; although somewhat "forgotten" today, it's "just as relevant as it was in the post-McCarthy '50s", "giving you plenty to think about" as it "profiles American prejudices."

Bad Education 🅵
23 | 26 | 23 | 24

2004 | Directed by Pedro Almodóvar | With Gael García Bernal, Fele Martínez, Daniel Giménez Cacho | 106 minutes | Rated R

"Bad boy" director Almodóvar proves he's at the "head of the class" with this "visually hypnotic", "gender-bending" mystery that pays homage to both "film noir" and "Hitchcock"; boasting a "bravura" performance by rising star Bernal (who's just as "sexy in drag"), this "out-there" flick is rife with "racy", "taboo"-smashing material (e.g. "drugs", "transvestites", "priest abuse") and "not for the easily offended."

Badlands
25 | 27 | 24 | 24

1973 | Directed by Terrence Malick | With Martin Sheen, Sissy Spacek, Warren Oates | 95 minutes | Rated PG

The "banality of evil" is dissected in this "dark, disturbing" depiction of a true-life teen crime spree; playing "shallow", "disaffected" lovers on the run, a "very young" Spacek and Sheen are "first rate", while Malick's "trademark sweeping cinematography" acts as "visually stunning" counterpoint to the "bitingly tragic" story; in short, it's "gutsy", "twisted" and "not nearly as well known as it should be."

Bad News Bears, The
18 | 16 | 19 | 15

1976 | Directed by Michael Ritchie | With Walter Matthau, Tatum O'Neal, Vic Morrow | 102 minutes | Rated PG

A "must-see for any Little Leaguer", this "cute" sports comedy pitches a story about a curmudgeonly drunk roped into coaching a "truly awful" kids' baseball team; though perhaps "better then than now" (with "foul but funny language" that might raise parental eyebrows), its sequels are definitely "bad news for moviegoers."

Bad Santa | 18 | 20 | 17 | 17 |

2003 | Directed by Terry Zwigoff | With Billy Bob Thornton, Tony Cox, John Ritter, Bernie Mac | 91 minutes | Rated R

"Rude, crude and awfully funny", this "fearless" black comedy toplines Thornton as a "burnt-out", "mean-spirited" Santa who robs department stores with his partner, a "potty-mouthed" elf; no question, it's "sick, sick, sick" and "definitely not for kids" ("it ain't rated R for nothing"), but "twisted" types label it the "perfect antidote to phony Christmas cheer."

Bad Seed, The ◑ | 22 | 23 | 25 | 20 |

1956 | Directed by Mervyn LeRoy | With Nancy Kelly, Patty McCormack, Eileen Heckart | 129 minutes | Not Rated

"Not for the faint of heart", this "very creepy" thriller is the story of a "perky little deranged girl" who's the "world's most evil child" (think "Ted Bundy in a pinafore"); "unsettling and unforgettable" in its time, it's still "way, way over the top", and even if the Broadway play "had a better ending", this one will positively "send chills down your spine."

Ball of Fire ◑ | 26 | 28 | 24 | 23 |

1941 | Directed by Howard Hawks | With Gary Cooper, Barbara Stanwyck, Oskar Homolka, Dana Andrews | 111 minutes | Not Rated

Fired-up admirers praise the "classic" hilarity in this "delightful" screwball comedy, wherein "sassy" burlesque queen Stanwyck holes up with "eight straight-laced" linguists to school them in "early '40s slang"; add Cooper in a "droll", "deadpan" turn as a "timid bookworm", and sparks fly as the "splendid cast" lets fly with the "witty" repartee.

Bambi | 26 | - | 25 | 26 |

1942 | Directed by David Hand | Animated | 70 minutes | Rated G

"Don't forget those tissues" before settling into this dear coming-of-age story that's best remembered for the "absolutely heart-wrenching" "death of Bambi's mother", a "cruel lesson in life" that will "make you think twice about showing it" to young children; otherwise, it's arguably the "most beautiful" example of vintage Disney animation, "warm and fuzzy" but "not mawkish."

Bananas | 23 | 20 | 22 | 19 |

1971 | Directed by Woody Allen | With Woody Allen, Louise Lasser, Carlos Montalban | 82 minutes | Rated PG-13

"For Allen purists mostly", this "early" comic romance "relies heavily on sight gags and slapstick humor" in its "anarchic" story of a nebbish turned "Latin American dictator" that's a "zany" satire to some, but "intermittently funny shtick" to others; P.S. hang on for a "young" Sylvester Stallone's cameo as a "thug on the subway."

Band Wagon, The | 26 | 21 | 20 | 26 |

1953 | Directed by Vincente Minnelli | With Fred Astaire, Cyd Charisse, Nanette Fabray | 111 minutes | Not Rated

A "worthy companion to *Singin' in the Rain*", this "solid musical" comedy boasts the "most romantic moment in movie history" – the "hauntingly

lovely 'Dancing in the Dark' number" – performed by Astaire and
Charisse in "top form"; thanks to its "fantastic music" and "delightful
cast", nostalgists sigh "they don't make 'em like this anymore."

Bang the Drum Slowly   23 | 25 | 24 | 18

1973 | Directed by John Hancock | With Michael Moriarty, Robert De Niro,
Vincent Gardenia | 96 minutes | Rated PG

Moriarty and De Niro deliver "two moving performances" in this memorably "sad" drama about a hayseed baseball catcher with a terminal
illness and the star pitcher who befriends him; both a "real tearjerker"
and a "powerful story of friendship", it's a "well done", "humbling"
experience that still has "staying power."

Barbarella   13 | 9 | 11 | 15

1968 | Directed by Roger Vadim | With Jane Fonda, John Phillip Law,
Anita Pallenberg, Milo O'Shea | 98 minutes | Rated PG

Über-"babe" Fonda "pushes the boundaries of sexuality" (at least the
1968 boundaries) with her "zero-g striptease" and other "amusing"
outfit-free antics in this "campy" sci-fi "cult classic"; if you can just
"forget the story" and the "terrible", "bad-high-school-play" production
values, you'll have "great fun" with all that young Jane "eye candy."

Barbershop   20 | 20 | 20 | 18

2002 | Directed by Tim Story | With Ice Cube, Cedric the Entertainer,
Eve | 102 minutes | Rated PG-13

An "old-time barbershop where everyone hangs out" is the centerpiece of this "enjoyable, day-in-the-life" comedy that may be "set in a
black neighborhood" but will "appeal to all hair colors"; Cedric the
Entertainer's "timing steals the show", and even if the "Rosa Parks"
and "Jesse Jackson" gibes seem "politically incorrect", the picture
ultimately offers a "solid message about community."

Barefoot Contessa, The   24 | 25 | 23 | 23

1954 | Directed by Joseph L. Mankiewicz | With Humphrey Bogart,
Ava Gardner, Edmond O'Brien | 128 minutes | Not Rated

"Romantic to the nth degree", this "enjoyable" drama centers on a
"ravishing" performance by the "amazing Ava" as a "gorgeous" inge-
nue who rises to "old Hollywood" stardom and ultimately marries into
minor royalty; if some say the "thin plot" reveals feet of clay, it's still
loaded with "elegance" and "real quality" – "those were movies!"

Barefoot in the Park   23 | 24 | 22 | 21

1967 | Directed by Gene Saks | With Robert Redford, Jane Fonda,
Charles Boyer, Mildred Natwick | 106 minutes | Rated G

Channeling "how delightful the first rush of true love is", this "light"
romantic comedy is the "cute tale" of newlyweds who "try on marriage
in a small NY flat"; there's "great chemistry" between the "beautiful"
leads and Neil Simon's script is "witty", even if some say its "strong
period quality" makes the film feel "a bit dated" today.

Barfly   18 | 21 | 17 | 16

1987 | Directed by Barbet Schroeder | With Mickey Rourke, Faye Dunaway,
Frank Stallone | 100 minutes | Rated R

"Down and out" in LA the Charles Bukowski way, this "painful look" at
"burnt-out alcoholics" stars Rourke and Dunaway as "rummies on the
skids" uttering "heavy dialogue" over "tacky/cool" background music;

some swat it for being "relentlessly depressing", but for most it's a "gritty look at the fringes of society" with some "great acting" as a bonus.

Barry Lyndon
20 | 18 | 21 | 27

1975 | Directed by Stanley Kubrick | With Ryan O'Neal, Marisa Berenson, Leon Vitali | 184 minutes | Rated PG

"Kubrick's classic adaptation" of the Thackeray novel depicts the "rise and fall of an Irish lad whose luck finally runs dry" with "amazing period detail" and "gorgeous photography"; but although this "thing of beauty" is a "feast for the eyes", the "acting's from hunger" and the "dull, plodding" pace leaves some sighing "what you see isn't what you get."

Barton Fink
20 | 24 | 19 | 22

1991 | Directed by Joel Coen | With John Turturro, John Goodman, Judy Davis, Michael Lerner | 116 minutes | Rated R

"Delightfully weird", this Coen brothers drama about a gone-Hollywood playwright with a colossal case of writer's block "alternates between fascinating and frustrating" given a "surreal", "terribly odd" storyline that's "brain candy" for intellectuals; despite "fantastic acting" from an "exceptional" Turturro and "absolutely sinister" Goodman, this "out-there" picture is "not for everyone."

Basic Instinct
19 | 19 | 20 | 19

1992 | Directed by Paul Verhoeven | With Michael Douglas, Sharon Stone, Jeanne Tripplehorn | 123 minutes | Rated R

Aside from Stone's notorious "uncrossed legs" "money shot", this "leering erotic thriller" offers enough "noir-esque dialogue" and "gratuitous sex" to make for one "highly provocative" "hormone movie"; though detractors deem it "unintentionally funny trash", "mired in leftover '80s hedonism", fans find it "surprisingly entertaining" – just "don't make the mistake of watching it with your parents."

Basquiat
17 | 20 | 19 | 17

1996 | Directed by Julian Schnabel | With Jeffrey Wright, Benicio Del Toro, David Bowie | 108 minutes | Rated R

It "feels as though you've lived, not just watched", this "insightful biopic" about the rise and fall of a "promising prodigy imploding" in the NY art scene; directed by fellow artist Schnabel, "excellently scored" by ex-Velvet Undergrounder John Cale and featuring a "beautifully cast" Bowie as pop conduit Andy Warhol, it's a "dark", tragic ride that "ends abruptly – like Basquiat's life did."

Batman
20 | 19 | 19 | 24

1989 | Directed by Tim Burton | With Michael Keaton, Jack Nicholson, Kim Basinger | 126 minutes | Rated PG-13

The "first of the bat franchise", this "brilliantly shot" flick reflects the "dark side of the comic book" thanks to the "dynamic duo" of "visionary" director Burton and "top-notch" "caped crusader" Keaton; Jack's an "awesome" Joker and the *Blade Runner*-esque Gotham City is "realized to stunning effect", so even if the "sequels stink", this one "rocks."

Batman Begins
23 | 21 | 23 | 26

2005 | Directed by Christopher Nolan | With Christian Bale, Michael Caine, Katie Holmes | 141 minutes | Rated PG-13

After a "worrisome decline" into "cartoonish goofery", the Batman franchise is "back on track" with this "quality" revival, a "rollicking ride" that revels in the "dark" tone of the "original comic book" as it recounts the Caped Crusader's "early years"; as for acting, the "brooding" Bale "soars" in the lead role, shedding new "insight" into his character's "inner turmoil", though romantic interest Holmes is deemed the "weak link."

Batman Returns
| 16 | 17 | 15 | 21 |

1992 | Directed by Tim Burton | With Michael Keaton, Danny DeVito, Michelle Pfeiffer | 126 minutes | Rated PG-13

The "last of the dark deco Batman" pictures, this "freak show of a sequel" is "another atmospheric Burton production" that keeps Keaton as the caped crusader and is "spiced up" by a "sizzling" Pfeiffer playing an "S&M version of Catwoman"; spoilsports say "they should've stopped" after the original, bemoaning what happens when "marketing takes over a movie."

Battle of Algiers, The ❶🅵
| 28 | 24 | 27 | 26 |

1967 | Directed by Gillo Pontecorvo | With Jean Martin, Yacef Saadi | 117 minutes | Not Rated

"Terrorism and military response" are the up-to-the-minute subjects of this "decades-ahead-of-its-time" feature delineating the Algerian struggle for independence from French rule; the "riveting" footage is "so lifelike" that it "looks like a documentary", but even as a "docudrama" it remains "timely, essential" viewing.

Beaches
| 22 | 23 | 22 | 21 |

1988 | Directed by Garry Marshall | With Bette Midler, Barbara Hershey, John Heard | 123 minutes | Rated PG-13

Alternately "heartwarming and heartbreaking", this "major chick flick" (a "10-hanky" special) captures the "intensity of friendship" as it recounts the "lifelong" alliance of "two opposites": the "always passionate" Midler and the more "detached" Hershey; hard-hearted sorts yawn it's a "sappy soap opera", but others say when you need a "good cathartic cry", this "guilty pleasure" is the "one to watch."

Beau Geste ❶
| 25 | 23 | 25 | 22 |

1939 | Directed by William A. Wellman | With Gary Cooper, Ray Milland, Robert Preston | 120 minutes | Not Rated

"Heroic heroes and villainous villains" populate this "ultimate" war picture about "friendship and honor" that's "perhaps the best Foreign Legion movie" ever made; ok, there are "no special effects" and it might seem "corny" today, but it still supplies plenty of "first-class adventure" right up to that "majestic ending."

🆉 Beautiful Mind, A ✉
| 26 | 28 | 25 | 25 |

2001 | Directed by Ron Howard | With Russell Crowe, Ed Harris, Jennifer Connelly | 134 minutes | Rated PG-13

"What *Rain Man* did for autism", this "absorbing" Oscar winner about a "brilliant mathematician's" battle with mental illness "does for schizophrenia", revealing the "thin line between genius and insanity"; "phenomenally acted" by Russell Crowe and Jennifer Connelly, it "celebrates the triumph of the human spirit" – though foes say its "Hollywoodized" script might "stray too far from historical accuracy."

	OVERALL	ACTING	STORY	PROD.

Beauty and the Beast ⊙🄵   28 | 25 | 27 | 28

1947 | Directed by Jean Cocteau | With Jean Marais, Josette Day, Marcel André | 93 minutes | Not Rated

Enter a "highly stylized universe" in this "hallucinatory" take on the classic "fairy tale" that's both "dreamlike" and "complex" owing to "Cocteau's wit and imagination"; "still unsurpassed by more lavish productions", this "amazing visual feast" demonstrates the artistry possible with "ancient technology" – and enough "sexuality beneath the surface" to keep things throbbing.

Beauty and the Beast   26 | - | 25 | 27

1991 | Directed by Gary Trousdale, Kirk Wise | Animated | 84 minutes | Rated G

A "sensational score" complements the cast of "lovable characters" in this "magical milepost" that "set the bar for a new wave of animated classics"; told with a "fresh approach", it has an "intelligent" "heroine with chutzpah" trilling "catchy", "singable songs" that will "keep tots of all ages entranced"; in short, this "modern masterpiece" – the first animated film ever nominated for Best Picture – is nothing less than "Disney at its high-flying best."

Becket ✉   26 | 29 | 26 | 26

1964 | Directed by Peter Glenville | With Richard Burton, Peter O'Toole, John Gielgud | 148 minutes | Not Rated

"Big drama writ large", this biopic about England's King Henry II and his "deep bond with Thomas Becket" features the "brilliant teaming" of "two high-powered actors" – the "winning" O'Toole and "wonderful" Burton – in "histrionic, bellowing performances"; sure, it's "a bit talky", but otherwise this "beautifully filmed period piece" is living proof of the way "history should be experienced."

Bedazzled   20 | 19 | 21 | 16

1967 | Directed by Stanley Donen | With Dudley Moore, Peter Cook, Raquel Welch | 104 minutes | Not Rated

This "immensely clever" "takeoff on the Faust legend" relocated to "swinging '60s London" is a "wickedly funny" comedy full of "vintage Brit humor" and "witty" "double entendres" in its story of "poor dweeb Moore selling his soul" to the devil in exchange for "true love"; ok, it may be "slow in spots", but it's still "far superior to the 2000 remake."

Beethoven   16 | 14 | 16 | 16

1992 | Directed by Brian Levant | With Charles Grodin, Dean Jones, Bonnie Hunt, Stanley Tucci | 87 minutes | Rated PG

"Dog lovers" dig this "cute" exercise in "good, clean family fun" about a "slobbery", "scene-stealing" St. Bernard who wreaks havoc in the house while deftly avoiding the clutches of an evil vet; though grumps growl about the "average acting", "predictable storyline" and "laboratory villains", "kids love it" – enough said.

Beetlejuice   20 | 19 | 21 | 22

1988 | Directed by Tim Burton | With Michael Keaton, Geena Davis, Alec Baldwin, Winona Ryder | 92 minutes | Rated PG

"Netherworld antics" animate this "demented haunted-house comedy", a "bizarre" yet "enchanting" flick from "twisted" director Burton that's "endlessly inventive and endearingly funny"; built around a "genius" turn by Keaton as the "wonderfully disgusting" title character, it's also notable for a "macabre" turn from Ryder as a very "unusual teenager."

Before Night Falls
| 22 | 26 | 22 | 20 |

2000 | Directed by Julian Schnabel | With Javier Bardem, Johnny Depp, Olivier Martinez | 133 minutes | Rated R

Based on the true life story of "gay Cuban poet" Reinaldo Arenas, this "historically significant" biodrama is a "serious" reminder not to "take freedom for granted" as it details the hero's struggles against an "oppressive regime" bent on "silencing" him; look for an "excellent" Bardem in a "beautiful", "fully realized" performance.

Before Sunrise
| 23 | 23 | 22 | 21 |

1995 | Directed by Richard Linklater | With Ethan Hawke, Julie Delpy | 105 minutes | Rated R

A "thinking person's" romance, this "bittersweet gem" examines a "passionate meeting of the minds" between Hawke and the "enchanting" Delpy as "star-crossed" Euroailing students who hook up for a single night; the duo's "winning chemistry" is framed by "beautiful" Viennese backdrops, and "what might have been" will dawn on those who catch the "10-years-later follow-up", *Before Sunset*.

Before Sunset
| 21 | 23 | 20 | 21 |

2004 | Directed by Richard Linklater | With Ethan Hawke, Julie Delpy | 80 minutes | Rated R

After their one-night "chance encounter" in *Before Sunrise*, Hawke and Delpy – now "older and somewhat wiser" – meet again in "atmospheric" Paris for a one-day "second chance" in this "intelligent romance"; while their "meandering" conversation seems to "drag" for some, it's like a "fairy tale" for those mesmerized by the stars' "amazing chemistry."

Being John Malkovich
| 22 | 24 | 24 | 22 |

1999 | Directed by Spike Jonze | With John Cusack, Cameron Diaz, John Malkovich, Catherine Keener | 112 minutes | Rated R

"'Original' does not even begin to describe" this "surreal romp" that mixes "dark fantasy" with "smart comedy" in its "off-the-wall" story of a regular guy who finds a portal that takes him "inside the head" of actor John Malkovich; though it "rewards rather than insults the audience's intelligence", it's definitely "not for everybody", being either "engrossing", "audacious fun" or "confusing as hell."

Being Julia
| 23 | 27 | 21 | 24 |

2004 | Directed by István Szabó | With Annette Bening, Jeremy Irons | 104 minutes | Rated R

Bening "steals the show" with her "luminous" portrayal of a "fading English actress undertaking one last fling" with a young Yank in this "enjoyable" Brit "comedy of manners" based on the Somerset Maugham novella; overall, it's a "fluffy period piece" perhaps best suited for devotees of the "theatuh", but it's still "worth watching" all the way through for that "deliciously wicked climax."

Being There
| 26 | 27 | 25 | 23 |

1979 | Directed by Hal Ashby | With Peter Sellers, Shirley MacLaine, Melvyn Douglas | 130 minutes | Rated PG

"Politics and hypocrisy" get a skewering in this "classic allegory" about a "slow-thinking" gardener who proves that "80 percent of life is just showing up"; "Sellers glows" in this "faithful" adaptation of Jerzy Kosinski's story, which "requires patience with its slow pace" but does "allow you to form your own conclusions."

Bell, Book and Candle
22 | 22 | 22 | 21

1958 | Directed by Richard Quine | With Kim Novak, James Stewart, Jack Lemmon | 106 minutes | Not Rated

Stewart and Novak "have fun with witchcraft" in this romantic comedy based on the Broadway hit about a "man falling for a woman who's a witch"; fans claim that this "old chestnut" was responsible for many cats being "named Pyewacket" and note that the "enchanting" title refers to the Roman Catholic rite of exorcism.

Belle de Jour 𝔽
24 | 25 | 23 | 23

1968 | Directed by Luis Buñuel | With Catherine Deneuve, Jean Sorel | 101 minutes | Rated R

Deneuve was "never sexier" than in this "marvelously perverse" French drama, a peek at the "dark side" of a "chichi housewife" pent up in "bourgeois" wedlock whose "S&M fantasies" compel her to take a "side job" at the local bordello; more "Dali painting" than *Playboy* centerfold, it's a "stylish", "complex" window into director Buñuel's "surreal world", and the leading lady's "intense" turn spices up the "slow" spots.

Bells Are Ringing
24 | 24 | 22 | 22

1960 | Directed by Vincente Minnelli | With Judy Holliday, Dean Martin, Fred Clark | 127 minutes | Not Rated

A "funny" Broadway musical becomes a "fine vehicle" for the "wonderful" Holliday in this story of a singing switchboard girl hung up on a playwright (the slightly "out-of-his-league" Martin); yet despite a "classic" score and a "famous song" ('The Party's Over'), some say this "stage-bound" production's "outdated."

Bells of St. Mary's, The ◑
24 | 25 | 23 | 23

1945 | Directed by Leo McCarey | With Bing Crosby, Ingrid Bergman | 126 minutes | Not Rated

Bergman and "ring-a-ding Bing" take turns "tugging your heart" in this "*Going My Way* sequel", a "heartwarming" drama (and "Christmas fave") about a crooning clergyman sent to a parochial school's rescue with a message of "selfless giving"; the "old-fashioned sweetness" strikes a "treacly" note for cynics, but "sentimental" sorts still delight in its "keep-a-hanky-handy" style of filmmaking that's "now extinct."

Bend It Like Beckham
26 | 24 | 25 | 23

2003 | Directed by Gurinder Chadha | With Parminder K. Nagra, Keira Knightley, Jonathan Rhys-Meyers | 112 minutes | Rated PG-13

"Bend it like anything you want" – this "thoroughly entertaining", "cross-cultural feel-good movie" about an "Indian girl in England who wants to play soccer" scores with its "empowering" storyline and "fantastic ensemble acting"; a "true delight", it's the "best ethnic-themed movie since *My Big Fat Greek Wedding*" – "but no TV series, please."

Ben-Hur ✉
26 | 23 | 25 | 28

1959 | Directed by William Wyler | With Charlton Heston, Jack Hawkins, Stephen Boyd | 212 minutes | Rated G

Unleashed four decades "before *Gladiator*", this "bigger than big" sword-and-sandals "masterpiece" features Heston exuding "hammy", bare-chested "bravura" as a Judean prince betrayed into Roman slavery only to seek payback via "breathtaking" bouts of action (including that "stunner" of a "chariot race"); a major Oscar magnet, it epitomizes the "grand Hollywood historical epic", built on "biblical" bedrock.

Benji
19 | 16 | 18 | 17

1974 | Directed by Joe Camp | With Patsy Garrett, Peter Breck | 86 minutes | Rated G

The "must-see" flick for the "mid-'70s" single-digit demo, this fetching "doggy adventure" features a star turn from a "cute", shaggy-browed mutt who trots to the rescue after his young owners are kidnapped; nostalgists recall a "sappy" but "wonderful" "childhood favorite", albeit with "low-rent" production values.

Benny & Joon
21 | 24 | 21 | 19

1993 | Directed by Jeremiah Chechik | With Johnny Depp, Mary Stuart Masterson, Aidan Quinn | 98 minutes | Rated PG

"Misfits find true love" in this "quirky" romance featuring the early "Depp in his element", exuding "priceless subtlety" as he "channels Buster Keaton" and Charlie Chaplin routines to win over his "kooky", "special-needs" pal Masterson; ok, it's "more than a little strange", but when "different" is this "engaging", "who needs normal?"

Best in Show
24 | 25 | 23 | 22

2000 | Directed by Christopher Guest | With Christopher Guest, Eugene Levy, Catherine O'Hara | 90 minutes | Rated PG-13

"Three woofs" and "four paws up" for this "quirky riot" of a mocku-mentary about a "gaggle of fanatical dog show participants" and their "pedigreed pooches"; the wacky repartee makes for a "beautifully in-appropriate", "laugh-a-minute satire" that "can be viewed 100 times without becoming dog-eared."

☑ Best Years of Our Lives, The ⊠◑
28 | 27 | 28 | 25

1946 | Directed by William Wyler | With Myrna Loy, Fredric March, Dana Andrews, Teresa Wright | 172 minutes | Not Rated

"Have the Kleenex handy" – there's no denying the "pure heart" of this "compelling" drama exploring the "uneasy readjustment" of WWII "vets coming home" to Main Street USA; its all-around "riveting" act-ing and "no-miss script" perfectly capture the "next-door" post-war mood, taking Best Picture (plus six more Oscars) and resonating as a "quintessentially American period piece."

Beverly Hills Cop
20 | 19 | 19 | 19

1984 | Directed by Martin Brest | With Eddie Murphy, Judge Reinhold, John Ashton | 105 minutes | Rated R

This action/comedy "breakthrough" is a "star vehicle" for Murphy, cast as an "inner-city" flatfoot with a "trademark laugh" who upstages his "goofy" El Lay counterparts in pursuit of a friend's killer; though the typically "'80s" foolery and "cheesy storyline" have cooled over time, this "hoot" still works as "feel-good" fare to fill a "Saturday afternoon."

Beyond the Sea
19 | 22 | 19 | 20

2004 | Directed by Kevin Spacey | With Kevin Spacey, Kate Bosworth, John Goodman | 118 minutes | Rated PG-13

A bona fide "labor of love", this "enjoyable" bio of '50s bopper Bobby Darin was directed, co-written and enacted by the "many hat"-wearing

Spacey, who's his "usual riveting self" – and even does his own "first-rate singing"; still, sinkers say Kevin's "too old for the part" and compare this "vanity project" to "singing into a hairbrush in front of a mirror."

Bicycle Thief, The ✉❶🅵

OVERALL	ACTING	STORY	PROD.
27	26	27	24

1949 | Directed by Vittorio De Sica | With Lamberto Maggiorani, Enzo Staiola | 93 minutes | Not Rated

"Poetry put on film", this early slice of "Italian neorealism" is "so sad" but so "beautifully executed" that it's ultimately "not a downer"; using "nonprofessional actors" in a drama of a father and son searching impoverished post-war Rome for the stolen bike that's key to their livelihood, De Sica tugs hearts with a "timeless pathos" that's most "affecting" for its "charm and simplicity."

Big

23	24	24	22

1988 | Directed by Penny Marshall | With Tom Hanks, Elizabeth Perkins, Robert Loggia | 104 minutes | Rated PG

Getting literal with its "inner child", this "cute" "kid-in-a-man's-body" comedy stars a "winning", "never-so-lovable" Hanks, who "makes the movie" as a 13-year-old who "becomes an adult overnight" and gains entrée to NYC's corporate playground; though some of the "fantasy" is "on the sappy side", a large contingent calls it "most rewatchable."

Big Business

19	20	18	18

1988 | Directed by Jim Abrahams | With Bette Midler, Lily Tomlin, Fred Ward | 97 minutes | Rated PG

Playing "two sets of twins" separated at birth, "Midler and Tomlin and Midler and Tomlin" star in this "hilariously cheesy" mistaken identity comedy set in NY's Plaza Hotel; a "guilty pleasure" for fans of '80s "polyester clothes and big hair", it "doesn't really hold up" for others who sniff it's "silly" and suggest that "Bette should stick to music."

Big Chill, The

23	24	22	21

1983 | Directed by Lawrence Kasdan | With Glenn Close, William Hurt, Kevin Kline, Jeff Goldblum, Mary Kay Place, JoBeth Williams, Tom Berenger | 105 minutes | Rated R

Trace the tracks of their tears as this '60s-era "nostalgia" trip tries to "define a generation" via a "superb ensemble", an "iconic soundtrack" and the "soul-searching" premise of "boomers regathering" at a friend's funeral (fun fact: Kevin Costner "plays the stiff"); anyone bummed by the "contrived" setup and "smug" "yuppie angst" can still groove to the "perfect" tune selection.

Big Clock, The ❶

25	25	25	23

1948 | Directed by John Farrow | With Ray Milland, Charles Laughton, Maureen O'Sullivan | 95 minutes | Not Rated

"Nice and twisty", this "classic noir" stars Ray Milland as a crime magazine editor in a "real predicament" after witnessing "his publisher killing his lover"; the "suspenseful" story was filmed again in 1987 as *No Way Out*, but pundits say the original "dances rings around" the remake.

Big Daddy

17	16	17	17

1999 | Directed by Dennis Dugan | With Adam Sandler, Joey Lauren Adams, Jon Stewart | 93 minutes | Rated PG-13

Big on "typical" Sandler "guy" appeal, this "untraditional comedy" about a "man-boy trying to be a father" has enough "cute child interaction" to make it one of the star's "most accessible" vehicles (it "mercifully lacks the crude humor" of his usual work); true believers find it "hard not to laugh", though some pan it as a "nonsensical" outing that "gives stupid a bad name."

Big Easy, The

22 | 22 | 22 | 20

1987 | Directed by Jim McBride | With Dennis Quaid, Ellen Barkin, Ned Beatty, John Goodman | 108 minutes | Rated R

Emitting the "same sweaty humidity as its New Orleans locale", this "steamy", "sultry" drama is the story of a "less than perfect cop" and an "easy-on-the-eyes" assistant D.A. who meet during a "police corruption investigation"; Quaid's at his "bad-boy best", Barkin's "sizzlin'" and their "explosive chemistry" comes to a boil in "one of the best love scenes" ever filmed.

Big Fish

22 | 24 | 23 | 25

2003 | Directed by Tim Burton | With Ewan McGregor, Albert Finney, Billy Crudup, Jessica Lange | 125 minutes | Rated PG-13

The "guy equivalent of a chick flick", this "bittersweet" story of a "complicated father-and-son relationship" reels in sentimentalists with equal parts of "whimsy and schmaltz"; "less twisted" than director Burton's usual fare, it still has its "oddball" moments via a "patchwork", *Forrest Gump*-like script, and if cynics yawn it's "sappy" and "slow", many more laud its "vivid imagery and good message" – plus, it's a relief to "see McGregor without a light saber" for a change.

Big Heat, The ❶

25 | 25 | 24 | 22

1953 | Directed by Fritz Lang | With Glenn Ford, Gloria Grahame, Lee Marvin, Carolyn Jones | 90 minutes | Not Rated

"Considered daring in its time", this "ultimate noir picture" features a rogues' gallery of hard-boiled "tough guys" and gals in a story about an honest cop "obsessed with getting revenge" following his wife's murder; though tepid types say the heat's "cooled off over the years", there's "one horrifying scene" involving a pot of "scalding hot coffee" that's still quite a "shocker."

Big Lebowski, The

20 | 22 | 19 | 20

1998 | Directed by Joel Coen | With Jeff Bridges, John Goodman, Julianne Moore, Steve Buscemi | 117 minutes | Rated R

The brothers Coen "strike again" with this "shaggy-dog" comedy, an "homage to slobs" that gets rolling when Bridges' "aging" "slacker/stoner character" and his "bizarre bowling buddies" become embroiled in a surreal kidnapping; though an "acquired taste" and certainly "strange for its own sake" ("dude, where's my plot?"), it has "cult" followers citing "quotable" lines and swearing "you'll laugh."

Big Night

24 | 26 | 23 | 23

1996 | Directed by Campbell Scott, Stanley Tucci | With Stanley Tucci, Tony Shalhoub, Minnie Driver | 107 minutes | Rated R

"Yum": this "quirky", "thoroughly enjoyable" dramatic "feast" tracks two "Italian immigrant brothers" in their "endearing" effort to keep their restaurant and culinary "vision" alive on the '50s-era Jersey coast; hailed as an "overlooked gem", its slow-simmering pace allows admirers to "savor" "brilliant performances" that are rivaled only by "stunning food shots" – "don't catch it on an empty stomach."

	OVERALL	ACTING	STORY	PROD.

☒ Big Sleep, The ◑ — 27 | 27 | 24 | 24

1946 | Directed by Howard Hawks | With Humphrey Bogart, Lauren Bacall, Martha Vickers | 114 minutes | Not Rated

"Whodunit? who cares?" as long as the legendary Bogie and Bacall keep up the "snappy" patter and "heavy-lidded" "chemistry" in this "dizzying" film noir "classic" featuring Bogart as "fast-talking" gumshoe Philip Marlowe prowling Raymond Chandler territory (1940s Los Angeles at its most "atmospheric"); if the notoriously "incomprehensible plot" is seriously in need of a clue, at least the "crackling" pace and "salty" repartee always "entertain and enthrall."

Bill & Ted's Excellent Adventure — 15 | 10 | 15 | 13

1989 | Directed by Stephen Herek | With Keanu Reeves, Alex Winter, George Carlin | 90 minutes | Rated PG

"Two goof-offs" about to flunk out of high school time-travel to the past in a desperate attempt to graduate in this "totally tubular" slacker comedy, a budding "cult classic" that just may be "better than you remember it"; sure, this "sophomoric", "truly mindless" flick could have "typecast Keanu" forever, and even if it's "not very good, it's still lots of fun, dude."

Billy Elliot — 25 | 26 | 25 | 23

2000 | Directed by Stephen Daldry | With Julie Walters, Jamie Bell | 110 minutes | Rated PG-13

It takes *Swan Lake* to break the "working-class shackles" of a Northern England mining town in this "coming-of-age" drama about a "boy who loves ballet" and his hardscrabble dad; behind the "thick British accents", fans discover a "captivating" if "unlikely tale" propelled by "talent, desire" and lots of "fancy footwork", with an "uplifting" finale that's apt to inspire "a good cry."

Billy Liar ◑ — 22 | 26 | 23 | 20

1963 | Directed by John Schlesinger | With Tom Courtenay, Julie Christie, Wilfred Pickles | 98 minutes | Not Rated

A prime example of British "kitchen-sink realism", this "poignant comic gem" relates the story of a daydreamer–cum–pathological liar itching to escape his humdrum, blue-collar existence; in the "challenging" title role, Courtenay's a "charmer", but the picture is stolen by the "scrumptious young" Christie in her first major film role.

Biloxi Blues — 21 | 22 | 22 | 20

1988 | Directed by Mike Nichols | With Matthew Broderick, Christopher Walken, Penelope Ann Miller | 106 minutes | Rated PG-13

WWII-era "basic training" gets the Neil Simon treatment in this "fair adaptation" of his "semi-autobiographical" stage comedy about a raw recruit confronted with a "crazed drill sergeant" in the "sweltering" South; a "sweet" "sequel of sorts to *Brighton Beach Memoirs*", it's "not momentous" but does manage to muster some "spirit of the times."

Birdcage, The — 22 | 25 | 22 | 22

1996 | Directed by Mike Nichols | With Robin Williams, Nathan Lane, Gene Hackman, Dianne Wiest | 117 minutes | Rated R

Reset in South Beach, director Nichols' "slick" take on the "classic" French farce *La Cage aux Folles* soars "over the top" on the wings of the "perfect comedic combination" of Williams and Lane, cast as a pair of "flamboyant" gay cabaret owners obliged to "play it straight" for their son's "uptight" in-laws-to-be; busy with burlesque and "insight", it's widely welcomed as a "laugh-out-loud" "blast", though holdouts chirp "stick with the original."

Birdman of Alcatraz ◑

22 | 25 | 22 | 20

1962 | Directed by John Frankenheimer | With Burt Lancaster, Karl Malden, Thelma Ritter | 147 minutes | Not Rated

Lancaster is "at the top of his game" in this saga of "a man, a prison and some birds", the "fascinating" bio of Rock lifer Robert Stroud who struggles under the screws' authority but "finds love and friendship" when he becomes a famed ornithologist; it's generally judged a "keeper" as a "gritty" but "entertaining" penal drama that's also a "touching" "examination of survival."

Birds, The

24 | 20 | 24 | 25

1963 | Directed by Alfred Hitchcock | With Tippi Hedren, Rod Taylor, Jessica Tandy | 119 minutes | Rated PG-13

"Nature strikes back, Hitchcock style", in this "improbably terrifying" "nail-biter" about "birds gone mad" that "still packs enough of a punch" to leave the timid "traumatized"; though critics aren't chirping about the "hokey", "no-rhyme-or-reason" plot that takes "too long to get going", ultimately you'll "never think of pigeons in the same way" after a gander at this one.

Birdy

23 | 25 | 22 | 21

1984 | Directed by Alan Parker | With Matthew Modine, Nicolas Cage | 120 minutes | Rated R

Much "emotional" flutter marks this "haunting" drama that "gets into the psyches" of a "pair of outcasts": Modine as a "traumatized" Vietnam-era vet with a "disturbing" fixation on "birdlike" behavior and a "brilliant" Cage as the childhood friend out to revive him; thanks to the leads' "breadth and heart", it's a "neglected minor classic" nested within a "surreal" story – "this film can fly."

Birth of a Nation, The ◑

25 | 20 | 19 | 27

1915 | Directed by D.W. Griffith | With Lillian Gish, Mae Marsh, Henry B. Walthall | 190 minutes | Not Rated

A "masterful" technical feat that could be the "most influential movie ever made", Griffith's "landmark" silent epic "wrote the book" on "camera movement" and "cinema as storytelling" while offering a "morally irresponsible" version of Reconstruction replete with "blatantly racist" "stereotyping" and the "Ku Klux Klan presented as heroes"; so even though this work marks the "birth of the feature" film, be prepared for a storyline that's a "mess" – "even by 1915" standards.

Bishop's Wife, The ◑

24 | 24 | 24 | 23

1947 | Directed by Henry Koster | With Cary Grant, Loretta Young, David Niven | 105 minutes | Not Rated

Although "less well known" than some of its "holiday movie" peers, this "Christmasy" romance stars Grant as a "guardian angel" blessed with "elegance and style" ("duh!") who's sent to "restore faith" to a clergyman and his spouse but "falls in love" along the way; overall, it's an "amusing, touching" display of "old-fashioned" "star power" that sentimental souls will "never forget."

	OVERALL	ACTING	STORY	PROD.

Blackboard Jungle ◑ — 23 | 24 | 22 | 19

1955 | Directed by Richard Brooks | With Glenn Ford, Anne Francis, Vic Morrow, Sidney Poitier | 101 minutes | Not Rated

See "the '50s in a new way" via this "gritty" drama, a standout of the "juvenile delinquent genre" set in an "inner-city school" where idealistic teacher Ford is forced to "tame" a horde of punks; notable for Hollywood's "first use of a rock 'n' roll" soundtrack, it may "feel a bit dated", though cynics shrug "schools haven't changed" that much.

Black Hawk Down — 23 | 21 | 23 | 26

2001 | Directed by Ridley Scott | With Josh Hartnett, Ewan McGregor, Tom Sizemore | 144 minutes | Rated R

It's "hard to watch, but it's even harder to turn away" from this "astoundingly gripping" (and "surprisingly accurate") account of a 1993 Mogadishu "military misadventure", which pitted a handful of U.S. Army Rangers against a huge enemy force; "Scott puts you on the ground with the soldiers" in all its "gory", "graphic" and "grueling" detail; indeed, even peaceniks agree this "salute to our servicemen" "doesn't simplify or sensationalize" combat.

Black Orpheus ✉🅵 — 26 | 23 | 25 | 25

1959 | Directed by Marcel Camus | With Marpessa Dawn, Breno Mello | 100 minutes | Rated PG

"Brazilian backdrops" and "bossa nova" rhythms cast their "spell" over Greek legend in this "enchanting", "lyrical" foreign flick, an "exotic retelling" of the Orpheus and Eurydice myth transposed to "modern-day Rio" during Carnival; "sexy", "lush" and full of "beautiful shots" of "cinema verité" revelry, it takes its Dionysian devotees to Hades and back in "unmatched" style – and oh, that "moving-in-your-seat" soundtrack!

Black Stallion, The — 24 | 20 | 23 | 25

1979 | Directed by Carroll Ballard | With Mickey Rooney, Kelly Reno, Teri Garr | 118 minutes | Rated G

Equestrians of "all ages" ponder the "bond between boy and horse" in this "captivating" family film about an Arabian steed who's shipwrecked with a youngster on a desert island only to be entered in a turf race after they're rescued and resettled to a Western ranch; though saddled with a "somber" side, it "wins the roses" with a "skillful blend" of "breathtaking" scenery and "luminous cinematography."

Blade — 18 | 15 | 19 | 21

1998 | Directed by Stephen Norrington | With Wesley Snipes, Stephen Dorff, Kris Kristofferson | 120 minutes | Rated R

A "moody" plotline whetted with "extreme action" makes for a "bloody good time" in this "style-laden" comic-book redo, with Snipes showing some "edge" as a "half-human, half-vampire" superhero who uses his "ninja" skills to "fight the underworld"; though the spectacle is so "slick" that it "created a franchise", those after something sharper may be "disappointed."

⤤ Blade Runner — 26 | 22 | 25 | 27

1982 | Directed by Ridley Scott | With Harrison Ford, Rutger Hauer, Sean Young, Daryl Hannah | 117 minutes | Rated R

This "awesome" "blueprint" for "modern sci-fi" is a "visually stunning" picture best watched with "your brain switched on"; an ultra-"stylish" "noir take" on LA as a 21st-century "dystopia" where "commercialism and biotech run amok", it's also a "hard-boiled" "morality play" with one of "Ford's best acting jobs" as a PI "hunting cyborg replicants while falling in love with one"; connoisseurs run right for the "superior director's cut."

☑ Blazing Saddles
`25` `22` `23` `23`

1974 | Directed by Mel Brooks | With Cleavon Little, Gene Wilder, Harvey Korman, Madeline Kahn | 93 minutes | Rated R

"You'll never look at a horse the same way" after a peek at this "hilarious", "decidedly un-PC" comedy via Mel Brooks, an "off-the-wall" Wild West "spoof" that "insults everyone" with a mix of "slapstick", "eminently quotable one-liners" and "tasteless" routines (like the sound effects-ridden "campfire scene"); most call it "enjoyable" if "overdone."

Blood Diamond
`25` `26` `25` `26`

2006 | Directed by Edward Zwick | With Leonardo DiCaprio, Djimon Hounsou, Jennifer Connelly | 143 minutes | Rated R

"You'll rethink your jewelry purchases" after a look at this "engaging" production mining the "horror of the African diamond trade" for "socially relevant" drama and featuring an "intense" DiCaprio as an "unlikable" smuggler whose "hint of a golden heart" helps a father – the "spectacular" Hounsou – find his kidnapped son; "violent" action scenes drive home the "savagery" of the conflict while indicting the "wealth-obsessed" culture that nurtures it.

Blood Simple
`24` `25` `25` `22`

1984 | Directed by Joel Coen | With Frances McDormand, John Getz, Dan Hedaya | 97 minutes | Rated R

"Complex" is more like it as the Coen brothers' first feature "pumps new blood" into the "low-budget crime thriller" in this "brilliant" "film noir homage" filled with "wicked" "thrills delivered with a drawl"; it's a "twisty", "nerve-jangling" tale of betrayal and revenge in a dusty Texas town, told with a "quirky" slant that "foreshadows" the filmmakers' "masterpiece, *Fargo*."

Blow
`22` `24` `22` `22`

2001 | Directed by Ted Demme | With Johnny Depp, Penélope Cruz, Ray Liotta | 124 minutes | Rated R

Both the "glamour and the consequences of drug trafficking" are depicted in this "gritty" true story charting the "rise and fall" of George Jung, the "premier coke dealer" of the '70s; as usual, Johnny's the "definition of cool", Penélope not as much ("lacks Deppth"), while the picture's "glorification of hedonism" leaves some "disappointed" by its "glossy Hollywood undertone."

Blowup
`26` `23` `25` `25`

1966 | Directed by Michelangelo Antonioni | With David Hemmings, Vanessa Redgrave, Sarah Miles | 111 minutes | Not Rated

"Forget *Austin Powers*", baby, "this is the *real* Swinging London": a "riveting existential thriller" that tracks a happening fashion photographer obsessed with both Redgrave and a "mysterious death in a park"; hipsters hail it as an "enigmatic" (or "infuriating") milestone of the "alienation genre" possessed by the "spirit of the '60s" – and that tasty "period flavor" is still "too cool for words."

	OVERALL	ACTING	STORY	PROD.

Blue Angel, The ❶🅵

| | 25 | 27 | 24 | 22 |

1931 | Directed by Josef von Sternberg | With Marlene Dietrich, Emil Jannings | 99 minutes | Not Rated

Behold the "magnificent Dietrich" "at her best" in this "Weimar-era" German drama, the story of "naughty Lola", a garter-flashing chanteuse who "seduces an old fool" of a schoolmaster and expedites his "descent into the gutter"; though it's a "dated" dose of "ennui and moral rot" in a "world now lost", fräulein Marlene's "tour-de-force", career-launching turn is "music to the eyes."

Blues Brothers, The

| | 22 | 19 | 19 | 21 |

1980 | Directed by John Landis | With John Belushi, Dan Aykroyd, John Candy | 133 minutes | Rated R

"Ignore the plot" and "get out the popcorn" for this "good-time" comedy, powered by Belushi and Aykroyd on a "full tank of gas" as sibs Jake and Elwood, who accept a "mission from God" to provoke "hilarity" and find out "how many cars they can wreck"; if it's (ahem) "not a critics' choice", those with a hankering for "hot" "soul 'n' blues" numbers liberally chased with "dumb fun" insist "you gotta love it."

Blue Velvet

| | 22 | 23 | 20 | 23 |

1986 | Directed by David Lynch | With Kyle MacLachlan, Isabella Rossellini, Dennis Hopper | 120 minutes | Rated R

"One sick puppy of a movie", this pretty "kinky" yet totally "enthralling" look at the "seedy underbelly" "beneath the surface of suburbia" is "love-it-or-hate-it" filmmaking from the "warped" mind of "surrealist auteur Lynch"; despite applause for Hopper's "creepy" portrayal of the "gas-inhaling pervert" ("worth seeing for the Pabst Blue Ribbon scene alone"), sensitive souls find the flick "ugly, pointless" and "not as good as its reputation."

Bob and Carol and Ted and Alice

| | 17 | 19 | 17 | 17 |

1969 | Directed by Paul Mazursky | With Natalie Wood, Robert Culp, Elliott Gould, Dyan Cannon | 104 minutes | Rated R

"Remember the '60s?" – this "social satire" of wannabe swingers experimenting with free love "captures the era to a T", though what was once "hip 'n' happening" seems more "quaint" today; still, many find themselves "laughing at the outfits, the decor", the "dated" dialogue and that "priceless" ending.

Bodyguard, The

| | 14 | 13 | 15 | 16 |

1992 | Directed by Mick Jackson | With Kevin Costner, Whitney Houston | 130 minutes | Rated R

This "melodramatic" romance finds Whitney testing her "star potential" as a "diva" pop singer ("what range!") who falls for Costner's "hot hunk" of a bodyguard; some endorse it as "watchable fluff", but just as many seek protection from a "witless yawner" whose "only redeeming quality" is its "hit songs."

Body Heat

| | 24 | 25 | 25 | 23 |

1981 | Directed by Lawrence Kasdan | With William Hurt, Kathleen Turner, Richard Crenna, Mickey Rourke | 113 minutes | Rated R

"Whew!" this "palpably steamy" "noir thriller" stars "what-a-babe" Turner as a trophy wife who "burns up the screen" as she seduces "small-town lawyer" Hurt into a "spiraling" web of "deceit" that "keeps you guessing" to the last frame; in short, it's a sexed-up "version of the old help-me-kill-my-husband story", a kind of *"Double Indemnity* for a new generation."

Bonnie and Clyde
25 | 25 | 24 | 25

1967 | Directed by Arthur Penn | With Warren Beatty, Faye Dunaway, Gene Hackman, Estelle Parsons | 111 minutes | Not Rated

More a piece of "film history than real history", this "stunning" 1930s "crime-spree" biopic "broke a lot of old rules" in its "revisionist" take on the title characters, real-life "losers" reconceived by Beatty and Dunaway as the "screen's best-ever antiheroes"; the "letter-perfect" cast, "impeccable" direction and "gorgeously gory" photography all add up to way-"ahead-of-its-time" moviemaking, even if the "indelible images" of the "bloody ballet at the end" unsettle the squeamish.

Boogie Nights
19 | 21 | 19 | 19

1997 | Directed by Paul Thomas Anderson | With Mark Wahlberg, Burt Reynolds, Julianne Moore | 152 minutes | Rated R

Set in the '70s "disco era", this "dead-on look" at the "ins and outs (so to speak) of the porn industry" features "inspired performances" – "Burt returns!", "Marky Mark grows up!" – even if the "XXX film stars" portrayed "don't have much going on upstairs"; though the "sex-drugs-and-roller-skates" plot is "shamelessly entertaining" for the "first 2/3" of the picture, the "violent", "depressing" final act can be "draining."

Born Free
24 | 19 | 24 | 23

1966 | Directed by James Hill | With Virginia McKenna, Bill Travers, Geoffrey Keen | 95 minutes | Rated PG

The "theme song alone" is enough to set off "shameless weeping" as this "well-told" flick unfolds, focusing on a family in "wild Africa" and their effort to "protect the lioness Elsa"; a "major tearjerker", it remains "vivid" for boomers who "loved it as a child" even though it's "so sad."

Born on the Fourth of July ✉
20 | 21 | 20 | 20

1989 | Directed by Oliver Stone | With Tom Cruise, Kyra Sedgwick, Willem Dafoe | 145 minutes | Rated R

"Cruise excels" in one of Stone's "most accomplished works", a "potent", "well-done" bio of Vietnam vet Ron Kovic that's an "intense", "heart-wrenching" study of "flag-waving patriotism"; though it draws fire for being "contrived" and "overwrought", it does offer convincing "proof that Tom can act."

Born Yesterday ✉◗
26 | 28 | 25 | 23

1950 | Directed by George Cukor | With Judy Holliday, Broderick Crawford, William Holden | 103 minutes | Not Rated

"Still magical today", this "zany" screwball comedy has to do with a "not-so-dumb blonde" who undergoes a *My Fair Lady*–like transformation and "breaks out of her bimbo chains"; thanks to a unique voice and "great timing", the "perfectly cast" Holliday won an Oscar for her "pure gold" turn, a "pièce de résistance" that the 1993 remake "can't match."

Bottle Rocket
22 | 20 | 21 | 17

1996 | Directed by Wes Anderson | With Owen Wilson, Luke Wilson, James Caan | 92 minutes | Rated R

Anderson's "offbeat" directorial debut, this "charmer" of a comedy sends off "quirky" fireworks, letting the "Wilson boys" rock as "would-be gangsters" on the run whose "hijinks-laden" exploits can be "surprisingly funny"; the "obviously low-budget" production "doesn't always gel", but it remains an "overlooked precursor" of "what was to come."

Bourne Identity, The
20 | 19 | 20 | 21

2002 | Directed by Doug Liman | With Matt Damon, Franka Potente, Chris Cooper | 119 minutes | Rated PG-13

An "amnesiac" CIA assassin struggles to recover his identity in this "adrenaline-rush" thriller based on the Robert Ludlum best-seller that features "riveting action" scenes (including "one of the better car chases in recent memory"), but only "decent chemistry" between the leads; though Matt's performance provokes debate – "cool and capable" versus "lightweight" – in the end the scenic European "locations redeem the picture."

Bourne Supremacy, The
21 | 21 | 21 | 23

2004 | Directed by Paul Greengrass | With Matt Damon, Joan Allen, Julia Stiles | 108 minutes | Rated PG-13

Damon is "re-Bourne" as a "secret agent turned wanted man" out for "payback" in this "sharp-shooting sequel", a "spy caper with a brain" that's "as good as the original", packing fresh "cat-and-mouse action", "high-tech twists" and "gorgeous" Euro backdrops; its "herky-jerky" camera coverage can be "dizzying", though, so "take Dramamine" during those "fantastic" car chases that are one "wicked ride."

Bowling for Columbine
22 | - | 21 | 19

2002 | Directed by Michael Moore | Documentary | 120 minutes | Rated R

Moore's "provocative" yet "surprisingly funny" docudrama is a "punch in the jaw to anyone who is completely pro-gun"; "even if the events were staged, the message massaged and the view decidedly one-sided", it's still an "important movie" that "everyone should see", so "watch it before passing judgment" – "you'll have something to talk about for hours."

Boys Don't Cry ✉
23 | 27 | 23 | 21

1999 | Directed by Kimberly Peirce | With Hilary Swank, Chloë Sevigny, Peter Sarsgaard | 118 minutes | Rated R

Turning a "dark situation" into a "tough" study of "intolerance", this "disturbing" drama is a "faithful telling of the story of Teena Brandon", a small-town girl who "dresses and acts the part" of a boy, leading to "powerful" complications; though the Oscar-winning Swank is "beyond convincing", the "brutal" ending is "not easy to watch", but "will stay with you" – "unfortunately, it's true."

Boys from Brazil, The
24 | 26 | 25 | 22

1978 | Directed by Franklin J. Schaffner | With Gregory Peck, Laurence Olivier, Steve Guttenberg, James Mason | 123 minutes | Rated R

"Old Nazis" plan new terror via a brood of "Hitler clones" in this "taut thriller" starring the "powerful" Olivier as a war-criminal tracker who goes "mano a mano" with Peck's "evil Dr. Mengele"; it's a trove of "delightfully creepy" scenes ("loved the Dobermans"), and the "over-the-top" scenario still holds up given that a "genetic-engineering nightmare" is "even scarier now."

	OVERALL	ACTING	STORY	PROD.

Boys on the Side
15 | 18 | 15 | 16

1995 | Directed by Herbert Ross | With Whoopi Goldberg, Mary-Louise Parker, Drew Barrymore | 117 minutes | Rated R

"Girl power" is alive and well in this "epitome of a chick flick" charting the offbeat adventures of three gals headed cross country; the "touching" story, one part road movie and one part feminist tract, proves that "friendship is a great thing", while also demonstrating that "Drew can act if she picks the right material."

Boyz N the Hood
23 | 22 | 24 | 21

1991 | Directed by John Singleton | With Ice Cube, Cuba Gooding Jr., Laurence Fishburne | 107 minutes | Rated R

The "gangsta flick" that "sets the bar" for the competition "keeps it real" as it takes a "hard-core" look at ghetto "gang wars in South Central" LA; an "important" breakthrough with some "surprising acting turns", it's a "fantastic first film" from Singleton, whose later work doesn't "get anywhere near this one."

☒ Braveheart ✉
26 | 24 | 25 | 27

1995 | Directed by Mel Gibson | With Mel Gibson, Sophie Marceau, Catherine McCormack | 177 minutes | Rated R

"It's got everything" say fans of this "awe-inspiring" medieval "history lesson" about an "underdog" Scottish hero ("Mel in a kilt" and "war paint") "knocking heads" in an anti-Brit "rebellion"; the "gory" battles, "heartfelt" acting and "huge scope" help justify Gibson's Best Director win, even if some warn of three "long", "melodramatic" hours.

Brazil
24 | 23 | 23 | 27

1985 | Directed by Terry Gilliam | With Jonathan Pryce, Robert De Niro, Bob Hoskins | 131 minutes | Rated R

Even as "fantasy", Monty Python alum Gilliam's "twisted", "utterly original" vision of a "part-Orwell, part-Python" future is "a little out there"; it demands "perseverance" – what with its "baffling" "whirlwind" of "bizarre" effects and chin-scratching "black comedy" plot about one man's struggle with a "Kafka-esque" "bureaucracy" – but rewards those who hang in there with a "totally crazy ride."

Breach
23 | 26 | 24 | 23

2007 | Directed by Billy Ray | With Chris Cooper, Ryan Phillippe, Laura Linney | 110 minutes | Rated PG-13

Based on the "actual events" surrounding the case of Robert Hanssen, the notorious FBI agent caught "spilling the beans to the Soviets", this "taut" espionage thriller pits the "brilliant" Cooper against an "amazing" Phillippe in a "chess game of the minds" that has you "engaged from the get-go"; don't expect any "over-the-top pyrotechnics" or "easy answers" here, just good old "edge-of-your-seat tension" that doesn't quit "even if you know the ending."

☒ Breaker Morant
27 | 27 | 27 | 24

1980 | Directed by Bruce Beresford | With Jack Thompson, Edward Woodward, Bryan Brown | 107 minutes | Rated PG

"Guy's-flick" fans salute this "solid Aussie" drama of "kangaroo" justice, a "small masterpiece" in its "gripping" depiction of "betrayal" at a military trial during the Boer War; told with "moving realism", it tackles the "question of morals in warfare" using a "top-notch" cast to "demonstrate bravery" and "bravura", turning the fate of "appointed scapegoats" into an "inspiration."

☑ Breakfast at Tiffany's
26 | 26 | 24 | 24

1961 | Directed by Blake Edwards | With Audrey Hepburn, George Peppard, Patricia Neal | 115 minutes | Rated PG

In the "role she was born to play", a "mesmerizing" Hepburn brings Truman Capote's "messed-up" "free spirit" Holly Golightly to life in "peerless style"; fans find everything about it "irresistible" – "Henry Mancini's divine score", Audrey's "timeless clothes", the "love-letter-to-NY" cinematography – and call this "dream-making, heartbreaking" tribute to the "power of romance" their "all-time favorite."

Breakfast Club, The
22 | 21 | 22 | 19

1985 | Directed by John Hughes | With Emilio Estevez, Anthony Michael Hall, Judd Nelson, Molly Ringwald | 92 minutes | Rated R

Any "child of the '80s" is apt to "know all the lines" of this "engaging" high school yukfest, a "Gen-X" "time capsule" about a group of "Brat Pack all-stars" "stuck in detention"; a "hoot" with a "sensitive" side, it's rerun "ad infinitum", since it "speaks to teenagers in a way that *American Pie* will never be able to."

Breakfast on Pluto
19 | 24 | 18 | 20

2005 | Directed by Neil Jordan | With Cillian Murphy, Liam Neeson, Stephen Rea | 135 minutes | Rated R

Thanks to Murphy's "beyond amazing" turn as a "hapless Irish trannie" seeking "self-actualization" in the '70s U.K., this "edgy" drama whips IRA "turmoil", "tongue-in-cheek" repartee, "T-Rex" and a "totally bitchin' wardrobe" into one "fabulous" eye-opener; but while its story of a "tragicomic innocent" is "compelling", a few feel the "odd flights of fancy" lie somewhere "between involving and cloying."

Breaking Away ✉
24 | 21 | 24 | 20

1979 | Directed by Peter Yates | With Dennis Christopher, Dennis Quaid, Daniel Stern | 100 minutes | Rated PG

A "rousing ride", this *Rocky*-esque "Hoosier tale" is a "coming-of-age" drama on two wheels, with Christopher leading a cast of "cutie-pie" "underdogs" as a cyclist who pedals straight into a "town-and-gown" "class conflict"; it's cheered on as a "big-hearted" "buddy film" that delivers a "socko" bike race finale.

Breaking the Waves
23 | 27 | 20 | 20

1996 | Directed by Lars von Trier | With Emily Watson, Stellan Skarsgård | 153 minutes | Rated R

"Be prepared" for "emotionally devastating" doings in this "raw" drama of "delusion" and "doomed romance" about a "dimwitted girl" who "sacrifices everything for her paralyzed husband"; most pronounce it "strange" yet "so well done it's painful" (the "musical interludes give one time to weep"), though foes call it a "silly" parable that's a most "depressing" picture of "female martyrdom."

Breathless ❶🄵
25 | 24 | 21 | 23

1961 | Directed by Jean-Luc Godard | With Jean-Paul Belmondo, Jean Seberg | 87 minutes | Not Rated

"So hip" and as "refreshing" now as at its debut, this French "New Wave masterpiece" breathes "pure pleasure" into a "silly gangster story" with "luscious" leads Belmondo and Seberg as lovers on the lam (even the late-'50s Paris setting is a "terrific character"); while scholars speak of genre-"defining" technical feats – the "jump cut is born!" – most simply find it "charming" and way "ahead of its time."

Bride of Frankenstein, The ◑

25 | 21 | 23 | 23

1935 | Directed by James Whale | With Boris Karloff, Colin Clive, Elsa Lanchester | 75 minutes | Not Rated

Bolt-necked Frankie gets "his one shot at love" in this "excellent sequel" to the hoary "'30s horror classic", wherein Karloff reprises his signature role with "panache" and Lanchester's shocked fiancée simply has "great hair"; fright fiends cherish the "creepy" results as "campy", "funny" and not a little "whacked."

Bride Wore Black, The ☒

▽ 25 | 26 | 25 | 22

1968 | Directed by François Truffaut | With Jeanne Moreau, Michel Bouquet, Jean-Claude Brialy | 107 minutes | Not Rated

The "original *Kill Bill*", this psychological thriller based on the Cornell Woolrich novel stars a "sterling" Moreau as a widow hell bent on avenging her husband's murder; it's an out-and-out "homage to Hitchcock" and plain that director Truffaut "knows the territory well", even engaging Hitch favorite Bernard Herrmann as its composer.

☑ Bridge on the River Kwai, The ✉

28 | 28 | 27 | 28

1957 | Directed by David Lean | With William Holden, Alec Guinness, Jack Hawkins | 161 minutes | Rated PG

Those "stiff upper lips" do some "memorable" whistling in director Lean's "grand", "engrossing" Japanese POW camp epic, an "old-fashioned" yarn about the "timeless themes" of "honor", "conviction" and the "madness" of war; a lock for the top Oscars of 1957, it "succeeds" mightily with "great performances" – led by a "hubris"-afflicted Guinness – enhanced by "splashy" scenery and an "explosive ending."

Bridges of Madison County, The

19 | 23 | 20 | 20

1995 | Directed by Clint Eastwood | With Clint Eastwood, Meryl Streep, Annie Corley | 135 minutes | Rated PG-13

Director/leading man Eastwood unveils his "gentle side" in this "bittersweet" romance recounting the "middle-aged" passion between a "roving" photographer and a "lonely housewife"; some cite the "banal", "snail's-pace" plot as a big "yawn", but to fans it's "lovably sappy" – and "way better" than the "treacly" book.

Bridget Jones's Diary

21 | 23 | 22 | 21

2001 | Directed by Sharon Maguire | With Renée Zellweger, Hugh Grant, Colin Firth | 97 minutes | Rated R

This "everygirl" "chick flick" is a "charming" romance starring the "fab" Zellweger, doing a "knockout job" in the title role as a "twentysomething singleton" "desperately seeking a spouse" but plagued by "faux pas", "weight gain" and a "perfect cad" of a boss; followers find it "hilarious yet true" but won't commit as to whether it "nails the book" or not.

Bridge to Terabithia

22 | 22 | 22 | 24

2007 | Directed by Gabor Csupo | With Josh Hutcherson, Anna Sophia Robb, Zooey Deschanel | 95 minutes | Rated PG

Roping together "imaginative" fantasy and "touching" drama, this "well-done" coming-of-ager about a pair of pre-teen "outsiders" who "find each other" in a "make-believe" world hews "very close to the book" it's based on and boasts "delightful" work by leads Hutcherson and Robb; still, parents caution the "shocking climax" may take a toll on tots.

⑦ Brief Encounter ◐   27 | 29 | 27 | 25
1946 | Directed by David Lean | With Celia Johnson, Trevor Howard, Stanley Holloway | 86 minutes | Not Rated

For a "truly romantic" fix, this "quiet" "masterpiece of yearning" from David Lean is "right up there" in the running as the "definitive tearjerker"; the "never better" Johnson and Howard play "ordinary people" whose meeting on a train develops into a "short but intense" "connection", with swells of Rachmaninoff to seal the deal; in brief, an "unforgettable" trip.

Brigadoon   24 | 21 | 22 | 24
1954 | Directed by Vincente Minnelli | With Gene Kelly, Van Johnson, Cyd Charisse | 108 minutes | Not Rated

A Lerner and Loewe "stage show turned into a movie", this "lesser-known" MGM musical is set in a mythical Scottish town that can be visited by outsiders only once every 100 years; though some criticize the "corny" concept, "phony accents" and "cardboard back-lot" sets, most "suspend disbelief" once the music starts and the "magical" Kelly and Charisse begin "dancing in the heather."

Brighton Beach Memoirs   22 | 23 | 23 | 20
1986 | Directed by Gene Saks | With Jonathan Silverman, Blythe Danner, Judith Ivey | 108 minutes | Rated PG-13

Pre-war Brooklyn "lives on in folklore" via this "nostalgic" coming-of-age drama that kicks off author Neil Simon's "autobiographical" trilogy with "bittersweet" reminisces of '30s "Jewish culture"; the "period-piece" POV can be "schmaltzy", but the "three-dimensional portrayals" from a "talented cast" leave "little to kvetch about."

Bringing Down the House   19 | 21 | 17 | 19
2003 | Directed by Adam Shankman | With Steve Martin, Queen Latifah, Eugene Levy, Joan Plowright | 105 minutes | Rated PG-13

Steve and Queenie are a "modern day George and Gracie" in this "laugh-out-loud" comedy about a "staid" lawyer and an "outrageous" bank robber who meet in an online chat room; the script may be "vulgar" with too many "outdated racial stereotypes", but at least it's "equal opportunity offensive" – and it's "nice to see plus-size girls get their props."

Bringing Up Baby ◐   27 | 27 | 24 | 24
1938 | Directed by Howard Hawks | With Katharine Hepburn, Cary Grant | 102 minutes | Not Rated

"One continuous roar", director Hawks' "screwiest of screwball comedies" is propelled at a "frenetic pace" by the Hepburn-Grant "chemistry" and a "tons-of-fun" scenario touching on "dinosaur bones, crazy rich folk" and a lost leopard; it's an old-school "madcap" "champ", and fans of "farce" still bring it up as the "funniest movie ever."

Bring It On   17 | 15 | 16 | 16
2000 | Directed by Peyton Reed | With Kirsten Dunst, Eliza Dushku, Gabrielle Union | 98 minutes | Rated PG-13

"One for the tweens", this "frothy" high-school comedy about "rival cheerleading squads" brings on "bouncy" pom-pommer Dunst, depending on "team spirit" as she copes with "cliques" and "cattiness" on the way to a "competitive" showdown; for sure, the plot's strictly "cookie-cutter", but "turn your brain off" and you just may feel like "15 again."

Broadcast News
23 | 25 | 22 | 20

1987 | Directed by James L. Brooks | With William Hurt, Albert Brooks, Holly Hunter | 127 minutes | Rated R
"Appearance over substance" is the subject of this "smart" "send-up of the media" about a "love triangle" in a "career-driven", *Network*-esque TV newsroom that hums with "behind-the-scenes" one-upmanship; nominated for a slew of Oscars (but winner of none), this "ahead-of-its-time" comedy remains "totally engaging", due to the efforts of its "sharp-as-a-tack" cast.

Broadway Danny Rose ◑
22 | 22 | 22 | 20

1984 | Directed by Woody Allen | With Woody Allen, Mia Farrow, Nick Apollo Forte | 84 minutes | Rated PG
Woody and Mia (in rosier days) light up this comedy about a "Mafia tootsie who melts" for the "ultimate mensch", a small-time talent agent clinging to the "underbelly" of "borscht-belt" showbiz; although infused with a "NY sensibility", some say the "shaggy-dog" plot "doesn't quite deliver."

Brokeback Mountain ✉
24 | 26 | 23 | 26

2005 | Directed by Ang Lee | With Heath Ledger, Jake Gyllenhaal, Michelle Williams, Anne Hathaway | 134 minutes | Rated R
Widely pegged as the "gay cowboy movie", this "star-crossed" "Romeo-and-Romeo" romance is as "controversial" as they come, yet its "gimmick-free" rendition of "forbidden love" "avoids sensationalism" thanks to an "understated" performance by Ledger (and an "underrated" one by Gyllenhaal), backed up by "stunning scenery", a "ravishing score" and "Angst" Lee's "heartfelt", Oscar-winning direction; ultimately, this "timeless" film has had a "real cultural influence", even if it's best remembered for the "most spoofed line of the year": "I wish I knew how to quit you."

Broken Flowers
16 | 20 | 15 | 17

2005 | Directed by Jim Jarmusch | With Bill Murray, Julie Delpy, Sharon Stone | 106 minutes | Rated R
Murray's "dry delivery" and director Jarmusch's "minimalism" are the "thin" soil for this "oddball", "low-key" indie drama about a "middle-aged Everyman" who "hits the road" to "revisit the women in his life" in order to find the "son he never knew"; "subtle" smarts aside, many say "enough already" of a "slow trip" made even more "infuriating" by an "arty ending."

Brother Bear
21 | - | 21 | 23

2003 | Directed by Aaron Blaise, Bob Walker | Animated | 85 minutes | Rated G
"Sweet" yet "not overly sentimental", this "politically correct" Disney feature tells the tale of a boy turned into a bear, learning to "respect all living things" along the way; despite "old-fashioned" animation and a "slow-moving" pace, it redeems itself with a "message of love"; P.S. a pair of moose voiced by SCTV's McKenzie brothers provide a breath of "over-the-top" relief for grown-ups.

	OVERALL	ACTING	STORY	PROD.

Brother from Another Planet, The
`23` `22` `23` `19`

1984 | Directed by John Sayles | With Joe Morton, Steve James, Bill Cobbs | 108 minutes | Rated R

"Truly original for its time", this "low-budget" "cult favorite" via John Sayles examines "race relations and urban life" in its "offbeat" story of a black extraterrestrial who lands in Harlem; despite the sci-fi underpinnings, it's more of a "funny social commentary" about "what it means to be human", with a mute title character (the very "likable" Morton) and one of the "greatest on-screen card tricks ever."

Brothers McMullen, The
`19` `19` `19` `16`

1995 | Directed by Edward Burns | With Edward Burns, Mike McGlone, Jack Mulcahy | 98 minutes | Rated R

"Indie darling" Burns' "low-budget" first flick is an "engaging" drama that serves up a "slice of Irish-American life", tracking a trio of "working-class" brothers through their amorous ups and downs; though some find this tale of "loyalty and commitment on Long Island" a tad "amateurish", this "little gem" generated "big buzz" – so "what happened to this guy?"

Bruce Almighty
`18` `20` `18` `19`

2003 | Directed by Tom Shadyac | With Jim Carrey, Jennifer Aniston, Morgan Freeman | 101 minutes | Rated PG-13

"Heaven help us": Carrey of the renown "rubber face" portrays an "ordinary man" turned Supreme Being and actually "delivers laughs" plus a "positive message" in this "enjoyable", "lighthearted" chuckler co-starring the "lovable" Aniston and "elegant" Freeman; a warning to those who pray for "something edgy": this one might feel like "religion class."

Buck Privates ◑
`22` `19` `16` `18`

1941 | Directed by Arthur Lubin | With Abbott & Costello, the Andrews Sisters | 84 minutes | Not Rated

A coupla clowns go to boot camp and "frivolity" ensues in this "classic Abbott and Costello" comedy, which "evokes an era" thanks to the "duo's rapid-fire patter" and USO-worthy tunes by the "Andrews Sisters at their peak"; despite "patchwork" plotting, it "ranks up there" in Bud and Lou's oeuvre and works as a swell "Sunday morning" indulgence.

Buddy Holly Story, The
`21` `23` `21` `20`

1978 | Directed by Steve Rash | With Gary Busey, Don Stroud, Charles Martin Smith | 113 minutes | Rated PG

Busey hits the "top of the charts" with his "flawless" singing impersonation of "pioneering rocker" Buddy Holly in this "convincing" biopic that charts the star's "rise to greatness" on the strength of seminal songs and "iconic glasses" that "invented geek chic"; indeed, the '50s "maverick spirit" is so "bravura", you wish they could "rewrite history" for a "happier ending."

Buena Vista Social Club
`25` `-` `24` `24`

1999 | Directed by Wim Wenders | Documentary | 101 minutes | Rated G

"Revelatory – and danceable" – this documentary is a "love letter to a vanishing breed" of musicians, "aging" vets of the "Afro-Cuban jazz" scene who volunteer "personal histories" of "trials and tribulations" in the "shadow of Castro", interspersed with "irresistible" live jams; it "builds slowly" in a haze of "washed-out tropical colors" to a narrative of "great charm" and "insight", backed by a soundtrack that's as "captivating" as they come.

Bug's Life, A

24	-	22	26

1998 | Directed by John Lasseter, Andrew Stanton | Animated | 96 minutes | Rated G

"Even parents" bug out on the "mind-blowing creativity" of the Disney/Pixar team's "step-ahead animation" in this "cute" parable of "insect politics" rendered in "sharp, colorful" computer graphics that "look incredible", even if the "social satire" is "geared for kids"; most maintain it's "superior to *Antz*" and advise sticking around for the fake outtakes as the credits roll (the "best part").

Bugsy

18	19	18	19

1991 | Directed by Barry Levinson | With Warren Beatty, Annette Bening, Harvey Keitel, Ben Kingsley | 135 minutes | Rated R

"Long but fascinating", this bio of mobster Bugsy Siegel (the "gangster who created Las Vegas out of desert dust") is a "graphic" film about high-rolling "lowlifes"; though a few yawn it's a "Beatty vanity project", at least the "bewitching cinematography" makes the already "beautiful cast even more ravishing"; fave line: "why don't you run outside and jerk yourself a soda?"

Bull Durham

22	22	22	20

1988 | Directed by Ron Shelton | With Kevin Costner, Susan Sarandon, Tim Robbins | 108 minutes | Rated R

"Life and love in minor-league baseball" equal "diverting" comedy in this "funny and realistic" sports pic, juiced by "sexy", "laid-back acting" from Sarandon and Costner, a "great pair" out to take the "American spirit" into extra innings; fans cheer it on as a "smart home run" that's "one of the best" of the hardball yarns.

Bullets Over Broadway

21	23	21	21

1994 | Directed by Woody Allen | With John Cusack, Dianne Wiest, Jennifer Tilly, Chazz Palminteri | 98 minutes | Rated R

A "quirky, colorful" shot of "period" atmosphere, this "backstage comedy" concerns a Jazz Age dramatist and a "gangster who rewrites his Broadway play"; it's "likable" enough for its "witty dialogue" and "over-the-top" cast, though as usual for a "post-*Hannah*" Allen opus, some wish it were "just a little funnier."

Bullitt

22	20	20	24

1968 | Directed by Peter Yates | With Steve McQueen, Robert Vaughn, Jacqueline Bisset | 113 minutes | Rated PG

Arguably "the mother of all cop films", this "solid" action thriller stars an "icy-cool" McQueen, "acting by not acting" as a no-bull SFPD detective who takes on a corrupt system; set in Frisco "before too many high-rises" arrived, it's famed for a "definitive car chase" ("whee!") that's "still the best" after "countless" knockoffs, though some find the ride "pretty straightforward" plotwise.

Bus Stop

21	21	20	20

1956 | Directed by Joshua Logan | With Marilyn Monroe, Don Murray, Eileen Heckart | 96 minutes | Not Rated

Proving herself "at home on the range", Monroe brings "depth" to romantic comedy as a "vulnerable" "Western chantoosie" with "impossible dreams" adrift in an otherwise "slightly sappy" tale of a cowpoke's "crazy love"; though Marilyn proves she's more than "just a pretty face", skeptics of her "serious actress" mode say they "want to get off."

Butch Cassidy & the Sundance Kid ✉ | 26 | 26 | 25 | 25 |

1969 | Directed by George Roy Hill | With Paul Newman, Robert Redford, Katharine Ross | 110 minutes | Rated PG

"Compulsive charmers" Newman and Redford play a pair of wise-cracking, "magnetic" "antiheroes" trying to stay ahead of the law in this "outstanding" Western "buddy movie", loaded with "adventure and humor"; it fuses a "snappy" script, Burt Bacharach soundtrack and "too many classic scenes to count" into a "sentimental favorite" that's "never boring" from start to "unforgettable" finish.

Butterfield 8 ✉ | 23 | 26 | 24 | 23 |

1960 | Directed by Daniel Mann | With Elizabeth Taylor, Laurence Harvey, Eddie Fisher, Dina Merrill | 109 minutes | Not Rated

A "bombshell" call girl with a "taste for the good life" and "fabulous furs" falls for a "rich, married heartbreaker" in this "expertly done" drama that landed Taylor her first Oscar; no question, Liz "sizzles", but some say this "dated", sanitized version of the 1935 John O'Hara novel is "hardly one for the ages."

Butterflies Are Free | 21 | 23 | 21 | 20 |

1972 | Directed by Milton Katselas | With Goldie Hawn, Edward Albert, Eileen Heckart | 109 minutes | Rated PG

"Great casting" floats this "charming comedy" from Broadway to the big screen, with a "young Goldie" playing a "goofy free spirit" out to "befriend/seduce" a blind attorney; while the "realities of disability" are "touching", it's the "priceless chemistry" that has most aflutter.

Bye Bye Birdie | 19 | 18 | 18 | 20 |

1963 | Directed by George Sidney | With Janet Leigh, Dick Van Dyke, Ann-Margret | 112 minutes | Rated G

The high "fun quotient" bolsters this "upbeat" musical from the "long-ago world" of 1963, a look at the hoopla surrounding an Elvis-like singer's farewell gig before he goes off to the army; though Ann-Margret is "one heck of a talented sex kitten" doing some athletic song-and-dance numbers that - whew! - "stay with you", detractors wave it off as "cheesy" fare that's "woefully dated now."

Cabaret ✉ | 26 | 25 | 25 | 27 |

1972 | Directed by Bob Fosse | With Liza Minnelli, Michael York, Joel Grey | 124 minutes | Rated PG

Comprised of equal parts "love, angst", "singing, dancing and Nazis", this "seminal modern musical" set in pre-WWII Berlin is a "touchstone" of the genre that "hasn't lost its luster"; old chums cheer Fosse's "superb direction" and the "starmaking performances" from Minnelli and Grey (who all took home Oscars), and even though the mood of the piece can career from "dark" to "raunchy", it's always "fun to watch."

Cabinet of Dr. Caligari, The ◐ | 26 | 21 | 24 | 26 |

1921 | Directed by Robert Wiene | With Conrad Veidt, Werner Kraus | 67 minutes | Not Rated

"They don't get any freakier" than this "fascinating antique", a "men-acingly atmospheric" silent horror flick that uses "German expressionism" and "twisted sets" to kindle a "nightmare" tale of murder told by a "tortured mind"; "stark, powerful" and "spooky" right down to the pioneering "surprise ending", it's "still being imitated" and still makes many modern chillers "look lame."

Cabin in the Sky ◗

	OVERALL	ACTING	STORY	PROD.
	24	23	23	22

1943 | Directed by Vincente Minnelli | With Ethel Waters, Eddie "Rochester" Anderson, Lena Horne | 98 minutes | Not Rated

A "rare major studio release with an all African-American cast", this "classic musical" is worth seeing since nearly "every black actor or singer of the era was in it"; the rather "dated" plot – something to do with a husband's temptation and its consequences – pales in comparison to the "wonderful music", including "gems" like 'Taking a Chance on Love' and 'Happiness is a Thing Called Joe.'

Cactus Flower

21	22	20	20

1969 | Directed by Gene Saks | With Walter Matthau, Ingrid Bergman, Goldie Hawn | 103 minutes | Rated PG

This "cute" if "dated" comedy about the affairs of a philandering dentist might be "romantic fluff", but it's redeemed by a "strong cast", particularly the "radiant" Bergman and the "delightful", Oscar-winning Hawn "in her screen debut"; sticklers say "even Matthau can't save" the "weak story", though "he does try."

⊿ Caddyshack

24	20	19	19

1980 | Directed by Harold Ramis | With Chevy Chase, Rodney Dangerfield, Bill Murray | 99 minutes | Rated R

"Dumb as it is", this "goofy" comedy of "golfers gone amok" is a "classic" of "un-ironic" (some say "sophomoric") humor featuring a "priceless" ensemble cast and a fake gopher; "ok, it's a guy thing", but it "stands the test of time" as "oft-quoted" "mindless fun."

Caine Mutiny, The

27	28	26	23

1954 | Directed by Edward Dmytryk | With Humphrey Bogart, Jose Ferrer, Van Johnson | 124 minutes | Not Rated

This "briny" blend of "powerful wartime story" and "engrossing" courtroom drama gets its ballast from Bogart's "brilliant", "pull-out-all-the-stops" turn as Queeg, the "demented sea captain" compulsively "click, click, clicking" a set of "steel balls"; the "classic script" follows a "totally believable" high-seas rebellion to a court-martial and is "must-see" material for maritime mavens.

Calendar Girls

23	25	23	22

2003 | Directed by Nigel Cole | With Helen Mirren, Julie Walters, John Alderton | 108 minutes | Rated PG-13

"Older can be beautiful" is the "serious message behind the tea and scones" of this comic tale of "plucky", middle-aged English gals who pose for a nude calendar to raise funds for a cancer center; the "talent-laden cast" does a "charming" job with this "female version of *The Full Monty*", and let's face it, "who doesn't love Helen Mirren naked?"

Camelot

21	21	23	23

1967 | Directed by Joshua Logan | With Richard Harris, Vanessa Redgrave, Franco Nero | 179 minutes | Rated G

Lerner and Loewe's Broadway musical of the "well-worn" King Arthur legend receives "faithful" treatment in this tale of pomp and "passion in medieval England"; admirers of the "gorgeous" sets and "beautiful music" sing its praises as a "magical" "diversion", though dissenters dis the "ponderous" "excess" and note "no one in the cast can carry a tune."

Camille ◑

26 | 26 | 25 | 26

1937 | Directed by George Cukor | With Greta Garbo, Robert Taylor, Lionel Barrymore | 109 minutes | Not Rated

The "epitome of classic romance", this ultra-"tragic love story" stars "Garbo at her peak" playing a 19th-century Parisian courtesan with a cough who falls for a rather naïve young man; although Taylor is "marginal in an admittedly thankless role", his leading lady's "charm" and "breathtaking beauty" is "fascinating" enough to keep admirers enthralled; P.S. "have plenty of Kleenex on hand."

Candidate, The ✉

20 | 22 | 22 | 20

1972 | Directed by Michael Ritchie | With Robert Redford, Peter Boyle, Melvyn Douglas | 109 minutes | Rated PG

A "prescient" civics lesson, this political drama tracks a "social activist seduced into selling his soul" when he runs for the Senate from California; a "most convincing" Redford leads the pack of "top-notch performances" as the novice campaigner who's "in far over his head", presenting an "accurate" if "cynical view" of the process that registers as "timely" over 30 years later.

Cannonball Run, The

17 | 14 | 15 | 16

1981 | Directed by Hal Needham | With Burt Reynolds, Roger Moore, Farrah Fawcett, Dom DeLuise | 95 minutes | Rated PG

"Zany, not brainy", this "sophomoric" comedy sends a "mugging" Reynolds and "half of 1981 Hollywood" on a "race across America" with "fast cars, hot women" and miles of "mindless fun" in lieu of an "actual plot"; though "incredibly cheesy" and "showing its age", it's still loaded with "good laughs", especially if you "don't want to think too hard."

Cape Fear ◑

25 | 26 | 26 | 23

1962 | Directed by J. Lee Thompson | With Gregory Peck, Robert Mitchum, Polly Bergen | 105 minutes | Not Rated

It's high tide for "rage and revenge" in this "doozy" of a noir thriller, a real "nail-biter" starring Peck as an upright dad who "gets down in the gutter" to protect his family from a "deeply frightening" ex-con at large in the marsh and "as evil as they come"; most rate it "scarier than the remake", "without the histrionics."

Cape Fear

20 | 24 | 21 | 20

1991 | Directed by Martin Scorsese | With Robert De Niro, Nick Nolte, Jessica Lange, Juliette Lewis | 128 minutes | Rated R

Count on "fear for sure" as Scorsese's "well-done" redo of the killer '62 thriller heads for "over-the-top territory", working up "sustained suspense" as a "terrifying" De Niro "has a ball" portraying a vengeance-bent "wacko"; it's an "edge-of-your-seat" ride, with the "cameos" from the "previous cast" that are a "nice touch."

⧉ Capote ✉

26 | 29 | 24 | 25

2005 | Directed by Bennett Miller | With Philip Seymour Hoffman, Catherine Keener, Chris Cooper | 114 minutes | Rated R

Not content to do a mere "uncanny impression", "genius" Hoffman delves "inside the mind" of "flamboyant" writer Truman Capote to render the "iconoclast" "in all his complexity" – while nabbing a "well-deserved" Oscar along the way – in this "fascinating" biopic, a behind the scenes look at the writing of Tru's "watershed" book *In Cold Blood*; abetted by Keener's "sturdy" supporting turn, this "world-class study" also works well as a "meditation on journalistic ethics."

Captain Blood ◑ | 23 | 21 | 20 | 21 |

1935 | Directed by Michael Curtiz | With Errol Flynn, Olivia de Havilland, Basil Rathbone | 119 minutes | Not Rated

Avast, there's "salty" "popcorn fun" aplenty in this "smashing" swash-buckler, featuring "Flynn's first starring role" as an enslaved wretch who becomes a "devil-may-care" pirate of the Caribbean; armchair bucca-neers jump on board for the "roguish" baddies, "high-seas action" and "men in tights", not minding that the old vessel is "on the creaky side."

Captains Courageous ✉◑ | 25 | 26 | 24 | 21 |

1937 | Directed by Victor Fleming | With Spencer Tracy, Freddie Bartholomew, Lionel Barrymore | 115 minutes | Not Rated

Fashioned from a Kipling tale that's "every boy's dream of excitement", this "tearjerker"-cum–adventure story stars Bartholomew as a bratty rich kid who's rescued at sea and matures under the helm of a salty sailor, the Oscar-winning Tracy; the lad's "touching" transformation is conveyed through "phenomenal" acting that's "too often forgotten."

Carlito's Way | 22 | 25 | 22 | 22 |

1993 | Directed by Brian De Palma | With Al Pacino, Sean Penn, Penelope Ann Miller | 145 minutes | Rated R

Scarface cohorts De Palma and Pacino go "gangster" again in this "tight, tense" crime thriller about a Latino drug lord just out of prison who's "trying to go straight but not getting there"; with the principals "in peak form" (Penn "steals the show" as a "slimy, coke-addicted" lawyer), it's a "cool", if "underrated" look at the underworld with a "subtle" slant.

Carmen Jones | 23 | 23 | 23 | 23 |

1954 | Directed by Otto Preminger | With Dorothy Dandridge, Harry Belafonte, Pearl Bailey | 105 minutes | Not Rated

A "modern", "Americanized" version of Bizet's "classic" *Carmen*, this "beautiful reimagining" was a "breakthrough for its time" given its all-black cast, led by the "sassy" Dorothy and "hot" Harry; while the con-cept's "superb" and the music "beautiful", it's docked a few points since the stars' songs were dubbed by "real opera singers."

Carnal Knowledge | 22 | 26 | 21 | 21 |

1971 | Directed by Mike Nichols | With Jack Nicholson, Candice Bergen, Art Garfunkel, Ann-Margret | 98 minutes | Rated R

"Literate people talk dirty" in this "bitter but engrossing" look at "two self-absorbed buddies who measure life in terms of their sexual con-quests", and though these "pretty sad characters" can be "hard to watch", the "perfect cast" expertly evokes its theme of "innocence lost"; still, the jaded jeer what was "bold for its time" is now rather "tame."

Carousel | 24 | 22 | 22 | 25 |

1956 | Directed by Henry King | With Gordon MacRae, Shirley Jones, Cameron Mitchell | 128 minutes | Not Rated

"Girl meets wrong boy" at the traveling show in this silver screen go-round of Rodgers and Hammerstein's "sentimental" musical, which draws on a "lovely" score and "fine cast" of "first-rate" singers to spin a tale that's "romantic, sad" and "not always pretty"; while it's regarded as a "neglected great" to devotees, it's also seen as a squandering of "talent" on a "corny", "tarnished-with-age" storyline.

Carrie

22 | 22 | 23 | 21

1976 | Directed by Brian De Palma | With Sissy Spacek, Piper Laurie, Amy Irving, John Travolta | 98 minutes | Rated R

"Stephen King done right", this "bloody good" horror pic headlines Spacek as a "bug-eyed" "telekinetic outcast" (with a "nut bar" of a mom) who repays the "casual cruelty of high-schoolers" with a prom-night "flip-out" that's gorier than a bucket of "pig's blood"; with "character-oriented" carnage that's a cut above "shock schlock", it's "white knuckles all the way" to that "grabber" of an ending.

Cars

24 | - | 23 | 27

2006 | Directed by John Lasseter, Joe Ranft | Animated | 116 minutes | Rated G

Disney/Pixar's "well-oiled" animation outfit rigs a "familiar fish-out-of-water story" ("*Doc Hollywood*", anyone?) to "talking cars" and rolls out this "delightful" joyride featuring "exceptional" renderings and "adorable" vocal characterizations by Owen Wilson, Paul Newman and comic Larry The Cable Guy; parents appreciate the "great" soundtrack and "offbeat" cultural references – real lifesavers when the young 'uns "watch it for the 30th time."

☑ Casablanca ✉◑

29 | 28 | 28 | 27

1942 | Directed by Michael Curtiz | With Humphrey Bogart, Ingrid Bergman, Paul Henreid, Claude Rains | 102 minutes | Rated PG

We'll always have the "magic" of this "most compelling" of romances, a showcase for "legendary" turns from an "enigmatic" Bogart, "radiant" Bergman and "top-shelf" supporting cast set against the "unforgettable" backdrop of WWII occupied North Africa; the "fast-paced" plot of passion and "intrigue" is an "unsurpassed" model of good, "old-fashioned storytelling" and a bona fide "runner-up to Shakespeare" for "classic lines" – there's no choice but to "play it again and again."

Casino

21 | 24 | 21 | 22

1995 | Directed by Martin Scorsese | With Robert De Niro, Sharon Stone, Joe Pesci | 178 minutes | Rated R

A crash course in "pre-corporate casino management", this "flashy" crime saga of "mob life" in "seedy Vegas" relates a "dark" tale that deals out "violence, drugs and self-loathing" in spades; proponents lay their money down for De Niro as a dapper hood, Pesci's "insane mob guy" bit and a "sizzling" Stone proving she "can actually act"; still, those who yawn it's "way too long" say bets are off, since they could be "watching *Goodfellas* instead."

Casino Royale

23 | 22 | 21 | 26

2006 | Directed by Martin Campbell | With Daniel Craig, Eva Green, Mads Mikkelsen, Judi Dench | 144 minutes | Rated PG-13

A "strong reboot for the franchise", this "excellent prequel" based on Ian Fleming's first 007 novel goes "back to basics" with "fewer gadgets" and "more brains" to give the long-running series a "needed jolt"; "blond Bond" Daniel Craig's "blue-collar" take on the character makes him a "worthy successor to Connery, Sean Connery", and though the picture "bogs down in the card scenes", it's worth seeing for that "amazing opening foot chase" alone.

Casper
15 | 14 | 15 | 19

1995 | Directed by Brad Silberling | With Christina Ricci, Bill Pullman, Cathy Moriarty | 100 minutes | Rated PG

The "special effects are worth the ticket price" of this "typical family movie" that's also notable for its "really cute" title character, a ghost who's referred to as 'living impaired'; though some say the "sappy" storyline's "charmless", at least it's "not annoyingly adorable."

Cast Away
20 | 25 | 18 | 23

2000 | Directed by Robert Zemeckis | With Tom Hanks, Helen Hunt | 143 minutes | Rated PG-13

"Hanks does Crusoe" in this "well-made" adventure based on Tom's "almost-one-man show" as a "pudgy FedEx" pilot marooned after a crash landing and forced to "slim down", don a "loincloth" and start "talking to a volleyball"; though "feeling his loneliness" may be "inspiring", foes say the action's beached by "slow-moving" stretches and a "trite" windup that's too "predictable."

Cat Ballou ✉
21 | 22 | 19 | 20

1965 | Directed by Elliot Silverstein | With Lee Marvin, Jane Fonda, Michael Callan | 97 minutes | Not Rated

"Not your typical Western", this comic oater "with a heart" stars Fonda as a righteous lady outlaw but is stolen by Oscar-winner Marvin, who horses around in two roles, including that of a whiskey-addled gunslinger; a "hoot in its day", it's nearing its ninth life but is still "fun to watch."

Catch Me If You Can
23 | 24 | 25 | 24

2002 | Directed by Steven Spielberg | With Leonardo DiCaprio, Tom Hanks, Christopher Walken | 141 minutes | Rated PG-13

Spielberg's "witty, fast-paced" "cat-and-mouse game" ("based on a true story" about a charming con man) is "mischievous fun from the opening credits until the final frame", with "lots of '60s color" and "awesome acting" by the "engaging DiCaprio" and "rock-solid" Hanks; it's an "exciting, wild ride" that shows us "sometimes crime *does* pay."

Cat on a Hot Tin Roof
25 | 27 | 24 | 23

1958 | Directed by Richard Brooks | With Elizabeth Taylor, Paul Newman, Burl Ives | 108 minutes | Not Rated

"Man, these people have problems": "steamy Liz" "in that white slip" and a "dynamite" Newman "couldn't possibly look better" as they "burn up the screen" in this "sex-soaked" Tennessee Williams drama of "love, rejection" and "Southern family politics"; the "towering" Ives presides as the ragin' Big Daddy, adding an "incredibly interesting" *Lear*-like thread to all that "eye candy."

Cat People ◑
23 | 20 | 21 | 22

1942 | Directed by Jacques Tourneur | With Simone Simon, Kent Smith, Tom Conway, Jane Randolph | 73 minutes | Not Rated

"More scary than many modern films", this "wonderfully weird" "low-budget" horror flick tells the story of a "tortured soul" who believes "she's cursed to become a killer panther"; it may be "relatively tame by today's standards" (and "not for *Friday the 13th* fans"), but does achieve an "eerie tension" via its "mysterious characters", "dark sets" and "incredible use of light and shadow."

Cat People
16 | 17 | 18 | 18

1982 | Directed by Paul Schrader | With Nastassja Kinski, Malcolm McDowell, John Heard, Annette O'Toole | 118 minutes | Rated R

"Pretty on the eye if fuzzy on the brain", this "atmospheric" remake of the 1942 "Simone Simon cult classic" is a "stylish but forgettable" fantasy having to do with panthers and "sexual politics"; fans purr about its "creepy", "feline performances" and "nifty special effects", but seen-it-alls say the "David Bowie theme song" is the "best thing about this movie."

Celluloid Closet, The
25 | - | 25 | 24

1995 | Directed by Robert Epstein, Jeff Friedman | Documentary | 102 minutes | Rated R

Learn to "appreciate" certain classics in a "whole new" way via this documentary "revelation" that traces "gay themes and undercurrents" in Hollywood history using film clips and "insightful" interviews from celebs like Lily Tomlin; it takes an "unsparing look at prejudice" that's also a "very entertaining" glimpse into a "crowded closet" – even if some wish there were more than "mild surprises behind the door."

Changing Lanes
16 | 19 | 17 | 17

2002 | Directed by Roger Michell | With Ben Affleck, Samuel L. Jackson | 99 minutes | Rated R

A freeway fender-bender turns into "road rage" of epic proportions in this "fast-moving" "urban melodrama" pitting an "affluent", "smarmy" lawyer against a "poor, down-and-out" dad, both suffering from "too much testosterone" and bent on one-upmanship; admirers like its "small scope" and Jackson's "fine" performance but not the "just-along-for-the-ride" Affleck or that "wussy", "cop-out" ending.

Charade
26 | 25 | 26 | 25

1963 | Directed by Stanley Donen | With Cary Grant, Audrey Hepburn, Walter Matthau | 113 minutes | Not Rated

Expect "plenty of plot twists" in this "quintessential romantic comedy/thriller" (the "best Hitchcock flick that Hitchcock didn't make") about the scramble for a missing fortune; its very "easy-on-the-eyes" stars, "luscious Paris" scenery, magical "Mancini melodies" and "Audrey's fab wardrobe" make for "perfect" moviemaking – "murder was never so much fun."

Chariots of Fire ✉
26 | 25 | 25 | 25

1981 | Directed by Hugh Hudson | With Ben Cross, Ian Charleson, Ian Holm | 123 minutes | Rated PG

Remembered for "running off with" a Best Picture Oscar, this "inspiring" drama paces itself in "superb" style as it follows the "trials and triumph" of a British track team bound for the 1924 Olympics; thanks to "uplifting" legwork and a very "hummable" soundtrack, it breaks the tape as a "never boring" movie.

| | OVERALL | ACTING | STORY | PROD. |

Charlie and the Chocolate Factory — 18 | 20 | 20 | 24

2005 | Directed by Tim Burton | With Johnny Depp, Freddie Highmore, Helena Bonham Carter | 115 minutes | Rated PG

Burton's "edgy imagination" molds this "ambitious reimagining" of the family classic into an "eye-popping" "morality tale" about a poor kid's visit to a candyland run by the "warped" Depp (who channels his version of Willy Wonka with enough "Michael Jackson" to "give you the willies"); though "truer to Roald Dahl's book" than the original, some say this go-round is "less sweet" – all that "dementia" adds up to "empty calories."

Charlie's Angels — 13 | 11 | 10 | 17

2000 | Directed by McG | With Cameron Diaz, Drew Barrymore, Lucy Liu, Bill Murray | 98 minutes | Rated PG-13

"Girl power" gets a glam "MTV" makeover replete with "booty-licious" babes and "high-flying action" in this "fluffy", "nonsensical" send-up of the '70s TV series about foxy femme crime-fighters; no doubt, "it doesn't have the best acting ever" ("did Murray lose a bet?") and the "storyline's completely far-fetched", but charitable souls say it's "good when you want something mind-numbing."

Charlotte's Web — 23 | 22 | 25 | 24

2006 | Directed by Gary Winick | With Dakota Fanning | 97 minutes | Rated G

There are "no surprises" in this "delightful rendering" of E. B. White's "classic" farm fable, just "sweet" storytelling made "magical" by the "amazing" Fanning and a barnyard bunch brought to life by "believable" effects and "wonderful" celeb voice work ("Julia Roberts is fabulous as Charlotte"); though an itsy-bitsy minority maintains the 1973 animated version "can't be beat", most exalt this "much-needed break" from today's family-unfriendly fare.

Charly ✉ — 21 | 25 | 22 | 17

1968 | Directed by Ralph Nelson | With Cliff Robertson, Claire Bloom, Leon Janney | 103 minutes | Rated PG

A bright idea grafting drama onto a "believable" sci-fi scenario, this "original" flick gives Best Actor honoree Robertson a chance to "shine" in his "best performance" as a "man who goes from retardation to genius and back again" after a round of brain surgery; tutor Bloom adds romantic interest to make the doings "touching" – "if a bit sappy" for cynics.

Chasing Amy — 20 | 19 | 20 | 17

1997 | Directed by Kevin Smith | With Ben Affleck, Joey Lauren Adams, Jason Lee | 111 minutes | Rated R

Director Smith's trademarks – "Jersey-speak", "coarse humor", "semi-realistic situations" – are all apparent in this "offbeat" romantic comedy, featuring Affleck in the role of a comic-book scribe bewitched by a lesbian with a "nails-on-chalkboard" voice; it "rocks" fans with an "entertainingly different" mix of "smart" talk and "slacker cool", but foes claim it's a "sentimental" ode to "geek life" that's "not really funny."

Cheaper By the Dozen — 22 | 22 | 23 | 19

1950 | Directed by Walter Lang | With Clifton Webb, Jeanne Crain, Myrna Loy | 85 minutes | Not Rated

Set at the turn of the last century, this "warm family comedy" relates the "wonderful", fact-based story of a pair of efficiency experts bringing up 12 "cute" children, with a "droll" Webb stealing the show as the "pompous" head of the brood; sure, it strays into "precious" territory but oldsters attest it "wears well over time."

Cheaper By the Dozen

17 | 18 | 16 | 18

2003 | Directed by Shawn Levy | With Steve Martin, Bonnie Hunt, Piper Perabo, Hilary Duff | 98 minutes | Rated PG

For a "good, old-fashioned movie experience", try this "wholesome" comedy about a "big crazy family" uprooted by dad and mom's new jobs; granted, it's "very different" from the original 1950 flick and "not really a remake except for the number of children", but the "kids are cute" and there are "some funny moments"; best scene: that "breakfast disaster of epic proportions."

☑ Chicago ✉

27 | 26 | 25 | 29

2002 | Directed by Rob Marshall | With Renée Zellweger, Catherine Zeta-Jones, Richard Gere, Queen Latifah | 113 minutes | Rated PG-13

"Bob Fosse would have been proud" of this "absolutely brilliant" adaptation of his boffo Broadway "tale of murder, greed and corruption" in 1920s Chicago; "astounded" surveyors swear this "razzle-dazzle" "visual masterpiece" "deserved every Oscar it won" thanks to its "phenomenal acting", "sexy cinematography", "spine-tingling music" ("who knew the big three could sing?") and "major dance moves that'll leave you gasping for air"; even critics who complain of "miscasting" and "MTV camerawork" hope it sparks a "return to old-fashioned movie musicals."

Chicken Little

19 | - | 17 | 22

2005 | Directed by Mark Dindal | Animated | 81 minutes | Rated G

Disney lays a *War of the Worlds* spin on a "classic" children's fable and hatches some "good clean fun" in this "cute" cartoon featuring "excellent" animation and some "amusing" moments; the scattered nuggets of adult "belly laughs" earn parental praise, though a few critics chirp it "should have spent a little more time in the incubator."

Chicken Run

23 | - | 23 | 27

2000 | Directed by Peter Lord, Nick Park | Animated | 84 minutes | Rated G

Pure "poultry in motion", this "ingenious", "touching" barnyard saga uses "fantastic" claymation to portray a "darn appealing" bunch of British fowl and their "valiant struggle" to get off the farm; "subtle references" make it a "hilarious take" on all the *Stalag 17*–style POW pics, so while kids can enjoy the "innocent" animated escapade, it "doesn't chicken out" on "tongue-in-cheek", grown-up undertones; in an eggshell, a "good run for the money."

Children of a Lesser God ✉

23 | 25 | 22 | 21

1986 | Directed by Randa Haines | With Marlee Matlin, William Hurt, Piper Laurie | 119 minutes | Rated R

This "touching" drama "does justice to the original play" on the strength of "sexy, compelling" turns from Hurt as a speech teacher at a school for the deaf and Best Actress winner Matlin, "signing throughout" as a hearing-impaired woman with a complex past; expect "moving scenes" as their intimacy develops, and though an "enjoyable" intro to the "deaf community", it might be a "little overdramatized."

Children of Men
22 | 24 | 22 | 24

2006 | Directed by Alfonso Cuarón | With Clive Owen, Julianne Moore, Michael Caine | 109 minutes | Rated R

Dubbed *"Blade Runner* for Generation X", this "dystopian" vision of a "not-too-distant future" in which "women can no longer conceive" bears the fruits of a "fine" production and Owen's "outstanding" turn as an "unwilling hero" whose daunting task is to "save the human race"; references to "war", "totalitarianism" and "immigration" sharpen the "contemporary bite", leaving it to Caine's "unconventional" cameo as a "hippie pothead" to provide some "levity."

☑ Children of Paradise ❶🅵
28 | 27 | 27 | 26

1946 | Directed by Marcel Carné | With Arletty, Jean-Louis Barrault, Pierre Renoir | 190 minutes | Not Rated

Filmed in France "under the noses of the Nazis", this "legendary" romance "lovingly re-creates 1840s Paris" in a "multilayered" story of a "lovesick" mime's passion for a vampish stage siren; built on "profound" themes and "stylized" performances (that come off as "melodramatic" but are rich with "beauty and feeling"), it "continues to fascinate" as a "masterpiece of world cinema" and the big screen's "greatest tribute to live theater."

Children's Hour, The ❶
24 | 26 | 24 | 22

1961 | Directed by William Wyler | With Audrey Hepburn, Shirley MacLaine, James Garner, Miriam Hopkins | 107 minutes | Not Rated

"Way ahead of its time", this "groundbreaking" adaptation of the Lillian Hellman play examines "scandal and reputation", specifically what happens after a "malicious child" fingers two schoolteachers as lesbians; despite a "predictable" ending and subject matter that's "tragic" verging on "depressing", the "performances still pack a wallop."

China Syndrome, The
22 | 25 | 24 | 20

1979 | Directed by James Bridges | With Jack Lemmon, Jane Fonda, Michael Douglas | 122 minutes | Rated PG

The going gets "scary" as a nuclear power facility heads for meltdown in this "intelligent thriller" with a "solid" cast, including a "terrific" Lemmon as the plant supervisor and "Fonda at her peak" as a frustrated TV reporter; the "could-happen" story is "well-crafted", but conservatives contend that the "melodramatic" matchup of "bad-guy corporate players" against "good-guy idealists" makes it into the "definitive liberal" "message film."

☑ Chinatown ✉
27 | 28 | 26 | 26

1974 | Directed by Roman Polanski | With Jack Nicholson, Faye Dunaway, John Huston | 131 minutes | Rated R

This "taut drama" about "stolen water" and "bottled-up emotion" in 1930s LA is a "nearly perfect" exercise in "Technicolor film noir" that's simultaneously "funny, bleak and knowing"; credit the "dynamite" cast, "ravishingly beautiful" cinematography and "superb script" (that ends with a "shocking", "untypical-Hollywood ending") for its success; most memorable scene: Dunaway's "slap"-happy "she's-my-sister-she's-my-daughter" tour de force.

	OVERALL	ACTING	STORY	PROD.

Chocolat
22 | 24 | 22 | 23

2000 | Directed by Lasse Hallström | With Juliette Binoche, Alfred Molina, Johnny Depp | 121 minutes | Rated PG-13

A "yummy escape" "bordering on a fairy tale", this "funny" romance finds "lovely" "rebel spirit" Binoche pitted against "petty-minded villagers" when she opens a chocolate shop in a French hamlet and takes up with Depp; the blend of a "beautiful setting" mixed with some "uplifting whimsy" makes for one "tasty bonbon."

☑ Christmas Carol, A ◐
27 | 26 | 28 | 23

1951 | Directed by Brian Desmond Hurst | With Alastair Sim, Kathleen Harrison, Mervyn Johns | 86 minutes | Not Rated

"Sim is the best Scrooge ever" in this Dickens of a "holiday delight", a "magical adaptation" of the "timeless" fable concerning a rich old paragon of "grouchiness" transformed by a Yuletide visit from a posse of ghosts; cherished as "superb" family fare that "inspires" without drowning in the "happily-ever-after tone" of other versions, it has fans replaying it "religiously" because there's "no way" to do "Christmas without it."

Christmas Story, A
26 | 23 | 27 | 22

1983 | Directed by Bob Clark | With Peter Billingsley, Melinda Dillon, Darren McGavin | 94 minutes | Rated PG

A "sweet but not sugary" look at the "debacle that's Christmas in America", this "irresistible" family fave takes a "fond glimpse back" with a "funny-till-it-hurts" "exposition of a '40s childhood" centered on a kid bent on a "BB gun" under the tree; "most rewatchable" and "quotable" thanks to its "excellent cast and script", it's "good clean fun" for all ages and now widely deemed a seasonal "must."

Chronicles of Narnia: The Lion, the Witch & the Wardrobe
23 | 21 | 24 | 26

2005 | Directed by Andrew Adamson | With Georgie Henley, Skandar Keynes, Tilda Swinton | 140 minutes | Rated PG

C.S. Lewis' "classic" children's fantasy novel is "faithfully" rendered on celluloid by way of this "masterful production", a veritable "feast for the eyes" whose mane highlights include "lovely" performances, "beautiful" costumes and "spectacular" special effects ("you can almost touch Aslan"); its "religious overtones" court controversy, however, with defenders declaring the "Christian themes are dealt with appropriately" and skeptics suggesting "it feels like a sermon."

Cider House Rules, The ✉
22 | 24 | 23 | 22

1999 | Directed by Lasse Hallström | With Tobey Maguire, Charlize Theron, Michael Caine | 126 minutes | Rated PG-13

Presenting "life choices" in a '30s-era Maine orphanage, this "thought-provoking tearjerker" is a story of "compassion" with some "tough subject matter sneaked in" that gives Maguire his "breakout role" and proves "Caine really can act"; despite a few objections to the "cloying" tone and "watered-down" treatment of John Irving's novel, "satisfied" customers rule it an "absorbing" "feel-good" flick that "doesn't pander to the Hallmark crowd."

| | OVERALL | ACTING | STORY | PROD. |

Cincinnati Kid, The
24 | 25 | 22 | 22

1965 | Directed by Norman Jewison | With Steve McQueen, Edward G. Robinson, Ann-Margret, Karl Malden | 102 minutes | Rated PG

This "gritty" drama that "predates today's poker craze" still "antes up" "real entertainment" thanks to a "royal flush of a cast" led by the "never-cooler" McQueen, whose portrayal of a "professional card sharp" pays off in a "riveting, big-game sequence"; though basically "*The Hustler* with cards", bettors wager it's one of the all-time "best gambling flicks."

Cinderella
26 | - | 25 | 26

1950 | Directed by Clyde Geronimi, Wilfred Jackson, Hamilton Luske | Animated | 74 minutes | Rated G

"You know the drill": "breathtaking" animation from "Disney's golden age" merges with the stuff "countless girlish dreams" are made of in this "beautiful fantasy" about an "overworked, abused orphan" who bags her Prince Charming, with a little help from her fairy godmother and some "industrious", very finely feathered friends; if "short on characterization", it remains an "old-fashioned favorite" that's a shoe-in to be a "classic for generations to come."

Cinderella Liberty
19 | 23 | 20 | 17

1973 | Directed by Mark Rydell | With James Caan, Marsha Mason, Kirk Calloway | 117 minutes | Rated R

"Great chemistry" between the leads buoys this "honest" but "often-overlooked" romance about a lonesome shore-patrol swabbie who falls for a "tender-hearted prostitute" and becomes a real father figure to her "mixed-race son"; an "excellent" Caan plays well against Mason's "sympathetic" portrayal of the "hooker who doesn't know any other way to live"; all in all, a shipshape effort.

ⓩ Cinderella Man
25 | 27 | 25 | 25

2005 | Directed by Ron Howard | With Russell Crowe, Renée Zellweger, Paul Giamatti | 144 minutes | Rated PG-13

The "dreary" "look of the Great Depression" permeates this "superbly crafted" sports biopic 'bout James Braddock, the "down-on-his-luck pug" who "battled back" from poverty and injury for a "shot at the heavyweight title"; given its "superb" combo of the "incredibly believable" Crowe and "wonderful" Giamatti, fans feel this "worthy" contender "should have been a bigger hit."

Cinema Paradiso ✉🄵
26 | 26 | 26 | 25

1988 | Directed by Giuseppe Tornatore | With Philippe Noiret, Jacques Perrin | 123 minutes | Rated R

This Italian "heart-warmer" is an "endearing" look at "love and loss" as well as a "nostalgic valentine" to the "magic of cinema"; based on the "utterly charming" story of a "projectionist in the local movie house" who "mentors a fatherless child", it rolls a "colorful" cast, "*bellissimo*" camerawork and a "lovely" score into an "engrossing", frankly "sentimental" film.

ⓩ Citizen Kane ✉◑
28 | 27 | 27 | 28

1941 | Directed by Orson Welles | With Orson Welles, Joseph Cotten, Agnes Moorehead, Everett Sloane | 119 minutes | Rated PG

"Loosely based on the life of William Randolph Hearst", this "magnum opus" about a "ruthless megalomaniac" who "mourns the loss of his innocent childhood" is an "undisputed masterpiece" that's "often imitated, never duplicated" and "as fresh as ever"; starring and directed by wunderkind Welles, it "revolutionized the cinema" and forever changed the meaning of the word "rosebud" – "by comparison, all other films are home movies."

City Hall 18 | 22 | 18 | 18

1996 | Directed by Harold Becker | With Al Pacino, John Cusack, Bridget Fonda, Danny Aiello | 111 minutes | Rated R
Hopefully not "what real politics is like", this crime thriller lets "Pacino and Cusack excel" as a populist "NYC mayor" and his deputy attempting to do some damage control after a police shooting unravels "big-city corruption" between officialdom and the mob; supporters say "don't fight it", but even the "can't-go-wrong" cast flounders with the "disappointing" storyline.

City Lights ❶ 28 | 28 | 26 | 25

1931 | Directed by Charles Chaplin | With Charles Chaplin, Virginia Cherrill | 87 minutes | Not Rated
"Humor, pathos and poignancy" make this silent "Chaplin masterpiece" glow with "old-fashioned sentimentality" as the Little Tramp's "devotion for a blind flower girl" leads to a series of "classic" sequences; from famed bits like the "balletic boxing match" to the "heartbreaking" closing, this early flicker is a testament to a master "on top of his game."

City of God 🄵 26 | 25 | 26 | 25

2003 | Directed by Kátia Lund, Fernando Meirelles | With Matheus Nachtergaele, Seu Jorge | 130 minutes | Rated R
"Even those who are allergic to subtitles" will be more than "captivated" by this "shattering portrait" of "street kids in Brazil" who "grow up to become a gang of murderous drug dealers"; it's a "harrowing, gut-wrenching" "tour de force" that's "dynamically acted" by "nonactors" and made "edgy and fresh" by "hypnotic visuals"; the "extreme violence and brutality" may "leave you feeling ill", but "you can't look away."

City Slickers 20 | 20 | 20 | 19

1991 | Directed by Ron Underwood | With Billy Crystal, Daniel Stern, Jack Palance | 112 minutes | Rated PG-13
"Yee-haw!"; a "super" Crystal rides high in this "tons-of-fun" "buddy comedy" about three NYers who go west for a dude-ranch vacation and wind up having a "midlife crisis during a cattle drive"; the "right-on" cast (particularly the "just-too-funny Palance") has a way with "wisdom and great one-liners", rounding up applause for "good fun" that doesn't shy from its "moving" side.

Claire's Knee 🄵 23 | 24 | 22 | 23

1971 | Directed by Eric Rohmer | With Jean-Claude Brialy, Aurora Cornu, Laurence de Monaghan | 105 minutes | Rated PG
The "antithesis of an action movie", this "insightful" look at "erotic desire done without conventional sex scenes" tells the story of a "midlife crisis"-bound Frenchman "obsessed with, well, the title says it all"; knockers rap all the "cerebral ooh-la-la" as too "talky", though admirers insist this "sweet paean to romantic longing" is "probably the high point of Rohmer's career."

Clash of the Titans
18 | 14 | 20 | 17

1981 | Directed by Desmond Davis | With Harry Hamlin, Judi Bowker, Laurence Olivier, Maggie Smith | 118 minutes | Rated PG

"Hamlin looks great in next to nothing" as he battles everyone from Medusa to a two-headed dog in this "campy" "sandal saga" based on classical Greek mythology; despite plenty of "star power", cynics nix the Olympian "bad acting" ("was Olivier just feeding his ego as Zeus?"), and the "dated" special effects split voters: modernists yawn "cheesy", but nostalgic types salute FX legend Ray Harryhausen, whose "claymation monsters" and "stop-motion animation" are "always entertaining."

Clear and Present Danger
20 | 21 | 22 | 20

1994 | Directed by Phillip Noyce | With Harrison Ford, Willem Dafoe, Anne Archer | 141 minutes | Rated PG-13

Clearly "popcorn fodder", this "provocative action" flick is "one of the better Clancy adaptations", with Ford in "fine form" reprising his role as "what-a-man" CIA agent Jack Ryan going *mano a mano* with a Colombian dope cartel; though some call it "escapist", it's so "exciting", you can't help but root for this "smart movie hero" who "kicks butt."

Cleopatra
19 | 18 | 19 | 25

1963 | Directed by Joseph L. Mankiewicz | With Elizabeth Taylor, Richard Burton, Rex Harrison | 192 minutes | Not Rated

"Grand, gaudy and tons of fun", this epic bio of the queen of the Nile (renowned for "breaking all production-cost records") is either a "guilty pleasure" or an "incredible waste of time"; devotees dig its "huge scale", over-the-top "entertainment" value and Liz's "exquisite" beauty, but cynics nix the flick's "bloated" look and "draggy" pace, advising that you "hit the clicker" immediately after Cleo's "showstopping entrance into Rome."

Clerks ◑
23 | 17 | 22 | 16

1994 | Directed by Kevin Smith | With Brian O'Halloran, Jeff Anderson, Marilyn Ghigliotti | 92 minutes | Rated R

"Crude" acting and "bottom-of-the-barrel production" values are redeemed by "wicked black humor" and "inspired", "raunchy" dialogue in this "microbudget indie" effort, a "fast-paced" comedy that pumps life into the "dead-end job" scene with a "realistic" look at "minimart" wage slavery; the "first foray" in Smith's "New Jersey series", it's a "slacker" "cult classic" that's "painfully funny" but unsafe for the "squeamish."

Client, The
17 | 19 | 19 | 18

1994 | Directed by Joel Schumacher | With Susan Sarandon, Tommy Lee Jones, Brad Renfro | 120 minutes | Rated PG-13

Ok, it's "not great literature or art", but this adaptation of the John Grisham best-seller makes for a "good evening of entertainment" with its "linear story" of a youngster fleeing mobsters *and* the FBI; though too "predictable" for some, the "enjoyable Sarandon" and "impressive Renfro" keep things "interesting" enough.

Cliffhanger
15 | 12 | 15 | 19

1993 | Directed by Renny Harlin | With Sylvester Stallone, John Lithgow, Janine Turner | 113 minutes | Rated R

"*Rocky* on the rocks" sums up this "usual Stallone" action vehicle, with Sly heading a mountain rescue team beset by "nasty guys" crash-landed in the mountains; its "panoramic" backdrops and "nail-biter" sequences definitely "keep guys on the couch", but the "wooden performances" and a "quick freefall" into "implausibility" lead some to dub it a "dud" – "too bad there wasn't an avalanche."

Clockwork Orange, A

25 | 24 | 24 | 25

1971 | Directed by Stanley Kubrick | With Malcolm McDowell, Patrick Magee | 137 minutes | Rated R

"Not for the weak of heart", this "ingenious Kubrick" cult parable is a "bold", "nightmarish" "mix of sex, ultraviolence" and "mind control" set in a "freaky", "futuristic" Britain; following the travails of "unhinged" "bad boy" McDowell (the "sinister yet strangely likable" head of a "vicious gang of droogies") through his "chilling" crimes to his "brainwashing" rehab, it threads "brilliant visuals" and "twisted" "social satire" into "riveting", "artful stuff" – helped by a bit of the old "Ludwig van."

Close Encounters of the Third Kind

24 | 22 | 25 | 27

1977 | Directed by Steven Spielberg | With Richard Dreyfuss, François Truffaut, Teri Garr | 135 minutes | Rated PG

"It's ok to believe in UFOs" thanks to this "landmark" sci-fi "spectacle", a "mesmerizing", "believable contact film" wherein Spielberg's "sense of wonder" first embraces the "aliens-come-to-earth" formula; the "hopeful" plotline involves a race to "figure it all out" when strange signals arrive from the sky, and the result is a "mind-blowing" "visual treat" with plenty of "heart" (and "mountains of mashed potatoes") that delivers a "jaw-dropping" climax with a "sentimental streak" a light-year wide.

Closer

19 | 23 | 18 | 19

2004 | Directed by Mike Nichols | With Jude Law, Julia Roberts, Natalie Portman, Clive Owen | 104 minutes | Rated R

"Possibly the worst first-date movie ever", this "chilly", "caustic" look at four "seriously flawed" folks involved in a "love trapezoid" is a "feel-bad flick" alright, even if defenders "love that Clive" as well as the "intelligent direction" and "brutally honest" script; but many find the "dirty talk", "unlikable characters" and "joyless" mood too "uncomfortable to watch."

Clueless

21 | 19 | 20 | 20

1995 | Directed by Amy Heckerling | With Alicia Silverstone, Paul Rudd, Brittany Murphy | 97 minutes | Rated PG-13

Totally "sneaky-smart", this "lively" "update of *Emma*" with a "*90210*" twist is a "winning" comedy about LA's "spoiled rich" kids and stars a "delightful", "not-quite-acting" Silverstone, who juggles romantic uncertainty, a variety of "Valley catch phrases" and a "'90s" wardrobe "to die for"; despite a few hints of "fluff" – "whatever" – it offers "pure enjoyment" as a "pivotal teen movie" and some of the "sharpest" "bubblegum" out there.

Coach Carter

21 | 22 | 21 | 20

2005 | Directed by Thomas Carter | With Samuel L. Jackson | 136 minutes | Rated PG-13

"Reliably cool" Jackson hits nothin' but net with this "inspiring" tale ("based on a true story") of a "get-tough" high school hoops coach who leads his "underdog" squad to the Big Game; sure, the "feel-good" outcome may be "a bit predictable", but at the final buzzer fans cheer the "valuable" stay-in-school message, not to mention those "slam 'n' jam" B-ball scenes.

Coal Miner's Daughter ⊠

| | 24 | 27 | 23 | 22 |

1980 | Directed by Michael Apted | With Sissy Spacek, Tommy Lee Jones, Levon Helm | 125 minutes | Rated PG

Kentucky moonshine and "bravura performances" brighten this "charming biopic" of country crooner Loretta Lynn, led by the Oscar-winning Spacek as the daughter of Appalachia who "makes it huge" in Nashville; a down-home, "down-to-earth fairy tale", its "realistic portrayal" of a star's "rise to fame" and bout with burnout plays like an "interesting" C&W take on *Behind the Music*.

Cocoanuts, The ➊

| | 24 | 22 | 19 | 19 |

1929 | Directed by Robert Florey, Joseph Santley | With the Marx Brothers, Kay Francis | 96 minutes | Not Rated

Never mind the "technical primitiveness", this first Marx Brothers comedy is as "zany" as their later work; though this "crude" rendering of the sibs' Broadway show is burdened with "trite musical numbers" and a "weak" story involving Florida real estate, die-hard Marxists say ya "gotta love" it as an "intriguing mess" that's at worst a guarantee of "better things to come."

Cocoon

| | 20 | 21 | 21 | 20 |

1985 | Directed by Ron Howard | With Don Ameche, Wilford Brimley, Hume Cronyn | 117 minutes | Rated PG-13

"Old duffers" meet "pod people" in this "warm" sci-fi tale, which spins a "clever story" of an intergalactic meet-up between extraterrestrials and Florida rest-home residents, whose backyard pool becomes a fountain of youth; the "delightful" setup and "complete characters" give some of Hollywood's elder statesmen room to "romp", while director Howard makes it all "credible" – if a bit too "warm and cuddly" for some.

Coffee and Cigarettes ➊

| | 18 | 20 | 16 | 19 |

2003 | Directed by Jim Jarmusch | With Roberto Benigni, Cate Blanchett, Iggy Pop, Tom Waits, Bill Murray | 95 minutes | Rated R

Filmed episodically over 17 years, this collection of 11 black-and-white vignettes depicting conversations over caffeine and ciggies is a "hit-or-miss" proposition: sometimes "brilliant", sometimes "monotonous"; fans single out Blanchett's "amazing" double role and that "hoot" of a scene pairing Bill Murray with Wu-Tang Clan, but ultimately this one's "more for Jarmusch fans than for the general public."

Cold Mountain

| | 22 | 24 | 22 | 26 |

2003 | Directed by Anthony Minghella | With Jude Law, Nicole Kidman, Renée Zellweger | 152 minutes | Rated R

The "cinematic equivalent of a coffee table book", this "beautifully shot" Civil War saga of separated lovers "adapted from Homer's *Odyssey*" stars a "smokin'" Law opposite a "too-beautiful" Kidman, ever the "fashion plate" when she's "supposed to be starving"; never mind the "long" running time, "watching-the-grass-grow" pacing and controversy over Renée's Oscar win ("much deserved" vs. "Granny Clampett"), at the least, this one is certainly "worth falling asleep on the sofa for."

	OVERALL	ACTING	STORY	PROD.

Collateral
`21` `24` `21` `22`

2004 | Directed by Michael Mann | With Tom Cruise, Jamie Foxx, Jada Pinkett Smith | 120 minutes | Rated R

Cruise sports a silver hairdo and plays "against type" as a "psychopathic" contract killer pitted against Foxx's "unassuming everyman" for one "nightmare evening" in this "taut" thriller from "master-of-moods" auteur Mann; devotees say the "incongruous plot", "tacked-on romance" and "generic conclusion" are "forgivable" due to the "morally challenging" situations – and "LA never looked so beautiful and dangerous."

Collector, The
`23` `26` `25` `22`

1965 | Directed by William Wyler | With Terence Stamp, Samantha Eggar | 119 minutes | Not Rated

A "deeply disturbed recluse" kidnaps a "lovely young woman" in this "chilling story of obsession" adapted from John Fowles' "devastating" first novel; "terrific acting by Stamp and Eggar" keeps folks "fascinated", and if this "creepy stalker film" can be "hard to watch" at times, it's still "wonderfully done."

Color of Money, The ✉
`16` `21` `16` `17`

1986 | Directed by Martin Scorsese | With Paul Newman, Tom Cruise, Mary Elizabeth Mastrantonio | 119 minutes | Rated R

Something different from Martin Scorsese, this "generation-later" "follow-up to *The Hustler*" details how a washed-up billiards baron molds an up-and-comer into his protégé; though somewhat "predictable", "excellent acting" from the "powerhouse Cruise" and the "finely tuned", Oscar-winning Newman "saves it."

Color Purple, The
`26` `27` `26` `25`

1985 | Directed by Steven Spielberg | With Whoopi Goldberg, Danny Glover, Oprah Winfrey | 154 minutes | Rated PG-13

A "heartfelt" reading of Alice Walker's "breakthrough" best-seller, this "moving" drama of "empowerment" "really hits home" with its depiction of a "post-slavery black family" in the Deep South and a wronged woman's "redemption and liberation"; the "breathtaking" lenswork, "Goldberg's best-ever showing" and a "brilliant" supporting cast make for a "teary" "triumph" that some cite as "Oscar's biggest snub."

Colors
`20` `22` `20` `19`

1988 | Directed by Dennis Hopper | With Sean Penn, Robert Duvall, Maria Conchita Alonso | 120 minutes | Rated R

"One of the first" looks at the LA gang scene, this "intense" crime flicker takes on the Crips-vs.-Bloods face-off "from the perspective of the police", i.e. Duvall and the colorful "young" Penn as, respectively, a "senior officer and a rookie"; though "worth seeing" for its "superb cast" alone, the "run-of-the-mill cop" plot "doesn't fulfill its lofty social-commentary" promise.

Coming Home ✉
`23` `26` `23` `21`

1978 | Directed by Hal Ashby | With Jane Fonda, Jon Voight, Bruce Dern, Penelope Milford | 126 minutes | Rated R

"Jon and Jane are magic together" in this "ultimate anti-war message" drama–cum–love triangle involving a paraplegic Vietnam vet, an "inconveniently married" hospital volunteer and a gung-ho marine; expect "moving performances" (Voight and Fonda took home Oscars)

and "loads of emotion" that manage to convey a "coming of age for both the characters – and the times."

Coming to America
18 | 18 | 17 | 17

1988 | Directed by John Landis | With Eddie Murphy, Arsenio Hall, James Earl Jones | 116 minutes | Rated R

"Multiple-character tour de force" showcasing the talents of "total riot" Murphy and "hilarious" Hall in a "goofy", "fish-out-of-water" comedy about an African prince who logically "heads to Queens" to find a royal mate; hard-core groupies who can "repeat the whole movie by heart" reveal their favorite scene: "pre-*ER* Eriq Le Salle's Soul Glow" routine.

Con Air
14 | 15 | 14 | 18

1997 | Directed by Simon West | With Nicolas Cage, John Cusack, John Malkovich, Steve Buscemi | 115 minutes | Rated R

"Hardened criminals" en route to a "high-security prison" skyjack their plane in this "popcorn action flick" that's a "no-brainer" if you're ready for an "enjoyably obnoxious" experience; foes protest this "testosteronefest" has "little plot" and "just-collecting-a-paycheck" acting, but worst of all is Cage's "horrific mullet."

Conan the Barbarian
16 | 9 | 15 | 18

1982 | Directed by John Milius | With Arnold Schwarzenegger, James Earl Jones | 129 minutes | Rated R

The flick that "brought Arnold to everyone's attention", this "archetypal sword-and-sorcery fantasy" about a "barbarian butt-kicker" is "all a teenage boy could want" in a movie, conjuring up a pulpy, "no-holds-barred world of lust and vengeance"; even though Schwarzenegger's "acting isn't that great" – it was "before he learned to talk" – his "muscles are expressive" enough.

Confessions of a Dangerous Mind
19 | 23 | 19 | 20

2003 | Directed by George Clooney | With Sam Rockwell, Drew Barrymore, George Clooney | 113 minutes | Rated R

"Odd but oddly compelling", this bio of "game show guru" Chuck Barris is a "real eyebrow-raiser", intercutting his antics as host of *The Gong Show* with his "secret life" as a "CIA hit man"; while the dual careers are too "preposterous" and "bizarro" for many to swallow ("puh-leeze"), some confess the picture "grows on you the more you watch it" – what it lacks in logic, "it makes up for in nerve."

Conformist, The 🅵
26 | 26 | 27 | 26

1971 | Directed by Bernardo Bertolucci | With Jean-Louis Trintignant, Stefania Sandrelli, Dominique Sanda | 115 minutes | Rated R

Director "Bertolucci is at his absolute best" in this "supercool, super-stylized" Italian psychological drama set in the '30s about an "emotionally troubled civil servant" turned "fascist agent"; nonconformists warn "beware the dubbed version" but concur that Vittorio Storaro's "haunting" cinematography transcends dialogue; hottest moment: that "erotic tango" between Sanda and Sandrelli.

Constant Gardener, The
23 | 26 | 23 | 24

2005 | Directed by Fernando Meirelles | With Ralph Fiennes, Rachel Weisz | 129 minutes | Rated R

The "politically pertinent" topic of pharmaceutical companies' alleged "exploitation of third-world citizens" forms the "fascinating" backdrop of this "tautly woven" thriller–cum–"haunting" love story featuring the "ever dependable" Fiennes as an "uptight English diplomat" who unravels a "mystery" involving his activist wife (the "fabulous" Weisz); based on John Le Carré's "complex" novel, it's undoubtedly "more exciting than its title might suggest", and provides plenty of "food for thought."

Contact   20 | 21 | 20 | 22

1997 | Directed by Robert Zemeckis | With Jodie Foster, Matthew McConaughey, Tom Skerritt | 153 minutes | Rated PG

This "thinking person's" sci-fi flick asks the "Big Question" – "are we alone" in the universe?; true believers cite the "excellent special effects", "fascinating" story and a fine Foster "near the top of her form", but the alienated dismiss it as "long-winded" and "preachy", opting to "read Carl Sagan's excellent book" instead.

Contempt 🅵   25 | 24 | 22 | 24

1964 | Directed by Jean-Luc Godard | With Brigitte Bardot, Michel Piccoli, Jack Palance, Fritz Lang | 104 minutes | Not Rated

The "struggle between commerce and artistic integrity" gets the Godard treatment in this "scathing" "movie about movies" that details a screenwriter's struggle to adapt James Joyce's *Ulysses* and keep his marriage from unraveling; with a "full-throttle" Palance and a "coquettish" Bardot on board, "stunning" Mediterranean vistas in CinemaScope and a "cameo from director Fritz Lang", it's a fine example of "classic French New Wave" that's "showy, smart" and "enjoyably pretentious."

Contender, The   19 | 23 | 20 | 19

2000 | Directed by Rod Lurie | With Joan Allen, Gary Oldman, Jeff Bridges, Christian Slater | 126 minutes | Rated R

In this Clinton White House-ish "Washington soap opera" (with enough "twists and turns" to keep you "guessing till the end"), a "scrappy" female pol "stays true to her principles" at great cost to her reputation and career; though Allen is "superb" and Bridges would make a "fine" real-life prez, some pundits protest the drama's "tackling of big issues" as "overblown melodrama."

Conversation, The   25 | 26 | 25 | 23

1974 | Directed by Francis Ford Coppola | With Gene Hackman, John Cazale, Frederic Forrest | 113 minutes | Rated PG

A "brilliant" thriller about a "paranoid" surveillance specialist who comes undone, this "little-known" Coppola feature features a "virtuoso performance by Hackman", whose gradual "deterioration is amazing" (there's also an appearance by a very young Harrison Ford); though a bit "slow-moving", the script is so "superbly constructed" that "if this flick doesn't put you on edge, nothing will."

Cooler, The   22 | 27 | 22 | 21

2003 | Directed by Wayne Kramer | With William H. Macy, Maria Bello, Alec Baldwin | 101 minutes | Rated R

"Losing is winning" for the perpetually "unlucky" title character in this "quirky" dramedy about a Vegas shill hired by a casino to "jinx high-rollers' winning streaks"; an "unglamorous" spin on the usual gambling yarn, it boasts "riveting acting" and a "believable love story", though some say the "gratuitous violence" and Macy's "racy" nude scenes are more of a "crapshoot."

	OVERALL	ACTING	STORY	PROD.

Cool Hand Luke
26 | 27 | 24 | 22

1967 | Directed by Stuart Rosenberg | With Paul Newman, George Kennedy, Strother Martin | 126 minutes | Not Rated

"One of the best movie lines ever" ('what we have here is a failure to communicate') and a "famous hard-boiled egg eating scene" make this "damn great" Deep South prison drama memorable – not to mention the "consummate pro" Newman playing a cool con on a "chain gang", abetted by Kennedy, who nabbed an Oscar for his supporting work.

Cool Runnings
18 | 16 | 21 | 17

1993 | Directed by Jon Turteltaub | With John Candy, Doug E. Doug, Leon, Malik Yoba | 98 minutes | Rated PG

Granted, it might be "silly", but this "cute", "underrated" comedy "based on the true" tale of the '88 Olympics' "Jamaican bobsled team" is "fun for the whole family" (despite "a bit too much profanity"); cheerleaders say its "come-from-behind" story will "touch anyone's heart", particularly those who "miss John Candy."

Corpse Bride, The
20 | - | 19 | 25

2005 | Directed by Tim Burton, Mike Johnson | Animated | 76 minutes | Rated PG

From the "macabre" mind of Tim Burton and in the spirit of "*The Nightmare Before Christmas*" comes this "ghoulishly entertaining" fairy tale pulsing with "eye-popping" stop-motion animation and "raucous" musical numbers; make no bones about it, Johnny Depp's voicing of a "groom who's stolen away to the world of the dead" is an added "pleasure", though some maligners mourn the "trite" story.

Counterfeit Traitor, The
25 | 25 | 26 | 23

1962 | Directed by George Seaton | With William Holden, Lili Palmer, Hugh Griffith | 140 minutes | Not Rated

"Based on a true story", this "classy" (albeit "forgotten") WWII spy thriller revolves around a Swedish "quisling" blacklisted by the Allies after trading with the Nazis; in the title role, the "dashing" Holden is in his "gracefully aging prime", though some say the "deeply moving" Palmer steals the show as his "noble" confederate.

Count of Monte Cristo, The
19 | 20 | 22 | 22

2002 | Directed by Kevin Reynolds | With James Caviezel, Guy Pearce, Richard Harris | 131 minutes | Rated PG-13

"Revenge is sweet" in this "well-crafted" swashbuckler about a man wrongfully imprisoned plotting epic payback; fans like its "old-fashioned", "golden-age-of-Hollywood" approach ("great swordplay", "excellent production values", "enough romance to keep the girls interested"), but foes yawn that this "500th remake of the Dumas classic" is "nothing new" and "not particularly engaging."

Cousin, Cousine 🄵∅
21 | 20 | 21 | 19

1975 | Directed by Jean-Charles Tacchella | With Marie-Christine Barrault, Victor Lanoux | 95 minutes | Rated R

This "sweet but naughty" French farce about romantically involved cousins-by-marriage offers a "refreshing" take on family dynamics; while some say it's "much better than the American" remake (*Cousins*), those suffering from memory lapses "can't recall anything" except – zut alors! – Barrault's "naked breasts."

	OVERALL	ACTING	STORY	PROD.

Crash ✉

26 | 27 | 26 | 25

2005 | Directed by Paul Haggis | With Sandra Bullock, Don Cheadle, Matt Dillon, Brendan Fraser, Terrence Howard, Ludacris, Thandie Newton, Ryan Phillippe | 113 minutes | Rated R

"Everyone's a little bit racist" according to this "provocative" treatment of "prejudice in America", a Best Picture Oscar grabber about "intertwined lives" in LA that "damn near hits the mark" in its attempts to "break down stereotypes" and "make you rethink your values"; with a "dream-team cast" enlivening the "incredible writing", expect to collide with some "tough", "wonderfully unpredictable" scenes that deliver a "powerful message."

Cries and Whispers 🅵

26 | 28 | 24 | 26

1972 | Directed by Ingmar Bergman | With Harriet Andersson, Liv Ullmann, Ingrid Thulin | 106 minutes | Rated R

"Compelling is an understatement" when it comes to this "tortured masterpiece", a "raw", "close-in study of three sisters and their prickly relationship" that's "quintessential Bergman"; although it's "well acted" and "handsomely mounted", its depiction of "pain" is so "hard to watch" that some ask "are you sure 'angst' isn't a Swedish word?"

Crimes and Misdemeanors

26 | 26 | 25 | 24

1989 | Directed by Woody Allen | With Woody Allen, Mia Farrow, Anjelica Huston, Martin Landau | 107 minutes | Rated PG-13

"Crime does pay" in this "deeply serious" Allen dramedy with dual plotlines, one about a murderous philanderer, the other a "socially inept" filmmaker; "ruthlessly truthful", it manages to be alternately "scathing", "thought-provoking" and "hilarious", with "dead-on casting" and an "expert" scenario to boot.

Crimson Tide

21 | 24 | 22 | 22

1995 | Directed by Tony Scott | With Denzel Washington, Gene Hackman, George Dzundza | 116 minutes | Rated R

"Gripping", "tightly plotted" action flick relating the "macho machinations aboard a submarine" as two officers square off over a nuclear launch that could trigger an "unprovoked war"; given the "smart", "thought-provoking" acting of "big-screen titans" Washington and Hackman, you can expect a "first-rate" ride, even if some shrug it off as a "*Hunt for Red October* wannabe."

Crocodile Dundee

17 | 14 | 17 | 16

1986 | Directed by Peter Faiman | With Paul Hogan, Linda Kozlowski | 98 minutes | Rated PG-13

This "surprise hit from Down Under" is a classic "fish-out-of-water" comedy about a transplanted Aussie "clashing with the ways of the modern world"; though critics split on Hogan's appeal – "charming" vs. "better in Subaru commercials" – overall, it's "lightweight" fun.

Crossing Delancey

23 | 23 | 23 | 21

1988 | Directed by Joan Micklin Silver | With Amy Irving, Peter Riegert, Sylvia Miles | 97 minutes | Rated PG

This "romantic comedy with a Jewish twist" earns *mazel tovs* for its "endearing" story of "intellectual" striver Irving, set up with "pickle vendor" Riegert thanks to "old-school matchmaking" from her "meddling" Lower East Side bubbe; despite crossing into "schmaltzy" territory, it's "well acted" and "relevant for all those single gals" who hope "all's well that ends well."

Crouching Tiger, Hidden Dragon ✉ 🄵 | 24 | 23 | 21 | 28 |

2000 | Directed by Ang Lee | With Chow Yun-Fat, Michelle Yeoh, Zhang Ziyi | 120 minutes | Rated PG-13

Whether it's a "kung fu chick flick", a "thinking person's" martial arts film or "'chop-socky' translated into art", this "surreal" fantasy is full of "eye-popping fight sequences" that are half "ballet", half "Bruce Lee"; most memorable for its "strong female characters" and that "encounter in the bamboo forest", it's nothing less than a "breath of fresh air on the stale movie landscape."

Cry-Baby | 17 | 16 | 15 | 16 |

1990 | Directed by John Waters | With Johnny Depp, Amy Locane, Susan Tyrrell | 85 minutes | Rated PG-13

"Kinda dumb" in a "classic B-movie" way, this "wacko" John Waters comedy set in 1950s Baltimore tells the story of a "boring square" who decides she's "tired of being good" and falls for a "troublemaking greaser"; given its "similarities to *West Side Story*", some call it the director's "most mainstream" work, but a few babies cry about "caricatures rather than characters" and "emoting rather than emotion."

Crying Game, The ✉ | 22 | 24 | 24 | 20 |

1992 | Directed by Neil Jordan | With Stephen Rea, Miranda Richardson, Jaye Davidson | 112 minutes | Rated R

"Violence and pathos" are served in the "right amounts" in this "disturbing" British drama about an "IRA recruit who's not really committed to his cause"; most famed for its whopper of a "surprise twist" (that leaves some "still flabbergasted"), this "intense vision of terrorism" offers enough nuanced "questions about race, sex and country" to justify a Best Screenplay Oscar.

Curious George | 19 | - | 19 | 21 |

2006 | Directed by Matthew O'Callaghan | Animated | 86 minutes | Rated G

"Belly laughs for the diaper set" abound in this "cuddly" animated feature (based on the "beloved storybook") that tells the tale of the "man in the yellow hat" and the "cutest monkey ever" with enough "simple innocence" to be "completely safe" for all ages; some say all that "kid stuff" can be "kinda boring", but "preschoolers" will be "glued to the screen."

Damned, The | 23 | 24 | 21 | 23 |

1969 | Directed by Luchino Visconti | With Dirk Bogarde, Helmut Berger, Ingrid Thulin, Charlotte Rampling | 157 minutes | Rated R

Steel yourself for "decadence on parade" in this "sick, slick" look at a family of "jaded" German industrialists who ally themselves with the Nazis on the eve of WWII; both "absorbing and repellent in equal measure", it's "kinky" alright, though "outstanding production values" and the "beautiful Rampling" make it more palatable for general audiences.

Damn Yankees | 24 | 23 | 23 | 24 |

1958 | Directed by George Abbott, Stanley Donen | With Gwen Verdon, Tab Hunter, Ray Walston | 111 minutes | Not Rated

This screen adaptation of the Faust-influenced Broadway musical recounts how a "man makes a pact with the devil" to guarantee that the

"Washington Senators win the pennant"; reprising their stage roles, Walston is at his "evil best" as Lucifer, while the "too-rarely-seen" Verdon gets what she wants as his sidekick, Lola; it's a "perfect evocation of the national optimism of the '50s" with a "great score" and a bonus: "Bob Fosse's mambo."

Dancer in the Dark
`22` `23` `20` `22`

2000 | Directed by Lars von Trier | With Björk, Catherine Deneuve, David Morse | 140 minutes | Rated R

A "musical like no other", this "dynamic" if "depressing" film "pushes the genre to the limit" in its account of an immigrant Czech "factory worker going blind who finds redemption only in music"; while foes find it "difficult to watch" – "even painful" – artistes laud its "wondrously strange" feel and praise pop star Björk's "amazing acting chops" and "compelling" vocal work.

Dances with Wolves ✉
`23` `20` `22` `25`

1990 | Directed by Kevin Costner | With Kevin Costner, Mary McDonnell, Graham Greene | 183 minutes | Rated PG-13

For once, American Indians are portrayed in a "human light" in this "picturesque, sweeping epic" about a Civil War soldier who goes West, joins the Sioux and finds love along the way; although "beautifully shot" and quite the Oscar magnet (seven statuettes, including Best Picture), this "guy flick that women love" has critics citing a "monotonous", way-"too-long" running time.

Dangerous Liaisons ✉
`24` `26` `24` `26`

1988 | Directed by Stephen Frears | With Glenn Close, John Malkovich, Michelle Pfeiffer | 119 minutes | Rated R

"Malkovich quietly chews up the scenery" opposite "perfectly evil" "ice queen" Close in this "flawless" drama set in "decadent", 17th-century France rife with "treachery, betrayal and sexual games" among the "upper classes" ("no wonder the peasants revolted"); still, its "sumptuous production" and Oscar-winning screenplay make the "manipulating" characters more palatable.

Dangerous Lives of Altar Boys, The
`19` `21` `19` `19`

2002 | Directed by Peter Care | With Kieran Culkin, Jena Malone, Emile Hirsch, Jodie Foster | 104 minutes | Rated R

"If you're into comic books or went to Catholic school", this "coming-of-age" drama "captures the essence" of "teen angst" among "mischievous" parochial kids and boasts an "inventive" visual style "mixing live action" with "cool" cartoon segments; it showcases Culkin's "great promise", and if skeptics shrug at "discombobulated" plotting, acolytes applaud a "solidly crafted" effort.

Daredevil
`14` `14` `14` `19`

2003 | Directed by Mark Steven Johnson | With Ben Affleck, Jennifer Garner, Colin Farrell | 103 minutes | Rated PG-13

"Ben Affleck in tights" may be a "big draw in Greenwich Village", but he's pretty "disappointing" everywhere else as the title character of this action/adventurer based on Marvel Comics' blind superhero, a lawyer by day turned freelance vigilante at night; despite the "delicious" Garner, "over-the-top" Farrell and "high-energy", Hong Kong-style fight sequences, most advise "watch *Spiderman* instead."

	OVERALL	ACTING	STORY	PROD.

Dark Crystal, The
24 - 24 26

1982 | Directed by Jim Henson, Frank Oz | With puppet characters | 93 minutes | Rated PG

"Sinister muppets" take the stage in this "classic" "all-puppet feature", a "magical fairy tale" with an "otherworldly good and evil" storyline that represents the "culmination of Jim Henson's imagination"; while the "stunning visuals" please crowds, some warn that the "dark" plot "may be too scary" for smaller fry.

Dark Victory ◑
25 27 23 23

1939 | Directed by Edmund Goulding | With Bette Davis, George Brent, Humphrey Bogart | 104 minutes | Not Rated

"Sensational" Bette at her "Warner Brothers peak" "turns camp into classic" in this melodramatic "tearjerker" about an heiress who's got everything – including a brain tumor; sob sisters say it's "worth every hanky" for Davis' "valiant" turn (one of the "best performances of 1939") and keep their eye out for a "young Ronald Reagan" in a supporting role.

Darling ✉◑
22 25 20 21

1965 | Directed by John Schlesinger | With Julie Christie, Dirk Bogarde, Laurence Harvey | 128 minutes | Not Rated

Get a "glimpse of the Swinging '60s" via this "quintessential" story of a "self-absorbed" "model/party girl" who "makes it to the top" only to find "there's nothing there"; if the film feels "a bit dated", at least it's "cast to perfection" – the "smashing", Oscar-winning Christie is "at the height of her beauty and acting powers" here.

Das Boot 🄵
28 26 26 27

1982 | Directed by Wolfgang Petersen | With Jürgen Prochnow, Herbert Grönemeyer | 149 minutes | Rated R

When it comes to "underwater über alles" action, it's hard to top this "sweaty, claustrophobic" saga of "doomed German sailors" engaged in a "battle of egos" in a U-boat at the "bottom of the ocean"; though it's almost an "anti-recruiting film" given its "harrowing" realism, it exhibits enough "depth" to prove that "fear has no nationality" – you'll almost "root for" the Nazis.

Dave
21 22 22 20

1993 | Directed by Ivan Reitman | With Kevin Kline, Sigourney Weaver, Frank Langella | 110 minutes | Rated PG-13

"Kline's adorable, as usual" in this "funny" political satire about an average "doofus" who looks so much like the President that he's asked to pinch-hit and winds up putting "faith back in government"; a latter-day "Mr. Smith Goes to Washington", this comedy has a "serious message", though conspiracy theorists say the message is "proof that liberals really do run Hollywood."

David Copperfield ◑
▽ 27 26 27 25

1935 | Directed by George Cukor | With Freddie Bartholomew, W.C. Fields, Lionel Barrymore | 130 minutes | Not Rated

"One of the gems" of the Hollywood versions of "classic novels", this "wonderfully atmospheric", "very Dickensian" production may be a bit "creaky", though ultimately most of its "scenes are truly effective"; credit the "brilliant acting" from the MGM "repertory company", an "inspired" bunch headed up by Fields, whose "agile, hilarious" performance as Mr. Micawber is a "joy to watch."

Da Vinci Code, The
19 | 18 | 21 | 22

2006 | Directed by Ron Howard | With Tom Hanks, Audrey Tautou, Ian McKellen | 149 minutes | Rated PG-13

Despite "all the hype", surveyors split on this "glossy" adaptation of Dan Brown's mega-popular "page-turner" about a "human" Jesus who "married Mary Magdalene": admirers call it a "well-crafted" thriller packed with "fun puzzles", "magnificent" European settings and "intriguing" "intellectual banter", but contras say the "hard-to-follow" story "leaves little room" for the actors to strut ("Hanks is sleepwalking"), feeling that what was "fast-paced" in the novel is "lumberingly slow" here; ultimately, the "book was better" – "aren't they always?"

Dawn of the Dead
19 | 12 | 19 | 17

1978 | Directed by George A. Romero | With David Emge, Ken Foree, Scott Reiniger, Gaylen Ross | 128 minutes | Rated R

"It's not just another day at the mall" as director Romero (*Night of the Living Dead*) brings his zombie franchise "back to life" via this "graphic gorefest" about survivors of an "apocalyptic nightmare" trapped in a shopping center besieged by hordes of the "walking dead"; a "morbidly funny" "critique of consumerism" with plenty of "heart and guts" (not to mention "cheesy" effects and "bad acting"), this is "seminal" horror.

Day After Tomorrow, The
16 | 14 | 14 | 24

2004 | Directed by Roland Emmerich | With Dennis Quaid, Jake Gyllenhaal, Emmy Rossum, Ian Holm | 124 minutes | Rated PG-13

"Weather is the enemy" in this "high-gloss" sci-fi "thrill ride" with a "virtuous environmental message" underlying its story of a "killer ice age" ironically brought on by "global warming"; alright, the "impressive special effects" are a "helluva lot of fun" (notably the "destruction of all your favorite landmarks"), but critics "cringe" at the "bad science", "hammy acting" and "check-your-brain-at-the-door" plot; for many, this one's "not a disaster movie", simply a "disaster."

Day at the Races, A ◑
24 | 21 | 20 | 19

1937 | Directed by Sam Wood | With the Marx Brothers, Maureen O'Sullivan, Margaret Dumont | 111 minutes | Not Rated

The "Marx Brothers at their zenith of zaniness" horse around in this "very funny" comedy about a veterinarian turned human doctor; though some say it's a "slightly second-tier" also-ran (only "sporadically funny" and even a tad "racist"), it was nevertheless one of the boys' "biggest box office hits."

Day for Night ✉🅵
27 | 25 | 25 | 25

1973 | Directed by François Truffaut | With Jacqueline Bisset, Valentina Cortese, Jean-Pierre Léaud | 115 minutes | Rated PG

"Truffaut's homage to American filmmaking", this "quintessential movie about making movies" "perfectly captures" all the "behind-the-scenes" "neuroses" and "joy" from an insider's point of view; though it shows the director "at his lightest", the "magical" result was both "charming" and "wacky" enough for it to take home a Best Foreign Language picture Oscar.

Day of the Jackal, The
25 | 24 | 27 | 22

1973 | Directed by Fred Zinnemann | With Edward Fox, Michael Lonsdale, Delphine Seyrig | 145 minutes | Rated PG

"Grip the edge of your seat and hang on" for a "fast-paced" game of "cat and mouse" as this "riveting" thriller follows the race to foil a "legendary" hit man's "plot to assassinate Charles de Gaulle"; a "top-notch cast" and "true-to-the-book intelligence" keep things "tense until the very end", so fans of "crackling suspense" call it the "real deal" – and wonder "why they bothered to remake it."

Day of the Locust, The
20 | 21 | 21 | 21

1975 | Directed by John Schlesinger | With Donald Sutherland, Karen Black, Burgess Meredith, William Atherton | 144 minutes | Rated R

"Hollywood's penchant for crushing dreams" gets the John Schlesinger treatment in this "dark" adaptation of Nathanael West's "cautionary satire" about down-and-out types scrambling to make it big in Tinseltown during the Depression; it's "powerful, disturbing" stuff with "fine" work from Sutherland and an ending so "frightening" that many "still can't be in a crowd without thinking about it."

Days of Heaven
23 | 21 | 20 | 25

1978 | Directed by Terrence Malick | With Richard Gere, Brooke Adams, Sam Shepard | 95 minutes | Rated PG

"Underseen but not underappreciated", this "gorgeous" if "bleak" drama detailing a love triangle between two dirt-poor migrant workers and a loaded landowner "broke new ground" in its use of "beautiful cinematography" to take the place of conventional exposition; though it "speaks volumes without much dialogue", low-attention-span types yawn "not terribly compelling."

☒ Days of Wine and Roses ◑
27 | 28 | 25 | 24

1962 | Directed by Blake Edwards | With Jack Lemmon, Lee Remick, Charles Bickford | 117 minutes | Not Rated

For a "tough look" at a "serious issue", this "harrowing" drama about the "ravages of alcoholism" was a "huge breakthrough in its day" and remains "relevant" thanks to "tear-your-heart-out" performances from Lemmon and Remick as "desperate" young marrieds "lost in the bottom of the bottle"; "Henry Mancini's haunting title song" won the Oscar and "says it all."

Day the Earth Stood Still, The ◑
25 | 20 | 26 | 21

1951 | Directed by Robert Wise | With Michael Rennie, Patricia Neal, Sam Jaffe | 92 minutes | Rated G

"Fifties-era real-life fears about the fate of humanity" are the backbone of this "Cold War sci-fi" flick about a "benevolent alien" invasion of Washington, DC; sure, the "less-is-more special effects" seem "dated" and "primitive by today's standards", but the "underlying message" – "world peace or else!" – makes this one "very enlightened for its time."

Dazed and Confused
22 | 19 | 20 | 18

1993 | Directed by Richard Linklater | With Jason London, Rory Cochrane, Sasha Jenson | 103 minutes | Rated R

Revolving around the "shameless" antics of teenagers "getting loaded, laid and in trouble" on the "last day of school", this "coming-of-age" flick recalls "*American Graffiti*" transposed to the 1970s and induces "big laughs" from "characters you quickly fall in love with"; throw in a "killer soundtrack", and it's just the ticket for a "brainless afternoon."

Dead Again
22 | 24 | 24 | 22

1991 | Directed by Kenneth Branagh | With Kenneth Branagh, Andy Garcia, Emma Thompson | 107 minutes | Rated R

There are "good twists and mind tricks" aplenty in this "stylish, pseudo-noir thriller" about a detective drawn into a decades-old murder mystery; deadheads dig its "riveting performances", "Dali-esque imagery" and that "wonderful twist at the end", swearing you'll never look at a "pair of scissors" the same way after seeing this "over-the-top" "nail-biter."

Dead Calm
20 | 21 | 21 | 19

1989 | Directed by Phillip Noyce | With Nicole Kidman, Sam Neill, Billy Zane | 96 minutes | Rated R

A "married couple" yachting "on the high seas" are terrorized by an "over-the-top psychopath" in this "creepy open-water thriller" that delivers "nail-biting" chills plus an "early look at La Kidman" enduring "desperation" (and "frightfully mismanaged hair"); it's a dead-on "popcorn flick" that'll "make you jump" – and also "think twice about chartering a boat."

Dead Man Walking ✉
23 | 26 | 23 | 21

1995 | Directed by Tim Robbins | With Susan Sarandon, Sean Penn, Robert Prosky | 122 minutes | Rated R

"Based on a true story", this "enlightening" study of capital punishment is also a "profound lesson in human compassion" thanks to "poignant" turns from a "riveting" Penn as a "condemned killer" and the Oscar-winning Sarandon as a nun bent on leading him to "redemption"; although "unsettling and disturbing" overall, the picture "provides both sides of the death-penalty argument" in an "objective", "unflinching" manner.

Dead Men Don't Wear Plaid ◑
20 | 20 | 18 | 22

1982 | Directed by Carl Reiner | With Steve Martin, Rachel Ward | 89 minutes | Rated PG

Martin's "satirical look at noir films" involves the "clever use of old footage" (featuring stars like Humphrey Bogart, Ingrid Bergman and Lana Turner) that's intercut into a "silly" story about a deadbeat, '40s-era detective; fans of splice comedies say this one was way "ahead of its time", long before "mashups and remixes", though a few opine it's only "fun for movie buffs and a curiosity for everyone else."

⚡ Dead Poets Society ✉
24 | 25 | 24 | 23

1989 | Directed by Peter Weir | With Robin Williams, Robert Sean Leonard, Ethan Hawke | 128 minutes | Rated PG

"Living with rules" vs. "living with passion" gets the big-screen treatment in this "uplifting" drama about an "inspirational teacher" who admonishes his students with a ringing "'carpe diem!'"; thanks to the Oscar-winning screenplay and Williams' ultra-"convincing" turn as the "influential mentor", many say this "wake-up call" of a movie should be "mandatory classroom viewing."

	OVERALL	ACTING	STORY	PROD.

Dead Ringers
18 | 23 | 19 | 19

1988 | Directed by David Cronenberg | With Jeremy Irons, Geneviève Bujold | 115 minutes | Rated R

Ok, it's "beyond weird", but this "cold, clinical" tale of "twin gynecologists" "descending into madness" strikes followers of things "depraved" as a "deliciously creepy" picture, given its fascination with "prescription drugs", "kinky sex" and some mighty "bizarre" surgical instruments; despite Irons' "astounding dual performance", very vocal opponents call it "really offensive" with "no redeeming value", maybe the "ickiest movie ever"; proceed at your own risk.

Dead Zone, The
21 | 23 | 24 | 19

1983 | Directed by David Cronenberg | With Christopher Walken, Brooke Adams, Martin Sheen, Tom Skerritt | 103 minutes | Rated R

"Twilight Zone fans" dig the "spooky" premise of this supernatural thriller, starring an "eerily sympathetic" Walken as an "inadvertent psychic" whose "disturbing" ability to foresee the future sets up a dead reckoning with a presidential contender; the "budget's a little low", but supporters say this is "one of the better Stephen King adaptations."

Death in Venice
24 | 26 | 24 | 24

1971 | Directed by Luchino Visconti | With Dirk Bogarde, Marisa Berenson, Bjorn Andresen, Silvana Mangano | 130 minutes | Rated PG

"Delicious but depressing", this "exquisitely sad meditation on love and loss" adapted from the Thomas Mann novella stars a "memorable" Bogarde as a man who becomes obsessed by a boy while on holiday in circa-1910 Venice; though the scenery's certainly "beautiful to look at" (and the "take-your-breath-away" Mahler soundtrack equally "haunting"), the film's "slow" pace and long, "languid" shots make some shrug "gorgeous but tedious."

Death on the Nile
19 | 20 | 23 | 21

1978 | Directed by John Guillermin | With Peter Ustinov, Bette Davis, Angela Lansbury | 140 minutes | Rated PG

"Everyone looks properly shifty-eyed and guilty" in this "decent" enough adaptation of the Agatha Christie whodunit that takes place on a cruise down the River Nile; though foes grouse it's a "lightweight" "follow-up to Murder on the Orient Express", cast with "out-of-work actors", fans find it "suspenseful" enough and single out the "outrageous" Lansbury and Oscar-winning costumes for praise.

Deathtrap
22 | 24 | 25 | 20

1982 | Directed by Sidney Lumet | With Michael Caine, Christopher Reeve, Dyan Cannon | 116 minutes | Rated PG

Mystery "mindbenders" don't come more "clever" than this "amusing" take on the Broadway "whodunit" that "keeps you guessing and guessing" ("mostly incorrectly") in its story of a blocked playwright planning murder most foul in order to pilfer a script; "masterful casting" offsets any stagey "static", while all the "twists" are "wickedly absorbing."

Death Wish
16 | 14 | 17 | 15

1974 | Directed by Michael Winner | With Charles Bronson, Hope Lange, Vincent Gardenia | 93 minutes | Rated R

"Brash, politically incorrect and extremely macho", this '70s "revenge fantasy" was quite "scary" (and controversial) in its time, given its story of a "do-gooder" architect turned vicious "vigilante" after the murder of his wife; in the role that made him a star, Bronson is "more bad-ass than Clint Eastwood ever was", although four sequels later some say "he should have stopped after the first one."

Deconstructing Harry
16 | 19 | 17 | 17

1997 | Directed by Woody Allen | With Woody Allen, Richard Benjamin, Kirstie Alley, Judy Davis | 96 minutes | Rated R
"Uncompromising self-examination" is the heart of this "dark" Woody Allen film about a "neurotic" novelist who uses his life as fodder for his writing; though the finicky fuss about his "treatment of women" and "abundance of dirty-mouthed" talk, fans call it his "strongest work in the last decade"; favorite character: Robin Williams' (literally) "unfocused" actor.

Deep, The
17 | 16 | 17 | 19

1977 | Directed by Peter Yates | With Robert Shaw, Jacqueline Bisset, Nick Nolte | 123 minutes | Rated PG
From the "same era" that gave us *Jaws* comes this "underwater" adventure about "dangerous sunken treasure", a damp "guilty pleasure" best remembered for that "infamous" image of "Jackie Bisset in a sopping-wet T-shirt"; though "not a match" for Peter Benchley's best-selling novel, it's still "solid", "cheesy fun."

Deep Impact
15 | 14 | 15 | 19

1998 | Directed by Mimi Leder | With Robert Duvall, Téa Leoni, Elijah Wood, Vanessa Redgrave | 120 minutes | Rated PG-13
Impending "mass destruction" (via a comet plummeting toward the earth) is the subject of this "world-coming-to-an-end" "disaster flick", a "strangely moving" endeavor portraying "people preparing for a known death"; though there are comparisons to *Armageddon*'s "similar storyline", "this one has heart, a brain and a bonus – no bad Bruce Willis performance."

Deer Hunter, The ✉
26 | 28 | 24 | 24

1978 | Directed by Michael Cimino | With Robert De Niro, Christopher Walken, Meryl Streep, John Cazale, John Savage | 183 minutes | Rated R
"Ordinary guys from an ordinary American town" undergo the "ravages" of Vietnam in this "unforgettable war film", a "deeply moving", "epic-in-every-way" work that netted five Oscars (including Best Picture); brace yourself for "tough-as-nails" performances from De Niro and Walken, some "profound" if "heavy-handed symbolism" plotwise and a wrenching "Russian roulette scene" that will "leave you drained"; P.S. it also features "someone new named Streep."

Deliverance
25 | 26 | 25 | 23

1972 | Directed by John Boorman | With Jon Voight, Burt Reynolds, Ned Beatty, Ronny Cox | 109 minutes | Rated R
This "allegorical nightmare" about four "city slickers" on a "weekend canoe trip" "did for camping in the woods what *Jaws* did for swimming in the ocean", mainly because of that infamous "squeal-like-a-pig" "rape scene" (to the tune of "those damn 'Dueling Banjos'"); more important, it also "proves that thought and testosterone can coexist" and "debunks the long-held myth that Reynolds can't act."

De-Lovely

`20` `22` `19` `22`

2004 | Directed by Irwin Winkler | With Kevin Kline, Ashley Judd | 125 minutes | Rated PG-13

"You can hum along (if you're old enough)" to the "wonderful score" of this Cole Porter biopic, an "informative" effort that doesn't shy away from the composer's "messy" love life; while some are "de-sappointed" by the "movie-of-the-week" screenplay and "gimmicky" musical numbers "decimated by modern singers", at least Kline's "usual fine performance" "gets the beguine begun."

☒ Departed, The ✉

`26` `28` `25` `26`

2006 | Directed by Martin Scorsese | With Leonardo DiCaprio, Matt Damon, Jack Nicholson, Mark Wahlberg | 151 minutes | Rated R

Scorsese brought home a "well-deserved and long-overdue" Oscar for directing this "dynamite" Boston "crime opera", a "complex" cops 'n' mobsters flick that's "overflowing with superstars" (though "Jack steals the show") but so "violent" that "your ears will ring from the gunshots"; set to an "excellent" soundtrack and featuring a finale that will have you "picking your jaw up off the floor", this "instant classic" simply "delivers on all cylinders."

Desk Set

`25` `27` `23` `23`

1957 | Directed by Walter Lang | With Katharine Hepburn, Spencer Tracy, Gig Young, Joan Blondell | 103 minutes | Not Rated

Set in the "dawn of the computer age", this "brisk" romantic comedy brings the "battle of the sexes into the workplace" by pitting "efficiency expert" Tracy against "research librarian" Hepburn; while the "two pros" display "perfect chemistry" and "flawless timing", a few say it's "not their finest hour" – though "Kate's wardrobe" alone makes it "worth the rental" for fashionistas.

Desperately Seeking Susan

`15` `13` `14` `13`

1985 | Directed by Susan Seidelman | With Rosanna Arquette, Madonna, Aidan Quinn | 104 minutes | Rated PG-13

This "quintessential '80s" flick set in NYC's SoHo has to do with a case of mistaken identity but is best known as Madonna's "breakout vehicle" (despite Arquette's "underappreciated" starring role); though the verdict on the Material Girl's thespian abilities is lukewarm – she "basically plays herself" – the picture's still "fun."

Destry Rides Again ◑

`25` `25` `23` `23`

1939 | Directed by George Marshall | With Marlene Dietrich, James Stewart, Mischa Auer | 94 minutes | Not Rated

A "surprisingly modern approach to the code of the Old West", this "funny" oater tells the tale of a "reluctant", "soft-spoken" lawman aiming to tame a corrupt town; there's "strong chemistry" between Stewart's "aw-shucks" deputy and Dietrich's "heart-of-gold" floozy, not to mention a "classic saloon fight" and an "irresistible" song – 'The Boys in the Backroom' – later "parodied in *Blazing Saddles*."

Detective, The

`20` `21` `19` `19`

1968 | Directed by Gordon Douglas | With Frank Sinatra, Lee Remick, Ralph Meeker, Jack Klugman | 114 minutes | Not Rated

"Anything with Frank in it has to be good", and "one of the best" in his acting oeuvre is this "powerful" crime story about a NYPD vet who reopens a murder case and uncovers corruption in the seedy side of the city; it's a "winner in the dramatic department", but some detect a "depressing" tone that leaves "a bad feeling" about New York, New York.

Devil's Advocate, The | 19 | 19 | 20 | 20 |

1997 | Directed by Taylor Hackford | With Keanu Reeves, Al Pacino, Charlize Theron | 144 minutes | Rated R

"Lawyers as the devil's minions" is this thriller's "delightfully sinister" setup, with a "creep-a-delic" Pacino in "hammy overdrive" as a "modern-day Satan" ("be very afraid") who leads legal eagle Reeves into temptation with a "Faust-like offer he can't refuse"; it's "required viewing for young attorneys", even if a few feel the plot is "one helluva mess."

Devil Wears Prada, The | 22 | 25 | 21 | 23 |

2006 | Directed by David Frankel | With Meryl Streep, Anne Hathaway, Emily Blunt, Stanley Tucci | 109 minutes | Rated PG-13

Streep's "absolutely delicious" as an "ice queen" "boss from hell" in this "haute couture comedy" delineating the "cutthroat world" of fashion journalism; although the "off-the-rack" storyline strikes some as "more Gap than Prada", the picture is a must-see "if you're into shoes and belts", and "so much better" than the "second-rate book"; best moment: the "coat montage."

Diabolique ❶🅵 | 26 | 25 | 28 | 23 |

1955 | Directed by Henri-Georges Clouzot | With Simone Signoret, Véra Clouzot | 116 minutes | Not Rated

"Leave it to the French" to serve up this "nasty little thriller" about a murderous love triangle set in a boarding school that "scares the socks" off surveyors; granted, it "looks pretty primitive today", but ultimately "Signoret still smolders", the "clever plot twists" keep coming and "whoa, what an ending!"

Dial M for Murder | 25 | 24 | 27 | 24 |

1954 | Directed by Alfred Hitchcock | With Ray Milland, Grace Kelly, Robert Cummings | 105 minutes | Rated PG

A "jilted husband seeks revenge on his philandering wife" in this "taut" Hitchcock thriller, a "stagey story" transformed into a "suspenseful" movie (fun fact: it was "originally shot in 3-D"); actingwise, "Kelly shines", Milland is "subtly sinister" and Cummings "drags down every scene he appears in."

Diamonds Are Forever | 20 | 18 | 18 | 21 |

1971 | Directed by Guy Hamilton | With Sean Connery, Jill St. John, Charles Gray | 125 minutes | Rated PG

"007 goes Vegas, baby" in this sixth installment of the series, chock-full of the usual "gadgets" and gals, including the "hot", high-"cheek-boned" St. John; in his next-to-last appearance as the stirred-but-never-shaken spy, Connery's at his "dashing, womanizing best" while Gray, as a "hilarious Howard Hughes type", makes a "great villain"; still, Fleming fanatics fret it's "one of the sillier" in the canon.

Diary of a Mad Housewife ∅ | 20 | 24 | 21 | 19 |

1970 | Directed by Frank Perry | With Richard Benjamin, Carrie Snodgress, Frank Langella | 104 minutes | Rated R

This "satire about urban living" examines the disintegration of a loveless marriage between a "self-absorbed" man and a woman "lacking in self-esteem"; Snodgress is "perfection", but Benjamin (the "ultimate night-mare husband") elicits the most heated response: a few want to "punch him" by the end of the movie; best scene: the "elevator sequence."

Diary of Anne Frank, The ◑

| 23 | 23 | 26 | 21 |

1959 | Directed by George Stevens | With Millie Perkins, Shelley Winters, Richard Beymer | 180 minutes | Not Rated

"Every young person should see" this true story of a Jewish family hiding from the Nazis in an Amsterdam attic that "brings to life a dark time in history"; "man's inhumanity to man" is depicted "from a child's point of view" and "though we know the outcome", the "suspense" is truly "heartbreaking."

Dick Tracy

| 13 | 13 | 13 | 20 |

1990 | Directed by Warren Beatty | With Warren Beatty, Madonna, Al Pacino, Glenne Headly | 105 minutes | Rated PG

It's "visually stunning", it's "star-studded", it's got "great Sondheim songs" – but this "classy", "colorful" adaptation of the long-running comic strip is still "nothing special" due to a "vapid" script and an overall sense of "wretched excess"; the good news: this could be "Madonna's best film appearance."

Die Another Day

| 19 | 17 | 16 | 23 |

2002 | Directed by Lee Tamahori | With Pierce Brosnan, Halle Berry, Toby Stephens | 133 minutes | Rated PG-13

Equipped with "everything you expect from a James Bond film", this 20th installment sports "cool gadgets", "fast cars", "easy-on-the-eyes" stars and "Schwarzenegger-like one-liners" in a story that has something to do with the "current political crisis with North Korea"; despite quibbles about an "absurd plot" and "too many CGI effects", diehards declare there's nothing wrong with the "yummy" Halle and her "homage-to-Ursula-Andress" bikini.

Die Hard

| 23 | 19 | 22 | 24 |

1988 | Directed by John McTiernan | With Bruce Willis, Bonnie Bedelia, Alan Rickman | 131 minutes | Rated R

This "flawless" "granddaddy of the '80s action" flick spawned "countless imitations but no equals" thanks to its "thrill-a-minute" mix of suspense, explosions and "comic one-liners"; die-hard diehards tout Willis' "ass-kicking" turn as a "loser whom fate requires to be a hero" as well as "chic bad guy" Rickman, who supplies the "cool quips and fashion tips."

Diner

| 25 | 25 | 23 | 22 |

1982 | Directed by Barry Levinson | With Steve Guttenberg, Mickey Rourke, Kevin Bacon, Ellen Barkin | 110 minutes | Rated R

Levinson's first Baltimore drama "centers on the lives of a group of '50s high school grads" "who spent their youth in diners"; a "finely observed" "guy flick" that's both "smart and funny", it features a "wonderful ensemble cast" that delivers the snappy patter so "brilliantly" it served as a "springboard" for the careers of "many future stars."

Dinner at Eight ◑

| 27 | 27 | 24 | 25 |

1933 | Directed by George Cukor | With Marie Dressler, John Barrymore, Jean Harlow | 113 minutes | Not Rated

It seems as if "every star at MGM appears" in this frothy dramedy about a social-climbing hostess' "high society" dinner party where nothing goes as planned; look for plenty of "art deco sparkle" productionwise, a "joy" of a script and "suave, understated" performances from Dressler and John Barrymore; biggest surprise: Harlow's "snappy" turn as a gum-popping, gold-digging hussy.

Dinner Rush
▽ | 23 | 24 | 23 | 22 |

2000 | Directed by Bob Giraldi | With Danny Aiello, Edoardo Ballerini, Kirk Acevedo | 99 minutes | Rated R

A "great flick for foodies", this "well-done" indie drama unfolds over one night at a trendy Manhattan eatery where the cast of characters includes low-down gangsters, high-strung chefs, put-upon waiters and spoiled food critics; maybe it's "not as endearing as *Big Night*", but fans savor the "excellent" Aiello – and that "nice twist" at the end.

Dinosaur
| 19 | - | 17 | 24 |

2000 | Directed by Eric Leighton, Ralph Zondag | Animated | 82 minutes | Rated PG

"Kids interested in dinosaurs" dig this Disney flick for its "extraordinary animation", "wonderful music" and "fabulous" meteor shower scene; but despite some "exciting moments", soreheads lament that it's "lacking in the plot department" and not much more than a "dull remake of *The Land Before Time*."

Dirty Dancing
| 21 | 17 | 20 | 20 |

1987 | Directed by Emile Ardolino | With Patrick Swayze, Jennifer Grey, Jerry Orbach | 96 minutes | Rated PG-13

Whether it's a "girls'-night-in" or a "Sunday afternoon vacation", this "cult classic" is the cinematic equivalent of "comfort food" and even works as an "excellent date movie"; its "heart-melting story" centers on the romance between "hot, sexy teen dream" Swayze and "cute gamine" Grey, who "shake their booties" just "like the Solid Gold dancers" used to do to pop hits in a "'60s Catskills resort."

Dirty Dozen, The
| 21 | 19 | 22 | 20 |

1967 | Directed by Robert Aldrich | With Lee Marvin, Ernest Borgnine, Charles Bronson | 145 minutes | Not Rated

This "delightful" war adventure exudes a "healthy dose of cynicism" in telling the tale of a "merry band of cutthroats" "brought together to do good in WWII"; the "early-in-their-careers" actors are "awesome", "super-macho" types, while the "rough-and-tumble", action-packed plot still seems "fun after all these years."

Dirty Harry
| 21 | 18 | 20 | 19 |

1971 | Directed by Don Siegel | With Clint Eastwood, Harry Guardino, Reni Santoni | 102 minutes | Rated R

Clint's at his "steely-eyed, gravelly voiced best" in this "modern cop" flick that "struck a chord in the '70s" and "created a fast-and-furious" subgenre "solid" enough to "spawn a host of imitators"; throw in some "great views of San Francisco" and a moodily "muted jazz score" and you just might "feel lucky, punk."

Dirty Pretty Things
| 23 | 24 | 24 | 21 |

2003 | Directed by Stephen Frears | With Chiwetel Ejiofor, Audrey Tautou, Sergi López | 97 minutes | Rated R

London's illegal "immigrant underworld" goes under the microscope in this "atmospheric", "suspenseful" crime thriller detailing "shady goings-on" (think prostitution, drug dealing and "macabre" trafficking in human organs) at a "swanky UK hotel"; the "low-budget look" works well with the "gritty performances", "thought-provoking" scenario and "unexpected ending."

Dirty Rotten Scoundrels `22` `24` `22` `20`

1988 | Directed by Frank Oz | With Steve Martin, Michael Caine, Glenne Headly | 110 minutes | Rated PG

Up there in the "pantheon of silly", this "inspired" farce (remade from 1964's *Bedtime Story*) has the "perfect cast": Martin and Caine as "competing con men" on the French Riviera "trying to outdo each other" in a Lothario's challenge to "grift an heiress"; the "fencing" between the "two pros" yields "high hilarity" and "quotable scenes galore."

Discreet Charm of the Bourgeoisie, The ✉ 🎬 `24` `23` `23` `22`

1972 | Directed by Luis Buñuel | With Fernando Rey, Delphine Seyrig, Stéphane Audran | 102 minutes | Rated PG

"Controversial" in its day, this Oscar-winning "satirical portrait of the French bourgeoisie" tells the "elliptical" tale of "six people in search of a hot meal" who are "confounded at every turn" by bizarre goings-on; Buñuel serves up enough "dream-within-a-dream sequences" to turn this dark comedy into a "thoughtful, surreal delight" that further enhances his reputation as the "Dali of cinema."

Diva 🎬 `24` `20` `24` `24`

1982 | Directed by Jean-Jacques Beineix | With Wilhelmenia Fernandez, Frederic Andrei | 123 minutes | Rated R

Perhaps the "greatest opera/action flick ever", this "oh-so-stylish" French thriller creates a "complicated world" about a "scooter-riding kid" obsessed by a "reclusive soprano"; "glorious to look at", with "wonderful images of Paris", it's most memorable for that "fast-paced motorcycle chase" in the Métro.

Divine Secrets of the Ya-Ya Sisterhood `16` `20` `17` `17`

2002 | Directed by Callie Khouri | With Sandra Bullock, Ellen Burstyn, James Garner, Ashley Judd | 116 minutes | Rated PG-13

A "disappointing adaptation of an amazing book", this Southern-fried "quintessential chick flick" tells the tale of a complicated "mother-and-daughter relationship" with "not a whit of the sass or charm of the novel"; though many find the performances "terrific" ("older actresses rock"), the "schmaltzy", *"Fried Green Magnolias"* script strikes some sisters as "more yo-yo than ya-ya."

Divorce Italian Style ✉🅞🎬 `24` `25` `23` `22`

1962 | Directed by Pietro Germi | With Marcello Mastroianni, Daniela Rocca, Stefania Sandrelli | 104 minutes | Not Rated

"Mastroianni's a hoot" playing an "unfortunately married man" "lusting for greener pastures" in this *"molto bene"* comedy set way back when divorce was illegal in Italy; its "silly but sweet" Oscar-winning screenplay is both a "condemnation of the law" as well as a "nice satire", and if it "loses a little in translation", it compensates with black-and-white cinematography that's "lusher than most color films."

D.O.A. ◑

22 | 22 | 26 | 21

1950 | Directed by Rudolph Maté | With Edmond O'Brien, Pamela Britton, Luther Adler | 83 minutes | Not Rated

"One of the best opening lines" – "I want to report a murder . . . mine" – sets in motion the "intriguing plot" of this "elaborate time-runs-backward" drama in which an "innocent man must find his own killer before he dies"; set against a backdrop of "great location shots of LA and San Francisco", it's "gritty, bleak" noir that's "compelling as hell", even if a few deadbeats declare it "promises more than it delivers."

☑ Doctor Zhivago ✉

27 | 26 | 26 | 28

1965 | Directed by David Lean | With Omar Sharif, Julie Christie, Geraldine Chaplin, Rod Steiger | 197 minutes | Rated PG-13

Lean's "timeless" – others say "long" – Oscar-winning evocation of Boris Pasternak's "sweeping" novel of "love and war" is the "epic to end all epics", merging "brilliant historical storytelling" with "romantic extravaganza"; set during the Russian Revolution, it "humanized the USSR during the Cold War" due to the "tear-jerking" relationship between Christie and Sharif – though its "balalaika"-heavy theme song and the scenes in that "winter wonderland" of an "ice palace" resonate most.

Dodgeball

16 | 16 | 15 | 16

2004 | Directed by Rawson Marshall Thurber | With Vince Vaughn, Ben Stiller, Christine Taylor, Rip Torn | 92 minutes | Rated PG-13

A "sophomoric spoof of the sporting world", this "manic" comedy fields a "Frat Pack" "matchup" of "deadpan" Vaughn vs. "sadistic meathead" Stiller, playing owners of "dueling gyms" who use the "goofball playground game" to settle a score; fans of "crude slapstick" say "don't dodge this one", but other spectators "may want to duck."

Dog Day Afternoon ✉

24 | 27 | 22 | 20

1975 | Directed by Sidney Lumet | With Al Pacino, John Cazale, Chris Sarandon, Charles Durning | 124 minutes | Rated R

This "funny/sad" true tale of a botched "bank heist" committed by "hapless" amateurs is transformed into a "deep, character-driven" example of director Lumet "at his best"; expect "great performances from the entire cast" (from the nervous bank tellers "right down to the pizza delivery guy"), with particular kudos to an "ass-kicking" Pacino and a "brilliant" Sarandon as his gay lover.

Dogville

21 | 25 | 20 | 21

2004 | Directed by Lars von Trier | With Nicole Kidman, Harriet Andersson, Lauren Bacall, Paul Bettany | 178 minutes | Rated R

Decidedly "not for everyone", this avant-garde "morality play" about a woman on the run taken in by a small town is "risky", "controversial" stuff, starting with its "minimalist", stagelike setting and "terribly long" running time; some growl it's too "self-important" (and maybe even "anti-American"), but those willing to "plunge in" find it "daring" and "thought-provoking" – "art films don't get much artier than this."

Donnie Brasco

20 | 24 | 22 | 20

1997 | Directed by Mike Newell | With Al Pacino, Johnny Depp, Anne Heche | 127 minutes | Rated R

In this true story, an undercover FBI agent "befriends the man he's supposed to entrap" and takes you "inside the inner workings of the mob" to reveal a "more realistic side to the underworld"; a "sympathetic", "nuanced" Pacino does the "gangster-as-loser" thing right, while Depp's titular turn is similarly "excellent"; like the 'family' it portrays, this one "never lets go of you."

Donnie Darko
22 | 23 | 23 | 21

2001 | Directed by Richard Kelly | With Jake Gyllenhaal, Drew Barrymore, Mary McDonnell | 113 minutes | Rated R

"*Harvey*" meets "*Psycho*" in this indie "cult favorite" that combines "trippy sci-fi" FX with "John Hughes high-school angst" in its story of a "delusional" teen who sees visions of "demonic bunny rabbits"; sure, you might "need a few viewings to understand it" (after which it may still "make no sense"), but its "huge fan base" goes bonkers over the "original" script, "top-notch soundtrack" and the "solid" Jake, in the breakout role that made him a star.

Don't Look Back ◑
25 | - | 22 | 23

1967 | Directed by D.A. Pennebaker | Documentary | With Bob Dylan, Joan Baez, Donovan | 96 minutes | Not Rated

This "revealing" "slice of musical history" "captures the young Bob Dylan in all his contradictory charm and churlishness" as an "artist in transition" and is an "indelible" "reminder of what all the fuss was about"; perhaps the "most referenced" rockumentary ever, "it's improved with time" and includes one of the "first music videos" ever: the famed cue-cards clip for 'Subterranean Homesick Blues.'

Don't Look Now
24 | 26 | 24 | 24

1974 | Directed by Nicolas Roeg | With Julie Christie, Donald Sutherland | 110 minutes | Rated R

"Venice at its most eerie" is the backdrop for this "disturbing" psychological thriller with an "atmosphere of dread" so pervasive that you'll be "on the edge of your gondola" throughout; based on a Daphne du Maurier story about "grieving parents" mourning the death of their child, it weaves a "blind clairvoyant" and a "murderous dwarf" into its "thoroughly adult" web – and tops things off with "one of the best sex scenes in the history of cinema."

Door in the Floor, The
19 | 23 | 19 | 19

2004 | Directed by Tod Williams | With Jeff Bridges, Kim Basinger, Jon Foster | 111 minutes | Rated R

"Nice looking and well acted", this "textured" adaptation of "the first third of John Irving's novel *A Widow for One Year*" relates the "sad, bleak" tale of a successful, "self-centered author whose marriage has fallen apart"; Bridges is "brilliant" ("when is he going to win an Oscar?"), Basinger the "same vulnerable mess, as usual", and although the picture certainly "has its moments", some slam it as "ultimately unengaging."

Do the Right Thing
23 | 23 | 22 | 21

1989 | Directed by Spike Lee | With Spike Lee, Danny Aiello, Ossie Davis, Ruby Dee | 120 minutes | Rated R

"Italian-American pizza parlor owners in Brooklyn" and the "African-American community who patronize the shop" clash "on the hottest day of the year" in this "anatomy of a race riot" from Spike Lee, who "deftly balances tragedy with comedy" to telegraph a "message as clear as black and white" that still "resonates years later."

	OVERALL	ACTING	STORY	PROD.

☒ Double Indemnity ◑ — 28 | 27 | 28 | 25

1944 | Directed by Billy Wilder | With Fred MacMurray, Barbara Stanwyck, Edward G. Robinson | 107 minutes | Not Rated

"From the chiaroscuro settings to the world-weary voice-over", Wilder's "refreshingly sour" slice of "hard-boiled" noir "sets the standard for the genre"; the story of "another dumb cluck done in by a woman", it features a "fast-talking" MacMurray, a "knockout" Stanwyck ("love the anklet") and a "fantastic" Robinson, with enough plot "twists" and sly "killer banter" to make it the cinematic equivalent of "bonded bourbon"; best scene: shopping at the "supermarket."

Double Jeopardy — 16 | 18 | 19 | 18

1999 | Directed by Bruce Beresford | With Tommy Lee Jones, Ashley Judd, Annabeth Gish | 105 minutes | Rated R

"Diverting" enough, this "clever" thriller finds Judd playing a "kick-ass bitch" wrongfully imprisoned for murder and hell-bent on "revenge"; legal eagles rule it's "completely implausible" (even its title "premise is false") and add that "Jones' cop thing is getting old", but it's "enjoyable nonetheless" if you like "a lot of twists."

Down and Out in Beverly Hills — 17 | 19 | 17 | 17

1986 | Directed by Paul Mazursky | With Nick Nolte, Richard Dreyfuss, Bette Midler | 103 minutes | Rated R

The "Jean Renoir classic" *Bondu Saved from Drowning* is "given an American spin" in this "spoof of the upper class", Beverly Hills–style, wherein a "bum interacts in the lives of a wealthy family" with "hilarious" results; Bette's "divine" as a "neurotic wife who undergoes an amazing transformation", and even if the humor verges on the "crude", it's still "winning" enough.

Down by Law ◑ — 24 | 23 | 23 | 22

1986 | Directed by Jim Jarmusch | With Tom Waits, John Lurie, Roberto Benigni | 107 minutes | Rated R

A "trio of unlikely fugitives" - a DJ, a pimp and an Italian tourist - takes it on the lam from a Louisiana slammer in this "odd", "brooding" comedy from indie king Jarmusch that's best remembered for "introducing Benigni" to American audiences; but even though this B&W "original" has attained "compulsory" "cult classic" status over time, a few say its "slow pace is not for everyone."

Down with Love — 18 | 19 | 17 | 23

2003 | Directed by Peyton Reed | With Renée Zellweger, Ewan McGregor, David Hyde Pierce | 101 minutes | Rated PG-13

"Not everyone's cup of tea", this "stylized homage" spoofs "Camelot-era" sex comedies with its "frothy" tale of a "lady-killer" journalist out to seduce a "wily" writer, and fans "dig the clothes" and the wink-wink "double entendres"; but foes fume "fluffy", citing a "thin" plot and "little chemistry" between the leads ("Doris and Rock did it better"), although Pierce "out-Tony Randalls Tony Randall."

Dracula ◑ — 24 | 21 | 23 | 20

1931 | Directed by Tod Browning | With Bela Lugosi, Helen Chandler, Dwight Frye | 75 minutes | Not Rated

Granted, the "special effects are nonexistent", but this "definitive Dracula" is still "scarier than anything made today", leaving "plenty of room for imagination" thanks to Lugosi's "riveting" take on the "immortal vampire"; though it uses music sparingly to evoke an "eerie atmosphere", a new, souped-up DVD with a "Philip Glass score" is highly touted; best line: "I never drink . . . *wine.*"

Dracula
20 | 19 | 22 | 25

1992 | Directed by Francis Ford Coppola | With Gary Oldman, Winona Ryder, Anthony Hopkins, Keanu Reeves | 130 minutes | Rated R
"You can sink your teeth" into Coppola's "highly underrated" "retelling of Bram Stoker's tale" of a "lovelorn", bloodthirsty Romanian count; "stylish" costumes, Oscar-winning sets, a "stunning" Oldman and the spectacle of "Tom Waits eating bugs" make for "visionary" moviemaking, even if some nix the "laughable miscasting" of Reeves.

Dr. Dolittle
16 | 17 | 17 | 18

1998 | Directed by Betty Thomas | With Eddie Murphy, Ossie Davis, Peter Boyle | 85 minutes | Rated PG-13
Both "kids and kids at heart" "crack up" over this "priceless" Murphy vehicle in which he "shines" playing a doc who can "talk to animals"; based vaguely on Hugh Lofting's "perennially popular" children's stories, this update employs state-of-the-art animatronics and computer graphics to make the animalspeak both realistic and "entertaining."

Dreamers, The
17 | 19 | 17 | 19

2004 | Directed by Bernardo Bertolucci | With Michael Pitt, Eva Green, Louis Garrel | 115 minutes | Rated NC-17
Themes of "cinematic and political freedom" (not to mention "graphic sex scenes") "keep your interest" in Bertolucci's "adults-only" drama set in the "tumultuous" Paris of 1968 that intercuts "actual footage" from classic films with a story of three "beautiful young idealists" involved in an "explicit" ménage à trois; whether it's a "fearless homage" to the "French New Wave" or a "pretentious" dose of "gratuitous porn" is one of the "challenging" issues raised.

Dreamgirls
23 | 24 | 22 | 26

2006 | Directed by Bill Condon | With Jamie Foxx, Beyoncé Knowles, Eddie Murphy, Jennifer Hudson | 131 minutes | Rated PG-13
This "glitzy" Motown musical chronicles the "roller-coaster" fortunes of a "Supremes"-like trio and marks the "breathtaking" big-screen debut of "*American Idol*" manqué Hudson, who "pours on the pathos" with an "exquisite" Beyoncé and "dy-no-mite" Murphy at her side; busting out "gorgeous" costumes to accompany the "top-notch" tunes, it "feels like being at a Broadway show – minus the ticket prices."

Dressed to Kill
20 | 22 | 19 | 20

1980 | Directed by Brian De Palma | With Michael Caine, Angie Dickinson, Nancy Allen | 105 minutes | Rated R
"Swirling camerawork, split screens, tracking shots that go on for miles" – yup, it's another "stylishly bloody" De Palma thriller, replete with "violent slashings, sensuous showers and sexual confusion" as it tells the adventures of a "happy hooker, an unhappy housewife and a shrink"; though an "inspiring" Angie provides the "sexy" "goose bumps", foes say it's "too derivative of Hitchcock."

	OVERALL	ACTING	STORY	PROD.

Driving Miss Daisy ✉ 24 | 27 | 23 | 22

1989 | Directed by Bruce Beresford | With Morgan Freeman, Jessica Tandy, Dan Aykroyd | 99 minutes | Rated PG

"Race relations" in the South and the "loss of dignity" that can come with aging are "wonderfully depicted" in this "heartwarming" story of an "unconventional friendship" between a matriarch and her chauffeur; the "sterling" Tandy and Freeman exhibit "incredible onscreen chemistry" (she drove home with an Oscar) in this "uplifting yet down-to-earth" drama.

Dr. No 23 | 20 | 22 | 23

1963 | Directed by Terence Young | With Sean Connery, Ursula Andress, Jack Lord | 110 minutes | Rated PG

The "first Bond outing" is a "lean and mean" thriller "unhindered by political correctness", with "fewer gadgets" and gals than usual (though the image of Andress in that "white bikini" is "seared forever onto many a man's brain"); while the "dashing" Connery "makes it all look effortless", "purists" note this "unadulterated" "template" is the "closest they ever came to Ian Fleming's vision."

☑ Dr. Strangelove ➊ 28 | 28 | 27 | 26

1964 | Directed by Stanley Kubrick | With Peter Sellers, George C. Scott, Sterling Hayden | 93 minutes | Rated PG

"Nuclear annihilation was never funnier" than in Kubrick's "stinging Cold War satire", a "chillingly comic" examination of "distressingly familiar government officials" and their "precious bodily fluids"; as members of "our military at work", Scott is "magnificent" and Sellers "phenomenal" (in "three, count 'em, roles"), while "Slim Pickens riding the bomb" remains one of the cinema's most indelible images; doomsday devotees dub it "apocalypse now and forever."

Drugstore Cowboy 19 | 21 | 19 | 18

1989 | Directed by Gus Van Sant | With Matt Dillon, Kelly Lynch, James Le Gros | 100 minutes | Rated R

Van Sant's grittily "accurate depiction" of narcotics addicts robbing drugstores for drugs is loaded with "precise, unexpected performances" and a surprise bonus: William Burroughs as a junkie ex-priest; though habit-ues hail it as a "highly original dark comedy", nonsupporters say it "doesn't hold up well."

☑ Duck Soup ➊ 27 | 25 | 23 | 22

1933 | Directed by Leo McCarey | With the Marx Brothers, Margaret Dumont | 70 minutes | Not Rated

"Hail, hail Freedonia" cry fans of the "anarchic" Marx foursome, whose trademark "lunacy" is at its "peak" in this "political satire" about a "mythical dictatorship"; "absurdly funny" – it includes the "legendary mirror scene with Groucho and Harpo" – it's the brothers' "finest hour" and voted top of the Marxes in this Survey.

Duel in the Sun 23 | 22 | 22 | 24

1946 | Directed by King Vidor | With Jennifer Jones, Gregory Peck, Joseph Cotten, Lillian Gish | 146 minutes | Not Rated

Producer David O. Selznick "goes for baroque" in this "overripe", "overacted", "overly long" horse opera about a "hot" half-breed and the two brothers who desire her; its "shockingly sexual" undercurrent led to its "nickname, *Lust in the Dust*", though what's "campy" and "over the top" for some is "epic" and "operatic" to others; no question, "they don't make 'em like this anymore."

Dumb and Dumber

	OVERALL	ACTING	STORY	PROD.
	15	16	12	14

1994 | Directed by Peter Farrelly, Bobby Farrelly | With Jim Carrey, Jeff Daniels, Lauren Holly | 106 minutes | Rated PG-13

No duh, the "title says it all" in this maiden effort from the Farrelly brothers, a "gross-out" "guilty pleasure" about a "moronic duo" "traveling cross country" with a briefcase stuffed with cash; fans say the "vulgar" antics (think "potty jokes", "disgusting noises") "grow on you", though foes sneer the "puerile", "not-for-adults" storyline makes for the "ultimate" in "lowbrow humor."

Dumbo

	24	-	23	24

1941 | Directed by Ben Sharpsteen | Animated | 64 minutes | Rated G

"Elephants fly" in this "short but sweet" animated Disney classic message movie "about the importance of being yourself"; though the politically correct disparage its "racist undertones" and find it "too sad" for smaller fry, fans laud its "fabulous", Oscar-winning score and "unforgettable sequences" – particularly the "tripped-out" "hallucination" of those pink pachyderms on parade.

Dune

	14	13	18	18

1984 | Directed by David Lynch | With Kyle MacLachlan, Francesca Annis, Jürgen Prochnow, Sting | 137 minutes | Rated PG-13

"Beautiful to look at but incoherent" plotwise, this "problematic" adaptation of Frank Herbert's "iconic" sci-fi novel is either a "heroic mess" or an "unjustly maligned" work that "gets better after repeated viewings"; many argue that the "complicated storyline" (something to do with warring factions in the far-off year of 10191) is practically "unfilmable", but whether the end result is worth seeing for director Lynch's trademark "high weirdness" or just a "waste of celluloid" is up to you.

Dying Gaul, The

	17	23	16	18

2005 | Directed by Craig Lucas | With Peter Sarsgaard, Campbell Scott, Patricia Clarkson | 101 minutes | Rated R

Art versus commerce is the "interesting premise" of this "edgy" drama wherein a "shattered gay man" sells a vaguely autobiographical screenplay to a Hollywood studio, only to undergo "betrayal heaped on betrayal" as it goes through rewrites; fans like the "never-saw-it-coming" ending and "terrific" cast "flexing their talent", but the blasé yawn the picture is "just not compelling" enough.

Easter Parade

	22	21	17	24

1948 | Directed by Charles Walters | With Judy Garland, Fred Astaire, Ann Miller | 107 minutes | Not Rated

"It isn't really Easter" till you've watched this "grand Irving Berlin musical" boasting 17 songs and "lots of frills upon it" – including Fred and Judy at their "singing and dancing best" in their "only screen appearance together"; the slender story has Astaire trying to make a star out of chorus girl Garland, but this "wonderful" MGM "showcase" transcends its plot with sheer star power.

	OVERALL	ACTING	STORY	PROD.

East of Eden
24 | 27 | 24 | 23

1955 | Directed by Elia Kazan | With James Dean, Julie Harris, Raymond Massey, Jo Van Fleet | 115 minutes | Not Rated

An "unforgettable" Dean eats "every actor on the set for breakfast" in his "searing" big-screen debut as the "proverbial bad seed" in this adaptation of John Steinbeck's tale of "sibling rivalry"; sure, there are also "beautiful" CinemaScope panoramas and an Oscar-winning turn from Van Fleet, but Jimmy makes it "memorable" – "to think he only made three films is amazing."

Easy Rider
23 | 23 | 20 | 20

1969 | Directed by Dennis Hopper | With Peter Fonda, Dennis Hopper, Jack Nicholson | 94 minutes | Rated R

"Sex, drugs and rock 'n' roll" explode on the silver screen in this "seminal" "road movie" that "defined a generation" by capturing the essence of the "tumultuous" '60s; famed for "Nicholson's starmaking performance" and Hopper's "manic", "revolutionary" direction, this "trippy" "time capsule" might have also "invented the music video" thanks to that "amazing soundtrack"; still, Gen-Y types protest it "doesn't hold up" today, unless you "get high" first.

Eat Drink Man Woman 🄵
25 | 24 | 24 | 24

1994 | Directed by Ang Lee | With Sihung Lung, Wu Chien-Lien, Yang Kuei-Mei, Wang Yu-Wen | 123 minutes | Not Rated

Gourmands eat up this "tasty" Taiwanese look at a "different culture" that tells the story of a traditional "Asian father who shows his love by cooking for his daughters"; director Lee's "visual feast" contrasts "ticklish relationships" with "stupendous food scenes" so adroitly that many "get hungry just thinking about it."

Eating Raoul
18 | 18 | 21 | 15

1982 | Directed by Paul Bartel | With Paul Bartel, Mary Woronov, Robert Beltran | 90 minutes | Rated R

"Not everyone can stomach" this "blacker-than-black" "bizarro" "cult" comedy, but there's agreement that its "absurd" plot (about a Moral Majority–esque couple luring swingers to their deaths) is the "trailer-park" version of *Sweeney Todd*; "kind of sick", this "deadpan" "low-budget" B movie is also kind of "fun" – and "for grown-ups only."

Educating Rita
18 | 21 | 19 | 18

1983 | Directed by Lewis Gilbert | With Michael Caine, Julie Walters | 110 minutes | Rated PG-13

Caine and Walters exhibit "great chemistry" in this "interesting" tale of an "alcoholic professor" who tutors a "working-class" gal; though the "pseudo-*Pygmalion*" plot "isn't quite convincing" for some, others relate perfectly to the "believable" title character, a "woman who won't allow herself to be held back by social class."

Edward Scissorhands
21 | 22 | 22 | 24

1990 | Directed by Tim Burton | With Johnny Depp, Winona Ryder, Dianne Wiest | 100 minutes | Rated PG-13

Burton's "oddball" opus spins a "delightfully bent" "love story" around an ultimate "outsider" – a "misfit boy with garden tools for hands" – living in "conformist suburbia"; "Depp shows he has the big-screen stuff" (and "makes a hell of a topiary"), while the "primary-colored" art direction creates an "alternative universe disturbingly close to home"; best line: Wiest's perky "Avon calling!"

Ed Wood ◑   20 | 23 | 19 | 21

1994 | Directed by Tim Burton | With Johnny Depp, Martin Landau, Sarah Jessica Parker | 127 minutes | Rated R

"Schlockmeister" director Ed Wood gets the Tim Burton treatment in this "loving tribute" that's also a "glimpse into grade Z filmmaking"; look for an "enthusiastic", "totally sympathetic" Depp in the title role opposite an Oscar-winning Landau as a "drugged-out" Bela Lugosi – "never before have the talentless been so brilliantly rendered by the talented."

Eight Below   22 | 19 | 24 | 24

2006 | Directed by Frank Marshall | With Paul Walker, Bruce Greenwood, Moon Bloodgood | 120 minutes | Rated PG

The "astounding canine cast" does the "best acting" in this live-action Disney adventure, an "uplifting" true story about a sled dog team's "struggle to survive" after the humans evacuate in the wake of a "monster snow storm"; though "weepy for sure", it's a "wholesome family flick" iced with enough "thrills" to ensure that you "won't be bored."

8½ ✉◑🎬   26 | 26 | 24 | 26

1963 | Directed by Federico Fellini | With Marcello Mastroianni, Claudia Cardinale, Anouk Aimée | 145 minutes | Not Rated

"Navel-gazing has never been more profound" than in this "semi-autobiographical" "Italian masterpiece" from the "extraordinary" Fellini about a blocked "director trying to make a film" by using his "life as material for his work"; told in "stream of consciousness", it also features "luscious" art direction and a "career-defining turn by Mastroianni" – no wonder many call this "heartfelt" flick the "definitive movie about movies."

Eight Men Out   24 | 24 | 25 | 23

1988 | Directed by John Sayles | With John Cusack, David Strathairn, D.B. Sweeney, Charlie Sheen | 119 minutes | Rated PG

A "black eye for baseball" gets a "dark" retelling in Sayles' "insightful" sports story, recounting the "legendary 1919 Black Sox scandal" that left eight players "forever banned" for "throwing the World Series"; with a "superb" ensemble cast (who "actually look like ballplayers") and an "uncanny re-creation" of "post-WWI" times, it's pitched as a "contender" for best diamond drama.

8 Mile   19 | 18 | 17 | 19

2002 | Directed by Curtis Hanson | With Eminem, Kim Basinger, Brittany Murphy, Mekhi Phifer | 110 minutes | Rated R

Take "Rocky", add "Purple Rain", "go to Detroit", and you've got this "quality" "retread" of the "poor-boy-claws-his-way-out-of-the-hood" story; while Eminem's "semi-autobiographical" performance is "raw and touching", this "gritty" flick (and its "7 mile"-long string of "F-words") gets truly "compelling" in the last "rap-off."

El Cid ∅   19 | 16 | 20 | 23

1961 | Directed by Anthony Mann | With Charlton Heston, Sophia Loren, Raf Vallone | 182 minutes | Not Rated

This early '60s epic is a "guy's delight" that finds Heston once again inhabiting the skin of a "larger-than-life" figure, this time the legendary

11th-century Spaniard who defended his country against the Moors; "lots of action" elates thrill-seekers, though foes lambaste it as "bombastic and overblown."

Election
22 | 24 | 22 | 20

1999 | Directed by Alexander Payne | With Reese Witherspoon, Matthew Broderick | 103 minutes | Rated R

"Student council elections" as an "allegory for real political life" underscore this "whip-smart" "black comedy" about a "goody two-shoes" "high-school overachiever" and a teacher bent on putting a stop to her rise; voters find "no fraud" in this "spot-on" "social satire", adding that "unless you were home-schooled, you'll relate."

Elephant
19 | 18 | 19 | 21

2003 | Directed by Gus Van Sant | With Alex Frost, Eric Deulen | 81 minutes | Rated R

"Wildly original", this "disturbing" examination of a "Columbine-esque" high-school massacre splits surveyors: fans praise the "dreamlike" plot, "cinema verité"–style photography and "moving" work by a cast of "nonprofessionals", but cynics say it's "insightless" and "boring"; both sides agree it's "tough to watch" and "definitely open to interpretation."

Elephant Man, The ◑
24 | 27 | 25 | 23

1980 | Directed by David Lynch | With Anthony Hopkins, John Hurt, Anne Bancroft | 125 minutes | Rated PG

The "dignity in deformity" is defined in this "unflinching" true story about a "Victorian-era" freak who "tests the compassion of a horrified society"; "brilliant acting and makeup" make it a "gloriously Gothic" "voyage into the human heart" – a "perfect match of director and material", it will "touch you deep inside."

Elf
21 | 21 | 20 | 20

2003 | Directed by Jon Favreau | With Will Ferrell, James Caan, Bob Newhart, Zooey Deschanel | 95 minutes | Rated PG

Imbued with the "real spirit of Christmas", this "surprisingly sweet-natured" holiday comedy stars "funny man Ferrell" as a "human being raised by elves" at the North Pole who travels to NYC to find his birth parents; granted, there's "nothing to tax your mind" in this "old-fashioned romp", but Will's a "hoot", "Deschanel looks gorgeous" and the "deadpan" Newhart is "consistently hilarious."

Elizabeth
24 | 27 | 23 | 26

1998 | Directed by Shekhar Kapur | With Cate Blanchett, Geoffrey Rush, Joseph Fiennes | 124 minutes | Rated R

"Captivating" Cate displays "unbelievable range" in this bio of England's "Virgin Queen" that follows her progress from "lusty young woman" to "ice-cold, calculating icon"; though it "feels like a fantasy version of Elizabeth I's life" to skeptics, fans swear it's "historically on the mark", with "beautiful sets", "excellent costume design" and a "gripping" plot.

Elmer Gantry ✉
25 | 27 | 24 | 23

1960 | Directed by Richard Brooks | With Burt Lancaster, Jean Simmons, Shirley Jones | 146 minutes | Not Rated

Disciples of this "rip-roaring" adaptation of the Sinclair Lewis novel testify that Lancaster's Oscar-winning, "fire-and-brimstone" performance as a "street preacher"-cum-"con man" in a "hypocritical" traveling ministry is the "best of his career" (while some "get religion" watching Jones' take on a jilted prostitute); its "excellent script" detailing a "flesh vs. the spirit" conflict also took home a statuette.

Elvira Madigan 🅵   20 | 19 | 20 | 24

1967 | Directed by Bo Widerberg | With Pia Degermark, Thommy Berggren | 91 minutes | Rated PG

Both "visually stunning" and "wonderfully dated", this Swedish sobfest recounts the "heartbreaking" affair between "two AWOL lovers" – a tightrope walker and a married army officer – who are "beautiful" and, of course, "doomed"; although memorable for its "lovely scenery" and the Mozart piano concerto it popularized, it's forgettable to those who see it as "tiresome" "romantic fluff."

Emma   22 | 23 | 23 | 24

1996 | Directed by Douglas McGrath | With Gwyneth Paltrow, Jeremy Northam, Greta Scacchi | 121 minutes | Rated PG

Jane Austen's "charming" story of "matchmaking at its best and worst" gets an "engaging" spin in this "delightful period piece" starring a "perfect" Paltrow opposite a "laconically charming" Northam; its "cheery" tone and dry "humor" make it a natural to "watch back-to-back with Clueless, since they're both based on the same novel."

Emmanuelle 🅵   16 | 14 | 14 | 15

1974 | Directed by Just Jaeckin | With Sylvia Kristel, Alain Cuny, Marika Green | 95 minutes | Rated R

Long before "Cinemax", this "leader" of "soft-core porn" features finds Kristel looking "very feminine" (and "sans silicone") in the part of a naive but libidinous diplomat's spouse out to explore the "erotic" possibilities available within R-rated limits; considered "sexy for its day", it remains "scenic in many ways" but rather "tame for this century."

Emperor's New Groove, The   20 | - | 18 | 20

2000 | Directed by Mark Dindal | Animated | 78 minutes | Rated G

A "selfish emperor becomes a llama" with humbling results in this "quirky", "overlooked cartoon" that effortlessly merges both "standard and CGI animation" with "superb voice acting"; sure, aesthetes complain of a "low-budget", "slapped-together" look, but most find it "highly entertaining" with "lots of great gags" and a script that's "actually funny."

Empire of the Sun   25 | 23 | 24 | 26

1987 | Directed by Steven Spielberg | With Christian Bale, John Malkovich | 154 minutes | Rated PG

Perhaps Spielberg's most "underappreciated" picture, this "touching story of a British child's internment in a World War II Japanese prison camp" is an "ambitious" epic replete with "dazzling" acting, "David Lean-worthy" imagery and an "especially moving John Williams score"; maybe the "storyline drags" a bit midway, but overall its "sheer power" supplies the "magic moments."

Enchanted April ∅   24 | 26 | 22 | 25

1992 | Directed by Mike Newell | With Joan Plowright, Miranda Richardson, Josie Lawrence | 95 minutes | Rated PG

For a "wonderfully rich pick-me-up", take a look at this "genteel" "getaway" of a movie about four "risk-taking" women who decide to "leave their dreary English lives behind" and are "transformed" during an April vacation in "lush, sunny" Tuscany; the perfect "antidote to winter", it's "more complex than it first appears", and Plowright's "terrific performance" will brighten any "rainy day."

Endless Summer, The
24 | - | 20 | 23

1966 | Directed by Bruce Brown | Documentary | 95 minutes | Not Rated

"Cowabunga" – this "quintessential" surfing documentary is a bona fide "'60s relic"-cum-"classic travelogue" that puts some in the mood to "grab a board and move to Hawaii"; ok, there's "not much of a storyline" (two surfers traveling the globe "in search of the perfect wave"), but armchair beachcombers seeking a "great escape" claim it "stands the test of time."

End of the Affair, The
20 | 24 | 20 | 22

1999 | Directed by Neil Jordan | With Ralph Fiennes, Julianne Moore, Stephen Rea | 102 minutes | Rated R

"Faith, love and loss" underlie this "terrific" adaptation of Graham Greene's "tragic romance" set in "rainy" WWII London about a "conflicted, adulterous Englishwoman" and her "jealous, angry lover"; this "difficult story" succeeds thanks to a "flashback"-heavy, "multi-layered" scenario and "wonderful screen chemistry" between a "powerful" Fiennes and a "smoldering" Moore modeling "glamorous slips and retro suits."

Enemy at the Gates
21 | 22 | 23 | 23

2001 | Directed by Jean-Jacques Annaud | With Jude Law, Ed Harris, Rachel Weisz, Joseph Fiennes | 131 minutes | Rated R

"Soviet Communists and Nazis" scrap on the Russian front in this "gripping" war pic, putting WWII's "hellish" siege of Stalingrad "on a very personal level", featuring Harris and Law as "two dueling snipers" with their sights set on "cleverly choreographed standoffs"; the "rousing action" and "engrossing characterizations" are "powerful stuff" that make this "violent", "sprawling" saga "worth the effort."

Enemy of the State
19 | 19 | 20 | 21

1998 | Directed by Tony Scott | With Will Smith, Gene Hackman, Jon Voight | 131 minutes | Rated R

"Privacy and civil liberties" issues take center stage in this ultra-"engaging", ultra-"paranoid" thriller about "Big Brother"-ish "government agents" pursuing a DC lawyer who's unwittingly holding an incriminating videotape; so "fast moving" that there's barely time to "catch your breath", it mixes "high-tech" effects with a "low-concept" idea to come up with something that's "very exciting" indeed.

English Patient, The ✉
22 | 24 | 21 | 25

1996 | Directed by Anthony Minghella | With Ralph Fiennes, Juliette Binoche, Kristin Scott Thomas | 160 minutes | Rated R

"Love it or hate it", there's no question that this "lush" WWII romance (winner of nine Oscars) boasts an "old-Hollywood scope", swoonworthy cinematography, "brilliant writing" and "magnetic" performances from Fiennes and Scott Thomas as star-crossed lovers "in the desert sands of North Africa"; but those who "agree with Elaine on *Seinfeld*" claim this patient requires "patience", thanks to a pace so "laborious" that it's "recommended for treating insomnia."

| | OVERALL | ACTING | STORY | PROD. |

Enron: The Smartest Guys in the Room   `25` `-` `26` `22`

2005 | Directed by Alex Gibney | Documentary | 109 minutes | Not Rated

Learn how "arrogant corruption" and "greed run amok" led to the collapse of energy trader Enron's "house of cards" in this "compelling" documentary that "reveals the downside of American corporate culture"; "full of information", it reduces a "complicated", "numbers-centered" scheme into an "easy-to-follow" account that manages to both "disgust and fascinate", without resorting to "Michael Moore hysteria."

Enter the Dragon   `23` `16` `17` `20`

1973 | Directed by Robert Clouse | With Bruce Lee, John Saxon, Jim Kelly | 98 minutes | Rated R

"Martial arts" mavens maintain that this "all-time best kung fu" flicker is "butt-kicker" Lee's "magnum opus", the "standard by which all karate films are judged"; sure, the "production's cheesy" and its "James Bond" "rip-off" plot is "unoriginal", but the "balletic, ballistic" fight scenes are so "spectacular" that this one "spawned many forgettable imitators" – not to mention many "video games."

Eraserhead ◑   `21` `17` `17` `19`

1977 | Directed by David Lynch | With Jack Nance, Charlotte Stewart | 90 minutes | Not Rated

Director Lynch's "trippy", "dread-inducing" debut is an "eerie glimpse of a marriage gone horribly awry" that "replicates the logic of a nightmare" (i.e. "you don't know what's going on half the time"); gird yourself for some "disturbing pictures, disturbing music" and "no discernable plot", but at least this "cult classic" is "willing to take risks."

Erin Brockovich ✉   `21` `23` `23` `21`

2000 | Directed by Steven Soderbergh | With Julia Roberts, Albert Finney, Aaron Eckhart | 130 minutes | Rated R

"Roberts proves her worth" with a "boffo", Oscar-winning turn in this "uplifting", "push-up bra"–laden true story about "standing up to a big corporation and winning"; ok, its "socially conscious", "don't-mess-with-the-little-people" screenplay might owe a lot to *Norma Rae*, but ultimately this "polished production" works as both a "star vehicle and a compelling story."

Escape from Alcatraz   `23` `22` `23` `21`

1979 | Directed by Don Siegel | With Clint Eastwood, Fred Ward, Patrick McGoohan | 112 minutes | Rated PG

"Actually filmed on The Rock", this "edge-of-your-seat thriller" based on a real-life "amazing escape" from the "infamous" prison stars Eastwood as a "likable bad guy" in one of his "best non-Western performances"; the "good pace" and "solid action" are "thoroughly entertaining", with some "socially conscious" commentary on the justice system thrown in to boot.

Escape from New York   `15` `13` `17` `18`

1981 | Directed by John Carpenter | With Kurt Russell, Lee Van Cleef, Ernest Borgnine | 99 minutes | Rated R

A "hoot and a half", this "tongue-in-cheek" action-adventurer is set in "post-apocalyptic" Manhattan that has morphed into a maximum security prison where the President is being held hostage; to the rescue

...comes Russell as Snake Plissken, a "cartoon character" but still a "very appealing hero", who manages to keep the "novel premise amusing" enough to make for some "silly", "cheesy fun."

Eternal Sunshine of the Spotless Mind   23 | 24 | 24 | 23

2004 | Directed by Michel Gondry | With Jim Carrey, Kate Winslet, Tom Wilkinson, Mark Ruffalo, Kirsten Dunst | 108 minutes | Rated R
A "one-of-a-kind experience", this "quirky, deeply romantic" fantasy follows a "balanced" Carrey and "winning" Winslet as broken-up lovers who biologically erase their memories of each other, then struggle to erase the erasure; though "not likely to be everyone's cup of tea", the "zany", "head-trip" script is "cerebral", "comical" and "complex" (given a "juggled time sequence" à la *Memento*), yet skillfully steered by director Gondry's "deft hand."

⌷ E.T. The Extra-Terrestrial   26 | 22 | 26 | 27

1982 | Directed by Steven Spielberg | With Dee Wallace, Henry Thomas, Drew Barrymore | 115 minutes | Rated PG
Arguably the "*Wizard of Oz* for a brand-new generation", this "irresistible" sci-fi "fairy tale" is the "endearing story of a boy", the "cutest alien of all time" and their attempts to "phone home"; there's agreement that Spielberg's "incredibly imaginative" "genius strikes again", managing to express "every human emotion in less than two hours", so gather the "entire family" along with a "big bowl of Reese's Pieces" and get ready for some "true magic."

Evil Dead, The   22 | 14 | 18 | 17

1982 | Directed by Sam Raimi | With Bruce Campbell, Ellen Sandweiss, Betsy Baker | 85 minutes | Rated NC-17
"Not for the weak-stomached", this "scary, scary, scary" "gorefest" with "abundant blood" and lots of "energy" is "dumb", "campy horror at its best"; alright, the acting's "questionable", the dialogue "lame", the story "hackneyed" and the effects very "low-budget", but it "blows Hollywood blockbusters away" because it's "so much fun."

Evita   19 | 17 | 21 | 24

1996 | Directed by Alan Parker | With Madonna, Antonio Banderas, Jonathan Pryce | 134 minutes | Rated PG
"Sleazy politics come alive" in this "visually rich" celluloid version of the Andrew Lloyd Webber stage musical based on the life of Argentina's Eva Peron, an all-singing, dialogue-free production that seems to some like an "extended MTV video"; though surveyors split on Madonna's title turn ("surprisingly good" vs. "doesn't have the chops"), the "smoldering", "powerful" Banderas is a hit and overall this "entertaining" epic is at the very least "watchable."

Excalibur   22 | 19 | 22 | 23

1981 | Directed by John Boorman | With Nigel Terry, Nicol Williamson, Helen Mirren, Nicholas Clay | 140 minutes | Rated R
The Holy Grail for "King Arthur junkies", this "grown-up version" of the round table legend is a "dark, moody" take on Camelot with "sumptuous" visuals, "racy love scenes" and a "Wagnerian" soundtrack that "set the bar" for "sensual" fantasy; forsooth, it's "long and self-important", but admirers exult over a "compelling" telling of a "tale you thought you knew."

	OVERALL	ACTING	STORY	PROD.

Exodus
23 | 23 | 26 | 25

1960 | Directed by Otto Preminger | With Paul Newman, Eva Marie Saint, Sal Mineo | 210 minutes | Not Rated

An "all-star cast" drives this story of the "founding of modern Israel", a "stunning", "satisfying" Preminger epic "faithfully" adapted from Leon Uris' best-seller; fans single out the star turn from a "too-gorgeous-for-words" Newman "in his prime", and if the plot has some "bathos" mixed into its "high drama", it's ultimately a "moving" moving picture.

Exorcist, The ✉
25 | 24 | 26 | 25

1973 | Directed by William Friedkin | With Ellen Burstyn, Max von Sydow, Linda Blair | 122 minutes | Rated R

"Horror and religion" collide in this "head-spinning", "nightmare-inducing" "shocker" about a child possessed by the devil that "grossed out America" with its "revolting" language and that infamous "pea-soup vomit scene"; though some say it's "slid into camp" over the years, most maintain it's still "one of the scariest ever" – but stick to the "original" cut that's much more "terrifying" than the recent 'restored' reissue.

Experiment in Terror ◑
25 | 24 | 25 | 23

1962 | Directed by Blake Edwards | With Glenn Ford, Lee Remick, Stefanie Powers, Ross Martin | 123 minutes | Not Rated

A rare thriller from Blake Edwards, this "little-known gem" is "one of the better woman-in-danger pictures" thanks to "chilling" performances by Remick as a "sexy" bank teller and Martin as an "asthmatic" extortionist; a jazzy Henry Mancini soundtrack and "mesmerizing" San Francisco settings (particularly that knockout windup at Candlestick Park) supply the atmosphere.

Eyes Wide Shut
13 | 15 | 12 | 19

1999 | Directed by Stanley Kubrick | With Tom Cruise, Nicole Kidman, Sydney Pollack | 159 minutes | Rated R

"Stanley Kubrick's final hurrah", this "would-be erotic thriller" about "marital infidelity" disappoints most voters, especially given the big "build-up before its release"; critics condemn Cruise's "cardboard-cutout" acting, the "plodding" plot, the "Chinese water torture" soundtrack and the director's "overall failure of vision" – but not the "polished, sexy" Kidman, who's the "only thing worth watching" in this "maddening" picture.

Eyewitness
23 | 24 | 23 | 21

1981 | Directed by Peter Yates | With William Hurt, Sigourney Weaver, Christopher Plummer | 103 minutes | Rated R

"Early starring roles" bear witness to the promise of "sexy" Bill and "stunning" Sigourney, who "both do excellent work" in this "absorbing" thriller about a janitor fixated on a TV newswoman, who meet after he discovers a murder victim; it's a "solid enough plot", and the "noir" atmosphere is enhanced by the "lovely" NYC settings.

Fabulous Baker Boys, The
20 | 22 | 18 | 19

1989 | Directed by Steven Kloves | With Jeff Bridges, Michelle Pfeiffer, Beau Bridges | 114 minutes | Rated R

"Sibling rivalry" gets "compelling" treatment in this "great date movie" about two "journeyman musicians" competing for the attentions of their "slinky, sexy" girl singer; the Bridges brothers exude the "art of cool" and Pfeiffer "slithers around so deliciously" that no one minds that this "slice-of-life" story "doesn't go anywhere", given the "enjoyable" ride; most memorable scene, no question: Michelle "draped over a piano" crooning 'Makin' Whoopee' – "who knew she could sing?"

Face/Off
18 | 19 | 18 | 21

1997 | Directed by John Woo | With John Travolta, Nicolas Cage, Joan Allen, Gina Gershon | 138 minutes | Rated R

"Hong Kong auteur" John Woo "goes Hollywood" in this "hyperkinetic" action flick that "fires on all pistons", despite an "unashamedly preposterous scenario" in which "over-the-top" archenemies Travolta and Cage "switch places" (and faces); be prepared for "twists and turns galore", "lots of violence" and enough "mindless fun" to put this one at the very top of your "guilty pleasures list."

Faces ❶
22 | 27 | 18 | 19

1968 | Directed by John Cassavetes | With John Marley, Gena Rowlands, Lynn Carlin, Seymour Cassel | 130 minutes | Rated PG-13

The "beginning of independent filmmaking as we know it", this "ultra-low-budget" drama really "put Cassavetes on the map as a director" with its "revealing" insights on infidelity and the meaninglessness of life; it "remains as avant-garde" as ever thanks to the "fierce performances" alone, and is just the thing "when you want to take a breather from feel-good fare."

Fahrenheit 451
21 | 19 | 25 | 19

1966 | Directed by François Truffaut | With Oskar Werner, Julie Christie, Cyril Cusack | 110 minutes | Not Rated

"Truffaut's first English-language picture" is an "excellent adaptation" of Ray Bradbury's "Big Brother"-ish sci-fi novel, a "social commentary" about "censorship by book burning" in the not-too-distant future (the title is the temperature at which paper ignites); though zealots praise the "thoughtful" presentation of an "important topic", nonbelievers flame it as "plodding" and suggest you "read the book" instead.

Fahrenheit 9/11
21 | - | 22 | 19

2004 | Directed by Michael Moore | Documentary | 122 minutes | Rated R

Conveyed "with all the subtlety of a carpet bombing", Moore's "unapologetically biased" polemic against George W. Bush's "policies and leadership" elicits passionate praise and bitter condemnation alike, with defenders calling it a "daring exposé" of the "real truth" and foes crying it's a "complete fraud on every level"; though unlikely to "change your opinion", it's still a "must-see for anyone remotely interested in what's going on in the Washington world of today."

Fail-Safe ❶
24 | 25 | 26 | 21

1964 | Directed by Sidney Lumet | With Henry Fonda, Walter Matthau, Larry Hagman | 112 minutes | Not Rated

The "Cold War gets hot" in this "chilling", "hypnotic" nuclear-war melodrama about an American President forced to make some "horrifying choices" as an atom bomb hurtles its way toward Moscow; devotees note that the storyline is strikingly similar to that of *Dr. Strangelove* (though decidedly laugh-free) but insist its "what if?" plot is especially "gripping – and hopefully not prophetic."

Failure to Launch
15 | 17 | 16 | 16

2006 | Directed by Tom Dey | With Matthew McConaughey, Sarah Jessica Parker, Kathy Bates | 97 minutes | Rated PG-13

This "light" comedy lifts off with McConaughey as a "dreamy" slacker "still living with his parents", who hire Parker (in full *Sex and the City* persona") to "coax" him out of the nest; with "few surprises" other than a "TMI" take of "Terry Bradshaw in the buff", it's either a "disposable date movie" or a "dud" that "should have been scrubbed."

Fame
21 | 18 | 21 | 20

1980 | Directed by Alan Parker | With Irene Cara, Lee Curreri, Eddie Barth, Laura Dean, Gene Anthony Ray | 134 minutes | Rated R

"Little girls who sing in front of the mirror" relate to this "feel-good" musical set in "NY's High School of Performing Arts", where "talented", "leg warmer–wearing teenagers" spend their days "dancing in the streets" and "struggling for fame"; ok, it's a bit "overdone" and "very dated now", but "crank up the volume" and you'll "enjoy the energy" all the same.

Family Man, The
16 | 17 | 18 | 17

2000 | Directed by Brett Ratner | With Nicolas Cage, Téa Leoni, Don Cheadle | 125 minutes | Rated PG-13

A "harried, unmarried exec wakes up with a new life and family" in this "what-if?" picture, an "update of *It's a Wonderful Life*" that may be "a bit far-fetched" but still "questions all the choices we make"; Leoni is "adorable", Cage "more affecting than expected" and despite the "slow" pace, most leave "believing wholeheartedly in true love."

Family Stone, The
16 | 19 | 16 | 18

2005 | Directed by Thomas Bezucha | With Sarah Jessica Parker, Diane Keaton, Rachel McAdams, Dermot Mulroney | Rated PG-13

A "type-A girl" meets her boyfriend's "type-B family" at Christmastime in this "mildly entertaining" dramedy that lies somewhere between "heartwarming", "heart-wrenching" and "girlie" "fluffy fluff"; while most agree on the "first-class talent" (including "national treasure" Keaton and a "fun" Parker playing against type as a "cold bitch"), there are catcalls for the "unlikable characters", "flip-flopping" storyline and that too "tidy ending."

Fanny and Alexander ✉ **F**
26 | 25 | 25 | 26

1982 | Directed by Ingmar Bergman | With Pernilla Allwin, Bertil Guve, Gunn Wallgren | 188 minutes | Rated R

"Proof that Bergman wasn't miserable all the time", this "semi-autobiographical look back at his childhood" in Sweden "told from two siblings' point of view" features the "master" "at his most accessible"; sure, the "pacing's slow" and the film "long" (in fact, it's a pared-down version of a six-hour TV miniseries), yet the overall "visual magnificence" makes for something "rich and interesting."

☒ Fantasia
28 | - | - | 29

1940 | Directed by Ben Sharpsteen et al | Animated | 120 minutes | Rated G

Disney's "magnificent merger" of "mind-blowing" animation with a symphonic orchestra conducted by "maestro Leopold Stokowski" is a piece of "unbeatably creative" "eye candy" that's "never been equaled"; though a "flop when it first came out", it was later revived as

| | OVERALL | ACTING | STORY | PROD. |

a "'60s head movie" (thanks to trippy sequences like those "dancing hippos in tutus" and "Mickey Mouse as the sorcerer's apprentice"); modernists maintain this "original music video" remains a "perfect way to introduce a child to classical" sounds.

Fantasia 2000 — | 24 | - | - | 27 |

1999 | Directed by James Algar et al | Animated | 75 minutes | Rated G
The "perfect companion" to the 1940 "classic", this "worthy" sequel marrying animation to music of great composers is "terrific Disney" that might be "more for adults than kids" for a change; it "keeps the spirit of the original beautifully" (right down to the "cloying celebrity" intros to each vignette), and although the "flamingo-with-the-yo-yo" scene enthralls many, the "best segment" is "'Rhapsody in Blue' via Al Hirschfeld."

Fantastic Four — | 14 | 13 | 14 | 19 |

2005 | Directed by Tim Story | With Ioan Gruffudd, Jessica Alba, Chris Evans, Michael Chiklis | 106 minutes | Rated PG-13
The "first family of comics" comes to life in this "CGI"-centric ac-tioner celebrating the "tight-costumed" quartet of "superhuman misfits" as they "fight the evil Dr. Doom"; though "inoffensive" "summer bubblegum" for some, foes fume that the "simplistic story" and "plastic" acting make for a "fantastic bore" that's "hard to watch" for "anyone over eight."

Fantastic Voyage — | 19 | 12 | 23 | 21 |

1966 | Directed by Richard Fleischer | With Stephen Boyd, Raquel Welch, Edmond O'Brien | 100 minutes | Rated PG
"Outrageous in its day", this sci-fi fantasy for "thinking" folks "still wows" the wide-eyed with its story about scientists shrunken and then "injected into a human body" to repair a blood clot; despite "wooden acting" and a "dumb ending", the "special effects are im-pressive for its time" – and Raquel sure looks swell in and out of that skintight diving outfit.

Farewell My Concubine 🄵 — | 25 | 26 | 24 | 26 |

1993 | Directed by Chen Kaige | With Leslie Cheung, Gong Li, Zhang Feng-Yi | 171 minutes | Rated R
"Worthy of David Lean on every level", this "sumptuous", "epic achievement" traces a complex friendship between two Peking Opera singers over a "fascinating sweep of history" from the '30s to the '70s; "stunning both visually and emotionally", it boasts "superb acting" and "outstanding scenery", but make sure to sit up straight: its "over-long" running time can be "draining."

Far From Heaven — | 24 | 27 | 23 | 26 |

2002 | Directed by Todd Haynes | With Julianne Moore, Dennis Quaid, Dennis Haysbert | 107 minutes | Rated PG-13
Haynes' "gorgeous homage to director Douglas Sirk's '50s melodra-mas" takes a "grippingly bittersweet" look at the "reality of the subur-ban picket-fence dream" and "genteel Northern racism"; though the pace is "slow" and the story "a little weak", it remains a "must-see" thanks to "flawless performances" from Moore and Quaid as well as "colorful", "stunning cinematography" that "captures the time period with brilliance" – the "costumes alone are close to heaven."

☒ Fargo ✉

25	27	25	25

1996 | Directed by Joel Coen | With Frances McDormand, William H. Macy, Steve Buscemi | 98 minutes | Rated R

This "comic noir" treatment of "crime in the heartland" shows "how funny Minnesota can be" in the hands of the Coen brothers, who "spin a folksy", violent yarn that makes the "outrageous seem everyday" and the "mundane interesting"; but the pièce de résistance is McDormand's "deadpan", Oscar-winning turn as a "pregnant" "crime-stopper" whose "goofy dialogue" alone is – "you betcha" – worth the price of admission.

Fast Times at Ridgemont High

22	19	21	18

1982 | Directed by Amy Heckerling | With Sean Penn, Judge Reinhold, Jennifer Jason Leigh | 92 minutes | Rated R

One of the "crown jewels of the teen-comedy" genre, this "totally killer" "coming-of-age" "favorite" is an indelible "snapshot of the '80s" that made a star of Penn in the immortal role of "surfer stoner dude" Jeff Spicoli; adapted from Cameron Crowe's book, it showcases a "sprawling cast in interweaving stories" (like a kind of "teenage Nashville") and, among other things, "inspired a generation of in-school pizza orderers"; best "gratuitous scene": "Phoebe Cates on the diving board."

Fatal Attraction

22	23	23	21

1987 | Directed by Adrian Lyne | With Michael Douglas, Glenn Close, Anne Archer | 119 minutes | Rated R

"Anyone contemplating an extramarital affair" should take a hard look at this "genuinely creepy" "cautionary tale", dominated by a "demented" Close as a "licentious hubby's worst nightmare"; though the plot "goes overboard" and Douglas "plays the same character as in 47 other movies", the picture had tremendous "cultural impact" in its day and is "still hair-raising" – particularly the "yikes"-inducing "boiled-bunny" scene.

Father of the Bride ◑

23	25	21	20

1950 | Directed by Vincente Minnelli | With Spencer Tracy, Joan Bennett, Elizabeth Taylor | 92 minutes | Not Rated

Hollywood legends Tracy (in the "harried" title role) and Taylor (as the bride) walk down the aisle together in this "heartwarming" chestnut about the "havoc surrounding the planning of a wedding"; while most vow it's something that "all fathers and daughters should watch" together, a few pronounce it "dated and slow."

Father of the Bride

20	20	19	20

1991 | Directed by Charles Shyer | With Steve Martin, Diane Keaton, Martin Short | 105 minutes | Rated PG

"Faster-moving than the original", this "thoroughly engaging" comedy captures the "chaos of wedding planning" thanks to a "hilarious" Martin (as the "clueless dad") and an equally "hysterical" Short; sure, it can be "tame" and rather "silly", but ultimately it goes down "like soothing chocolate pudding"; better yet, it "won't inflict pain on guys", even though it's a bona fide "chick flick."

Fear and Loathing in Las Vegas

15	20	15	18

1998 | Directed by Terry Gilliam | With Johnny Depp, Benicio Del Toro, Craig Bierko | 119 minutes | Rated R

"You'll either love or loathe" this "whirlwind cult film", a "faithful adaptation" of Hunter S. Thompson's "unadaptable" book detailing his "psychedelic" escapades in Las Vegas; despite kudos for Depp and Del Toro's "bizarre but authentic" performances, loathers find the film "essentially unpleasant" with "no plot", just a bunch of "idiots doing drugs."

Ferris Bueller's Day Off

| 23 | 22 | 23 | 21 |

1986 | Directed by John Hughes | With Matthew Broderick, Alan Ruck, Mia Sara | 98 minutes | Rated PG-13

"Every teenager's fantasy" of "ditching high school" for the day is re-alized in this "brilliant comedy" about a "sly slacker" on the loose in Chicago who "gets away with everything" and "does it with style"; the "smug-mugged" Broderick exudes "bravado" in the role that "launched his career", while "underappreciated" director Hughes off-handedly produces a picture so "influential" that it "belongs in a time capsule of the '80s."

Fever Pitch

| 20 | 19 | 21 | 19 |

2005 | Directed by Bobby Farrelly, Peter Farrelly | With Drew Barrymore, Jimmy Fallon | 103 minutes | Rated PG-13

"Sports and love" are the themes of this "surprisingly tame outing" from the Farrelly brothers, a "feel-good" romantic comedy about an al-pha gal who falls for an "obsessed" Red Sox fan; even though the "chemistry's believable" between the "watchable" Fallon and the "adorable as always" Barrymore, the overall call is "harmless" – "not a home run", but maybe a "solid triple."

Few Good Men, A

| 23 | 26 | 23 | 22 |

1992 | Directed by Rob Reiner | With Tom Cruise, Jack Nicholson, Demi Moore, Kevin Bacon | 138 minutes | Rated R

"Star-driven", "crackerjack courtroom drama" about a military murder investigation that's both "intelligent and entertaining"; no question, there are more than a few good performances, especially the "adorable-as-ever" Cruise in a "gritty", change-of-pace role playing against Nicholson's "riveting" if "pompous" marine colo-nel, who delivers the picture's most "infamous line: 'you can't handle the truth.'"

Fiddler on the Roof

| 26 | 25 | 27 | 26 |

1971 | Directed by Norman Jewison | With Topol, Leonard Frey, Norma Crane | 181 minutes | Rated G

One of the "last of the epic musicals", this "uplifting" adaptation of the "Broadway classic" finds "wide-screen resonance" in its "memorable" score and "elaborate production" values; despite the unmusical subject matter (19th-century "Jews fleeing the pogroms"), it's still a "joyous" film that's as "moving as a moving picture can be."

Field of Dreams

| 22 | 21 | 23 | 22 |

1989 | Directed by Phil Alden Robinson | With Kevin Costner, Amy Madigan, Ray Liotta, James Earl Jones | 107 minutes | Rated PG

"Even non-sports fans can love" this "feel-good" fantasy/drama about "baseball, ghosts" and "one man's search to find himself" in an Iowa cornfield; its "realistic sporting sequences, great storyline" and "touching" Costner turn ("before he lost it") make for a flick that "gets better every time you see it"; even those who find it too "sentimental" agree it's a "must-see for any father and son."

	OVERALL	ACTING	STORY	PROD.

Fifth Element, The
19 15 19 23

1997 | Directed by Luc Besson | With Bruce Willis, Gary Oldman, Milla Jovovich | 126 minutes | Rated PG-13

"Hyperkinetic", "loud" and "fast-paced", this "slick" sci-fi "actionfest" is about as substantial as a "big ball of cotton candy, but a hoot nonetheless"; sure, "Willis saves the planet – again" – but in this "loopy" "send-up of the genre", the "tongue-in-cheek" plot plays a distinct second fiddle to the "visually spectacular" effects; still, shirkers shrug it off as a "messy example of why more isn't always better."

50 First Dates
18 18 19 19

2004 | Directed by Peter Segal | With Adam Sandler, Drew Barrymore, Rob Schneider | 99 minutes | Rated PG-13

"Comedy power couple" Sandler and Barrymore have the "chemistry" down pat in this "surprisingly touching", "well-thought-out" romance about a womanizer enthralled by a woman with short-term memory loss (i.e. she can't remember what she did on her last date); fans sigh it's "sweet" and "light-hearted", foes say "juvenile" and "farfetched", but at least they "didn't cop out with a cheap Hollywood ending."

Fight Club
23 25 24 24

1999 | Directed by David Fincher | With Brad Pitt, Edward Norton, Helena Bonham Carter | 139 minutes | Rated R

"Love-it-or-hate-it" moviemaking is alive and well in this "testosterone-ridden" "cult classic" that uses "top-notch effects", "twisted humor" and a "killer" soundtrack in its depiction of "ultraviolent, disenfranchised males"; an "amazing Norton" and "underrated Pitt" provide the fireworks in this "gore"-drenched drama, with a "surprise finish" that's either "mind-blowing" or "nonsensical", depending on who's talking.

Finding Forrester
22 24 22 20

2000 | Directed by Gus Van Sant | With Sean Connery, Rob Brown | 136 minutes | Rated PG-13

Plenty of "feel-good" "male bonding" turns up in this "inspirational" "cross-race" drama, with Connery as a literary "curmudgeon" playing "unlikely mentor" to an "inner-city kid" who's pushing to "surmount the odds" at a tony prep school; it works thanks to "excellent acting" that elevates the "clichéd" themes, though some find Van Sant's *Good Will Hunting* "very similar."

☑ Finding Nemo
28 – 25 29

2003 | Directed by Andrew Stanton, Lee Unkrich | Animated | 100 minutes | Rated G

"No matter what your age", you'll be "riveted to your seat" by this "Pixar masterpiece" about a "neurotic father fish searching for his son" in a "beautifully rendered undersea world"; voters insist it's "one of the best animated films of all time", blending "superb visual effects" with a "touching" yet "hilarious script" (laced with "adult references that the tots will miss") and "fully developed, brilliantly voiced characters."

Finding Neverland
25 27 24 26

2004 | Directed by Marc Forster | With Johnny Depp, Kate Winslet, Julie Christie | 106 minutes | Rated PG

"Even if you're a rock-hearted cynic", get out your handkerchiefs for this "pixie dust-coated", "semi-biographical" reflection on *Peter Pan* playwright J.M. Barrie's "fantastic imagination" and the people who inspired it; "do-no-wrong" Depp and Winslet "fly high" with "stellar performances", though most agree it's the "adorable child" actors who "steal the show" demonstrating the "simple power of play."

Finian's Rainbow
| | 21 | 21 | 20 | 22 |

1968 | Directed by Francis Ford Coppola | With Fred Astaire, Petula Clark, Tommy Steele, Keenan Wynn | 141 minutes | Rated G
This "last musical" starring "lighter-than-air Fred Astaire" was "directed by Francis Ford Coppola, of all people", who supplies an "inventive" take on the genre in this story of Irish folks (and a leprechaun) transplanted to a small Southern town; although "dated" to a few, it's "underrated" to others.

Firewall
| | 15 | 16 | 16 | 17 |

2006 | Directed by Richard Loncraine | With Harrison Ford, Paul Bettany, Virginia Madsen | 105 minutes | Rated PG-13
With Ford putting his "aging bones back into action" as a high-tech security exec out to rescue his kidnapped family, this thriller heats up suspense at a "slow simmer" spiced up with "cyber-twists" for "IT geeks"; still, cynics nix the "ho-hum" momentum and advise the star to shed the "same ol'" roles and "start acting your age."

Firm, The
| | 17 | 17 | 20 | 18 |

1993 | Directed by Sydney Pollack | With Tom Cruise, Jeanne Tripplehorn, Gene Hackman | 154 minutes | Rated R
"Nail-biters" say this "slick" adaptation of John Grisham's "solid" best-seller about an "honest lawyer and his evil employers" succeeds mainly because of its "quirky supporting performances"; but foes argue this "not-too-thrilling thriller" "rarely lives up to the book", particularly since they went and "changed the ending."

First Blood: Rambo
| | 18 | 13 | 19 | 18 |

1982 | Directed by Ted Kotcheff | With Sylvester Stallone, Richard Crenna, Brian Dennehy | 97 minutes | Rated R
A "great kick-butt movie" "bolstered by a muscular score", this "simplistic but satisfying revenge tale" about a Vietnam vet harassed by small-town cops "delivers some punch"; the "studly", "steroidal" Stallone makes a bloody decent "action god", if not a silver-tongued thespian ("he should never talk"), though compadres caution it's his "last good movie before getting lost in sequel land."

First Wives Club, The
| | 17 | 19 | 18 | 17 |

1996 | Directed by Hugh Wilson | With Bette Midler, Goldie Hawn, Diane Keaton, Maggie Smith | 102 minutes | Rated PG
The "heavyweight talent" of its "all-star cast" made this "lightweight battle-of-the-sexes farce", a revenge comedy pitting "strong women" against "rotten men", into a big hit at the box office; still, foes say it's as "fluffy as Goldie's lips", citing a "ridiculous plot" that's an "embarrassment for all involved"; P.S. it's "not a good date movie" either.

Fish Called Wanda, A
| | 23 | 24 | 22 | 21 |

1988 | Directed by Charles Crichton | With John Cleese, Jamie Lee Curtis, Kevin Kline | 108 minutes | Rated R
It's easy getting hooked on this "nonstop", "kitchen-sink comedy" about a heist perpetrated by a "bumbling gang" portrayed by a "few chaps of

Python fame" as well as the "show-stealing", Oscar-winning Kline; be prepared for "lots of giggles", but "forget political correctness", as "stutterers" and some unfortunate "goldfish" are gleefully abused.

Fisher King, The
21 | 24 | 21 | 21

1991 | Directed by Terry Gilliam | With Jeff Bridges, Robin Williams, Mercedes Ruehl, Amanda Plummer | 137 minutes | Rated R
Grail-seekers gravitate to this "strange" mix of "comedy, fantasy and drama", a "powerful" story of a high-flying radio shock jock who falls to earth only to be rescued by a homeless man; some find the plot "a little too out there", but loyal subjects say the "incredible visual effects in the Grand Central Station" scene alone "make it worth watching."

Fistful of Dollars, A
19 | 17 | 18 | 17

1967 | Directed by Sergio Leone | With Clint Eastwood, Marianne Koch, Mario Brega | 99 minutes | Rated R
The "pasta flows" in this "early spaghetti Western" as Clint "defines coolness" with his "prototypical" "Man With No Name" caught between two rival families; though a "couple notches down from *The Good, the Bad and the Ugly*" ("maybe something was lost in the translation"), this "classic" is "still fun" on a rainy day.

⚡ Fitzcarraldo
27 | 26 | 26 | 27

1982 | Directed by Werner Herzog | With Klaus Kinski, Claudia Cardinale | 158 minutes | Rated PG
"Absolute perseverance" verging on "outlandish obsession" is the theme of this "bizarre" story of a "quixotic" fellow determined to "build an opera house in the South American jungle"; "awe-inspired" types say "you've never seen anything like it", starting with that "scene of a ship being carried over a mountain", done with "no special effects"; N.B. check out *Burden of Dreams*, the making-of documentary.

Five Easy Pieces
24 | 27 | 22 | 21

1970 | Directed by Bob Rafelson | With Jack Nicholson, Karen Black, Lois Smith | 96 minutes | Rated R
"Nicholson's at the height of his powers" in this "deliberately paced character study" about "disaffection", "wasted ambition and dreams" that's a "must-see" for die-hard Jack fans; it "captures the restlessness of its era" with an expert "mix of comedy and serious drama" – and offers explicit instructions on "how not to be a waitress" in that "unforgettable chicken-salad sandwich" scene.

5,000 Fingers of Dr. T., The
20 | 17 | 21 | 24

1953 | Directed by Roy Rowland | With Tommy Rettig, Hans Conried, Peter Lind Hayes | 88 minutes | Not Rated
"Imaginative, absurd, trippy and a million other crazy things", this "ahead-of-its-time" musical "written by Dr. Seuss" depicts a "bizarre world" where a boy battles a piano teacher bent on world domination; though this "quirky little masterpiece" boasts a "growing cult following", it might be a little too "dark" and "frightening" for smaller fry.

Flags of Our Fathers
23 | 23 | 23 | 26

2006 | Directed by Clint Eastwood | With Ryan Phillippe, Jesse Bradford, Adam Beach | 132 minutes | Rated R
As an "elegiac" tribute to "our military heroes", Clint's snapshot of the "real history" behind the "Iwo Jima flag-raisers" – subjects of the "fa-

nous photo" that "won World War II" – focuses on the "flipside of heroism" to document the "brutal realities" encountered "both on and off the battlefield"; the ensemble cast is "outstanding", the action scenes "gritty" (if a bit "hard to follow") and the "insights" into "government propaganda" especially resonant "in today's climate."

Flashdance

| | 16 | 14 | 15 | 18 |

1983 | Directed by Adrian Lyne | With Jennifer Beals, Michael Nouri | 96 minutes | Rated R

"Break dancing, leg warmers and sweatshirts worn off the shoulder" got their start in this "breakthrough" musical about a "Cinderella"-esque steel worker by day, exotic dancer by night, yearning to be a ballerina; granted, the "politically incorrect" story is "somewhat lacking", yet this "guilty pleasure" features a "soundtrack that nails the early '80s" and was "one of the highest grossing films" of its time – "what a feeling", indeed.

Fletch

| | 19 | 18 | 18 | 16 |

1985 | Directed by Michael Ritchie | With Chevy Chase, Joe Don Baker, Tim Matheson | 98 minutes | Rated PG

This "goofball" "cult" comedy represents "Chase's peak" in his "ultimate" role as an "undercover reporter who changes his ID more often than his underwear"; fools for "tomfoolery" swear it's "possibly the most quotable movie" ever, thanks to a flurry of "great one-liners" that only get "funnier every time you see it."

Flight of the Phoenix, The

| | 25 | 26 | 24 | 21 |

1965 | Directed by Robert Aldrich | With James Stewart, Richard Attenborough, Peter Finch | 147 minutes | Not Rated

"Jimmy Stewart can fly anything" and does in this post-*Spirit of St. Louis* adventure flicker about a desert plane crash that leaves its survivors facing a "seemingly hopeless future"; "realistically shot" and "brilliantly acted", it's a "feel-good", "can-do" kind of picture "without violence" that "really stays with you."

Flightplan

| | 18 | 21 | 17 | 19 |

2005 | Directed by Robert Schwentke | With Jodie Foster, Peter Sarsgaard, Sean Bean | 98 minutes | Rated PG-13

After clearing for a "promising takeoff", this "head-scratcher" thriller finds Foster in "stressed single mom" mode ("à la *Panic Room*"), "frantic" to convince sky marshal Sarsgaard she's "lost her daughter" aboard a "supersized plane"; those leery of "plot holes" so big that "you could practically fly a 747 through" should plan on a "bumpy ride", but with a "terrific" Jodie "keeping you guessing", it's still intermittently "engrossing."

Fly, The

| | 20 | 18 | 22 | 18 |

1958 | Directed by Kurt Neumann | With Vincent Price, David Hedison, Patricia Owens | 94 minutes | Not Rated

The "golden age of B movies" lives on in this wonderfully "camp classic" about a scientist "who pushes the envelope too far and becomes a fly"; fans buzz it remains "truly horrifying", especially that "unforgettable" shot of our hero "stuck in the spider's web" (*"help me!"*) that makes up for any quaintness in the execution."

Fly, The
16 | 17 | 17 | 20

1986 | Directed by David Cronenberg | With Jeff Goldblum, Geena Davis | 96 minutes | Rated R

A "reinterpretation, not a rehash" of the "campy original", this "graphic, gruesome" remake explores Cronenberg's "obsession about the relationship between biology and technology"; sure, "special effects rule the day" here, yet there's also an "effective" love story amid the otherwise "dark" doings.

Fly Away Home
22 | 20 | 24 | 24

1996 | Directed by Carroll Ballard | With Anna Paquin, Jeff Daniels, Dana Delany | 107 minutes | Rated PG

Get out your "biggest bowl of popcorn" for this "deeply felt family film" about a young girl, her estranged dad and the flock of baby geese she takes under her wing; fans "honk" about its "captivating story" and "beautiful" Canadian scenery, saying it's "not just for kids", but rather a "quite uplifting", "lovely movie for all."

Flying Down to Rio ◑
23 | 19 | 16 | 25

1933 | Directed by Thornton Freeland | With Dolores del Rio, Gene Raymond, Fred Astaire, Ginger Rogers | 89 minutes | Not Rated

It was made as a Dolores del Rio vehicle, but this "often overlooked" musical is best remembered as the "first pairing" of "scene stealers" Fred and Ginger who are "pure heaven" performing the "infectious" 'Carioca'; most choose to "forget the plot" and "fast-forward to the dance routines", particularly the "girls-dancing-on-airplane-wings" number.

Fog of War, The
26 | - | 25 | 23

2003 | Directed by Errol Morris | Documentary | 95 minutes | Rated PG-13

"Controversial" former U.S. Secretary of Defense Robert S. McNamara recounts his involvement in WWII and the Cuban missile crisis, as well as his role as one of the "architects of the Vietnam War", in this "eye-opening", Oscar-winning documentary that's "amazingly relevant considering the current political climate"; director Morris' "fascinating yet maddening" work underscores McNamara's "brilliance and fallibility" while "neither condemning nor excusing him entirely."

Footlight Parade ◑
23 | 21 | 18 | 25

1933 | Directed by Lloyd Bacon | With James Cagney, Joan Blondell, Ruby Keeler, Dick Powell | 104 minutes | Not Rated

A "low-budget troupe" of show folk struggles to stay afloat during the Depression in this "zany" musical that's worth seeing for "Busby Berkeley's grand production numbers", as well as the chance to "watch James Cagney" cut a rug; maybe the "dated" story's just "so-so", but the "amazing" dance routines (including 'By a Waterfall', 'Honeymoon Hotel' and 'Shanghai Lil') are nothing short of "electric."

Footloose
17 | 15 | 16 | 17

1984 | Directed by Herbert Ross | With Kevin Bacon, Lori Singer, John Lithgow, Dianne Wiest | 107 minutes | Rated PG

A "town that's banned dancing" is the setting for this "classic '80s rebellion flick", a "guilty pleasure" that "started it all for Kevin Bacon" and is best remembered for its hit-heavy soundtrack and "jumping" theme song; though "silly fluff" to detractors, it's "all-around fun" for "toe-tappers" who "take it for what it is."

For a Few Dollars More

23 | 21 | 21 | 20

1967 | Directed by Sergio Leone | With Clint Eastwood, Lee Van Cleef, Gian Maria Volontè | 130 minutes | Rated R

"No one's tougher than Clint" (who "doesn't smile once" but sure "looks good in a poncho") in this "tasty spaghetti western", the second installment in the Man With No Name trilogy; even though the dialogue's "dubbed", the characters "cardboard" and the bounty-hunter plot "weird", this "guilty pleasure" is still "fun" – and "oh, that music!"

Forbidden Planet

25 | 18 | 25 | 24

1956 | Directed by Fred M. Wilcox | With Walter Pidgeon, Anne Francis, Leslie Nielsen | 98 minutes | Rated G

Its long-before-digital FX "may seem quaint" today, but this "top-notch psychological thriller" represents the "true start of the sci-fi genre" to many; despite a compelling storyline "based on Shakespeare's *Tempest*" and some halfway decent acting from the humans, "Robby the Robot is the real star" here.

Foreign Correspondent ◑

24 | 22 | 24 | 22

1940 | Directed by Alfred Hitchcock | With Joel McCrea, Laraine Day, Herbert Marshall, George Sanders | 120 minutes | Not Rated

One of Hitchcock's "forgotten movies", this "crackling" espionage drama set on the eve of WWII follows a political reporter across Europe, and is worth seeing for its "terrific set pieces" (the "famous windmill scene", those "umbrellas in the rain"); still, a minority finds the "pro-American" sentiment a tad "too preachy", saying the director is "more the master of propaganda than the master of suspense" here.

⚡ Forrest Gump ✉

24 | 26 | 24 | 25

1994 | Directed by Robert Zemeckis | With Tom Hanks, Robin Wright, Gary Sinise | 142 minutes | Rated PG-13

"Even macho guys" get misty over this "sentimental" story of "hope and perseverance" that explores recent American history through the "unlikely eyes" of a "simple-minded", Zelig-like hero (the "triumphant", Oscar-winning Hanks); though picky viewers find "not much assortment in this box of chocolates", they're overruled by "enchanted" believers who say its "basic good-heartedness" makes it "remarkably touching."

Fort Apache ◑

23 | 22 | 23 | 22

1948 | Directed by John Ford | With John Wayne, Henry Fonda, Shirley Temple, Ward Bond | 125 minutes | Not Rated

This "great" Golden-Age-of-Hollywood Western is the first of the Ford trilogy that both mythologized and humanized the cavalry; Fonda's effectively "cast against type" as a by-the-numbers commander who takes over a frontier fort and can't connect with his men or the local Indians, while Wayne is "perfect" as the more understanding captain with whom he clashes; tame for the TV generation, its fight scenes are "remarkable for its era."

Fortune Cookie, The ◑

23 | 25 | 22 | 21

1966 | Directed by Billy Wilder | With Walter Matthau, Jack Lemmon | 125 minutes | Not Rated

The first (and many say the "best) pairing of the Lemmon-Matthau combo", this biting black comedy via Billy Wilder takes aim at our litigious society in its story of a sports cameraman faking an injury in exchange for insurance money; a "top-notch script" intertwining "big laughs" and "nonstop snickers" keeps things moving at a fast clip, even if the ending "veers uncomfortably between drama and humor."

48 HRS.
| | 19 | 18 | 18 | 17 |

1982 | Directed by Walter Hill | With Nick Nolte, Eddie Murphy, Annette O'Toole | 92 minutes | Rated R

The "blueprint" for "buddy action flicks", this "entertaining" crime thriller about a "white cop teaming up with a black convict" features "stroke-of-genius" casting pairing Nolte and Murphy; ok, it's "brainless fun" and a "little too violent", but worth catching for Eddie's "starmaking" screen debut alone – especially his "great rendition of 'Roxanne.'"

42nd Street ◐
| | 24 | 18 | 20 | 26 |

1933 | Directed by Lloyd Bacon | With Ruby Keeler, Ginger Rogers, Bebe Daniels | 89 minutes | Not Rated

Alright, it's a "bit corny by modern standards", but this "brassy" "mother of all backstage musicals" showcases choreographer "Busby Berkeley at his glossy best" applying his "inventive" genius to all those "dancing feet"; "every actress' dream" come true, it's a real "classic", so just ignore the "hackneyed" plot and Keeler's "clunky" footwork.

40 Year Old Virgin, The
| | 19 | 20 | 19 | 18 |

2005 | Directed by Judd Apatow | With Steve Carell, Catherine Keener, Paul Rudd | 116 minutes | Rated R

Alright, the title portends a hopeless "one-trick pony", but funnyman Carell actually "pulls it off", delivering "loads of laughs" and even some "surprising charm" as a "sweet", middle-aged "nerd" chasing his first score in this "wickedly funny" sex farce; no surprise, prudes protest the "unapologetically vulgar" content and complain the story takes "too long" to climax; P.S. "body wax", anyone?

For Whom the Bell Tolls
| | 25 | 26 | 26 | 22 |

1943 | Directed by Sam Wood | With Gary Cooper, Ingrid Bergman, Katina Paxinou | 170 minutes | Not Rated

Fans swear this adaptation of Hemingway's Pulitzer Prize–winner about an American fighting fascism in '30s Spain "gets every single nuance right", starting with its "poignant", "old-fashioned love story" right down to the very convincing battle sequences; though a minority dubs it "schmaltz in macho drag", it strikes a chord as a "true classic."

For Your Eyes Only
| | 18 | 16 | 18 | 21 |

1981 | Directed by John Glen | With Roger Moore, Carole Bouquet, Topol, Julian Glover | 127 minutes | Rated PG

A "solid" entry in the Bond blitz, this spy flicker focuses less on "supergadgets" and more on Moore, leading many to label it his "best" outing as the ever-suave 007; the "realistic villains", "exotic locations" and "jaw-dropping" ski chases entice "even die-hard nonfans" – although the "fight scenes are never believable."

Foul Play
| | 21 | 19 | 20 | 19 |

1978 | Directed by Colin Higgins | With Goldie Hawn, Chevy Chase, Dudley Moore | 116 minutes | Rated PG

Goldie "at her giggly best" and a "terrific" Chevy make a "charming couple" in this "lightweight murder mystery" that's a "takeoff on Hitchcock's

| | OVERALL | ACTING | STORY | PROD. |

The Man Who Knew Too Much"; its "international-assassination-plot" seesaws between "hilarity and suspense", while Moore steals the show as a lecherous swinger with a memorably equipped bachelor pad.

Fountainhead, The ❶ — 22 | 22 | 23 | 22

1949 | Directed by King Vidor | With Gary Cooper, Patricia Neal, Raymond Massey | 114 minutes | Not Rated

Ayn Rand's mammoth novel "brought to life", this Hollywood version fortunately "doesn't take six months to watch" as it profiles an independent, "Frank Lloyd Wright"-esque architect intent on being a "genuine individual"; foes find it too talky and "hokey" (except for the "delicious deal") and advise you "read the book before seeing the movie."

Four Brothers — 17 | 18 | 18 | 18

2005 | Directed by John Singleton | With Mark Wahlberg, Tyrese Gibson, André Benjamin, Garrett Hedlund | 109 minutes | Rated R

"Tough guys with hearts" flaunt their "badass style" in this "gritty" action drama about a quartet of "misfit foster brothers" primed for "revenge" and "lots of gunplay" after their "non-biological mother" is murdered; it's near kin to a "typical" "B-level shoot 'em up", but "intense" doses of "realistic inner-city turmoil" ensure "you won't fall asleep."

400 Blows, The ❶🅵 — 27 | 26 | 25 | 24

1959 | Directed by François Truffaut | With Jean-Pierre Léaud, Robert Beauvais | 94 minutes | Not Rated

"Anyone who survived adolescence" can relate to this French "coming-of-age" film, a "semi-autobiographical" effort that marked Truffaut's directorial debut; as his "great alter ego", Léaud "depicts the pain and joy of growing up" in a winsomely "giddy" turn, though the picture earned its "place in film history" by "breaking a lot of rules" while demonstrating a "true love of movies."

Four Seasons, The — 21 | 23 | 21 | 21

1981 | Directed by Alan Alda | With Alan Alda, Carol Burnett, Rita Moreno, Jack Weston, Sandy Dennis | 107 minutes | Rated PG

Director/star Alda's comedy of "real life" is a "well-done character study" about three married couples who compare "quippy" notes on "divorce and middle age" when they meet for quarterly "joint vacations"; it's seasoned with "spectacular locations" and "endearing" moments perfectly synched to a "Vivaldi score", though cynics call it "sappy" *Big Chill* for 50-year-olds."

Four Weddings and a Funeral — 21 | 21 | 21 | 20

1994 | Directed by Mike Newell | With Hugh Grant, Andie MacDowell, Kristin Scott Thomas | 117 minutes | Rated R

This "entertaining" marriage of "sweet and savvy" wrings "unexpected" laughs out of the "ups and downs of modern love" and "every bad wedding" you've ever endured; notable for "putting Hugh Grant on the map", it also boasts a "sparkling script" and a "quirky" ensemble cast, though the less said about the "wooden" MacDowell the better.

Fox and the Hound, The — 18 | – | 19 | 18

1981 | Directed by Ted Berman, Richard Rich, Art Stevens | Animated | 83 minutes | Rated G

As the title canines become unlikely pals, kids can learn about the "meaning of friendship" from this "cute" Disney film, but it's not all

tail-wagging "family" fun: the "bittersweet" tone "tugs at those heart
strings with no mercy", and bashers bark at the "copy-machine" qual
ity of the early '80s animation.

Fracture
22 | 26 | 22 | 22

2007 | Directed by Gregory Hoblit | With Anthony Hopkins, Ryan Gosling,
David Strathairn, Rosamund Pike | 112 minutes | Rated R
Up-and-comer Gosling goes "toe to toe" with "scene-stealing" Si
Anthony and "holds his own" in this "smart" "cat-and-mouse" crim
thriller deploying a "decent formula" to "Hitchcockian" effect; if th
truckload of "twists and turns" don't leave you "wondering how it ends'
at least the "witty" repartee between the leads will "hold your attention.

Frances
23 | 28 | 23 | 22

1982 | Directed by Graeme Clifford | With Jessica Lange, Kim Stanley
Sam Shepard | 140 minutes | Rated R
"Disturbing" but still "quite fine", this "harrowing" bio of "Hollywoo
nonconformist" Frances Farmer pulls no punches exploring the ac
tress' "demons" and "society's response to her mental illness"; in th
title role, Lange is "magical" (and "matched by Stanley as her mother"),
but this one's "not for the timid" given its ultimately "desperate" tone

Frankenstein ◑
25 | 21 | 25 | 23

1931 | Directed by James Whale | With Boris Karloff, Colin Clive, Mae
Clarke | 71 minutes | Not Rated
The "granddaddy of all horror films" adds a touch of "pathos" an
"camp" to its story of a mad scientist who "goes against nature" an
builds a creature "prone to violence"; beyond monster-mashing,
also explores the "theme of loneliness" via Karloff's "heartbreaking
ghoul, and though "a bit overacted", it's still "goose-bumps time whe
Colin Clive shouts 'it's alive!'"

Frankie & Johnny
20 | 23 | 20 | 19

1991 | Directed by Garry Marshall | With Al Pacino, Michelle Pfeiffer
Nathan Lane, Kate Nelligan | 118 minutes | Rated R
"Pfeiffer and Pacino show their chops" in this "unconventional" romanc
that gets "honest" about "real relationship" tangles between a "charm
ing" short-order cook and a "weary waitress"; maybe Michelle's "a li
tle too glam for this", but the performances are "convincing enough
to make for a "sweet tale of love and second chances."

Freaks ◑
23 | 18 | 22 | 19

1932 | Directed by Tod Browning | With Wallace Ford, Leila Hyams,
Olga Baclanova | 64 minutes | Not Rated
"Dated" perhaps, but "as creepy as ever", this "subversive" look a
"circus sideshow" performers still shocks 75 years later since it cast
"actual human oddities" – real midgets, pinheads and Siamese twins
in leading roles; "banned for years" after its initial release and "hardl
politically correct", it's either "exploitative", "sympathetic" or
"nightmare-inducing" "train wreck" that "you can't take your eyes off of.

Freaky Friday
18 | 17 | 21 | 16

1976 | Directed by Gary Nelson | With Barbara Harris, Jodie Foster,
John Astin | 95 minutes | Rated G
A "kooky" idea – a teenage girl and her mom trade bodies for a day
powers this "fun" '70s "family film" that's a step up from the "usua

body-swapping" comedies; thanks to a "smart script" and "brilliant" performances from Harris and Foster, some mothers and daughters watch it together for a "great bonding experience."

Freaky Friday
21 | 22 | 20 | 20

2003 | Directed by Mark Waters | With Jamie Lee Curtis, Lindsay Lohan, Mark Harmon | 97 minutes | Rated PG

"Nicely adapted to the 21st century", this "surprisingly entertaining" remake of the '70s comedy about mother-and-daughter body-swapping is "in many ways better than the original" thanks to "smart, funny" performances by the "spirited" Lindsay and "still-a-babe" Jamie Lee; it's just the ticket when "you don't feel like thinking too hard", with plenty of "family appeal" that extends beyond the "Disney Channel crowd."

Freedom Writers
22 | 23 | 23 | 20

2007 | Directed by Richard LaGravenese | With Hilary Swank, Patrick Dempsey, Scott Glenn | 123 minutes | Rated PG-13

Alright, the "fish-out-of-water-teacher-teaching-rough-urban-youths" story is as "clichéd" as they come, but this "inspirational" iteration earns high marks thanks to its "true-life" source material and Swank's "home-run" swing as a "creative" pedagogue who urges her "challenging" students to "pour their hearts out in journals"; extra credit is awarded for the "attempt to show the real side of growing up poor and non-white in America."

Free Willy
17 | 14 | 18 | 18

1993 | Directed by Simon Wincer | With Jason James Richter, Lori Petty | 112 minutes | Rated PG

"Everyone cries at the end" of this "family favorite", the "touching" story of an unhappy street kid who befriends an unhappy "killer whale" to "inspiring" results; it's "captivating" enough to work as a good "babysitter" for the kiddies, though seen-it-all types find it too "simplistic and message-laden."

French Connection, The ✉
25 | 26 | 25 | 24

1971 | Directed by William Friedkin | With Gene Hackman, Roy Scheider, Fernando Rey | 104 minutes | Rated R

Famed for the "most harrowing car chase ever", this "seminal hard-boiled cop drama" is a "fast-paced" "exposé of the drug underworld" that's also "superbly cast and acted", starting with Hackman's "explosive", Oscar-winning turn as the tough-talking 'Popeye' Doyle; sure, it might seem "dated" to modernists, but that's "only because it's aped so frequently."

French Lieutenant's Woman, The
22 | 25 | 21 | 23

1981 | Directed by Karel Reisz | With Meryl Streep, Jeremy Irons, Hilton McRae | 127 minutes | Rated R

"Streep is fantastic" as always in this "original" romance detailing parallel relationships: one involving an upper-class gentleman and a lower-class lass in Victorian England, the other between the contemporary actors playing them; granted, Harold Pinter's scenario might be "a bit confusing at the get-go", but ultimately this "excellent" adaptation of John Fowles' novel is both "really cool and worthwhile."

Frenzy
20 | 20 | 22 | 21

1972 | Directed by Alfred Hitchcock | With Jon Finch, Barry Foster, Anna Massey, Billie Whitelaw | 116 minutes | Rated R

Alfred Hitchcock's "familiar obsession with mistaken identity" is the basis of this "violent" tale about a "necktie murderer" on the loose in London; "wonderful location settings" and renowned set pieces (the "stairway backtracking shot", the corpse in the sack of potatoes) draw applause, yet even though it's "more graphic than his earlier films", some moan the master is "well past his prime" here.

Frequency
19 | 20 | 22 | 19

2000 | Directed by Gregory Hoblit | With Dennis Quaid, James Caviezel | 118 minutes | Rated PG-13

Sure, it might be "unbelievable", but this "time-travel" tale generates lots of "surprise" with its "truly original story" about a young man who talks to his late father via ham radio; despite "metropolis-size plot holes", it's still "touching", with a baseball subplot that's "especially fun" for fans of NY's 1969 "Miracle Mets."

Freshman, The
21 | 22 | 21 | 20

1990 | Directed by Andrew Bergman | With Marlon Brando, Matthew Broderick, Penelope Ann Miller | 102 minutes | Rated PG

"Devotees of The Godfather" can't refuse this "lighthearted comedy" centering on a "priceless" "Don Corleone send-up", with a "self-mocking" Brando playing a "straight-faced parody" of his signature role "to the hilt"; the "screwball" plot about "boyish" student Broderick inadvertently "involved with the mob" is "silly", but even as a "one-gag" gig, this one's definitely "funny."

Frida
25 | 27 | 25 | 27

2002 | Directed by Julie Taymor | With Salma Hayek, Alfred Molina | 123 minutes | Rated R

"Fiery" Hayek "put her heart and soul" into this "underrated little" bio of "eccentric" Mexican artist Frida Kahlo, "and it shows"; she delivers her "finest performance", capturing the "pain, grief and personal tragedy that the painter expressed in her art" against a "visually stunning tapestry" of "color and texture" in which her "actual paintings come to life"; "wonderful" acting by Molina and an "amazing soundtrack" are more reasons "not to miss it."

Friday Night Lights
21 | 21 | 21 | 20

2004 | Directed by Peter Berg | With Billy Bob Thornton, Derek Luke, Jay Hernandez | 118 minutes | Rated PG-13

"Football fanatics" feel the "mojo" of this "gritty", "documentary-style" look at a Texas town's "bigger than life" devotion to high school gridiron; as an "embattled" coach preaching "love for the game", Thornton shows his "versatility", but some Monday morning quarterbacks are "unimpressed with the character development" and the "headache-inducing" camerawork.

Friday the 13th
16 | 9 | 15 | 13

1980 | Directed by Sean S. Cunningham | With Betsy Palmer, Adrienne King, Harry Crosby | 95 minutes | Rated R

The "granddaddy of modern-day horror films", this "cult slasher flick" "spawned an entire franchise" of "wretched sequels" that don't hold a

candle to its "unrelenting creepiness"; set in a summer camp populated by "stupid, horny teenagers" who "scream a lot", it might "suc-
ceed more on a comedic level" today, but that "twist at the end" still
"scares the hell" out of everybody.

	OVERALL	ACTING	STORY	PROD.

Fried Green Tomatoes

| 23 | 25 | 23 | 22 |

1991 | Directed by Jon Avnet | With Kathy Bates, Jessica Tandy, Mary
Stuart Masterson | 130 minutes | Rated PG-13

"Southern-fried memories" are the basis of this "heartwarming"
dramedy detailing how a "pathetic excuse for a woman" transforms
herself into a "take-charge wonder"; its "sweet story" might feature a
dash of "male bashing", but it's "genuinely touching and involving" –
no wonder many fried-food fans find this "feel-good" "tear-jerking"
"chick flick" so gosh darn "yummy."

Friendly Persuasion

| 24 | 25 | 25 | 23 |

1956 | Directed by William Wyler | With Gary Cooper, Dorothy McGuire,
Anthony Perkins | 140 minutes | Not Rated

"One for thy heart", this story of "Civil War Quakers" "trying to be pacifists" is an "all-around solid" picture thanks to a "strong storyline"; its
"endearing characters" include the ultra-"believable" Cooper (the
"Harrison Ford of his time") as well as a "moving" McGuire and Perkins.

Friends with Money

| 16 | 20 | 15 | 17 |

2006 | Directed by Nicole Holofcener | With Jennifer Aniston, Joan
Cusack, Catherine Keener, Frances McDormand | 88 minutes | Rated R

Aniston goes "indie" in this "chick flick with a brain", a "moody" LA
comedy featuring Jen as a singleton "doormat" who's "barely getting
by", while her married pals cope with issues that "money can't cure";
maybe the "nuanced" ensemble work is "underappreciated", but
skeptics still see a "meandering character sketch" that amounts to a
"whiny downer" for the "Sundance crowd."

Fritz the Cat

| 16 | - | 15 | 17 |

1972 | Directed by Ralph Bakshi | Animated | 78 minutes | Rated X

"Soft-core kitty porn" fans tout this "risqué" "stoner's delight", an "artifact of the underground comics scene" that's best remembered as the
first X-rated animated feature; critical cats call it too "dumbed-down
and diluted" (Fritz's "creator, R. Crumb, supposedly disliked it"), but
admit it "has its funny moments" provided your "drugs haven't worn off."

From Dusk Till Dawn

| 18 | 16 | 17 | 20 |

1996 | Directed by Robert Rodriguez | With Harvey Keitel, George
Clooney, Quentin Tarantino, Juliette Lewis | 108 minutes | Rated R

"Awesome schlock" sucks "gorefest" fans into this "crass" crime/
horror trip, a "lurid" tale of "gun-toting" baddies making a getaway to
a Mexican roadhouse that's actually a "den of vampires"; it's a "roller-
coaster" of "gratuitous exploitation" with plenty of "cheap thrills", but
buzz-killers yawn maybe the "title refers to the running time."

From Here to Eternity ✉◐

| 26 | 27 | 24 | 24 |

1953 | Directed by Fred Zinnemann | With Burt Lancaster, Montgomery
Clift, Deborah Kerr, Frank Sinatra, Donna Reed | 118 minutes | Not Rated

Based on James Jones' "powerful" novel, this "gold standard" of war
dramas depicts military life in Honolulu's Pearl Harbor just before the

Japanese attack; the "all-star cast" (including an Oscar-winning "Ol' Blue Eyes") and a "technically brilliant" production make this a "compelling classic" – though it's best remembered for Burt and Deborah's iconic "kissing-on-the-beach" scene.

From Russia With Love   23 | 21 | 23 | 23
1964 | Directed by Terence Young | With Sean Connery, Robert Shaw, Lotte Lenya, Daniela Bianchi | 115 minutes | Rated PG
Ride the "Orient Express from Istanbul to Venice" – with plenty of stops for "exotic locales", "scantily clad" gals and "great fight scenes" – in this early James Bonder; the "formula never works better" thanks to an "incomparable" Connery pitted against "non-cartoon" villains, especially Lenya at her most "sadomasochistic."

Front, The   23 | 23 | 25 | 21
1976 | Directed by Martin Ritt | With Woody Allen, Zero Mostel, Andrea Marcovicci | 95 minutes | Rated PG
The "one great Woody movie" that he "didn't direct", this "dark comedy" is a "flashback" to the dark days of "McCarthyism in the '50s" starring Allen as a "reluctant hero" shilling scripts penned by "blacklisted writers" (though "Mostel steals the show" as a comedian pressured into the "witch hunt"); suitably "sharp and cynical", it does deliver a "powerful message" that "may still have resonance today."

Front Page, The ◑   24 | 24 | 25 | 20
1931 | Directed by Lewis Milestone | With Adolphe Menjou, Pat O'Brien, Edward Everett Horton | 101 minutes | Not Rated
Based on the timeless stage comedy from Ben Hecht and Charles MacArthur, this zany satire of tabloid journalism is propelled by a fast-moving plot delivered with rapid-fire, overlapping dialogue; since it's an early talkie, it hasn't aged well, but the story was well-regarded enough to inspire three remakes, including *His Girl Friday*, arguably the best of the bunch.

Fugitive, The   23 | 24 | 24 | 23
1993 | Directed by Andrew Davis | With Harrison Ford, Tommy Lee Jones, Sela Ward, Julianne Moore | 127 minutes | Rated PG-13
From the "ultimate adrenaline rush" of the opening "train wreck" to the "smashing grand finale", you'll be perched "on the edge of your seat" throughout this "thinking person's action flick", based on the "long-ago" TV series about a doctor unjustly accused of murder who's trying to clear his name; the "cat-and-mouse" plot lends a "Hitchcockian" feel to the proceedings, while Ford and Jones deliver "pitch-perfect performances."

Full Metal Jacket   24 | 25 | 22 | 25
1987 | Directed by Stanley Kubrick | With Matthew Modine, Adam Baldwin, Vincent D'Onofrio | 116 minutes | Rated R
"Kubrick does Vietnam" in this "intense" war picture that's really "two amazing films in one": first up is the "disturbingly funny" depiction of "boot-camp" basic training, followed by an abrupt about-face to the "total hell" of the front-line war; "first-rate production and acting" keep things "compelling" throughout, even if peaceniks feel the "uneven" second half is a tad too "violent."

	OVERALL	ACTING	STORY	PROD.

Full Monty, The   22 | 22 | 24 | 19

1997 | Directed by Peter Cattaneo | With Robert Carlyle, Mark Addy, Tom Wilkinson | 91 minutes | Rated R

Out-of-work, out-of-shape blokes put together a "Chippendale's-type" strip act as a "creative response to unemployment" in this "riotous" English comedy that mixes "bumps and grinds" with "serious social themes"; its "enthusiastic" if "unknown" ensemble cast shake their booties to a "terrific" pop soundtrack, though most prefer it "with subtitles" to decipher those "British accents."

Funny Face   24 | 24 | 21 | 25

1957 | Directed by Stanley Donen | With Audrey Hepburn, Fred Astaire, Kay Thompson | 103 minutes | Not Rated

"Cinderella" goes to Paris in this "fashion industry musical" wherein a "gracefully aging", "debonair" Astaire turns a "bookish" Hepburn into an "ethereal", "luminous" supermodel; despite "no story to speak of", it's "thoroughly enchanting" thanks to "magic" dancing and Gershwin's "s'wonderfully" "dreamy" score; best number: Thompson's "steal-the-movie" rendition of 'Think Pink.'

Funny Girl ✉   26 | 25 | 24 | 26

1968 | Directed by William Wyler | With Barbra Streisand, Omar Sharif, Walter Pidgeon | 151 minutes | Rated G

"Hello, gorgeous!"; Babs' "big movie debut" in one of the "last great traditional Hollywood musicals" made her the "greatest star" thanks to some "chutzpah", some "charm" and a voice "like buttah"; indeed, her Oscar-winning turn as comedienne Fanny Brice is so "socko" that it's easy to ignore the "schmaltzy" plot about the "man who got away."

Funny Lady   15 | 17 | 14 | 18

1975 | Directed by Herbert Ross | With Barbra Streisand, James Caan, Omar Sharif | 136 minutes | Rated PG

This "not-as-good follow-up to *Funny Girl*" (they should have "quit while they were ahead") strikes some as a Streisand "vanity production" trying to "milk the success" of the original, with "everything in excess – except the story and acting"; on the positive side, there are a couple of "sparkling Kander and Ebb" tunes.

Funny Thing Happened on the Way to the Forum, A   22 | 22 | 21 | 20

1966 | Directed by Richard Lester | With Zero Mostel, Phil Silvers, Buster Keaton | 99 minutes | Not Rated

For "comedy tonight", try this "total farce" of a musical that depicts Ancient Rome as a freewheeling toga party; sure, "Zero's the greatest" at provoking "laugh after laugh", but fans of the stage version find it "stupid" "schlock" with "a lot lost in the translation to the screen."

Fury ◐   ▽ 25 | 25 | 25 | 23

1936 | Directed by Fritz Lang | With Spencer Tracy, Sylvia Sidney, Bruce Cabot | 90 minutes | Not Rated

"Paranoia master" Lang's first American film, this "chilling depiction of mob violence and collective hysteria" remains "as fresh today as it was in 1936" thanks to the director's "skillful manipulation of sympathies"; a "nice and bitter" Tracy is its lynchpin, playing a "morally ambiguous" everyman caught up in a "social tragedy."

F/X

21 | 19 | 23 | 21

1986 | Directed by Robert Mandel | With Bryan Brown, Brian Dennehy, Diane Venora | 109 minutes | Rated R

Go "behind the scenes" into the "world of effects masters" via this "fun romp" of a thriller about a movie-set special "F/X man" relying on some "imaginative tricks" after he's framed for murder and takes it on the run; though "somewhat implausible" and now "dated" by "CGI", it's "loaded" with "unpredictable twists and turns" to "keep things moving" effectively.

Gallipoli

25 | 25 | 25 | 24

1981 | Directed by Peter Weir | With Mel Gibson, Mark Lee, Bill Kerr, David Argue | 110 minutes | Rated PG

A "fresh-faced" Gibson "comes of age" as an actor in this "oh-so-sad war movie" about a "disastrous WWI" battle in Turkey that points out the "pointlessness" of combat; "one of the best of the Australian New Wave" films, it winds up with a "10-hanky tragic ending" that "tugs at the heartstrings without being corny."

Game, The

22 | 22 | 24 | 22

1997 | Directed by David Fincher | With Michael Douglas, Sean Penn, Deborah Unger | 128 minutes | Rated R

"Fincher fans rejoice" at the director's "psych thriller follow-up" to *Seven*, a "gripping mind-bender" featuring Douglas as a "wealthy, overworked" broker who gets a "disturbing birthday present" from brother Penn: a ticket to a "twisted", real-life game; as an "unpredictable rush" it's "suspenseful to the last drop", but be prepared to play by "loopy" rules ("I'm still confused").

◪ Gandhi ⊠

27 | 28 | 27 | 27

1982 | Directed by Richard Attenborough | With Ben Kingsley, Candice Bergen, Edward Fox | 188 minutes | Rated PG

"Big Hollywood at its best", this "meticulously detailed" bio of the Indian leader is *The Ten Commandments* of the '80s", "long but riveting" and "emotionally wrenching"; Kingsley's "searing", Oscar-winning portrayal of the figure "who brought the British Empire to its knees" is the movie's "glorious centerpiece", and if a few find it "ponderous" and "overblown", there's no debate that it "captures the spiritual essence of the man perfectly."

Gangs of New York

21 | 23 | 20 | 25

2002 | Directed by Martin Scorsese | With Leonardo DiCaprio, Daniel Day-Lewis, Cameron Diaz | 166 minutes | Rated R

The "corrupt world" of "Civil War-era New York" is the backdrop for this "bloody good" "love and revenge" picture via Martin Scorsese that's "overwhelming visually" but "wholly uneven" plotwise; cynics skewer the "unnecessary violence", "moldy love story" and "way too long" running time, while fans counter Day-Lewis' "vivid" performance is the picture's "saving grace"; in sum, "flawed, but worth it."

Garden of the Finzi-Continis, The ⊠🄵

25 | 24 | 27 | 25

1971 | Directed by Vittorio De Sica | With Dominique Sanda, Lino Capolicchio, Helmut Berger | 94 minutes | Rated R

"Complacency leads to disaster" in this "haunting" WWII drama about "upper-class Italian Jews" who "close their eyes to the looming

evil" of fascism by believing that "money and position will insulate
them"; "gripping and emotional", it's notable for making the "beautiful" young Sanda a star.

Garden State

OVERALL	ACTING	STORY	PROD.
22	23	21	20

2004 | Directed by Zach Braff | With Zach Braff, Natalie Portman, Peter
Sarsgaard | 102 minutes | Rated R

Think of it as "*The Graduate* for a new century": this "quirky" dramedy
directed, written and starring Zach Braff is pitched to "disillusioned
twentysomethings" with its depiction of the ultimate "quarter-life crisis sufferer"; despite mixed notices for the "enchanting" (or "annoying") Portman and catcalls for that "fake Hollywood ending", it's worth
renting for the "kick-ass soundtrack" alone.

Gaslight ✉️◐

26	27	26	24

1944 | Directed by George Cukor | With Ingrid Bergman, Charles Boyer,
Joseph Cotten | 114 minutes | Not Rated

Anything but light, this "high-tension" thriller stars a "glowing",
Oscar-winning Bergman as a newlywed who thinks she's "going
insane – or is she?"; "mesmerized" fans say the "original" storyline
"maintains the suspense to the end", helped by an atmospheric
"Victorian setting" and a particularly "villainous villain" in Boyer.

Gattaca

20	20	23	22

1997 | Directed by Andrew Niccol | With Ethan Hawke, Uma Thurman,
Jude Law | 101 minutes | Rated PG-13

Sci-fi spliced with "smarts", this "stylish" "dystopian vision" is a "compelling" look at a "scary future" where mere human Hawke bargains
with "co-conspirator" Law to upgrade into the ranks of the "genetically
engineered" elite; though "slow-moving", it's got the "philosophical"
DNA to "make you think" about the dawn of "designer babies."

Gauntlet, The

17	17	18	18

1977 | Directed by Clint Eastwood | With Clint Eastwood, Sondra Locke |
109 minutes | Rated R

Catch the "pre-sensitive Clint" in a typical "clenched-jaw cop role" in
this "not bad" action flick about a "*Dirty Harry*-ish" lawman with an
uncharacteristically "weak" streak who's double-crossed after being
assigned to "protect prostitute crime witness" Locke; it's a "watchable
shoot 'em up" with a "savage climax", though both "credibility" and
acting ability are "stretched thin" here.

Gay Divorcee, The ◐

25	23	20	25

1934 | Directed by Mark Sandrich | With Fred Astaire, Ginger Rogers,
Edward Everett Horton | 107 minutes | Not Rated

"No one could dance like Fred and Ginger", and this footloose '30s musical "whirls" with production numbers "par excellence" as Rogers
plays a spouse untying the knot in high style as Astaire duly falls into
step; the "silly story" is trumped by the "dreamy" tunes and, of course,
that terpsichorean team-up "can't be beat."

General, The ◐

28	27	26	27

1927 | Directed by Clyde Bruckman, Buster Keaton | With Buster Keaton,
Marion Mack | 75 minutes | Not Rated

One of the "most remarkable" silent films, this pioneering effort "establishes gags still used today" in its story of a Civil War–era Southern

engineer in relentless, hapless pursuit of a stolen locomotive; the "Great Stoneface's" most "ambitious" work, it also incorporates some "amazing physical comedy" that must be "seen to be believed."

Gentleman's Agreement ✉️◐

26	27	27	24

1947 | Directed by Elia Kazan | With Gregory Peck, Dorothy McGuire, Celeste Holm | 118 minutes | Not Rated

A once-"controversial exposé" of "American anti-Semitism", this "earnest" "message drama" offers Peck in a "wonderfully emotional" turn as an investigative reporter who passes himself off as Jewish and becomes a first-hand witness to "subtle prejudice"; if the final result seems a bit "dated" and "simplistic" today, it's still "interesting" as an early attempt at social criticism.

Gentlemen Prefer Blondes

23	21	20	24

1953 | Directed by Howard Hawks | With Jane Russell, Marilyn Monroe, Charles Coburn | 91 minutes | Rated PG

You'll probably prefer Monroe's "ingenious, ingenuous" "dumb blonde" to the "nonexistent storyline" in this "guilty-pleasure" musical comedy, a "deliciously over-the-top" story of "gold diggers" on the make made all the more vivid in "spectacular Technicolor"; it's "one for the time capsule", if only for Marilyn's "dazzling", iconic rendition of 'Diamonds Are a Girl's Best Friend.'

George of the Jungle

17	16	16	17

1997 | Directed by Sam Weisman | With Brendan Fraser, Leslie Mann, Thomas Haden Church | 91 minutes | Rated PG

Young chimps and big apes who "remember the cartoon" have "goofy fun" with this comedy featuring "Fraser in a loincloth" as a "moronic" secondhand Tarzan; cynics say Disney grabs for the vine and "falls short", but it is "surprisingly entertaining", even if the theme ditty will stay "in your head for days."

Georgy Girl ◐

23	25	21	20

1966 | Directed by Silvio Narizzano | With Lynn Redgrave, James Mason, Alan Bates, Charlotte Rampling | 99 minutes | Not Rated

An "ever optimistic ugly duckling" takes on "London in the Swinging '60s" in this "bittersweet comedy" that makes you "laugh and cry" as you "root for the protagonist"; starring a "moving", "before-Weight-Watchers" Redgrave as the "odd person out", it "still holds up" over 40 years later, but beware: the "theme song will stick in your head for days."

Getaway, The

22	22	21	21

1972 | Directed by Sam Peckinpah | With Steve McQueen, Ali MacGraw, Ben Johnson | 122 minutes | Rated PG

"Steve and Ali sizzle" with their "on-screen (and off-screen) love affair" in this "essential" "crime spree road trip" flick about an ex-con and his missus "on the run"; McQueen is his "usual stoic yet likable self", MacGraw's deliciously "icy" and director Peckinpah provides enough "slo-mo" action to make for "exciting B-movie" thrills.

Get Shorty

20	22	21	20

1995 | Directed by Barry Sonnenfeld | With John Travolta, Gene Hackman, Rene Russo, Danny DeVito | 105 minutes | Rated R

Travolta brings his "*Pulp Fiction* cool and charisma" to this "zippy" crime farce about a "loan shark who comes to Hollywood" and goes native among "eccentric mobsters" and "movie business" types; with no shortage of "tongue-in-cheek satire", it proves that an Elmore Leonard story "done right" can be "more fun than a week in Vegas."

Ghost ✉ | 21 | 21 | 22 | 21 |

1990 | Directed by Jerry Zucker | With Patrick Swayze, Demi Moore, Whoopi Goldberg | 128 minutes | Rated PG-13
There's "action for the boys and romance for the girls" in this comic "tearjerker" that's got "hot date movie" written all over it; sure, its story of a dead man watching over his surviving lover is "improbable" (and "sappy and manipulative", according to cynics), yet Moore and Swayze make it seem so "sexy", while the "priceless", Oscar-winning Goldberg "delivers the laughs."

Ghost and Mrs. Muir, The ◑ | 24 | 25 | 25 | 22 |

1947 | Directed by Joseph L. Mankiewicz | With Rex Harrison, Gene Tierney, George Sanders | 104 minutes | Not Rated
This "timeless" fantasy details the unlikely "love story" between a widow and a "crusty old" sea captain who's "full of life" – even though he's a ghost; the "otherworldly" romance that ensues avoids being "sentimental goop" thanks to "superb performances" from Tierney, Harrison and little "eight-year-old Natalie Wood."

Ghostbusters | 21 | 18 | 21 | 23 |

1984 | Directed by Ivan Reitman | With Bill Murray, Dan Aykroyd, Sigourney Weaver, Harold Ramis | 107 minutes | Rated PG
"Kooky, spooky" and flat-out "funny", this "classic '80s" "sci-fi comedy" about 'paranormal investigators' banishing ghosts from NYC is "one of the best stupid movies ever", so "not much thinking is required"; "wonderful special effects" and a brilliantly "sarcastic Murray" are its highlights, though its most lasting achievement is that it "made the word 'slime' into a verb."

Ghost World | 23 | 26 | 22 | 21 |

2001 | Directed by Terry Zwigoff | With Thora Birch, Steve Buscemi, Scarlett Johansson | 111 minutes | Rated R
A "witty" look at two "nonconformist" girls in a "homogenized" suburb, this "random" comedy is a "nice departure from the typical teen angst film"; the "quirky" characters sport "great thrift-store clothes", while the "phenomenal Buscemi" is "pitch-perfect."

Giant ✉ | 24 | 23 | 24 | 24 |

1956 | Directed by George Stevens | With Elizabeth Taylor, Rock Hudson, James Dean, Dennis Hopper | 201 minutes | Rated G
As "sprawling" as the Lone Star state itself, this "all-out wonderful" Texas "epic" about money, love and oil "burns with star power", featuring some mighty "big names" – Liz, Rock and Jimmy (in his last role) – "in their prime"; cynics say this "way too long" example of "Hollywood bloat" is just "cornball hooey", but fans insist this "colossal '50s production" "holds your interest."

Gigi ✉ | 24 | 23 | 23 | 26 |

1958 | Directed by Vincente Minnelli | With Leslie Caron, Maurice Chevalier, Louis Jourdan | 119 minutes | Rated G
"Thank heaven" for this "fine rendering" of Lerner and Loewe, an "unorthodox love story" about a "turn-of-the-century" Parisian courtesan

and the client who wants to marry her; winner of nine Oscars, this "stunner" boasts a "radiant" Caron, suave Jourdan, "*amusant*" Chevalier and "top-notch production values", so even if the end result might look like a "lavish" wad of "cotton candy", "just give in" and enjoy it.

Gilda ◖

24 | **23** | **21** | **23**

1946 | Directed by Charles Vidor | With Rita Hayworth, Glenn Ford, George Macready | 110 minutes | Not Rated

Noir was never more "delectable" than in this "solid" love triangle starring a "delicious" "Hayworth in her signature role" as the "glamorous", hair-tossing Gilda; though her "modified striptease" in the 'Put the Blame on Mame' number is the "only reason to see it" for some, others find enough "mystery and suspense" to make it "memorable."

Gimme Shelter

25 | **-** | **21** | **22**

1970 | Directed by Albert Maysles, David Maysles, Charlotte Zwerin | Documentary | With The Rolling Stones | 91 minutes | Rated R

Originally commissioned by the Rolling Stones as a "simple concert" flick, this "rockumentary" took on a "darker side" after filmmakers inadvertently recorded a "real murder" at the group's infamous Altamont gig; the result is a "grim, gritty look" at the "turbulent '60s" "spiraling out of control", with a "complicated storyline" and "classic" soundtrack that put modern "music videos to shame"; hottest moment: the "amazing" Tina Turner at the mike.

Girl, Interrupted

18 | **22** | **18** | **18**

1999 | Directed by James Mangold | With Winona Ryder, Angelina Jolie, Brittany Murphy | 127 minutes | Rated R

"Haunting if overwrought" drama providing a "hair-raising glimpse" inside a mental institution headlining a "convincing" Ryder as a "troubled" patient, though Jolie "steals the show" (and an Oscar) portraying the "sexiest crazy person" ever captured on film; fans insist it's a "compelling" "emotional trip", but others say it's so insanely "soapy" that it "should have been a 'Cosmo' article."

Girl with a Pearl Earring

21 | **23** | **19** | **25**

2003 | Directed by Peter Webber | With Colin Firth, Scarlett Johansson, Tom Wilkinson | 95 minutes | Rated PG-13

A "true art movie", this "beautifully photographed" period piece set in 17th-century "bourgeois Holland" is based on a Vermeer painting (and a recent novel) of the same name and explores the artist's "possible relationship" with a "lovely muse" played by Johansson, "who wows with her nearly wordless performance" as his "shy", "entrancing" servant; though the "slow" pacing is "like watching paint dry", enough "sexual tension abounds" to keep the interest level up.

⧉ Gladiator ✉

23 | **23** | **22** | **27**

2000 | Directed by Ridley Scott | With Russell Crowe, Joaquin Phoenix, Oliver Reed, Richard Harris | 155 minutes | Rated R

"Everything a big Hollywood blockbuster should be", this "old-fashioned" "sword-and-sandal" extravaganza features lots of "action, adventure and backstabbing" in its story of a Roman general turned wretched slave; the "intense", Oscar-winning Crowe oozes "testosterone" and the "lavish re-creation of Ancient Rome" brings the "Coliseum to life", but thumbs-downers dismiss it as "bombastic beefcake."

	OVERALL	ACTING	STORY	PROD.

Glengarry Glen Ross
23 | **27** | **22** | **20**

1992 | Directed by James Foley | With Al Pacino, Jack Lemmon, Ed Harris, Alec Baldwin | 100 minutes | Rated R

"High-pressure" real-estate salesmen "with an axe about to fall on their jobs" get the David Mamet treatment in this "dark", "lacerating drama" about the "predatory world of business"; its "talky", expletive-laden scenario can be "intensely disturbing", but ultimately it "shows what can be done with a small cast, limited sets and Godzilla talent."

Gloria
22 | **26** | **22** | **20**

1980 | Directed by John Cassavetes | With Gena Rowlands, John Adames, Buck Henry | 123 minutes | Rated PG

A "retired gun moll" and a six-year-old orphan go "on the run from the mob" in this "gritty" Cassavetes drama that manages to be both hard-boiled and "surprisingly moving" (with a "mystery ending" to boot); similarly, "tough cookie" Gena ranges from "fierce" to "maternal" in the "kick-butt" title turn.

Glory
25 | **26** | **26** | **26**

1989 | Directed by Edward Zwick | With Matthew Broderick, Denzel Washington, Morgan Freeman | 122 minutes | Rated R

Based on the "true tale" about the "first black Civil War regiment and the white Union officer who led them", this "period piece" is a fine "evocation of a story few people know"; expect "great battle scenes", even if it "doesn't end the way you want it to."

☑ Godfather, The ✉
29 | **29** | **29** | **29**

1972 | Directed by Francis Ford Coppola | With Marlon Brando, Al Pacino, Diane Keaton, Robert Duvall, James Caan, John Cazale | 175 minutes | Rated R

Perhaps the "best three hours you can spend sitting still", this "ultimate gangster film" and "cultural phenomenon" is ranked both Top Overall and Most Popular film in this Survey; an "absolutely flawless" "American epic", it recounts the "operatic" lives of the Corleone family via an "intricate" plot, "bravura photography" and "iconic performances" from Brando and Pacino; in fact, the end result is so "killer" that "nothing else comes close – except maybe the sequel"; favorite line: "leave the gun, take the cannoli."

☑ Godfather Part II, The ✉
29 | **29** | **28** | **29**

1974 | Directed by Francis Ford Coppola | With Al Pacino, Robert Duvall, Diane Keaton, Robert De Niro, John Cazale | 200 minutes | Rated R

A "real rarity – a sequel as good as the original" – this "true masterpiece" "stands on its own laurels" as it "delves deeper into the Corleone family" saga; a "moody meditation on the emptiness of power", its "complex" plot "masterfully intercuts" two stories separated by a half-century into a "taut", "heartbreaking tale of innocence lost", and though "never overshadowing its big brother", it just might be "even more subtle and sublime"; most chilling moment: the "kiss between Michael and Fredo."

Godfather Part III, The
16 | **18** | **16** | **21**

1990 | Directed by Francis Ford Coppola | With Al Pacino, Diane Keaton, Talia Shire, Andy Garcia | 161 minutes | Rated R

"Conspiracy, mayhem, opera, revenge": the "prime American" crime "saga" concludes with this "flawed" but "watchable" sequel as

Pacino's don Michael aims to take the Corleones legit, despite beefs from both the old guard and his own clan; though it's a "must-see" for diehards, some say the "forced" plotting and "miscasting" ("two words: Sofia Coppola") are a "disgrace to the Family"; in short, it doesn't fill the "enormous shoes" of I and II.

Gods and Monsters ✉ | 23 | 27 | 23 | 22

1998 | Directed by Bill Condon | With Ian McKellen, Brendan Fraser, Lynn Redgrave | 105 minutes | Rated R

McKellen's "brilliant" performance is the backbone of this "innovative biopic" detailing an "encounter between a hedge clipper and a has-been" moviemaker that's based on the life of 1930s "gay director" James Whale; partisans point to the Oscar-winning script as proof of why "indie films are such a delight."

Gods Must Be Crazy, The | 22 | 17 | 23 | 18

1981 | Directed by Jamie Uys | With Marius Weyers, Sandra Prinsloo, N!xau | 109 minutes | Rated PG

"Consumerism meets primitive African bushmen" when a Coke bottle "falls out of the sky" in this "cult" "culture-clash" comedy that "proves you don't need a big Hollywood budget" to be "original and witty"; despite bare-bones production and middling acting, this "diamond in the rough" still exhibits "universal appeal" thanks to "creative" ideas and "more sight gags than the Marx Brothers."

Godzilla ◑ | 16 | 10 | 16 | 14

1956 | Directed by Terry Morse, Ishiro Honda | With Raymond Burr, Takashi Shimura | 80 minutes | Not Rated

The menace of the atom age hovers over this sci-fi "classic" about a colossal, radiation-spawned lizard who rises up to become the "prototypical city-destroying" beast, doing the "monster mash" through a model-train-gauge Tokyo; "laugh if you want" at the "camp-to-the-max" "Japanese footage" (with "Burr spliced in"), but the "bleak, creepy" A-bomb "echoes" throughout still have a "hold over our imaginations."

Going My Way ✉◑ | 24 | 23 | 22 | 21

1944 | Directed by Leo McCarey | With Bing Crosby, Barry Fitzgerald, Risë Stevens | 126 minutes | Not Rated

"Sing along with Bing" in this "hokey but pleasant" musical drama showcasing Crosby "at his best" as a "popular priest" with heavenly pipes who converts a parish house choir to his feel-good philosophy; though multiple Oscars came its way, it looks "very dated" now since they "stopped making" this brand of "engaging schmaltz" "long ago."

Gold Diggers of 1933 ◑ | 25 | 19 | 16 | 26

1933 | Directed by Mervyn LeRoy | With Joan Blondell, Ruby Keeler, Dick Powell, Ginger Rogers | 96 minutes | Not Rated

An attempt to "cheer up" Depression-wracked America, this "wonderfully dated" "art deco musical" about down-and-out show people putting on a revue is best remembered for choreographer Busby Berkeley's "endlessly inventive" dance routines that evoke "joy and naughtiness" – along with a "bittersweet undercurrent of desperation"; don't-miss moment: "Ginger Rogers' pig latin version of 'We're in the Money.'"

		OVERALL	ACTING	STORY	PROD.

GoldenEye

19 | 19 | 19 | 23

1995 | Directed by Martin Campbell | With Pierce Brosnan, Sean Bean, Famke Janssen | 130 minutes | Rated PG-13

"Born to play the part" of the "never-fazed secret agent", Brosnan brings the 007 "franchise" "back from the dead" with a "suave" turn opposite Janssen's "great villainess" in this "modern Bond" flick; though the "convoluted storyline" about globe-busting weaponry in post-Soviet Russia is a "little clunky", overall it "gets the job done" with "outstanding action", "amazing special effects" and a "refreshing lack of hokeyness."

☒ Goldfinger

26 | 23 | 25 | 25

1964 | Directed by Guy Hamilton | With Sean Connery, Honor Blackman, Gert Frobe | 112 minutes | Rated PG

Rated the Top 007 picture in this Survey, this "classic" has it all: "formidable villains", the "coolest gadgets", an "out-of-this-world", "robbing-Fort-Knox" plot, a "fabulous theme song" "belted out by Shirley Bassey" and perhaps the "best-named" babe of them all, the one-and-only "Pussy Galore"; most memorable exchange: "do you expect me to talk? - no, Mr. Bond, I expect you to *die*!"

Gold Rush, The ◑

28 | 28 | 25 | 26

1925 | Directed by Charles Chaplin | With Charles Chaplin, Mack Swain | 82 minutes | Not Rated

Chaplin's "amazing talent" (as a writer, director and actor) is evident in this "brilliant" silent flicker, featuring the Little Tramp as a prospector "fighting the elements in the Klondike" and "overcoming all hurdles to get the girl" – and the gold; rife with "classic sequences" (the "bread-roll dance", the boiled "shoe for dinner", the cabin teetering on the edge of a cliff), it doesn't need dialogue "to evoke both laughter and pathos" – indeed, over 80 years later, many report a "lasting emotional impact."

Gone in Sixty Seconds

14 | 14 | 14 | 18

2000 | Directed by Dominic Sena | With Nicolas Cage, Angelina Jolie, Giovanni Ribisi, Robert Duvall | 117 minutes | Rated PG-13

"If you're a car person" revving for a "speed fix", this "flashy" action flick provides a "wild ride" as Cage and company get busy boosting 50 "hot" autos in a single night; but "slick chase scenes" aside (the "cars are the stars"), those who steer clear of "throwaways" with a "high cheese" factor just "wish it were over that fast."

☒ Gone with the Wind ✉

28 | 27 | 27 | 29

1939 | Directed by Victor Fleming | With Clark Gable, Vivien Leigh, Leslie Howard, Olivia de Havilland, Hattie McDaniel, Butterfly McQueen | 238 minutes | Rated G

A bona fide piece of "American pop culture", this Civil War melodrama based on Margaret Mitchell's "beloved" book is a "timeless", "sweeping" saga of love and loss in dwindling Dixieland; frankly, legions of admirers "do give a damn", rating it an "epic with a capital E" for its incredibly "beautiful production", "amazing" costumes and "perfect cast", especially Gable's "dashing" Rhett and Leigh's "performance of a lifetime" as the "feisty", "fiddle-dee-deeing" Scarlett; sure, it's a "long sit", yet in the end this "gorgeous triumph" "still thrills."

	OVERALL	ACTING	STORY	PROD.

Goodbye, Columbus
19 | 19 | 20 | 19

1969 | Directed by Larry Peerce | With Richard Benjamin, Ali MacGraw, Jack Klugman | 102 minutes | Rated PG

Based on Philip Roth's once-provocative novella, this frank romantic comedy "might seem dated" now, but nostalgists remember its "good performances", especially MacGraw's tour-de-force turn as a "crush"-worthy "Jewish princess"; foes say that it "should have been better" considering the source material.

Goodbye Girl, The ✉
21 | 23 | 20 | 20

1977 | Directed by Herbert Ross | With Richard Dreyfuss, Marsha Mason, Paul Benedict | 110 minutes | Rated PG

"Exactly what a romantic comedy should be", this "feel-good movie" is about a "likable", lovelorn single mom forced to share an apartment with an unlikable, "lovable actor"; one of "Neil Simon's best" screenplays, this surprise hit garnered a clutch of Oscar nominations and won one for Dreyfuss' "charismatic" turn.

Goodbye, Mr. Chips ✉◐
25 | 27 | 25 | 23

1939 | Directed by Sam Wood | With Robert Donat, Greer Garson, Paul Henreid | 114 minutes | Not Rated

More proof for the theory that "1939 was the best film year ever", this "touching" tale depicting 40 years in the life of everyone's "favorite" British schoolmaster is an unabashedly "sentimental story that will leave nary an eye dry"; credit "wonderful turns" from both Garson and Donat for making this "classic" "withstand the test of time."

☒ Goodfellas
27 | 27 | 26 | 25

1990 | Directed by Martin Scorsese | With Robert De Niro, Ray Liotta, Joe Pesci | 146 minutes | Rated R

"Not for the faint of heart", "mob-master" Scorsese's "harrowing modern gangster" classic careens from "hysterically funny to terrifyingly violent" owing to an "electrifying" screenplay based on the true story of "'made' guys and greed" that reveals "mobsters as human beings" - albeit "vicious and heartless" ones; "beautiful lensing" and "stellar performances" make this one boil with "brutal power."

Good Girl, The
18 | 22 | 17 | 17

2002 | Directed by Miguel Arteta | With Jennifer Aniston, Jake Gyllenhaal, Zooey Deschanel, John C. Reilly | 93 minutes | Rated R

"Escaping the dreariness of real life" is the theme of this "downbeat" dramedy about a "disillusioned" shopgirl living in "Nowheresville" and "dreaming of better things"; it's "better than it had any right to be" thanks to Jake's "childish charm" and Jen's "nuanced" work, even if foes find it "slow going" and saddled with an "oversupply of angst."

Good Morning, Vietnam
22 | 24 | 22 | 22

1987 | Directed by Barry Levinson | With Robin Williams, Forest Whitaker, Bruno Kirby | 119 minutes | Rated R

Get a "different perspective on the Vietnam war" from this "bittersweet" tale of an army radio DJ in Saigon that "strikes just the right balance between comedy and drama", capturing the "reality" while still provoking beaucoup "laughs"; Williams "at his manic best" not only supplies the expected "hilarious ad-libbing" but shows off some "impressive acting skills" too.

	OVERALL	ACTING	STORY	PROD.

☑ Good Night, and Good Luck ◗ — 25 | 27 | 24 | 26

2005 | Directed by George Clooney | With David Strathairn, George Clooney, Robert Downey Jr. | 93 minutes | Rated PG

"History doesn't get much better" than this recreation of the "tense", "smoke-filled" ambiance of CBS's 1950s-era newsroom, scene of an "intriguing showdown" between Senator Joseph McCarthy and broadcaster Edward R. Murrow ("they don't make journalists like that anymore"); crackling with "sharp dialogue" and blessed with a "sterling cast" led by the "phenomenal" Strathairn, it raises enough "thoughtful criticism" to incite "discussion about government censorship."

Good, the Bad and the Ugly, The — 24 | 21 | 23 | 23

1967 | Directed by Sergio Leone | With Clint Eastwood, Lee Van Cleef, Eli Wallach | 161 minutes | Rated R

A "delicious spaghetti Western" drenched in "tasty dramatic marinara sauce", this Clint-essential "Man-With-No-Name" oater about a trio of Civil War–era gunmen battling over Confederate treasure is a "true classic"; sure, Eastwood's "penetrating glare" is "hypnotic", but some say Wallach "steals the show" by injecting some "subtle comedy" into the mix, while composer Ennio Morricone's "memorable score" will "stick in your head for days."

☑ Good Will Hunting ✉ — 24 | 25 | 24 | 22

1997 | Directed by Gus Van Sant | With Robin Williams, Matt Damon, Ben Affleck | 126 minutes | Rated R

Written by the "then-unknown" team of Damon and Affleck, this "intelligent" drama is built on an "uplifting", "powerful" screenplay about a "troubled petty criminal" who's coincidentally a "brilliant math genius"; its "searing yet subtle" performances include an Oscar-winning turn from Williams at his "most moving", and though the ill-willed badmouth it as "predictable", overall most folks "like them apples."

Goonies, The — 23 | 19 | 23 | 21

1985 | Directed by Richard Donner | With Sean Astin, Josh Brolin, Corey Feldman | 114 minutes | Rated PG

One of the "best kids' adventures ever", this "smart, finely crafted" "family movie" about a gang of "pre-teen treasure hunters" who wield "go-go gadgets" and thwart bad guys is a fun "roller-coaster ride" "for all ages" (and a bona fide "nostalgia" trip for "Gen-Xers"); ok, it may have "some flaws", but at least it "doesn't take itself too seriously."

Gorillas in the Mist — 19 | 21 | 20 | 21

1988 | Directed by Michael Apted | With Sigourney Weaver, Bryan Brown, Julie Harris | 129 minutes | Rated PG-13

"African jungles" supply the "beautiful setting" in this bio of primatologist Dian Fossey, the story of a complex woman who abandons humanity in favor of a group of endangered mountain gorillas; Weaver delivers a "great performance", the special effects blend real and artificial apes seamlessly and the "ending will stay with you."

Gosford Park ✉ — 23 | 27 | 21 | 25

2001 | Directed by Robert Altman | With Clive Owen, Alan Bates, Maggie Smith, Helen Mirren, Kristin Scott Thomas | 137 minutes | Rated R

"Agatha Christie meets Upstairs, Downstairs" in this "jolly good show" of a "whodunit" that's an "insightful", "behind-the-scenes skewering of the British class system" set in a "'30s country estate"; "one of Altman's best", it boasts "rich atmosphere", "scintillating dialogue" and a "bloody great" ensemble cast all "acting up a storm", and if contrarians complain about its "convoluted", "hard-to-follow" plot, fans claim it "gets better every time you see it."

Gothika

| | 17 | 19 | 17 | 19 |

2003 | Directed by Mathieu Kassovitz | With Halle Berry, Robert Downey. Jr., Penélope Cruz | 98 minutes | Rated R

Surveyors split on this "supernatural thriller" in which a shrink in a psycho ward wakes up one day to find herself an inmate accused of murder: fans praise the "heebie-jeebie"-inducing cinematography and "keeps-you-guessing" plot, but foes find "very few scares" in this "standard" effort – even the "hot Halle can't heat it up."

⮀ Graduate, The ✉

| | 27 | 27 | 26 | 24 |

1967 | Directed by Mike Nichols | With Dustin Hoffman, Anne Bancroft, Katharine Ross | 105 minutes | Rated PG

The "benchmark coming-of-age comedy", this "knowing" look at a "confused young man" and his "older seductress" is the "definitive '60s alienation" flick and "somehow never ages"; credit its "witty script", Mike Nichols' "ahead-of-its-time direction", a "groovy" Simon-and-Garfunkel soundtrack and "superb" turns from the "fab" Hoffman and the "unforgettable" Bancroft as – "koo-koo-ka-choo" – Mrs. Robinson; best word: "plastics."

Grand Canyon

| | 18 | 21 | 18 | 18 |

1991 | Directed by Lawrence Kasdan | With Danny Glover, Kevin Kline, Steve Martin, Mary McDonnell | 134 minutes | Rated R

In this ambitious "meaning-of-life" drama, director Kasdan brings together a group of "average people leading average lives" to tell some "extraordinary stories" about "destiny and hope"; though some find the "fragmented", "confusing" result too "out there", most allow that this "surprisingly moving" moving picture "just misses being great."

Grand Hotel ✉◑

| | 25 | 26 | 24 | 25 |

1932 | Directed by Edmund Goulding | With Greta Garbo, John Barrymore, Joan Crawford, Lionel Barrymore | 112 minutes | Not Rated

"Intertwined lives" are the basis of this star-studded "early MGM talkie", one of the first multicharacter dramas set in a hotel; in addition to its "sumptuous" production and "literate" screenplay, it's endured thanks to a "brilliant" cast, particularly an "amazing Crawford", the "show-stealing" Barrymores and the "breathtaking Garbo", who utters her most famous line here: "I vant to be alone."

Grand Illusion ◑🄵

| | 28 | 28 | 27 | 26 |

1938 | Directed by Jean Renoir | With Jean Gabin, Erich von Stroheim, Pierre Fresnay | 114 minutes | Not Rated

"It's no illusion": this "compelling" WWI "masterpiece" has "inspired generations" with its "crushing portrayal of the futility of war" and is "still as powerful as ever"; director Renoir "shows how it should be done" in this "ahead-of-its-time" picture that's on "everyone's greatest list" simply because it "touches on every human emotion."

☑ Grapes of Wrath, The ✉◑ | 28 | 28 | 28 | 25 |

1940 | Directed by John Ford | With Henry Fonda, Jane Darwell, John Carradine | 128 minutes | Not Rated

"Every frame is a work of art" in this "faithful rendition" of Steinbeck's "eloquent" novel about dispossessed Depression-era farmers living through "desperate" times; quite possibly "Ford's best", it's a "classic for a reason" and "ranks high on the list of great American films" as an "important statement about life" and the "depth of man's sorrow."

☑ Grease | 23 | 19 | 21 | 23 |

1978 | Directed by Randal Kleiser | With John Travolta, Olivia Newton-John, Stockard Channing | 110 minutes | Rated PG

"Fun" is the word for this "campy" comedy "classic", a "high-energy" "adaptation of the Broadway musical" that's a "'70s take on a "hokey '50s" story enacted by some of the "oldest high-school students ever"; still, the "hunky Travolta" and "stunning Newton-John" "light up the screen", and the "slick production" numbers are so "irresistible" that "cult followers" watch this "guilty pleasure" "over and over."

Great Dictator, The ◑ | 26 | 27 | 25 | 23 |

1940 | Directed by Charles Chaplin | With Charles Chaplin, Jack Oakie, Paulette Goddard | 124 minutes | Not Rated

The normally "silent Chaplin" "fearlessly" takes "aim at Hitler" in this rare talkie, a "scathing satire of fascist tyranny" in which he "plays two roles": a Jewish barber and "rabid" dictator Adenoid Hynkel, a "brilliant parody" of Der Führer; although "overly sentimental" and "preachy" to some, most find this "masterpiece of physical comedy" "thought-provoking and perpetually relevant."

☑ Great Escape, The | 27 | 26 | 27 | 26 |

1963 | Directed by John Sturges | With Steve McQueen, James Garner, Richard Attenborough | 169 minutes | Not Rated

"Guy movies don't get any better" than this "absorbing" "prison break" flick "based on a true escape" from a WWII "German war camp"; featuring McQueen backed up by an "all-star" ensemble, it also boasts "excellent writing", a "hummable score" and "flawless action" scenes, including the "best motorcycle scene ever filmed"; though on the "long" side, it's "worth every minute."

☑ Great Expectations ◑ | 27 | 27 | 28 | 26 |

1947 | Directed by David Lean | With John Mills, Valerie Hobson, Alec Guinness, Jean Simmons | 118 minutes | Not Rated

A "pip of a movie", David Lean's "superb realization" of Dickens' novel about an orphan and his mysterious benefactor is a "masterpiece in every sense of the word"; it's "hauntingly shot" in "living black and white", and memorable moments include the "stunning graveyard sequence", Miss Havisham's "cobwebby wedding table" and "wonderful early performances by Simmons and Guinness"; in sum, "when they talk about a classic, this is what they mean."

Great Gatsby, The | 22 | 22 | 24 | 23 |

1974 | Directed by Jack Clayton | With Robert Redford, Mia Farrow, Bruce Dern, Karen Black, Sam Waterston | 144 minutes | Rated PG

"Wealth doesn't buy happiness" in this "opulent" adaptation of Scott Fitzgerald's classic 1920s novel that's sure "gorgeous to look at" but otherwise splits surveyors: fans feel its "gangster-in-love" story is "wonderfully mounted" and the "hot blond" Redford and "luminous" Farrow are "superbly cast", but opponents say "overblown", "shallow" and distinctly "bottom drawer, old sport."

Great Race, The 20 | 18 | 20 | 20
1965 | Directed by Blake Edwards | With Jack Lemmon, Tony Curtis, Natalie Wood, Peter Falk | 150 minutes | Not Rated
Director Edwards revs up the engines in this "kitschy" "family" comedy about a turn-of-the-century auto race from NY to Paris, with plenty of "must-see" settings along the way; a tip-top cast supplies "over-the-top" performances, but the pièce de résistance is the "best pie fight in movie history"; in a word, it's a "hoot."

Great Santini, The 22 | 27 | 21 | 21
1979 | Directed by Lewis John Carlino | With Robert Duvall, Blythe Danner, Michael O'Keefe | 115 minutes | Rated PG
This intense "dissection" of a "dysfunctional family" offers a "look inside the mind" of a "domineering" marine - "outstandingly" played by the "frighteningly good Duvall" - who treats his wife and kids like soldiers under his command; you'll "love him or hate him (or maybe both)", but in any event his "imperfect life" will "stay with you."

Great White Hope, The 25 | 27 | 25 | 23
1970 | Directed by Martin Ritt | With James Earl Jones, Jane Alexander | 103 minutes | Rated PG-13
"Way before Darth Vader", Jones is rematched with his "Broadway hit" role and delivers a "phenomenal" performance as a "Jack Johnson-esque heavyweight champion" whose devotion to Alexander is "doomed by racism and resentment"; in a unanimous decision, judges say this "riveting" drama "captures an era" with "tremendous emotion" and packs a "powerful punch."

Greed ❶∅ ▽ 28 | 27 | 27 | 29
1925 | Directed by Erich von Stroheim | With Gibson Gowland, ZaSu Pitts, Jean Hersholt | 140 minutes | Not Rated
Originally "exceedingly long" (clocking in at 10 hours), this silent "tour de force" from Erich von Stroheim is famous for the studio's "hatchet job" to trim it to a commercially viable length; still, even in a "truncated" form, this "dark masterpiece" about a down-and-out dentist and his lottery-winning wife remains an exercise in "gritty realism", right down to that "stunning finale" in Death Valley.

Green Mile, The 23 | 25 | 23 | 24
1999 | Directed by Frank Darabont | With Tom Hanks, David Morse, Michael Clarke Duncan | 188 minutes | Rated R
Stephen King's "harrowing" serial novel comes to the screen in this "disturbing drama" that "tugs at your emotions" with its "touching depiction" of "humanity at its best and worst"; despite "fine acting", this "very long" Mile makes some "wish it was an hour shorter."

Gremlins 19 | 14 | 20 | 20
1984 | Directed by Joe Dante | With Zach Galligan, Phoebe Cates, Hoyt Axton | 106 minutes | Rated PG
This "black comedy" features a "cuddly", "too-cute-for-words" pet who breeds "scary" offspring when exposed to bright light, water or

being "fed after midnight"; although "lots of fun", some parents warn "proceed with caution": it has a "dark side", i.e. those "mean-spirited", "nightmare"-inducing gremlins who are too violent for smaller fry.

Grey Gardens
25 | - | 23 | 22

1976 | Directed by Albert Maysles, David Maysles et al | Documentary | 100 minutes | Rated PG

Deserving its own "special place in the cult classic hall of fame", this "disturbing" documentary about "aristocrats sliding downward into poverty and neglect" captures the "bickering and bantering" between an "eccentric" mother and daughter living together in a "crumbling old mansion" (not incidentally, they happen to be "Jackie O's relatives"); all agree it's "totally engrossing", yet what's "hysterically amusing" for some is a "too sad" look at "mental illness" for others.

Greystoke: The Legend of Tarzan
15 | 14 | 17 | 19

1984 | Directed by Hugh Hudson | With Christopher Lambert, Andie MacDowell, Ian Holm | 130 minutes | Rated PG

Don't expect much monkey business in this "lush" drama, a "compelling retelling" of Edgar Rice Burroughs' ape-man tale that adds class-system critique and "animal welfare overtones" to the mix; there's plenty of "gorgeous" scenery as Lambert's jungle-bred hunk is introduced into English aristocracy, but even though it's "pretty to look at", many see an "overlong mess."

Grifters, The
22 | 26 | 23 | 21

1990 | Directed by Stephen Frears | With Anjelica Huston, John Cusack, Annette Bening | 119 minutes | Rated R

Despite "soulless characters" and a "cynical" theme, this very "adult" piece of "hard-core film noir" is a "first-class" study of "lowlife culture" (the "twisted" plot concerns a "mommy and her long-lost son who are reunited" only to "go down in flames"); while the "film gels" around the "powerhouse work of all three leads", some say the "real star" is Donald Westlake's "superb" script.

Grindhouse
21 | 19 | 18 | 23

2007 | Directed by Quentin Tarantino, Robert Rodriguez | With Kurt Russell, Rose McGowan, Freddy Rodriguez | 191 minutes | Rated R

This "clever homage" to the "spatter-and-gore" cinema of the '70s ("campy" coming attractions and all) offers an "over-the-top" double feature: Rodriguez's "schlocky" zombie-fest, *Planet Terror*, and Tarantino's "talky" but still "awesome" car-stunt showcase, *Death Proof*; at three-plus hours running time, it "may be too much for one sitting", though turns by a "gun-legged" McGowan and the "fantastic" Russell as a "cold-blooded serial killer" keep the juices flowing.

Grosse Pointe Blank
22 | 21 | 22 | 19

1997 | Directed by George Armitage | With John Cusack, Minnie Driver, Alan Arkin, Dan Aykroyd | 107 minutes | Rated R

A "must-see" for Cusack fans, this "totally original" cult comedy finds the star "as charming as ever" playing a "nice-guy contract killer" who's returned to suburbia for his high school reunion only to be embroiled in a "showdown between competing assassins"; "dark premise" or not, it scores points with "every thirtysomething" for its "snarky black humor" and "rockin' '80s soundtrack."

	OVERALL	ACTING	STORY	PROD.

Groundhog Day
22 | 20 | 24 | 20

1993 | Directed by Harold Ramis | With Bill Murray, Andie MacDowell, Chris Elliott | 101 minutes | Rated PG

An "intelligent existential romp", this "literate comedy" has an "original concept": a "jerk" is forced to "live the same day over and over until he gets it right" and "becomes a lovable man"; ok, it's a "one-joke premise" that gets "tedious", but for most it "works like a charm" thanks to the "hilarious" Murray, who exchanges his "usual smart-ass" persona for something "surprisingly deep."

Grumpy Old Men
21 | 24 | 20 | 20

1993 | Directed by Donald Petrie | With Jack Lemmon, Walter Matthau, Ann-Margret | 103 minutes | Rated PG-13

Though "made for the *Murder, She Wrote*" set, this "lighthearted comedy" works for both "young and old", reuniting the "classic Matthau-and-Lemmon" team playing retired Minnesotans "vying for the affections" of a "comely" new neighbor (the "not-hard-to-watch Ann-Margret"); sure, "we've seen it all before", but these "well-loved icons" still provoke a "ton of laughs."

Guess Who's Coming to Dinner ✉
25 | 27 | 25 | 22

1967 | Directed by Stanley Kramer | With Spencer Tracy, Sidney Poitier, Katharine Hepburn | 108 minutes | Not Rated

"Daring for its day", this '60s "commentary on race relations" is the "final film of Hollywood's finest couple", "class acts Hepburn and Tracy", at their most "powerful"; sure, its "controversial subject" of "interracial marriage" might seem a bit "stagy" and "dated" now, but its "poignant and charming" treatment assures that the "issues remain" relevant.

☑ Gun Crazy ◐
27 | 24 | 27 | 22

(aka Deadly Is the Female)

1949 | Directed by Joseph H. Lewis | With Peggy Cummins, John Dall | 86 minutes | Not Rated

"Eat your heart out, *Bonnie and Clyde*" – this "tight little thriller" about "gun-toting lovers on the run" is film noir at its most "brilliant" and "economical", despite its "B-list stars" and "zero-budget" budget; there's plenty of "subtly kinky" innuendo too, but it's best remembered for an "influential" robbery sequence, shot in one take from the backseat of a car.

Gunfight at the O.K. Corral
20 | 21 | 20 | 21

1957 | Directed by John Sturges | With Burt Lancaster, Kirk Douglas, Rhonda Fleming | 122 minutes | Not Rated

Always "entertaining", this Western recounts the famed 19th-century shoot-out between rival gangs in Tombstone, AZ; despite two Hollywood icons "playing off each other wonderfully" – the rugged Lancaster and the cleft-chinned Douglas – foes fume this "too-long" production doesn't "move the way it should."

Gunga Din ◐
25 | 24 | 25 | 24

1939 | Directed by George Stevens | With Cary Grant, Victor McLaglen, Douglas Fairbanks Jr | 117 minutes | Not Rated

This "rousing adventure flick" from "Hollywood's golden age" recounts the "golden age of the British Empire" via the "story of three soldiers in imperial India" and the titular native lad who befriends them; some snappy "byplay between Grant, McLaglen and Fairbanks" makes it a "buddy film" prototype, though a few are troubled by the "superior", "racist attitude" of the colonialists.

Gung Ho
17 | 16 | 18 | 15

1986 | Directed by Ron Howard | With Michael Keaton, Gedde Watanabe, Mimi Rogers, George Wendt | 112 minutes | Rated PG-13

"Cultural clashes" drive this "light-hearted comedy" as Keaton engineers a "Japanese firm's takeover" of an auto factory only to discover that blue-collar "American spirit" gets fusty Far East execs to "loosen up"; it "transports you" to the "mid-'80s" for "a few laughs", but otherwise this "archive of stereotypes" just "doesn't hold up."

Guns of Navarone, The
23 | 22 | 24 | 23

1961 | Directed by J. Lee Thompson | With Gregory Peck, David Niven, Anthony Quinn | 158 minutes | Rated PG

"Even people who hate war movies love" this "star-studded" production about WWII Allied commandos plotting to destroy Nazi artillery; "pounding" suspense and a "splendid cast" put this action-adventurer "head-and-shoulders above" the rest – and that "climactic sequence" will have you "holding your breath."

Guys and Dolls
24 | 21 | 24 | 24

1955 | Directed by Joseph L. Mankiewicz | With Marlon Brando, Jean Simmons, Frank Sinatra | 150 minutes | Not Rated

"Brando sings!" in this "colorful" musical rendition of the "Damon Runyon stories" about "gamblers, evangelists" and racehorses, all dolled up into one "heavyweight" extravaganza set around Times Square, rife with "catchy tunes" and "showstopping" numbers; foes think Marlon's "miscast", pointing to his "bored", "sexually smug" rendition of 'Luck Be a Lady.'

Gypsy
20 | 21 | 22 | 22

1962 | Directed by Mervyn LeRoy | With Rosalind Russell, Natalie Wood, Karl Malden | 143 minutes | Not Rated

"Stripper Gypsy Rose Lee's life" is the basis of this "terrific" musical biography about the "original backstage mother" and her "passionate" efforts to mold her kids into stars; ok, it's "kind of windy" and Wood (in the title role) "doesn't really strip", while the "brilliant miscasting" of a "shrill" Russell leads many to say the part "should have gone to Ethel Merman", who delivered the "real goods" on Broadway.

Hair
20 | 18 | 21 | 21

1979 | Directed by Milos Forman | With John Savage, Treat Williams, Beverly D'Angelo | 121 minutes | Rated PG

The groovy "Broadway musical" that "defined the psychedelic '60s" gets a "terrific" big-screen transfer in this story of a draftee bound for Vietnam dallying with Central Park hippies; even though "Treat's a treat" in a role that "epitomizes the loving craziness" of the time, some say the "flower-child imagery" is "sadly faded."

Hairspray
19 | 17 | 18 | 18

1988 | Directed by John Waters | With Divine, Ricki Lake, Sonny Bono, Ruth Brown, Debbie Harry | 91 minutes | Rated PG

"Grab a can of Aquanet" and get ready to "shake a tailfeather": this "hilariously campy" story of a "fat girl who lives to dance" is underground director Waters' "mainstream" ode to his "beloved Baltimore" and his "most family-friendly" flick (it even "unflinchingly looks at racism"); though "Divine's divine" and the "absolutely perfect" Lake wears her "big hair" well, devotees hedge it's "kind of tame, but still fun."

Halloween

22 | 16 | 20 | 19

1978 | Directed by John Carpenter | With Donald Pleasence, Jamie Lee Curtis | 91 minutes | Rated R

"Changing the face of horror movies forever", this "almost bloodless chiller shows that gore doesn't equal terror" as it depicts a "masked psycho stalker" who preys on "rowdy teens"; despite "zero-budget" production values and so-so acting (but mighty "great screaming by Jamie Lee"), this "influential" "slasher" flick spawned a slew of sequels.

Hamlet ✉◑

27 | 29 | 28 | 24

1948 | Directed by Laurence Olivier | With Laurence Olivier, Eileen Herlie, Basil Sydney, Jean Simmons | 153 minutes | Not Rated

"Probably the best Shakespeare film ever made with the greatest Shakespearean actor", this Oscar-winning epic is a "brilliantly visual" take on the Bard's "greatest drama"; director/producer/star Olivier does Hamlet as a blond "as only he can do it", and if the action scenes are less vivid than in other versions, overall it's still "unfailingly great."

Hamlet

24 | 26 | 26 | 25

1996 | Directed by Kenneth Branagh | With Kenneth Branagh, Julie Christie, Derek Jacobi | 242 minutes | Rated PG-13

This oft-done (maybe "overdone") Shakespearean tragedy gets "expansive" treatment from "modern master" Branagh, who uses the Bard's full text, resulting in a "four-hour adaptation"; though "engrossing, suspenseful" and "beautifully reimagined" to fans, those who say "enough already" call it "*too much* of a good thing."

Hand That Rocks the Cradle, The

16 | 16 | 17 | 16

1992 | Directed by Curtis Hanson | With Annabella Sciorra, Rebecca De Mornay | 110 minutes | Rated R

It's De Mornay who "rocks" as the "world's most warped nanny" nursing a "psychopathic" grudge in this "well-done" thriller, a "real nail-biter" despite "huge plot holes" and "overwrought" situations; the ultimate in "working-mom paranoia", it delivers a "chilling" moral: "always check references!"

Hannah and Her Sisters ✉

24 | 25 | 23 | 23

1986 | Directed by Woody Allen | With Mia Farrow, Barbara Hershey, Dianne Wiest | 103 minutes | Rated PG-13

A "nice balance of jokes and philosophy", this "pertinent" romantic comedy about three sisters and their "struggle with the meaning of life" "brims with so much heart" that many call it "Allen's most life-affirming" picture; featuring "all-around wonderful" acting, it's a "valentine" to "NYers in all their neurotic glory" that manages to "convey a message without tempering the laugh-out-loud humor."

Hannibal

15 | 21 | 14 | 19

2001 | Directed by Ridley Scott | With Anthony Hopkins, Julianne Moore, Ray Liotta, Gary Oldman | 131 minutes | Rated R

Sure, it's "not the same without Jodie", but this "grisly" *Silence of the Lambs* sequel lets the "fascinating" Hopkins chew the scenery as a refined psycho dreaded for his "wry comments" – "bon appétit!" – and "unspeakable" cravings; buckets of "baroque gore" help distract from the "inferior story", yet many say it "crosses the line" into a "pointless ickfest" with a "tasteless (no pun intended)" climax better suited to *Fear Factor*."

Happiness
23 | 25 | 22 | 20

1998 | Directed by Todd Solondz | With Jane Adams, Jon Lovitz, Philip Seymour Hoffman | 134 minutes | Not Rated

Forget the "truly ironic title": this extremely "dark" "feel-bad" comedy is *American Beauty* with a lot more acid" and so "unrelentingly bleak" that it's "not for the faint of heart"; given some "taboo subject matter", the unhappy call it a "sicko train wreck" that's "probably the worst first-date movie ever", but fans tout its "brave" if "perverted" take on the "middle classes."

Happy Feet
21 | - | 19 | 25

2006 | Directed by George Miller, Warren Coleman, Judy Morris | Animated | 108 minutes | Rated PG

The "penguins look so real, you almost forget they're animated" in this "warm and fuzzy" cartoon featuring "toe-tappin'" music and "large laughs" courtesy of "reliable" voice-veteran Robin Williams, who "of course steals the show" in multiple roles; as for the flick's "environmental message", surveyors stand at opposite poles: allies applaud the "valuable lessons" while detractors deem it too "heavy-handed."

Hard Day's Night, A ◑
24 | 19 | 19 | 24

1964 | Directed by Richard Lester | With The Beatles, Wilfrid Brambell | 87 minutes | Rated G

"Before there was MTV", there was this "best rock movie ever", an "ahead-of-its-time" "groundbreaker" shot with documentary-style "quick edits" that brilliantly convey the "lunacy" and the "pure joy of Beatlemania" in the "days of innocence"; it's "still a film of wonder", and, of course, there's that "incredible soundtrack" of "Fab Four" classics.

Harder They Come, The
▽ 25 | 19 | 21 | 20

1973 | Directed by Perry Henzell | With Jimmy Cliff, Carl Bradshaw, Janet Barkley | 98 minutes | Rated R

Get a "non-tourist view of Jamaica" via this "engrossing" drama, a "reggae-scored" Kingston import starring Cliff as a "wannabe singing star who turns to crime" under pressure of "racism and classism"; there's a "subtle message about power" in "post-colonial" culture" at work here, but its cult appeal has to do with "one of the greatest soundtracks" ever.

Harold & Kumar Go to White Castle
19 | 17 | 17 | 16

2004 | Directed by Danny Leiner | With John Cho, Kal Penn, Paula Garcés | 88 minutes | Rated R

"Whoa, dude": "sophomoric stoner comedies" get a "whole new twist" (starting with the "long-overdue casting" of "Asians in the leads") in this "buddy" tale of "potheads" with the "munchies" on an "all-night journey" to score a "case of sliders"; the "gross-out humor", "pointless plot" and "cameo by Doogie Howser" are "so freakin' funny" that many are left "hungry for more."

	OVERALL	ACTING	STORY	PROD.

Harold and Maude `25 25 25 21`
1972 | Directed by Hal Ashby | With Ruth Gordon, Bud Cort, Vivian Pickles | 91 minutes | Rated PG

Ok, it "starts with a hanging", but this "counterculture cult classic gets funnier", managing to be both "morbid" and "absurdly wonderful" in its "May-December story" of a "death-obsessed" kid who finds love with a "free-spirited old lady"; while "not for everyone", this "original" features a "phenomenal" Gordon and a "gem" of a "Cat Stevens soundtrack."

Harry Potter and the Chamber of Secrets `24 22 24 27`
2002 | Directed by Chris Columbus | With Daniel Radcliffe, Rupert Grint, Emma Watson, Kenneth Branagh | 161 minutes | Rated PG

This "rare spectacular sequel" is "much darker and scarier than the first", but "fantastic fantasy fare for the family" nevertheless and an "excellent adaptation of the book" "within the limits of time"; the special effects are "amazing", of course, and "the young stars have grown into their roles and do an even better job" this time around, but fans who "can't wait for the next one" admit that "Dumbledore is going to be tough to replace."

Harry Potter and the Goblet of Fire `24 22 25 27`
2005 | Directed by Mike Newell | With Daniel Radcliffe, Rupert Grint, Emma Watson, Gary Oldman | 157 minutes | Rated PG-13

"Dragons", a giant "maze" and "puberty" spell trouble for Harry and the Hogwart gang in this "fine addition" to a series that's "progressed beyond the kids movie" milieu and ventured into "darker" territory thanks to the maturing Potter's "increasing angst"; a "faithful compression" of Rowling's tome, it summons more "impressive" effects wizardry and "strong acting", keeping the franchise "on fire" as the wand passes to future episodes.

Harry Potter and the Prisoner of Azkaban `24 22 25 27`
2004 | Directed by Alfonso Cuarón | With Daniel Radcliffe, Rupert Grint, Emma Watson | 141 minutes | Rated PG

Rowling's third installment in the "beloved" series of children's books about a triumvirate of young wizards is "as wonderful and fanciful as the others", with particularly "fabulous production values"; featuring just the "right touch of menace and darkness" to win over "older moviegoers", it has appeal for all ages, but since the "kids are growing up", some wonder "will Harry have a beard in the next one?"

☑ Harry Potter and the Sorcerer's Stone `24 23 25 27`
2001 | Directed by Chris Columbus | With Daniel Radcliffe, Rupert Grint, Emma Watson | 152 minutes | Rated PG

It's "Hogwarts brought to magic life": this "reverent" screen adaptation of the ultra-"popular children's book" about a school for young witches and wizards is simply "spellbinding" – nothing less than a "21st-century *Wizard of Oz*"; fans zero in on the "eye-popping special effects", "outstanding" ensemble cast and "perfect" scenario that "gets every character right", "just like you imagined them"; still, the "length and scariness factors" might mean it's "wasted on little kids."

	OVERALL	ACTING	STORY	PROD.

Harvey ◑

26 | 27 | 25 | 22

1950 | Directed by Henry Koster | With James Stewart, Josephine Hull, Peggy Dow | 104 minutes | Not Rated

"So sweet and genuine that it's never become dated", this ever "classic comedy" concerning an "adorable sot" and his "imaginary six-foot rabbit" is such an "enchanting, grown-up fairy tale" that the "word 'heartwarming' was coined for it"; "delightful performances" elevate this "feel-good" flick into the "can't-miss" category.

Hatari!

21 | 17 | 18 | 23

1962 | Directed by Howard Hawks | With John Wayne, Hardy Kruger, Elsa Martinelli | 157 minutes | Not Rated

"Great African location shots" and a "fab" Henry Mancini score make this "somewhat forgotten" action/adventurer "better than its reputation" (even if its rather "dull" plot about "wild animal" trappers lacks "political correctness"); though it's a "lesser" vehicle for the "bigger-than-life" Wayne, at least the "beautiful photography" supplies some real "entertainment value."

Heartbreak Kid, The

20 | 20 | 21 | 19

1972 | Directed by Elaine May | With Charles Grodin, Cybill Shepherd, Jeannie Berlin, Eddie Albert | 106 minutes | Rated PG

"Not your traditional romantic comedy", this "biting satire" tells the story of a "NY Jewish guy" who falls for a Midwestern "shiksa goddess" – while on his honeymoon; it's "hysterical" albeit "cringe-making" stuff, with Grodin appropriately "smarmy" in his "bulldoggish pursuit" of the "unobtainable" Shepherd, but the "fabulous" Berlin (director May's daughter) steals the picture, leaving many with a "complex about egg salad sandwiches."

Heartburn

19 | 24 | 19 | 19

1986 | Directed by Mike Nichols | With Meryl Streep, Jack Nicholson, Jeff Daniels, Maureen Stapleton | 108 minutes | Rated R

The "ups and downs of married life" are dissected in this "comedic" yet "acidic" story of "revenge" that's a "thinly veiled account" of writer Nora Ephron's relationship with "Watergate reporter" Carl Bernstein; still, some say the "slight" story is "unworthy" of its "divine" stars, and outside of a memorable "Key lime pie", much of the movie is "tripe."

Heart Is a Lonely Hunter, The ∅

25 | 27 | 24 | 22

1968 | Directed by Robert Ellis Miller | With Alan Arkin, Sondra Locke, Stacy Keach, Chuck McCann | 123 minutes | Not Rated

If you're in the mood for a "tearjerker", among the "best of its kind" is this "beautifully told" drama featuring Arkin "hitting all the right notes" as a "deaf-mute saint" who comes to a Southern town and alters "lonely" local lives; the cast is "incredible" at conveying "unspoken dialogue", and the poignant "parable" provides a "tug at the heartstrings" "you'll never forget."

Heat

22 | 25 | 19 | 22

1995 | Directed by Michael Mann | With Al Pacino, Robert De Niro, Val Kilmer, Jon Voight | 171 minutes | Rated R

"Both the cop and robber are heroes" in this "operatic" crime epic, a "star-studded killfest" that's cinematically historic, since "legends" Pacino and De Niro are "finally on-screen together" (their "face-to-face" "coffeehouse scene" is a "knockout"); yet "despite a captivating cast and storyline", "they could have done a better job in the editing room" – "there's a perfect two-hour movie" lurking in this sprawling, 171-minute marathon.

Heathers
21 | 19 | 22 | 18

1989 | Directed by Micheal Lehmann | With Winona Ryder, Christian Slater, Shannen Doherty | 102 minutes | Rated R

The "pinnacle of '80s dark humor" – maybe even "before its time" – this "out-there" "black comedy" is "twisted" and "proud of it" as it provides an important lesson in "teen peer pressure": "popularity can kill"; though "not for everyone" (especially the "lighthearted or light-stomached"), it did "launch Slater's and Ryder's careers", and the "deliciously biting dialogue is full of comebacks you wish you'd thought of."

Heaven Can Wait
24 | 24 | 24 | 22

1943 | Directed by Ernst Lubitsch | With Gene Tierney, Don Ameche, Charles Coburn | 112 minutes | Not Rated

The famed "Lubitsch touch" is rendered in Technicolor in this "witty, unsentimental" comedy about a deceased playboy at the gate of Hell hoping to be admitted by listing his many transgressions; it's a "clever" yet "charming" trifle about how "life doesn't meet up to one's expectations", with a "devilishly nice ending."

Heaven Can Wait
21 | 19 | 22 | 19

1978 | Directed by Warren Beatty, Buck Henry | With Warren Beatty, Julie Christie, Dyan Cannon | 101 minutes | Rated PG

An "enjoyable remake of *Here Comes Mr. Jordan*", this comedy-fantasy mix of true love and the afterlife is kind of "far-fetched, but it works"; sure, "Buck Henry's script is as good as the original" and a "likable" Beatty at least "tries to be sincere", but the "hysterical" Charles Grodin "steals the show."

Heavenly Creatures
24 | 25 | 26 | 24

1994 | Directed by Peter Jackson | With Kate Winslet, Melanie Lynskey, Clive Merrison | 99 minutes | Rated R

One part "fantasy", one part "true crime", this "absolutely riveting" drama about two teens plotting "matricide" is a "surreal", "haunting descent into the imagination" as it details an "attachment that turns deadly"; Winslet's "career-launching" performance is so "astounding" that some say "*this* is the movie" that the *Titanic* star "should have gotten an Oscar nomination for."

Heaven's Gate
14 | 15 | 14 | 19

1980 | Directed by Michael Cimino | With Kris Kristofferson, Christopher Walken, Sam Waterston, Isabelle Huppert | 219 minutes | Rated R

The "gorgeous fiasco" that nearly "bankrupted a studio", this infamously "overambitious" Western inflates the Johnson County War between homesteaders and rich cattlemen in 1890 Wyoming into a "beautifully filmed" but "plodding" epic with performances ranging from "wonderful" (Walken) to "wooden" (Kristofferson); in retrospect, it's "not as bad as its reputation", but heaven knows the gait is "interminable."

	OVERALL	ACTING	STORY	PROD.

Heavy Metal
20 | - | - | 21

1981 | Directed by Gerald Potterton | Animated | 86 minutes | Rated R

"Based on the sci-fi comic book of the same name", this "cult" cartoon "classic" is a novel "departure for animation", given its "adult-oriented" content and "heavy metal" score; some shrug it "wavers between entertaining and dull", since this "strung-together anthology" of hard-rock-flavored "vignettes" is more than "a little choppy" (it "makes no sense without alcohol").

Hedwig and the Angry Inch
21 | 23 | 21 | 20

2001 | Directed by John Cameron Mitchell | With John Cameron Mitchell, Michael Pitt, Miriam Shor | 95 minutes | Rated R

Positively "not for the Pat Robertson crowd", this "offbeat indie musical" details the adventures of a "semi-transgendered wannabe rock star" – "yes, you read that right" – with "Farrah hair" and a "Ziggy Stardust"-esque stage act; based on the "off-off Broadway cult hit", it seems destined to become a "midnight movie" staple thanks to its "giddy, gritty" plot and "kick-ass music."

Heiress, The ✉️●
27 | 28 | 27 | 26

1949 | Directed by William Wyler | With Olivia de Havilland, Montgomery Clift, Miriam Hopkins | 115 minutes | Not Rated

There's "not a weak link" in this "haunting" "old-world" version of Henry James' *Washington Square*, with Oscar winner de Havilland leading an "aces" cast in a "multilayered" turn as a "plain-Jane heiress yearning to be loved" by "gold digger" Clift over the veto of her "stern" father; indeed, her "riveting" makeover "from wallflower to woman" generates "expertly crafted" drama.

Hello, Dolly!
20 | 19 | 20 | 23

1969 | Directed by Gene Kelly | With Barbra Streisand, Walter Matthau, Michael Crawford | 146 minutes | Rated G

This "big, over-the-top" musical concerning a turn-of-the-century matchmaker is a "colorful" romp with all the "beautiful music from the Broadway show"; but goodbye Charlies call it an "overblown spectacle", citing "one of the most unappealing romantic couplings imaginable": a "miscast" Streisand ("who knew Dolly Levi was 25 years old?") playing opposite an "embarrassing" Matthau.

Hell's Angels ●
▽ 24 | 19 | 19 | 26

1930 | Directed by Howard Hughes | With Ben Lyon, James Hall, Jean Harlow | 127 minutes | Rated PG

"Howard Hughes' great aeronautic epic" set during WWI is worth seeing for its "amazing dogfight footage" as well as its "impressive", "big-budget" depiction of a Zeppelin raid over London; but some note that another "bombshell" – the "platinum blonde" Harlow in "her first major film role" – nearly "steals the show away from the brilliant camera work."

Help!
19 | 16 | 15 | 20

1965 | Directed by Richard Lester | With The Beatles, Leo McKern, Eleanor Bron | 90 minutes | Rated G

"Sing along with the hits from 1965" that enliven this "zany musical comedy", a "perfectly enjoyable" if "silly John-Paul-George-and-Ringo romp" that's really not much more than a "platform to take advantage of the Beatles' popularity"; still, the "story's ok" ("at least there's a plot this time"), the international "locations are great" and, "of course, the soundtrack is terrific."

Henry & June
20 | **22** | **20** | **21**

1990 | Directed by Philip Kaufman | With Fred Ward, Uma Thurman, Maria de Medeiros | 136 minutes | Rated NC-17

"Not for the prudish", this "lushly produced" drama explores the libidinous "literary underbelly" of Paris in the '30s, where burgeoning bohemian scribe Henry Miller, his alluring wife June and their groupie Anaïs Nin indulge in a steamy triangle fueled by "curiosity and lust"; an ultra-"erotic lesbian love scene" helped tag this "perverse gem" with the "first NC-17 rating" ever.

Henry V
26 | **28** | **27** | **26**

1989 | Directed by Kenneth Branagh | With Kenneth Branagh, Derek Jacobi | 137 minutes | Rated PG-13

"Brush up on your Shakespeare" via this "revisionist" adaptation of the Bard's "difficult" history play about an English monarch at war with France; "both spectacular and approachable", it makes the 17th-century dialogue "completely understandable to modern ears", and first-time director Branagh's "lavish, lusty" brio is so "brilliant" that many acolytes ask "Sir Laurence who?"

Hercules
17 | **-** | **17** | **21**

1997 | Directed by Ron Clements, John Musker | Animated | 92 minutes | Rated G

To "Disney-fy" Greek mythology risks the wrath of Zeus, but this "witty" animated saga is "elevated" Olympusward by a "strong voice cast", "great songs" and enough "jokes for adults" to make for "stylish family fun" with "an edge"; like its brawny hero fending off superhuman foes, it "stands up well" and marks a "departure from the usual formula."

Hero 🔳
25 | **22** | **23** | **27**

2004 | Directed by Zhang Yimou | With Jet Li, Zhang Ziyi | 99 minutes | Rated PG-13

"Not your typical martial-arts movie", this Chinese "homage to *Rashomon*" told from multiple perspectives in "non-linear" format explodes with "luscious visuals", "chop-'em-up kung fu" fight scenes and even some "noble" performances ("Jet Li can act!"); still, while fans see a "thought-provoking" epic, a few Sinophobes can't help but read a "propaganda" message in the "nationalist storyline."

Hidalgo
20 | **21** | **21** | **23**

2004 | Directed by Joe Johnston | With Viggo Mortensen, Omar Sharif | 136 minutes | Rated PG-13

"*The Little Engine That Could* meets *Lawrence of Arabia*" with "not quite epic" results in this "old-fashioned" story about an "underdog" cowboy undertaking a 3,000-mile horse race across the North African desert; while the scenery's "sumptuous" and Viggo's a "god", neighsayers say the plot's "weak" and the running time "a little long."

High Anxiety
21 | **19** | **19** | **19**

1977 | Directed by Mel Brooks | With Mel Brooks, Madeline Kahn, Cloris Leachman | 94 minutes | Rated PG

"Hitch would have laughed" at this "totally goofy" comic homage from the "totally insane" Mel Brooks that's a "send-up" of the Hitchcockian oeuvre, particularly *Psycho* and *Vertigo*; only problem is, "you must know the material he's spoofing in order to get the jokes" or else this "silly" picture "doesn't really hang together."

High Fidelity
21 | 23 | 20 | 19

2000 | Directed by Stephen Frears | With John Cusack, Jack Black, Todd Louiso, Iben Hjejle | 113 minutes | Rated R

Cusack is "pitch perfect" as an "underachieving record-store owner who can't commit" in this "funny, biting" romantic comedy that "lives up to" its source material, the Nick Hornby novel; "people obsessed with list-making" tick off its virtues – an "excellent soundtrack", the spot-on "music-snob jokes", "Jack Black's breakout moment" as a "hilariously obnoxious clerk" – and rate this "rare straddle between a chick flick and a guy movie" as one of the "top five date movies" ever made.

Highlander
19 | 15 | 21 | 19

1986 | Directed by Russell Mulcahy | With Christopher Lambert, Sean Connery, Roxanne Hart | 116 minutes | Rated R

A "cult following" favors this highly "original" fantasy flick, a "good vs. evil" face-off between "immortal warriors" settling "centuries-old" scores; though the acting's "adequate at best", the "awesome swordplay", "cool" effects and Queen's "rockin' soundtrack" make for an "entertaining" combo – just "don't bother" with the "subpar" sequels.

⊿ High Noon ⊠❶
28 | 26 | 26 | 25

1952 | Directed by Fred Zinnemann | With Gary Cooper, Grace Kelly, Lloyd Bridges | 85 minutes | Not Rated

Voted the "best classic Western" in this Survey, this "tense drama" filmed in "real time" "breaks the mold" by combining all the "grit of the West" with a "strong comment on the McCarthyist '50s" and a touch of "Greek drama" on the side; as the "single-minded sheriff" with high moral "principles", Cooper took home an Oscar, though many admit they're drawn to this timeless "allegory" for its "theme song" alone; in short, it's "absolutely tops" – nothing else "comes close."

High Plains Drifter
18 | 19 | 20 | 19

1972 | Directed by Clint Eastwood | With Clint Eastwood, Verna Bloom, Marianna Hill | 105 minutes | Rated R

"Perennial badass" Eastwood plays a "violent" "avenging angel" in this "powerful" if by-the-numbers Western in which "everyone gets what they deserve"; connoisseurs say it's Clint's "defining moment", though the less enamored rate it an "acquired taste", "not up to the standard of some of his others."

High Sierra ❶
25 | 26 | 24 | 23

1941 | Directed by Raoul Walsh | With Humphrey Bogart, Ida Lupino, Alan Curtis | 100 minutes | Not Rated

Hard-boiled with a heart, this "gritty gangster pic" features a sneering Bogie in a "part made for him" as a "bad crook gone worse" who puts on a "tough" front to cover up the sentimental sap underneath; noir connoisseurs call it "dated but great", heaping high praise on Lupino's incredibly "hot" performance.

	OVERALL	ACTING	STORY	PROD.

High Society
23 | 22 | 22 | 23

1956 | Directed by Charles Walters | With Bing Crosby, Grace Kelly, Frank Sinatra, Celeste Holm | 107 minutes | Not Rated

"What a swell party" is this Cole Porter "musical rendition of *The Philadelphia Story*", a "sophisticated comedy of manners" set in a "Newport mansion" inhabited by some "fantastic talent": a "gorgeous Grace", "swingin' Bing" and "delightful Sinatra"; sure, the original might be "far superior" plotwise, but fans dub this "softer" take the "Tiffany" of the singing-and-dancing genre.

Hilary and Jackie
21 | 26 | 22 | 21

1998 | Directed by Anand Tucker | With Emily Watson, Rachel Griffiths, David Morrissey | 121 minutes | Rated R

"Poignant and touching", this "overlooked" biodrama tells the true story of the prickly "relationship between two sisters", one a cellist who's "battling MS" as well as other "personal" demons; "outstanding lead performances from Watson and Griffiths" lend appeal to more than just "classical music fans", though some say it can be "difficult to watch", given the "tragic" storyline.

Hiroshima, Mon Amour ❶🅕
25 | 24 | 24 | 23

1960 | Directed by Alain Resnais | With Emmanuelle Riva, Eiji Okada | 90 minutes | Not Rated

Simultaneously "harrowing and beautiful", this "inventive", "intellectual" drama "explores the tragedies of war and the meaning of memory" by intercutting an "interracial love story" with "documentary footage" of the ruins of Hiroshima; though too "enigmatic" and "arty" for some ("I really want to like it, but . . ."), others tout the "cinematic importance" of this French New Wave "masterpiece."

His Girl Friday ❶
26 | 28 | 24 | 22

1940 | Directed by Howard Hawks | With Cary Grant, Rosalind Russell, Ralph Bellamy | 92 minutes | Not Rated

"Pay attention" now: the "superfast-moving plot" "comes at you at 100 mph" in this "biting" screwball comedy that's a "wonderful adaptation" of "*The Front Page*"; Grant and Russell "snap and crackle" as a "newspaper editor and star reporter chasing the story of a lifetime – and each other" – and if the "breakneck speed" of this zippy "rollercoaster ride" can be "exhausting", the payoff is "absolute hilarity."

History Boys, The
22 | 24 | 22 | 21

2006 | Directed by Nicholas Hytner | With Richard Griffiths, Dominic Cooper, Samuel Barnett | 109 minutes | Rated R

Proving why the "English rarely disappoint" is this "jolly good" stage-to-screen transfer about eight "erudite" Ox-bridge hopefuls and their "idiosyncratic" instructors, with "beautiful" performances from the "original theatrical cast" ("Griffiths especially"); expect some "profound" insights into "teaching and learning", though even admirers admit the "quirky" spin on "child molestation" borders on "disturbing."

History of the World: Part I
22 | 19 | 21 | 20

1981 | Directed by Mel Brooks | With Mel Brooks, Gregory Hines, Madeline Kahn, Dom DeLuise, Harvey Korman | 92 minutes | Rated R

Mel's "in fine form" in this "raunchy" "romp through history", comprised of a "salacious" string of "winking" comedy sketches including a "Moses spoof", "standup at Julius Caesar's Palace" and a "musical version of the Inquisition"; if it's "dated (no pun intended)" and "not quite" Brooks' best, given all the "scattershot brilliance" it's "too bad there's no Part II."

History of Violence, A   22 | 25 | 22 | 22
2005 | Directed by David Cronenberg | With Viggo Mortensen, Maria Bello, Ed Harris, William Hurt | 96 minutes | Rated R
Examining the "brutal violence underlying a serene landscape", this "taut", "pitch-perfect" thriller from David Cronenberg asks the question "do you really know anyone?" in its story of a "quiet family man" who may be a "cold-blooded killer"; Viggo's "awesome" as the "ambiguous average Joe", "Hurt's a hoot" in a minor, "scene-stealing" turn and that "blatant" "stairway sex scene" is just plain "hot."

Hitch   21 | 21 | 20 | 20
2005 | Directed by Andy Tennant | With Will Smith, Eva Mendes, Kevin James | 118 minutes | Rated PG-13
A "charismatic" "date doctor" tutoring a "down-on-his-luck guy" on the "NYC singles scene" loses his cool in the face of true love in this "light" romantic comedy; while a tad "trite and silly" for those who disparage the "no-brainer" "Hollywood heart-tugger" ending, it's "no disappointment" for chuckleheads thanks to that "unforgettable dance scene."

Hitchhiker's Guide to the Galaxy, The   17 | 17 | 19 | 20
2005 | Directed by Garth Jennings | With Martin Freeman, Mos Def, Zooey Deschanel, Sam Rockwell | 109 minutes | Rated PG
The "crazy universe of Douglas Adams' cult smash novel" gets the big-screen treatment in this "wacky" comedy about an "Everyman" interacting with "weird" intergalactic characters; but despite the picture's "boffo effects" and "zany wit", the "grafted-on love story" gets a thumbs-down from the book's "disappointed" devotees and the "silly" shenanigans leave others "lost" ("should have taken the bus").

Hoffa   19 | 23 | 20 | 19
1992 | Directed by Danny DeVito | With Jack Nicholson, Danny DeVito, Armand Assante | 140 minutes | Rated R
DeVito's laborious, "uneven" drama delivers a "real dose of reality" as it traces the rise and demise of notorious union boss Jimmy Hoffa, who uses rough justice and mob connections to win the Teamsters their due; though it's "very well-acted and photographed", critics call it an overlong, "flawed" piece of work.

Holes   23 | 23 | 24 | 22
2003 | Directed by Andrew Davis | With Sigourney Weaver, Jon Voight, Tim Blake Nelson | 117 minutes | Rated PG
The "wonderful children's book" about a boy punished for a crime he didn't commit has been "faithfully adapted" into this "excellent movie for the whole family"; a "creative, interesting story", "outstanding" performances by "old pros" and "young actors" alike and an "awesome soundtrack" that will keep "the kids singing all week" add up to a "highly entertaining" two hours.

| | OVERALL | ACTING | STORY | PROD. |

Holiday ◑
27 | 27 | 25 | 23

1938 | Directed by George Cukor | With Katharine Hepburn, Cary Grant, Doris Nolan, Lew Ayres | 95 minutes | Not Rated

"Nonconformity" and "high society" collide in this "glorious" romantic comedy about a "charming" average Joe on the verge of marrying into a wealthy family; "crisp" dialogue, "wonderful character actors" and "radiant" stars make this somewhat "overlooked" Kate-and-Cary vehicle the perfect choice when you "can't watch *Bringing Up Baby* or *The Philadelphia Story* one more time"; P.S. "who knew Grant could do such a good backflip?"

Holiday Inn ◑
23 | 20 | 20 | 23

1942 | Directed by Mark Sandrich | With Bing Crosby, Fred Astaire, Marjorie Reynolds | 100 minutes | Not Rated

"Crooner Bing" and "hoofer Astaire" are "rivals" in this "lively" "musical romance" that's chock-full of "Irving Berlin favorites" but most remembered for introducing 'White Christmas'; sure, the plot's pretty "lightweight", but at least the songs of this "holiday bonbon" will "stick in your brain well into the new year."

Hollywood Ending
15 | 18 | 16 | 17

2002 | Directed by Woody Allen | With Woody Allen, Téa Leoni, George Hamilton, Debra Messing | 112 minutes | Rated PG-13

Ok, it has "a few memorable bon mots", but otherwise this "Woody-Allen-on-cruise-control" comedy about a has-been director who goes "hysterically blind" is "pretty bland" stuff; most say his shtick is "wearing a bit thin" (casting himself opposite "women a third of his age" is distinctly "unfunny") and feel he's "not having fun" anymore: "what happened?"

Home Alone
19 | 17 | 20 | 19

1990 | Directed by Chris Columbus | With Macaulay Culkin, Joe Pesci, Daniel Stern | 103 minutes | Rated PG

"Every parent's nightmare" – and "every child's fantasy" – this "ultimate sleepover movie" made Culkin a star as a "self-sufficient kid who defends himself against robbers" after his vacation-bound family accidentally "leaves him at home"; though its "loony premise" is "full of sight gags", some warn it can be too "violent" for smaller fry: "this is Bugs Bunny vs. Yosemite Sam for real."

Home at the End of the World, A
18 | 22 | 19 | 18

2004 | Directed by Michael Mayer | With Colin Farrell, Robin Wright Penn, Dallas Roberts, Sissy Spacek | 97 minutes | Rated R

Three "offbeat" characters – a gay man and a straight couple – make up the nontraditional family at the heart of this "touching" drama that "got little attention" on its theatrical release; Farrell's "brave", "bittersweet" performance as a "boy-man who just wants everyone to love him" garners kudos even if some find the end result too "sentimental" and "disingenuous" – Michael Cunningham's "book is better."

Honey, I Shrunk the Kids
16 | 14 | 18 | 19

1989 | Directed by Joe Johnston | With Rick Moranis, Matt Frewer, Marcia Strassman | 101 minutes | Rated PG

A "cute", "creative idea" that "grows on you", this "wacky family" comedy concerns a "friendly mad scientist" dad whose "experiments go awry" when his kids are zapped down to sub-pint size; with "inventive" special effects to "overcome lame acting", it's "always good for some laughs", though most shrink from the "next two installments."

Hook
17 | 18 | 17 | 21

1991 | Directed by Steven Spielberg | With Robin Williams, Dustin Hoffman, Julia Roberts | 144 minutes | Rated PG

Presenting "Peter Pan if he grew up", this "clever" '90s "twist" on the adventure finds Williams' cynical adult Peter activating his "inner child" for a rematch with Hoffman's "memorable" Hook; if often a "pleasure to watch", it's also panned as a "bloated", "PC version" of the fairy tale and "one of Spielberg's rare mistakes."

Hoop Dreams
26 | - | 26 | 23

1994 | Directed by Steve James | Documentary | 170 minutes | Rated PG-13

"Two young athletes who dream of NBA fame" as a way "to escape the inner city" are the subjects of this "gritty" documentary, a "slam-dunk exposé" of "naive boys" that's "quite moving" if a "tad long"; "superb editing" makes it feel more like a "drama" than a real-life story, but don't look for a "Hollywood ending": this one's so "devastatingly real", it just might "break your heart."

Hoosiers
23 | 22 | 24 | 19

1986 | Directed by David Anspaugh | With Gene Hackman, Barbara Hershey, Dennis Hopper | 114 minutes | Rated PG

A modern-day "David and Goliath on the basketball court", this "inspirational" "classic of the small-town-team-rises-up genre" is a "corporate team builder" kind of flick; as the "motivational" but "down-and-out coach trying to make a comeback in the boonies", Hackman captures the spirit of "rural" hoops culture and supplies this "underdog story" with some "real heart."

Hope and Glory
26 | 26 | 26 | 25

1987 | Directed by John Boorman | With Sarah Miles, Ian Bannen, Sebastian Rice-Edwards, Sammi Davis | 113 minutes | Rated PG-13

It's "chins up" in Boorman's "nostalgic" drama set in WWII England, a "touching" tale told "through a boy's eyes" about a family escaping the London blitz to decamp in "small-town" Britannia; with "endearing honesty" that balances humor with the "heavy subject" of war, this "priceless gem" also boasts a "stellar" cast "mostly made up of unknowns."

Horse Feathers ◑
24 | 22 | 20 | 18

1932 | Directed by Norman Z. McLeod | With the Marx Brothers, Thelma Todd | 68 minutes | Not Rated

"One of the Marxes' zaniest comedies" showcases the boys in "peak form" in a college setting, in which Groucho is the incoming university president; expect the usual "breezy lunacy" "based on years of vaudeville antics" – especially the "hilarious" "French-farcical wooing of Todd" – and ignore that "abrupt ending."

Horse Whisperer, The
17 | 19 | 18 | 20

1998 | Directed by Robert Redford | With Robert Redford, Kristin Scott Thomas, Sam Neill | 169 minutes | Rated PG-13

"Redford and horses" are "so right" together in this "tearjerker" romance, with Bob taking a "real star turn" as a Montana cowpoke whose way with the "healing process" sweeps city gal Scott Thomas right out of her saddle; it's all "uplifting", "tender" and "lovingly" shot, and if some bridle at the "boring", "interminable" pace, stay awake and you'll "learn a lot about horses."

▣ Hotel Rwanda

| 28 | 28 | 28 | 26 |

2004 | Directed by Terry George | With Don Cheadle, Sophie Okonedo, Joaquin Phoenix, Nick Nolte | 121 minutes | Rated PG-13

A "heartwrenching" reminder of the "horrors" committed during the 1994 Rwandan genocide ("a modern-day Holocaust"), this "true story" of a hotel manager who "helped save 1,200 lives" eschews "preachy" moralizing and overt carnage in order to emphasize the "redemptive" notion that "courage can turn the tide"; the "magnificent" Cheadle and "brilliant" supporting cast "do a great service" to this "important piece of history", inspiring "much hope" that such an "appalling" tragedy "doesn't happen again."

Hot Fuzz

| 24 | 23 | 23 | 23 |

2007 | Directed by Edgar Wright | With Simon Pegg, Nick Frost, Timothy Dalton | 121 minutes | Rated R

The "brill" blokes behind *Shaun of the Dead* are back with this "way cool" spoof of "American buddy-cop movies", mixing "witty dialogue", "absurd" plot twists and "sick humor" (including "one of the most gruesome deaths ever shown in movies"); a "John Woo–worthy" gunfight and walk-ons by "favorite Brits" like Bill Nighy and Jim Broadbent add to the "nonstop" laughter.

Hound of the Baskervilles, The ❶

| 22 | 22 | 25 | 20 |

1939 | Directed by Sidney Lanfield | With Basil Rathbone, Nigel Bruce, Richard Greene | 80 minutes | Not Rated

Critics call this the "most successful" take on Arthur Conan Doyle's "classic" thriller, featuring Rathbone's "quintessential" Sherlock Holmes sleuthing around an English castle; it's "must" viewing for detective fans, complete with "campy" ambiance and "over-the-top" emoting.

Hours, The ✉

| 25 | 28 | 24 | 25 |

2002 | Directed by Stephen Daldry | With Nicole Kidman, Julianne Moore, Meryl Streep, Ed Harris | 114 minutes | Rated PG-13

There's "no action, only acting" in this "intelligent, challenging" adaptation of the "brilliant" book about three women of different generations whose "not perfect" lives are linked by a Virginia Woolf novel – and the "acting by all three leading ladies" "deserved an Oscar" (Kidman "won by a nose"); "don't watch it if you're in a good mood", however, because it's "hopelessly depressing" and "so slow moving it should have been called *The Days*."

House of Flying Daggers ▣

| 24 | 22 | 21 | 27 |

2004 | Directed by Zhang Yimou | With Takeshi Kaneshiro, Zhang Ziyi, Andy Lau | 119 minutes | Rated PG-13

"Exhilarating fight sequences" and "feast-for-the-eyes" scenery team up with a "tearjerker" story of "star-crossed lovers" in this "outstanding" Chinese epic from "virtuoso" director Zhang that kicks the martial arts genre to "new heights"; still, visual beauty aside, not everyone's flying high over the kung-fusing plot (with "more twists and turns than the Yangtze River"), ditto the seemingly "interminable" ending.

	OVERALL	ACTING	STORY	PROD.

House of Games
24 | 23 | 27 | 21

1987 | Directed by David Mamet | With Lindsay Crouse, Joe Mantegna, Lilia Skala | 102 minutes | Rated R

"Cold characters and clipped conversations" make this "mind-bending thriller" pure Mamet "at his most manipulative"; its "twisty" con-game plot (something like "*The Sting*, all grown-up") "keeps you guessing", and though the dialogue reminds some critics of "cartoons talking", it's "chilling on many levels", with a "head-spinning" ending that stays with you "long after the movie's over."

House of Sand and Fog
23 | 27 | 22 | 23

2003 | Directed by Vadim Perelman | With Jennifer Connelly, Ben Kingsley, Shoreh Aghdashloo | 126 minutes | Rated R

A "brilliant rendering" of the "moral stand-off" between a "slacker who loses her home" and a "desperate" Iranian who purchases it for his exiled family, this "taut", "heart-wrenching" drama explores "everything that the American dream is – and isn't"; "balanced directing" and "amazingly nuanced performances" turn this inherently "dour material" into a "gripping", "haunting" tragedy.

House of Wax
21 | 18 | 21 | 20

1953 | Directed by Andre de Toth | With Vincent Price, Frank Lovejoy, Phyllis Kirk | 90 minutes | Rated PG

"Look out for the giant vat of wax!": this "entertaining" "horror melodrama" was one of the first flicks made in 3-D, but modern-day fans say it's "still fun" "even without the glasses"; featuring a "priceless Price", a "chiller"-diller story and "atmospheric", "gaslight-era" settings, it's ever the "stuff of nightmares" and always "spooky."

Howards End ✉
22 | 26 | 21 | 25

1992 | Directed by James Ivory | With Anthony Hopkins, Emma Thompson, Helena Bonham Carter | 140 minutes | Rated PG

"Another Merchant-Ivory masterpiece", this "period piece" adaptation of the E.M. Forster novel concerns a "snobby upper-class" British family scheming to cut an interloper out of their mother's will; though Anglophiles laud the lovely cinematography and appearances by "some of the best actors of our time" (including a "superb" Hopkins and Oscar-winning Thompson), phobes fret it's "way too slow."

☑ How Green Was My Valley ✉◗
27 | 26 | 26 | 26

1941 | Directed by John Ford | With Walter Pidgeon, Maureen O'Hara, Anna Lee, Donald Crisp | 118 minutes | Not Rated

Director Ford's "gentler side" is showcased in this "sentimental", "soulful" story of a Welsh mining family over the course of 50 years; renowned as the movie that "beat out *Citizen Kane*" for the year's Best Picture Oscar, it may seem a tad "corny" to modernists, but traditional types laud its "compassion, humanity" and "old-fashioned values."

How the Grinch Stole Christmas
17 | 18 | 19 | 23

2000 | Directed by Ron Howard | With Jim Carrey, Jeffrey Tambor, Christine Baranski | 105 minutes | Rated PG

Dr. Seuss gets the "grand production" treatment in this "enjoyable" comedy featuring "great visuals" and a "scary" Carrey as a "perfect Grinch" plotting Yuletide vengeance on the "über-commercialized" "world of the Whos"; while it's hailed as a "holiday keeper" that stands "heart to heart" with the "classic cartoon", some viewers see a "heavy-handed" effort that's a few sizes too "overinflated."

How the West Was Won ✉

OVERALL	ACTING	STORY	PROD.
23	21	22	25

1963 | Directed by John Ford, Henry Hathaway, George Marshall | With Gregory Peck, Henry Fonda, James Stewart, George Peppard, Carroll Baker, Eli Wallach | 162 minutes | Rated G

A "true epic" that feels like "five films in one", this "sprawling Western" boasts an "all-star cast" hitting the trail to follow "compelling storylines" ranging from the Civil War to a prairie-schooner drive, all in blazing "Cinerama"; the "long overview" of the "taming" of the territories makes for a grand, "sweeping tale" that's "plenty entertaining", but see it in "wide-screen" or else "don't bother."

How to Lose a Guy in 10 Days

19	20	19	19

2003 | Directed by Donald Petrie | With Kate Hudson, Matthew McConaughey | 116 minutes | Rated PG-13

"Cute" Kate "carries on her mother's legacy" in this romantic comedy, a kind of "Losing Mr. Goodbar" story about a journalist trying to get dumped so she can write about it; maybe it's a "total chick flick" with a "typical Hollywood ending", but both leads are so "likable" and "easy on the eyes" that it also works as a "surprisingly good" date movie.

How to Marry a Millionaire

22	20	19	22

1953 | Directed by Jean Negulesco | With Betty Grable, Marilyn Monroe, Lauren Bacall | 95 minutes | Not Rated

"Fabulous gowns and mink coats are the stars" of this "rather entertaining" romantic comedy, a "guilty pleasure" about three gold diggers on the loose in Manhattan; "Lauren and Marilyn are charming in their own ways", while its "fascinating look" at women's roles in "'50s society" makes many feminists sigh "thank goodness for progress."

Hud ✉◐

26	28	24	24

1963 | Directed by Martin Ritt | With Paul Newman, Melvyn Douglas, Patricia Neal, Brandon De Wilde | 112 minutes | Not Rated

"Stud muffin" Newman is at his "bad boy best" playing a "black-hearted" cowboy in this "truly adult" "modern Western" about a "struggle between a father and son"; sure, "Neal got the Oscar" (as did "heartbreaker Douglas" and that "gorgeous black-and-white cinematography"), but in the end, Paul's "cool" anti-hero gets the most reaction.

Hudsucker Proxy, The

22	22	21	23

1994 | Directed by Joel Coen | With Tim Robbins, Jennifer Jason Leigh, Paul Newman | 111 minutes | Rated PG

"Big business" and the "bootstrappy American dream" are satirized in this "sly satire" via the Coen brothers about a "plucky mailroom clerk" who "invents the hula hoop" ("ya know, for kids") and becomes president of the company; despite a "refreshingly cynical" script peppered with "dialogue so crisp you can hear the gum smacking", a few find it a bit "odd", though it's certainly "never dull."

Hunchback of Notre Dame, The ◐

26	26	26	24

1939 | Directed by William Dieterle | With Charles Laughton, Cedric Hardwicke, Maureen O'Hara | 116 minutes | Not Rated

One of the more "remarkable" adaptations of the much-filmed Victor Hugo novel of 15th-century Paris, this "timeless" picture about a hunchback's love for a gypsy girl garners praise for its "terrific story and wonderful production"; in the flashy title role, the "spectacular" Laughton gives Lon Chaney's 1923 silent performance a run for its money; best word: "sanctuary!"

Hunchback of Notre Dame, The

	OVERALL	ACTING	STORY	PROD.
	19	-	19	21

1996 | Directed by Gary Trousdale, Kirk Wise | Animated | 91 minutes | Rated G

"Disney does Victor Hugo" in this "underrated" bell-ringer that's "edgier than most animated fluff" and thus "more rewarding" for adults, given its "opera"-esque feel and "dark subtleties"; but cynics nix it as a bit "too sinister for children" and fear that the "forgettable songs" and "stupid talking gargoyles" must have the author "turning in his grave."

Hunger, The

20	21	20	20

1983 | Directed by Tony Scott | With Catherine Deneuve, David Bowie, Susan Sarandon | 100 minutes | Rated R

Deliciously "scary and erotic", this "stylish" "modern-day vampire film" "gets the blood moving" with a "to-die-for cast", including a "surprisingly effective Bowie" opposite Deneuve and Sarandon as two very "hot" vamps ("Buffy wouldn't stand a chance against them"); a pop Goth score by Bauhaus jazzes up the atmospherics, but ultimately this one's best remembered for that notorious "lesbian" interlude.

Hunt for Red October, The

24	24	25	24

1990 | Directed by John McTiernan | With Sean Connery, Alec Baldwin, Scott Glenn | 134 minutes | Rated PG

The "first and best Jack Ryan thriller", this "entertaining" "Cold War guy flick" about a "renegade Russian submarine captain" combines "heart-pounding" suspense with "characters you can root for" (i.e. the "powerhouse" Connery and "holding-his-own" Baldwin); the "twisting plot" supplies enough "white-knuckle" moments to make it every bit "as good as the book."

Hurricane, The

21	26	21	21

1999 | Directed by Norman Jewison | With Denzel Washington, Liev Schreiber | 145 minutes | Rated R

Denzel's "excellent", "Oscar-worthy" performance is the glue in this true story about a hardscrabble middleweight boxer wrongly convicted of a triple murder; alternately "exciting and poignant", the script "really emphasizes human emotion", but it's Washington's "tremendous" performance that makes this miscarriage-of-justice movie so moving.

Husbands and Wives

22	24	21	20

1992 | Directed by Woody Allen | With Woody Allen, Mia Farrow, Judy Davis, Sydney Pollack, Juliette Lewis | 108 minutes | Rated R

A "complex exploration of relationships", this "biting" dramedy examines two married couples breaking up "in a way that only Woody Allen can pull off"; expect the usual "fantastic ensemble cast" (notably the "glorious" Davis) and the usual "May/December romance" subplot, along with a twist: "jittery", hand-held camerawork that "takes some getting used to."

	OVERALL	ACTING	STORY	PROD.

Hush . . . Hush, Sweet Charlotte ◑
24 | 26 | 23 | 23

1964 | Directed by Robert Aldrich | With Bette Davis, Olivia de Havilland, Joseph Cotten, Agnes Moorehead | 133 minutes | Not Rated

Playing a "faded Dixie belle" with a "Lizzie Borden" rep, Davis "demonstrates the fine art of overacting" in this "Gothic horror classic" made as a follow-up (but not a sequel) to *Whatever Happened to Baby Jane?*; it's a "campy, creepy" ride revolving around a long-ago murder and its consequences that "holds your attention throughout."

Hustle & Flow
23 | 26 | 21 | 21

2005 | Directed by Craig Brewer | With Terrence Howard, Anthony Anderson, Taryn Manning, Ludacris | 116 minutes | Rated R

This "gritty", "gutter-to-glory" story of a Southern "street hustler" chasing "rap star" dreams has a simple message: "it's tough out there for a pimp"; "emerging star" Howard turns in a "hard-to-the-bone" performance that morphs an "unlovable" character into "someone you root for", while his chief co-star – that "catchy soundtrack" – will "stick in your head for days."

Hustler, The ◑
25 | 26 | 24 | 22

1961 | Directed by Robert Rossen | With Paul Newman, Jackie Gleason, Piper Laurie | 134 minutes | Not Rated

"Dark, tense and beautifully delivered", this "ultimate movie about winning" is also a "love poem to the game of pool", featuring "Newman on a roll" opposite Gleason in a rare dramatic turn that nearly "steals the picture"; it's "convincing", "gripping" stuff, and though Paul reprised the character of Eddie Felson in *The Color of Money*, connoisseurs claim this first take is so "much better."

I Am Sam
21 | 25 | 21 | 21

2001 | Directed by Jessie Nelson | With Sean Penn, Michelle Pfeiffer, Dakota Fanning | 132 minutes | Rated PG-13

Nary an emotion's left untouched in this "enjoyable, if predictable tearjerker" about a "mentally handicapped man's struggle to raise his child"; while it does "make one ponder the rights of the retarded", it's basically "a Barney movie for grown-ups" abetted by an "amazing soundtrack of Beatles remakes"; what saves it are the "luminous performances" from a "poignant" Penn and Fanning as "his darling daughter" ("I want one like her").

Ice Age
23 | - | 21 | 25

2002 | Directed by Chris Wedge, Carlos Saldanha | Animated | 81 minutes | Rated G

The "oddest combination" of ice-age mammals sets out to save a little girl in this "cute", "cross-generational animated flick" featuring a "perfectly chosen" "all-star" vocal cast (e.g. Ray Romano as a "whiney" woolly mammoth); although it's "not up to the current high animated film standards", the "laugh-out-loud-funny" script and "well-done graphics" certainly "won't leave you cold."

Ice Age: The Meltdown
21 | - | 19 | 24

2006 | Directed by Carlos Saldanha | Animated | 91 minutes | Rated PG

With a "cute" nod to "Noah's Ark", this "enjoyable", "family"-friendly animated sequel dishes out "lots of laughs" ("even for adults") as it sends a "mishmash" of "prehistoric animals" fleeing from the watery "doom" wrought by a "melting glacier"; if a few cynics smell a "warmed-over rehash" of the original, at least the "impressive visuals" help the adventure "stay fresh."

Ice Storm, The
22 | 25 | 20 | 21

1997 | Directed by Ang Lee | With Kevin Kline, Joan Allen, Sigourney Weaver | 112 minutes | Rated R

Defrosting the "suburban '70s" with "dead-on insight", this "affecting drama" (from Rick Moody's novel) finds a "top-notch cast" acting out a "painful account" of "dysfunctional families" and "sexual awakening" among white-bread "upper-middle class" types; though certainly "chilling" ("brrr-r-r-r"), it's hailed as a "small masterpiece" that's "worth watching" so long as you don't mind things "dark and depressing."

Identity
18 | 20 | 19 | 20

2003 | Directed by James Mangold | With John Cusack, Ray Liotta, Amanda Peet, John Hawkes | 90 minutes | Rated R

"Ten strangers are stuck in a rained-out motel" – and "one of them is a killer" – in this "tricky", "twisty" thriller that owes a lot to "Agatha Christie's *10 Little Indians*"; though there's plenty of "razzle-dazzle" and an "amazing ensemble cast", the "surprise ending" is debatable: either "well thought out" or a "disappointing" "audience-cheater" that's "too clever for its own good."

Igby Goes Down
20 | 23 | 19 | 19

2002 | Directed by Burr Steers | With Kieran Culkin, Claire Danes, Jeff Goldblum, Amanda Peet, Ryan Phillippe | 97 minutes | Rated R

"Hints of *Catcher in the Rye*" permeate this "quirky" coming-of-ager featuring the "terrific" Culkin ("Macaulay, eat your heart out") as a Caulfield-esque "dispossessed teen" coping with his "rich, dys-functional family" and other "messed-up" metropolitans; its "touching moments" and "fabulously dark" flourishes unfold at a "slow" pace that "loses energy" at times, so stay alert to "pick up where it's going."

Illusionist, The
23 | 24 | 24 | 25

2006 | Directed by Neil Burger | With Edward Norton, Paul Giamatti, Jessica Biel | 110 minutes | Rated PG-13

A "lush production" lit up by "gorgeous" cinematography reproduces the "old-world charm" of "fin de siècle" Vienna in this "clever", "lyrical musing on love and magic" starring the "brilliant" Norton as a "sly" soothsayer smitten by a nobleman's dame; the "intricate" plot "pleases and teases", with some appropriately "enchanting" contribu-tions by Giamatti and Biel.

Il Postino 🎬
24 | 25 | 24 | 24

1995 | Directed by Michael Radford | With Massimo Troisi, Philippe Noiret | 108 minutes | Rated PG

A "charming" mix of "poetry and postal services", this "small trea-sure" "could only have been made in Italy", given its "lyrical", "hum-ble" airs; the "sweet tale" of a "simple" postman "with the heart of a poet", it manages to be both a "great love story" and a "haunting" tale of "inspiration", with "bravura" acting and "beautiful scenery" that come together for "winning" moviemaking.

| | OVERALL | ACTING | STORY | PROD. |

Imitation of Life
21 22 23 22

1959 | Directed by Douglas Sirk | With Lana Turner, John Gavin, Sandra Dee | 125 minutes | Not Rated

Bring "two boxes of Kleenex" before viewing this melodramatic Turner vehicle, a "classy" if "campy" "B movie" about a black woman who passes for white; a remake of the 1934 Claudette Colbert "tearjerker", this time around it's "all gussied up in pretty color" with the "racial theme toned down", leading realists to rate it a "ridiculous", "sudsy" soap opera.

I'm No Angel ◑
23 22 21 21

1933 | Directed by Wesley Ruggles | With Mae West, Cary Grant | 87 minutes | Not Rated

Mae's a "hoot" in this "made-to-order vehicle" about a "brazen" sideshow performer and the many men in her life, including a hot millionaire whom she sues for breach of promise; the "risqué dialogue" showcases her sexy, "sassy sense of humor", though the picture's most famous line – "Beulah, peel me a grape" – isn't racy, just plain "hilarious."

Importance of Being Earnest
21 23 23 22

2002 | Directed by Oliver Parker | With Rupert Everett, Colin Firth, Frances O'Connor, Reese Witherspoon | 97 minutes | Rated PG

This "undemanding" production of Oscar Wilde's "comedy of mistaken identities, romance and your typical weekend at an English manor" scores with "gorgeous sets" and "wonderful" acting from a "cast that looks like they're enjoying themselves"; but purists who prefer the "perfect 1952 version" insist the "magically funny play didn't need 'opening up'" by the screenwriter.

In America
26 27 25 24

2003 | Directed by Jim Sheridan | With Paddy Considine, Samantha Morton, Djimon Hounsou | 107 minutes | Rated PG-13

Sheridan's "beautiful" retelling of the "immigrants-come-to-NY" story is brought to life by an "exceptional ensemble" cast in this "small movie with a big heart"; while its "bittersweet" scenario of a poor Irish family trying to "rebuild after the tragic loss" of a child has many "crying like babies", it's executed so "brilliantly" that even the dry-eyed concur it's "without a single false moment."

In & Out
17 19 17 17

1997 | Directed by Frank Oz | With Kevin Kline, Joan Cusack, Matt Dillon, Tom Selleck | 90 minutes | Rated PG-13

"Is he gay or not?", that is the question: a Midwestern drama teacher protests too much after being outed at the Oscars in this "lighthearted" comedy that's like an extended *Saturday Night Live* skit"; though "well-acted" by an ace "ensemble cast", it's Kline's "inspired" lead – capped by a "scene-stealing boogie session" – that's the "very funny" payoff.

In Cold Blood ◑
25 26 26 22

1967 | Directed by Richard Brooks | With Robert Blake, Scott Wilson, John Forsythe | 134 minutes | Rated R

Brooks' "brilliant" adaptation of Truman Capote's "true-crime" "spellbinder" is "one of the most chilling films" about random murders ever made ("remember when not showing blood was more scary than showing it?"); shot "in almost documentary style" and all the more frightening thanks to Quincy Jones' evocative score, it "still works today" as "powerful" albeit "disturbing" moviemaking.

Inconvenient Truth, An

OVERALL	ACTING	STORY	PROD.
24	-	24	22

2006 | Directed by Davis Guggenheim | Documentary | 100 minutes | Rated PG

Self-described "Once Future President of the U.S." Al Gore sounds the alarm on the "global warming crisis" in this "informative" documentary that's "surprisingly entertaining" given that it's essentially a "glorified PowerPoint presentation" with a few "feel-good interludes" about the climate crusader's "life and career"; as polarizing as they get, it's either a "wake-up call" or a "real snooze", so if you "don't like the message or the messenger", "save your money" for something else.

Incredibles, The

26	-	25	28

2004 | Directed by Brad Bird | Animated | 115 minutes | Rated PG

"Not everyone can be Batman", and this animated Pixar satire "with brains" depicts the everyday "humdrum" lives of "has-been superheroes" suddenly drawn into an "edge-of-your-seat" rescue; it's "not just for kids" what with its "existential take on superherodom", though its "stunning animation" and "witty" set pieces (the "Jack Jack attack", that "show-stealing costumer") appeal to "all ages"; in fact, its "old-fashioned" message – the "family comes first" – makes many "love cartoons again."

Indecent Proposal

15	16	17	17

1993 | Directed by Adrian Lyne | With Robert Redford, Demi Moore, Woody Harrelson | 117 minutes | Rated R

With a "provocative premise" that "spawned countless water-cooler debates", this drama features a "still-hot" Redford offering "down-on-their-luck" marrieds Harrelson and Moore an "improbable proposal": a "cool million" for a one-night dalliance with Demi; consensus calls it "much ado about not much" since many a missus "wouldn't even need the million" – or "two hours to think about it."

Independence Day

19	16	18	24

1996 | Directed by Roland Emmerich | With Will Smith, Bill Pullman, Jeff Goldblum | 145 minutes | Rated PG-13

"E.T. with an attitude", this "ultimate flying-saucer movie" might be a "remake of War of the Worlds" and "splashy trash" with a "plot as thin as a dime" that's "all noise and no substance", but at least it "doesn't take itself too seriously"; so grab some "popcorn" and hold on for a "helluva lot of fun."

Indiana Jones and the Last Crusade

24	23	23	26

1989 | Directed by Steven Spielberg | With Harrison Ford, Sean Connery, Denholm Elliott | 127 minutes | Rated PG-13

"Almost as good as the first" installment, this third foray in the "Indy adventure" series is a "search-for-the-Holy-Grail" tale that alternates "lighthearted humor" with plenty of "gee-whiz", "close-call action sequences"; Ford is the "perfect hero", but Connery (as his dad) "takes the cake" in this fond salute to "old-fashioned Saturday afternoon movie serials" "brought up to date."

| | OVERALL | ACTING | STORY | PROD. |

Indiana Jones and the Temple of Doom
22 | 21 | 21 | 25

1984 | Directed by Steven Spielberg | With Harrison Ford, Kate Capshaw, Quan Ke Huy | 118 minutes | Rated PG

"Ford rules the day and saves the world" – again – in this "take-me-away" action/adventure story, the "follow-up to *Raiders*" that "goes more for shock value than the original" (though as exhilaratingly "over the top" as ever); still, doomsayers say its "hooey"-heavy plot and "dark feel" can be "far too grisly for younger viewers", dismissing it as a "blip in the trilogy"; most indelible image: those "chilled monkey brains."

Indochine ✉🅵
23 | 25 | 23 | 25

1992 | Directed by Régis Wargnier | With Catherine Deneuve, Vincent Perez | 152 minutes | Rated PG-13

A "haunting", "epic" tale of French Indochina, this Foreign Language Oscar winner details an "enthralling romance" played out against the background of a country in turmoil; as a "beautiful" plantation owner, Deneuve "looks smashing in great clothes", though some say the end result is a "little too picture perfect."

I Never Sang for My Father ∅
27 | 27 | 27 | 23

1970 | Directed by Gilbert Cates | With Melvyn Douglas, Gene Hackman, Estelle Parsons | 92 minutes | Rated PG

Guys get their own "tearjerker" thanks to this stage drama adaptation that "hits home" with its "knowing depiction" of a "tortured son" forced to care for his widower father; the "excellent" Hackman's "controlled exasperation" in dealing with Douglas' "family patriarch" makes for a refrain that's manfully "maudlin" but rings "so true."

Inherit the Wind ◑
26 | 28 | 27 | 22

1960 | Directed by Stanley Kramer | With Spencer Tracy, Fredric March, Gene Kelly | 128 minutes | Rated PG

"You'll go ape" for this "superb" "fictionalized account of the Scopes monkey trial", based on the true story of a teacher trying to bring Darwin into his Tennessee classroom; a "magnificent Tracy and March" are "at the top of their game" trying to "reconcile creationism with evolution" in this "relevant thought-provoker" that many call the "ultimate in intelligent courtroom drama."

In Her Shoes
18 | 20 | 19 | 18

2005 | Directed by Curtis Hanson | With Cameron Diaz, Toni Collette, Shirley MacLaine | 130 minutes | Rated PG-13

Sibling "bonding" is the theme of this "sweet" dramedy built on the comic "chemistry" between careerist Collette and "ditzy" sis Diaz, who get "second chances" when their long-lost granny turns up; most stand by it as "lightweight" but "enjoyable" "rainy-day fare", but those who fall "out of step" cite a "sappy" scenario with "not enough sole."

In-Laws, The
24 | 24 | 24 | 20

1979 | Directed by Arthur Hiller | With Peter Falk, Alan Arkin, Richard Libertini | 103 minutes | Rated PG-13

If you have any "weird" relatives-by-marriage, you'll "laugh out loud" at this "sidesplitting" comedy pitting a "chameleonic Falk" against a "befuddled Arkin" ("one of the great pairings of the cinema") as about-to-be in-laws; "totally unpredictable", it's "worth watching" if only to "find out where *Meet the Parents* came from."

	OVERALL	ACTING	STORY	PROD.

Innerspace

15 | 15 | 18 | 17

1987 | Directed by Joe Dante | With Dennis Quaid, Martin Short, Meg Ryan, Kevin McCarthy | 120 minutes | Rated PG

Far-out FX and "likable" characters keep this "charming" entry in the "comedy sci-fi category" inneresting as Quaid's top-gun pilot is shrunken and inadvertently sent into the bloodstream of nerdy clerk Short; the "cute-as-always" Ryan rounds out the cast for an excursion that's lightweight but "quite funny" as crackpot "fantasy" goes.

Inside Man

23 | 25 | 23 | 23

2006 | Directed by Spike Lee | With Denzel Washington, Clive Owen, Jodie Foster | 129 minutes | Rated R

A "clever bank robber" undertakes an "elaborate" heist and tries to elude the "embattled cop" sent after him in this "intense" thriller driven by a "tight", "fast-paced" script that "keeps you guessing until the end"; featuring a "top-flight" cast led by the "sensational" duo of Denzel and Clive, it marks a "graceful" foray into "mainstream commercial" fare for Spike Lee.

Insider, The

25 | 28 | 25 | 23

1999 | Directed by Michael Mann | With Al Pacino, Russell Crowe, Christopher Plummer | 157 minutes | Rated R

Crowe turns in a "quietly intense" performance (while Pacino is intense but definitely not quiet), in this dramatic thriller about a tobacco company "whistle-blower" trying to "do the right thing no matter what the consequences"; although a "disillusioning behind-the-scenes look" at "big business, the media and public opinion", it's "absolutely riveting" and an "inspirational" profile in "courage."

Insomnia

18 | 22 | 18 | 19

2002 | Directed by Christopher Nolan | With Al Pacino, Robin Williams, Hilary Swank, Martin Donovan | 118 minutes | Rated R

There's "a lot of high-powered talent" on board this "above-average" "mainstream thriller" about a "wayward cop investigating a murder in Alaska", where the "round-the-clock sunshine" and "tense" goings-on keep him wide awake; as the "droopy-eyed" protagonist, Pacino sure looks "tired" and Williams is a "surprisingly good bad guy", yet those who "expected more" yawn it's so "forgettable" that they "had no trouble sleeping right through it."

Interiors

23 | 25 | 22 | 23

1978 | Directed by Woody Allen | With Geraldine Page, Diane Keaton, Mary Beth Hurt, Maureen Stapleton | 93 minutes | Rated PG

"Nuanced performances" and "brilliant cinematography" are the highlights of this Woody Allen "homage to Ingmar Bergman", a "thoughtful" drama that examines "family dynamics" and "sibling rivalry" in the wake of a divorce; though some say the director should "stick to comedy", others counter this "wonderfully depressing" flick "didn't get its due when first released."

Interpreter, The

20 | 23 | 20 | 22

2005 | Directed by Sydney Pollack | With Nicole Kidman, Sean Penn | 128 minutes | Rated PG-13

A "United Nations interpreter overhears something she shouldn't and ends up under Secret Service protection" in this "promising" if "predictable" political thriller; while Kidman does the "classic movie hero-ine" thing well and Penn "seems to get better with age", the real star of the picture might be the "awe-inspiring" UN – this is the "first film shot inside the building."

Interview with the Vampire
19 | 19 | 20 | 22

1994 | Directed by Neil Jordan | With Tom Cruise, Brad Pitt, Antonio Banderas, Christian Slater | 123 minutes | Rated R

"Cover up your neck"; this "entertaining Gothic horror flick about a maladjusted trio of immortal vampires" is "almost as good" as Anne Rice's "overwrought" best-selling book; sure, it might be "too beauti-ful" for words and they "could have cut out some of the gore", but with "pretty boys" Brad, Tom and Antonio playing "yummy bloodsuckers", "what's not to like?"

In the Bedroom
22 | 26 | 20 | 21

2001 | Directed by Todd Field | With Sissy Spacek, Tom Wilkinson, Marisa Tomei | 130 minutes | Rated R

"Less is more" in this "intense" drama about murder, revenge and family "dysfunction" that's the kind of picture in which the "si-lences say more than any of the dialogue" (though there's nothing wrong with the dialogue); though "Spacek and Wilkinson are su-perb" and "first-time director" Field "does an amazing job", critics sigh it's a "made-for-Lifetime movie" that's "dark, depressing and 20 minutes too long."

In the Company of Men
20 | 23 | 21 | 17

1997 | Directed by Neil LaBute | With Aaron Eckhart, Stacy Edwards, Matt Malloy | 95 minutes | Rated R

A "manipulative", "seriously despicable" loser abuses his "power over men and women alike" and "plays them for fools" in this "nasty little" drama that unflinchingly depicts the "evil that lurks in the hearts of men"; even those who "left the movie with a scowl" and "felt like they needed a shower" afterward admit being "strangely affected" by this "underwatched work."

In the Heat of the Night ✉
24 | 27 | 24 | 22

1967 | Directed by Norman Jewison | With Sidney Poitier, Rod Steiger, Warren Oates | 109 minutes | Rated PG

The "faint smell of honeysuckle hangs over" this "excellent" crime drama, a "brave statement on race relations" about a "black Yankee cop" suspected of murder in a small Southern town; it "generated a fair amount of controversy in its day" and was quite the Oscar magnet, taking home five statuettes including Best Picture and Best Actor for the "perfect Steiger."

In the Line of Fire
20 | 20 | 21 | 19

1993 | Directed by Wolfgang Petersen | With Clint Eastwood, John Malkovich, Rene Russo | 128 minutes | Rated R

"Eastwood is perfect" as an "aging but resourceful" Secret Service agent – "vulnerable, tough and world-weary" – battling a "would-be Presidential assassin" in this "solid action" thriller; throw in a "truly creepy" Malkovich as the "coldly reptilian" villain and you have a "completely engrossing" flick that's more than "effective", right up to the "suspenseful climax."

In the Name of the Father

	OVERALL	ACTING	STORY	PROD.
	23	25	24	21

1993 | Directed by Jim Sheridan | With Daniel Day-Lewis, Emma Thompson, Pete Postlethwaite | 133 minutes | Rated R

This "shattering" look at "desperate times" in Northern Ireland is a "riveting" true story about a "father and son jailed for a crime they did not commit"; "Day-Lewis is mesmerizing" and "totally believable" in this "troubling" account of "love and respect" amid a "terrible civil war."

Intolerable Cruelty

	15	18	15	17

2004 | Directed by Joel Coen | With George Clooney, Catherine Zeta-Jones, Geoffrey Rush, Billy Bob Thornton | 100 minutes | Rated PG-13

The Coen brothers go "mainstream" in this reworking of the "old war-between-the-sexes theme", a sporadically "snappy" screwball comedy involving a gold digger and a divorce attorney; critics complain "it's not Coen enough", citing a "rambling" story that "drags in parts", and even "gorgeous" George and "luscious" Catherine can't elevate its overall "tolerable" ratings.

Intolerance ◑

	▽ 27	23	24	28

1918 | Directed by D.W. Griffith | With Lillian Gish, Mae Marsh, Constance Talmadge | 178 minutes | Not Rated

"D.W. Griffith's apology" for the racist subtext in his earlier film, *Birth of a Nation,* is this "monumental" silent "landmark", which intercuts four tales of intolerance set respectively in Babylon, Calvary, 15th-century France and contemporary California; the result is "grandiosity glorified" on a scale of "sheer staggering size" never seen before, and arguably the birth of "epic" filmmaking.

Invasion of the Body Snatchers ◑

	24	19	25	19

1956 | Directed by Don Siegel | With Kevin McCarthy, Dana Wynter, Larry Gates | 80 minutes | Not Rated

"Don't fall asleep!"; this '50s slice of "paranoid science fiction" posits that there are "alien pod people among us" "plotting to take over our hearts and minds"; alright, it's a "classic Red Scare parable", but "still perfectly effective today" despite "wooden acting" and that studio-enforced optimistic ending.

Invasion of the Body Snatchers

	19	18	21	18

1978 | Directed by Philip Kaufman | With Donald Sutherland, Brooke Adams, Jeff Goldblum | 115 minutes | Rated PG

You'll be "looking for pods in the basement" after seeing this "thought-provoking", "very different" remake of the "classic" sci-fi thriller about an insidious alien invasion; this time around, the McCarthyist subtext has been replaced by 'Me Decade' pop psychobabble, and even if "less fun" than the original, it's still pretty darn "scary."

Invincible

	21	21	23	20

2006 | Directed by Ericson Core | With Mark Wahlberg, Greg Kinnear, Elizabeth Banks, Kevin Conway | 105 minutes | Rated PG

Basically *"Rocky"* transposed to the gridiron, this "feel-good" football flick based on the "true story" of Vince Papale (a South Philly bartender who earned a spot with the Eagles in the '70s) "follows all the formulas" until you're "cheering for the underdog" on cue; "strong" performances by Kinnear and a "bicep"-baring Wahlberg score extra points.

	OVERALL	ACTING	STORY	PROD.

Invisible Man, The ◑
22 | 20 | 21 | 20

1933 | Directed by James Whale | With Claude Rains, Gloria Stuart, William Harrigan | 71 minutes | Not Rated

"Fabulous effects" ("especially for its time") and some slyly "campy" moments make this "classic" creature feature worthy of "every movie lover's repertoire"; the tale of an inventor whose invisibility serum transforms him into a crazed killer, it stars an engrossing Rains in the "scary" title role, whose amazing acting has more to do with vocalizing than visibility.

Ipcress File, The
24 | 24 | 26 | 23

1965 | Directed by Sidney J. Furie | With Michael Caine, Nigel Green, Guy Doleman, Sue Lloyd | 109 minutes | Not Rated

"Caine rocks" in an "early" role as a distinctly non-Bond British agent in this "totally engaging" Cold War spy thriller, centering on a "heart-pounding" hunt for a top-secret file through a "bleak" underworld of brainwashing and betrayal; based on the Len Deighton novel, its "exciting" intelligence proves that "classic espionage never gets old."

Iris
24 | 28 | 22 | 22

2001 | Directed by Richard Eyre | With Judi Dench, Kate Winslet, Jim Broadbent | 90 minutes | Rated R

This "beautifully done" bio of English writer Iris Murdoch and her "spiral" into "frightening illness" shines with "amazing acting" and bookish wit; "flashbacks" follow her from a "sweet" Oxford courtship to later years when the "superb" Dench "realistically portrays" the onset of Alzheimer's in a "sad but finally uplifting" tribute to "true" fidelity.

Irma La Douce
21 | 23 | 20 | 21

1963 | Directed by Billy Wilder | With Shirley MacLaine, Jack Lemmon, Lou Jacobi | 147 minutes | Not Rated

A surprisingly "sweet" comedy from the acerbic Billy Wilder, this story of an honest Parisian cop who falls for a prostitute, becomes her unwilling pimp, then schemes to keep her off the streets is "funny and well done"; MacLaine plays the "hooker with a heart of gold" perfectly, while Lemmon mugs winningly in a dual role.

I, Robot
18 | 17 | 19 | 23

2004 | Directed by Alex Proyas | With Will Smith, Bridget Moynahan | 115 minutes | Rated PG-13

Master sci-fi author Isaac Asimov's futuristic "classic" of "robots turning against man" gets a "blockbuster" buff-up in this "fast, fun" action flick full of "dazzling effects", "over-the-top" stunts and "cool set design"; Smith does his "typical" routine as a "wise-cracking" cop, though that glimpse of his "bare" ro-butt in the shower is definitely "worth the money."

Iron Giant, The
24 | - | 25 | 25

1999 | Directed by Brad Bird | Animated | 86 minutes | Rated PG

"Markedly different from other animated films", this story of a "quirky boy and an enormous robot from outer space" is both a "sly satire of the '50s" and a "message" flick about "tolerance and non-violence"; "criminally underrated" (it "slipped through the cracks due to poor marketing"), it's "entertaining and deserves to be seen."

| | OVERALL | ACTING | STORY | PROD. |

Italian Job, The
22 | 19 | 21 | 24

2003 | Directed by F. Gary Gray | With Mark Wahlberg, Edward Norton, Charlize Theron | 111 minutes | Rated PG-13

The "Mini Cooper is the real star" of this "edge-of-your-seat" remake that "fires on most, if not all, cylinders", as a "fast-moving", "action-packed" "heist film" "filled with plot twists, maniacal car chases", "high-tech gadgets" and "timely pop-culture references"; while "not at all thought-provoking", it's "everything a summer movie should be."

☑ It Happened One Night ✉❶
28 | 28 | 26 | 25

1934 | Directed by Frank Capra | With Clark Gable, Claudette Colbert | 105 minutes | Not Rated

"Gable and Colbert are swell together" in this "great Depression spirit-lifter", the "mother of all screwball comedies" about a "wisecracking tabloid reporter" and a "snooty heiress" "on the run"; the first picture to "sweep all the major Oscars", it was also considered rather "racy for its time": indeed, Gable's baring of his chest in the "walls of Jericho" sequence sent the "undershirt industry" into a tizzy.

It's a Mad Mad Mad Mad World
24 | 21 | 22 | 23

1963 | Directed by Stanley Kramer | With Spencer Tracy, Milton Berle, Sid Caesar, Buddy Hackett, Mickey Rooney, Ethel Merman, Edie Adams, Jonathan Winters | 192 minutes | Rated G

The ultimate "car comedy", this "sprawling gut-buster" features a "huge cast" of "crème de la crème" comedians in an "every-man-for-himself" "race to find a hidden fortune"; sure, it's a "long long long long movie", but it's "still terrifically entertaining" with plenty of "silly slapstick" and "great cameos" to keep things lively; best moment: "Jonathan Winters tearing up the gas station."

☑ It's a Wonderful Life ❶
27 | 27 | 27 | 25

1946 | Directed by Frank Capra | With James Stewart, Donna Reed, Henry Travers | 130 minutes | Not Rated

"Nobody tells a story like Capra", and this "inspirational" film "strikes a fundamental chord with lots of people" via its "small-town" tale about a "good guy" coping with "hard times" and proving "how one life can make a difference"; sure, it's a "little schmaltzy" and "surprisingly dark", but most say "it's a wonderful picture" and "Christmas wouldn't be Christmas without it" – even if you've seen it a "million times" on TV.

I Want to Live! ✉❶
24 | 27 | 25 | 23

1958 | Directed by Robert Wise | With Susan Hayward, Simon Oakland, Theodore Bikel | 120 minutes | Not Rated

For "Susan Hayward at her most Susan Hayward", check out her "scenery-chewing", Oscar-grabbing turn in this "gut-wrenching" true story about a "tough cookie" "party girl" headed for the gas chamber; though cynics hiss this overheated "potboiler" as "extremely dated", more feel it's "not easily forgotten", particularly its still "effective" "anti-death penalty" theme.

I Was a Male War Bride ❶
21 | 24 | 20 | 20

1949 | Directed by Howard Hawks | With Cary Grant, Ann Sheridan | 103 minutes | Not Rated

Maybe it's "pretty standard" and "not in the pantheon of romantic comedies", but this "amusing little movie" is still "watchable" thanks to the "debonair" Grant as a WWII French army captain who falls for an American lieutenant (the "nice" Sheridan); it's best remembered for its sequences of "Cary in drag" – even in a skirt, he's as "irresistible" as ever.

Jackass: The Movie | 13 | 9 | 7 | 11 |

2002 | Directed by Jeff Tremaine | With Johnny Knoxville, Bam Margera, Steve-O, Chris Pontius | 87 minutes | Rated R

Fans of "sheer stupidity" fall for this "dumb", "title-says-it-all" flick based on the MTV series, in which a few "sick", "not-too-bright lads" perform "idiotic stunts" and "crude sight gags" for your amusement; while too "moronic" for highbrows and not for those "squeamish about paper cuts and bodily fluids", it's "absolutely hilarious" to its "brainless" cult followers, who report that "alcohol helps" make it even funnier.

Jacob's Ladder | 19 | 22 | 21 | 20 |

1990 | Directed by Adrian Lyne | With Tim Robbins, Elizabeth Pena, Danny Aiello | 115 minutes | Rated R

Step up for some "disturbing images that may stick around" "longer than you want" courtesy of this "unsettling" psychological thriller, featuring Robbins as a Vietnam vet back on the Brooklyn home front and afflicted with "paranoia" and "truly creepy" hallucinations; "cerebral" sorts salute the "mind-altering" scenario with a "haunting twist at the end", but for a few "all the unpleasantness" is just "not top rung."

Jagged Edge | 22 | 22 | 22 | 20 |

1985 | Directed by Richard Marquand | With Glenn Close, Jeff Bridges, Peter Coyote | 108 minutes | Rated R

This "entertaining murder" thriller tells the tale of a "grisly homicide, a sensational trial and a forbidden love affair"; "great performances" from "'80s diva" Close (as a lawyer with principles) and Bridges (as the client endowed with troubling "charm") keep it so "exciting" that you'll be "guessing to the very end."

Jailhouse Rock ◑ | 18 | 15 | 14 | 19 |

1957 | Directed by Richard Thorpe | With Elvis Presley, Judy Tyler, Mickey Shaughnessy | 96 minutes | Not Rated

The "only really good Elvis movie (and that's not saying much)", this "cheesy classic" about an ex-con turned crooner is "worth the price of admission alone" for its "big musical number" featuring chorus boys in prison stripes and the King in all his "hip-swiveling" glory; favorite lyric: "if you can't find a partner, use a wooden chair."

James and the Giant Peach | 20 | - | 20 | 24 |

1996 | Directed by Henry Selick | Animated | 79 minutes | Rated PG

"Fantastic effects", a kinetic visual style and bushels of "charm" give this "quirky" cartoon a "different look from the typical animated movie"; the story of a boy and a house-size fruit, it blends "live-action" shots with animation, though the result is "too edgy" and "bizarre" for those who claim Roald Dahl's "book is much better."

Jane Eyre ◑ | 25 | 27 | 26 | 22 |

1944 | Directed by Robert Stevenson | With Orson Welles, Joan Fontaine, Margaret O'Brien | 97 minutes | Not Rated

A "moody rendition of the Brontë novel", this "damn good" Gothic romance concerns a "frail" governess, a rich landowner and a houseful of dark secrets; expect plenty of "gloom and doom from the get-go" followed by atmospheric "shadows" and "Orson scowling" throughout – but as for that "disappointingly contrived ending", blame the author, not Hollywood.

Jarhead   17 | 20 | 17 | 20

2005 | Directed by Sam Mendes | With Jake Gyllenhaal, Jamie Foxx, Peter Sarsgaard | 123 minutes | Rated R

"War isn't fun" in this "troublingly accurate depiction of what Marines experienced on their tour of duty" during the first Gulf War – i.e. "waiting" and "boredom" (it's "not a good movie for action"); as a "gung-ho enlistee", Gyllenhaal is "believable", but the "labored pace" and "meandering" plot makes it "surprisingly uninvolving" for many: a "movie about soldiers doing nothing isn't that interesting to watch."

☒ Jaws   26 | 22 | 25 | 26

1975 | Directed by Steven Spielberg | With Roy Scheider, Robert Shaw, Richard Dreyfuss | 124 minutes | Rated PG-13

"Sink your teeth" into this "classic summer" scarefest that "gets the adrenaline pumping", since it's got "everything": "horrifying shark attacks", "missing limbs", "crackling" John Williams music and even "fully developed characters"; it "launched the Spielberg juggernaut" by cleverly "making you fear what you don't see", and if the title character looks a bit dated today, the "seasick" wonder "will it ever be safe to go back in the water?"

Jean de Florette ☐   27 | 27 | 26 | 26

1987 | Directed by Claude Berri | With Yves Montand, Gérard Depardieu | 120 minutes | Rated PG

"As Balzacian as French cinema can get", this "epic" drama about farmers feuding over a natural spring in the "pastoral paradise of Provence" is "stunningly beautiful" and "totally compelling"; since it's only the "first half of a genuinely tragic tale", "make sure to see *Manon of the Spring*" (its sequel) afterward to get the full scope of this truly "unforgettable story."

Jeremiah Johnson   23 | 21 | 23 | 22

1972 | Directed by Sydney Pollack | With Robert Redford, Will Geer, Stefan Gierasch | 108 minutes | Rated PG

"One of the earliest Westerns to change the movie stereotypes of Indian ways", this saga relates the story of an American soldier turned "mountain man" and his pitched, emotional battle with Crow Nation warriors; a precursor of *Dances with Wolves*, it showcases Redford "at his best" and is a "classic" to true believers.

Jerk, The   22 | 21 | 19 | 18

1979 | Directed by Carl Reiner | With Steve Martin, Bernadette Peters, Catlin Adams | 94 minutes | Rated R

Starting out with "one of the best lines ever" – "I was born a poor black child" – this "absolutely hysterical" "rags-to-riches-to-rags" comedy captures the "wacky early Steve Martin" in all his "zany" glory (along with ample support provided by Peters as his "sweetly naive love interest"); some surveyors say it's "silly", but "that's exactly the point."

Jerry Maguire 21 | 22 | 21 | 20

1996 | Directed by Cameron Crowe | With Tom Cruise, Cuba Gooding Jr., Renée Zellweger, Jonathan Lipnicki | 138 minutes | Rated R

A "gutsy sports agent" "sees the light" and "rediscovers his soul" in this "crowd-pleasing" dramedy that blends "football and love" into an "honest", "better-than-average" brew; in the "tailor-made" title role, "Tom terrific" plays "Mr. Show Me the Money" with excellent backup from the Oscar-winning Gooding and "little kid" Lipnicki (who "steals the movie"); best line: "you had me at hello."

Jesus Christ Superstar 21 | 18 | 22 | 21

1973 | Directed by Norman Jewison | With Ted Neeley, Carl Anderson, Yvonne Elliman | 108 minutes | Rated G

"Old flower children" find religion in this "visually arresting" "rock opera", a "fantastic" depiction of "Christ's humanity" featuring "hottie" Neeley in the title role and possibly the "best Andrew Lloyd Webber score" ever; heretics say it's "overindulgent" and "not as good as the stage show", speculating that the "cast was stoned the entire time" and thus it all "made sense to them."

Jewel of the Nile, The 19 | 19 | 19 | 20

1985 | Directed by Lewis Teague | With Michael Douglas, Kathleen Turner, Danny DeVito | 106 minutes | Rated PG

Alternately "rugged and romantic", this sequel to *Romancing the Stone* features Douglas, Turner and DeVito reprising their roles as "adventure-seekers" on a misguided Arabian treasure hunt who "end up toppling a government"; as a "tongue-in-cheek romp" it's a "fun rental", but those who miss the "excitement of the original" grade it "more paste than jewel."

Jezebel ✉◑ 25 | 27 | 23 | 23

1938 | Directed by William Wyler | With Bette Davis, Henry Fonda, George Brent, Fay Bainter | 103 minutes | Not Rated

"Bette does *Gone with the Wind*" in this familiar-sounding "period piece" about an "obstinate Southern belle who defies a way of life about to be blown away"; the "melodramatic" plot may be a bit "over-baked", but Davis' Oscar-winning turn as a "most delicious bitch" is sheer "perfection"; most "legendary" moment: the "red dress scene."

JFK 19 | 20 | 20 | 21

1991 | Directed by Oliver Stone | With Kevin Costner, Kevin Bacon, Tommy Lee Jones, Gary Oldman | 189 minutes | Rated R

This "riveting", "revisionist" "conspiracy theory" drama about "what really happened on November 22, 1963" is, at the very least, a look at "what might have happened"; zealots swear it "makes a pretty good case" and delivers some "pull-out-all-the-stops" punches, but debunkers dub it "powerful paranoia" with "too many ifs, buts and maybes to be credible"; in the end, "whether truth or fiction", it remains as "controversial" as ever.

Johnny Guitar ∅ 19 | 20 | 18 | 19

1954 | Directed by Nicholas Ray | With Joan Crawford, Sterling Hayden, Mercedes McCambridge | 110 minutes | Not Rated

Think "Mildred Pierce in a cowboy hat" to get the gist of this "bizarre" Western rife with "sexual innuendo" and "Freudian overtones", courtesy of "tough-as-nails" saloonkeeper Crawford and her "tightly wound foil", land baron McCambridge; it may be the "strangest", "butchest" oater ever made, but for "camp" followers, it's "utterly fascinating" – and "unintentionally funny."

Journey to the Center of the Earth

| 19 | 16 | 21 | 18 |

1959 | Directed by Henry Levin | With James Mason, Pat Boone, Arlene Dahl | 132 minutes | Rated G

"Bernard Herrmann's score lends enchantment" to this very "enjoyable" production based on "Jules Verne's fantastical tale" of underground exploration that's a "fun" sci-fi "romp" worth seeking out in a "widescreen" format; sure, it's a tad "hokey", but kids like its "Disney-esque" flavor and "superior special effects."

Joy Luck Club, The

| 25 | 25 | 26 | 24 |

1993 | Directed by Wayne Wang | With Ming-Na Wen, Tamlyn Tomita, Lauren Tom, Rosalind Chao | 139 minutes | Rated R

Both an "intergenerational" drama and a "class-A weeper", this "evocative" rendering of Amy Tan's best-seller traces the "interwoven stories" of four Chinese women and their daughters with "complex insight"; admirers who identify with this "real look at family dynamics" that "transcends all cultures" declare it "a joy to watch."

Judgment at Nuremberg ⊠❶

| 26 | 27 | 25 | 22 |

1961 | Directed by Stanley Kramer | With Spencer Tracy, Burt Lancaster, Richard Widmark | 178 minutes | Not Rated

Based on the "historic" 1948 Nazi war criminal trials, this "excellent courtroom drama" "asks some tough questions" and boasts "uniformly fine" players "often cast against type", as well as a "brilliant", Oscar-winning script; though the issues it raises are "unsettling", it remains a "relevant flick that everyone should see."

Jules and Jim ❶🄵

| 24 | 26 | 24 | 23 |

1962 | Directed by François Truffaut | With Jeanne Moreau, Oskar Werner, Henri Serre | 100 minutes | Not Rated

One of the "milestones of the French New Wave", this charming "Truffaut masterpiece" is the "ultimate" "love triangle", wherein Moreau's "enigmatic beauty" makes her the "elusive muse" of two best friends; the "chemistry" between the players is "haunting and lyrical", and though that "bad-dream" ending is mighty "sad", the "fascinating story" proves "how complicated life can be."

Julia ⊠

| 25 | 27 | 25 | 24 |

1977 | Directed by Fred Zinnemann | With Jane Fonda, Vanessa Redgrave, Jason Robards | 118 minutes | Rated PG

"Fonda and Redgrave are radiant" in this "fascinating" drama, a "superb pairing of two actresses" cast as playwright Lillian Hellman and her "beloved childhood friend" Julia, a lefty resisting the Nazis in '30s Europe; fans applaud the "nervous" suspense and "moving" moments in this "frightening portrayal" of fraught times.

Juliet of the Spirits 🄵

| 25 | 26 | 22 | 26 |

1965 | Directed by Federico Fellini | With Giulietta Masina, Mario Pisu, Sandra Milo | 142 minutes | Not Rated

"Fellini's first color feature", this "dreamlike" tale is the story of an unhappy housewife who escapes her "dreary marriage" and slides into "fantasy" after a séance; it "still haunts" fans who dub it a "vivid" look at the power of "imagination", thanks to the performance of the director's "likable" real-life wife Masina, along with a "surrealistic platter" of "fascinating" character actors.

Jumanji
18 | 18 | 19 | 22

1995 | Directed by Joe Johnston | With Robin Williams, Bonnie Hunt, Kirsten Dunst | 104 minutes | Rated PG

"You'll see rolling dice in a whole different light" after a look at this "smartly done" adventure fantasy about a "mysterious board game" that swallows a young boy and coughs him up a quarter-century later – "along with a number of rampaging animals"; despite a "very cool concept" with "lots of action" and "loud CGI effects", it's "too scary for younger children" and ultimately might be a "better theme-park ride than movie."

Junebug
21 | 25 | 19 | 19

2005 | Directed by Phil Morrison | With Embeth Davidtz, Alessandro Nivola, Amy Adams | 106 minutes | Rated R

A "rural" North Carolina family welcomes home the "son who got away" and his new "Blue State" bride in this "sleeper" dramedy whose "excellent" ensemble cast – notably the "sensational" Adams – manages to produce a "vivid", "lovingly" realized "slice of Southern life"; for most, the "non-formulaic" storyline is a "quirky delight", though a few fret it "rambles around with no discernible point."

Jungle Book, The
24 | 21 | 25 | 24

1942 | Directed by Zoltan Korda | With Sabu, Joseph Calleia, Rosemary DeCamp | 109 minutes | Not Rated

Talk to the animals: this "great children's movie" is a picturesque take on the Kipling yarn of Mowgli, a lad reared by wolves who returns to village life only to face mercenary types hot on the scent of hidden riches; it's a wild eyeful of "classic" family fare that even outdoes "one of the best Disneys", the Mouse House's animated version made 25 years later.

Jungle Book, The
23 | - | 23 | 24

1967 | Directed by Wolfgang Reitherman | Animated | 78 minutes | Rated G

Kipling's "Tarzan-like character and all his friends" pop up in this "charming" Disney cartoon that "makes an impression" with a "crowd-pleasing" story full of "family fun"; it might not be the studio's "best animation", but its "enchanting" soundtrack has enough "delightful songs" to make for a thing of "pure joy."

Jurassic Park
22 | 16 | 22 | 27

1993 | Directed by Steven Spielberg | With Sam Neill, Laura Dern, Jeff Goldblum | 127 minutes | Rated PG-13

"Humans are upstaged by dinosaurs" in this sci-fi "thrill ride" from the "astounding" Spielberg set in an extinct-creatures-come-to-life theme park that's "every child's dream come true"; don't expect much from the "lame story" and "weak" actors (nothing more than "dinochow"), but hold on for "white-knuckle", "roller-coaster" pacing and "astounding special effects" so "truly frightening" that they "might scare younger viewers."

	OVERALL	ACTING	STORY	PROD.

Just Like Heaven
19 | 20 | 19 | 19

2005 | Directed by Mark Waters | With Reese Witherspoon, Mark Ruffalo | 95 minutes | Rated PG-13

A slice of "date movie" heaven comes with this "fluffy" romantic comedy, provided "you're willing to ride along" with its "offbeat premise": a "cynical" man hooking up with the disembodied "spirit of a woman"; "couch-cuddling" couples ignore the "cutesy" script's "predictability."

Karate Kid, The
19 | 16 | 20 | 17

1984 | Directed by John G. Avildsen | With Ralph Macchio, Pat Morita, Elisabeth Shue | 126 minutes | Rated PG

"*Rocky* for teenagers", this "classic" "underdog-wins-the-day story" matches a "kid finding it hard to fit in" with a martial-arts "mentor" who teaches him control through "discipline and loyalty"; balancing "solid values" with "doses of action", this "not-typical teen movie" has the "coming-of-age" thing down pat while being "inspiring" and "entertaining throughout."

Key Largo ◗
26 | 26 | 23 | 23

1948 | Directed by John Huston | With Humphrey Bogart, Edward G. Robinson, Lauren Bacall | 101 minutes | Not Rated

"Tough guys and dolls bring back the golden Warner Brothers days" in this "hard-hitting" noir showcase about a group held hostage by a "super-rat" of a gangster – until "anti-hero" Bogart shows up; near the "top of Huston's body of work", it features a "highly suspenseful" plot, "stellar performances" and some "vintage" Bogie and Bacall moments – "'nuff said."

Kid Stays in the Picture, The
21 | - | 22 | 20

2002 | Directed by Nanette Burstein, Brett Morgen | Documentary | 93 minutes | Rated R

The "rise and fall" of legendary producer/studio head Robert Evans (*Chinatown, The Godfather, Rosemary's Baby*) gets the big-screen treatment in this "stylish documentary", an "only-in-America story" that's "narrated by the subject himself"; although "self-congratulatory propaganda" to some, most find it a "fascinating", "inside" look at moviemaking – "if you can get past Evans' enormous ego", that is.

Kill Bill Vol. 1
23 | 22 | 21 | 25

2003 | Directed by Quentin Tarantino | With Uma Thurman, Lucy Liu, Vivica A. Fox, Sonny Chiba | 111 minutes | Rated R

"Violence and gore abound" in this "over-the-top", "occasionally ridiculous" first installment of Quentin Tarantino's two-part salute to "comic strips", "spaghetti westerns" and "grindhouse kung fu flicks"; starring a "butt-kicking" Uma as a "revenge"-seeking "killing machine", it's "not for everyone" what with all the "spurting blood", "flying limbs" and "gross sound effects", but thrill freaks purr its "adrenaline" rush is simply "cool as heck" – provided you "check your brains at the door" before viewing.

Kill Bill Vol. 2
25 | 24 | 24 | 26

2004 | Directed by Quentin Tarantino | With Uma Thurman, David Carradine, Michael Madsen, Daryl Hannah | 136 minutes | Rated R

A continuation that "improves upon the original", this "gentler cousin" of the "obscenely graphic" *Vol. 1* features "less red food coloring" and more "character development", while remaining a "wickedly referential" homage to martial arts movies; as the ever-vengeful assassin, Thurman still "burns bright" and despite "trademark" Tarantino dialogue that gets a bit "long-winded", fans say there's a "true heart beating at the center of all the fighting" that lends "emotional heft" to both parts.

Killers, The ◑   25 | 25 | 25 | 23

1946 | Directed by Robert Siodmak | With Burt Lancaster, Ava Gardner, Edmond O'Brien | 105 minutes | Not Rated

"Lancaster makes a powerful film debut" backed up by an "outstanding" Gardner in this "riveting" flick "expanded from the Hemingway short story" about a mysterious small-town murder and its aftermath; it gets to the "core of film noir" through a burbling mix of "moral ambiguity, sexual tension and crime."

Killing, The ◑   25 | 24 | 25 | 24

1956 | Directed by Stanley Kubrick | With Sterling Hayden, Coleen Gray, Elisha Cook Jr. | 85 minutes | Not Rated

"Long before Quentin Tarantino", this "hardened noir" from the "early Kubrick" elevated a "B-list cast" and "run-of-the-mill" racetrack robbery story into a "nail-biting knockout" that typifies "taut" pacing and "tough-guy" attitude; an "overlooked" but "influential" effort with a diced-up structure that's "ahead of its time", it's a killer calling card from "one of the masters."

Killing Fields, The   26 | 26 | 27 | 25

1984 | Directed by Roland Joffé | With Sam Waterston, Haing S. Ngor, John Malkovich | 141 minutes | Rated R

"Friendship is tested by war" in this "harrowing" true story "told through the eyes of a journalist" relating the "atrocities in Cambodia" and the "horrors of the Khmer Rouge" following the U.S. pullout from Vietnam; "worthy Oscar-winner Ngor" (a real-life survivor of this "holocaust") turns in an "honest" performance that "will move you to tears" and "make you think" a lot.

Kind Hearts and Coronets ◑   26 | 28 | 26 | 24

1949 | Directed by Robert Hamer | With Alec Guinness, Dennis Price, Valerie Hobson | 106 minutes | Not Rated

For "quintessential" "English humor" that "gets better with each viewing", check out this "matchless black comedy" about the disinherited scion of a noble family who tries to achieve dukedom through serial murder; in an inspired twist, his victims – all eight of them – are played by the one-and-only Alec Guinness, whose spot-on performance squarely places this one on the "forever best list."

King and I, The ✉   27 | 26 | 25 | 27

1956 | Directed by Walter Lang | With Yul Brynner, Deborah Kerr, Rita Moreno | 133 minutes | Rated G

The "'Shall We Dance' scene" alone is "worth the price of admission" to this regally "sumptuous" version of Rodgers and Hammerstein's "terrific, old-fashioned" Broadway musical; though it may be "historically inaccurate", "who cares?" given the "stunning production", "gorgeous score" and "totally engaging" team of the "lovely Kerr" "getting to know" Oscar-winner Brynner.

	OVERALL	ACTING	STORY	PROD.

King Kong ◑   25 | 15 | 24 | 24
1933 | Directed by Merian C. Cooper, Ernest B. Schoedsack | With Fay Wray, Robert Armstrong, Bruce Cabot | 100 minutes | Rated PG

This "granddaddy of all monster flicks" "still rules the roost" as an "essential piece of cinema history" and the inspiration for "countless" imitators; ok, the "stop-motion" special effects are "Stone Age stuff by today's standards", but this "warped beauty-and-the-beast saga" remains memorable for its "indelible" imagery, that iconic "climax atop the Empire State Building" and most of all for the "irreplaceable" Fay Wray, "filmdom's finest screamer."

King Kong   20 | 18 | 19 | 26
2005 | Directed by Peter Jackson | With Naomi Watts, Jack Black, Adrien Brody | 187 minutes | Rated PG-13

"Less would have been more" in this "bloated remake" of the '30s classic about a "big monkey coerced into show business" that many dub more "video game" than movie; though fans can't help but "love the big furball" and are awed by the "mega-bucks" production, "slow pacing" and endless "monkeying around before the inevitable climb up the Empire State Building" add up to one "way-too-long" flick; in sum, director Jackson should either "hire an editor" or "stick to Middle-Earth."

King of Comedy, The   23 | 26 | 23 | 21
1983 | Directed by Martin Scorsese | With Robert De Niro, Jerry Lewis, Sandra Bernhard | 101 minutes | Rated PG

"Sharp, insightful and totally original", this pitch-black comedy about a wannabe comedian and the talk-show host he stalks is a different kind of "De Niro psycho flick" that's "complex and unsettling"; as the stalkee, Lewis is both "funny and sad" ("maybe the French do know something"), and the picture is the "most underrated of Scorsese's career."

King of Hearts ▣   26 | 26 | 26 | 24
1967 | Directed by Philippe de Broca | With Alan Bates, Geneviève Bujold, Pierre Brasseur, Adolfo Celi | 100 minutes | Not Rated

One of the "best anti-war flicks", this "satiric" allegory tells of a WWI soldier's attempt to dismantle a bomb set in a village solely inhabited by "insane asylum inmates"; while some snort its "pacifist" message is too "simplistic" and "heavy-handed", more say this "cult classic" is a "thought-provoking" indictment of the "madness of war."

King Solomon's Mines   20 | 18 | 20 | 22
1950 | Directed by Compton Bennett, Andrew Marton | With Stewart Granger, Deborah Kerr | 103 minutes | Not Rated

"Location filming on the beautiful African continent" is the raison d'être of this H. Rider Haggard "chestnut" that's "hardly the most realistic" action flick, but a "good enough rendition" for most; it delivers some "romance" (via its "matinee idol" marquee names) and some "camp" (that "noble savages" subtext), but whether it's truly "Indiana Jones *before* Indiana Jones" is your call.

Kings Row ◑   22 | 20 | 22 | 21
1942 | Directed by Sam Wood | With Ann Sheridan, Robert Cummings, Ronald Reagan, Betty Field | 125 minutes | Not Rated

A "curiosity" that proves "Reagan could really act", this "dark" drama follows the "trials and tribulations" of folks in "small-town America" via a "predictable but well-done" chronicle of sundry amorous entanglements; even foes admit that the "soap opera" plot "keeps you interested", though for many the "only memorable thing" is the Great Communicator's most unforgettable line: "where's the rest of me?"

Kinky Boots
23 | 24 | 22 | 23

2006 | Directed by Julian Jarrold | With Joel Edgerton, Chiwetel Ejiofor | 107 minutes | Rated PG-13

There's "off-kilter British comedy" afoot in this "sweet, funny" story of a failing shoe manufacturer that hires a design-savvy transvestite to lift it up by the bootstraps; with a "little moralizing" about "tolerance" and a lot of "charming fluff", it delivers "quirky", "feel-good" fare "in the same vein as *The Full Monty*."

Kinsey
22 | 26 | 22 | 22

2004 | Directed by Bill Condon | With Liam Neeson, Laura Linney, Chris O'Donnell, Peter Sarsgaard | 118 minutes | Rated R

"Kinky", "controversial" sex therapist Alfred Kinsey is the subject of this "racy", "pulls-no-punches" biopic that details "how the sexual revolution started" as well as "how far we've progressed and how far we have to go"; Neeson is "arousing" and Linney ever the "acting goddess", but overall what's "provocative and poignant" to some is "sterile and congratulatory" to others; P.S. "don't watch it with your parents."

Kissing Jessica Stein
21 | 20 | 21 | 19

2001 | Directed by Charles Herman-Wurmfeld | With Jennifer Westfeldt, Heather Juergensen, Tovah Feldshuh | 97 minutes | Rated R

"Single women relate" to this "new-age chick flick", a "quirky romantic comedy" about a "funny, likable" gal "discouraged by the dating scene" who embarks on a lesbian affair; it's rendered in such a "sensitive" way that it "transcends moral objections" (i.e. it "won't offend your mother"), and even if "not profound", it's sure "sweet and solid."

Kiss Kiss Bang Bang
20 | 22 | 20 | 20

2005 | Directed by Shane Black | With Robert Downey Jr., Val Kilmer, Michelle Monaghan | 102 minutes | Rated R

This "tongue-in-cheek" film noir "send-up" is "fast, slick and darkly funny" thanks to a "twisted", "*Pulp Fiction*"-esque plot played at full tilt by an "on-the-money" cast, starting with the "superb" Downey as a thief-turned-thespian-turned-private eye on the loose in LA; loyalists lament "nobody saw this movie", while critics contend the whole enterprise is a bit "too impressed with itself."

Kiss Me Deadly ◐
24 | 20 | 23 | 21

1955 | Directed by Robert Aldrich | With Ralph Meeker, Albert Dekker, Paul Stewart, Marian Carr | 104 minutes | Not Rated

"Cold War propaganda has never been more frightening" than in this "mesmerizing" example of "classic film noir" rife with girls, guns and "cynicism", topped off with some "nuclear paranoia"; based on Mickey Spillane's lurid best-seller, it "bears repeat viewing" thanks to Aldrich's "superb direction", a "memorable ending" and that famous "suitcase", later "paid homage to in *Pulp Fiction*."

	OVERALL	ACTING	STORY	PROD.

Kiss Me Kate
`24` `21` `24` `25`

1953 | Directed by George Sidney | With Howard Keel, Kathryn Grayson, Ann Miller | 109 minutes | Not Rated

"Cole Porter's Broadway smash" gets the "Hollywood treatment" in this "sparkling film version" that's a reworking of "*The Taming of the Shrew*"; even though the "principals lack star power", you can still "brush up on your Shakespeare" nicely with "great musical numbers" and "exciting dancing", which come together famously in Miller's "knock-'em-dead" turn in 'Too Darn Hot.'

Kiss of Death ❶
`23` `24` `22` `22`

1947 | Directed by Henry Hathaway | With Victor Mature, Brian Donlevy, Richard Widmark, Coleen Gray | 98 minutes | Not Rated

A "decent ex-con" hoping to lead a straight life fends off a "very bad man" from his criminal past in this "classic" noir best remembered for Widmark's Oscar-nominated, big-screen debut as "chilling" hit man Tommy Udo ("you'll remember his cackle forever"); creepiest scene: when the "old lady in the wheelchair" meets her fate.

Kiss of the Spider Woman ✉Ø
`22` `25` `22` `21`

1985 | Directed by Hector Babenco | With William Hurt, Raul Julia, Sonia Braga | 120 minutes | Rated R

An "odd couple" – a political activist and a gay pederast – inhabit the same prison cell in this "intense drama" based on the Manuel Puig novel that deals with "love, corruption and redemption"; though "worth seeing" for its "moving" script and Hurt's Oscar-winning turn, it may be "too much" for mainstream audiences.

Klute ✉
`20` `23` `21` `19`

1971 | Directed by Alan J. Pakula | With Jane Fonda, Donald Sutherland, Roy Scheider | 114 minutes | Rated R

Oscar-winner Fonda stars as an "unhappy hooker" in this "heart-pounding" thriller, where she's "stalked by a killer" but protected by an "excellent" Sutherland as the cop who humanizes her; it "avoids all the clichés" of the genre via a chillingly matter-of-fact script, and if a bit "forgotten", at least Jane's shag "hairdo" is memorable.

Knife in the Water ❶🅵
`24` `23` `24` `22`

1963 | Directed by Roman Polanski | With Leon Niemczyk, Jolanta Umecka, Zygmunt Malanowicz | 94 minutes | Not Rated

Polanski's "breakthrough" movie achieves "suspense in a boat" via its story of a married couple who invite a hitchhiker along on their sailing expedition; despite a "small cast" and "obvious low budget", the "mesmerizing" result achieves "Hitchcock-level tension", no mean feat considering that it was the director's first feature.

Knight's Tale, A
`18` `17` `17` `20`

2001 | Directed by Brian Helgeland | With Heath Ledger, Rufus Sewell, Shannyn Sossamon, Paul Bettany | 132 minutes | Rated PG-13

A "man of humble birth" yearning to lance a lot schemes to become a tournament knight in this "inoffensive" medieval action comedy loosely based on Chaucer's *Canterbury Tales*; expect some boldly "modern" twists – namely that "'70s rock music" soundtrack – though what's "purposeful anachronism" to some strikes others as just "a bit silly."

K-Pax

OVERALL	ACTING	STORY	PROD.
16	21	18	17

2001 | Directed by Iain Softley | With Kevin Spacey, Jeff Bridges | 120 minutes | Rated PG-13

"Alien or human?" is the "perplexing" question at the heart of this sci-fi-inflected drama starring the "stellar" K-Spacey as a psych patient who claims to be an E.T. and "keeps you guessing" whether he's for real or "really mad"; it "starts off with potential" and has some "nice moments", but the ultimate diagnosis is "could have been more interesting."

Kramer vs. Kramer ✉

OVERALL	ACTING	STORY	PROD.
23	26	23	21

1979 | Directed by Robert Benton | With Dustin Hoffman, Meryl Streep, Justin Henry | 105 minutes | Rated PG

"All about the acting", this "riveting drama" won Oscars for Hoffman and Streep as a married couple undergoing the "trauma of divorce and child custody"; overturning the "gender-biased view of parenting", its depiction of a growing "father-son" bond is the core of the story, though its "heart-wrenching" theme "hits you hard" – "there are no winners" in this split-up.

Kung Fu Hustle 🄵

OVERALL	ACTING	STORY	PROD.
23	20	21	24

2005 | Directed by Stephen Chow | With Stephen Chow, Yuen Wah, Qiu Yuen | 95 minutes | Rated R

"Move over Jackie Chan!": this "wildly imaginative" piece of "chop-socky" merges "mind-boggling fight choreography" with "genre-blending" aplomb in its tale of "unlikely heroes" facing off against mobsters; its "spaghetti-western-meets-*Crouching-Tiger*"approach is equal parts "Bruce Lee, Wile E. Coyote and Quentin Tarantino", with a dash of "Bob Fosse" thrown in for good measure.

La Bamba

OVERALL	ACTING	STORY	PROD.
20	21	21	19

1987 | Directed by Luis Valdez | With Lou Diamond Phillips, Esai Morales, Rosanna DeSoto | 108 minutes | Rated PG-13

The "passionate" spirit of '50s Chicano rocker Ritchie Valens, whose "brief life" was "cut too short" by a tragic plane crash, "comes through strongly" in this "haunting" biopic; fronted by a "spot-on" Phillips, it also draws applause for exploring "immigrant family" themes, but ultimately it's the "fantastic *música* that will "touch your heart."

Labyrinth

OVERALL	ACTING	STORY	PROD.
22	19	22	23

1986 | Directed by Jim Henson | With David Bowie, Jennifer Connelly | 101 minutes | Rated PG

This "trippy" fairy tale from the "weird" mind of Muppetmaster Henson uses both puppets and live actors to tell its story of a young girl trying to rescue her kidnapped brother from an "evil" Goblin King; credit the "whimsical" blend of "out-there" visuals and "catchy" tunes crooned by the "magnetic" Bowie for its longstanding rep as one of the "most rewatchable movies" ever.

La Cage aux Folles 🄵

OVERALL	ACTING	STORY	PROD.
24	26	25	22

1979 | Directed by Edouard Molinaro | With Michel Serrault, Ugo Tognazzi, Remy Laurent | 100 minutes | Rated R

"Funnier than the American remake", the "Broadway musical" and the "two sequels", this "absurd" French farce is "light-years ahead of its time" telling the story of two gay blades forced to "play it straight" in order to impress prospective in-laws; "overacted to perfection" by a "unbeatable" cast, it defines flaming "frivolity", even if a few cluck it's become "a bit faded" with time.

ⓩ L.A. Confidential ✉ | 26 | 27 | 25 | 26 |
1997 | Directed by Curtis Hanson | With Kevin Spacey, Russell Crowe, Guy Pearce, Kim Basinger | 138 minutes | Rated R

"Every nuance is perfect" in this "steamy" period crime drama, an "explosive exposé" about "crooks, hookers" and "police corruption" in '50s LA that's "sharp", "detailed" and "violent as hell"; though it "made a star of Crowe", the overall "dead-on casting" advances the "case for an ensemble acting award", while the "smart", Oscar-winning script has "all the grit" of a "film noir" classic, boosted by "21st-century production values."

Ladder 49 | 19 | 21 | 19 | 22 |
2004 | Directed by Jay Russell | With Joaquin Phoenix, John Travolta | 115 minutes | Rated PG-13

"Hunky" Phoenix and Travolta suit up to battle blazes in this "stirring tribute to firefighters", which impresses with "frightening" inferno scenes and "tugs at the heartstrings" with its "introspective" looks at "camaraderie" and "sacrifice"; most feel its themes carry special "poignancy in post-9/11" times, though a few hose it for being a bit "predictable and corny."

La Dolce Vita ⓞⒻ | 25 | 25 | 23 | 25 |
1961 | Directed by Federico Fellini | With Marcello Mastroianni, Anita Ekberg, Anouk Aimée | 167 minutes | Not Rated

"Celebrity-obsessed culture" goes under the microscope in this "scandalous" study of "decadence", "damnation and redemption" as seen in '60s Rome through the eyes of a jaded gossip columnist (Mastroianni "at his best") fed up with the "sweet life"; arguably "Fellini's most famous" film, it's a "decidedly unglamorous look at glamour" that "introduced the word 'paparazzi'" into the world lexicon; most iconic scene: "Ekberg in the Trevi Fountain."

Lady and the Tramp | 26 | - | 24 | 25 |
1955 | Directed by Wilfred Jackson, Hamilton Luske, Clyde Geronimi | Animated | 75 minutes | Rated G

Puppy love gets a "gorgeous vintage Disney" spin in this "cute" canine romance awash in "lush animation" and lensed in "beautiful" CinemaScope; doggy devotees adore its fetching characters, "endearing story" and "great songs" ("highlighted by Peggy Lee's" sultry rendition of 'He's a Tramp'), though the most unforgettable moment has to be its "famous spaghetti kiss."

ⓩ Lady Eve, The ⓞ | 28 | 28 | 27 | 26 |
1941 | Directed by Preston Sturges | With Barbara Stanwyck, Henry Fonda, Charles Coburn | 97 minutes | Not Rated

"Steamy innuendo" and "wacky pratfalls" coexist in this "smart" Preston Sturges "romp" about a "scheming con artist" out to snare an "unsuspecting" "wealthy geek", aided by an "outstanding supporting cast" of "cardsharps"; a "sassy", "shameless" Stanwyck does "that sultry thing" so well that Fonda's "bumbling rube" "doesn't stand a chance" in this "slyly amusing" screwball comedy that many pronounce "perfect."

· Lady from Shanghai, The ◑

25 | 23 | 22 | 26

1948 | Directed by Orson Welles | With Orson Welles, Rita Hayworth, Everett Sloane | 87 minutes | Not Rated

"Another Orson Welles achievement", this "bravura" "B movie" is "completely enjoyable" for many, thanks to some memorable "stand-out scenes": the "shootout in the hall of mirrors", "Rita Hayworth speaking Chinese"; still, skeptics shrug the plot is a "confusing mess" that "looks like it's been cut to death."

Ladykillers, The

21 | 23 | 21 | 20

1956 | Directed by Alexander Mackendrick | With Alec Guinness, Cecil Parker, Peter Sellers, Katie Johnson | 97 minutes | Not Rated

"Inspired lunacy" from Britain's Ealing Studios, this "really funny" black comedy tells the story of a band of "incompetent" con artists planning a heist but "done in by a sweet little old lady"; the "marvel-ous" cast includes a "first-rate" Guinness and a "just-starting-out" Sellers, but many say the picture's "stolen" by Katie Johnson, who's a "brilliant foil" as the elderly dowager.

Ladykillers, The

15 | 19 | 16 | 18

2004 | Directed by Ethan Coen, Joel Coen | With Tom Hanks, Irma P. Hall, Marlon Wayans | 104 minutes | Rated R

"Trying to recapture the magic of *O Brother, Where Art Thou?*", the Coen brothers again head to the Deep South for this "flat" remake of the British black comedy that has some "good single laughs" but ulti-mately seems "another lame attempt by Hollywood to co-opt a classic film"; playing a "witty" if "uncharacteristically evil" con man, the "over-the-top" Hanks doesn't fare well either: despite a "great set of false teeth", he's "no Alec Guinness."

Lady Sings the Blues

22 | 23 | 23 | 23

1972 | Directed by Sidney J. Furie | With Diana Ross, Billy Dee Williams, Richard Pryor | 144 minutes | Rated R

"Sad yet real", this biography of songbird Billie Holiday moves to the tempo of the "commanding" Miss Ross' body-and-soul performance; following Lady Day from hard times to the big time to her "strung-out" decline, it "holds you from beginning to end", though for diva devotees it's Diana who's the "best part."

Lady Vanishes, The ◑

25 | 24 | 26 | 23

1938 | Directed by Alfred Hitchcock | With Margaret Lockwood, Michael Redgrave, Dame May Whitty | 97 minutes | Not Rated

A first-class ticket to "intrigue", this "crackerjack Hitchcock classic" finds the master at his "most fleet" and "fascinating", cooking up a "sublime combination" of the comic and the thrilling; its story of a strange disappearance on a train full of "memorable characters" is such "sheer entertainment" that even those who "know the ending" "never tire" of jumping back aboard.

La Femme Nikita 🄵

23 | 22 | 24 | 23

1991 | Directed by Luc Besson | With Anne Parillaud, Jean-Hugues Anglade, Jeanne Moreau | 115 minutes | Rated R

The "intelligent foreign film" gets a "violent jolt of adrenaline" in this "fast-paced", "thought-provoking" "tough chick" flick about a punk junkie turned pro assassin; as the "kick-ass" lead, the "mesmerizing

Parillaud performs "spectacular stunts" that "hold your attention" so completely that it's more than "worth the effort to read the subtitles."

Lara Croft: Tomb Raider
13 | 13 | 12 | 19

2001 | Directed by Simon West | With Angelina Jolie, Jon Voight, Iain Glen, Daniel Craig | 100 minutes | Rated PG-13

A "popular video game" character akin to a "female Indiana Jones" bungees onto the silver screen via this "slick" but "mindless" action vehicle for "eye-candy" queen Jolie; with "cool gadgets", "beautiful locales" and Angie's "great bodysuit" making up the "deluxe" visuals, seekers of "guilty viewing pleasure" shrug "who cares about story?"

Last Detail, The
22 | 26 | 22 | 19

1973 | Directed by Hal Ashby | With Jack Nicholson, Randy Quaid, Otis Young | 103 minutes | Rated R

"Pull up your socks" – this "accurate depiction of Navy life" (that includes plenty of "poetic cursing") details a young sailor's trip to a military prison, escorted by two enlisted men who decide to show him one last good time along the way; though "not a happy story", it's "well worth seeing" for a glimpse of an "early Jack" at "his most free-form."

Last Emperor, The ✉
26 | 24 | 25 | 28

1987 | Directed by Bernardo Bertolucci | With John Lone, Joan Chen, Peter O'Toole | 160 minutes | Rated PG-13

"Truly an epic, and a darned good one" at that, this "sweeping", "large-scale" bio tells the story of China's "final monarch" from his ascent to the throne at age three through war, occupation and "revolutionary changes" in his kingdom; credit "lavish" sets, "spectacular scenery" and "outstanding" acting by Lone and O'Toole for its winning an impressive "nine Academy Awards"; P.S. several versions exist, but all are on the "long" side.

Last King of Scotland, The ✉
25 | 29 | 24 | 25

2006 | Directed by Kevin Macdonald | With Forest Whitaker, James McAvoy, Kerry Washington, Gillian Anderson | 123 minutes | Rated R

"Perfectly capturing the charisma and paranoia" of Ugandan dictator Idi Amin, Whitaker's "transcendental", Oscar-winning performance is an "indelible achievement" that brings a "barbarous" chapter in African history to light; told from the perspective of a "fictionalized" doctor, it features several depictions of "gruesome" violence, including "one of the most horrific torture scenes ever."

Last Metro, The 🄵
24 | 25 | 23 | 23

1981 | Directed by François Truffaut | With Catherine Deneuve, Gérard Depardieu, Jean Poiret | 131 minutes | Rated PG

"Love and loyalty" are the underlying themes of this "wistful" tale of a French theatrical troupe staging a play in Nazi-occupied Paris; it's "vintage Truffaut" with "beautiful" work from the "haunting" Deneuve, and might work best as a "double bill with Day For Night", the same director's "tribute to movies and movie folk."

Last of the Mohicans, The
22 | 22 | 22 | 25

1992 | Directed by Michael Mann | With Daniel Day-Lewis, Madeleine Stowe, Russell Means | 122 minutes | Rated R

For a "realistic portrayal of the French and Indian War", this "historical adventure set in the battle-torn American colonies" doesn't stint on the "barbarism", though it's tempered by "beautiful scenery" and an "incredible score"; "evil villains and larger-than-life heroes" make for a "wonderful realization of James Fenimore Cooper's book."

L.A. Story
20 | 20 | 20 | 19

1991 | Directed by Mick Jackson | With Steve Martin, Victoria Tennant, Sarah Jessica Parker | 95 minutes | Rated PG-13

"Every LA stereotype is played for laughs" in this "on-point" romantic comedy that's a "biting" if "loving put-down" of the "outrageous city" where people "really do drive down the road to get the mail"; Martin's "effortlessly intelligent" script throws "wacky" curves – and foretells the Starbucks invasion with its priceless "half-caff-triple-shot-no-foam-cappuccino" scene.

Last Picture Show, The ❶
23 | 23 | 23 | 22

1971 | Directed by Peter Bogdanovich | With Timothy Bottoms, Jeff Bridges, Cybill Shepherd, Ben Johnson | 118 minutes | Rated R

This "gritty portrait of a small Texas town on the brink of extinction" is "stunningly realized" in Bogdanovich's "masterpiece" that captures the loss so well "you can practically hear the death rattle"; the "birthplace of many new stars", it features some mighty "raw performances" from its "marvelous ensemble", a "strong script" and ultra-"realistic production values"; in short, it's a "lovely" if "sad" tribute to "something intrinsically American."

La Strada ✉❶🎞
27 | 28 | 26 | 25

1956 | Directed by Federico Fellini | With Giulietta Masina, Anthony Quinn, Richard Basehart | 108 minutes | Not Rated

Set in a "traveling circus", Fellini's "parable of goodness thwarted by cruelty" pairs a "strongman who's all muscle and no heart" with a "peasant girl who's nothing but heart"; the "waiflike" Masina is "luminous" opposite a "surprisingly good" Quinn, and combined with "beautiful imagery" and "sad" "music that will stay with you", it's plain to see why this "masterwork" won the very first Best Foreign Film Oscar.

Last Samurai, The
23 | 23 | 22 | 27

2003 | Directed by Edward Zwick | With Tom Cruise, Ken Watanabe, Tony Goldwyn | 154 minutes | Rated R

"*Shogun*" meets "*Dances with Wolves*" in this "rousing" epic, wherein a haunted, "drunken Civil War vet" goes to feudal Japan to fight the samurai and is instead taken hostage by their "honor and spirit"; while Cruise garners an equivocal appraisal ("bang-up job" vs. "doesn't cut it"), "Watanabe wildly outshines him" as the "noble, betrayed" samurai leader; despite "slow pacing" and way "too much blood", this "clash of cultures" still swells with "sweeping vistas", "beautiful cinematography" and "amazing fight scenes."

Last Seduction, The
22 | 24 | 22 | 20

1994 | Directed by John Dahl | With Linda Fiorentino, Peter Berg, Bill Pullman | 110 minutes | Rated R

"Fiorentino sizzles" as a "bad"-to-the-bone "femme fatale" in this "deliciously wicked" neo-noir crime thriller about a "very sexy" gal who rips off her husband and takes cover with a love-struck doofus; sure, it's "low budget" and there may be more than a few "holes in the plot", but "man, what a ride!"

	OVERALL	ACTING	STORY	PROD.

Last Tango in Paris
17 | 20 | 15 | 19

1973 | Directed by Bernardo Bertolucci | With Marlon Brando, Maria Schneider | 129 minutes | Rated NC-17

Definitely not about dance lessons, this "evocative blend" of the "romantic" and the "erotic" presents a "graphically sexual" Parisian pas de deux between a "compelling" Brando and a limber Schneider; scenes that "seemed steamy then" may come off as "pointless" now, but Marlon's "at his best" "mumbling in two languages" and dreaming up "risqué" ways to "use butter."

Last Temptation of Christ, The
22 | 23 | 25 | 22

1988 | Directed by Martin Scorsese | With Willem Dafoe, Harvey Keitel, Barbara Hershey | 164 minutes | Rated R

"Controversial" with a big C, this "intriguing" drama "reexamines Christian faith" by portraying "one of the most humanizing perspectives on Jesus" ever filmed; of course, those "rigid on the Scriptures" consider it blasphemous (and it's still not available in certain video chains to this day), but believers say this "absorbing", "important" Scorsese drama must "be seen to be criticized."

Last Waltz, The
26 | - | 20 | 26

1978 | Directed by Martin Scorsese | Documentary | With The Band | 117 minutes | Rated PG

In the running for "best concert movie of all time", this renowned documentary "captures the end of a rock 'n' roll era" in its recording of The Band's last gasp, abetted by a musical "dream team" that includes, among others, Bob Dylan, Eric Clapton, Joni Mitchell, Muddy Waters, Neil Young and Van Morrison; it's "clearly a labor of love from Scorsese" that "shouldn't be this good, but it is."

Laura ◑
27 | 25 | 27 | 26

1944 | Directed by Otto Preminger | With Gene Tierney, Dana Andrews, Clifton Webb | 88 minutes | Not Rated

A "suspenseful, elegant whodunit with a twist" – the "detective falls in love with the murder victim" – this "chic" take on film noir provides plenty of "romantic goose bumps" owing to the simmering "chemistry" between the "brooding" Andrews and "exquisite" Tierney; throw in some "haunting music" and a "nicely paced" if somewhat "silly plot", and the result is "Preminger's best flick."

Laurel Canyon
18 | 24 | 17 | 20

2003 | Directed by Lisa Cholodenko | With Frances McDormand, Christian Bale, Kate Beckinsale | 103 minutes | Rated R

A "dysfunctional family" is dissected in this "quirky" drama pitting an "aging hippie" record producer against her "conservative" son, who's moved back in with her; the "radiant" McDormand "carries the film" as the "hot, smart" mama, though she's up against a "predictable", "unfulfilling" story that "doesn't quite come together."

Lavender Hill Mob, The ✉◑
25 | 26 | 23 | 22

1951 | Directed by Charles Crichton | With Alec Guinness, Stanley Holloway | 78 minutes | Not Rated

"Wittily whimsical", this British comic "gem" helped introduce Alec Guinness – an "actor's actor with the most expressive raised eyebrow in film" – to America; the caper-gone-awry story involving a milquetoast bank clerk who dreams up the "perfect crime" is "delightfully funny" thanks to its "wonderful" script.

L'Avventura 🌓🄵

| 24 | 23 | 22 | 25 |

1961 | Directed by Michelangelo Antonioni | With Gabriele Ferzetti, Monica Vitti, Lea Massari | 145 minutes | Not Rated

A real art-house "landmark" and one of "Antonioni's most accessible" films, this "minimalist masterwork" follows a jaded playboy as he hunts for his missing mistress on a Mediterranean isle; its "stark visual and intellectual" values are hailed as "revolutionary", though literalists wading through the "ennui" come up "baffled and confused."

🄯 Lawrence of Arabia ✉

| 29 | 28 | 27 | 29 |

1962 | Directed by David Lean | With Peter O'Toole, Omar Sharif, Alec Guinness | 222 minutes | Rated PG

The "biggest epic of them all", this bio of WWI British soldier T.E. Lawrence "sets the standard for large-scale filmmaking" with its "stunning" desert cinematography, "suspense by the duneful" and "stupendous cast", led by the "perfect" O'Toole; thanks to Lean's "painterly techniques", the "background is as consistently amazing as the foreground" in this "gold standard" of an Oscar magnet that "demands to be seen on the big screen."

League of Their Own, A

| 20 | 20 | 22 | 20 |

1992 | Directed by Penny Marshall | With Geena Davis, Tom Hanks, Madonna, Lori Petty, Rosie O'Donnell | 128 minutes | Rated PG

"There's no crying in baseball", though this "nostalgic gem" about a WWII women's team has fans praising its "fantastic" ensemble cast ("even Madonna is good"); "bringing back the innocence" of simpler times, this "piece of history" might have a "sentimental epilogue", but its "feel-good" aura makes it "highly rewatchable."

Leaving Las Vegas ✉

| 20 | 24 | 18 | 18 |

1995 | Directed by Mike Figgis | With Nicolas Cage, Elisabeth Shue, Julian Sands | 111 minutes | Rated R

"Disturbing" and "depressing", this "tragic love story" between a "suicidal alcoholic" and a "burned-out prostitute" is still "brilliant in all aspects", leaving viewers "emotionally drained"; while giddy fans agree the "damn good" Cage "deservedly won the Oscar" for his "best work thus far", soberer sorts call this "feel-bad" flick the "ultimate downer."

Legally Blonde

| 19 | 20 | 17 | 19 |

2001 | Directed by Robert Luketic | With Reese Witherspoon, Luke Wilson | 96 minutes | Rated PG-13

The near-unanimous verdict on this "*Clueless*-goes-to-law school" comedy: "cute-as-a-button" Witherspoon is "irresistible" as a "Valley Girl" "bursting the stereotype" and proving that "anyone can achieve their dream"; though most jurors decree that "even an intellectual can like" this "pink puffball of a movie", some say "there ought to be a law" against such "derivative piffle."

Legend

| 18 | 15 | 18 | 22 |

1986 | Directed by Ridley Scott | With Tom Cruise, Mia Sara, Tim Curry, David Bennent | 94 minutes | Rated PG

"Fantasy" fanatics adore this "mythical" tale of a quest to rescue an "innocent princess" and free the "last remaining unicorn" by a group of "bumbling elves" and a "forest boy"; while it's atmospheric enough to be a "guilty pleasure" for some, "dippy" dialogue makes it a "winner in the unintentional humor" department for others.

Legends of the Fall
20 | 21 | 20 | 23

1994 | Directed by Edward Zwick | With Brad Pitt, Anthony Hopkins, Aidan Quinn, Julia Ormond | 133 minutes | Rated R

This "sweeping epic" set in "untamed 19th-century America" chronicles "one family's struggle in times of political turmoil" and the "moving" story of a woman "tragically passed between three brothers"; sure, a few label it "pretentious" and "no threat to the best Westerns", but there are no complaints about the "fantastic scenery" – and "nothing beats Pitt riding in on that horse!"

Lemony Snicket's
A Series of Unfortunate Events
18 | 20 | 19 | 23

2004 | Directed by Brad Siberling | With Jim Carrey, Liam Aiken, Emily Browning | 107 minutes | Rated PG

Brimming with "visually pleasing" sets and costumes à la "Tim Burton", this "dark yet heartwarming" orphan tale is distilled from the popular children's book series; while the kid actors fit their parts "to a tee", super-"ham" Carrey's "scenery-devouring" turn as villainous Count Olaf splits surveyors: supporters say it's "overacting at its best" but foes fume it "drags the movie down."

Lenny ◑
24 | 27 | 23 | 21

1974 | Directed by Bob Fosse | With Dustin Hoffman, Valerie Perrine | 111 minutes | Rated R

"Blue comic" Lenny Bruce gets the Bob Fosse scrutiny in this "knockout", "ahead-of-its-time" biopic that's alternately "depressing and funny"; the amused applaud the "virtuoso" Hoffman, "excellent" Perrine ("who knew?") and "gritty" black-and-white cinematography that perfectly "captures the kind of seedy clubs" where the "self-destructive" comedian got his start.

Leopard, The 🇫
25 | 27 | 24 | 27

1963 | Directed by Luchino Visconti | With Burt Lancaster, Claudia Cardinale, Alain Delon | 187 minutes | Rated PG

"Historical sweep", "stunning visuals" and "personal reverie" combine in this "magnificent period piece" from Luchino Visconti, a "sumptuous" epic set in 19th-century Italy detailing the rise of Garibaldi and subsequent "decline of the aristocracy"; despite a "sluggish pace" and mixed marks for Lancaster's title turn as an Italian prince, "awesome" production values and the finale's "lauded" ballroom sequence make this one a "must-see" for cineasts.

Lethal Weapon
21 | 19 | 20 | 21

1987 | Directed by Richard Donner | With Mel Gibson, Danny Glover, Gary Busey | 112 minutes | Rated R

"Top-notch" action peppered with "plenty of laughs" establishes this "classic buddy" flick as the "first and best of the franchise" (three sequels and counting); as "hard-bitten, job-weary" LA detectives, Gibson and Glover are "at the top of their form" with such "tremendous chemistry" that the picture became the "model for '80s cop movies", a "classic" of the genre.

Letter, The ◐ ▽ 25 | 28 | 26 | 25

1940 | Directed by William Wyler | With Bette Davis, Herbert Marshall, Gale Sondergaard | 95 minutes | Not Rated

"Bette shines" as a cool customer in torrid British Malaya in this "superb" drama based on Somerset Maugham's story of a planter's wife who goes postal on her paramour; replete with "tinkling chimes and clouded full moons", the "exotic ambiance" lends "scary impact" to the proceedings, while Davis' "incredible" chops set the "standard for judging acting to this day."

☑ Letters from Iwo Jima 🅵 27 | 27 | 26 | 28

2006 | Directed by Clint Eastwood | With Ken Watanabe, Kazunari Ninomiya, Tsuyoshi Ihara | 141 minutes | Rated R

The "incomparable" Eastwood "brilliantly" bookends *Flags of Our Fathers* with this "eloquent" foreign-language epic, dubbed "one of the best WWII films ever" for its "humane" and ultimately "heartbreaking" depiction of the Japanese during their "doomed" final days on Iwo Jima; with the "fabulous" Watanabe leading an "outstanding" cast through "beautifully filmed" but "gruesome" battle scenes, this "remarkable achievement" dares to suggest that "we are all the same."

Letter to Three Wives, A ✉◐ 24 | 23 | 25 | 23

1949 | Directed by Joseph L. Mankiewicz | With Jeanne Crain, Linda Darnell, Ann Sothern, Kirk Douglas | 103 minutes | Not Rated

Three "country-club-set" women stuck on a boat trip "have an entire day to figure out" which one of their husbands "will be leaving town with the local seductress" in this "golden oldie" chick flick that "really takes you back"; Mankiewicz's "solid" script and direction both nabbed Academy Awards, leading some to label it the "witty precursor" to his later Oscar-winner, *All About Eve*.

Liar Liar 16 | 17 | 16 | 16

1997 | Directed by Tom Shadyac | With Jim Carrey, Maura Tierney, Justin Cooper | 87 minutes | Rated PG-13

Critics quibble over this "Carrey vehicle" about a lawyer compelled to tell the truth for 24 hours for the sake of his child; while some laud the star's "hilarious", "effective" performance shaded with some "poignant, non-hammy" moments, cynics nix the "not believable" (verging on "boring") story.

License to Kill 14 | 13 | 13 | 17

1989 | Directed by John Glen | With Timothy Dalton, Carey Lowell, Robert Davi, Talisa Soto | 133 minutes | Rated PG-13

Dalton's second turn as 007 is also "thankfully his last" as this "grim" Bonder bucks the franchise formula to show the normally suave spy "losing his cool" and going on a mission to "get even" with a drug lord; the violence is "too graphic" and the tone overly "mean spirited" gripe critics who lament "there's no fun in this one."

Life Aquatic with Steve Zissou, The 16 | 19 | 14 | 19

2004 | Directed by Wes Anderson | With Bill Murray, Owen Wilson, Cate Blanchett, Anjelica Huston | 119 minutes | Rated R

"Quirk"-meister Anderson captains this "esoteric" undersea "parody of Jacques Cousteau" (and *Moby Dick*") that's awash in "droll" humor, "visual candy" and "great actors", chiefly the "brilliant" Murray; all

	OVERALL	ACTING	STORY	PROD.

told, what's "imaginative filmmaking" to some feels like "flat" "self-in-dulgence" to a majority who can't fathom "what all the fuss is about."

Lifeboat ◑

	25	26	25	22

1944 | Directed by Alfred Hitchcock | With Tallulah Bankhead, William Bendix, Walter Slezak | 96 minutes | Not Rated

"Can a one-set movie hold your attention?": this "fascinating Hitchcock" war-era thriller does, providing "more drama per square inch", since the "entire picture takes place in a small lifeboat"; among the "bickering crew of castaways", Bankhead is "superb, dahling", but blink and you'll miss the director's "inspired" cameo.

Life Is Beautiful ✉🄵

	27	27	27	25

1998 | Directed by Roberto Benigni | With Roberto Benigni, Nicoletta Braschi | 118 minutes | Rated PG-13

Simultaneously "heart-wrenching" and "uplifting", this story about an Italian family's attempt to shelter their son from the Holocaust is a "bittersweet fable about the triumph of the human spirit"; Oscar-winner Benigni provides an "emotional roller-coaster ride" with some "inspired comedic" touches, and though some "uncomfortable" viewers suggest a "trivialization" of a very serious subject, most agree "if you don't shed a tear, you're not human."

Life of Brian

	23	21	23	20

1979 | Directed by Terry Jones | With Monty Python | 94 minutes | Rated R

"Profane, sacrilegious and really funny", this "hysterical" "cult classic" about a Holy Land sad sack mistaken for the Messiah is "as bitingly original as has ever been made" and "probably one of God's favorites"; only "Monty Python at their finest" could "get away with" the final scene that "sends you off singing 'Always Look on the Bright Side of Life.'"

Life of David Gale

	21	24	22	20

2003 | Directed by Alan Parker | With Kevin Spacey, Kate Winslet, Laura Linney | 130 minutes | Rated R

Expect a "great shocker at the end" of this "compelling" capital punishment drama, "but getting there has some pretty dull moments"; "surprised" surveyors "love the twists and turns", while those who "figured things out ahead of time" find the story "predictable" and "contrived", but "interesting nonetheless."

Like Water for Chocolate 🄵

	25	24	25	25

1993 | Directed by Alfonso Arau | With Lumi Cavazos, Marco Leonardi | 123 minutes | Rated R

"Ahh, food and sex" make a "lip-smacking" combination in this "mouthwatering" Mexican "foodie classic" that serves up an "eccentric" love story that's "as pleasing to the eye as it is to the palate"; "deliciously true to the novel", it offers "magical realism at its best" and, "like a warm dessert", leaves one feeling so "content and hopeful" that many show up for "another helping."

Lili ∅

	24	24	23	24

1953 | Directed by Charles Walters | With Leslie Caron, Mel Ferrer, Jean-Pierre Aumont | 81 minutes | Rated G

Walking a tightrope between "deep whimsy" and "endearing" drama, this ringside look at an "innocent" orphan follows "ultimate waif"

Caron as she joins the circus; enlivened by "one song" and some occasional dancing, the story is almost "too cute", but an "outstanding" cast ensures it will "turn on the tears every time."

Lilies of the Field ✉️◗   25 | 26 | 24 | 23

1963 | Directed by Ralph Nelson | With Sidney Poitier, Lilia Skala, Stanley Adams | 94 minutes | Not Rated

With his "flawless" performance in this "quiet, simple" tale about a handyman who helps refugee nuns build a chapel, Poitier became the first African-American to win a lead-role Oscar and also helped "open up racial dialogue" in the Civil Rights era; the film's many admirers hail a "sweet story" told with "heart and charm" that delivers a "lesson in dignity and trust."

Lilo & Stitch   23 | - | 22 | 24

2002 | Directed by Chris Sanders, Dean DeBlois | Animated | 85 minutes | Rated PG

"Different from the usual Disney stuff", this "adorable" animated tale features a "spunky" orphaned Hawaiian girl who adopts a "lovable" blue 'dog' that turns out to be a space alien; it's a "heartwarming story" with "great life lessons" about "love", the "meaning of family" and "finding your place in the world", as well as "laughs from beginning to end" and an Elvis-infused soundtrack; "beautiful watercolor backdrops" give the film its "distinctive look."

Limelight ◗   24 | 25 | 22 | 23

1952 | Directed by Charles Chaplin | With Charles Chaplin, Claire Bloom, Buster Keaton, Nigel Bruce | 137 minutes | Rated G

"Chaplin's last great film", this "poignant" look at a British ballerina and a music hall clown draws mixed responses; foes call it "dated corn" and protest its "overstated" "self-indulgence", but fans counter it's "sensitive" stuff, and certainly worth watching to see "two giants of the silent film era [Charlie and Buster Keaton] on-screen together."

▣ Lion in Winter, The ✉️   28 | 29 | 27 | 26

1968 | Directed by Anthony Harvey | With Peter O'Toole, Katharine Hepburn | 134 minutes | Rated PG

Hepburn and O'Toole give "performances so brilliant your eyes will hurt" as "two titans battling each other and history" in this "intelligent, delicious" drama that reigns as "one of the best historical films ever made"; indeed, this "masterful" look at Henry II and Eleanor of Aquitaine (the original "dysfunctional royal family") is so "superb" that it earned Kate her third Oscar, as well as statuettes for its "sparkling" screenplay and score.

Lion King, The   25 | - | 25 | 27

1994 | Directed by Roger Allers, Rob Minkoff | Animated | 89 minutes | Rated G

Hakuna Matata!: this "crowning achievement" garners roars of approval as one of "Disney's best" thanks to its "breakthrough animation techniques", "toe-tapping" music and "exceptional voice characterizations by Matthew Broderick and Jeremy Irons"; though this "heartwarming" tale about an exiled lion cub (sort of the "same story as *Bambi*") is "touching" and often "comedic", the film has some bona fide "scary moments" and "may be too intense" for smaller fry.

	OVERALL	ACTING	STORY	PROD.

Little Big Man
24 | 25 | 24 | 23

1970 | Directed by Arthur Penn | With Dustin Hoffman, Faye Dunaway, Chief Dan George | 147 minutes | Rated PG

A "rousing" Wild West "saga", this "memorable period piece" concerns a "Forrest Gump–like" character with a knack for popping up at "famous historical moments"; plaudits go to its "engrossing blend of humor and drama" and "great" performances by George and Hoffman ("truly the man of 1,000 faces") – indeed, it's "one of the best looks at Native Americans" ever portrayed in moviedom.

Little Caesar ◐
24 | 26 | 23 | 22

1931 | Directed by Mervyn LeRoy | With Edward G. Robinson, Douglas Fairbanks Jr., Glenda Farrell | 79 minutes | Not Rated

"Crime doesn't pay" in this "seminal" gangster flicker, a "fictionalized" version of the Al Capone story starring "true Hollywood tough guy" Robinson, who brings some "Greek tragedy" to the role of a "moiderous bum" on the way up ("Tony Soprano, eat your heart out"); it's a "gritty", "fast-paced" ride that's best remembered for its immortal last line: "mother of mercy, is this the end of Rico?"

Little Children
24 | 27 | 23 | 23

2006 | Directed by Todd Field | With Kate Winslet, Patrick Wilson, Jennifer Connelly, Jackie Earle Haley | 130 minutes | Rated R

"Brilliant" Winslet and "easy-on-the-eyes" Wilson play "desperate" stay-at-home parents consumed by "forbidden attraction" in this "American Beauty"–esque study of suburban "infidelity" and "discontent"; though a "pedophilia" subplot adds a decidedly "dark" touch, Haley's "standout" supporting turn as a "creepy sex offender you actually feel bad for" drives home the picture's "powerful message about the consequences of your actions."

Little Foxes, The ◑
26 | 28 | 26 | 25

1941 | Directed by William Wyler | With Bette Davis, Herbert Marshall, Teresa Wright, Dan Duryea | 116 minutes | Not Rated

All the "power" of Lillian Hellman's "bitter little" stage drama is apparent in this "excellent" film adaptation via William Wyler, a showcase for "Bette at her bitchy best" as the mercenary missus in a shifty Southern family; the sly scheming and deadly betrayal make for a bang-up "lesson in acting."

Little Mermaid, The
24 | - | 23 | 25

1989 | Directed by Ron Clements, John Musker | Animated | 82 minutes | Rated G

This "first of the great second wave of Disney classics" manages to "hold its own against Cinderella and Snow White", what with its delightful cartoon "critters", "witty dialogue" and "upbeat", Oscar-winning music that "made animation sing again"; sure, feminists discern a "sexist message" ("why does the woman have to change for the man?"), but in the end "how could you not love this adorable redheaded mermaid?"

Little Miss Sunshine ✉
24 | 26 | 24 | 23

2006 | Directed by Jonathan Dayton, Valerie Faris | With Abigail Breslin, Greg Kinnear, Steve Carell, Toni Collette, Alan Arkin | 101 minutes | Rated R

"Wackiness" abounds when a "totally dysfunctional family" hops aboard a sputtering VW van en route to a beauty pageant in this "hilarious" but "dark"-edged road-trip comedy that's akin to an "indie version of *National Lampoon's Vacation*"; harnessing the talents of a "fine" ensemble cast – Carell is "fabulous", Breslin a "real find" and Arkin a "foul-mouthed treasure" – it's topped off with a "memorable" dance sequence that will "leave you squirming in your seat."

Little Princess, A
24 | 22 | 25 | 25

1995 | Directed by Alfonso Cuarón | With Liesel Matthews, Eleanor Bron | 97 minutes | Rated G

"Shirley Temple's version has nothing on" this "sumptuous", "perfectly played" family fable of a "pampered" boarding-school lass with "mystical" leanings who goes from "riches to rags and back" after her dragoon dad is declared dead during WWI; though it attracts less than the "attention it deserves", loyalists label it a "top-flight tearjerker."

Little Shop of Horrors
19 | 19 | 20 | 21

1986 | Directed by Frank Oz | With Rick Moranis, Ellen Greene, Steve Martin | 94 minutes | Rated PG-13

If "campy" "sci-fi musicals" ring your bell, this "twisted" tale about a boy, a girl and a "smart-ass, man-eating plant" (based on an old Roger Corman B-movie) "ranks right up there with *The Rocky Horror Picture Show* as a cult classic"; credit the "great cast" and "humorously dark score" for the ensuing "goofy fun"; most "priceless" moment: Martin's "sadistic dentist" treating "masochist patient" Bill Murray.

Little Women
21 | 23 | 24 | 21

1994 | Directed by Gillian Armstrong | With Winona Ryder, Susan Sarandon | 115 minutes | Rated PG

Surveyors are split on this "feminist" adaptation of Louisa May Alcott's classic novel about a Civil War–era family: partisans of George Cukor's 1933 version dismiss this remake as "unnecessary", harrumphing that "Ryder can't compare to Katharine Hepburn", yet others swear it's "worth watching" for Sarandon's performance alone; there's no debate, however, that its "great message" – about a "family loving each other no matter what" – is "very well done."

Live and Let Die
19 | 17 | 20 | 21

1973 | Directed by Guy Hamilton | With Roger Moore, Jane Seymour, Yaphet Kotto | 119 minutes | Rated PG

Expect "beautiful women, fast cars", "snakes, voodoo and Yaphet Kotto" in this "exotic" James Bond caper set in the Caribbean and the "sultry South"; "nonstop" action sequences ("particularly the bayou boat chase"), "humor that's shaken (not stirred)" and Moore's first 007 impersonation make it worth watching – even if Sean Connery loyalists label it the "beginning of the decline."

☑ Lives of Others, The ✉🅕
28 | 28 | 28 | 27

2007 | Directed by Florian Henckel von Donnersmarck | With Ulrich Mühe, Martina Gedeck, Sebastian Koch | 137 minutes | Rated R

A "fascinating yet chilling" peek "behind the Iron Curtain", this "near-perfect" drama exhibits the "stifling of artistic expression" in "pre-glasnost" East Germany, a "real-life police state" where "Big Brother" is always "listening in"; winner of the Oscar for Best Foreign Language Film, it features a "universally excellent" cast and its "suspenseful" script, highlighting the "best and worst of humanity", "keeps you guessing until the last scene."

Living Daylights, The
14 | 14 | 14 | 18

1987 | Directed by John Glen | With Timothy Dalton, Maryam d'Abo, Jeroen Krabbé, Joe Don Baker | 130 minutes | Rated PG

There's heated debate about Timothy Dalton's first stab at James Bond, with fans saying his "underrated", "hard-edged" performance is "very true to Ian Fleming", while foes fume his "brooding", "gritty" take does the character a "disservice" (007 "doesn't have to be politically correct"); as for the plot, it's the usual over-the-top thrill ride involving a defecting Russian general, an American arms dealer and a drop-dead gorgeous cellist/assassin.

Local Hero
26 | 24 | 26 | 23

1983 | Directed by Bill Forsyth | With Burt Lancaster, Peter Riegert, Peter Capaldi | 111 minutes | Rated PG

"The little people triumph over the money people" in this "understated but brilliant" comedy contrasting the differences between a "quaint Scottish town" and the "corporate world"; its "engaging characters", "quirky" storyline and Mark Knopfler's "great soundtrack" make for such "bighearted", "whimsical" fun that many argue it "deserves a larger following."

Lock, Stock and Two Smoking Barrels
23 | 22 | 25 | 23

1998 | Directed by Guy Ritchie | With Jason Flemyng, Dexter Fletcher, Nick Moran | 105 minutes | Rated R

"First-time director" Ritchie does a "brilliant job co-opting every gangster flick cliché" in this "violent but riveting" thriller that's a "Cockney" take on *Pulp Fiction*; agreed, it's "hard to understand the accents", but the "acting, setting and soundtrack are dead-on" and "super plot surprises" abound; all in all, this "fun romp with guns" is "lean", mean and "wonderfully produced."

Lolita ◑
24 | 24 | 24 | 23

1962 | Directed by Stanley Kubrick | With James Mason, Sue Lyon, Shelley Winters, Peter Sellers | 152 minutes | Not Rated

Though this "fine adaptation of the Nabokov classic" might be somewhat "sanitized" ("it was made in 1962, after all"), it's still "slyly dirty" enough for its very adult subject, a middle-aged man's obsession with a barely teenaged girl; though ageists argue Lyon is "too old" for the title role, there still are plenty of "choice moments" supplied by an "extremely funny" Sellers and Winters, who "gives the performance of her life."

Lone Star
25 | 25 | 25 | 22

1996 | Directed by John Sayles | With Kris Kristofferson, Matthew McConaughey, Chris Cooper | 135 minutes | Rated R

Director Sayles' "overlooked masterpiece" is a "flawless murder mystery that digs deep into the American psyche" and "takes a hard look at race relations"; following the discovery of a buried skeleton in a small Texas town, the plot goes through "more twists and turns than the Rio Grande" but still "works on multiple levels" as it "seamlessly interweaves multiple characters" – and that "ending will make your jaw drop."

| | OVERALL | ACTING | STORY | PROD. |

Longest Day, The ◐
24 | 20 | 25 | 26

1962 | Directed by Ken Annakin, Andrew Marton et al | With John Wayne, Rod Steiger | 180 minutes | Rated G

As far as "war-as-spectacle" epics go, this "sweeping" saga of the Normandy invasion sets the "standard by which all others are measured"; D-day devotees dig the "superb dedication to detail" and "all-star cast" that "really gets into their characters" thanks to a script that "includes the point of view of everyone involved"; still, foes snipe "too many cameos" turn it into a "cattle call."

Longest Yard, The
17 | 15 | 18 | 16

1974 | Directed by Robert Aldrich | With Burt Reynolds, Eddie Albert, Michael Conrad | 121 minutes | Rated R

A "guy's movie" Hall of Famer, this "prison football comedy" stars Reynolds as a pro quarterback sent to the big house only to "lead a Heisman-quality cast" of roughneck convicts in a game against the guards; scoring many "memorable lines", it has "Mean Machine" mavens ruling it "arguably the best" pigskin pic ever.

Longest Yard, The
17 | 16 | 17 | 18

2005 | Directed by Peter Segal | With Adam Sandler, Chris Rock, Burt Reynolds, Nelly | 113 minutes | Rated PG-13

A "decent remake of an already good film", this "mildly amusing" sports comedy about a prison football team "rehashes" the original, adding a "more modern soundtrack" and "cameos galore"; still, foes fret this "formulaic" flick "fumbles on every level", starting with Sandler, who's "unbelievable as a quarterback" – "once a waterboy, always a waterboy."

Longtime Companion
23 | 25 | 25 | 21

1990 | Directed by Norman René | With Campbell Scott, Mary-Louise Parker, Bruce Davison | 100 minutes | Rated R

"Love and heartbreak" are the themes of this "groundbreaking" film that follows seven gay men throughout a "specific time and place": '80s Manhattan during the "first wave of AIDS"; "just as devastating today as when first released", it "gives legitimacy" to a former "forbidden subject" but "doesn't pander or trivialize the issues" thanks to the "heartfelt performances", notably the "standout" Davison and "up-and-coming" Parker.

Looking for Mr. Goodbar ∅
18 | 21 | 19 | 18

1977 | Directed by Richard Brooks | With Diane Keaton, Tuesday Weld, Richard Gere | 135 minutes | Rated R

Powered by Keaton's "brilliant" turn as a "sexually repressed" teacher by day who "trolls the bars by night", this "sobering tale of '70s promiscuity" is a "dark primer for single women" that "sends chills down your spine" – with a "gruesome ending" delivered "like a sledgehammer upside the head."

Lord of the Flies ◐
23 | 21 | 25 | 20

1963 | Directed by Peter Brook | With James Aubrey, Tom Chapin, Hugh Edwards | 90 minutes | Not Rated

The last word in youth gone wild, this "powerful" take on novelist William Golding's "modern classic" finds a pack of marooned British schoolboys slipping into "disturbing" behavior as barbarity overtakes breeding; the "realistic" style makes for an "unsettling" drama with bonus "social commentary buried within", though some savage the "incompetent acting" and sniff "read the book instead."

Lord of the Rings, The
15 | - | 22 | 16

1978 | Directed by Ralph Bakshi | Animated | 132 minutes | Rated PG
Graphics guru Bakshi's animated take on Tolkien is no "Fritz the Hobbit": it's "true to the books" in presenting the elfin Frodo's "epic" face-off with the forces of evil (even if it's "too bad" the "truncated storyline" "breaks off halfway" into the trilogy); but others say that this "muddled" "travesty" often "looks ridiculous" – "thank God for Peter Jackson."

☑ Lord of the Rings: The Fellowship of the Ring
27 | 25 | 27 | 29

2001 | Directed by Peter Jackson | With Elijah Wood, Ian McKellen, Viggo Mortensen, Sean Astin, Liv Tyler | 178 minutes | Rated PG-13
This "enthralling", "true-to-the-book" retelling of Tolkien's classic epic "transcends the genre" and "sets the benchmark for fantasy films to come" with its "lovingly crafted" visualization of Middle Earth; despite a somewhat "slow beginning", "three hours of brilliant bliss" ensue that are "exhilaratingly" perfect, "right down to the hairy Hobbit feet."

☑ Lord of the Rings: The Return of the King ✉
28 | 26 | 27 | 29

2003 | Directed by Peter Jackson | With Elijah Wood, Ian McKellen, Viggo Mortensen, Sean Astin, Liv Tyler | 201 minutes | Rated PG-13
Jackson "should be knighted" for this "history-making", Oscar-grabbing finale to the "superlative trilogy", a "paean to the goodness of good" in the Fellowship's "united allegiance against evil"; it "lives up to the hoopla" from its two "faithfully rendered" predecessors thanks to "mythic sweep and grandeur" and a "cast obviously devoted to the picture"; in sum, this "masterpiece" is a "cinematic monument" to Tolkien's original fantasy, capped by a "long ending" that nonetheless draws a "big round of applause."

☑ Lord of the Rings: The Two Towers
27 | 25 | 26 | 29

2002 | Directed by Peter Jackson | With Elijah Wood, Ian McKellen, Viggo Mortensen, Sean Astin, Liv Tyler | 179 minutes | Rated PG-13
There's "much less exposition" and much "more testosterone" in the second "gripping" installment of the Tolkien trilogy, which "starts right where the last one ended"; grab a "comfortable chair" and brace yourself for three hours of "flawless special effects" ("Gollum rocks"), "wonderful" acting by "hot guys", "epic battles the likes of which have never before been captured on celluloid" and an "amazing storyline" that really "does justice" to the book.

Lost Highway
16 | 18 | 15 | 19

1997 | Directed by David Lynch | With Bill Pullman, Patricia Arquette, Balthazar Getty | 135 minutes | Rated R
"Something different with a capital D", this "stylish nightmare" from David Lynch relates the "surreal" story of a husband's "journey into madness and jealousy"; hard-core fans find it "beautifully shot" and "totally addictive", but most everyone else says the "convoluted", "weird-with-a-side-dish-of-weird" plot "doesn't make a bit of sense."

| | OVERALL | ACTING | STORY | PROD. |

Lost Horizon ◐
25 | 24 | 26 | 22

1937 | Directed by Frank Capra | With Ronald Colman, Jane Wyatt, Margo, Sam Jaffe | 138 minutes | Not Rated

A "nostalgic reminder of Hollywood's Golden Age", this "moving" adaptation of James Hilton's best-seller still "casts a spell" thanks to an "irresistible" conceit, the utopia known as "Shangri-la"; sure, this "fairy tale" of a picture may seem rather "quaint" and "dated" now, but Colman's performance is "as contemporary as if it were made today."

Lost in America
20 | 20 | 21 | 17

1985 | Directed by Albert Brooks | With Albert Brooks, Julie Hagerty, Garry Marshall | 91 minutes | Rated R

Brooks' "seriously underrated" satire about a yuppie couple who chuck it all and hit the road is dryly "hilarious" filmmaking boasting what may be the "funniest first 45 minutes in movie history"; though a few lost souls protest the "premise doesn't quite get there", the majority reports the "situations, characters and jokes are all in sync."

Lost in Translation ✉
21 | 24 | 19 | 21

2003 | Directed by Sofia Coppola | With Bill Murray, Scarlett Johansson | 102 minutes | Rated R

"Not much happens" in this "poignant" look at a young woman and a "has-been" movie star who meet out of "boredom and insomnia" in a Tokyo hotel; admirers say it's "eminently watchable" thanks to "talented" writer/director Coppola (it must "run in the family") as well as the "surprising chemistry" between the "world-weary" Murray and "enigmatic" Johansson; still, "baffled" viewers want to know "what the hoopla is all about" – and especially "what he whispers at the end"; best scene: the "Suntory commercial."

Lost Weekend, The ✉◐
25 | 27 | 24 | 22

1945 | Directed by Billy Wilder | With Ray Milland, Jane Wyman, Phillip Terry | 101 minutes | Not Rated

"Strong" stuff served neat, this "smart", sobering drama depicts the "terrifying inner world" of an alcoholic who "lives only" for the bottle, starring Milland in a "top-shelf", Oscar-winning turn as a barfly on a bender careening from double bourbons to detox to the d.t.'s; some maintain it "should be required viewing" at AA meetings – it's the "scariest movie of all time if you drink."

Love Actually
22 | 23 | 21 | 22

2003 | Directed by Richard Curtis | With Hugh Grant, Liam Neeson, Colin Firth, Laura Linney, Emma Thompson, Alan Rickman, Keira Knightley, Bill Nighy | 135 minutes | Rated R

"Intertwining" vignettes of lovesick Londoners meeting up "cute" and breaking up "sad" form the core of this "walk-away-smiling" romantic comedy; while Brit chick flick fans are "delighted" by the "great ensemble" with a nod to the "charming" Grant, those finding it "not that good actually" zap its "saccharine" script as barely "tolerable fluff."

Love Bug, The
18 | 15 | 16 | 17

1969 | Directed by Robert Stevenson | With Dean Jones, Michele Lee, Buddy Hackett | 107 minutes | Rated G

"They don't get much sillier" than this "imaginative" Disney "oldie" about Herbie, a "sweet"-talking VW bug that supplies boomers with plenty of "fond memories"; it still "stands the test of time" well enough for it to be a perennial "rainy-afternoon" rental.

Love in the Afternoon ◐ | 24 | 25 | 21 | 22 |

1957 | Directed by Billy Wilder | With Gary Cooper, Audrey Hepburn, Maurice Chevalier | 130 minutes | Not Rated

An "old-fashioned" romance set in "misty" Paree, this "witty" Wilder "treat" stars Coop as an "American playboy" who goes "mad with desire" for the much-younger Hepburn; if the "age difference" between the "odd couple" might seem "unspannable", the "bright cast" shows lots of "chemistry" – "isn't love grand?"

Love Is a Many-Splendored Thing | 22 | 23 | 22 | 21 |

1955 | Directed by Henry King | With Jennifer Jones, William Holden | 102 minutes | Not Rated

"What drama! what heartbreak!" sigh admirers of this "classic" romantic "tearjerker", an "ahead-of-its-time" tale about an affair between a "liberated" Eurasian woman and a conflicted American war correspondent; ok, it's a little "soppy" and "Jones isn't believable as a Eurasian", but the "breathtaking" Hong Kong scenery and "memorable", Oscar-winning theme song "make the whole thing worth it."

Love Song for Bobby Long, A | 19 | 23 | 19 | 19 |

2004 | Directed by Shainee Gabel | With John Travolta, Scarlett Johansson, Gabriel Macht | 119 minutes | Rated R

Travolta pours all he's got into his "fearless" performance as an "unlikable", "aging drunk" forced to live with a teen "misfit" in this "soapy" drama set in N'Awlins; filmed at a "slow" tempo that intensifies the overall "depressing vibe", the picture ultimately splits surveyors: it's either a "lovable sleeper" or a "tedious" soporific.

Love Story | 19 | 18 | 20 | 18 |

1970 | Directed by Arthur Hiller | With Ali MacGraw, Ryan O'Neal, Ray Milland | 99 minutes | Rated PG

"Get out the Kleenex" – this "three-hanky chick flick" about a "rich boy, a poor girl" and an incurable disease is applauded for its "adorable" leads, the "cute" O'Neal and "divine" MacGraw; critics of this "shameless" "schmaltz"-fest sneer that "love means having to say you're sorry every five minutes", but even they admit "35 years of soggy-eyed females can't be wrong."

Love! Valour! Compassion! | 21 | 24 | 23 | 22 |

1997 | Directed by Joe Mantello | With Jason Alexander, Stephen Spinella, John Glover | 108 minutes | Rated R

Adapted from Terrence McNally's "Broadway smash", this "well-acted" dramedy follows eight gay men over three weekends in the country; alternately "funny, touching and sad", it's a "social commentary about the early years of the AIDS epidemic", but the compassionate claim it's "only peripherally about homosexuality" and really more about "the power of the human heart."

Lucky Number Slevin | 21 | 22 | 22 | 21 |

2006 | Directed by Paul McGuigan | With Josh Hartnett, Morgan Freeman, Ben Kingsley, Lucy Liu, Bruce Willis | 109 minutes | Rated R

Tapping a "pulp vein" rich in "snappy dialogue" and "body bag"-stuffing violence, this "enjoyable" gangster thriller features a roster of "top-shelf" talents playing "juicy roles"; factor in a "cerebral", mistaken-identity storyline with "lots of twists and turns", and there's plenty to "hold your interest" – even if the big payoff reminds some of *The Usual Suspects."*

Lust for Life
23 | 25 | 23 | 23

1956 | Directed by Vincente Minnelli | With Kirk Douglas, Anthony Quinn, James Donald | 122 minutes | Rated PG

Kirk's "at his most tormented" as "revolutionary painter" Vincent van Gogh in this "powerful" biopic canvassing the "disturbed" Dutchman's "complex" life, along with his stormy friendship with Paul Gauguin (the Oscar-winning Quinn); a "colorful, vibrant" production filmed at many of the "original locations" where the master worked, it immortalizes a "genius" who was "never appreciated in his lifetime."

M ⊙🎞
26 | 26 | 26 | 23

1931 | Directed by Fritz Lang | With Peter Lorre, Ellen Widmann, Gustaf Gründgens | 99 minutes | Not Rated

Still "frightening seven decades later", this crime thriller features Lorre as a "nervous, sweaty little child killer" in a "riveting" performance that evokes "horror and pity at the same time"; set in "'30s Berlin" "plunging headlong into fascism", it's known for its "expressionistic" camerawork and montage sequences that "set the benchmark for film editing."

MacArthur
21 | 24 | 22 | 21

1977 | Directed by Joseph Sargent | With Gregory Peck, Dan O'Herlihy, Ed Flanders | 130 minutes | Rated PG

"You really believe he's the General" claim fans of Peck's "superb" work in this profile of Douglas MacArthur, the soldier/politician whose "extraordinary career" and famously "imperious manner" made him "one of the most iconic – and flawed – figures of the 20th century"; though a "10-hour miniseries" might better serve the subject, this "solid" effort remains an "insightful" window into a "fascinating" life.

Madagascar
21 | - | 19 | 24

2005 | Directed by Eric Darnell, Tom McGrath | Animated | 86 minutes | Rated PG

"NYC zoo animals" fly the coop and end up "in the wilds of Africa" in this "wholesome" animated feature rendered in "eye-popping colors", and with enough "zaniness for kids" (and "'in' jokes" for adults) to keep viewers of all ages happy; sure, its "uneven" storyline eventually gets "tangled" in its own nets, so it's a good thing those "penguins steal the show."

Mad Max
20 | 17 | 19 | 19

1980 | Directed by George Miller | With Mel Gibson, Joanne Samuel, Hugh Keays-Byrne | 93 minutes | Rated R

"Raw" and thrillingly "underproduced", this "seminal" tale of "post-apocalyptic", "Darwinian doom" is one of the "all-time great low-budget fantasies", done with "conviction and style"; it pits a "fabulous Mel in tight black leather" against some "truly bad bad guys" and is so "ultimately effective" that it spawned two sequels (though connoisseurs claim the first is "the best").

	OVERALL	ACTING	STORY	PROD.

Mad Max Beyond Thunderdome
17 | 16 | 17 | 21

1985 | Directed by George Miller, George Ogilvie | With Mel Gibson, Tina Turner, Bruce Spence | 107 minutes | Rated R

For "early Mel Gibson" ("before he went nuts"), check out this final installment in the Mad Max trilogy about a "post-apocalyptic world" where the survivors are entertained in Thunderdome, a latter-day blood-and-circuses arena; sure, the pace is "fast", the mayhem "inventive", the villains "inspired" and Tina simply "the best", yet many still say "like most Part Threes", this one's "disappointing."

Madness of King George, The
22 | 26 | 23 | 24

1994 | Directed by Nicholas Hytner | With Nigel Hawthorne, Helen Mirren, Ian Holm | 107 minutes | Rated PG-13

"Insightful", "worthwhile" bio of the "mad, irascible" British monarch who, among other things, lost the American colonies; though "history buffs" declare the "accuracy is debatable", there's no debate about Hawthorne's "superb" performance (that "almost makes George III sympathetic"), nor that it's "visually stunning", with an Art Direction Oscar as proof.

Magdalene Sisters, The
25 | 26 | 26 | 23

2003 | Directed by Peter Mullan | With Anne-Marie Duff, Dorothy Duffy, Eileen Walsh, Nora-Jane Noone | 119 minutes | Rated R

"Quite an eye-opener", this Irish "exposé" tells the true story of young women "deemed immoral" and committed to asylums to "pay for their sins" "in the name of religion"; its "documentary-like style" and a strong cast of "little-known actors" make for "raw" filmmaking that "stays in your mind."

Magnificent Ambersons, The ❶∅
25 | 26 | 22 | 24

1942 | Directed by Orson Welles | With Joseph Cotten, Dolores Costello, Anne Baxter, Agnes Moorehead | 88 minutes | Not Rated

"In the shadow of *Citizen Kane*" stands Welles' "visually brilliant" but oft-"overlooked" follow-up, this "turn-of-the-century" drama detailing the "downfall of an Indiana family" whose spoiled scion can't "keep up with the times"; some magnificence is lost due to the "damage done by the studio's re-editing", but admirers say this "90% masterpiece" is still "brilliant filmmaking."

Magnificent Obsession
22 | 22 | 21 | 22

1954 | Directed by Douglas Sirk | With Jane Wyman, Rock Hudson, Barbara Rush, Agnes Moorehead | 108 minutes | Not Rated

"Tissue anyone?" – those yearning to "drown in suds" tout this "ultimate soap opera", the "twisted" story of a jaded playboy's attempts to win the heart of a blind woman whom he's wronged; while the "florid acting", "melodramatic" goings-on and "eye-popping color" lead cynics to dub it "*Magnificent Hokum*", analytical types say its "value lies in what it tells us about the times in which it was filmed."

Magnificent Seven, The
26 | 22 | 25 | 23

1960 | Directed by John Sturges | With Yul Brynner, Steve McQueen, Eli Wallach, Charles Bronson | 128 minutes | Not Rated

"Gunfighter cool" is alive and well in this "magnificent remake" of *The Seven Samurai* that "stands on its own" despite being "translated into a Western" and cast with "big stars of the '60s"; those who "never tire of watching it" "enjoy the adventure", "love the score" and attempt to "memorize the dialogue" that's become "fodder for countless movie trivia questions."

Magnolia   20 | 23 | 18 | 21

1999 | Directed by Paul Thomas Anderson | With Tom Cruise, Julianne Moore, Philip Seymour Hoffman, Jason Robards Jr., John C. Reilly | 188 minutes | Rated R

"Love-it-or-hate-it" filmmaking from auteur Anderson that's either a "compelling" study of "intersecting lives" in the San Fernando Valley or a "never-ending" "letdown" about a "bunch of dysfunctional people"; still, the direction is "energetic" and "Cruise actually acts", though some ask "what's up with the frogs?"

Maid in Manhattan   14 | 14 | 13 | 16

2002 | Directed by Wayne Wang | With Jennifer Lopez, Ralph Fiennes, Natasha Richardson | 105 minutes | Rated PG-13

"Warm and fuzzy" says it all about this "modern day Cinderella" story, a romantic comedy about a hotel chambermaid with a "great booty" who lands a "JFK Jr.–esque bachelor" (wags tag it *"Pretty Cleaning Woman"*); while it's certainly "harmless" enough "airline entertainment", cynics say "sappy", citing "no chemistry" between the leads, the "all-glammed-up-but-nowhere-to-go" J. Lo and "uncomfortable-looking" Fiennes.

Malcolm X   23 | 26 | 23 | 23

1992 | Directed by Spike Lee | With Denzel Washington, Angela Bassett, Al Freeman Jr | 194 minutes | Rated PG-13

In this "galvanizing", "probing" bio, the "transformation" of Malcolm X from "young hustler" to "outspoken" Civil Rights leader is portrayed by an "emotional" Washington in such a "bravura", "sympathetic" way that many say he was "robbed of an Oscar"; still, this "profound" film is a "time capsule of black American style" that resolutely "captivates and educates."

Mallrats   18 | 16 | 18 | 15

1995 | Directed by Kevin Smith | With Shannen Doherty, Jeremy London, Jason Lee, Claire Forlani, Ben Affleck | 94 minutes | Rated R

Director Smith's "sound" follow-up to *Clerks* mines the mall for "silly", "low-budget amusement", capturing a generation of "bored losers" who mouth "memorable", "profanity-laced" dialogue in comic "pratfalls"; though "not as good" as its predecessor (there's "not much of a storyline"), it's got enough "Jedi mind tricks" up its sleeve to touch the "'90s child in us all."

☒ Maltese Falcon, The ◑   28 | 27 | 27 | 25

1941 | Directed by John Huston | With Humphrey Bogart, Mary Astor, Peter Lorre | 101 minutes | Not Rated

The "stuff movies should be made of", this "vintage noir gem" boasts an "unforgettable Bogie" as the "hard-boiled detective" Sam Spade, plus a "blue-ribbon" supporting cast of "creeps and crooks", all searching for a mysterious "rara avis"; although its "taut script" that "runs like a Swiss watch" and "keeps you guessing to the end" is "often imitated", this "perfect rendering" of Dashiell Hammett's novel has been "never duplicated."

| | OVERALL | ACTING | STORY | PROD. |

Mambo Kings, The
20 | 21 | 20 | 20

1992 | Directed by Arne Glimcher | With Armand Assante, Antonio Banderas, Cathy Moriarty | 104 minutes | Rated R

Aficionados of this "sexy" chronicle of two Cuban musicians' "rollicking" immigrant experience in '50s NY simply "don't know whom to love more": Antonio or Armand – two equally "talented", "gorgeous" specimens; not just a "pleasure to watch", however, the film also drums up enough "incredible" Latin tunes to spice up the already "well-done" proceedings.

Man and a Woman, A ✉🄵
24 | 24 | 24 | 24

1966 | Directed by Claude Lelouch | With Anouk Aimée, Jean-Louis Trintignant | 102 minutes | Not Rated

For "romance par excellence", this "touching", "very French" '60s "classic" is served with "panache" and is "still worth seeing" today – indeed, the "music alone can make you fall in love"; detailing an affair between a widow and widower, it stars a "beautiful Aimée" opposite "Trintignant at his best"; "see it with someone special" and you may produce your own little sequel.

Man Called Horse, A
22 | 23 | 22 | 22

1970 | Directed by Elliot Silverstein | With Richard Harris, Judith Anderson | 114 minutes | Rated R

An "English aristocrat is captured by Sioux Indians and becomes one of them" in this "moving" Western made two decades before *Dances with Wolves* and featuring the "intense" Harris in one of his "greatest roles"; a warning for "weak stomachs": be prepared for some "pretty gruesome moments", chiefly the "sadomasochistic", "purple nipple" initiation scene.

☒ Manchurian Candidate, The ◑
27 | 26 | 28 | 25

1962 | Directed by John Frankenheimer | With Frank Sinatra, Laurence Harvey, Angela Lansbury | 126 minutes | Rated PG-13

As "perfectly paranoid" "Cold War" filmmaking, this provocative "conspiracy thriller" about Korean War–era "brainwashing" still packs a "wallop" due to a "twist"-laden script and a "take-your-breath-away" ending; Sinatra and Harvey are "electrifying", but the real revelation is Lansbury as an "evil", solitaire-playing mommy.

Manchurian Candidate, The
18 | 21 | 19 | 19

2004 | Directed by Jonathan Demme | With Denzel Washington, Meryl Streep, Liev Schreiber | 129 minutes | Rated R

"Cleverly updated" by substituting "corporate conspiracies" for "Cold War paranoia", this remake of the "classic" '60s political thriller is "different enough to be interesting", yet ultimately many wonder "why mess with perfection?"; even if Denzel "does his best" and Meryl "gives Angela Lansbury a run for her money", this "unnecessary" effort "doesn't hold a candle to the original."

☒ Man for All Seasons, A ✉
28 | 28 | 27 | 27

1966 | Directed by Fred Zinnemann | With Paul Scofield, Wendy Hiller, Robert Shaw | 120 minutes | Rated G

"Intelligent in a quiet way", this "literate" historical drama about the "conflict between conscience and convenience" between Henry VIII and Sir Thomas More garnered six Oscars, including Best Actor for the "magnificent Scofield"; a "rare film about integrity", "loyalty and betrayal", it's as a "reminder of the days when the movies enlightened."

Man from Elysian Fields, The
21 | 23 | 21 | 21

2002 | Directed by George Hickenlooper | With Andy Garcia, Mick Jagger, Julianna Margulies | 106 minutes | Rated R

A "struggling writer" turns gigolo to make ends meet in this "sexy, stylish" variation on the "Faust legend"; although Garcia is a bit "one-note" and the "story falls off at the end", the big "surprise" here is Jagger, who "makes the whole thing worthwhile" portraying a "dapper", high-end pimp.

Manhattan ◑
26 | 24 | 23 | 24

1979 | Directed by Woody Allen | With Woody Allen, Diane Keaton, Michael Murphy, Mariel Hemingway | 96 minutes | Rated R

"Even NYers get all mushy" about this "love letter to the Big Apple" filmed in "fantastic black and white" and set to a thrilling "Gershwin soundtrack"; a romance laced with "angst", it appeals to those who like their "philosophy mixed with a little comedy" and is "more fully realized than *Annie Hall*"; in a nutshell, "it can be fun to be depressing."

Manhunter
21 | 21 | 25 | 20

1986 | Directed by Michael Mann | With William Petersen, Kim Greist, Brian Cox, Joan Allen | Rated R

As the "first filmed version" of Thomas Harris' novel *Red Dragon*, this "scary" prequel to *The Silence of the Lambs* is "relatively unknown" but may be "better" than its 2002 remake thanks to a "slick" production showcasing director Mann's "brilliant visuals"; nope, "Anthony Hopkins isn't in it", but Cox's "different" spin on Hannibal Lecter makes this picture "well worth a look."

Man on Fire
21 | 25 | 21 | 22

2004 | Directed by Tony Scott | With Denzel Washington, Dakota Fanning, Christopher Walken | 146 minutes | Rated R

"Revenge" is the emotion driving this "intense" thriller starring a "prime Denzel" as "one bad mother" bodyguard who turns "vigilante" after his charge is kidnapped; critics find the beginning "compelling" enough, but say the second half disintegrates into a "mindless shoot-'em-up" further muddied by "hyperactive" camerawork; "no lasting impact" is the final verdict.

Man on the Moon
16 | 22 | 15 | 17

1999 | Directed by Milos Forman | With Jim Carrey, Danny DeVito, Courtney Love | 118 minutes | Rated R

Carrey is "better as Andy than Andy himself" in this "affecting" bio of spaced-out '70s comic Andy Kaufman, whose "funny but strange" routines conclude with an early curtain after he succumbs to cancer; though it's heckled as a "disappointing, disjointed" portrait that "doesn't shed much light" on its "complicated" subject, it's still "entertaining" for Dada comedy fans.

Man Who Came to Dinner, The ◑
26 | 27 | 26 | 24

1942 | Directed by William Keighley | With Bette Davis, Ann Sheridan, Monty Woolley | 112 minutes | Not Rated

Fans of "smart, hilarious" comedy relish the "unforgettable feast" in this screen treatment of Kaufman and Hart's stage play à clef, with

Woolley "stealing the movie" as a "pompous radio personality" who visits a Midwestern household and "won't go home" after becoming wheelchair-bound; mixing "acid wit" with "fast-paced" dialogue, it's a "not-to-be-missed" "scream" from the "old school."

Man Who Fell to Earth, The
18 | 18 | 20 | 17

1976 | Directed by Nicolas Roeg | With David Bowie, Rip Torn, Candy Clark | 140 minutes | Rated R

Followers of this "way-ahead-of-its-time" sci-fi fantasy about an extraterrestrial "searching for water" to save his planet say it's "still relevant", citing its "inventive" storyline and "perfect casting" ("Bowie has no trouble playing a trippy alien"); however, some dismiss it as an "incoherent", "unwatchable mess" that's too "creepy and weird."

Man Who Knew Too Much, The
24 | 24 | 25 | 24

1956 | Directed by Alfred Hitchcock | With James Stewart, Doris Day, Brenda de Banzie | 120 minutes | Rated PG

A "Hitchcock remake of an earlier Hitchcock" thriller, this "more commercial" version plays up the "amazing ordinariness" of its "everyman" stars as they seek their kidnapped son; for most, it's "very exciting" – especially the "unbearably suspenseful" "scene in Royal Albert Hall" – though a few "could do without" Day's "cornball" rendition of 'Que Sera, Sera' (which still snagged a Best Song Oscar).

Man Who Shot Liberty Valance, The ◑
25 | 24 | 25 | 23

1962 | Directed by John Ford | With John Wayne, James Stewart, Vera Miles, Lee Marvin, Edmond O'Brien | 123 minutes | Not Rated

The formidable Ford's "darkest Western" is illuminated by a "star-studded" cast featuring "all-time bad guy" Lee Marvin in his "finest performance", with "dynamic" backup from Wayne and Stewart; though a bit "claustrophobic" (it was filmed "mostly on Hollywood soundstages"), this is still "mythic" moviemaking that "works like a huge, sprawling novel"; biggest surprise: "Wayne loses the girl."

Man Who Wasn't There, The ◑
21 | 25 | 19 | 25

2001 | Directed by Joel Coen | With Billy Bob Thornton, Frances McDormand, James Gandolfini | 116 minutes | Rated R

This "quirky, haunting" take on vintage film noir ("as only the Coen brothers can re-create it") charts the last days of a "hapless" small-town barber whose "decline is a metaphor" for nothing less than "modern alienation"; the "stylistically incredible" cinematography is "so colorful you forget it's filmed in black and white", while Thornton's titular turn nearly manages to "out-Bogart Bogart."

Man Who Would Be King, The
25 | 26 | 26 | 25

1975 | Directed by John Huston | With Sean Connery, Michael Caine, Christopher Plummer | 129 minutes | Rated PG

Based on Kipling's "epic of friendship and heroism", this "classic adaptation" is a "ripsnorting", "good-time adventure" chronicling the perils of a pair of "opportunistic" "British rogues" on a "grand lark" in 19th-century colonial India; the combination of "sweeping vistas", "incandescent chemistry" between Connery and Caine and a "haunting ending" make for a "buddy flick that rises way above the genre."

	OVERALL	ACTING	STORY	PROD.

Man with the Golden Arm, The ❶
24 | 26 | 25 | 22

1955 | Directed by Otto Preminger | With Frank Sinatra, Eleanor Parker, Kim Novak | 119 minutes | Not Rated

Proof that "Sinatra was as good an actor as he was a singer", this "grim" look at one man's "drug problem" stars an "excellent" (Oscar-nominated) Frankie as a professional card dealer/"recovering heroin addict" who falls into a "downward spiral" after being discharged from rehab; some users find it rather "dated", but most warn it's a "harrowing", "fasten-your-seatbelts" ride.

Man with the Golden Gun, The
18 | 17 | 17 | 20

1974 | Directed by Guy Hamilton | With Roger Moore, Christopher Lee, Britt Ekland | 125 minutes | Rated PG

"Moore almost redeems himself" in his second stab at 007 ("much better than his debut"), though Lee steals the show as a "droll" assassin boasting "three nipples" as well as a golden gun; still, despite the sizzle supplied by Ekland and some "great Asian scenery", foes dismiss it as a "disjointed, inferior" misfire in the Bond canon.

Marathon Man
24 | 27 | 24 | 22

1976 | Directed by John Schlesinger | With Dustin Hoffman, Laurence Olivier, Roy Scheider | 125 minutes | Rated R

"Just when you thought it was safe to go back to the dentist" comes this "nasty" little thriller about a "totally mad", "tooth-drilling" "Nazi on the loose" hell-bent on retrieving ill-gotten loot; the "huffing, puffing" Hoffman is "superlative" as a man "drawn into something way beyond his control", while set pieces like the "whining drill" scene and the "diamond-swallowing" finale raise enough "goose bumps" to make most "swear off checkups for life."

❏ March of the Penguins
26 | - | 25 | 28

2005 | Directed by Luc Jacquet | Documentary | 85 minutes | Rated G

The "majestic" emperor penguins who "struggle to survive and procreate" in the "hostile", "frigid ice fields" of Antarctica will "melt your heart" in this "superlative" documentary, an "entertaining, educational" dramatization of the "tuxedo-clad" critters' life cycle; mixing "breathtaking" footage with Freeman's "perfectly voiced" narration, it may paint an overly "anthropomorphized" picture – "they're just birds" – but somehow it manages to make "human problems seem petty" by comparison.

Maria Full of Grace ❏
25 | 26 | 25 | 22

2004 | Directed by Joshua Marston | With Catalina Sandino Moreno, Yenny Paola Vega | 101 minutes | Rated R

The "horrific plight" of women desperate to "wean themselves from poverty" by becoming "pawns in the drug trade" is the "untold story" brought to light by this "raw", "impactful" indie; newcomer Moreno shows she's "full of talent" in the role of a Colombian cocaine mule, and while her near-"suicidal" mission "puts you through a wringer", it's worth it for the film's "unbleached message of hope."

Mark of Zorro, The ❶
22 | 19 | 22 | 19

1940 | Directed by Rouben Mamoulian | With Tyrone Power, Linda Darnell, Basil Rathbone | 94 minutes | Not Rated

This "rousing adventure" tale of "double identity and romance" has "hardly dated" thanks to the "dashing", buckle-swashing Power's "sexy swordfighting"; "lady-in-distress" Darnell is "unbelievably lovely", "fop" Rathbone "as dastardly as ever" and a "marvelous" Alfred Newman score provides the cinematic coup de grace.

Marnie
OVERALL	ACTING	STORY	PROD.
21	21	22	21

1964 | Directed by Alfred Hitchcock | With Tippi Hedren, Sean Connery, Diane Baker | 130 minutes | Rated PG

A "rich man falls for a compulsive thief" in this "tense" psychological thriller from Alfred Hitchcock starring a "young", "yummy" Sean opposite a very "blonde" Tippi (the last-minute "Grace Kelly replacement"); still, critics call this "second-rate" effort the master of suspense's "last gasp", citing "murky, pseudo-Freudian goings-on" and a "bored-looking" cast.

Marriage of Maria Braun, The 🇫
25	25	24	23

1979 | Directed by Rainer Werner Fassbinder | With Hanna Schygulla, Klaus Löwitsch, Ivan Desny | 120 minutes | Rated R

This "scathing portrait" of "survival in postwar Germany" traces its gritty heroine's determined climb up the economic ladder with some "bitingly funny" scenes that demonstrate "you can't bury the past", no matter how hard you try to disguise it; "extraordinary" work from Fassbinder and the "brilliant" Schygulla make up for that "letdown of an ending."

Married to the Mob
17	17	16	16

1988 | Directed by Jonathan Demme | With Michelle Pfeiffer, Matthew Modine, Dean Stockwell | 103 minutes | Rated R

'Family' fare à la Jonathan Demme, this "quirky" comedy stars a "gorgeous" Pfeiffer playing a "small-time mobster's wife" parting with The Life after a dishonored don rubs out her hubby; "silly" but "easy to watch", it features a "fine" ensemble cast "having a great time" as well as a "don't-miss-it" cameo from "Alec Baldwin's chest hair."

Marty ✉◑
25	27	24	21

1955 | Directed by Delbert Mann | With Ernest Borgnine, Betsy Blair, Esther Minciotti | 91 minutes | Not Rated

Ok, the story of a "sloppy butcher" who finds love with a "mousy clerk" might "never play", but this "poignant" Paddy Chayefsky drama proved naysayers wrong, garnering four Oscars (including Best Actor for Borgnine, who's "perfect" as an ordinary Brooklyn schmo); shot in black and white, its "realistic style" "never gets old" – but be prepared for a feeling of "hopelessness" throughout.

🔢 Mary Poppins ✉
27	24	25	27

1964 | Directed by Robert Stevenson | With Julie Andrews, Dick Van Dyke, David Tomlinson | 140 minutes | Rated G

Mix a "perky" Julie (as an "odd" nanny with "magical powers") with a "cheeky" Dick, "fantastic animation" and "catchy tunes", add a "spoonful of sugar" and the result is a "super-duper" Disney "treat"; a "technical marvel of its time", this "jolly" production "makes you feel good at any age" and serves as a dandy "introduction to musicals for kids."

MASH ✉
26	25	26	24

1970 | Directed by Robert Altman | With Donald Sutherland, Elliott Gould, Sally Kellerman | 116 minutes | Rated PG

"War is hell (and funny)" in this "groundbreaking" "black" satire about a dysfunctional Korean War medical unit that still "holds up" as "one of the smartest comedies ever written" – "once you get past all the blood", that is; maybe the "last third" goes "downhill" during the "lame" football game, but there's no doubt this is "Altman's breakthrough."

Mask

| | 21 | 24 | 23 | 19 |

1985 | Directed by Peter Bogdanovich | With Cher, Sam Elliott, Eric Stoltz | 120 minutes | Rated PG-13

Proof that "Cher can act", this "touching tearjerker" showcases the diva in "top form" as a single biker mom "in a tough situation with a challenged kid" who's horribly disfigured; as the "grotesque" teen who just "wants to be treated normally", an "amazing" Stoltz radiates enough "inner beauty" to remind the rest of us "how lucky we are."

Mask, The

| | 17 | 18 | 15 | 20 |

1994 | Directed by Chuck Russell | With Jim Carrey, Cameron Diaz, Peter Riegert | 101 minutes | Rated PG-13

A bedraggled schmo finds a magical mask that transforms him into a swinging, macho hero in this "entertaining" comedy that might hinge on a "ridiculous concept" but nevertheless "works" (thanks to Carrey's "funny" performance); though "kinda stupid" to brainiacs, fans are wowed by the "dazzling effects", including the "luminous Diaz", who makes her "delightful" screen debut here.

Mask of Zorro, The

| | 18 | 17 | 18 | 21 |

1998 | Directed by Martin Campbell | With Antonio Banderas, Catherine Zeta-Jones | 136 minutes | Rated PG-13

This "big-budget" spin on the "Zorro legend" provokes dueling opinions: zealots admire its "old-school movie style" ("great swordfights", "breathtaking" production values) and ask "is there a better-looking cast ever assembled?"; but critics parry it's "lightweight fluff" that might work well with "popcorn" but "doesn't hold a candle to the 1940 version."

Master and Commander: The Far Side of the World

| | 23 | 24 | 22 | 27 |

2003 | Directed by Peter Weir | With Russell Crowe, Paul Bettany | 138 minutes | Rated PG-13

For "textbook adventure filmmaking" sailing over the "bounding main", set your sights on this "visually extraordinary" nautical epic depicting "cat-and-mouse" high-sea games during the Napoleonic War; the all-male cast includes the "great-as-usual" Crowe backed up by a "strong" Bettany, but despite "incredible battle scenes", "magnificent storms" and "stellar" special effects, mutineers say the "thin" storyline and "endless frigate jargon" simply "don't hold water"; other seafarers, however, "look forward to another installment."

Match Point

| | 22 | 23 | 22 | 22 |

2005 | Directed by Woody Allen | With Jonathan Rhys Meyers, Scarlett Johansson, Matthew Goode | 124 minutes | Rated R

Breaking from his usual "silly slapstick", Woody Allen channels both "Hitchcock" and "Theodore Dreiser" to serve up this "mesmerizing", "keeps-you-guessing" London thriller whose "chilling portrait of a social climber" examines "the role of luck in life"; further assuring the film's place in the sun are the "outstanding" Rhys Meyers and "sumptuous" Scarlett, who simmer with "intense chemistry."

Matchstick Men

OVERALL	ACTING	STORY	PROD.
20	24	21	19

2003 | Directed by Ridley Scott | With Nicolas Cage, Sam Rockwell, Alison Lohman | 116 minutes | Rated PG-13

A "neurotic" con artist "with more tics than a time bomb" shows his "soft" side when he plays dad to a "junior swindler" in this "smart", "dark"-edged comic caper featuring "excellent" performances from Cage and the "stardom"-bound Lohman; it "takes a while" to get going, but don't fret – the "surprise twist" at the end will "hook you."

⊿ Matrix, The

OVERALL	ACTING	STORY	PROD.
25	19	25	28

1999 | Directed by Andy Wachowski, Larry Wachowski | With Keanu Reeves, Laurence Fishburne, Carrie-Anne Moss | 136 minutes | Rated R

"Move over, *Star Wars*"; not even Reeves' "leaden" acting can sink this "mind-bending, reality-rocking" movie that "raised the bar on special effects" and "revolutionized hand-to-hand combat in filmmaking"; even if its "intricate" plot (something about a computer hacker turned "humanity's last hope") verges on "incoherence", this "sci-fi shoot-'em-up for people with brains" just "gets better every time you see it."

Matrix Reloaded, The

OVERALL	ACTING	STORY	PROD.
21	17	18	26

2003 | Directed by Andy Wachowski, Larry Wachowski | With Keanu Reeves, Carrie-Anne Moss, Laurence Fishburne, Hugo Weaving | 138 minutes | Rated R

The "conceptual novelty's gone", the "story is not as compelling as the original" and it "could have benefited from some editing", yet the "sexier" second installment of the "groundbreaking" sci-fi trilogy is still "worth a watch" for its "eye candy galore" – "off-the-charts special effects", "take-your-breath-away fight scenes" and a "car-chase scene that just blows your mind"; now if only there were "a *Matrix for Dummies* to explain what happened."

Matrix Revolutions, The

OVERALL	ACTING	STORY	PROD.
15	14	13	23

2003 | Directed by Andy Wachowski, Larry Wachowski | With Keanu Reeves, Laurence Fishburne, Carrie-Ann Moss | 129 minutes | Rated R

This "less than stellar end" to the martial-arts/sci-fi trilogy features the same "over-the-top CGI effects" and "garbled-but-intriguing philosophy" as the preceding installments, but this time out there's "too much action and not enough thought"; in fact, it's such a "letdown" to a series that "started with so much potential" that many think "they should have stopped after the first one."

Maverick

OVERALL	ACTING	STORY	PROD.
18	20	17	19

1994 | Directed by Richard Donner | With Mel Gibson, Jodie Foster, James Garner | 127 minutes | Rated PG

As TV shows morphed into movies go, this "laid-back Western" based on ABC's '50s series "works well" by loading the deck with "escapism", "modern twists" and Gibson as a "tall, dark stranger" who's "having more fun than the audience"; but it's the "effortless style" of Garner (the original Maverick) that wins big.

McCabe & Mrs. Miller

OVERALL	ACTING	STORY	PROD.
23	23	23	24

1971 | Directed by Robert Altman | With Warren Beatty, Julie Christie, Shelley Duvall | 120 minutes | Rated R

Decidedly "not for conventional Western" fans, this "brilliantly directed", "postmodern deconstruction" of the genre "eliminates the clichés" and "faithfully re-creates what the West was really like": namely, "harsh, cruel and lacking true heroes"; despite one major drawback – "you can't understand what anyone is saying" – it's more than evident that the leads are "impossibly in love."

Mean Girls
20 | 19 | 20 | 19

2004 | Directed by Mark Waters | With Lindsay Lohan, Rachel McAdams, Tina Fey | 97 minutes | Rated PG-13

The "*Heathers* of the new millennium", this "smart teen comedy" brings back "painful high school memories" of the "trauma of trying to fit in" at a time when "social status seems so important"; as the new kid on the block, "goddess" Lohan demonstrates she's definitely "going places" and Tina Fey's "witty" script "hits the nail on the head" – even if the "sappy" finale is a tad too "preachy" for many.

Meaning of Life, The
24 | 22 | 20 | 20

1983 | Directed by Terry Jones, Terry Gilliam | With Monty Python | 107 minutes | Rated R

"Lunacy abounds" in this "wonderfully outrageous" Monty Python flick rolling "music, comedy and philosophy" vignettes that attempt to answer life's big questions into one "screamingly funny" (if sometimes "retch-covered") package; marking the British troupe's "last spurt" of cinematic collaboration, it suffers the occasional "second-rate" segment but endures as a "classic" that "shines in comparison to what else is out there."

Mean Streets
24 | 27 | 23 | 22

1973 | Directed by Martin Scorsese | With Harvey Keitel, Robert De Niro | 110 minutes | Rated R

"Gritty and graphic before that became the norm", Scorsese's breakout drama of hoods in the 'hood "rings with truth" as a "definitive slice of NY", with Keitel out to "make it in the mob" in spite of "Catholic guilt" and ties to De Niro's "unforgettable" loose-cannon "loser"; it's a "grim" but "passionate" study of streetwise style, including some "pioneering" use of "oldies but goodies" on the soundtrack.

Meatballs
18 | 15 | 17 | 14

1979 | Directed by Ivan Reitman | With Bill Murray, Harvey Atkin, Kate Lynch | 99 minutes | Rated PG

A pre-"*Caddyshack*" Murray plays a wisecracking "summer camp counselor everyone would love to have" in this "underrated", lowbrow "comedy staple", later "ruined" by three sequels; ok, it might be a "little dated" and "poor production quality" detracts, but overall it conveys the "experience every camper hopes for."

Mediterraneo ✉🄵∅
21 | 21 | 20 | 23

1991 | Directed by Gabriele Salvatores | With Diego Abatantuono, Claudio Bigagli | 96 minutes | Rated R

Sure, this "sweet" comedy about a group of WWII Italian soldiers "stranded" on a Greek isle is a "trifle", but the "beautiful cinematography" and "sweep-you-away" soundtrack nicely complement its assortment of "cute characters"; some report the story "drags in some parts" (resulting in "awkward" scenes), but it offers enough "great escapism" to make for a primo "date flick."

	OVERALL	ACTING	STORY	PROD.

Meet John Doe ◑
24 | 26 | 23 | 22

1941 | Directed by Frank Capra | With Gary Cooper, Barbara Stanwyck, Edward Arnold, Walter Brennan | 123 minutes | Not Rated

Cooper and Stanwyck are a "joy to watch" in this "classic" Capra fanfare for the "common man" that mixes some "social commentary" into its tale of an "honest" hobo who's recruited by a newspaper to "threaten suicide" in the name of America's "lost ideals" – and ends up capturing the nation's "attention and hearts"; despite the film's "heroic" intentions, "politics are still corrupt", but the "warm, fuzzy dream" that "things can be better" never looked so "convincing."

Meet Me in St. Louis
26 | 24 | 23 | 26

1944 | Directed by Vincente Minnelli | With Judy Garland, Margaret O'Brien, Mary Astor | 113 minutes | Not Rated

Clang, clang, clang, here comes Garland "at her radiant finest" as a girl who "adores the boy next door" in this musical "treasure" about a "turn-of-the-century" American family; fans laud its "sumptuous" Technicolor production and "unforgettable" tunes, while brainiacs hint it's "darker and deeper than its rep suggests."

Meet the Fockers
18 | 21 | 17 | 19

2004 | Directed by Jay Roach | With Robert De Niro, Ben Stiller, Dustin Hoffman, Barbra Streisand | 115 minutes | Rated PG-13

There's "major star wattage" on display in this *Meet the Parents* sequel, starting with the "oy vey" pairing of "big names" Dusty and Babs, who "steal the show" along with a can of "whipped cream"; otherwise, this "crude" comedy about in-laws interacting for the first time earns mixed marks: it's either a "one-trick movie" with "too many potty jokes" or else "hilarious", "verging on ridiculous – what's wrong with that?"

Meet the Parents
19 | 21 | 19 | 19

2000 | Directed by Jay Roach | With Robert De Niro, Ben Stiller, Blythe Danner | 108 minutes | Rated PG-13

"Every guy's worst nightmare" about being introduced to his "prospective in-laws" comes true in this very "watchable" comedy that succeeds mainly because of the "brilliant pairing of Stiller and De Niro"; though the unamused frown it "relies too much on slapstick" and repeats the "same joke for two hours straight", most say it "pinpoints" an "all-too-real" situation.

Meet the Robinsons
22 | - | 21 | 25

2007 | Directed by Stephen J. Anderson | Animated | 102 minutes | Rated G

A "brainy orphan's search for his parents" takes a "deliriously zany" turn into "*Back-to-the-Future*" territory in this "clever" Disney 'toon featuring a "heartwarming" moral about the "meaning of family" and some "great" visuals (the "T-Rex scene is worth the price of admission" alone); while "not the best" animated flick you'll ever meet, it's good enough to "keep the kids from killing each other for 90 minutes."

Melinda and Melinda
17 | 21 | 18 | 18

2005 | Directed by Woody Allen | With Radha Mitchell, Will Ferrell, Chloë Sevigny | 100 minutes | Rated PG-13

"Two versions of the same tale" – one comic, one tragic – form the framework for this "intriguing" Woody Allen flicker about a "nervous" adulteress adrift in "ultrasophisticated Manhattan"; fans feel the

Woodman "flits between the two stories with ease", but those who re-title it *"Monotonous and Monotonous"* advise he "join the 21st century" ("who can afford those apartments?") or else "retire."

Melvin and Howard ⊠   22 | 23 | 22 | 19
1980 | Directed by Jonathan Demme | With Paul Le Mat, Mary Steenburgen, Jason Robards | 95 minutes | Rated R

A "small movie that landed in a big way", this "wacky" riff on the "Howard Hughes myth" tells the tale of a milkman who befriends a bum, who's really a gazillionaire, who wills the milkman a fortune; it's "funny", "off-the-wall" stuff that's "uplifting without being preachy or schmaltzy" and might be best enjoyed "as a companion piece to *The Aviator*."

Member of the Wedding, The ◑   25 | 27 | 26 | 25
1952 | Directed by Fred Zinnemann | With Ethel Waters, Julie Harris, Brandon De Wilde | 93 minutes | Not Rated

"One of the most touching films ever", this "sweet" slice of Americana adapted from (and "capturing the essence of") Carson McCullers' play delineates a Southern household's "moving dynamic" between an alienated youngster, her black housekeeper and her soon-to-be-married brother; fans sing the praises of its "remarkable" cast, singling out the "soaring" Harris and the "remarkable" Waters, whose on-screen rendition of the hymn 'His Eye Is on the Sparrow' is "thankfully preserved forever."

⊡ Memento   26 | 25 | 27 | 25
2000 | Directed by Christopher Nolan | With Guy Pearce, Carrie-Anne Moss | 113 minutes | Rated R

"Bring your brain to the theater, you'll need it" for this "exquisitely existential" "mind-bender" about a man who loses his "short-term memory" following his wife's murder; it "turns traditional narrative on its head" by telling the story "in reverse" – so it may "require several viewings to get it all straight"; though there's applause for the "stunning" Pearce, befuddled folks "still trying to figure it out" wail it's too "gnisufnoc."

Memoirs of a Geisha   21 | 23 | 21 | 26
2005 | Directed by Rob Marshall | With Zhang Ziyi, Ken Watanabe, Gong Li, Michelle Yeoh | 145 minutes | Rated PG-13

"Beautiful costumes" and "breathtaking" cinematography ("every shot feels like a painting") shine in this "poignant", "rags-to-silks" period drama that offers a rare glimpse inside the "closed society" of Japan's geishas; despite some grumbling that "Chinese actors playing Japanese" characters may be "politically incorrect", overall most find the experience "transporting", albeit at a "slow" clip.

Men in Black   21 | 20 | 21 | 24
1997 | Directed by Barry Sonnenfeld | With Tommy Lee Jones, Will Smith, Linda Fiorentino | 98 minutes | Rated PG-13

"Wisecracking" Smith and "deadpan" Jones show "great chemistry" as they battle "slime, aliens and explosions" in this "action-packed" sci-fi "blockbuster" that's "delicious fun"; a "kids' movie for adults", it's a "hugely enjoyable spoof" that some find "silly" and may be a "little gross."

Men in Black II

OVERALL	ACTING	STORY	PROD.
14	16	12	20

2002 | Directed by Barry Sonnenfeld | With Tommy Lee Jones, Will Smith, Rip Torn, Lara Flynn Boyle | 88 minutes | Rated PG-13

An "overload of special effects", a "cast on autopilot" and "no real storyline" are the classic symptoms of "sequel syndrome" afflicting this "mediocre" encore to the hit sci-fi comedy; fortunately, a "few amusing sight gags" (i.e. the "worth-a-laugh Michael Jackson cameo") and the "short" running time "make it bearable."

Metropolis ◗

27	22	24	28

1927 | Directed by Fritz Lang | With Alfred Abel, Gustav Froelich, Brigitte Helm | 153 minutes | Not Rated

A "visionary" film of "magnitude, imagination and depth", this "sci-fi social commentary" about "oppression and uprising" set in a "futuristic city" "still retains its visual impact" seven decades later; indeed, Lang's "man-versus-machine" story (embodied by a "fetishized woman robot") remains "revolutionary in every sense of the word" – this is a "movie everybody should watch at least once."

Metropolitan

20	19	20	17

1990 | Directed by Whit Stillman | With Carolyn Farina, Edward Clements, Christopher Eigeman | 99 minutes | Rated PG-13

The "young and the privileged" in "present-day NY" get the Jane Austen treatment in this "charming" "coming-of-age" comedy with an "exciting young cast" spouting "intensely dry", "droll" dialogue; those fascinated by "rich kids and their problems" say it's one part "Woody Allen", one part "George Plimpton."

Midnight Cowboy ✉

26	28	24	24

1969 | Directed by John Schlesinger | With Dustin Hoffman, Jon Voight, Sylvia Miles | 113 minutes | Rated R

"Still as gritty as ever", this "unvarnished look at NYC street life" is a "touching" if "depressing" depiction of a pair of "down-and-out" losers "spiraling downward" that turns the "buddy-flick concept" on its ear; the first "X-rated" film to take Best Picture honors (and since re-rated), it continues to wow with "inner beauty", "haunting music" and "brilliant" turns from Hoffman and Voight – and that "ending on the bus is unforgettable."

Midnight Express ✉

24	24	25	22

1978 | Directed by Alan Parker | With Brad Davis, Randy Quaid, John Hurt | 120 minutes | Rated R

This "frighteningly realistic" drama about a not-so-innocent American abroad imprisoned for smuggling hash "should be required viewing for teens and travelers", even though this "eye-opener" might "induce nightmares for years to come"; it probably "did more to stop kids from doing drugs" than all of "Nancy Reagan's efforts" combined.

Midnight Run

23	25	23	21

1988 | Directed by Martin Brest | With Robert De Niro, Charles Grodin, Yaphet Kotto | 126 minutes | Rated R

For a "quintessential" buddy flick, try this "wild", "witty" action comedy about a "white-collar crook" and the bounty hunter who "tries to bring him in alive" that runs strong on the "great chemistry" of "old pros" De Niro and Grodin, the "funniest odd couple since Oscar and Felix"; add in some "quirky" supporting players (a "fleet of FBI agents", "inept mobsters" and other "eccentrics"), and there's "never a dull moment."

Midsummer Night's Sex Comedy, A
18 | 20 | 19 | 19

1982 | Directed by Woody Allen | With Woody Allen, Mia Farrow, Julie Hagerty, José Ferrer | 88 minutes | Rated PG

"Funny" albeit "fairly forgettable", this "romantic Woody Allen romp" follows three turn-of-the-century couples over a weekend in the country; one part "Shakespeare" satire, one part ode to Bergman's *Smiles of a Summer Night*, it's altogether "silly" stuff and if "far from the director's best", it's "pleasant enough for a Saturday afternoon."

Mighty Aphrodite
18 | 21 | 18 | 18

1995 | Directed by Woody Allen | With Woody Allen, Mira Sorvino, Michael Rapaport | 98 minutes | Rated R

Maybe "not as incisive" as Allen's "best", this "minor Woody" work still exudes "inventive charm" in its story of a man seeking the biological mother of his adopted child; throw in an "inspired Greek chorus" providing commentary and Sorvino's Oscar-winning turn as a "ditzy hooker", and the result is "painless fun."

Mighty Wind, A
23 | 26 | 21 | 23

2003 | Directed by Christopher Guest | With Bob Balaban, Christopher Guest, John Michael Higgins, Eugene Levy | 91 minutes | Rated PG-13

"You'll have almost as much fun as the cast" watching this "hysterical mockumentary" about the "'60s folk music scene" full of "priceless material", a "hilarious cast of characters" and "lots of hidden humor"; while "not as good as *Best in Show*", "anything by Guest is better than most everyone else's work."

Mildred Pierce ✉◐
26 | 25 | 25 | 24

1945 | Directed by Michael Curtiz | With Joan Crawford, Jack Carson, Ann Blyth, Eve Arden | 111 minutes | Not Rated

Oscar-winner Crawford is in "full weeper bloom" (with "shoulder pads for days" and "star lighting to make sure you get the point") in this noir "sudser" based on the James M. Cain novel about a "mother who sacrifices everything for her daughter"; "camp" followers crack up over Arden's "witty repartee" (which "would put any drag queen to shame") and "rent it as a double feature with *Mommie Dearest* for full impact."

Miller's Crossing
22 | 23 | 22 | 22

1990 | Directed by Joel Coen | With Gabriel Byrne, Albert Finney, Marcia Gay Harden | 115 minutes | Rated R

"Don't give the high hat" to this "subtle", "criminally underrated" early Coen brothers "gem" about a gangland war between Irish and Italian mobsters that proves "betrayal can come back to haunt you"; devotees declare it "deserves to be up there with *Goodfellas*", given the worthiness of the "broody" Byrne, "knockout Finney" and "deliciously tangled" plot "larded with obscure underworld slang."

☑ Million Dollar Baby ✉
27 | 28 | 25 | 26

2004 | Directed by Clint Eastwood | With Clint Eastwood, Hilary Swank, Morgan Freeman | 132 minutes | Rated PG-13

What begins as a boxing "Cinderella story" about a "guilt-racked coach" mentoring a "determined female fighter" takes a "sharp turn" and becomes a "profound" meditation on "significant moral dilemmas" in this "knockout" Oscar magnet from "powerhouse" actor/director Eastwood; a "flawless Swank" and "quietly brilliant" Freeman round out the cast in this "simple", "less-is-more" production, with a "surprise" ending that "leaves you breathless."

Minority Report
21 20 22 25

2002 | Directed by Steven Spielberg | With Tom Cruise, Colin Farrell, Samantha Morton, Max von Sydow | 145 minutes | Rated PG-13

"Cruise and Spielberg are a great combo" in this "intelligent, exciting" sci-fi thriller with "stunning visual effects" and "a mind-bending premise" – catching murderers before they commit the actual crime; though the "original, chilling storyline" "moves at lightning speed", it's "hard to follow at times", making it more difficult to detect the "holes in the plot"; bottom line: "better than the box office would indicate."

Miracle
24 23 26 24

2004 | Directed by Gavin O'Connor | With Kurt Russell, Patricia Clarkson | 135 minutes | Rated PG

Although most already "know the ending", this "feel-good" "insider's look" at the U.S. hockey team's quest for gold at the 1980 Olympics keeps athletic supporters "riveted" with its taut "they-shoot-they-score" script; indeed, Kurt's "commanding performance" and the "realistic moments on and off the ice" keep its "inspirational" themes resonating long afterwards – "way to go, team."

Miracle of Morgan's Creek, The ◐
23 22 25 21

1944 | Directed by Preston Sturges | With Eddie Bracken, Betty Hutton, William Demarest | 99 minutes | Not Rated

From the "fabulous" Preston Sturges comes this "raucous farce" starring Betty Hutton as Trudy Kockenlocker, an "unwed mother-to-be who can't remember who the father is" ("they're still debating how the story got past the Hollywood production code"); admirers say this "crackerjack comedy" is all about the "tremendous dialogue" and only "grows richer with age" – capped by an "ending that should be enshrined in the Movie Hall of Fame."

Miracle on 34th Street ✉◐
25 23 26 23

1947 | Directed by George Seaton | With Maureen O'Hara, Natalie Wood, Edmund Gwenn | 96 minutes | Not Rated

It "can't be Christmas" without a screening of this "schmaltzy", "charming fantasy" that embodies a "child's belief in Santa Claus" so well that it's become an enduring "seasonal favorite" for "every generation"; true believers say the Oscar-winning screenplay is the key behind this "perfect" "holiday classic" that puts the remakes to shame.

Miracle Worker, The ✉◐
25 28 24 22

1962 | Directed by Arthur Penn | With Anne Bancroft, Patty Duke, Victor Jory, Inga Swenson | 106 minutes | Not Rated

"Beautifully transferred from stage to screen" by director Penn, this "moving" account of deaf-and-blind Helen Keller and her teacher Annie Sullivan garnered Oscars for both leads (who reprised their Broadway roles); while Duke is undeniably "superb", it's Bancroft who "dominates" this "fiercely acted", "exceptional" film; most memorable moment: at the water pump.

Misery ✉

| | 21 | 24 | 23 | 19 |

1990 | Directed by Rob Reiner | With James Caan, Kathy Bates, Richard Farnsworth | 107 minutes | Rated R

This "freaky" yarn about an injured writer "rescued" from a snowstorm by a "seriously deranged" fan is a "hobbling", "cracking-with-tension" experience that really "packs a wallop"; Oscar-winner Bates is beyond "mesmerizing" as the seriously "obsessed", "sledgehammer-swinging" captor opposite Caan's "excellent", hapless hostage, though diehards say the real credit goes to Reiner's "great hand when it comes to directing Stephen King stories."

Misfits, The ◑

| | 21 | 24 | 21 | 22 |

1961 | Directed by John Huston | With Clark Gable, Marilyn Monroe, Montgomery Clift, Thelma Ritter, Eli Wallach | 124 minutes | Not Rated

The "swan song of Gable and Monroe" (and the "last movie" for both), this "bittersweet" romance between a Reno divorcée and an aging cowboy has a big theme at its heart, the demise of the Old West; while Arthur Miller's script is "thought-provoking" and there's plenty of "chemistry" between the leads, some say this "famously troubled production" ("were they all as dead tired as they appeared?") has "taken on an aura it doesn't deserve."

Miss Congeniality

| | 15 | 16 | 15 | 16 |

2000 | Directed by Donald Petrie | With Sandra Bullock, Michael Caine, Benjamin Bratt | 109 minutes | Rated PG-13

Action comedy meets "chick flick" in this "lighthearted send-up" of beauty-contest culture starring Bullock at her most "adorable" as a "tomboy FBI agent" who goes undercover as cheesecake in a national pageant; ok, it's "slight" and "sophomoric", but in the eyes of most beholders it's "endearing fun" – despite the absence of "Bert Parks."

Missing ✉

| | 24 | 26 | 25 | 22 |

1982 | Directed by Costa-Gavras | With Jack Lemmon, Sissy Spacek, John Shea | 122 minutes | Rated PG

Based on "actual events in South America", this fictionalized account of a U.S.-sanctioned military coup and its bloody aftermath is a "riveting" yet "moving" political thriller with a "devastating" message: "governments lie"; given "strong" performances by Lemmon and Spacek that "save it from being too preachy", many wonder why this Best Picture nominee is so "unheralded" and "overlooked" 25 years later.

Missing, The

| | 18 | 22 | 18 | 19 |

2003 | Directed by Ron Howard | With Tommy Lee Jones, Cate Blanchett | 137 minutes | Rated R

Helmer Howard goes for grit in this "entertaining" if "somewhat disturbing" Western that adds a "supernatural" slant to a "familiar" abducted-child storyline ("isn't this The Searchers in disguise?"); in spite of "great acting on all parts" and some "gorgeous scenery", those with reservations claim the "slow pace" sends things "a little off the mark."

Mission, The

| | 24 | 24 | 22 | 25 |

1986 | Directed by Roland Joffé | With Robert De Niro, Jeremy Irons, Liam Neeson | 126 minutes | Rated PG

"Beautifully shot", Oscar-winning cinematography nearly steals the show in this "intriguing drama" about an 18th-century struggle between missionaries and mercenaries over the riches of South America; even though evangelist Irons and reformed slave trader De Niro turn out their usual "amazing" work, unfazed foes feel Ennio Morricone's "soundtrack is far better" than the picture itself.

Mission: Impossible
| 16 | 15 | 15 | 21 |

1996 | Directed by Brian De Palma | With Tom Cruise, Jon Voight, Ving Rhames | 110 minutes | Rated PG-13
Many "convoluted" plot "twists" make this "tense", "James Bond-ish" action/adventure flick a "watchable" if "highly confusing" picture; while diehards "drool" over the "never-looking-better" Tom in an "all-black DKNY-ish outfit" performing "amazing stunts", purists pronounce it "not as good as the TV show" and bawl "bring back Peter Graves."

Mission: Impossible II
| 15 | 14 | 15 | 21 |

2000 | Directed by John Woo | With Tom Cruise, Dougray Scott, Thandie Newton, Ving Rhames | 123 minutes | Rated PG-13
There's "lots of flash but not much else" in this "slick" second installment of the franchise pairing "wannabe tough guy" Cruise ("before his freak-out") with Woo's directorial "bravado" for a "fast-paced" Ethan Hunt spy adventure; while "easier to follow" than the original, most still maul the "dull, Bond retread" plot and those impossibly "unrealistic" action scenes.

Mission: Impossible III
| 18 | 17 | 16 | 23 |

2006 | Directed by J.J. Abrams | With Tom Cruise, Philip Seymour Hoffman, Michelle Monaghan | 126 minutes | Rated PG-13
There's "never a dull moment" in this "whiz-bang", "megabucks" sequel that's voted the "best of the trilogy" given its "nonstop action", "believable love interest" subplot and Hoffman's "steal-the-show" performance as the "ultimate bad guy"; though critics complain about "not enough story" (adding "there's no such thing as a good movie with a colon in the title"), at least "Cruise appears saner here than in real life", performing "lots of jumping around" stunts but thankfully "none off couches."

Mississippi Burning
| 23 | 24 | 23 | 22 |

1988 | Directed by Alan Parker | With Gene Hackman, Willem Dafoe, Frances McDormand | 128 minutes | Rated R
A "story that needed to be told", this "powerful" depiction of '60s "racial unrest" focuses on an investigation of the murder of three Civil Rights workers; yet despite an "all-too-real glimpse of life in the Deep South", critics say it overemphasizes "white hate" to the point that there are few "speaking parts for black actors."

Missouri Breaks, The
| 16 | 20 | 17 | 18 |

1976 | Directed by Arthur Penn | With Marlon Brando, Jack Nicholson, Randy Quaid, Harry Dean Stanton | 126 minutes | Rated PG
Set in central Montana's river-carved badlands (aka the Missouri Breaks), this "unusual" Western about a gang of horse thieves features "excellent work by Nicholson" but is nearly "overacted" to oblivion by – "yikes!" – a "bloated" Brando in "one of the weirdest performances ever put on film"; ultimately, the flick "isn't for all tastes", though some find its "off-kilter" approach rather "fascinating."

	OVERALL	ACTING	STORY	PROD.

Mister Roberts

	27	27	24	23

1955 | Directed by John Ford, Mervyn LeRoy | With Henry Fonda, James Cagney, Jack Lemmon | 123 minutes | Not Rated

A Broadway hit transposed to the big screen, this "heartfelt" story about the misadventures of a WWII supply ship crew delivers "wonderful acting all around", from the "unforgettable" Cagney to the "perfect" Fonda and "no-slouch" Lemmon; a "great wartime comedy with a serious side", it leaves even tough guys with a "lump in their throat."

Modern Times ◑

	28	26	26	25

1936 | Directed by Charles Chaplin | With Charles Chaplin, Paulette Goddard | 87 minutes | Not Rated

"Timelessly funny and resonant", this "man-vs.-machine" story runs on a "blend of slapstick and pathos" guaranteed to make you "smile . . . though your heart is breaking"; there's "little dialogue" (save for Chaplin's "singing waiter" "gibberish number"), but his "heartwarming" performance and sharp "swipes at the age of technology" transcend words; in short, this one's a "must-see in *these* times."

Mommie Dearest

	17	19	16	17

1981 | Directed by Frank Perry | With Faye Dunaway, Diana Scarwid, Steve Forrest | 129 minutes | Rated PG

Right up there in the "camp classic" pantheon is this look at "ice lady" Joan Crawford and her adopted daughter Christina that's notorious for Dunaway's "uncanny", "over-the-top" title performance, a truly "scary" imagining of the "horror of being a fading star"; though some call it "exploitive", "bitter stuff", others insist it's "absorbing" and sometimes "terribly funny"; most quoted line: *no more wire hangers!*"

Mona Lisa Smile

	16	19	16	18

2003 | Directed by Mike Newell | With Julia Roberts, Kirsten Dunst, Julia Stiles, Maggie Gyllenhaal | 117 minutes | Rated PG-13

Set "in the days before women's lib", this "female version of *Dead Poets Society*" tells the story of a "strong-willed", 1950s college professor hoping to inspire her Stepford-esque students; though some call it "superficial", "watered-down feminism for the masses", side benefits include "authentic period touches", "beautiful costumes" and a "who's who of top young actresses stealing scenes from Queen Julia."

Money Pit, The

	16	17	17	16

1986 | Directed by Richard Benjamin | With Tom Hanks, Shelley Long, Alexander Godunov, Maureen Stapleton | 91 minutes | Rated PG

Hanks and Long find themselves "in over their heads" as spouses saddled with the "fixer-upper from hell" in this "silly" comedy taking "what every homeowner experiences" to levels of "frustrating insanity"; but those who feel it liens toward "lackluster" recommend you hold out for the "original version, *Mr. Blandings Builds His Dream House.*"

Monkey Business ◑

	26	24	21	22

1931 | Directed by Norman Z. McLeod | With the Marx Brothers, Thelma Todd | 77 minutes | Not Rated

This "early" Marx Brothers' "Hollywood vehicle" is both "solidly entertaining" and "suitably anarchic" as the sibs stow away on a luxury line and much "hilarious" "shipboard mayhem" ensues; though maybe "not quite their best" work, this "could be their looniest" of all – especially Harpo's "Punch and Judy" riff.

Mon Oncle ✉🅵   26 | 25 | 22 | 23

1958 | Directed by Jacques Tati | With Jacques Tati, Jean-Pierre Zola | 110 minutes | Not Rated

A trove of "very French" folly to "tickle your brain" and "set you giggling", this "delightful" comedy has Tati reprising his "sad-sack" Hulot act as he "bumbles through life" in a series of "superb gags and set pieces"; his "everyman-as-a-buffoon" shtick is a trusty "chuckle producer", while the underlying "commentary on modernity gone awry" is "really funny" too.

Monsieur Verdoux ◑   ▽ 25 | 25 | 23 | 22

1947 | Directed by Charles Chaplin | With Charles Chaplin, Martha Raye, Isobel Elsom | 124 minutes | Not Rated

Cynics who say "Chaplin's little tramp is too sentimental" relish this "wicked" comedy of murders, a "dark, dark, dark" tale in which Charlie plays a "serial-killing", modern-day "bluebeard"; admirers say it's way "ahead of its time", some find it "too preachy at the end", but most agree this "overlooked" work is still "very moving."

Monsoon Wedding 🅵   24 | 23 | 23 | 23

2002 | Directed by Mira Nair | With Naseeruddin Shah, Lillete Dubey, Shefali Shetty, Vasundhara Das, Parvin Dabas | 114 minutes | Rated R

A "feast for the funny bone, eyes and mind", this "charming" dramedy about a "dysfunctional" Indian family and the wedding of their daughter "proves that all families are the same no matter the ethnicity"; it's "a bit slow", but the "colorful cinematography" and "fantastic music" will make you "want to see it again."

Monster ✉   24 | 29 | 24 | 22

2003 | Directed by Patty Jenkins | With Charlize Theron, Christina Ricci | 109 minutes | Rated R

"Frighteningly believable" and thus "tough to watch", this bio of serial murderess Aileen Wuornos "pushes all the emotional buttons" thanks to a "complete immersion" in the role by the Oscar-winning, "makeup"-slathered Theron (with ample backup from the "unsung" Ricci as her girlfriend); though "not as gruesome as it could have been", this "downer" does deliver enough imagery so "violent" that many vow to "never pick up a hitchhiker again."

Monster-in-Law   15 | 17 | 15 | 17

2005 | Directed by Robert Luketic | With Jennifer Lopez, Jane Fonda, Michael Vartan | 101 minutes | Rated PG-13

Ending her 15-year "retirement" from the silver screen, J-Fo meets J-Lo in this "by-the-numbers" comedy about a "Barbara Walters type" who "channels all her energies" into squashing her son's engagement; if the "story holes" and "flat jokes" aren't scary enough, you can count on it to "put the ever-living fear of weddings into you."

Monster's Ball ✉   22 | 26 | 21 | 21

2001 | Directed by Marc Forster | With Billy Bob Thornton, Halle Berry | 111 minutes | Rated R

A "redneck" prison guard and the widow of an inmate he helped execute fall in love in this "disturbingly good" drama, a "gritty depiction" of "two lost souls"; the "slow-moving" story sometimes seems "strained", but is redeemed by the acting" of a deglamorized, Oscar-winning Berry and a "solid" Thornton, who display "great chemistry" during that "steamy sex scene."

Monsters, Inc. — 26 | - | 25 | 28
2001 | Directed by Peter Docter, David Silverman, Lee Unkrich | Animated | 92 minutes | Rated G

"Pixar does it again" with this "innovative" "animation gem" that "shows kids that the monsters in their closets are really harmless"; this time around, the "*Toy Story*" tech team alloy an "original" plot, "amazing attention to detail" and "ugly" but "cute" characters to create an "endearing" entertainment that works "for adults" too; P.S. the "blow-you-away" "flying door" sequence has got "theme-park ride" written all over it.

Monty Python & the Holy Grail — 26 | 22 | 23 | 21
1975 | Directed by Terry Gilliam, Terry Jones | With Monty Python | 91 minutes | Rated PG

By dint of "sheer tasteless genius", this "absurdly wacky" "burlesque of the King Arthur legend" turns "historic reverence" on its ear and rules among "true" Pythonettes as the "movie of a thousand quotes" ("bring out your dead!"); granted, it may be comprised of a series of "strung-together skits" involving "killer bunnies" and "knights who say 'ni'", but the array of "knee-slapping" characters provides enough "lunacy to last the ages."

Moonlight Mile — 17 | 22 | 17 | 18
2002 | Directed by Brad Silberling | With Jake Gyllenhaal, Dustin Hoffman, Susan Sarandon | 117 minutes | Rated PG-13

A "young man makes peace" with his murdered fiancée's "grieving family" and "falls in love" again in this "touching" drama based on the writer-director's "real-life" experience; though there's ample praise for the "three super leads" who milk the "tough" material's "every dysfunctional second", critics contend that the "wanting script" drags down what "could have been spectacular."

Moonraker — 16 | 14 | 15 | 20
1979 | Directed by Lewis Gilbert | With Roger Moore, Lois Chiles, Richard Kiel | 126 minutes | Rated PG

A "stiff" Roger Moore pursues the usual mad villain in this 007 picture that has a hard time living up to its "dynamite credits sequence"; most agree the "silly" scenario is "quite a stretch", what with metal-mouth "Jaws finding love" and a "laughable space battle" that "tries to cash in on *Star Wars*" but "plays more like a Bond spoof."

ℤ Moonstruck ✉ — 24 | 25 | 24 | 22
1987 | Directed by Norman Jewison | With Cher, Nicolas Cage, Olympia Dukakis | 102 minutes | Rated PG

Both "Italians and wannabe Italians" fall for this "totally charming" "romp" that shows how "love can be found in the least likely places" – even Brooklyn; a "phenomenal" Cher and Cage (making *amore* at such "full throttle" that the "heat between them could peel wallpaper") combine with a "dead-on", "star-studded" ensemble to keep this "romance classic" shining bright; fave scene: the "snap-out-of-it" slap.

	OVERALL	ACTING	STORY	PROD.

Moscow on the Hudson
19 | 20 | 20 | 18

1984 | Directed by Paul Mazursky | With Robin Williams, Maria Conchita Alonso | 115 minutes | Rated R

A "Soviet circus performer" bids the Motherland goodbye and "defects to NYC" in this "patriotic" Reagan-era comedy that doubles as a "tender tribute to the immigrant experience"; if post–Cold War audiences find the "need-for-freedom" shtick a bit "corny", at least Williams' "fine" performance supplies some "soul."

Mosquito Coast, The
16 | 19 | 18 | 18

1986 | Directed by Peter Weir | With Harrison Ford, Helen Mirren, River Phoenix | 117 minutes | Rated PG

A "refreshingly different" Ford stars in this "intriguing" adaptation of the Paul Theroux novel in which a utopian inventor "forsakes American civilization" to live with his family in the jungle, only to descend into "fanaticism" and beyond; while the "awesome" Phoenix is a bonus, skeptics swat the flick as "boring" and gnat very memorable.

Mothman Prophecies, The
15 | 16 | 16 | 16

2002 | Directed by Mark Pellington | With Richard Gere, Laura Linney, Debra Messing, Will Patton | 119 minutes | Rated PG-13

"Loosely based on real events", this "psychological ghost story" plays to the "X-Files crowd" with its "spooky" tale of a West Virginia town visited by an "eerie" apparition that can "predict tragedy" before it strikes; some see "potential" given the "solid" cast and "creepy" ambiance, but the "confusing" plot and "slow" pacing ultimately make for a "murky", "incoherent" film.

Motorcycle Diaries, The 🎬
23 | 25 | 23 | 24

2004 | Directed by Walter Salles | With Gael García Bernal, Rodrigo de la Serna | 128 minutes | Rated R

Witness the "seeds of social conscience" sprouting in "young Che Guevara" in this "poetic" road picture set amid "breathtaking South American scenery"; "ogle"-icious Bernal's "marvelous" turn as the future "legendary figure" stokes the revolutionary fire despite hitting a raw nerve with a few *capitalistas* who claim this "saintly" depiction fosters too much "undeserved attention."

Moulin Rouge
21 | 22 | 20 | 26

1952 | Directed by John Huston | With José Ferrer, Zsa Zsa Gabor, Colette Marchand | 119 minutes | Not Rated

"Drenched in color and the excitement of belle epoque Paris", this "original" look at the tortured life of artist Toulouse-Lautrec is the "lush" product of an era when "movies were movies"; Ferrer's "completely entertaining" performance as the "completely odd" painter is the glue here, even if his gloomy portrayal might be at odds with the "eye-candy" production values.

Moulin Rouge!
23 | 23 | 20 | 27

2001 | Directed by Baz Luhrmann | With Nicole Kidman, Ewan McGregor, Jim Broadbent | 127 minutes | Rated PG-13

This "dizzying, decadent" "fever dream of a musical" set in "bohemian Paris" earned a clutch of Oscar nominations and may have "single-handedly revived and re-created the genre" for the "new millennium"; the ever-"ravishing" Kidman "sheds her icy image" in a "kaleidoscopic" turn as a notorious "shady lady" smitten by a "naive poet", and it turns out "McGregor can sing", but naysayers call it a "confusing", "overedited" "mishmash" that's "all glitter, no substance."

Mouse That Roared, The
23	23	24	19

1959 | Directed by Jack Arnold | With Peter Sellers, Jean Seberg, David Kossoff | 83 minutes | Not Rated

"British humor has never been better" than in this "priceless" Cold War–era import about an impoverished nation that declares war on America, planning to lose in exchange for foreign aid; an "ingenious" satire that "pokes lots of holes" in a lot of targets, it's "worth seeing" for "Sellers' expert multiple performances alone."

Mr. & Mrs. Smith
16	17	15	19

2005 | Directed by Doug Liman | With Brad Pitt, Angelina Jolie, Vince Vaughn | 120 minutes | Rated PG-13

"Über-sexy" stars Pitt and Jolie make "one hell of an explosive couple" onscreen in this "over-the-top" action comedy made "infamous" by the leads' "headline"-hogging offscreen antics; but beyond the "Brangelina hype", it's mostly a "mindless" merger of *The War of the Roses* and *Prizzi's Honor*" gussied up with "nonstop" mayhem.

Mr. Blandings Builds His Dream House ◑
23	24	23	21

1948 | Directed by H.C. Potter | With Cary Grant, Myrna Loy, Melvyn Douglas | 94 minutes | Not Rated

"If you're thinking of building or remodeling your home", "there's no funnier movie" than this "timeless" "cautionary tale" that proves the "perils haven't changed in the last 50 years"; "fixer-uppers" laugh along with this amusing view of the "suburban dream gone askew", most notably "Myrna's painting-the-living-room" scene.

Mr. Deeds Goes to Town ✉◑
25	26	24	23

1936 | Directed by Frank Capra | With Gary Cooper, Jean Arthur, George Bancroft, Lionel Stander | 115 minutes | Not Rated

With "all the heart and soul" (and "schmaltz") that you expect from director "Capra-corn", this "sweet" tale of a "pixilated" eccentric who inherits a fortune and then tries to give it away is one of the "great populist films" of the '30s; thanks to the "feel-good" mood, "heart-warming ending" and Cooper's "trademark underplaying", it's become a "standard" and is "much superior" to Adam Sandler's remake, *Mr. Deeds*

Mr. Holland's Opus
21	22	21	19

1995 | Directed by Stephen Herek | With Richard Dreyfuss, Glenne Headly | 143 minutes | Rated PG

"Sweet, funny and insightful", this "uplifting" opus chronicles the career of a "reluctant" high-school music teacher "who makes a difference in the lives of his students" while "struggling to come to terms with his own deaf son"; though the hard-hearted fuss it's too "preachy", most swear this "inspirational" story is worth seeing for Dreyfuss' "superb" performance alone.

Mr. Hulot's Holiday ◑🄵
25	25	22	22

1954 | Directed by Jacques Tati | With Jacques Tati, Nathalie Pascaud | 86 minutes | Not Rated

Right "up there with Keaton and Chaplin", Tati's "irresistible" "comic masterpiece" is bound to "take away the worst blues" with some of the "best sight gags" delivered in "almost pure mime"; when its "hilariously" maladroit title character goes to a vacation retreat, whatever "could possibly go wrong does" and the payoff's a "quirky", "low-key" "laugh riot."

Mr. Mom ✉ | 18 | 18 | 20 | 17

1983 | Directed by Stan Dragoti | With Michael Keaton, Teri Garr, Martin Mull | 91 minutes | Rated PG

Mom and pop "switch roles" in this "fish-out-of-water" comedy detailing the misadventures of a "stay-at-home dad" reduced to "ironing grilled-cheese sandwiches" and "playing poker" with housewives for "shopping coupons"; but even though Keaton is a "likable" enough "slob" in the title role, rewinders report this "guilty pleasure" "doesn't hold up" to repeated viewings.

Mrs. Brown | 22 | 28 | 23 | 23

1997 | Directed by John Madden | With Judi Dench, Billy Connolly, Geoffrey Palmer | 103 minutes | Rated PG

"Not widely seen", this "intelligent" drama detailing the platonic relationship between Queen Victoria and her groomsman shows that "even the most hardened heart can be changed by love"; naturally, many say that the "amazing" Dench is "the reason to see it", given her "poignant" performance, though the "intriguing" plot and "subtle" work from Connolly are equally "wonderful."

Mrs. Doubtfire | 20 | 23 | 20 | 20

1993 | Directed by Chris Columbus | With Robin Williams, Sally Field, Pierce Brosnan | 125 minutes | Rated PG-13

This "laugh-out-loud" story of a man attempting to "win back his ex and kids" by impersonating a "nanny" manages to be "over-the-top", "subversive" and "endearing" all at once; sure, doubters snipe the "far-fetched" screenplay "can't decide if it's a farce or a tearjerker", but it's agreed that "riot" Williams is "at his manic best" when in "drag."

Mrs. Henderson Presents | 23 | 27 | 22 | 23

2005 | Directed by Stephen Frears | With Judi Dench, Bob Hoskins, Kelly Reilly, Christopher Guest | 103 minutes | Rated R

"Dench didn't earn her reputation for nothing", as demonstrated by her "marvelous" performance in this British comedy about an "eccentric" theater owner whose "nude cuties" revue helps stiffen public resolve during WWII; co-star Hoskins is equally "wonderful" in support, and the pairing of "top-notch humor" with "poignant" meditations on "love and loss" strikes a "crowd-pleasing" balance.

Mrs. Miniver ✉◑ | 25 | 27 | 24 | 24

1942 | Directed by William Wyler | With Greer Garson, Walter Pidgeon, Teresa Wright | 134 minutes | Not Rated

For "WWII without the combat scenes", check out the "civilian side" in this "stirring" saga of Britain during the Blitz, starring Garson as a "stiff-upper-lipped" homemaker who stoically endures everything from "harrowing air raids" to "Nazi paratroopers" in the kitchen; while cynics say it seems "more propaganda than entertainment", the film was an Oscar magnet, taking home six statuettes, including Best Picture and Best Actress.

	OVERALL	ACTING	STORY	PROD.

Mr. Smith Goes to Washington ◐
26 | 27 | 25 | 22

1939 | Directed by Frank Capra | With James Stewart, Jean Arthur, Claude Rains | 125 minutes | Not Rated

"As American as two slices of apple pie", Frank Capra's "rousing" "political fairy tale" about "one man's belief in goodness" and his eventual "triumph" "appeals to the idealist in each of us"; "corny", perhaps, but "you can't help but be moved" by Stewart waging the "filibuster to beat all filibusters" – and proving "you *can* beat City Hall."

Mulan
23 | – | 23 | 24

1998 | Directed by Tony Bancroft, Barry Cook | Animated | 88 minutes | Rated G

An "underrated" rarity, this "gorgeously realized" animated "Chinese folk tale" features a Disney heroine "who can carry a movie on her own"; its mix of "family honor" and "women power" make it "good for a girl's self-esteem", while "just the right balance of seriousness and humor" "sends its message without preaching."

Mulholland Dr.
20 | 22 | 19 | 22

2001 | Directed by David Lynch | With Naomi Watts, Laura Harring, Justin Theroux | 145 minutes | Rated R

"Another confusing but consuming Lynch production", this "intriguing", "utterly disquieting" "portrait of Hollywood losers" "requires contemplation" since it's "hard to follow"; sure, fans say its "smoldering" leads are so "beautiful" that their presence alone makes the film "visually worth it", but cynics feel "totally ripped off" by this "weird" "nonsense."

Mummy, The ◐
24 | 20 | 22 | 23

1932 | Directed by Karl Freund | With Boris Karloff, Zita Johann | 72 minutes | Not Rated

Fresh out of his Frankenstein boots, "master" of fear Karloff wraps himself around the role of an ancient Egyptian priest who's revived when foolhardy explorers open his crypt in this "standout" horror flick; indeed, Boris is "so very creepy" that many say this "original" version of the oft-filmed tale is still the "best."

Mummy, The
19 | 16 | 18 | 24

1999 | Directed by Stephen Sommers | With Brendan Fraser, Rachel Weisz | 124 minutes | Rated PG-13

Archeologists ravage Egyptian tombs to disastrous results in this "cornball" "modern B movie" featuring "fancy CGI effects" and a plot that lurches between "scary and funny"; but foes who dis its "ridiculous" premise suggest you "rent the original – *Raiders of the Lost Ark.*"

Mummy Returns, The
18 | 17 | 18 | 23

2001 | Directed by Stephen Sommers | With Brendan Fraser, Rachel Weisz, The Rock | 130 minutes | Rated PG-13

Wrapped in even more "neat FX" and "tongue-in-cheek" nods to "monster movies" than before, this "fast-paced" sequel sees the return of *The Mummy*'s "dependable" cast for another "old-fashioned adventure" in "pop" Egyptology by way of Indiana Jones; alright, it's "not an award-winner by any means", but for "brainless" fare, "you can't go wrong."

| | OVERALL | ACTING | STORY | PROD. |

Munich
23 | 24 | 23 | 24

2005 | Directed by Steven Spielberg | With Eric Bana, Daniel Craig, Geoffrey Rush | 164 minutes | Rated R

The "spiritually corrosive effects of revenge" come under Steven Spielberg's "soul-searching" lens in this "provocative", "action-packed" thriller modeled on the "real events" that followed the 1972 "massacre of Israeli Olympic athletes" by Palestinian terrorists; treating the "very sensitive issue" of the Middle East conflict in a "balanced" manner, it suggests there are "no easy answers", frustrating foes who prefer a less "muddy" moral message.

Muppet Movie, The
24 | 23 | 23 | 25

1979 | Directed by James Frawley | With Charles Durning, Austin Pendleton | 97 minutes | Rated G

"You're never too old" to enjoy this "goofy" but "utterly delightful" romp that might unleash your "inner kid" thanks to some "wonderful puppetry" abetted by an array of star-studded cameos from everyone from Milton Berle to Steve Martin; fans say it's the "best" of the Muppet oeuvre, crediting the "genius" of "national treasure" Jim Henson for the "successful transition" of *Sesame Street*'s denizens to the big screen.

Murderball
25 | - | 25 | 22

2005 | Directed by Henry Alex Rubin, Dana Adam Shapiro | Documentary | 88 minutes | Rated PG-13

"Leave your pity at the door" and hold tight for this "hard-hitting" documentary profiling the "fierce competitors" of "quadriplegic rugby", a "rough" wheelchair sport with a rep for "demolition derby" intensity; smashing the conventional "clichés about the disabled", it's a "non-sentimental" glimpse at a "seldom seen" group whose "guts, strength and love of life" are an "inspiration" to all.

Murder by Death
21 | 21 | 22 | 19

1976 | Directed by Robert Moore | With Peter Falk, Peter Sellers, Maggie Smith, Alec Guinness | 94 minutes | Rated PG

A "kooky lampoon that hits the spot", this Neil Simon–penned whodunit "spoof" places a "diverse" group of private eyes in a castle where murder ensues; given the efforts of a Charlie Chan–esque Sellers and a Bogart-channeling Falk, this "madcap" exercise is a "must-see satire for mystery lovers", even if some turn up evidence of too many "good actors playing useless parts."

Murder, My Sweet ◑
24 | 24 | 24 | 22

1944 | Directed by Edward Dmytryk | With Dick Powell, Claire Trevor, Anne Shirley, Otto Kruger | 95 minutes | Not Rated

For "Dick Powell without Ruby Keeler", check out his "breakout" role as the "tough" private dick Philip Marlowe in this adaptation of Raymond Chandler's *Farewell, My Lovely*; it's a "quintessential" piece of "early noir", replete with a "perfect femme fatale", "unsurpassed" dialogue and a world-weary, "wisecracking" outlook on life.

Murder on the Orient Express
23 | 23 | 26 | 24

1974 | Directed by Sidney Lumet | With Albert Finney, Lauren Bacall, Ingrid Bergman | 128 minutes | Rated PG

"Agatha Christie hasn't been done better" than in this "fascinatingly complex, lushly produced" Hercule Poirot mystery set onboard the

Orient Express; boasting a "crisply directed" "all-star" ensemble cast that "looks like they're having the time of their lives", this "luxuriously funny" "perfect thriller" certainly "won't bore you" – and "you'll never guess whodunit."

Music Man, The
25 | 24 | 25 | 26

1962 | Directed by Morton DaCosta | With Robert Preston, Shirley Jones, Buddy Hackett | 151 minutes | Rated G

Making an "exquisite, seamless transition from Broadway to the silver screen", this slice of "pure Americana" about a "traveling con man" let loose in River City, Iowa, hits "classic" notes with its "catchy" Meredith Willson score; thanks to a "tour-de-force" turn by a "mesmerizing" Preston, this "family treat" "never grows old."

Must Love Dogs
16 | 18 | 15 | 16

2005 | Directed by Gary David Goldberg | With Diane Lane, John Cusack, Elizabeth Perkins | 98 minutes | Rated PG-13

Taking a "lighthearted" look at the "horrors of dating after divorce", this "run-of-the-mill" chick flick boasts a "wonderful" cast led by two "rock stars of romantic comedy", the "charming" Lane and "endearing" Cusack; problem is, there's absolutely "no chemistry between them", and a "slow-paced", "dog-tired" script to boot.

Mutiny on the Bounty ✉◐
25 | 25 | 25 | 23

1935 | Directed by Frank Lloyd | With Charles Laughton, Clark Gable, Franchot Tone | 132 minutes | Not Rated

Despite being "a bit creaky" after all these years, this original version of a legendary clash of egos on the high seas remains "the one and only" simply because "you don't get acting like this anymore": Laughton is darn "grand" as "definitive villain" Captain Bligh, and "Gable is, well, Gable" as Mr. Christian, his second-in-command.

Mutiny on the Bounty
22 | 24 | 24 | 22

1962 | Directed by Lewis Milestone | With Marlon Brando, Trevor Howard, Richard Harris | 178 minutes | Not Rated

Ultra-"fabulous scenery" that will surely make you "want to move to Tahiti" and a "cast of thousands" collide in this "big-budget" MGM remake about an uprising at sea; Brando turns in "one of his most controversial roles" as a "foppish" Fletcher Christian, even if foes harrumph "I'll take Gable."

My Beautiful Laundrette
23 | 24 | 23 | 19

1985 | Directed by Stephen Frears | With Daniel Day-Lewis, Gordon Warnecke | 98 minutes | Rated R

This "highly original" drama of "modern London" puts race and assimilation through a "wonderfully up-front" spin cycle in its story of "smart", "entrepreneurial" immigrants vs. the nativist "lower classes"; amid the many "honest" moments that come out in the wash is the "daring" bond between Warnecke's go-getting Pakistani and Day-Lewis' tough hooligan, resulting in some "steamy gay kissing."

My Best Friend's Wedding
19 | 19 | 19 | 19

1997 | Directed by P.J. Hogan | With Julia Roberts, Dermot Mulroney, Rupert Everett | 105 minutes | Rated PG-13

There's "no thinking required" in this "enjoyable if predictable" "chick flick" about a single gal bent on preventing her best male friend from getting hitched; while a "surprisingly funny Roberts" and "yummy Everett" "chew up the scenery" entertainingly, those through with love find this "anti-romance" "contrived" and "obvious" – except for the "'Say a Little Prayer'" sing-along.

My Big Fat Greek Wedding   23 | 22 | 23 | 21

2002 | Directed by Joel Zwick | With Nia Vardalos, John Corbett, Lainie Kazan | 96 minutes | Rated PG

It "doesn't matter whether you are Greek, Jewish, Italian or Albanian" – "we all see our crazy relatives up on the screen" in this "absolutely hilarious" "feel-good" look at Hellenic matrimony featuring a "likable cast of characters that you grow to love despite all their quirks"; critics claim "too much big fat hype", but they're outvoted by fans who "will never look at Windex the same way again."

My Bodyguard   18 | 18 | 19 | 16

1980 | Directed by Tony Bill | With Chris Makepeace, Adam Baldwin, Matt Dillon | 96 minutes | Rated PG

The "ultimate teenage revenge fantasy", this "feel-good" flick about an "underdog" high-schooler who hires a tough classmate to protect him from a bully "rings true" with "anyone who was ever picked on"; sure, there's a "silly, irrelevant" subplot about "eccentric grown-ups", but overall this "endearing" "coming-of-age saga" is "well done."

My Brilliant Career   25 | 28 | 25 | 23

1979 | Directed by Gillian Armstrong | With Judy Davis, Sam Neill, Wendy Hughes | 100 minutes | Rated G

A "headstrong young woman" coming of age in 19th-century Australia must choose between a man or a career in this "wonderful" drama that's a bona fide "feminist favorite" ("it changed my life"); in the "brilliant performance" that made her a star, "Davis rules", and abetted by "lovely photography and scenery", the film's an "absorbing" testimony to "girl power."

My Cousin Vinny   22 | 24 | 21 | 19

1992 | Directed by Jonathan Lynn | With Joe Pesci, Ralph Macchio, Marisa Tomei | 120 minutes | Rated R

"Fuhgeddaboudit": this "laugh-out-loud", "quotable" "courtroom classic" about a novice "Noo Yawk lawyer" representing his cousin in an Alabama murder trial is a "cleverly written" comic look at "Southern justice"; a "perfect" Pesci "carries the show", amply assisted by Tomei, who earned a "well-deserved Oscar" just by "making a Brooklyn accent the sexiest sound around"; P.S. it works best with "ordered-in pizza."

My Darling Clementine ◑   25 | 27 | 23 | 24

1946 | Directed by John Ford | With Henry Fonda, Linda Darnell, Victor Mature, Walter Brennan | 97 minutes | Not Rated

"One of the all-time great Westerns", this "wonderfully humane" Ford oater strays from the "real history" behind the "shootout at the O.K. Corral" to pose an "idealized" Wyatt Earp against a "rich" backdrop of a frontier "on the verge of change"; fortified with "romance", "moody characters" (Doc Holliday "reciting Shakespeare") and, you bet, lots of "gunplay", it's a "rewarding" ride that exemplifies the "definition of 'classic.'"

My Dinner with Andre

	OVERALL	ACTING	STORY	PROD.
	21	21	18	19

1981 | Directed by Louis Malle | With Wallace Shawn, Andre Gregory | 110 minutes | Not Rated

Who'd have thought a movie that "consists entirely of a dinner conversation" between two acquaintances could keep you entertained for two hours?; although with talk "spanning every philosophical topic" that "captures the magic in the ordinary", Shawn and Gregory do just that; "remarkable for how little it works with", this "simple, unpretentious" art-house hit is "oddly fascinating" to those who wish their own dining companions "could be as interesting."

☑ My Fair Lady ✉

27	27	27	27

1964 | Directed by George Cukor | With Audrey Hepburn, Rex Harrison, Stanley Holloway | 170 minutes | Rated G

"Hollywood couldn't have done a better job" than this "grand, classy" version of Broadway's Lerner and Loewe musical "based on *Pygmalion*"; a "breathtaking" (but "dubbed") Hepburn is "incomparable" as the Cockney "guttersnipe turned into a lady", while Oscar-winner Harrison "at his tweedy best" plays her "superior yet vulnerable" teacher; "infectious" tunes and costumes that "leave you weak-kneed" ("those hats!") make this "luscious production" all the more "loverly."

My Favorite Year

22	25	22	20

1982 | Directed by Richard Benjamin | With Peter O'Toole, Mark Linn-Baker, Jessica Harper | 92 minutes | Rated PG

This "winning comedy" about the "early days of TV" involves a boozy matinee idol's appearance on a program that's a "great riff on the old Sid Caesar show"; although "O'Toole playing a drunk might not be a stretch", he "nails every nuance", turning this "affectionate period piece" into "one of the funniest movies no one has ever seen."

My Girl

20	18	19	18

1991 | Directed by Howard Zieff | With Dan Aykroyd, Jamie Lee Curtis, Anna Chlumsky | 102 minutes | Rated PG

Get out your handkerchiefs: this "make-you-cry" dramedy pulls out all the stops in its depiction of a motherless girl dealing with emotional awakening (and her father's new girlfriend); Chlumsky's "sweet", "heart-wrenching" turn nails the "innocence and complexity of childhood" so well that many would like to "have her as a daughter."

My Left Foot ✉

25	28	25	23

1989 | Directed by Jim Sheridan | With Daniel Day-Lewis, Brenda Fricker, Hugh O'Conor | 98 minutes | Rated R

It "could have been sappy and overly sentimental", but this "stereotype-smashing" true account of an Irish man born with cerebral palsy is "handled with unvarnished dignity" thanks to the Oscar-winning Day-Lewis, who "maintains the contorted body and emotional scars" of his condition so adeptly that "you forget you're watching an actor"; "very moving", this film's a "beacon of light for all."

My Life As a Dog 🇫

25	24	25	22

1987 | Directed by Lasse Hallström | With Anton Glanzelius, Melinda Kinnaman | 101 minutes | Rated PG-13

"For once, an adult really gets into a child's head" in this "enchanting" Swedish "coming-of-age" drama that devotees deem director

"Hallström's best"; the "puckish" lead is both "complex" and "cute", his fellow villagers "wacky" and the story "heart-tugging" without a "single false note" – no wonder many say it's "goose bump–worthy."

My Little Chickadee ❶
23 | 23 | 18 | 19

1940 | Directed by Edward F. Cline | With Mae West, W.C. Fields | 83 minutes | Not Rated

"Two comic pros" take on the Old West in this screwball oater about a fallen woman run out of town and the con man she weds; Mae's "priceless line delivery" works well against W.C.'s "vaudeville-era" gags – but since they "share very little screen time together" (interrupted by lengthy "pedestrian melodramatics"), some say the pairing of these screen legends "isn't as effective as one might hope."

My Man Godfrey ❶
25 | 25 | 23 | 21

1936 | Directed by Gregory La Cava | With William Powell, Carole Lombard, Eugene Pallette | 94 minutes | Not Rated

As an "unconventional love-struck heiress", Lombard displays "impeccable timing" opposite the "masterful" Powell as the "hobo hired to be the family butler" in this "ultimate screwball comedy"; of course, the "fast-paced", fast-talking "plot is absurd" (that's "precisely the point"), but the "charming" principals "make it look convincing."

My Night at Maud's ❶🅕
▽ 26 | 26 | 23 | 23

1970 | Directed by Eric Rohmer | With Jean-Louis Trintignant, Françoise Fabian, Marie-Christine Barrault | 105 minutes | Rated PG

A "movie about grown-ups for grown-ups", this "rewarding philosophical" drama examines the "concept of morality" in its story of a man attracted to two very different women; it's "mostly an extended conversation" with beaucoup "talk, talk and more talk", but intellectuals insist "all of it is worth listening to" (or reading about in the subtitles).

My Own Private Idaho
19 | 21 | 19 | 19

1991 | Directed by Gus Van Sant | With River Phoenix, Keanu Reeves, William Richert | 102 minutes | Rated R

"Beautiful boys" work the streets of Portland in this "original modern romance" about a "narcoleptic hustler" (Phoenix, in a "heartbreaking" turn) who falls for a "man he can never have"; once the plot drifts off into a "pretentious" takeoff of *Henry IV*, some say it becomes "overreaching" and downright "depressing", but still there are "enough good moments to make it worthwhile."

Mystic Pizza
17 | 18 | 17 | 15

1988 | Directed by Donald Petrie | With Annabeth Gish, Julia Roberts, Lili Taylor | 104 minutes | Rated R

"Female friendships" and young romance are examined in this "coming-of-age charmer" set in a New England pizza parlor, an "authentic slice of life" that's also a "great Sunday afternoon chick flick"; notable for being "Julia's first major movie", it's "fluffy", but its "sweetness" is "winning."

Mystic River ✉
26 | 28 | 25 | 25

2003 | Directed by Clint Eastwood | With Sean Penn, Tim Robbins, Kevin Bacon, Laurence Fishburne, Marcia Gay Harden, Laura Linney | 137 minutes | Rated R

"Lots of angst and anger" lie beneath this "bleak" tale of childhood buddies reunited as adults in the aftermath of a murder; it really "packs a wallop" thanks to a "pitch-perfect", "all-star" ensemble (with special kudos to Oscar winners Penn and Robbins for their "kick-in-the-gut" performances), not to mention Clint's "compelling" direction and "haunting score"; the only dissonant note is that "slightly off-the-mark" ending.

Naked Gun, The
20 | 17 | 17 | 18

1988 | Directed by David Zucker | With Leslie Nielsen, Priscilla Presley, George Kennedy | 85 minutes | Rated PG-13

This "laugh-a-minute" "cop spoof" from the minds behind *Airplane!* stars a "deadpan" Nielsen, who "raises the bar for satirical comedy" with his "terrific" performance; sure, the "brilliantly dumb characters" and "loopy overlapping dialogue" are equally "riotous", but ultimately "you have to be a guy to enjoy this much stupidity"; P.S. some find it "discomfortingly amusing" when O.J. Simpson appears.

Naked Lunch
17 | 19 | 17 | 18

1991 | Directed by David Cronenberg | With Peter Weller, Judy Davis, Ian Holm, Roy Scheider | 115 minutes | Rated R

Cronenberg's "well-meaning" adaptation of William Burroughs' iconic chronicle of "heroin-induced hallucinations" endured in a North African "expat community" injects a blend of the author's "bio and fiction" into a nightmarish hash of "mind-bending" imagery; "not for the faint of heart", it could "freak out" the uninitiated as well as bug beatniks who insist "this book can't be filmed."

Name of the Rose, The
22 | 24 | 24 | 23

1986 | Directed by Jean-Jacques Annaud | With Sean Connery, Christian Slater, F. Murray Abraham | 130 minutes | Rated R

The "cold, scary world" of the Middle Ages comes to life in this "excellent period mystery" drawn from Umberto Eco's "intricate" novel about a "monk who visits a monastery plagued by unexplained murders"; blessed by Connery's "top-notch" turn as a kind of "14th-century 007", it's an "entertaining" take on "religious conspiracy" that many find "superior to *The Da Vinci Code*."

Nanny McPhee
21 | 22 | 21 | 23

2006 | Directed by Kirk Jones | With Emma Thompson, Colin Firth, Angela Lansbury | 97 minutes | Rated PG

A "lonely" widower saddled with an "awful bunch" of "misbehaving children" dials "nanny 9-1-1" and receives "magical", "Mary Poppins"–esque relief in this "charming" fairy tale; Thompson is "fabulous" in the title role (her "makeup's unbelievable" too), and if the McPlot veers toward "formulaic", know that small fry are "sure to enjoy" it.

Napoléon ❶∅
▽ 29 | 22 | 22 | 29

1927 | Directed by Abel Gance | With Albert Dieudonné, Antonin Artaud | 235 minutes | Rated G

"Eye-popping even today", this bio of Napoléon Bonaparte from "audacious" director Gance is a "sweeping epic" from the silent era that had been truncated over time but then restored to its former glory; its "unsurpassed" camerawork includes shots made "from horseback" and on a "pendulum", but its "final triptych", predating widescreen photography, makes for a particularly "rousing" windup.

	OVERALL	ACTING	STORY	PROD.

Napoleon Dynamite
19 | 20 | 17 | 17

2004 | Directed by Jared Hess | With Jon Heder, Jon Gries | 82 minutes | Rated PG

"Gosh", the road to "cult classic" status was short for this "flippin' sweet" underdog comedy whose "deadpan" depiction of a carrot-topped, "tater tot"–chomping "born loser" pays "honest" homage to that "nerdy kid you went to school with"; voters "love it or hate it": lovers like its "quotable lines" ("vote for Pedro") and the "best dance scene ever", though foes fret it "goes nowhere and does nothing."

Nashville
23 | 23 | 22 | 24

1975 | Directed by Robert Altman | With Ronee Blakley, Keith Carradine, Lily Tomlin, Geraldine Chaplin, Karen Black, Shelley Duvall, Henry Gibson, Scott Glenn | 159 minutes | Rated R

It's the "wonderful ensemble" cast that makes this comic "portrait of '70s America" set in Nashville "richer and funnier with every viewing"; though some find it "frustrating" ("too many people talking at once"), "black humor" fans dub it "Altman's best", with enough "interesting characters" and "smart observations" to make it the "country cousin of *Gosford Park*."

National Lampoon's Vacation
22 | 17 | 20 | 17

1983 | Directed by Harold Ramis | With Chevy Chase, Beverly D'Angelo, Randy Quaid | 98 minutes | Rated R

"Bad taste has never been funnier" than in this "vacation-from-hell" comedy recounting a "dysfunctional family's" cross-country road trip; as the beleaguered dad, Chase is at the "pinnacle of his career", though many say he's upstaged by fleeting glimpses of white-"hot" "Christie Brinkley in a red sports car."

National Treasure
19 | 17 | 20 | 21

2004 | Directed by John Turteltaub | With Nicolas Cage, Jon Voight | 131 minutes | Rated PG

"Indiana Jones meets *The Da Vinci Code*" in this "helluva roller-coaster ride" hinged around a treasure map discovered "on the back of the Declaration of Independence" ("seriously") and other "far-fetched" clues geared toward "American history buffs"; granted, Nic may be "no Harrison Ford" and the flick an "utterly disposable" "no-brainer", but it's "ok for a little escapism" and works best with a "large bag of popcorn."

National Velvet
24 | 24 | 24 | 22

1945 | Directed by Clarence Brown | With Elizabeth Taylor, Mickey Rooney, Anne Revere | 123 minutes | Rated G

The movie equivalent of "comfort food", this "classic" "coming-of-age story" about a "girl and her horse" stars a "dazzlingly young Taylor" and a "scene-stealing" Rooney in a "feel-good" parable of "surmounting obstacles to make dreams come true"; maybe it's "corny", but any young lady "who ever dreamed of having a pony" can't help but "gush" over that climatic steeplechase race.

Natural, The
23 | 21 | 23 | 22

1984 | Directed by Barry Levinson | With Robert Redford, Robert Duvall, Glenn Close | 134 minutes | Rated PG

"Every Little Leaguer's favorite flick", this mix of "magic" and "major league baseball" stars a "rugged Redford" as a "middle-aged rookie" who hits a "chill"-inducing "home run into the lights"; though some sigh it's too "sentimental", fans cheer this "solid period drama" (and Randy Newman's "unforgettable score").

Natural Born Killers
14 | 16 | 14 | 17

1994 | Directed by Oliver Stone | With Woody Harrelson, Juliette Lewis, Robert Downey Jr., Tommy Lee Jones | 118 minutes | Rated R

Ok, it's director Stone's "most controversial work", but otherwise this "raw" (as in "bloody") look at how "mass murderers" are portrayed by the "mass media" galvanizes surveyors: admirers call it a "blistering social commentary" that's both "visionary" and "visually stunning", but sinkers say its "violence-as-a-cartoon" ethos is "gratuitous", "pointless" and ultimately "more stupid than thrilling."

Network ⊠
24 | 25 | 24 | 22

1976 | Directed by Sidney Lumet | With Faye Dunaway, William Holden, Peter Finch, Beatrice Straight | 120 minutes | Rated R

Even 30 years later, newscaster Howard Beale's "fateful cry, 'I'm mad as hell, and I'm not going to take it anymore'" is still "relevant" to proponents of this "prophetic" dramedy about television's "battle between news and entertainment"; "expertly written" by Paddy Chayefsky and "brilliantly acted" by Finch, Dunaway and Straight (who all won Oscars), this "biting" dark comedy has surveyors citing *Jerry Springer* and sighing "it's all true now."

Never on Sunday ◑
24 | 26 | 23 | 21

1960 | Directed by Jules Dassin | With Melina Mercouri, Jules Dassin | 91 minutes | Not Rated

A "sensuous" Mercouri became an international star after illuminating the screen in this "delightful" drama about an "earthy" Greek prostitute and an uptight American (played by director Dassin) who tries to pull a Pygmalion on her; although once "shocking" and now "delightfully dated", every-nighters could "watch it anytime – even on a Sunday."

Never Say Never Again
18 | 20 | 17 | 19

1983 | Directed by Irvin Kershner | With Sean Connery, Klaus Maria Brandauer, Barbara Carrera | 134 minutes | Rated PG

Live-and-let-diehards declare it's "fun to see Connery reprise the role that made him famous (and rich)" in this "rehash of *Thunderball*" featuring an "older" though "still studly" 007 who's "stunningly" teamed with Carrera; but foes say this "disappointing" picture "shouldn't be considered a Bond film", since it lacks the "appropriate music" and panache of producer Albert Broccoli.

New World, The
16 | 17 | 15 | 23

2005 | Directed by Terrence Malick | With Colin Farrell, Q'Orianka Kilcher, Christopher Plummer | 135 minutes | Rated PG-13

"Visual poet" Malick stays "true to form" with this "contemplative, brooding" look at the "life of Pocahontas" as a metaphor for the "broken love affair" between Native Americans and Virginia's first British colonists; but while fans faun over the "lush", "put-a-frame-around-it" imagery and 14-year-old Kilcher's "particularly good" performance, just as many malign the film's "slow" pace and "pretentious" airs.

	OVERALL	ACTING	STORY	PROD.

New York, New York
`19` `21` `18` `22`

1977 | Directed by Martin Scorsese | With Liza Minnelli, Robert De Niro, Mary Kay Place | 164 minutes | Rated PG

Minnelli's "perfectly cast" and in "flawless voice" in this "postmodern musical from Martin Scorsese" about married musicians yearning for "fame in the 1940s"; still, many moan "De Niro's character is so unlikable" that the "picture never works", resulting in a "forgettable muddle" – "except for a certain song."

Niagara
`21` `22` `20` `22`

1953 | Directed by Henry Hathaway | With Marilyn Monroe, Joseph Cotten, Jean Peters | 92 minutes | Not Rated

The movie that "made Monroe a star", this "twisted" Technicolor thriller is set back in the day when Niagara Falls was a "hot destination" for honeymooners; its "double-cross", "soap opera"–esque plot involves a "treacherous wife", a frustrated husband and a pair of naive newlyweds, but its most "unforgettable" moment is Marilyn's "famous walk" through a parking lot, which totally "overshadows" everything else in the picture.

Nicholas Nickleby
`22` `23` `24` `22`

2002 | Directed by Douglas McGrath | With Christopher Plummer, Jim Broadbent, Charlie Hunnam, Anne Hathaway | 132 minutes | Rated PG

"Escape to another era" and follow the "wholesome" adventures of a "down-on-his-luck" bloke who "rises to the top" in this "rich", "intelligently pared-down" rendering of Dickens' "very long novel"; "outstanding performances" by the "wonderfully odious" Plummer and fellow "fine talents" contribute to an overall "solid" production, leaving fans to ponder why "nobody saw it."

Night at the Opera, A ◑
`26` `25` `22` `22`

1935 | Directed by Sam Wood | With the Marx Brothers, Kitty Carlisle, Margaret Dumont | 96 minutes | Not Rated

"Inspired insanity" meets "Marxist lunacy" in this "nutty" comedy (the "origin of the term 'laugh riot'") from the brothers Marx, wherein Groucho persuades a social-climbing Dumont to invest in an opera production; fans fast-forward through the "saccharine musical moments" in favor of the "verbal dazzle" of the "contract routine", the "baseball-in-the-orchestra-pit" bit and, of course, that "not-to-be-believed stateroom scene."

Nightmare Alley ◐
▽ `22` `23` `21` `21`

1947 | Directed by Edmund Goulding | With Tyrone Power, Joan Blondell, Coleen Gray | 110 minutes | Not Rated

"Talk about a downer" – this "creepy" film noir flick depicts the "moral disintegration" of a "true charlatan", a carnival roustabout turned "phony nightclub spiritualist" who "goes too far to reach his dream"; Power "fearlessly proves he's not just another pretty face" with a "scary yet appealing" performance that's "stunning for its time."

Nightmare Before Christmas, The
`24` `-` `22` `28`

1993 | Directed by Henry Selick | Animated | 76 minutes | Rated PG

The "perfect antidote to the holidays" may well be this "magical", "macabre masterpiece" of stop-motion animation that ideally epitomizes the "bizarre genius" of producer Tim Burton; with a "cool story" – Halloween meets Christmas – "interesting characters" and "Danny Elfman's great score", it's a "must-see for kids of all ages."

Nightmare on Elm Street, A
19 | 14 | 19 | 18

1984 | Directed by Wes Craven | With John Saxon, Ronee Blakley, Johnny Depp | 91 minutes | Rated R

Built around the "concept that your nightmares are real", this "original splatter" flick "did for sleeping what *Jaws* did for swimming" thanks to Freddy Krueger, its "pizza-faced" villain who sports "knives for fingers"; over 20 years later, this "darn scary" picture is now recognized as a "modern horror classic."

☒ Night of the Hunter, The ❶
27 | 28 | 25 | 26

1955 | Directed by Charles Laughton | With Robert Mitchum, Shelley Winters, Lillian Gish | 93 minutes | Not Rated

Playing a "semi-psychotic preacher" "personifying pure evil", the "mesmerizing" Mitchum "terrorizes a bunch of kids" (and "invents tattooed knuckles") in this "strange" film noir frightfest; it's a "pity this was Laughton's only directorial" effort, given the "exquisite cinematography" and "unforgettable" performances that add up to "stunningly innovative cinema."

Night of the Iguana, The ❶
23 | 26 | 22 | 22

1964 | Directed by John Huston | With Richard Burton, Ava Gardner, Deborah Kerr, Sue Lyon | 125 minutes | Not Rated

This "beautiful rendering" of Tennessee Williams' play concerns a defrocked clergyman turned south-of-the-border tour guide who lusts after three women, but is probably better known as the "movie that put Puerto Vallarta on the map as a tourist destination"; fans say the script is so "sultry" that you can almost "see the heat coming off the screen" – check out "Ava Gardner and those beach boys."

Night of the Living Dead ❶
22 | 13 | 19 | 16

1968 | Directed by George A. Romero | With Duane Jones, Judith O'Dea, Russ Streiner | 96 minutes | Not Rated

Director Romero "does zombies right" in this "zero-budget" indie "landmark" that proves that even "schlocky" special effects, a "shabby story" and "bad acting" can produce what living dead–heads call the "scariest movie ever made"; the "grainy black-and-white film adds to the creepy aura", right down to the "freak-you-out", "pj-wetting" finale.

Night Shift
19 | 20 | 19 | 17

1982 | Directed by Ron Howard | With Henry Winkler, Michael Keaton, Shelley Long | 105 minutes | Rated R

A prostitution ring setting up shop in a NYC morgue is the "goofy concept" servicing this "sleeper" buddy comedy best remembered for Keaton's "hysterical", "star-making" debut as the "nutty" sidekick to Winkler's "stuck-in-a-rut" shlub; P.S. "look fast" for Kevin Costner appearing in a "bit part."

Nights of Cabiria ✉❶🎬
27 | 28 | 25 | 24

1957 | Directed by Federico Fellini | With Giulietta Masina, François Périer | 117 minutes | Not Rated

"Post-WWII Italy" as seen "through the eyes of a streetwalker" is the premise of this "simple, heartfelt" drama that's one of Fellini's "most moving" (and least "bizarre") films; as the "lovable girl of the streets", the "radiant" Masina is nothing less than a "female Charlie Chaplin", rendering an "amazing" performance that "ranges from tragedy to transcendence to flat-out comedy."

9½ Weeks
	OVERALL	ACTING	STORY	PROD.
	15	15	15	16

1986 | Directed by Adrian Lyne | With Mickey Rourke, Kim Basinger | 113 minutes | Rated R

"Groundbreaking for its time", this "steamy" rendering of an "obsessive relationship" remains a definite "third-date movie", what with the "twisted" Rourke and "hot! hot! hot!" Basinger engaged in "kinky sex" via blindfolds, "ice cubes" and peanut shells; still, bluenoses find it "dreary, numbing" "softcore porn" that's nowhere near "as sexy as *An Officer and a Gentleman.*"

1900 🇫
	22	25	21	25

1976 | Directed by Bernardo Bertolucci | With Robert De Niro, Gérard Depardieu, Burt Lancaster | 243 minutes | Rated R

This "sweeping epic" from Bernardo Bertolucci is a "sumptuous", "fascinating study of Italian society and politics in the first half of the 20th century"; "finely acted" by De Niro (playing an aristocrat) and Depardieu (as a proletariat labor leader), it might be "a bit long and self-indulgent", but most find its "operatic form" and "meticulous" camerawork completely "involving."

9 to 5
	18	18	19	17

1980 | Directed by Colin Higgins | With Jane Fonda, Lily Tomlin, Dolly Parton, Dabney Coleman | 110 minutes | Rated PG

"Every secretary's dream" of "getting even with the boss" comes true in this "silly comedy", a "feminist classic" with a "relevant message" (though chauvinists snicker it's "proof that women's lib can be sexist too"); still, its "strong" protagonists exhibit "amazing chemistry" and Parton's theme song sure is "catchy."

Ninotchka ◑
	25	27	24	23

1939 | Directed by Ernst Lubitsch | With Greta Garbo, Melvyn Douglas, Ina Claire | 110 minutes | Not Rated

This "great American comedy" depicts Soviet comrades seduced by capitalism, but is best known as the picture in which "Garbo laughs" for the first time on-screen; playing a "woman who follows her heart rather than the Communist manifesto", she's "smooth and sexy" spouting "incredibly funny dialogue" courtesy of scenarist Billy Wilder.

Norma Rae ✉
	24	27	24	21

1979 | Directed by Martin Ritt | With Sally Field, Beau Bridges, Ron Leibman, Pat Hingle | 110 minutes | Rated PG

A "stirring tale about ordinary people", this "uplifting" drama "based on a true story" is a "painfully accurate look" at a "courageous" mill worker's "fight for justice" when caught between "unions and management"; in the title role, the "superb" Field really "earned her Oscar", and the "image of her holding up that sign" has become iconically "indelible."

🄩 North by Northwest
	28	26	27	27

1959 | Directed by Alfred Hitchcock | With Cary Grant, Eva Marie Saint, James Mason | 136 minutes | Not Rated

"James Bond, eat your heart out" – "no one is cooler than Cary Grant" in this "incredibly stylish" Hitchcock thriller, a "twisting story of mistaken identity" set "all over the country" involving a "cool blonde", a "smooth villain" and a "malevolent crop duster"; despite some "holes in the script", there's distraction via that "exhilarating" climb down Mount Rushmore and the "double entendre" scenario (e.g. the "train entering a tunnel" at the climax).

North Country
22 | 26 | 22 | 21

2005 | Directed by Niki Caro | With Charlize Theron, Frances McDormand, Woody Harrelson, Sissy Spacek | 126 minutes | Rated R

"Boy, can Theron act" declare devotees of her "fine performance" as a miner fighting "sexual harassment in the Minnesota iron range" in this "powerful" drama inspired by "real events"; highlighting a "piece of history few know about", this "message film" risks "heavy-handedness" to stand as a "harsh reminder" of "how hard it is for women to earn a living."

North Dallas Forty
19 | 18 | 20 | 18

1979 | Directed by Ted Kotcheff | With Nick Nolte, Mac Davis, Charles Durning, Dayle Haddon | 119 minutes | Rated R

"Way before the steroids controversy" was this "ahead-of-its-time" depiction of the "dirty underside of pro football", a "pre-ESPN" flick starring Nolte as an "aging", "medicated" player ("boy, those needles look like they hurt"); the "tell-it-like-it-is" script "doesn't have a story-book ending", and many are convinced the team is a "thinly disguised version of the Dallas Cowboys" in their '70s heyday.

Nosferatu ◐
26 | 22 | 24 | 24

1922 | Directed by F.W. Murnau | With Max Schreck, Gustav von Wangenheim, Greta Schroeder | 84 minutes | Not Rated

"Still creepy after all these years", this "important German horror film" (an "unauthorized version of *Dracula*") is "one spooky" silent flick that can "evoke terror" thanks to the "genuinely scary Schreck"; it's the "most poetic of vampire films" and the "standard that others are measured against – and usually found lacking."

Nosferatu the Vampyre 🅵
22 | 24 | 22 | 25

1979 | Directed by Werner Herzog | With Klaus Kinski, Isabelle Adjani, Bruno Ganz | 107 minutes | Rated PG

A "stylish retelling" of the "familiar" Dracula story, this "great remake" via Werner Herzog owes a lot to the "mesmerizing", "out-there" Kinski who "stakes his claim" on the title role; "visually stunning" and imbued with a "strong political subtext", it's "reasonably creepy", but paced at such a "hypnotic crawl" that purists insist the Murnau original is "still the gold standard."

Notebook, The
23 | 24 | 24 | 23

2004 | Directed by Nick Cassavetes | With Ryan Gosling, Rachel McAdams, James Garner, Gena Rowlands | 123 minutes | Rated PG-13

Sweet enough to "dissolve a tooth", this "hauntingly beautiful" sob-o-rama based on the Nicholas Sparks best-seller might be the "ultimate chick flick", a "testament to the awesome power of love" as it endures "through the ages"; naturally, the dry-eyed cry "corny", but even they credit the "genuinely sad Alzheimer's storyline" for addressing an issue that's "not often given attention."

| | OVERALL | ACTING | STORY | PROD. |

Notes on a Scandal
24 28 23 23

2006 | Directed by Richard Eyre | With Judi Dench, Cate Blanchett, Bill Nighy | 92 minutes | Rated R

A "sad tale of obsessive love", this "disturbing" picture details "quite the touchy subject", a "pathetic spinster teacher" (Dench) enamored with a younger colleague (Blanchett) who "has a full life without her" – not to mention a "tawdry" secret of her own; it's "unsettling", "creepy" stuff that's "adult in the best way", with "wonderful" performances that will "scare the hell out of you."

Nothing Sacred
▽ **23 23 20 20**

1937 | Directed by William Wellman | With Carole Lombard, Fredric March | 75 minutes | Not Rated

The "notion of celebrity is lampooned" in this nutty screwball comedy, the story of a woman diagnosed with a terminal disease who's feted by a newspaper in exchange for her exclusive story – only to find out that she's been misdiagnosed; it's way "ahead of its time" in its arch analysis of the fame game alone.

No Time for Sergeants ◑∅
23 22 22 19

1958 | Directed by Mervyn LeRoy | With Andy Griffith, Myron McCornick, Nick Adams | 119 minutes | Not Rated

Managing to be "endearing without being annoying", Griffith "delivers the goods" in this "hilarious" comedy about a "dim hayseed who nearly destroys the U.S. Air Force", abetted by "perfect foil" Don Knotts; the infamous "toilet-seat scene" is a "display of American ingenuity" at its finest.

� Notorious ◑
27 27 26 26

1946 | Directed by Alfred Hitchcock | With Cary Grant, Ingrid Bergman, Claude Rains | 101 minutes | Not Rated

"Fetching" Ingrid Bergman "goes under the sheets for her country and gets Cary Grant as a reward" in this "brilliantly subversive" Hitchcock spy thriller featuring equal parts of "suspense", "suspicion", "hurt pride" and "Nazis too"; best remembered for the leads' "lingering, smoldering love scene", it also boasts "top-notch" supporting work from Rains, who has the best line: "mother, I'm married to an American agent."

Notting Hill
19 19 18 19

1999 | Directed by Roger Michell | With Julia Roberts, Hugh Grant, Rhys Ifans | 124 minutes | Rated PG-13

"Straight-up chick flick" about a "hair-flicking" movie star who finds love with an "endearing" bookseller; though rotters relate it's "formulaic" (with "Roberts playing herself" and Grant in his "stammering ingénue" mode), at least the supporting cast is "brilliantly funny"; the London scenery provides the "charm."

No Way Out
20 19 23 19

1987 | Directed by Roger Donaldson | With Kevin Costner, Gene Hackman, Sean Young | 114 minutes | Rated R

Perhaps "Costner's finest hour", this "entirely enjoyable military thriller" offers "wonderful intrigue" in its way-out plot, something to do with the KGB, the Pentagon, the backseat of a limousine and a classy call girl (the "very hot" Young); while coolly "tense" throughout, the "unexpected", "twisty" ending is still a "shocker."

⛶ Now, Voyager ◑   27 | 28 | 26 | 25

1942 | Directed by Irving Rapper | With Bette Davis, Paul Henreid, Claude Rains | 117 minutes | Not Rated

"Break out the hankies" – this "chick flick extraordinaire" features "the moon, the stars and Bette Davis", who effects an "appealing transformation" as an "old maid" defecting from a "demanding mother" to find kismet with a "perfect" Henreid; though the "two-cigarette scene" is decidedly un-PC today, it's become a "sacred" (and paradoxically "life-affirming") moment in this "classy" "mature love story."

Nurse Betty   15 | 18 | 15 | 15

2000 | Directed by Neil LaBute | With Renée Zellweger, Morgan Freeman, Chris Rock | 108 minutes | Rated R

"Entertaining" but "unconventional", this "quirky black comedy" toplines Zellweger as a "clueless blonde" soap opera buff pursued by vicious hitmen; foes find the wild mix of comedy and gore too "incongruous" and "unnecessarily violent" ("what planet did the screenwriter come from?"), and even fans admit it's "not for everyone" – just those who appreciate "inventive" filmmaking.

Nutty Professor, The   21 | 19 | 18 | 18

1963 | Directed by Jerry Lewis | With Jerry Lewis, Stella Stevens, Del Moore | 107 minutes | Not Rated

Jerry's "finest hour", this "can't-be-improved-upon" "wacky" comedy concerns a nerdy college prof who is transformed from Dr. Jerk-yll into Mr. Hyde after guzzling an exotic tonic; fans find it "sweet", foes shrug "typical Lewis shtick" and deep thinkers deem it a "metaphor for the monsters inside the greatest comedians."

Nutty Professor, The   15 | 18 | 14 | 18

1996 | Directed by Tom Shadyac | With Eddie Murphy, Jada Pinkett, James Coburn | 95 minutes | Rated PG-13

This "competent remake" of the Jerry Lewis comedy features Murphy in "amazingly versatile" mode, playing a seriously overweight professor (in a "great fat suit") in addition to six other minor characters; it may be "more sentimental and less sharp" than the original – and "probably not appreciated by the French" – but those "dinner table scenes" are "wet-your-pants funny."

O Brother, Where Art Thou?   22 | 23 | 22 | 24

2000 | Directed by Joel Coen | With George Clooney, John Turturro, Tim Blake Nelson, John Goodman | 106 minutes | Rated PG-13

"Who else but the Coen brothers could mix Greek mythology, bluegrass and George Clooney?" ask fans of this picaresque, "perversely funny" satire "based on Homer's *Odyssey*" that details the adventures of three Depression-era "hayseeds" who bust out of prison; though a bit too "highbrow" for some, the "beautiful period detail" and "best roots music soundtrack ever" keep this "sweet" if "strange" genre-bender accessible.

Ocean's Eleven   16 | 15 | 19 | 18

1960 | Directed by Lewis Milestone | With Frank Sinatra, Dean Martin, Sammy Davis, Jr., Peter Lawford | 127 minutes | Not Rated

A "guilty pleasure to be sure", this "original version" of the casino heist caper features the "Rat Pack at their best" in a fab "1960 Las Vegas"

	OVERALL	ACTING	STORY	PROD.

Polyester
19 | 16 | 17 | 16

1981 | Directed by John Waters | With Divine, Tab Hunter, Edith Massey | 86 minutes | Rated R

From "prince of prurience" John Waters comes this "rude" black comedy featuring the "cross-dressing diva" Divine opposite "sex symbol of yore" Tab Hunter; the only picture ever shot in "Odorama" (a "gimmick" involving "scratch-and-sniff cards"), it tells the "silly" story of a put-upon housewife and is ultimately "so over the top, you wind up back down at the bottom."

Portrait of a Lady, The
16 | 21 | 19 | 21

1996 | Directed by Jane Campion | With Nicole Kidman, Barbara Hershey, John Malkovich | 142 minutes | Rated PG-13

Fans of novelist Henry James say this interpretation of his 1881 opus concerning an American heiress in Europe is "not to be missed" even though it does "leave out some major elements of the story"; but many others – even Nicole buffs – claim sitting through this "strange, sad" portrait is a lot "like watching paint dry."

Poseidon Adventure, The
19 | 18 | 20 | 22

1972 | Directed by Ronald Neame | With Gene Hackman, Ernest Borgnine, Red Buttons | 117 minutes | Rated PG

A "boat flips over" and the "actors flip out" in this "topsy-turvy" "granddaddy of Hollywood all-star disaster flicks" that's "more fun in a campy way than you'd expect"; sure, the "phenomenal underwater footage" and "unforgettable (if not completely subtle) performances" are "entertaining" enough, but foes sneer this "kitschy" "sinking ship" defines the "true meaning of 'all wet.'"

Possession
17 | 19 | 19 | 18

2002 | Directed by Neil LaBute | With Gwyneth Paltrow, Aaron Eckhart, Jeremy Northam, Jennifer Ehle | 102 minutes | Rated PG-13

A "good but not great" adaptation of A.S. Byatt's "complex" book, this romance packs "two love stories in one", spanning the centuries to chronicle a pair of "present-day researchers" (Paltrow and Eckhart) and the "Victorian poets" (Ehle and Northam) that they're studying; while most agree there's "no charisma between the modern couple", there's debate about whether it's more *Masterpiece Theatre* or "trashy romance novel" overall.

Postcards from the Edge
18 | 23 | 19 | 18

1990 | Directed by Mike Nichols | With Meryl Streep, Shirley MacLaine, Dennis Quaid | 101 minutes | Rated R

Edgy types tout this "Hollywood insider story" as a "terrifically funny" look at the relationship between a "recovering-druggie" movie star and her scenery-chewing movie-star mom; though both the "biting" MacLaine and "brilliant" Streep "shine", fans say that the "sharp" script is as acidly "amusing" as they come.

Postman Always Rings Twice, The ◑
25 | 25 | 25 | 24

1946 | Directed by Tay Garnett | With John Garfield, Lana Turner, Cecil Kellaway | 113 minutes | Not Rated

Garfield and Turner "set off the smoke alarms" in this "steamy" slice of film noir, a "deliciously sinful" saga about a "married femme fatale", a "streetwise vagabond" and their simmering affair that "boils over into murderous passion"; though this "twisting" tale of "love, betrayal" and "homicide" is pretty "wonderful", one question remains "didn't people know about divorce in those days?"

Postman Always Rings Twice, The   20 | 23 | 22 | 19

1981 | Directed by Bob Rafelson | With Jack Nicholson, Jessica Lange, John Colicos | 122 minutes | Rated R

Maybe it's "not as good as the original", but this "decent" enough remake of the film noir classic features "real sex" scenes instead of "implied" ones, most notably that display of "countertop love" that inspired many to install "butcher blocks in their kitchens"; "Jack is as creepy as ever" and Jessica's "good" as well, though purists protest that "there's too much emphasis on sex at the expense of characterization" here.

Potemkin ◑   27 | 22 | 25 | 27

1925 | Directed by Sergei Eisenstein | With Aleksandr Antonov, Vladimir Barsky | 75 minutes | Not Rated

Over 80 years later, cineasts are still electrified by director Eisenstein's "influential" "triumph" that "put 'montage' into the film-making lexicon" and "forever set the standards for camerawork", detailing the failed 1905 uprising against the Czar, it's best known for its "often copied baby-carriage-on-the-Odessa-steps sequence" that "paved the way for edit-happy MTV directors"; indeed, it's so "exciting" that many insist it "should be mandatory moviegoing."

Prelude to a Kiss   16 | 16 | 17 | 15

1992 | Directed by Norman René | With Alec Baldwin, Meg Ryan, Kathy Bates | 105 minutes | Rated PG-13

A stage-to-screen transfer of Craig Lucas' play, this "quirky" love story involving a bride's "weird" body-swap with an elderly stranger sheds some "poetic" perspective on "interesting themes" like "identity and acceptance"; it may be "nothing to write home about", but count on the ever-"charming" Ryan to add some "sweet" notes to the "sentimental" script.

Prestige, The   22 | 24 | 23 | 24

2006 | Directed by Christopher Nolan | With Hugh Jackman, Christian Bale, Michael Caine, Scarlett Johansson | 130 minutes | Rated PG-13

Portraying "rival magicians" who "go to extremes" to win over audiences, Bale and Jackman "keep you enthralled" throughout this "dark" Victorian meditation on "pride", "obsession" and "love"; given a plot full of "twists and turns" that some find sleight-ly "tough to follow", "repeated viewings" are recommended, if only to savor David Bowie's "notable cameo" again and again.

Presumed Innocent   20 | 21 | 22 | 18

1990 | Directed by Alan J. Pakula | With Harrison Ford, Brian Dennehy, Raul Julia | 127 minutes | Rated R

Based on Scott Turow's best-seller, this "darkly powerful courtroom thriller" concerns a Philadelphia prosecutor whose life takes a "rollercoaster" turn after he's accused of murder; jurists say its "cliffhanger" storyline boasts a "perfect surprise ending" that "keeps you guessing up till the last frame."

	OVERALL	ACTING	STORY	PROD.

Pretty Baby
17 | 18 | 17 | 18

1978 | Directed by Louis Malle | With Brooke Shields, Keith Carradine, Susan Sarandon | 109 minutes | Rated R

Despite the "iffy" subject matter – "child prostitution in WWI-era New Orleans" – this "controversial" drama is "presented so matter-of-factly" that jaded folks "may find it a bit dull"; starring a "very young Brooke" (who's "just fine" in the title role), it's "beautifully filmed" in "soft focus" and "not exploitative", though a few "shocked" sorts say it "could never be made today."

Pretty in Pink
19 | 18 | 19 | 18

1986 | Directed by Howard Deutch | With Molly Ringwald, Harry Dean Stanton, Jon Cryer | 96 minutes | Rated PG-13

For a most "entertaining" "glimpse into the horrors of teenage dating", try this "Brat Pack" comedy "classic" starring Ringwald (at her late-80s "poutiest") as an "angst"-ridden gal from the "wrong side of the tracks" who falls for a "rich preppie"; ok, it's "sappy" and "not too original", but given all the "cute touches" and that "killer soundtrack", many call it a "guilty pleasure to the nth degree."

☑ Pretty Woman
23 | 22 | 22 | 22

1990 | Directed by Garry Marshall | With Richard Gere, Julia Roberts, Jason Alexander | 119 minutes | Rated R

Despite a premise somewhere between "Cinderella" and "Eliza Doolittle", this story of a "hooker with a heart of gold" who bags "Prince Charming" is a "happily-ever-after" romance that "put Julia (and her smile) on the map"; credit the "dizzying charisma" and "palpable chemistry between its stars" for its "believability", and though the "glamorization-of-prostitution" angle turns off bluenoses, "hopeless romantics" insist it will "steal your heart."

Pride and Prejudice ◑
25 | 25 | 26 | 23

1940 | Directed by Robert Z. Leonard | With Greer Garson, Laurence Olivier, Mary Boland | 118 minutes | Not Rated

A "lovely, headstrong heroine and a handsome haughty hero" make "sparks fly" in this "lush", "true-to-the-book" adaptation of the Jane Austen classic; "fabulous period costumes and sets" in high MGM style contribute to the "splendid" feel, while "Garson and Olivier play off each other wonderfully" – now, "that's style."

Pride & Prejudice
23 | 24 | 25 | 25

2005 | Directed by Joe Wright | With Keira Knightley, Matthew Macfadyen, Donald Sutherland | 127 minutes | Rated PG

"New insights into an old classic" flow from this "pared-down" yet "delightful" translation of Jane Austen's novel featuring a "radiant" Knightley as the "headstrong" heroine who finds a "sparring partner and true love" in "brooding English Lord" Mr. Darcy; a "lavish production" featuring "breathtaking scenery", "intelligent" dialogue and an "alluring soundtrack", it maintains a modern "freshness."

Pride of the Yankees, The ◑
22 | 22 | 23 | 20

1942 | Directed by Sam Wood | With Gary Cooper, Teresa Wright, Walter Brennan | 127 minutes | Not Rated

A "must" for both "baseball and Yankee fans", this "best sports" biopic virtually guarantees a "lump in the throat" as it delineates the life story of the "great Lou Gehrig" and his courage in the face of death; in the title role, Cooper is so effectively "self-effacing" that repeat viewers "cry every time" they hear his "farewell speech."

Primal Fear
22 | 25 | 23 | 21

1996 | Directed by Gregory Hoblit | With Richard Gere, Laura Linney, Edward Norton | 129 minutes | Rated R

The verdict's in: an "amazing" Norton "hits a home run" in his "stunning debut" as a "timid, stuttering" altar boy accused of killing an archbishop in this "unsettling" murder mystery/courtroom drama; otherwise, the "acting is on-point all around" (even "Gere is less dull than usual"), though the performances are nearly "blown away" by that "knock-you-for-a-loop" "surprise ending."

Primary Colors
16 | 19 | 17 | 17

1998 | Directed by Mike Nichols | With John Travolta, Emma Thompson, Kathy Bates | 143 minutes | Rated R

An "uncomfortable peek" into the '92 Presidential campaign, this "tight" political comedy stars a "right-on" Travolta as a "thinly disguised" Bill Clinton; though hindered by "unnecessary melodrama", this "underrated" picture works as a "good insider's view" of the "way things probably were – and you wish they weren't."

Prime
17 | 20 | 17 | 17

2005 | Directed by Ben Younger | With Meryl Streep, Uma Thurman, Bryan Greenberg | 105 minutes | Rated PG-13

A "Jewish therapist's son falls for her non-Jewish patient" ("oy vey!") in this "offbeat" romantic comedy starring the "magic" Meryl opposite "stunning" Uma and "endearing" newcomer Greenberg; it's a "funny" enough "dissection of love and maturity", though those hoping for a "Hollywood ending" are "disappointed" by its "true-to-life" finish.

Prime of Miss Jean Brodie, The ✉
25 | 28 | 24 | 23

1969 | Directed by Ronald Neame | With Maggie Smith, Robert Stephens, Pamela Franklin, Jane Carr | 116 minutes | Rated PG

Transposing "Dead Poets Society" to a '30s-era Scottish boarding school, this portrait of a "free-thinking teacher" is "worth revisiting" for Dame Maggie's "towering", Oscar-grabbing turn (which "does for Jean Brodie what Roz Russell did for Auntie Mame"); it's a "coming-of-age classic" crafted with "impressionable girls" in mind, despite its "heartbreaker" message: "idealism can be bad for you."

Prince of Egypt, The
19 | - | 19 | 23

1998 | Directed by Simon Wells, Brenda Chapman, Steve Hickner | Animated | 99 minutes | Rated PG

Voters part like the Red Sea over this "history/cartoon combo": fans insist it's a "fascinating modern Bible retelling" of the story of Moses' exodus with the Jews from Egypt, with "terrific animation" and "beautiful songs", but foes say it's an "overwrought" derivation of the "Disney formula" that "lacks" in all areas "except special effects."

Prince of Tides, The
19 | 21 | 21 | 20

1991 | Directed by Barbra Streisand | With Barbra Streisand, Nick Nolte, Blythe Danner | 132 minutes | Rated R

In this "interesting story" about a "Southern football coach, his dysfunctional family" and the "New York City psychiatrist who sorts it all out", the "convincing Nolte really gives his all"; yet despite the "lyricism" and "stunning scenery", some say the "self-important" Babs "never should have directed herself" in this "vanity" production.

❷ Princess Bride, The

27 | 23 | 27 | 24

1987 | Directed by Rob Reiner | With Cary Elwes, Mandy Patinkin, Robin Wright | 98 minutes | Rated PG

Despite the "chick-flick title", this "lighthearted" but "fractured fairy tale" defies any easy "categorization" and is admired by "even macho" guys for its "swordfights" and "verbal jousting"; thanks to an "intelligent" William Goldman script, "masterful" direction by Reiner and an "incredibly talented" cast, "finding a better movie is inconceivable."

Princess Diaries, The

18 | 19 | 17 | 18

2001 | Directed by Garry Marshall | With Julie Andrews, Anne Hathaway, Hector Elizondo | 114 minutes | Rated G

It's "every girl's dream" – to discover she's "actually a princess" (albeit of "some little country you've never heard of") – and this "wholesome" "mom-and-daughter" comedy follows newcomer Hathaway's transformation from "high-school dork" to crowned head amusingly enough; but even though this "feel-good" flick appeals to the "teenager inside us all", critics complain it's a "little flat for older audiences."

Prisoner of Second Avenue, The

22 | 25 | 21 | 20

1975 | Directed by Melvin Frank | With Jack Lemmon, Anne Bancroft, Gene Saks | 98 minutes | Rated PG

There's "a lot of hollering out the window" in this Neil Simon comedy about a frustrated worker who loses his job and has a "classic breakdown" in circa-1970 NYC; it's a "quintessential" Lemmon role (with Bancroft equally "awesome" as his put-upon wife), and if some dismiss it as a "not funny enough" "sitcom", at least it's a "well-acted one"; P.S. watch for a "fun cameo" from the then-unknown Sylvester Stallone.

Private Benjamin

17 | 19 | 17 | 16

1980 | Directed by Howard Zieff | With Goldie Hawn, Eileen Brennan, Armand Assante | 100 minutes | Rated R

"Goldie's golden" in this "funny, inspirational" comedy about a newly widowed Jewish princess who comes into her own after unwittingly enlisting in the army; a "lighthearted twist on women's liberation", it "shines" with "punchy" dialogue and a "charming" cast, particularly an acerbic Brennan and a "what-a-hunk" Assante as the romantic interest.

Prize Winner of Defiance, Ohio, The

22 | 24 | 23 | 22

2005 | Directed by Jane Anderson | With Julianne Moore, Woody Harrelson, Laura Dern | 99 minutes | Rated PG-13

"Based on a true story", this "nostalgic" drama stars the "amazing" Moore as a "saintly" '50s housewife who supports "10 kids and an alcoholic husband" by "winning jingle-writing contests"; given its "brilliant evocation" of a "time when you were somebody only if you were a man", many feel this entry "deserved more attention than it got."

Prizzi's Honor

21 | 24 | 21 | 19

1985 | Directed by John Huston | With Jack Nicholson, Kathleen Turner, Anjelica Huston | 130 minutes | Rated R

This "terrific black comedy about a dysfunctional mob family" anticipates The Sopranos with "cynical", "give-and-take" dialogue delivered by the "perfect cast" (a "bright" Jack and a "stellar", Oscar-copping Anjelica); one of John Huston's "last masterpieces", this "whacked-out gangster farce" wrings laughs via a "play-it-straight" script peppered with "in-jokes"; biggest conundrum: "do I ice her? do I marry her?"

☑ Producers, The ✉   26 | 26 | 26 | 23

1968 | Directed by Mel Brooks | With Zero Mostel, Gene Wilder, Kenneth Mars | 88 minutes | Rated PG

Flaunting "silly and shocking originality" long before the "Broadway hoopla", this "anarchic", "appallingly funny" comedy boasts Mostel and Wilder "at their best" as perps of a "Ponzi scheme" to produce an "unbelievably over-the-top" musical winningly titled *Springtime for Hitler* and cash in on its failure; it earns a standing ovation as "unrelenting", "inspired lunacy" from the "warped mind" of Mel Brooks that still "holds up" as a manic "masterpiece."

Producers, The   •   18 | 20 | 21 | 21

2005 | Directed by Susan Stroman | With Nathan Lane, Matthew Broderick, Uma Thurman, Will Ferrell | 134 minutes | Rated PG-13

Alright, there were "huge expectations" for this "movie musical based on a stage show based on a film comedy", but surveyors' reactions are mixed: "once-was-enough" types fret it "doesn't capture the charm of the original" picture (the "ghost of Zero Mostel hovers over every scene"), though fans say there are enough "catchy tunes" and big, "old-fashioned production numbers" (like the "old-ladies-and-the-walkers" routine) to make it a "lasting souvenir of a great Broadway show."

Professional, The   25 | 25 | 24 | 23
(aka Leon - The Professional)

1994 | Directed by Luc Besson | With Jean Reno, Gary Oldman, Natalie Portman | 110 minutes | Rated R

A "rare" example of a "well-executed" action flick, this "compelling" portrait of a hit man "with a heart of gold" who takes an orphan "under his wing" soars with its "unconventional" coupling of the "terrific" Reno with a "luminous" young Portman (in her feature film debut); count on "scary" Gary's "hyped-up bad cop" and some "wonderfully filmed" gunfight sequences to heighten the already "intense" mood.

Proof   18 | 22 | 20 | 18

2005 | Directed by John Madden | With Gwyneth Paltrow, Anthony Hopkins, Jake Gyllenhaal | 99 minutes | Rated PG-13

The thin line between "genius" and "madness" bisects this "intelligent" stage-to-screen adaptation starring Paltrow at her most "compassionate" as a "tortured" soul "suffering in the shadow" of her "brilliant" but "crazy" mathematician father; Hopkins is "mesmerizing as usual" in support of the "top-notch" script, though some suggest the "lethargic" pacing proves why this "treat for the intellect" is often "overlooked."

☑ Psycho ◑   28 | 26 | 27 | 27

1960 | Directed by Alfred Hitchcock | With Anthony Perkins, Vera Miles, John Gavin, Janet Leigh | 109 minutes | Rated R

"Generations of moviegoers started double-locking their bathroom doors" after one look at the "famous shower scene" in this "classic Hitchcock" "psycho-logical thriller" that was "quite a shocker in its day" and "still packs a wallop" – "without the gross violence of modern flicks"; standouts include Bernard Herrmann's "scariest film score ever" and Perkins' "twitchy", "tour-de-force" performance as the ultimate "mama's boy."

Psycho
14 | 14 | 18 | 14

1998 | Directed by Gus Van Sant | With Vince Vaughn, Anne Heche, Julianne Moore | 105 minutes | Rated R

Gus Van Sant's "shot for shot" remake of Hitchcock's "homage to the dysfunctional son" strikes many as "blasphemy", a "cut-and-paste" exercise that surely must have "Alfred twirling in his grave"; sure, Vaughn is "creepily seductive" in the title role, but many say there was "absolutely no need for a new version" – "wouldn't it have been cheaper to colorize the original?"

Public Enemy ◑
25 | 25 | 22 | 22

1931 | Directed by William Wellman | With James Cagney, Jean Harlow, Edward Woods, Mae Clarke | 84 minutes | Not Rated

"Cagney's spectacular" in this "classic '30s gangster flick" that made him a star in the role of a petty crook who evolves into a "dangerous" crime czar; the picture still delivers quite a punch, brimming with "energy", especially the famous scene in which the girlfriend gets it in the kisser with a grapefruit.

☑ Pulp Fiction ✉
26 | 26 | 25 | 25

1994 | Directed by Quentin Tarantino | With John Travolta, Samuel L. Jackson, Uma Thurman, Bruce Willis, Amanda Plummer, Tim Roth, Ving Rhames, Harvey Keitel | 154 minutes | Rated R

A "pioneer of plot shuffling" and "twisty chronology", this "propulsive", "in-your-face" thriller is a "true original" with an "unpredictable storyline" and "dialogue that's like a punch in the face"; recounting the affairs of some "charming hit men", it stars a "rogues' gallery of actors" in memorable bits ("Travolta's dancing", Uma's overdose, Plummer's "psychotic rant") played out with "dark humor", "intense violence" and "foul language"; not only did it "put Tarantino on the map", it's in a "genre all by itself."

Pumping Iron
17 | - | 18 | 15

1977 | Directed by George Butler, Robert Fiore | Documentary | With Arnold Schwarzenegger, Lou Ferrigno | 85 minutes | Rated PG

An "enlightening" look into the "world of competitive bodybuilding", this "muscle-bound" documentary "put working out on the map" but is better known for "introducing Arnold to the world" in all his "cocky", "competitive" glory, full of the "charisma" and "ambition" that led to his "running the state of California" – "talk about foreshadowing!"

Punch-Drunk Love
17 | 20 | 16 | 17

2002 | Directed by Paul Thomas Anderson | With Adam Sandler, Emily Watson, Philip Seymour Hoffman | 95 minutes | Rated R

"Not for everyone", this "quirky" "love story for losers" stars a "zombified" Sandler as an "angry, passive-aggressive type" who falls for an "adorable" if somewhat "weird" gal; foes find "more potential than payoff" here and say it's "about as self-important as movies get", while even fans admit it will "leave you scratching your head a little . . . kind of the way life does"; best line: "I beat up the bathroom."

Purple Rain   `14` `10` `11` `16`

1984 | Directed by Albert Magnoli | With Prince, Appolonia Kotero, Morris Day | 111 minutes | Rated R

Acknowledged as the flick that "catapulted an unknown into a superstar", this "modern musical" tells the story of a struggling singer, played by the one-and-only Prince; purple-xed types say this "two-hour music video" "hasn't aged well" (too much "bad acting" and "'80s fashion"), but most say its "amazing", Oscar-winning soundtrack reigns.

Purple Rose of Cairo, The   `21` `21` `24` `21`

1985 | Directed by Woody Allen | With Mia Farrow, Jeff Daniels, Danny Aiello | 84 minutes | Rated PG

The Woodman rises to the occasion with this "clever", "not-self-absorbed" comedy, a "bittersweet tale" featuring "Farrow's best" work as a Depression-era moviegoer whose "fantasy world" merges with "real life" when an RKO star walks off the screen into her life; the "imaginative" plot takes an "inside-out" look at "love of the movies", with a last reel calculated to "break your heart."

Pursuit of Happyness, The   `23` `25` `24` `22`

2006 | Directed by Gabriele Muccino | With Will Smith, Jaden Smith, Thandie Newton | 117 minutes | Rated PG-13

Open up and say "awww": this "heartstring-pulling" paean to the "American dream" will "grab you" with its "Alger"-esque plot and Will's "phenomenal" performance as a "dedicated father" who "never gives up" despite "life's hardships"; sure, "you know where it's going right from the beginning", but the fact that it's "based on a true story" keeps the "sappyness" in check.

▣ Queen, The ✉   `26` `29` `23` `25`

2006 | Directed by Stephen Frears | With Helen Mirren, Michael Sheen, Helen McCrory, James Cromwell | 103 minutes | Rated PG-13

The "private side" of the British monarchy gets a public airing in this "wholly absorbing" look at the "royal response to the death of Diana", Princess of Wales; in the title role, Oscar-winner Mirren gives a "beautiful" performance that goes "beyond the icy veneer" to "humanize" the "insulated" Queen and almost single-handedly crafts an "immensely entertaining" picture from "seemingly bland subject matter."

Quest for Fire   `17` `16` `17` `19`

1981 | Directed by Jean-Jacques Annaud | With Everett McGill, Ron Perlman, Rae Dawn Chong | 100 minutes | Rated R

An "ambitious attempt" to dramatize the daily life of "prehistoric man", from the "frightening" (think "cannibalism and warfare") to the "erotic and even funny", this "unique" saga follows "three brave warriors" as they traverse "untamed land" on a mission to save their tribe from extinction; despite the "lush production", some have a bone to pick with the "sedate pace" and non-subtitled, "grunt-and-groan" dialogue.

Quiet American, The   `24` `26` `24` `24`

2002 | Directed by Phillip Noyce | With Michael Caine, Brendan Fraser | 101 minutes | Rated R

Delivering a "powerful performance", Caine demonstrates why he's "legendary" in this "highly underrated" adaptation of the Graham Greene novel about "America's involvement in the early stages of the

Vietnam War"; a "terrific" Fraser, a "wonderful story" and a "lavish" re-creation of 1950s Saigon are more reasons why many say "it's a shame" this "sleeper wasn't promoted enough."

☑ Quiet Man, The ✉

27 | 25 | 25 | 27

1952 | Directed by John Ford | With John Wayne, Maureen O'Hara, Barry Fitzgerald | 129 minutes | Not Rated

"Every Irish cliché" is "alive and well" in this "romanticized" drama, starring the Duke as an American boxer who hangs up his gloves and settles in his Hibernian "ancestral home" only to be smitten by the "beautiful", "feisty" O'Hara; presenting a "postcard" Ireland populated by "enchanting townspeople", it's "witty" and – despite a wee bit o' "blarney" – judged "worthy of a yearly viewing."

Quiz Show

21 | 23 | 21 | 20

1994 | Directed by Robert Redford | With Ralph Fiennes, John Turturro, Rob Morrow | 133 minutes | Rated PG-13

"America's loss of innocence" is the subtext for this "intelligent" drama chronicling the '50s TV quiz-show scandals, a "blistering" commentary on the "mania for celebrity and money"; Turturro is the cast's "bright spot" as a bought-off contestant in a rigged highbrow showdown, and nostalgists prize the "vivid picture of the era", long before *Millionaire* – the "kicker is it really happened."

Rabbit-Proof Fence

26 | 25 | 26 | 24

2002 | Directed by Phillip Noyce | With Everlyn Sampi, Tianna Sansbury, Laura Monaghan, Kenneth Branagh | 94 minutes | Rated PG

Young Aboriginal girls "escape forced slavery" and trek 1,500 miles across the Australian outback to return home in this "heart-wrenching true story" "acted wonderfully" by "three unknowns"; "don't expect special effects", and make sure to "watch the credits and you'll see the real children, now in their 80s."

Radio

22 | 25 | 23 | 22

2003 | Directed by Michael Tollin | With Cuba Gooding Jr., Ed Harris | 109 minutes | Rated PG

"Small-scale" and proud of it, this "inspiring" sports drama recounts the true story of a "friendly football coach" who molds a "less fortunate", mentally disabled man into a popular mascot-cum-cheerleader (played by the "outstanding" Gooding); parents say its "old-fashioned, feel-good" scenario teaches "great life lessons for kids."

Radio Days

23 | 23 | 23 | 23

1987 | Directed by Woody Allen | With Mia Farrow, Julie Kavner, Dianne Wiest | 85 minutes | Rated PG

Tune in for "fond memories" to this "charming" "family comedy", an "affectionate period piece" set in late-'30s Rockaway Beach, where "childhood innocence, neurotic relatives" and golden-age radio fill the airwaves; touted for "top-to-bottom acting excellence", it's a "funny", "free-form" sampler of "Allen at his sunniest" and "most enjoyable."

Raging Bull ✉◑

26 | 28 | 24 | 26

1980 | Directed by Martin Scorsese | With Robert De Niro, Cathy Moriarty, Joe Pesci | 129 minutes | Rated R

Perhaps the "best boxing movie of all time", this "riveting" biopic charts the "rise and fall" of former middleweight champion Jake

LaMotta, whose toughest opponents were his own "self-destructive tendencies"; shot in "beautiful black and white", it features a "primo De Niro", and though it can be "as painful as an open wound" to watch, most feel this is "knockout" filmmaking.

Ragtime

21 | 23 | 23 | 23

1981 | Directed by Milos Forman | With Howard Rollins Jr., Elizabeth McGovern, Mandy Patinkin, James Cagney, Mary Steenburgen | 155 minutes | Rated PG

Based on "E.L. Doctorow's bravura novel", this "big production" takes on nothing less than the "Victorian era" with a "big storyline" that places fictional characters alongside such real-life figures as Stanford White, Evelyn Nesbit, Harry Houdini and Booker T. Washington; while some find it all "fascinating" and the cast "outstanding", others sigh it's too "longwinded" and "not as good as the book."

☑ Raiders of the Lost Ark

28 | 24 | 27 | 28

1981 | Directed by Steven Spielberg | With Harrison Ford, Karen Allen, Paul Freeman | 115 minutes | Rated PG

It doesn't get "more exciting" than this "benchmark" of "nonstop pulp-fiction action", Spielberg's "roller-coaster" homage to "Saturday matinee" serials that introduces the "rakish" Indiana Jones, a tweedy archaeologist with a "strapping-hero" alter ego who scraps with the Nazis over an "all-powerful artifact"; chock-full of "retro" delights like "tongue-in-cheek" humor, "improbable cliff-hanger escapes" and a "love interest" amid the "snakes, whips and guns", it's a "rousing blockbuster" that proves the "'80s weren't all bad."

Rainmaker, The

21 | 22 | 22 | 20

1997 | Directed by Francis Ford Coppola | With Matt Damon, Danny DeVito, Claire Danes, Jon Voight | 135 minutes | Rated PG-13

Proving again why he's one of the "best in the business", Coppola molds a "clichéd" John Grisham novel into a "moving" courtroom drama detailing the "seamy side of law practice"; a "fine" Damon and "hysterical" DeVito play "ambulance chasers" targeting a heartless insurance company opposite Voight, a "perfectly menacing" shark who enlivens the "excellent trial scenes."

Rain Man ✉

25 | 27 | 24 | 23

1988 | Directed by Barry Levinson | With Dustin Hoffman, Tom Cruise, Valeria Golino | 133 minutes | Rated R

This Best Picture winner is an unconventional "brothers bonding" drama driven by an Oscar-winning performance from Hoffman, who's "nothing short of incredible" as a full-grown "autistic savant" blessed with an endless supply of "quirky mannerisms" and "memorable lines"; Cruise shows off his own "acting chops" as the "scheming" sibling angling for half his inheritance, bringing on showers of "insight" that clear up to let a "feel-good" resolution shine through.

Raising Arizona

23 | 23 | 23 | 21

1987 | Directed by Joel Coen | With Nicolas Cage, Holly Hunter, John Goodman | 94 minutes | Rated PG-13

For a "completely original" and truly "bizarre" screwball comedy, check out this "hilarious white-trash" "cult classic" about a "childless", "criminal-class" couple (a policewoman married to a "failed convenience-store thief") that kidnaps a kid; Cage and Hunter are drolly "deadpan" delivering "dialogue that can't be beat", while the plot is typical Coen brothers: "goofy", "quirky" and gosh "darn funny."

Raisin in the Sun, A ◑

26 | 28 | 26 | 23

1961 | Directed by Daniel Petrie | With Sidney Poitier, Claudia McNeil, Ruby Dee, Diana Sands | 128 minutes | Not Rated

"Equal to" Lorraine Hansberry's award-winning Broadway play, this "groundbreaking" adaptation tells the story of a poor black family coping with a modest financial windfall; there's "emotional conflict" aplenty in its "dueling themes" of "racism, motherhood and manhood" and the "strong" cast is up to the challenge (particularly the "poignant Poitier"); pessimists say it's "sadly as applicable today as it was in the '60s."

Ran 🅕

27 | 25 | 27 | 29

1985 | Directed by Akira Kurosawa | With Tatsuya Nakadai, Mieko Harada, Daisuke Ryu | 160 minutes | Rated R

"Big, bold and beautiful", Kurosawa's "swan song" shows his "deft touch" intact in this "expansive retelling of *King Lear*" transformed into a "riveting" samurai "epic" involving a Shogun warlord whose decision to sheath his sword leads to intra-clan "betrayals"; suitably "Shakespearean" in scale, with "stunning" depictions of "feudal society" and "incredible battle scenes", it's "slow"-running pacewise but most hail it as "brilliant almost beyond belief."

Ransom

16 | 18 | 17 | 17

1996 | Directed by Ron Howard | With Mel Gibson, Rene Russo, Gary Sinise, Lili Taylor | 120 minutes | Rated R

"Gripping", "sustained suspense" is tempered with "much emotion" in this "dark" tale of a kidnapped child, starring "Mel in a suit" as a "conflicted" dad; though some bluff-callers deem it "overblown" and "formulaic", others swear by its "realistic" tension that's "scary to every parent out there."

🄴 Rashomon ◑🅕

29 | 27 | 29 | 25

1951 | Directed by Akira Kurosawa | With Toshiro Mifune, Machiko Kyo, Masayuki Mori | 88 minutes | Not Rated

Surely "truth is in the eye of the beholder", but most agree that Akira Kurosawa's "superb head-twister" of a Japanese drama should be "required viewing"; aided by "exquisite" camerawork and "fine medieval embellishments", it's a "simple story" about an ambush in the forest told from "four different points of view", proving that "self-interest" amounts to "nine-tenths of everything"; in sum, this "seminal" tale has been tirelessly "copied but never equaled."

Ray ✉

26 | 29 | 25 | 26

2004 | Directed by Taylor Hackford | With Jamie Foxx | 152 minutes | Rated PG-13

"Foxx almost disappears into the person of Ray Charles" in this "phenomenal" bio-"tribute" to the "legendary musician", nabbing a "well-deserved" Oscar for his "foot-stomping", "heartrending" portrayal of the superstar that's so convincing you'll "forget who you're really watching"; fans agree the "uncompromising" look at the soul man's "boozing, drugs and womanizing" is right on key, with additional hoorays going out to that "marvelous soundtrack."

Reality Bites

1994 | Directed by Ben Stiller | With Winona Ryder, Ethan Hawke, Janeane Garofalo | 99 minutes | Rated PG-13

"Escape with the losers" in this romantic comedy of "post-college" Gen-X existence as Winona and company find themselves "going no-where" but obliged to deal when faced with "job woes", tainted love and "utter annoyance with life"; vets of the day say as a "portrayal of MTV and other pop-culture" touchstones, "nothing represents the '90s more accurately."

Real Women Have Curves
21 | 22 | 21 | 19

2002 | Directed by Patricia Cardoso | With America Ferrera, Lupe Ontiveros, Ingrid Oliu, George Lopez | 90 minutes | Rated PG-13

Those with "less-than-supermodel bodies" – "which is about 99 per-cent of the population" – will especially enjoy this "inspirational" coming-of-age story about a "courageous" Latina teen "who isn't a size eight" "caught between family traditions and modern mores"; "there needs to be more movies" like this "celebration of women."

☒ Rear Window
28 | 27 | 28 | 27

1954 | Directed by Alfred Hitchcock | With James Stewart, Grace Kelly, Thelma Ritter | 112 minutes | Rated PG

"Voyeurism" meets "suspense" in this "snooper's dream" about a "wheelchair-bound" photographer "spying on his neighbors" and try-ing to "trap a killer" while fending off his girlfriend, who's tempting him into "another trap – marriage"; while the "crisp script" and "great NY set" draw huzzahs, fans tout its "perfectly cast" leads, the "solid" Stewart and "deeelicious" Kelly; so many find it "unsurpassed" that it was voted the top Hitchcock flick in this Survey.

☒ Rebecca ✉◑
27 | 27 | 27 | 25

1940 | Directed by Alfred Hitchcock | With Laurence Olivier, Joan Fontaine, Judith Anderson | 130 minutes | Not Rated

Based on Daphne du Maurier's "ultimate romance novel", "Hitchcock's first American film" is a "dark, moody" tale of a woman living in the shadow of her new husband's old wife; "haunting" and "eerily captivating", it showcases an "excellent" Olivier and a "gor-geous" Fontaine, but it's the "over-the-top" Anderson who's the real "hoot" here.

Rebel Without a Cause
24 | 24 | 21 | 22

1955 | Directed by Nicholas Ray | With James Dean, Natalie Wood, Sal Mineo | 111 minutes | Not Rated

A "lost generation lives on" in this "terse drama" of "disaffected youth" and "family conflict", which elevated Dean to "icon" status as a "rebellious" juvenile delinquent who leads a "great cast" as they cope with "hope, fear and love" in the "inchoate LA" of the '50s; if all that acting out is a bit "dated", most maintain it "lives up to its rep" as the "ultimate" ode to "teen alienation."

Recruit, The
17 | 20 | 18 | 19

2003 | Directed by Roger Donaldson | With Al Pacino, Colin Farrell, Bridget Moynahan | 115 minutes | Rated PG-13

"Nothing is what it seems" in this "keeps-you-guessing" spy thriller wherein a "secretive CIA" man attempts to enlist a promising recruit;

though Farrell "holds his own" as the protégé, some say Pacino's "patented screaming mentor role" is "starting to sound the same in every movie", and despite all the "twists and turns", the "ending's kind of weak."

Red Dragon
19 | 22 | 20 | 20

2002 | Directed by Brett Ratner | With Anthony Hopkins, Edward Norton, Ralph Fiennes, Harvey Keitel | 124 minutes | Rated R

"Better than *Hannibal*" but "not as good as *Silence of the Lambs*" is this "engaging" "prequel" wind-up of the "Lecter trilogy", a "suspenseful" thriller pitting a "stoic" G-man against a "disturbed murderer", and featuring the obligatory "mental chess match" with Hopkins' "good doctor" (albeit in a "minor role"); P.S. compare it with 1986's *Manhunter*, based on the same novel and often considered the "superior" version.

Red River ◐
26 | 25 | 25 | 27

1948 | Directed by Howard Hawks | With John Wayne, Montgomery Clift, Joanne Dru | 133 minutes | Not Rated

"Perhaps the grandest" Western of all, this cowpuncher "classic" breaks into a gallop when "lots of hunky men" saddle up for a dangerous cattle drive along the Chisholm Trail; Wayne "excels in an unsympathetic role" as a "stolid" rancher who turns against Monty, who "holds his own" as a buckaroo of "brooding sensitivity"; the result is a horn-lock that fans brand a grade-A prime "rewatcher."

Reds ✉
21 | 21 | 20 | 22

1981 | Directed by Warren Beatty | With Warren Beatty, Diane Keaton, Jack Nicholson | 194 minutes | Rated PG

Agitprop meets "epic romance" in this "impressive" bio of writers John Reed and Louise Bryant that chronicles their courtship and activities as bolshie sympathizers during the Russian Revolution; "Beatty's labor of love" celebrating "American radicalism", it's an "excellent re-creation" of the time, framed by "remembrances" of "largely forgotten men and women", but "major themes" or no, critics say this "big production" is "too long to keep you interested."

Red Shoes, The
26 | 24 | 24 | 26

1948 | Directed by Michael Powell, Emeric Pressburger | With Anton Walbrook, Moira Shearer | 133 minutes | Not Rated

With a tip of the slipper to Hans Christian Andersen, this "ageless" drama of "romance and ballet" "takes a fairy tale and creates magic" around the story of a young dancer who joins a celebrated troupe only to enter into a pas de deux with a composer; "sumptuous" staging and "dreamy choreography" make it a terpsichorean "benchmark", and fans "love every bit of it."

Red Violin, The ▣
24 | 23 | 24 | 24

1999 | Directed by François Girard | With Samuel L. Jackson, Greta Scacchi | 131 minutes | Rated R

A "symphony" recounting the "many tales of a violin's life", this "intricate" drama "follows the path" of a "fabulous instrument" from its creation in Renaissance Italy though various owners, countries and epochs, up to Jackson's encounter as a present-day appraiser; in spite of "art-house" airs, boosters bow to a "twisting" story that "keeps you guessing" – backed by a really "stunning" soundtrack featuring "real music by a real composer."

Remains of the Day, The

1993 | Directed by James Ivory | With Anthony Hopkins, Emma Thompson, Christopher Reeve | 138 minutes | Rated PG

"If you loved *Howards End*", you'll dig this "complex and entertaining" drama of "two fragile souls" on a British estate in the late '30s; "repressed" head butler Hopkins "puts duty above all else", even his yen for housekeeper Thompson, and both give "precise, controlled performances" filled with "gripping silences" to suit its "nuanced" story of "unfulfilled love", "class-system" bias and the "obtuseness of the upper crust" – just "don't expect action."

Remember the Titans

2000 | Directed by Boaz Yakin | With Denzel Washington, Will Patton, Wood Harris | 113 minutes | Rated PG

"Denzel is the man" to knock a ball team into shape while tackling "racial fault lines" in this "inspirational" family drama about a black high-school coach taking over a newly integrated football squad; if the "feel-good" theme of "tolerance and social understanding" on and off the field plays out as "hokey" and "about as deep as astroturf", fans "cheer anyway" for a "sleeper" that never fumbles its underlying "hope."

Rent

2005 | Directed by Chris Columbus | With Anthony Rapp, Adam Pascal, Rosario Dawson, Jesse L. Martin | 135 minutes | Rated PG-13

Of course, there's "nothing like the live Broadway show", but this stage-to-screen transfer of Jonathan Larson's "groundbreaking" musical actually "holds its own" thanks to the casting of "most of the original" players (albeit "aged" some years) for an "energetic" reprise of those "rousing" song-and-dance numbers; if a few critics charge the AIDS-themed storyline "loses its punch" in translation, most feel it's still as "poignant as ever."

Replacement Killers, The

1998 | Directed by Antoine Fuqua | With Chow Yun-Fat, Mira Sorvino | 87 minutes | Rated R

For a "good time" – "without too much stress on the ol' gray cells" – check out this "underrated" thriller about a conscience-stricken hit man unable to complete his latest hit; the picture was supposed to be "Hong Kong superstar" Yun-Fat's "ticket to American stardom", but unfortunately a "slim", "not exactly believable" scenario tricked up with plenty of "generic action" makes it play like "John Woo lite."

Repo Man

1984 | Directed by Alex Cox | With Harry Dean Stanton, Emilio Estevez | 92 minutes | Rated R

A "cult classic with a serious following", this "wacko" comedy "captures the nihilism of the '80s punk scene" in its story of lowlifes repossessing cars and chasing after UFOs; with lots of "throwaway gags", "quotable lines" and an "overlooked soundtrack", this "silly delight" is proudly "over the edge" and "hard to resist."

	OVERALL	ACTING	STORY	PROD.

Repulsion ◐   ▽ 25 | 27 | 24 | 23

1965 | Directed by Roman Polanski | With Catherine Deneuve, Ian Hendry | 105 minutes | Not Rated

Polanski's first English-language feature, this "disturbing" psychological thriller top bills an "unbeatable" Deneuve as an unstable young woman slowly descending into madness; although made on a shoestring budget, it's still really "frightening" in its "depiction of insanity from the inside out" and is already showing "definite cult potential."

Requiem for a Dream   25 | 27 | 24 | 25

2000 | Directed by Darren Aronofsky | With Ellen Burstyn, Jared Leto, Jennifer Connelly | 102 minutes | Not Rated

"Heavy" and "altogether devastating", this "bleak" "druggy" drama "spirals into the depths of hell" on the back of some "scary", strung-out imagery and Burstyn's "amazing" turn as a magenta-maned diet-pill popper with a none-too-swift junkie son; a "stomach-churning" depiction of "major drug use" that pushes Aronofsky to the "cutting edge" of "directing talents", it's "not subtle" but lingers like a "brilliant", "unnerving nightmare" – "be prepared" for some "grueling" going.

Requiem for a Heavyweight ◐   26 | 28 | 26 | 23

1962 | Directed by Ralph Nelson | With Anthony Quinn, Jackie Gleason, Mickey Rooney, Julie Harris | 95 minutes | Not Rated

Adapted from Rod Serling's Emmy-winning television play, this "knockout" drama is "one of the best fight films around", detailing a punch-drunk boxer's "gut-wrenching" decline; maybe it's turned "dated" and "preachy" over time, but for diversion there's always that "superb" ensemble cast, especially the "amazing" Quinn; N.B. look for cameos from real-life heavyweights Jack Dempsey and Muhammad Ali (billed here as Cassius Clay).

Rescuers, The   23 | - | 23 | 23

1977 | Directed by Wolfgang Reitherman, John Lounsbery, Art Stevens | Animated | 76 minutes | Rated G

A "must-see for every child", this animated Disney feature stars a pair of "adorable" mice bent on rescuing a kidnapped little girl; although maybe not at the top of the Mouse House pantheon, it's still "fun" with notable voicework from Bob Newhart, Eva Gabor and Geraldine Page.

Reservoir Dogs   24 | 25 | 24 | 22

1992 | Directed by Quentin Tarantino | With Harvey Keitel, Tim Roth, Michael Madsen, Steve Buscemi | 99 minutes | Rated R

The Tarantino "template" for a "new" style of crime thriller splices "hip, sharp" dialogue with "hard-core violence" as a "dream cast" sporting two-tone threads turns a jewel heist into a "riveting" "bloody spectacle"; the "clever" script relies on diced chronology, "sly riffs" on pop culture and "psychological twists" to lend heart to the "vicious" gang, though many howl the "nasty" bits ("ear removal", anyone?) are still "painful to watch."

Reversal of Fortune ✉   23 | 26 | 23 | 21

1990 | Directed by Barbet Schroeder | With Jeremy Irons, Glenn Close, Ron Silver | 120 minutes | Rated R

"You can't make this stuff up" – Oscar-winner Irons is "totally mesmerizing" in his "smarmy" take on the real-life Claus von Bulow, the high-society ladies' man accused of sending his heiress wife into an irreversible coma; Close and Silver also deliver the goods in this "solid" picture whose only drawback is "not having the ending that you want."

Rififi 🅞🄵
26 | 24 | 27 | 24

1956 | Directed by Jules Dassin | With Jean Servais, Carl Mohner, Robert Manuel | 115 minutes | Not Rated

Arguably the "first modern caper film", this "original" French take on film noir is loaded with "intrigue, gangsters and great scenes of Paris" as it details the plans to burgle a jewelry store; its "stunning" heist sequence – "totally silent for half an hour" – assures its "classic" status, and even if the "production quality seems dated now", ultimately it "still holds up after 50 years."

Right Stuff, The
26 | 24 | 26 | 26

1983 | Directed by Philip Kaufman | With Sam Shepard, Scott Glenn, Ed Harris | 193 minutes | Rated PG

"Exuberant", "involving" and "proud to be American", this "triumphant" drama "never flags" in launching Tom Wolfe's "snarky yet sincere" "epic of the space age" onto the big screen; a "retelling of true events" surrounding the evolution of test pilots into astronauts in the Mercury program, it takes "historical" stuff and pushes the envelope with "adventure, humor" and a cast that's "A-ok in every way."

Ring, The
19 | 18 | 20 | 21

2002 | Directed by Gore Verbinski | With Naomi Watts, Martin Henderson, David Dorfman, Brian Cox | 115 minutes | Rated PG-13

Viewers of a "mysterious videotape" receive a "spooky" call and "die seven days later" in this "genuinely scary" ghost story that delivers its "spine-tingling" chills without the "gross-out effects" common to the genre; cynical cinephiles say the "convoluted" story "falls apart" toward the end (*Ringu*, the "original Japanese version, is better"), but most are still "clutching their armrests" and vowing "never to answer the phone again."

Rio Bravo
24 | 22 | 21 | 22

1959 | Directed by Howard Hawks | With John Wayne, Dean Martin, Ricky Nelson | 141 minutes | Not Rated

"As Westerns go", this "entertaining" oater from the Hawks/Wayne team is an "expert reshuffling" of the plot elements of "*High Noon*", the story of a sheriff trying to hold a prisoner against a threatening mob virtually alone; though the picture was remade as *El Dorado* (and later as *Rio Lobo*), aficionados say the original is the "best version."

Risky Business
20 | 18 | 19 | 18

1983 | Directed by Paul Brickman | With Tom Cruise, Rebecca De Mornay, Bronson Pinchot | 98 minutes | Rated R

"Every boy's dream" comes true in this "smart, sexy" "coming-of-age" comedy, with Cruise as the high-schooler who turns chez suburbia into party central when his parents leave town – only to fall into "the arms of a beautiful hooker" and venture into the brothel business; it's a "funny" jibe at "upper-middle-class teenage life" with some "raging hormones" thrown in, and that celebrated scene of "Tom dancing in his Jockeys" is nothing short of "starmaking."

	OVERALL	ACTING	STORY	PROD.

River Runs Through It, A — 22 | 23 | 21 | 25

1992 | Directed by Robert Redford | With Brad Pitt, Craig Sheffer, Tom Skerritt | 123 minutes | Rated PG

Sounding "deep" waters with a "pastoral" tale of "life as we no longer know it", Redford's "elegiac" drama of "family bonds" takes a "moving", "candid" look at the sibling rivalry between two small-town minister's sons; the "smooth" pace is set by the stars' "subtle emotion" and "striking" cinematography that captures the "Montana wilderness" in all of its full "majesty", though some clock-watchers find the running time a bit "too slow."

Road to Perdition — 23 | 26 | 22 | 25

2002 | Directed by Sam Mendes | With Tom Hanks, Paul Newman, Daniel Craig, Jude Law | 117 minutes | Rated R

"Hanks proves his versatility" in this "evocative period piece", playing a "cold-blooded hit man" for the Irish mafia during the Depression; the "intense journey" is "impeccably done", with Newman in "stellar form", Oscar-winning cinematography that will "take your breath away" (notably that "tommy gun scene in the rain") and "top-notch screenwriting" that "stays true to the novel."

Road Warrior, The — 22 | 18 | 21 | 20

1982 | Directed by George Miller | With Mel Gibson, Bruce Spence, Mike Preston | 94 minutes | Rated R

"Road rage" kicks into overdrive in this "raw Aussie action flick", with "lean, mean" Gibson "at his baddest" as Mad Max, a "lone, reluctant cowboy" cruising a "post-apocalyptic" wasteland and upholding his "own brand of justice"; set in a "nihilistic" near-future when barbaric gangs comb the desert pestering decent folk for petrol, its combo of an "intriguing" setup and "incredible car stunts" makes it a "visceral" "cult favorite"; gas up.

Robe, The — 22 | 20 | 21 | 24

1953 | Directed by Henry Koster | With Richard Burton, Jean Simmons, Victor Mature | 135 minutes | Not Rated

"Burton reigns" as a Roman centurion who oversees the crucifixion, then wins Christ's robe in a dice game in this '50s "religious movie" that inspired a slew of biblical flicks; most memorable for being the first feature shot in CinemaScope, it's "big" in every way, though some ask "can it really be an epic without Charlton Heston?"

Robin and Marian — 20 | 23 | 20 | 21

1976 | Directed by Richard Lester | With Sean Connery, Audrey Hepburn, Robert Shaw | 106 minutes | Rated PG

In "Robin Hood's later years" he resumes his affair with Maid Marian in this "wistful wisp" of a tale worth seeing for the "casting" alone; the "sadness of time passing is palpable" (right down to that "darkly romantic ending"), and if it's mainly a "woman's film", there's still "enough swordplay" to keep the guys happy.

Robin Hood: Prince of Thieves — 16 | 14 | 17 | 18

1991 | Directed by Kevin Reynolds | With Kevin Costner, Morgan Freeman, Alan Rickman | 138 minutes | Rated PG-13

This retelling of the spurned-lord-turned-benevolent-thief legend is "surprisingly original", with a "super villain" and enough "tongue-in-cheek" antics to "keep it moving"; but Costner's "now-you-hear-it, now-you-don't English accent" and other "inaccuracies" make holdouts hold out for "Errol Flynn."

RoboCop
16 | 13 | 17 | 19
1987 | Directed by Paul Verhoeven | With Peter Weller, Nancy Allen, Ronny Cox | 103 minutes | Rated R

"Ruthlessly smart and satirical", this "novel" sci-fi adventure flick tells the story of a cop killed in the line of duty then brought back to life as a bio-mechanical robot; alternately "violent and hilarious", this "live-action comic book" is a "thought-provoking look" at a "techno vigilante" and a heck of a lot "better than it should have been."

Robots
20 | - | 19 | 24
2005 | Directed by Chris Wedge, Carlos Saldanha | Animated | 91 minutes | Not Rated

"Dazzling", "Rube Goldberg-esque" animation "keeps the whole family entertained" in this "simple", "heartfelt" 'toon about a young 'droid who "leaves home to chase a dream" in the big city; ok, the "ho-hum" "fish-out-of-water" plotline is "as mechanical as the characters", 'bot at least it's got an "uplifting", "you-can-do-anything-you-put-your-mind-to" message for the kids.

Rock, The
20 | 21 | 20 | 22
1996 | Directed by Michael Bay | With Sean Connery, Nicolas Cage, Ed Harris | 136 minutes | Rated R

Find out who's got the biggest "fireballs" in this very "noisy testosterone fix", bringing "slick", "edge-of-your-seat action" to Alcatraz as "crusty" ex-spy Connery and "bumbling" weapons-expert Cage penetrate the prison walls to stop a mad general from blitzing the Bay Area with nerve gas; fans find the pair "amazing together", and despite the highly "not-likely" scenario, the "awesome locale" and "great FX" ensure a "kick-ass" good time.

Rocky ✉
25 | 20 | 25 | 21
1976 | Directed by John G. Avildsen | With Sylvester Stallone, Talia Shire, Burt Young | 119 minutes | Rated PG

This "red-blooded" ring drama (and Oscar champ) "goes the distance" with an "underdog-makes-good" theme as "two-bit" boxer Sly "wins over everyone's heart" when he "gets his shot" at the title, works up "lots of sweat" and "finds true love" along the way; though part "hokey" "Hollywood fantasy", it's also a "stirring confidence-booster" that packs an everlasting "wallop."

Rocky Horror Picture Show, The
21 | 18 | 19 | 22
1975 | Directed by Jim Sharman | With Tim Curry, Susan Sarandon, Barry Bostwick | 100 minutes | Rated R

"Beyond weird" to the uninitiated, this "camp classic" rock 'n' roll musical is famed for the "floor show" put on at "midnight screenings" by costumed carousers who pronounce it the "best trash ever"; a "pure B-movie" spoof involving a pair of innocents who stumble into the lair of a "sweet transvestite", it's "silly" but "entertaining on its own bizarre level", so "get out your toast, rice and lighter" and "sing along" with this "legendary mess."

Roger & Me

24 | - | 24 | 20

1989 | Directed by Michael Moore | Documentary | 91 minutes | Rated R

"Laugh and cringe" at this salvo of "guerrilla filmmaking", an "eye-opening" documentary chronicling both the "disintegration" of a Michigan town after its GM plant pulls up stakes and "squeaky wheel" Moore's "quest to confront" the corporation's CEO; the "too-real" footage is "drop-dead funny" yet "sobering" ("rabbit lovers beware"), and if a few find the "irreverent" tone "annoying", progressives everywhere hail it as a "vital exposé" of the "new global economy."

Roger Dodger

18 | 22 | 18 | 16

2002 | Directed by Dylan Kidd | With Campbell Scott, Jesse Eisenberg, Isabella Rossellini | 104 minutes | Rated R

Playing the "biggest cad since Alfie", the "underappreciated" Scott is "socko" in this "sharp little indie" that ventures into "Neil LaBute" territory in its story of a "smarmy" adman instructing his "wide-eyed teenage nephew" in the "art of seduction"; despite "lots of talk", it's "never dull", though some find this "bitter, mean-spirited rant" "hard to watch."

Romancing the Stone

20 | 19 | 21 | 20

1984 | Directed by Robert Zemeckis | With Michael Douglas, Kathleen Turner, Danny DeVito | 105 minutes | Rated PG-13

This "poor man's *Raiders of the Lost Ark*" turns a "lighthearted" adventure into a "fast-paced crowd-pleaser", with Turner cast as a "nerdy" romance novelist who hooks up with "tongue-in-cheek hero" Douglas down South America way; the two are "quite the duo", and some "humorous action sequences" with archrival DeVito "trying to keep up" make for "durable escapism."

☑ Roman Holiday ✉◑

27 | 26 | 25 | 25

1953 | Directed by William Wyler | With Gregory Peck, Audrey Hepburn | 118 minutes | Not Rated

A "date movie without equal", this "frothy", "witty romance" presents a "radiant" Hepburn as the "rebellious" "gamine princess" with a "pixie cut" who plays hooky in the Eternal City, escorted by "charming", "not-so-hard-boiled reporter" Peck; helped along by "wondrous Roman scenery", their "coy" exchanges lead things on their natural "exhilarating" course, making for a "captivating fantasy" that draws to a "bittersweet", "refreshingly realistic" ending ("awww!").

Romeo and Juliet

26 | 24 | 27 | 26

1968 | Directed by Franco Zeffirelli | With Olivia Hussey, Leonard Whiting | 138 minutes | Rated PG

"Achingly beautiful", this "faithful Zeffirelli" reading renders the "grand" romance of star-crossed love so "accessible" that "even boys cry" during the tragic last act; the "classic" production stays "true to the Bard" with "so-cute" teenage actors and "gorgeous" sets, pleasing "purists" as the "definitive film version" and surviving as the odds-on favorite to be the Shakespeare everyone's "made to watch in school."

Romeo + Juliet

19 | 17 | 22 | 23

1996 | Directed by Baz Luhrmann | With Leonardo DiCaprio, Claire Danes, John Leguizamo | 120 minutes | Rated PG-13

Flash master Luhrmann presents the ageless romance "in a different light" in this "daring updating", a "kinetic visual feast" that aims to please the "MTV generation" with "pop music" and "creative" modern-day staging; Leo and Claire lend the lovers "teen-idol" allure, and if some sniff at "style over substance" and say the "acting seriously lacks", those who are "ok with extravagance" find it "effective" and "really cool."

Romy and Michele's High School Reunion　14 | 15 | 15 | 14

1997 | Directed by David Mirkin | With Mira Sorvino, Lisa Kudrow, Janeane Garofalo | 92 minutes | Rated R

Sorvino and Kudrow star as "airheads with hearts of gold" who dream of "impressing former classmates" at their high school reunion in this "silly" comic "tribute to nerds and outsiders" everywhere; it's definitely "not to be taken seriously", but for "brainless fun" set to a "great" '80s soundtrack, this "trifle" is, like, quite the "guilty pleasure."

Ronin　20 | 22 | 19 | 21

1998 | Directed by John Frankenheimer | With Robert De Niro, Jean Reno, Natascha McElhone, Jonathan Pryce | 121 minutes | Rated R

"It's all about the car chases" in this "gritty", "grown-up" thriller revved up by an "excellent ensemble" cast (led by the "subtly powerful Reno") and an "interesting" heist plot that "twists and turns" against "great European backdrops"; one of the "last hurrahs" from action genre pioneer Frankenheimer, it's "not a thinking person's film" – so don't fret over "what's in that suitcase."

Rookie, The　22 | 22 | 23 | 20

2002 | Directed by John Lee Hancock | With Dennis Quaid, Rachel Griffiths, Brian Cox | 127 minutes | Rated G

Quaid "hits a grand slam" as an over-the-hill major-league baseball rookie in this "feel-good movie for the whole family to enjoy" and "learn from"; it's a true story (with a "little Disney sprinkled on it") "that shows the importance of following your dreams" "even when it seems too late"; critics have just one quibble: it "drags on longer than a low-scoring doubleheader."

Room at the Top ⊠◑　24 | 27 | 24 | 23

1959 | Directed by Jack Clayton | With Simone Signoret, Laurence Harvey, Heather Sears | 115 minutes | Not Rated

Britain's "class struggle" is the subject of this "powerful" "drama of ambition" starring an "excellent" Harvey as an angry young man bent on improving his lot in life by wooing a naive heiress; along the way, he has some "provocative" moments with the "smoky" Signoret, who steals the picture (and copped a Best Actress Oscar) as his "sultry, world-weary" playmate.

Room with a View, A ⊠　26 | 26 | 24 | 27

1986 | Directed by James Ivory | With Maggie Smith, Helena Bonham Carter, Denholm Elliott | 117 minutes | Not Rated

"Florence looks like heaven" in this "crisp" costume drama about a "proper Victorian girl's" sightseeing tour that's considerably perked up by "friendships that form in a pensione", leading to her "romantic awakening"; the "brilliant acting" brings "wit and energy" to a "sunny" "study of class and character" that finds all kinds of room for "superb fin de siècle" touches and "seductive" shots of the Italian landscape.

	OVERALL	ACTING	STORY	PROD.

Rope
22 | 21 | 23 | 22

1948 | Directed by Alfred Hitchcock | With Farley Granger, James Stewart, John Dall | 80 minutes | Rated PG

"One word – Hitchcock" – draws film buffs to this "chilling" reworking of the Leopold and Loeb murder case that's told with a "compelling gimmick": it was "shot entirely on one set" and "runs in real time"; though a few snore "slow and stagy", at least the master's "eye to detail" makes it an "interesting curiosity."

Rose, The
19 | 23 | 18 | 18

1979 | Directed by Mark Rydell | With Bette Midler, Alan Bates, Frederic Forrest | 125 minutes | Rated R

The "mesmerizing" Miss M makes the "most stunning movie debut since Streisand" in this rock-chanteuse drama, a "homage" to the wild-at-heart chronicling the life and times of a "self-destructive Janis Joplin type" as she barrels down the road to ruin; groupies who insist Midler's "strong performance" should have "won the Oscar" find consolation in that "great title song."

Rosemary's Baby
24 | 25 | 25 | 22

1968 | Directed by Roman Polanski | With Mia Farrow, John Cassavetes, Ruth Gordon | 136 minutes | Rated R

A "glamorous horror" flick about a "naive" housewife duped into bearing "Satan's child", this "gut-wrenching classic" still "scares the hell out" of nearly everybody; "pro-choice" types tout Farrow's "amazing" turn (and "faaabulous haircut") as well as Polanski's "very faithful adaptation" of Ira Levin's novel, but everyone says that the "devilishly good", Oscar-winning Gordon "steals the show."

Roxanne
21 | 21 | 21 | 19

1987 | Directed by Fred Schepisi | With Steve Martin, Daryl Hannah, Rick Rossovich | 107 minutes | Rated PG

Schnoz aficionados consider this "amusing" romance the "quintessential Martin vehicle": a "modernization" of *Cyrano de Bergerac* concerning a fire chief cursed with a prodigious proboscis but blessed with a "grab bag of comic devices" with which he helps a surrogate court the highly "watchable" Hannah; though some find it too "cute", "God nose" it's a "good-natured" yarn with a "ton of heart."

Royal Tenenbaums, The
20 | 24 | 18 | 21

2001 | Directed by Wes Anderson | With Gene Hackman, Anjelica Huston, Ben Stiller, Gwyneth Paltrow | 109 minutes | Rated R

This "very black" yet colorful "character-driven" comedy delineates the "humorous side of dysfunctionality" within a "wacky family of overachievers"; while the "Oscar-worthy" script and "stellar ensemble cast" draw applause, some shrug it's a "movie about nothing" that's "too clever" and "cynical" – the "reviewers liked it more than I did."

Rudy
23 | 22 | 25 | 21

1993 | Directed by David Anspaugh | With Sean Astin, Jon Favreau, Ned Beatty | 116 minutes | Rated PG

"What *Hoosiers* is to basketball", this "inspiring" flick is to college football, "bringing grown men to tears" with its "sentimental" celebration of true-life "ultimate underdog" Rudy Ruettiger, an "undersized kid with an oversized heart" who famously tackled his "lifelong dream to play for Notre Dame"; fielding a stellar cast led by the "excellent" Astin, it will "have you chanting with the crowd" during the "feel-good" finale.

Rules of the Game, The ❶🅵 ▽ 27 | 24 | 25 | 26
1939 | Directed by Jean Renoir | With Marcel Dalio, Nora Gregor, Mila Parély | 110 minutes | Not Rated
"Always on the short list of the greatest films ever made" is this "scathing indictment of the French upper class" from "master" filmmaker Renoir, which "takes place at a weekend retreat in the country" and contrasts the romantic entanglements of both rich and poor alike; although "perfectly written, filmed and acted", it was not a hit in its initial release, and only garnered its rep after resurfacing at a film festival 20 years later.

Ruling Class, The 23 | 26 | 22 | 21
1972 | Directed by Peter Medak | With Peter O'Toole, Alastair Sim, Arthur Lowe, Harry Andrews | 154 minutes | Rated PG
Alternately "funny and disturbing", this black "social satire" takes on "the British upper class" in its story of a "delusional" fellow who becomes "the 14th Earl of Gurney" after the death of his father; the "bizarre" plot includes some "absurd song-and-dance routines" but "moves like lightning", and as the "bonkers" nobleman, O'Toole's "totally over the top."

Runaway Jury 20 | 22 | 21 | 20
2003 | Directed by Gary Fleder | With John Cusack, Gene Hackman, Dustin Hoffman | 127 minutes | Rated PG-13
"Liberal Hollywood goes after the gun industry" in this courtroom drama pitting a "jury-stacking lawyer" against a "righteous underdog"; ok, it "doesn't follow the storyline" of its John Grisham origins, but devotees dig watching "old pros Hackman and Hoffman square off" just the same – even if they appear together on-screen in "just one scene."

Runaway Train 21 | 22 | 20 | 21
1985 | Directed by Andrei Konchalovsky | With Jon Voight, Eric Roberts, Rebecca de Mornay | 111 minutes | Rated R
"Surprisingly" stimulating despite "cheapish production values", this "stark", "existential actioner" keeps onlookers "enthralled" with a "twist on the prison-break" scenario as a freight train carrying a pair of fugitive cons careens through the Alaskan wild ("bring a parka") while the law looks on; though "over the top" enough to nearly hop the rails, this "bleak masterwork" also offers "powerful" acting and "dark" themes.

Run Lola Run 🅵 23 | 21 | 24 | 24
1999 | Directed by Tom Tykwer | With Franka Potente, Moritz Bleibtreu, Herbert Knaup | 81 minutes | Rated R
There's "never a dull moment" in this "amped-up" German import involving the "sweat-dripping" effort of a fleet-footed fräulein to hustle a big pile of cash to save her boyfriend from a nasty mobster; "strongly driven" by an "adrenaline"-pumping "techno soundtrack" and "videogame" vibe, the "breathless" "nonlinear" narrative forges "different perspectives" and "time repeats" into a "pulse-pounding" "original" that's as "ultra-watchable" as it is "quirky."

| | OVERALL | ACTING | STORY | PROD. |

Running Man, The
17 | 13 | 19 | 18

1987 | Directed by Paul Michael Glaser | With Arnold Schwarzenegger, Maria Conchita Alonso, Yaphet Kotto | 101 minutes | Rated R

"Required viewing for anyone who wants to be on reality TV", this "cartoon-esque" action picture stars Ahnold as a contestant in a "futuristic" game show that "allows criminals to compete for their freedom" (think "*Family Feud* gone horribly wrong"); sure, it's a "guilty pleasure", but our survey says "Richard Dawson steals it as the host from hell."

Rush Hour
19 | 17 | 16 | 20

1998 | Directed by Brett Ratner | With Jackie Chan, Chris Tucker, Tom Wilkinson | 97 minutes | Rated PG-13

Formula "fluff" with "all the right moves", this actioner finds time for "comic relief" as a crime-fighting pair of "exact opposites" teams up to rescue a kidnapped kid; "high-kicking" Chan breaks out with some "inventive chop-socky sequences" and "exhilarating" stunts while playing it straight alongside outspoken "wild man" Tucker, so even if the "plot's not much", the "buddy pairing" offers enough crowd-pleasing "chemistry" to translate into "loads of fun."

Rush Hour 2
17 | 16 | 16 | 19

2001 | Directed by Brett Ratner | With Jackie Chan, Chris Tucker, Zhang Ziyi | 90 minutes | Rated PG-13

The lucrative recipe of "great martial arts" seasoned with "goofball" shtick skewering East-West "cultural differences" plates this second helping of "entertaining" action-comedy; true, there are "no surprises" as the reunited Chan and Tucker once again "kick butt" and deliver "laughs" playing a "mismatched pair" of crimestoppers, but most agree it's "not so bad" for an "overdone Hollywood ride."

Rushmore
23 | 25 | 22 | 22

1998 | Directed by Wes Anderson | With Jason Schwartzman, Olivia Williams, Bill Murray | 93 minutes | Rated R

A monument of "quality quirkiness", this "unabashedly unusual" comedy stars Schwartzman as an "arrogant and clever" but "dysfunctional" scholarship student at an elite prep school whose "coming of age" takes many a "droll" twist when he befriends a rich alumnus and falls for a teacher; the "smart", "character-driven" script is "expertly acted", leading to high marks for a "winning gem" with "real heart" "beneath the smarminess" – and how about that "killer soundtrack"?

Russians Are Coming, The Russians Are Coming, The
21 | 21 | 22 | 20

1966 | Directed by Norman Jewison | With Alan Arkin, John Phillip Law, Jonathan Winters | 120 minutes | Not Rated

Da, comrades, this "classic '60s comedy" is a "Cold War satire" that offers a "sweet take" on a paranoid period as a Red Navy sub goes aground off the Massachusetts coast and Soviet swabbie Arkin is sent into a Nantucket-like island community for a rescue boat, setting off rumors of an invasion; *Strangelove* it ain't, but the "very funny" situations are still "worth the time."

	OVERALL	ACTING	STORY	PROD.

Ruthless People

`20` `19` `19` `17`

1986 | Directed by David Zucker, Jerry Zucker, Jim Abrahams | With Danny DeVito, Bette Midler | 93 minutes | Rated R

Echt '80s in its send-up of "pure greed", this pretty "crass" but "side-splitting" black comedy gets going when a couple of "inept kidnappers" snatch Midler (carrying on at her "bitchy best") and demand ransom from DeVito, a "standout" as the "crude", double-dealing "spandex king" husband scheming to rid himself of a despised spouse; "lots of plot twists" ensue in a "silly", "hilarious" caper that anyone with a cynical side shouldn't overlook.

Ryan's Daughter

`22` `23` `22` `24`

1970 | Directed by David Lean | With Robert Mitchum, Trevor Howard, Sarah Miles, John Mills | 176 minutes | Rated PG

"Love and infidelity" are played out against a "magnificent Irish seacoast setting" in this "epic tearjerker" via David Lean, a "weak-in-the-knees romance" that's set to memorably "haunting music"; its "bracing scenery" and truly "powerful" story – depicting "love as steadfastness rather than a cheap emotion" – lead many to call it "underrated."

Saboteur ◐

`23` `21` `24` `23`

1942 | Directed by Alfred Hitchcock | With Robert Cummings, Priscilla Lane, Otto Kruger | 108 minutes | Not Rated

"Cross-country intrigue" underlies this "effective" Hitchcock "romp across America", wherein an "innocent man" is "unwittingly involved in an espionage plot"; maybe it's a bit "cheesy by today's standards", but even "Bob Cummings' wooden performance" is blown away by that "unforgettable finale" atop the "torch of the Statue of Liberty."

Sabrina ◐

`25` `25` `25` `23`

1954 | Directed by Billy Wilder | With Humphrey Bogart, Audrey Hepburn, William Holden | 113 minutes | Not Rated

Like an order of "first-class everything", this "delicious" "rags-to-riches" romance sparkles with "wit and couture" as an "ethereal" Hepburn plays a "beguiling", love-struck chauffeur's daughter in a "little black dress"; the "modern Cinderella" scenario finds Bogie in a "co-medic role" as an all-business heir determined to beat out his "younger playboy brother" for Audrey's affections; as for Harrison Ford's 1995 remake, loyalists "consider it blasphemy."

Sahara

`17` `16` `16` `20`

2005 | Directed by Breck Eisner | With Matthew McConaughey, Penélope Cruz, Steve Zahn | 124 minutes | Rated PG-13

An "amusing" if "minor-league Indiana Jones rip-off", this "carefree" adventure yarn based on Clive Cussler's best-seller grafts the search for a "Civil War battleship in Africa" onto an "enviro-sensitive" story of a catastrophic plague threatening the worlds' oceans; though Matthew, Penélope and the "exotic locales" make for "beautiful scenery", the end result is "pretty to look at, but not much else."

Salvador

`21` `24` `21` `20`

1986 | Directed by Oliver Stone | With James Woods, James Belushi, John Savage | 123 minutes | Rated R

Oliver Stone keeps it fairly "lucid" in this early drama, a "worthwhile" character study starring the Oscar-nominated Woods, who proves he "can flat-out act" playing a burnt-out photojournalist desperate to score freelance work in war-torn Central America; though *Platoon* (from the same director) took Best Picture honors that year, a few feel this one's the "better movie."

Same Time, Next Year
22 | 24 | 25 | 21

1978 | Directed by Robert Mulligan | With Ellen Burstyn, Alan Alda, Ivan Bonar | 119 minutes | Rated PG

Expect to go from "laughter to tears and back again" in this "decade-spanning romance", featuring "convincing" turns from Alda and Burstyn as a couple of "married lovers who meet once a year"; adapted from the stage, the "annual adultery" device tracks the two as they "change with the times", making for "sweet", "warm" entertainment – even if it does "promote affairs."

Sand Pebbles, The
24 | 26 | 25 | 24

1966 | Directed by Robert Wise | With Steve McQueen, Richard Crenna, Richard Attenborough, Candice Bergen | 179 minutes | Rated PG-13

An "epic of China" told from the point of view of Yank sailors knee-deep in the revolutionary turmoil of 1926, this "powerful, pertinent" war drama features "authentic hero" McQueen "smoldering in top form" as a "tough-guy" Navy mechanic "with a heart of gold", manning an American patrol boat; if the tale "meanders like the Yellow River", it's still a "must-see" for History Channel addicts.

Santa Clause, The
19 | 17 | 19 | 19

1994 | Directed by John Pasquin | With Tim Allen, Judge Reinhold, Wendy Crewson | 97 minutes | Rated PG

"Corny in a good way", this holiday comedy packages the "fantastic" with the "real world" when exec Allen takes over the reins from an abruptly retired Kris Kringle, mysteriously begins "fattening" and meets with complications in the custody of his young son; though it sleds along on a "sappy story", at least it's "original."

Saturday Night Fever
22 | 19 | 20 | 22

1977 | Directed by John Badham | With John Travolta, Karen Lynn Gorney | 118 minutes | Rated R

A paean to "polyester", this romance defines the "days of disco" with an "electric" Travolta as the blow-dried mook who lives to "look good" and "shake his groove thing" but has to boogie to "improve his life" when love comes to town; iconic "dance scenes" accentuate an "affecting" story with "dark" undercurrents that "perfectly evokes" "real life in Brooklyn" circa '77, even if some survivors of those "cheesy times" "feel embarrassed" about it now.

Satyricon 🇫
20 | 17 | 17 | 24

1969 | Directed by Federico Fellini | With Martin Potter, Hiram Keller, Capucine, Alain Cuny | 129 minutes | Rated R

"Nothing's sacred" in this "out-there" "hymn to decadence", a "provocative", "surreal" trip through Nero's Rome that's based on incomplete remnants of a satire by Petronius, which might explain its "oddly fragmented" structure ("can someone please tell me what it's about?"); definitely "not for everyone" (especially kids), this is "disturbing", ultra-"kinky" stuff – either "Fellini at his indulgent worst" or "awe-inspiring in its sheer extravagance."

Save the Last Dance | 17 | 17 | 17 | 17 |

2001 | Directed by Thomas Carter | With Julia Stiles, Sean Patrick Thomas, Kerry Washington | 112 minutes | Rated PG-13

This "modern star-crossed-lovers" saga stars Stiles as a suburban teen transferred to an inner-city school where she falls into an interracial "across-the-tracks romance"; though the "textbook" set-ups "could have been more inventive", the picture imparts a "good message", abetted by a "great soundtrack", some "fancy footwork" and a climactic "hip-hop 'n' classical ballet."

Save the Tiger ⊠ | 22 | 26 | 22 | 20 |

1973 | Directed by John G. Avildsen | With Jack Lemmon, Jack Gilford, Thayer David | 100 minutes | Rated R

"One of Lemmon's greatest performances" – an "Academy Award winner", in fact – is the lynchpin of this "well-done" portrait of a struggling businessman who considers arson (i.e. insurance fraud) as a means to "survive in the fashion industry"; also notable for Gilford's "strong" supporting work, this one is a "pleasure to see", so long as you can abide its "grim look at the travails of middle age."

☑ Saving Private Ryan ⊠ | 26 | 26 | 24 | 28 |

1998 | Directed by Steven Spielberg | With Tom Hanks, Tom Sizemore, Edward Burns | 170 minutes | Rated R

"As intense as it gets", Steven Spielberg's "celluloid monument" to WWII evokes the fear of war with "in-your-face" footage like the "devastating" opening, a "masterful" montage of "graphic" death and mayhem on a D-day beachhead; thereafter Hanks leads a "superbly" cast unit through no-man's-land on a "compelling" quest for a missing grunt, and despite sniping that "the story bogs down", it's a "wrenching" oh-"so-real" reminder that "war is hell."

Saw | 18 | 17 | 22 | 19 |

2004 | Directed by James Wan | With Leigh Whannell, Cary Elwes, Danny Glover | 100 minutes | Rated R

"Graphic" and "gruesome", this "edge-of-your-seat thriller" is definitely "not for the squeamish" ("don't eat beforehand") in its story of two men chained in a lavatory with a hacksaw – for sawing off their own legs – their only means of escape; while aficionados dis the "lousy acting" and a *Seven* rip-off" plot, many more praise its "real scares" and that "absolutely stunning ending" – "you won't see it coming."

Saw II | 19 | 16 | 19 | 19 |

2005 | Directed by Darren Lynn Bousman | With Tobin Bell, Shawnee Smith, Donnie Wahlberg | 93 minutes | Rated R

This "gory-as-it-gets" sequel features a "whole new gang" of human guinea pigs forced to "play a psychopath's games" in a "sick" house of horrors ("if this doesn't make your skin crawl, you must be dead"); maybe it's "not as, um, cutting edge" as the original, but devotees still dub it a "doozy" and "can't wait" for more.

Say Anything | 23 | 22 | 22 | 20 |

1989 | Directed by Cameron Crowe | With John Cusack, Ione Skye, John Mahoney | 100 minutes | Rated PG-13

"Teenage love is beautiful" in this "quintessential" '80s romance that had a "serious impact on Gen-X women" by making them "fall in love with Cusack", the "geek who gets the popular girl" from a "different class of society"; though naysayers suggest the "dad drama" subplot "slows things down", overall this "youth-in-angst" story has become the "touchstone of a generation"; most memorable prop: the "boom box."

Scarface
22 | 23 | 22 | 22

1983 | Directed by Brian De Palma | With Al Pacino, Steven Bauer, Michelle Pfeiffer | 170 minutes | Rated R

"Raw and fun all at once", this "benchmark" crime thriller about a Miami-based "Latin drug ring" is ultra-"intense" and "extravagantly bloody" ("close your eyes when they bring out that chainsaw!"); addicts attest that it's worth seeing for Pacino's "over-the-top" turn as the "kind of bad guy you could really like", but the unmoved sneer it's "ultimately unredeeming" – and too "profane" to boot ("how many times can you say the F-word?").

Scarlet Empress, The ◑
▽ 24 | 23 | 22 | 27

1934 | Directed by Josef von Sternberg | With Marlene Dietrich, John Lodge, Sam Jaffe, Louise Dresser | 104 minutes | Not Rated

"Spectacularly bizarre", this over-the-top take on the life of Catherine the Great is a "masterpiece of fantasy pretending to be biography" that's worth watching for its "dazzling" production values, period; La Dietrich enacts the title role in a "series of poses" lovingly lit by director von Sternberg, and even if it's "not *The Blue Angel*", this "delirious mess" is certainly "like nothing else you've ever seen."

Scarlet Street ◑
▽ 25 | 26 | 24 | 23

1945 | Directed by Fritz Lang | With Edward G. Robinson, Joan Bennett, Dan Duryea | 103 minutes | Not Rated

A "pathetic old man is caught in a sticky web of sex and murder" when he meets the ultimate femme fatale in Fritz Lang's "creepy" but "painfully brilliant" entry in the film noir canon; the pulpy goings-on may be "entertaining on a trashy level", but even if "you think you've remembered every plot twist" of the genre, this picture "really surprises."

Scenes from a Marriage 🅵
25 | 27 | 23 | 23

1973 | Directed by Ingmar Bergman | With Liv Ullmann, Erland Josephson, Bibi Andersson | 168 minutes | Rated PG

Originally a six-hour TV miniseries pared down to feature length, this still "powerful" portrayal of a "marriage breaking down" via Ingmar Bergman is a "real, poignant" tale told with such "rich execution" that it might "scare off all but the bravest from the altar"; though "hard to take for its intensity", this "talkathon" is worth seeing for its simply "astonishing performances."

Scent of a Woman ✉
21 | 25 | 21 | 21

1992 | Directed by Martin Brest | With Al Pacino, Chris O'Donnell, Philip Seymour Hoffman | 157 minutes | Rated R

Pacino's "bravura" Best Actor bit has him cast as a retired military man compensating for his visual impairment with an "abrasive personality" and "foghorn" pipes as he drags his "meek" preppy babysitter along for a wild weekend in the Naked City; where cynics see "hokum" that "tends to drag", fans of the "too-fabulous" Al find it worthwhile "for the tango scene" alone.

☑ Schindler's List ✉◑   29 | 29 | 28 | 29
1993 | Directed by Steven Spielberg | With Liam Neeson, Ben Kingsley, Ralph Fiennes | 197 minutes | Rated R

Embarking on a "tour-de-force" "journey through a dark period", Spielberg's "direct", "painful" wartime drama "crystallizes" the "real-life horror" of the Holocaust in "stunning quasi-documentary" black-and-white, with Neeson as the man of "moral conscience" dealing with the Nazis in "shattering" circumstances; "beyond moving" and "tough to watch" in spite of its "understatement" and "touches of grace", it's a top Oscar honoree that's all-but-unanimously cited as "unforgettable required viewing."

School of Rock   20 | 20 | 20 | 19
2003 | Directed by Richard Linklater | With Jack Black, Joan Cusack | 108 minutes | Rated PG-13

"Jack Black's manic zeal" takes center stage in this comedy about a "selfish wannabe" pop star who learns "selflessness" and turns a "bunch of buttoned-up prep schoolers" into "rock monsters"; it's "cute" and "sappy" in a "predictable", "family-friendly" way, but the "infectious energy" embodies the "irreverent spirit of classic rock" well enough to appeal to "young and old alike."

Score, The   17 | 21 | 18 | 18
2001 | Directed by Frank Oz | With Robert De Niro, Edward Norton, Marlon Brando, Angela Bassett | 124 minutes | Rated R

"Three generations of great method actors" – Norton, De Niro and an "over-the-top" Brando in his final film appearance – play criminals bent on burglarizing the Montreal Customs House in this "boilerplate" caper; though fans praise the "top-drawer" casting and that "really cool ending", it scores lower for its "slow" pace and "seen-it-all-before" storyline.

Scream   20 | 16 | 21 | 19
1996 | Directed by Wes Craven | With David Arquette, Neve Campbell, Courteney Cox | 111 minutes | Rated R

In an "aptly titled" entry, *Nightmare on Elm Street*'s Wes Craven "revives" the horror genre by aiming "clever potshots" at a host of hackneyed "slasher-film" clichés, lending a "humorously self-aware twist" to a "fast-paced" story of a "slice-and-dice" psycho at large among suburban teens; sure, the picture "makes fun of itself", but it's still "scary stuff" that sets a "bloody and gross" precedent for a "slew of imitators."

Scrooged   19 | 19 | 20 | 20
1988 | Directed by Richard Donner | With Bill Murray, Karen Allen, Carol Kane, Bobcat Goldthwait | 101 minutes | Rated PG-13

Dickens' *A Christmas Carol* gets a "modern" makeover complete with "dark" comedic notes via this "inspired" parody led by Murray playing a "cruel TV exec" in desperate need of a "morality lesson"; further boosted by an "excellent" supporting cast, "it's become a tradition" to include this one in the annual "holiday movie marathon."

Seabiscuit   25 | 25 | 25 | 26
2003 | Directed by Gary Ross | With Tobey Maguire, Jeff Bridges, Chris Cooper | 141 minutes | Rated PG-13

Set against the "backdrop of the Great Depression", this "winning" adaptation of Laura Hillenbrand's best-selling pony tale trots out an "old-fashioned" story about a "little horse that could"; "moving" turns from Maguire, Bridges and Cooper (as jockey, owner and trainer) and "beautifully photographed", "suspenseful" racing sequences evoke cheers, even if a few find this gelding's gait a tad "slow", saying "it misses greatness by a nose."

Sea of Love
20 | 23 | 21 | 19

1989 | Directed by Harold Becker | With Al Pacino, Ellen Barkin, John Goodman | 113 minutes | Rated R

"Pacino and Barkin sizzle like ham and eggs" in this "intense", "atmospheric" thriller about a "tortured cop" on the trail of a serial killer who becomes enmeshed in a "steamy" affair with a "hot" "temptress" or perhaps "suspect"; dancing around the old "did-she-or-didn't-she?" question, the "taut" script plants enough "seeds of doubt" along the way to keep things "interesting" till the windup.

⊠ Searchers, The
27 | 25 | 27 | 27

1956 | Directed by John Ford | With John Wayne, Jeffrey Hunter, Vera Miles | 120 minutes | Not Rated

"Not just a shoot-'em-up", this "thinking person's" Western boasts "peak" work from Wayne, who delivers a "gripping" portrayal of a "brooding" Civil War veteran obsessed with tracking down his niece, who's been abducted by Comanches; with its "spectacular" backdrops and "controversial" handling of "kinship and racism", it's much praised as "Ford's masterpiece", "perhaps the finest in the genre."

Secondhand Lions
22 | 25 | 22 | 22

2003 | Directed by Tim McCanlies | With Michael Caine, Robert Duvall, Haley Joel Osment | 109 minutes | Rated PG

A young boy spends the summer in the "middle of nowhere" with his "eccentric uncles" in this "family-friendly", "feel-good" flicker that teaches "moral lessons about integrity and honor", yet is still "fun to watch"; as two "grumpy old men" weaving "tall tales from truth", Caine and Duvall exhibit "perfect timing", despite a somewhat "corny", "predictable" premise.

Secretary
21 | 24 | 20 | 19

2002 | Directed by Steven Shainberg | With James Spader, Maggie Gyllenhaal | 104 minutes | Rated R

A "repressed" attorney "takes out his do-as-I-say delights on his all-too-willing secretary" in this "brilliant black comedy" (or is it a "kinky love story"?) that "makes you realize there's someone for everyone"; "hilarious characters", "interesting plot twists" and "superb acting" add up to an "ass-spanking good time."

Secret of NIMH, The
24 | - | 25 | 24

1982 | Directed by Don Bluth | Animated | 82 minutes | Rated G

From the all-pro pens of "former Disney artists" comes this "freaky", oft-"forgotten" "alternative to sugar-coated" animation, a "beautifully drawn gem" of a barnyard yarn about a mama mouse desperately seeking a new nest for her brood; the "captivating" depiction of farm life comes with "character development" and an "interesting" story designed to appeal to the "adult" in everyone.

Secrets and Lies

24 | 27 | 24 | 22

1996 | Directed by Mike Leigh | With Brenda Blethyn, Marianne Jean-Baptiste | 136 minutes | Rated R

Bad boy Leigh turns "accessible" in this "smart", "solid British drama" of "long-lost" family ties concerning a young black Londoner who "searches out her biological mother" only to find out that mum may be a working-class white woman; led by Blethyn's "pure, honest performance", the principals do a "terrific job" of making this tale "involving" and "heartbreaking."

Seduction of Joe Tynan, The

▽ 22 | 25 | 22 | 19

1979 | Directed by Jerry Schatzberg | With Alan Alda, Barbara Harris, Meryl Streep, Melvyn Douglas | 107 minutes | Rated R

Along with *The Candidate*, this "well-done" portrait of a "hard-charging", "Ted Kennedy–esque" Senator whose extramarital exploits roil both his private life and his public "ambitions" is required viewing for "anyone thinking of a career in politics"; scripted by and starring the "awesome" Alda, it also features an "incandescent" Streep in one of her earliest screen roles.

Sense and Sensibility ✉

26 | 27 | 26 | 26

1995 | Directed by Ang Lee | With Emma Thompson, Alan Rickman, Kate Winslet, Hugh Grant | 136 minutes | Rated PG

"Jane Austen would have liked" this "bittersweet" story of two husband-hunting sisters that "captures the true flavor" of her novel "with wit and honesty" largely due to a "strong", Oscar-winning script from the "so-fine" Emma Thompson; sensitive types tout the "beautiful" scenery, director Lee's "brilliant" job and an ensemble cast that "rises to the occasion" – "this is what moviemaking should be."

Serenity

23 | 22 | 23 | 24

2005 | Directed by Joss Whedon | With Nathan Fillion, Gina Torres, Alan Tudyk | 119 minutes | Rated PG-13

A big-screen adaptation of the "short-lived" "cult" TV series *Firefly*, this "enjoyable" sci-fi/Western spins an "innovative" outer-space adventure enlivened by "solid" FX and a "memorable" cast of "relative unknowns" armed with a payload of "witty lines"; advice to the "uninitiated": viewing the original show "isn't mandatory", but it might make the "convoluted" story less "confusing."

Sergeant York ✉◐

25 | 25 | 24 | 22

1941 | Directed by Howard Hawks | With Gary Cooper, Walter Brennan, Joan Leslie | 134 minutes | Not Rated

A "true story that needs no amplification", this "satisfying" biopic stars an Oscar-winning Cooper as the pacifist who became WWI's most decorated soldier after single-handedly dismantling an enemy regiment; a "complex" piece of pro-war propaganda, it's also a "great depiction" of a man of "quiet inner strength."

Serpico

23 | 26 | 24 | 21

1973 | Directed by Sidney Lumet | With Al Pacino, John Randolph, Tony Roberts | 129 minutes | Rated R

Honesty "doesn't pay" in this "gritty" true story starring a "superb" Pacino as a whistle-blowing NYPD do-gooder who becomes a "man alone" when his exposure of "cop corruption" threatens to bring down the whole city; if all the "raw emotion" can grow "frustrating" and the milieu seems "a bit dated", it remains arresting as a "compelling commentary on the times."

Servant, The ❶
25 | 27 | 25 | 23

1963 | Directed by Joseph Losey | With Dirk Bogarde, James Fox, Sarah Miles, Wendy Craig | 112 minutes | Not Rated
The "British class structure" gets the Harold Pinter treatment in this "dark", "nasty piece of work" detailing the "power struggle" between a "menacing butler" and his "decadent", weak-willed master; in the title role, the "peerless" Bogarde is so "appropriately creepy" that some consider "giving up their household staff."

Seven
23 | 23 | 24 | 23

1995 | Directed by David Fincher | With Brad Pitt, Morgan Freeman, Kevin Spacey | 123 minutes | Rated R
All the "elegant nastiness" of a "guided tour through hell" surfaces in this "macabre psychological thriller" about two big-city detectives on the trail of an "ingenious" serial killer who dreams up "genuinely disturbing" torments "based on the seven deadly sins"; an "unrelenting" dose of "creepy modern noir" at its "darkest", it's wickedly "riveting" and "impressive" but "hard-to-take" and "gruesome" – with "no happy ending."

Seven Beauties 🅵
26 | 26 | 25 | 24

1976 | Directed by Lina Wertmüller | With Giancarlo Giannini, Fernando Rey, Shirley Stoler | 115 minutes | Rated R
Wertmüller's "extraordinary" exploration of "survival in WWII" stars Giannini as a Chaplin-esque romeo trying to stay alive in a German concentration camp; a "brilliant" "amalgam of comedy and drama", it's a "powerful introduction to foreign filmmaking."

Seven Brides for Seven Brothers
24 | 20 | 21 | 25

1954 | Directed by Stanley Donen | With Howard Keel, Jane Powell, Russ Tamblyn | 103 minutes | Rated G
Ok, it's "low on feasibility", but this "down-home" musical of "seven eligible backwoodsmen looking for love" with a septet of hillbilly "Sabine women" strikes "pure gold" with its "great Johnny Mercer" tunes and "extraordinary" choreography; fans dig its "exuberant" production numbers so "athletic" they "make dance macho", particularly that "barn-raising scene."

Seven Days in May ❶
26 | 24 | 28 | 22

1964 | Directed by John Frankenheimer | With Burt Lancaster, Kirk Douglas, Fredric March | 118 minutes | Not Rated
"It could happen here", or so says this "riveting 'what-if' drama", a "scary" Cold War story about disgruntled Pentagon brass who lay plans for a "military takeover"; soldiering along with "well-plotted" plausibility and "Douglas and Lancaster turning up the star heat", it's a "powerful nail-biter" that "political junkies" consider – gulp – "as timely today as ever."

🆉 Seven Samurai, The ❶🅵
29 | 27 | 28 | 27

1956 | Directed by Akira Kurosawa | With Toshiro Mifune, Takashi Shimura | 203 minutes | Not Rated
Credited with "defining its own genre", Kurosawa's "awesome", "pivotal" Japanese adventure introduces the "original magnificent seven"

as old-time samurai "warrior-heroes" who rise to the defense of a village menaced by a "vicious band of marauders"; the "epic running time melts away" before the "exciting" display of "honor", "courage" and "classic swordplay", and though there are "countless" reworkings, connoisseurs claim this "way-cool prototype" is "far superior."

1776
22 | 22 | 24 | 23

1972 | Directed by Peter H. Hunt | With William Daniels, Howard da Silva, Blythe Danner | 142 minutes | Rated G

Put away the books and take an "entertaining shortcut" to U.S. history via this "faithful" rendering of the Broadway musical, a "patriotic pageant" wherein periwigged radicals assemble in Philly and wrangle over the Declaration of Independence, backed up by "wonderful music and lyrics"; it's a "smart", "informative" way to "put a face" on "those lovable founding fathers", and they turn out to be "such great singers" – "who knew?"

Seventh Seal, The ❶❶
27 | 27 | 26 | 26

1957 | Directed by Ingmar Bergman | With Max von Sydow, Gunnar Björnstrand, Nils Poppe | 96 minutes | Not Rated

An utterly foreign flick and staple of "college days", Bergman's "challenging" drama is a "dark allegory" with von Sydow as a "knight returning from the Crusades to plague-swept Europe" only to hunker down for a high-stakes "chess game with Death"; as a "cerebral" meditation on the "meaning of existence", it seals the deal with "some of the greatest visuals ever" and a "symbolic story" that "makes everything else look like a game of checkers."

7th Voyage of Sinbad, The
20 | 12 | 20 | 22

1958 | Directed by Nathan Juran | With Kerwin Mathews, Kathryn Grant, Torin Thatcher | 88 minutes | Rated G

"Amazing for its time", this "delightful" adventure "throwback" "makes myth real without computers" using '50s-era FX to summon up a host of "lovingly created monsters"; ok, the "Saturday-matinee" storyline is "standard cheese", but it's a "fondly remembered fantasy" for fans who happily "take it for what it is."

Seven Year Itch, The
23 | 23 | 20 | 20

1955 | Directed by Billy Wilder | With Marilyn Monroe, Tom Ewell, Evelyn Keyes | 105 minutes | Not Rated

Marilyn's billowing-dress "subway-grate scene" is the iconic moment in this "enjoyable" comedy, which finds "ordinary guy" Ewell "on his own" when the wife and kiddies split for summer vacation simultaneous with the arrival of his new neighbor, a most "memorable" Monroe in full "innocent-sexpot" mode, who brings on a major "midlife crisis"; sure, the repartee seems "dated and stagy", but it can still tickle the "funny" bone.

Sex, Lies and Videotape
19 | 20 | 20 | 18

1989 | Directed by Steven Soderbergh | With James Spader, Andie MacDowell, Peter Gallagher | 98 minutes | Rated R

Wounded libidos fight the "battles of the sexes" in this "fresh take" on the "deterioration of relationships", a "well-crafted" drama about a college chum visiting an unhappily married couple and getting some spicy tell-all on tape; it's an "intelligent" look at the "permissive age" heated up by erotic "suspense" more than "actual" on-screen whoopee, though those who spurn "loser" characters find it "hard to care about."

Shadow of a Doubt ◑
26 | 26 | 26 | 25

1943 | Directed by Alfred Hitchcock | With Teresa Wright, Joseph Cotten, Macdonald Carey | 108 minutes | Not Rated

Hitchcock's "first truly American film" (and his "personal favorite"), this "dark" thriller is set in a "sunny", "Norman Rockwell"–esque town that's home to a "young girl and her mysterious yet appealing uncle" who's suspected of murder; the "is-he-or-isn't-he" plot works thanks to the "spot-on" Cotten, whose performance is "chilling" enough for you to consider "background checks on your own family."

Shadow of the Vampire
20 | 25 | 20 | 23

2000 | Directed by E. Elias Merhige | With John Malkovich, Willem Dafoe, Cary Elwes | 92 minutes | Rated R

Maybe it's "not scary", but this "unusual", "behind-the-scenes" drama does apply a few shadowy "touches of horror" as it chronicles the "legendary production" of the fiendish '20s masterwork Nosferatu; Dafoe does a "great job" vamping as an undead actor with an "evil" hankering for hemoglobin, but foes call it a "disappointing" "art-house mess" that's "not sharp" enough to draw blood.

Shaft
▽ 17 | 16 | 18 | 15

1971 | Directed by Gordon Parks | With Richard Roundtree, Moses Gunn, Charles Cioffi | 100 minutes | Rated R

With its pimped-out portrayal of "'70s Harlem" – "Afros" and all – plus Roundtree's star turn as a "bad mother" private eye, this unabashedly "cheesy" action thriller is hailed as a pioneering entry in the "blaxploitation" genre; no question, it looks "outdated", but no one cares once Isaac Hayes' Oscar-winning title tune starts to play – can you dig it?

⊠ Shakespeare in Love ⊠
24 | 25 | 24 | 26

1998 | Directed by John Madden | With Gwyneth Paltrow, Geoffrey Rush, Joseph Fiennes, Judi Dench | 122 minutes | Rated R

"Whether it be true or not", this "lush, literate" romance is a "good-humored confection" that "lights up the screen" with "adorable" performances from Fiennes (an "ink-stained" Elizabethan scribe) whose "writer's block" is cleared by the "exquisitely attired" Paltrow (his not-so-secret admirer); a "rich" depiction of the age "laced with dialogue" from the plays, it's a "rip-roaring" ride that's "accessible at any level."

Shall We Dance ◑
25 | 22 | 20 | 25

1937 | Directed by Mark Sandrich | With Fred Astaire, Ginger Rogers, Edward Everett Horton | 109 minutes | Not Rated

"Fred and Ginger" meet "George and Ira" (Gershwin) in this "champagne-bubbly" romance between a Russian ballet star and an American hoofer; maybe the "weak plot" is just another "variation on the same storyline" from the series, but "who cares?" given that "iconic" choreography and "great chemistry" between its "elegant" stars.

Shall We Dance?
17 | 17 | 17 | 18

2004 | Directed by Peter Chelsom | With Richard Gere, Jennifer Lopez, Susan Sarandon | 106 minutes | Rated PG-13

A married "everyman" caught in the grip of an "innocent midlife crisis" takes ballroom dancing lessons to "spruce up his daily grind" in this "light" romantic comedy; ok, it's "nothing deep" and the original "Japanese version is better", but Gere and J-Lo "burn up the screen" with their two-steps, bringing some needed "sizzle" to this "piece of fluff."

Shampoo
16 | 16 | 15 | 16

1975 | Directed by Hal Ashby | With Warren Beatty, Julie Christie, Goldie Hawn, Lee Grant, Carrie Fisher | 109 minutes | Rated R
Starring a "state-of-the-art Warren Beatty at his prettiest", this bedroom farce unfolds over election day, 1968, and follows the "hysterical" ups and downs of a randy hairdresser bouncing around Beverly Hills; both Christie and Hawn are a "blast", the premise is "very funny" and the "bittersweet" ending is a "touching" surprise.

Shane
26 | 25 | 25 | 25

1953 | Directed by George Stevens | With Alan Ladd, Jean Arthur, Van Heflin | 118 minutes | Not Rated
There's "always a nuance to savor" in this "towering", "classic" Western, telling the "mythical American" tale of a "world-weary gunslinger forced out of retirement" when he sides with a homesteader family menaced by "ruthless cattle ranchers"; the "poignant" setup pays off with a "great finale" as Ladd walks tall in a showdown with "no-good" varmint Jack Palance, leading many oater voters to name it "best" in the West.

Shark Tale
19 | - | 18 | 23

2004 | Directed by Bibo Bergeron, Vicky Jenson, Rob Letterman | Animated | 90 minutes | Rated PG
A "whale-size list of celeb voices" (Robert De Niro, Renée Zellweger, Angelina Jolie) adds buoyancy to this aquatic-themed animated feature that desperately "wants to be *Finding Nemo*" but just "isn't in the same league"; still, it "tries hard" with a positive, "be-yourself" message for the kiddies and "cute sight gags" for their parents (e.g. the "characters' resemblance to the actors voicing them").

Shattered Glass
21 | 23 | 24 | 19

2003 | Directed by Billy Ray | With Hayden Christensen, Peter Sarsgaard, Chloë Sevigny | 95 minutes | Rated PG-13
A "smart surprise" reminiscent of "*All the President's Men*", this true story about a "gifted journalist who self-destructs" after "making up articles for the *New Republic*" is an "engrossing", behind-the-scenes look at "how the media manipulates what the public sees"; though it "drags a tad", Christensen delivers a "surprisingly mature performance" – "why couldn't he do that in *Star Wars*?"

Shaun of the Dead
22 | 19 | 22 | 20

2004 | Directed by Edgar Wright | With Simon Pegg, Kate Ashfield, Nick Frost | 99 minutes | Rated R
Leave it to "those crazy Brits" to concoct this "groovy" "send-up of zombie movies" combining equal doses of "campy fun" and "all-out horror bloodbath" to give you "giggles with your chills"; geeks advise watching some "George Romero flicks" first to "get all the references", but if that's not doable, "a few pints of ale" should be sufficient to prime your "brainnnssss."

	OVERALL	ACTING	STORY	PROD.

☑ Shawshank Redemption, The   28 | 28 | 28 | 27

1994 | Directed by Frank Darabont | With Tim Robbins, Morgan Freeman, Bob Gunton | 142 minutes | Rated R

Finding the "stirring" in the stir and big hearts in the big house, this "first-rate" "gripper" of a prison drama goes behind the walls of a "dismal" state pen to follow fellow lifers Robbins and Freeman on a "long, dark journey" that pits "friendship", "ingenuity and inner strength" against a "corrupt system"; besides the "marvelous acting", there's a last-reel "surprise" to add a "feel-good factor" and even some "hope."

She Done Him Wrong ◐∅   ▽ 22 | 22 | 19 | 18

1933 | Directed by Lowell Sherman | With Mae West, Cary Grant | 66 minutes | Not Rated

From the early days "when Hollywood still told it like it was", this "racy, pre-code" comedy is based on *Diamond Lil,* West's stage play about shady cabaret owners in the Gay Nineties; it's best remembered for Mae's immortal line – 'why don't you come up some time and see me?' – delivered to Cary Grant, who "looks like he's about 10 years old" here.

Sheltering Sky, The   16 | 19 | 15 | 21

1990 | Directed by Bernardo Bertolucci | With Debra Winger, John Malkovich, Campbell Scott | 138 minutes | Rated R

"Morocco never looked so beautiful" as in this "gorgeously filmed" adaptation of Paul Bowles' existential novel about a couple's aimless roaming around North Africa in the hope of rekindling their romance; many report it's "rambling" and "pretentious", with too much "sand" and not enough plot, so "to avoid disappointment, see the movie first and then read the book."

She's Gotta Have It ◐   21 | 19 | 20 | 17

1986 | Directed by Spike Lee | With Tracy Camilla Johns, Tommy Redmond Hicks, John Canada Terrell, Spike Lee | 84 minutes | Rated R

Spike's first feature, this "interesting" relationships comedy set in Brooklyn "keeps it real" with a "fresh" take on the age-old battle between "Mars and Venus", in this case, a woman with three beaus; true, this "seminal" indie production "has the feel of a student film" (it was shot in two weeks for $160,000), yet fans say it's a "brilliant" moviemaker's "great debut."

She Wore a Yellow Ribbon   24 | 22 | 23 | 25

1949 | Directed by John Ford | With John Wayne, Joanne Dru, John Agar, Ben Johnson | 103 minutes | Not Rated

Ford's second bugle blast in his "cavalry trilogy" finds the director "at his best" in a tribute to the "honor and tradition" of horse soldiers posted to the ever-fleeting frontier; the Duke is typically "bigger than life" as a stiff-brimmed but sympathetic old man about to hang up his hat after a career in Injun territory, all portrayed against boundlessly "beautiful" big-sky scenery – "what else does a Western need?"

Shine ✉   22 | 25 | 21 | 21

1996 | Directed by Scott Hicks | With Geoffrey Rush, Armin Mueller-Stahl, Lynn Redgrave | 105 minutes | Rated PG-13

"Mad musician makes good" in this "enlightening", "uplifting true story" about a gifted Australian pianist who succeeds in the shadow of an inflexible father but succumbs to a "harrowing" bout with schizophrenia – only to return to the bench for a midlife comeback; Rush's "compelling" turn keeps things uptempo, and if some dub it an "overrated curiosity", more offer bravos for a portrait that "shines" from first movement to last.

Shining, The

25 | 26 | 25 | 25

1980 | Directed by Stanley Kubrick | With Jack Nicholson, Shelley Duvall, Scatman Crothers | 146 minutes | Rated R

The "supernatural and psychotic" collide in this "revolutionary horror film", a "downright scary" story from the Stephen King novel about a "snowbound caretaker of an old hotel" running amok; though voters agree that the "elevator scene", "Diane Arbus twin girls" and "gloriously unhinged Nicholson" all shine, Duvall gets mixed marks: "intensely annoying" vs. "profoundly brilliant"; best line, no contest: "heeere's Johnny!"

Ship of Fools ❶

23 | 25 | 24 | 23

1965 | Directed by Stanley Kramer | With Vivien Leigh, Simone Signoret, José Ferrer, Lee Marvin, Oskar Werner, Elizabeth Ashley, George Segal, Michael Dunn | 149 minutes | Not Rated

A "touching but loaded adaptation" of the Katherine Anne Porter novel, this "clever" drama follows a clutch of characters "aboard an ocean liner" traveling from Mexico to Germany "on the eve of WWII"; while sinkers shrug it off as "hammy", "soap operatic" stuff (think *Grand Hotel* at sea), far more feel the "all-star" international cast is worth watching, notably the "memorable" Signoret, "standout" Werner and "heartbreaking" Leigh, who's "too convincing as a faded beauty."

Shipping News, The

18 | 21 | 17 | 21

2001 | Directed by Lasse Hallström | With Kevin Spacey, Julianne Moore, Judi Dench | 111 minutes | Rated R

Based on the best-selling book, this drama tells the "strange story" of a "hopeless mope" doing drudge work at a small-town gazette who gets a "second chance" when his wife dies and he ships out to the Newfoundland coast; though it's praised as "ultimately optimistic", foes torpedo the "overblown", "contrived" production as a "lackluster" Miramax bid for the Oscar race.

Shirley Valentine

24 | 24 | 23 | 20

1989 | Directed by Lewis Gilbert | With Pauline Collins, Tom Conti, Alison Steadman | 108 minutes | Rated R

A real "charmer" with a "Liverpudlian accent", this "spirited" comedy sends a "terrific message" with its "sweet midlife fantasy" of a "bored English housewife" who flees to the Aegean "looking for love" and nets Greek sailor Conti; adapted from the "superb" stage show, it "loses nothing in the translation" as a "wise" celebration of "independence and self-respect."

☑ Shoah �ƒ

28 | - | 28 | 26

1985 | Directed by Claude Lanzmann | Documentary | 563 minutes | Not Rated

"Not a film to watch casually", this documentary addresses the "horror of the Holocaust" through "first-hand accounts" as a "necessary antidote" to "one of the worst episodes in human history"; Lanzmann uses witnesses from both sides of the "barbed-wire fence" to record their "intense", "shattering" memories of an entire society's "complicity", and "emotions pour out" over "eight hours of painful viewing" that are "impossibly sad and difficult" – but "worth all of it."

Shoot the Piano Player ❶🅵

25 | 24 | 23 | 22

1962 | Directed by François Truffaut | With Charles Aznavour, Marie Dubois, Nicole Berger | 84 minutes | Not Rated

Beside the "great title", Truffaut's "stylized" sophomore effort is a "slightly weird" combination of Gallic satire and American gangster picture that features a "not-so-romantic view of Paris"; its "unusual" story of a former concert pianist (the "sexy" Aznavour) mixed up with hooligans may be "for movie lovers only", but cineasts advise "see it with small expectations and you'll be rewarded."

Shop Around the Corner, The ❶

24 | 25 | 25 | 23

1940 | Directed by Ernst Lubitsch | With Margaret Sullavan, James Stewart, Frank Morgan | 99 minutes | Not Rated

Lubitsch plies his signature touch to a "classic" romantic comedy template – "two people who don't like each other" falling in love – and cooks up this "tasteful but funny" production starring Stewart and Sullavan as "colleagues who spar at work" while sharing a passionate but "anonymous" postal correspondence on the side; like many "good old-fashioned" flicks, this one's been "remade and remade" (try "*You've Got Mail*"), but as usual, the imitators "can't beat" the original.

Shopgirl

18 | 21 | 18 | 18

2005 | Directed by Anand Tucker | With Steve Martin, Claire Danes, Jason Schwartzman | 104 minutes | Rated R

A "refreshing change from Hollywood's usual date movies", this "thinking person's romance" based on the Steve Martin novella delineates a bittersweet love triangle involving a shy, "Cinderella-like salesgirl" and "two Prince Charmings": a "scruffy slacker" and a "suave, middle-aged" millionaire; Danes is a "revelation" and the story "subtly nuanced", but some find it "uninvolving" and "rather bleak", noting that it "takes less time to read the better book."

Short Cuts

22 | 24 | 21 | 20

1993 | Directed by Robert Altman | With Julianne Moore, Jack Lemmon, Lily Tomlin, Jennifer Jason Leigh, Andie MacDowell, Robert Downey Jr. | 187 minutes | Rated R

A "must-see for anyone who loves storytelling", this "intelligent" Robert Altman drama is a patchwork of "several Raymond Carver short stories" woven into a "delightful film that really draws you in"; ok, it's "lengthy" and the story "doesn't really go anywhere" – maybe "that's the point" – but it's "essential viewing for LA residents" and for everyone else, it's worth seeing for its "star-studded" ensemble cast.

Shot in the Dark, A

23 | 22 | 20 | 20

1964 | Directed by Blake Edwards | With Peter Sellers, Elke Sommer, George Sanders | 102 minutes | Rated PG

Sort of a cub *Pink Panther*, this "laugh-aloud funny" comedy features a "brilliant" Sellers as the clueless Inspector Clouseau, bumbling his way through a "delicious red-herring salad" of a plot that finds him assigned to solve a murder pinned on a Parisian chambermaid; if the "charmingly quirky" setup has its "slow" moments, the "master" makes it watchable "for his accent alone."

Show Boat
23 | 20 | 24 | 25

1951 | Directed by George Sidney | With Kathryn Grayson, Ava Gardner, Howard Keel | 107 minutes | Not Rated

The "schmaltzy" but "fabulous" hit from the Broadway boards gets the "brightest Technicolor" treatment in this "sterling MGM musical" about a showgirl's "sentimental" entanglement with a riverboat gambler; the big wheel paddles along to "unforgettable" songs, "solid production numbers" and hoofers who "dance up a storm", and if purists prefer 1936's "glory-days" version, most can't help lovin' dat "beautiful, melodic" spectacle.

Showgirls
5 | 4 | 4 | 10

1995 | Directed by Paul Verhoeven | With Elizabeth Berkley, Kyle MacLachlan, Gina Gershon | 131 minutes | Rated NC-17

Alright already, "nobody expected Shakespeare", but this "sorry" saga of a stripper hell-bent on becoming a Vegas showgirl is one truly "tacky", "pointless" enterprise, with "absolutely no redeeming value" and an NC-17 rating to boot; for "camp" followers, however, it's "unintentionally funny" (sort of a "nudie" version of *All About Eve*) and "so awful it's wonderful"; biggest howler: the "swimming pool sex scene."

◪ Shrek
26 | - | 25 | 28

2001 | Directed by Andrew Adamson, Vicky Jenson | Animated | 90 minutes | Rated PG

They "added a category" on Oscar night to honor this "playfully creative original" that uses "exceptional" CGI animation and "great voicing" to rework a "hoary storyline" about an ogre saving a princess into "highly entertaining" fare; it challenges the "Disney fairy-tale formula" with adult-level "parody" and "inside jokes" underscored with a "positive message" for all.

Shrek 2
26 | - | 24 | 28

2004 | Directed by Andrew Adamson, Kelly Asbury, Conrad Vernon | Animated | 92 minutes | Rated PG

"Another ogre-achiever", this "worthy sequel" once again features "incredible animation so lifelike you forget it's animation", "star voice actors" (Mike Myers, Eddie Murphy, Cameron Diaz) and a "laugh-out-loud" love story that sends up classic fairy-tale films; the "sly" satire and "clever" dialogue are "as much fun for adults as for the kids", and new addition Antonio Banderas – "purrfect as Puss 'n' Boots" – nearly "steals the movie."

Shrek the Third
20 | - | 18 | 25

2007 | Directed by Chris Miller, Raman Hui | Animated | 92 minutes | Rated PG

Staunch shrekkies report "satisfying" viewing via this "fun" three-peat by Hollywood's profitably "adorable" ogre, who returns with an "excellent cast and animation (as always)" in tow for more "hilarious" misadventures; but some are less than enchanted, claiming the "hokey storyline" and excessively "crude" humor prove that the "third time's not always the charm."

	OVERALL	ACTING	STORY	PROD.

Sid & Nancy

18 20 18 16

1986 | Directed by Alex Cox | With Gary Oldman, Chloe Webb, David Hayman | 112 minutes | Rated R

An "absolutely demented but totally compelling love story", this "gripping" slice of "rock history" details the rise and fall of the "Sex Pistols' wildest member", featuring a "convincing Oldman" as Sid Vicious and the "scarily real" Webb as his "crazy girlfriend"; though the story of their downward, drug-laden spiral is not for the faint-hearted, groupies dig it 'cause it's "dark, ugly and vibrant all at once."

Sideways

23 26 22 22

2004 | Directed by Alexander Payne | With Paul Giamatti, Thomas Haden Church, Virginia Madsen, Sandra Oh | 123 minutes | Rated R

Oenophiles toast this "intoxicatingly hilarious" road tripper pitting Giamatti's "shlub" against Church's "crack-up" for a Bacchian weekend of "middle-aged angst"–inspired "debauchery" in "scenic California wine country"; the "literate", Oscar-winning script uncorks some "wonderfully painful" scenes that are "so real" it's "like watching a train wreck", though a few whine it's just a "mundane soaper" with as much depth as a "glass of merlot."

Signs

18 20 18 20

2002 | Directed by M. Night Shyamalan | With Mel Gibson, Joaquin Phoenix, Rory Culkin | 106 minutes | Rated PG-13

Farmer Mel finds weird "crop circles" in his cornfields in this "paranormal" thriller from M. Night Shyamalan that delivers a "good number of jump-out-of-your-seat moments"; some say it's a really a "religious movie disguised as science fiction" ("I've coughed up scarier things"), yet there's a "creepy realness" about it that keeps the mood "tense."

☑ Silence of the Lambs, The ✉

27 28 27 26

1991 | Directed by Jonathan Demme | With Jodie Foster, Anthony Hopkins, Scott Glenn | 118 minutes | Rated R

Every subsequent "psych-profiling" flick owes alot to this "profoundly creepy" thriller that combines "heart-thumping suspense" with "premier" performances as Foster, an FBI greenhorn on a serial-killer hunt, is drawn into "intense mind games" with the "soft-spoken" madman Hopkins; its "well-deserved Oscars" speak for its "twisted", "truly terrifying" achievement, though some say it "gives fava beans a bad name."

Silent Movie

20 20 19 20

1976 | Directed by Mel Brooks | With Mel Brooks, Marty Feldman, Dom DeLuise, Sid Caesar | 87 minutes | Rated PG

"Kudos" to Brooks for ditching dialogue and scoring "audience roars" with "clever" sight gags in this "entertaining" send-up of silent films; expect a parade of "star" cameos (Burt Reynolds, Liza Minnelli, Paul Newman), though the "best moment" belongs to mime Marcel Marceau, who utters the picture's "only spoken word."

Silkwood

22 26 25 21

1983 | Directed by Mike Nichols | With Meryl Streep, Kurt Russell, Cher, Craig T. Nelson | 131 minutes | Rated R

This "somewhat forgotten" drama generates a "great deal of tension" telling the fact-based story of a whistle-blowing nuclear plant worker who comes to a "mysterious end" when she tries to go public with hazardous goings-on at the facility; lit up by "terrific acting" from "marvelous" Meryl and "eye-opener" Cher, it's a "moving" picture of blue-collar good guys vs. white-collar baddies.

Silverado
24 | 24 | 23 | 24

1985 | Directed by Lawrence Kasdan | With Kevin Kline, Scott Glenn, Kevin Costner | 127 minutes | Rated PG-13

Boys, the "fun Western" rides again in this "well-made" "modern horse opera", a "true homage" that "throws in all the clichés" and delivers some "slick sequences" and "great one-liners" of its own; a "tremendous" cast "manages to upstage the glorious scenery", though it's best appreciated on the "biggest screen you can find."

Silver Streak
19 | 19 | 18 | 19

1976 | Directed by Arthur Hiller | With Gene Wilder, Richard Pryor, Jill Clayburgh | 114 minutes | Rated PG

"One of the best comedy teams on film" gets its "first pairing" in this "slick takeoff" on Hitchcock-style "train capers", featuring Wilder in the "amusing" role of an innocent railroaded in an art-world murder only to find himself on the run along with the "beyond-funny" Pryor; devotees call it "enjoyable" and "underappreciated."

Simple Plan, A
19 | 22 | 22 | 19

1998 | Directed by Sam Raimi | With Bill Paxton, Bridget Fonda, Billy Bob Thornton | 121 minutes | Rated R

B-movie maestro Raimi's "entry into respectable filmdom" is a "well-paced thriller" with a "convincing" scenario about a rustic threesome in the backwoods who stumble upon a wrecked plane and a bag of cash; "plot-twisting" and "suspense" ensue as lives "unravel" in a "tragic" parable of the "evils of ill-gotten gain" that makes it the *Treasure of the Sierra Madre* for the *Fargo* crowd.

Sin City
22 | 21 | 20 | 26

2005 | Directed by Frank Miller, Robert Rodriguez, Quentin Tarantino | With Bruce Willis, Mickey Rourke, Jessica Alba | 124 minutes | Rated R

This "sin-tillating" noir take on a pulp comic book series is "gritty" and "ultra-violent", with a "meandering" three-part storyline played out in a mix of black-and-white live action and colorful "comic animation"; Willis is "compelling", a "'roided-up Rourke" makes his "comeback" and a "scantily clad" Alba does tricks with a "lasso."

☑ Singin' in the Rain
28 | 26 | 25 | 28

1952 | Directed by Stanley Donen, Gene Kelly | With Gene Kelly, Donald O'Connor, Debbie Reynolds | 103 minutes | Rated G

"Giddy", "wet and wonderful", this "timeless" musical brightens the worst day with an "exuberant" "something-for-everyone" blend of "quintessential" song and dance, "satire" and a "sappy, funny love story"; the "flawless" Kelly plays a silent movie star in a "sweet send-up" of Hollywood's early talkie days and effortlessly executes the puddle-hopping "title number", leaving fans "awed."

Single White Female
16 | 18 | 17 | 15

1992 | Directed by Barbet Schroeder | With Bridget Fonda, Jennifer Jason Leigh, Steven Weber | 107 minutes | Rated R

"Watch your back!": this "roommate-from-hell thriller" "keeps you on edge" with its "sick vulgarity" and mounting "suspense"; though the

	OVERALL	ACTING	STORY	PROD.

trading-identities storyline might be "derivative", the picture's still "full of surprises" and "done well" enough to "make you think it could actually happen"; P.S. brace yourself for a particularly "nasty ending."

Sister Act
18 | 18 | 17 | 17

1992 | Directed by Emile Ardolino | With Whoopi Goldberg, Maggie Smith, Kathy Najimy | 100 minutes | Rated PG

Whoopi gets a witness protection program in this "engaging" "fish-out-of-water comedy" about a lounge diva who sings for the cops after her beau commits homicide, only to find herself stashed in "nun other than" a convent; the verdict: a "guilty pleasure" that rises above the "run of the mill" with "cool" musical interludes.

Sisterhood of the Traveling Pants, The
19 | 19 | 20 | 19

2005 | Directed by Ken Kwapis | With Amber Tamblyn, Alexis Bledel, America Ferrera, Blake Lively | 119 minutes | Rated PG

The "angst"-ridden "summer adventures" of four "very different" teen girls are sewn together by a "pair of magical pants" in this "charming" coming-of-ager featuring an "adorable" cast of young actresses; sure, it's a "tear-jerking" "chick flick if there ever was one", but its one-size-fits-all spirit means "even males" may be reaching for a "hanky."

Sisters
▽ 22 | 21 | 23 | 20

1973 | Directed by Brian De Palma | With Margot Kidder, Jennifer Salt, Charles Durning | 92 minutes | Rated R

"De Palma does Hitchcock" ("again") in this "tense", "really scary" thriller about a pair of "warped" Siamese twins, recently separated; filmed on Staten Island for what looks like a "$2.50 budget", it's most "memorable" for Bernard Herrmann's "excellent score" and some "great acting" from a "pre-Lois Lane" Kidder.

Six Degrees of Separation
21 | 24 | 23 | 20

1993 | Directed by Fred Schepisi | With Will Smith, Stockard Channing, Donald Sutherland | 112 minutes | Rated R

"Great performances" ensure this "intriguing" "stage-to-screen" drama "adjusts quite nicely" to celluloid as a "sublime" Channing offers an encore of her theatrical role opposite a "young" Smith in the "challenging" part of a "charming hustler" posing as Sidney Poitier's son; it draws applause as a "clever" critique of "moneyed values" that's "surprisingly strong."

16 Blocks
17 | 19 | 18 | 19

2006 | Directed by Richard Donner | With Bruce Willis, Mos Def, David Morse | 102 minutes | Rated PG-13

A pair of "strong performances" primes this "slick" action flick, starring an "older" Willis as a "boozy", "wrung-out" detective who kindles a "spark of decency" while escorting state's witness Mos Def (a "rapper who can act") through a "cop vs. cop" gauntlet; it's "well-filmed" and "suspenseful" (if "nothing profound"), though stretches of "implausible", "formula-driven" plotting can mean "16 blocks never felt so long."

Sixteen Candles
22 | 18 | 21 | 19

1984 | Directed by John Hughes | With Molly Ringwald, Justin Henry, Anthony Michael Hall | 93 minutes | Rated PG

"Ringwald will steal your heart" in this "sweet coming-of-age classic", a "day-in-the-life" comedy that conveys the "teen angst" of high school, "first love and puberty" as seen through the eyes of a 16-year-old "birthday girl whom everyone forgot"; though its "damn funny" "Brat Pack" cast "characterizes the '80s to a tee", modernists who love this "brilliant" send-up "can still relate to it."

⚡ Sixth Sense, The | 26 | 25 | 27 | 25 |
1999 | Directed by M. Night Shyamalan | With Bruce Willis, Haley Joel Osment, Toni Collette | 107 minutes | Rated PG-13
A "tricky" one, this mega-hit thriller "surprises even the most astute" with its "perfectly crafted story" of a troubled boy with an "unwelcome gift" who finds a friend in Willis, leading to "really spooky" plot developments; it's hailed as an "unpredictable" sensation that rewards with "white-knuckle jolts" and a "stunning" "O. Henry"-esque ending.

Slap Shot | 22 | 18 | 19 | 17 |
1977 | Directed by George Roy Hill | With Paul Newman, Michael Ontkean, Strother Martin | 122 minutes | Rated R
Right up there with the "funniest sports flicks", this puckish comedy finds "Newman on skates" as the "foul-mouthed coach" of a "dark horse" minor-league hockey team with a "strange way" of turning every face-off into a riot on ice; it "epitomizes the goonery" of the high-sticking '70s, resulting in "crazy", "profane" and "fairly violent" fare that hard-core fans "cannot live without."

Slaughterhouse-Five | 22 | 20 | 25 | 20 |
1972 | Directed by George Roy Hill | With Michael Sacks, Valerie Perrine, Ron Leibman | 104 minutes | Rated R
Countering the conventional wisdom that Kurt Vonnegut's "classic" novel is "impossible to translate to film", this "well-done adaptation" preserves the "powerful" punch of the book and is "worth watching for the curiosity factor alone"; recounting the "strange" adventures of one Billy Pilgrim, an everyman who becomes 'unstuck in time', it's a "wildly original" blend of "funny" fantasy and "heart-tugging reality."

Sleeper | 23 | 19 | 23 | 20 |
1973 | Directed by Woody Allen | With Woody Allen, Diane Keaton, John Beck | 89 minutes | Rated PG
Orwell's wake-up call has nothing on this "inspired sci-fi spoof", a "hilarious" comedy of a nebbishy NYer who's cryogenically preserved then "defrosted in the future"; "laced with fast-paced verbal" cracks, it's "vintage" Allen at his "goofiest" and "most slapsticky" in a romp that generates "nonstop laughs" – the "orgasmatron alone is worth the price of admission."

Sleepers | 22 | 25 | 23 | 22 |
1996 | Directed by Barry Levinson | With Kevin Bacon, Jason Patric, Robert De Niro, Brad Pitt | 147 minutes | Rated R
Years after a "terrible mistake" landed them in a "tough juvenile detention center" (where "abuse" was a staff specialty), four best friends exact "revenge" on their former tormentors in this "very dark" Levinson drama; though there's debate at to whether it's actually "based on actual events", most find the story "moving" enough and credit the "stellar" ensemble for conferring a "psychological" authenticity to the proceedings.

Sleeping Beauty
25 | - | 23 | 25

1959 | Directed by Clyde Geronimi | Animated | 75 minutes | Rated G

No snooze among the "old Disney greats", this "lushly animated" "princess movie" has a trio of good fairies protecting the titular knock-out from an evil spell by zapping her into a sound nap, interrupted only after her true love battles it out with filmdom's most fearsome dragon lady; the very wicked witch may be "too scary for the little ones", but most say this "classic" only "gets better with age."

Sleeping with the Enemy
17 | 18 | 18 | 17

1991 | Directed by Joseph Ruben | With Julia Roberts, Patrick Bergin, Kevin Anderson | 99 minutes | Rated R

"Harrowing scenes of spousal abuse" supply the "scary edge" in this "Julia Roberts vehicle" about a "murderous husband and the wife determined to get away from him"; though it strikes a few as "over-wrought and cartoonish", this thriller makes others "think long and hard" about a problem that could be "more common than we think."

Sleepless in Seattle
21 | 22 | 22 | 21

1993 | Directed by Nora Ephron | With Tom Hanks, Meg Ryan, Rosie O'Donnell | 105 minutes | Rated PG

Although pretty "predictable", this Ephron romance "works", renewing faith in the "soul-mate concept" as the "perfectly cast", "totally lovable" Hanks and Ryan make "a great match" in the story of a woman who pursues a lonely-hearts stranger cross country; sure, this "toothache-sweet trifle" is "a bit far-fetched" ("at least Harry *met* Sally"), but it's also a "funny", "male-tolerable chick flick" that's likely to spring eternal for "hopeless romantics."

Sleepy Hollow
17 | 18 | 17 | 23

1999 | Directed by Tim Burton | With Johnny Depp, Christina Ricci, Miranda Richardson | 105 minutes | Rated R

All your "decapitation entertainment needs will be fulfilled" in this "engrossing" rendition of Washington Irving's "headless horseman fable", a "funny but gory" ride from Tim Burton that's a "wonderful update of the Hammer horror films"; Depp is "daringly unconventional", and the "eye-popping" cinematography is "visually splendid" – so it's alright to nod off during that "big Hollywood action finale."

Sleuth
25 | 28 | 26 | 23

1972 | Directed by Joseph L. Mankiewicz | With Laurence Olivier, Michael Caine | 138 minutes | Rated PG

It's no mystery why this suspense thriller based on the Broadway smash adapts "wonderfully to film": "masters-at-work" Olivier and Caine offer "witty", "subtle" work as a cuckolded writer and his rival engaged in a calculated confrontation in an English country manor; the "creative" story builds "numerous plot twists" that cross and double-cross, and "two of the greatest" muster up some of the liveliest back-and-forth volleys ever seen "outside of Wimbledon."

Sliding Doors
21 | 21 | 24 | 20

1998 | Directed by Peter Howitt | With Gwyneth Paltrow, John Hannah, John Lynch | 99 minutes | Rated R

If you've ever "wondered what your life would be like if one detail had been slightly altered", this "quirky" but "poignant" romance offers a "clever" side-by-side examination of a woman's "parallel worlds" that not only offers "lots to think about" but will also "keep you hooked"; a "fab", "pre-Coldplay" Gwyneth shines in "dual" lead roles, while the "completely lovable" Hannah adds some "charm" to the mix.

Sling Blade ✉ 25 | 27 | 25 | 22

1996 | Directed by Billy Bob Thornton | With Billy Bob Thornton, Dwight Yoakam, J.T. Walsh | 135 minutes | Rated R

"Too convincing" in the role that lands him "on the map", "creepy Billy Bob" is "brilliantly believable" in this "tragedy from the real world" playing a slow-witted country boy who's sprung from the state booby hatch and taken in by a single mom; a "unique, touching" drama of man trouble, it "earns every accolade" with "excellent acting" and an "unforgettable punch" at the climax.

Smiles of a Summer Night ◑🄵 26 | 26 | 25 | 26

1957 | Directed by Ingmar Bergman | With Ulla Jacobsson, Eva Dahlbeck, Gunnar Björnstrand | 108 minutes | Not Rated

For "Bergman without the angst", check out his "rare venture" into romantic comedy, this "sumptuous" tale of love, desire and "what it means to be human" set in fin de siècle Sweden; probably the director's "lightest, most approachable" film, it was "most influential" to a generation of artists, and best known today as the inspiration for Sondheim's *A Little Night Music*.

Smokey and the Bandit 16 | 13 | 15 | 15

1977 | Directed by Hal Needham | With Burt Reynolds, Sally Field, Jackie Gleason | 96 minutes | Rated PG

This "good ol' boys car chase" comedy is a rootin' tootin' good "road movie" about a cross-country "race against time"; sure, it's "corny", "cheaply made" stuff based on what appears to be a completely improvised script, but in the end, it's plain that "everyone's having fun", particularly the "dynamite duo" of Reynolds and Field.

Snake Pit, The ◑ 25 | 28 | 25 | 24

1948 | Directed by Anatole Litvak | With Olivia de Havilland, Mark Stevens, Leo Genn, Celeste Holm | 108 minutes | Not Rated

"Daring for its time", this "hair-raising" depiction of conditions inside a mental institution was made during the postwar "heyday of psychoanalytic films" and is "still frightening" today; in addition to de Havilland's "sensitive", Oscar-nominated performance, many say it's most "memorable" for that "bird's-eye view" of the asylum's psycho ward.

Snatch 21 | 23 | 22 | 22

2000 | Directed by Guy Ritchie | With Benicio Del Toro, Dennis Farina, Brad Pitt | 104 minutes | Rated R

Fittingly "splashy" fare from Mr. Madonna, director Ritchie's sophomore effort is a "relentless crime comedy" with a substantial cast of "wild" London gangsters who follow "interacting storylines" in a "quick-witted" "mix-'em-up heist" caper centered around a stolen diamond; the results are "bloody hilarious", and though you might need "subtitles" to decipher Pitt's "crazy-man accent", at least it's "never boring."

| | OVERALL | ACTING | STORY | PROD. |

☑ Snow White & the Seven Dwarfs `27` `-` `26` `27`

1937 | Directed by David Hand | Animated | 83 minutes | Rated G

The "one that started it all", this "true classic" is the *Citizen Kane* of animation", the "first full-length feature" from the Disney drawing boards and "still the finest" of them all; this tale of a fair maiden hiding in the forest with a band of "cute little guys" to escape a "terrifying wicked queen" is a "masterpiece" of "charm, simplicity and beauty" that continues to "entertain generations" and leave 'em humming "hi ho, hi ho!"

Soldier's Story, A `26` `26` `25` `22`

1984 | Directed by Norman Jewison | With Howard E. Rollins Jr., Adolph Caesar, Denzel Washington | 101 minutes | Rated PG

Partially a "mystery" chronicling an "investigation into the murder of an African-American soldier on an army base" in the segregated South, this "powerful" drama also functions as an "important morality play" dealing with the "class issues facing black men" under white rule; enhanced by the "riveting performances" of Rollins, Caesar and a "then-young" Denzel, it's a "gripping" exercise building up to a "great twist at the end."

☑ Some Like It Hot ◑ `28` `27` `26` `26`

1959 | Directed by Billy Wilder | With Marilyn Monroe, Tony Curtis, Jack Lemmon, Joe E. Brown | 120 minutes | Rated PG

"Cross-dressing was never so hilarious" as in this "legendary" "laff riot" about "two patsies on the run from the mob" who don dresses and join an all-girl band as part of their escape plan; thanks to Wilder's "sure touch" and the "sidesplitting" script's "countless priceless scenes" ("Lemmon with the maracas", "Curtis' riff on Cary Grant", Monroe "running wild"), this is one hot contender for the "greatest comedy ever made" – with the "best closing line" in moviedom: "nobody's perfect."

Something's Gotta Give `23` `26` `22` `23`

2003 | Directed by Nancy Meyers | With Jack Nicholson, Diane Keaton, Keanu Reeves | 128 minutes | Rated PG-13

"People over 50 having sex" is the novel premise of this "middle-aged" romantic comedy positing that "growing old can be fun"; cynics nix the "lousy title" and "predictable", "sitcom-lite" plot, but the "*Architectural Digest*-worthy" settings and mighty "excellent chemistry" between Jack and Diane make it go down easy for "mature audiences"; just ignore the "lame", "too-bad-she-wound-up-with-the-wrong-guy" ending.

Something Wild `20` `20` `20` `19`

1986 | Directed by Jonathan Demme | With Jeff Daniels, Melanie Griffith, Ray Liotta | 113 minutes | Rated R

"You're never quite sure what's going on" when a "funky gal" meets a "conservative guy" in this "wild road movie", a "fast-paced", "fasten-your-seatbelt" ride that "starts funny", "ends tragically" and "constantly surprises at every turn"; the "pre-plastic surgery" Griffith "sizzles" as the "new wave femme fatale", Daniels "shines" as the good-natured chump and Liotta is just plain "scary as hell"; ultimately, the "title says it all" about this one.

Song of Bernadette, The ✉◑ | 22 | 24 | 22 | 21 |

1943 | Directed by Henry King | With Jennifer Jones, Charles Bickford, Gladys Cooper, Anne Revere | 156 minutes | Not Rated

This "uplifting", "inspirational" tale of a French peasant girl who claims to have seen a vision of the Virgin Mary features a "sympathetic", Oscar-winning performance by Jones that will make you "believe her, even if no one else in the film does"; overall, the picture's a relic of "less cynical" times and may be too "syrupy" for modern audiences, but "it can still touch your heart, if you let it."

Song of the South ∅ | 23 | - | 22 | 26 |

1946 | Directed by Wilfred Jackson, Harve Foster | Animated | With Ruth Warrick, James Baskett | 94 minutes | Rated G

Yup, it's "corny and dated", but "Disney's version of the Uncle Remus stories" is also "one of the earliest" to offer an "animation–live action mix" as a young boy encounters Brers Rabbit, Fox and Bear; its "controversial" stereotyping of plantation life means it's currently MIA on DVD, but fans say it will always be "tough to top 'Zip-A-Dee-Doo-Dah.'"

Sophie's Choice ✉ | 26 | 28 | 26 | 24 |

1982 | Directed by Alan J. Pakula | With Meryl Streep, Kevin Kline, Peter MacNicol | 150 minutes | Rated R

A "luminous" Streep with a "faint Polish accent" "shows her stuff" in this "haunting", highly "emotional" drama, which draws its "powerful story" from William Styron's novel about an Auschwitz survivor; though "wrenching" at points, it's a "compelling tour de force" that many see as Oscar-winner Meryl's "finest" hour.

☑ Sorrow and the Pity, The ◑🅵 | 29 | - | 28 | 25 |

1972 | Directed by Marcel Ophüls | Documentary | 251 minutes | Rated PG

The "truth about the Nazi occupation of France" is revealed in this "devastating" but "essential" documentary that shows how "even civilized countries can fall victim to fascism"; bien sûr, it's "a bit long" (clocking in at just over four hours) and its "chilling depiction of neighbor against neighbor" is "not easy to take", but it's "required viewing for historical revisionists everywhere" thanks to its "relentlessly tenacious" director.

Sorry, Wrong Number ◑ | 25 | 25 | 25 | 23 |

1948 | Directed by Anatole Litvak | With Barbara Stanwyck, Burt Lancaster | 89 minutes | Not Rated

This "real thriller" adapted from a famed radio play stars Stanwyck as an "invalid heiress" who overhears a murder plot over crossed telephone wires; it's "pretty much a one-woman show" that relies on flashbacks to keep in motion, and if some say the "static" story is "stretched too thin", more report "enough twists" to keep your "spine tingling."

Sounder | 26 | 27 | 26 | 25 |

1972 | Directed by Martin Ritt | With Cicely Tyson, Paul Winfield, Kevin Hooks | 105 minutes | Rated G

The "sadness and dignity" of life as a black sharecropper in the Depression-era South "still resonate" with those who grew up watching this "classic with a heart", a "beautifully crafted" story of "strength" over suffering highlighted by a boy's "poignant" odyssey to locate his imprisoned father; featuring the "wonderful", Oscar-nominated Winfield and Tyson – not to mention that "heartbreaking" dog – "it might be one of the best family films ever."

⚆ Sound of Music, The ✉   28 | 25 | 27 | 28

1965 | Directed by Robert Wise | With Julie Andrews, Christopher Plummer, Eleanor Parker | 174 minutes | Rated G

Everyone has an Alp-size "soft spot" for this "schmaltzy" Rodgers and Hammerstein musical, wherein a "charming" governess marries into a "do-re-mi" singing family and "stands on principle" after the Huns invade; the only Best Picture winner to feature "nuns, Nazis" and "kids in lederhosen", it's "shamelessly saccharine" but loved for its "uplifting" story, "fantastic" songs and "lush" scenery.

South Pacific   24 | 22 | 24 | 25

1958 | Directed by Joshua Logan | With Mitzi Gaynor, Rossano Brazzi, John Kerr | 151 minutes | Not Rated

"Incomparable music" washes up in a "tropical paradise" in this Rodgers and Hammerstein songfest, which finds American sea dogs and dames living and loving and singing along to "beautiful orchestrations" on a WWII Pacific atoll; though a huge hit in its day owing to those "eternal" tunes, some say it "doesn't hold up" anymore, pointing to the "filtered camera gels" that yield "gaudy Technicolor" tints.

South Park   20 | - | 19 | 16

1999 | Directed by Trey Parker | Animated | 81 minutes | Rated R

Don't "blame Canada" for this "tasteless" full-length treatment of the "rude, crude" TV series, a "very un-PC" "equal-opportunity offender" with a "raunchy" mix of "lowbrow" laffs and "catchy" musical interludes; "rated R for a reason", it's "unbelievably funny" but "not for the kiddies" or "faint-of-heart" adults.

Spaceballs   18 | 15 | 17 | 17

1987 | Directed by Mel Brooks | With Mel Brooks, John Candy, Rick Moranis | 96 minutes | Rated PG

"Brooks strikes again" in this "goofy takeoff on *Star Wars*" that skewers sci-fi as a couple of space cowboys rocket to the rescue of a princess, setting up "cornball" gags that are the "hysterical" stuff of Mel's genre parodies; though hard-core fans find it "gets funnier every time", those unamused by the "tired", "obvious" humor contend it's "hard to believe" this is the work of a "genius."

Space Jam   16 | - | 14 | 19

1996 | Directed by Joe Pytka | Animated | With Michael Jordan, Wayne Knight, Charles Barkley | 87 minutes | Rated PG

The "Looney Tunes get their own movie" in this "fun fantasy" in which Bugs and crew play b-ball with über-hoopster Jordan and other stars to free themselves from alien kidnappers; despite "so-so" acting and storytelling, the "surprisingly good" matching of animation and live action makes this one "fun for the whole family."

Spanglish   19 | 20 | 18 | 18

2004 | Directed by James L. Brooks | With Adam Sandler, Téa Leoni, Paz Vega, Cloris Leachman | 131 minutes | Rated PG-13

Cultures clash in this "more-serious"-than-you'd-expect film from James L. Brooks about a privileged, "dysfunctional" family turned upside down when a "beautiful" Latina becomes their housekeeper; though there's applause for Sandler's "serious acting chops", critics say Téa's "too over the top" as the "control-freak wife" and "aren't sure about the ending", nor the "after-school-special" script.

Spartacus

| 26 | 24 | 25 | 26 |

1960 | Directed by Stanley Kubrick | With Kirk Douglas, Laurence Olivier, Jean Simmons | 184 minutes | Rated PG-13

"Elevated" by its "sweeping vision" and "superb all-star cast", Kubrick's "impressive" epic headlines Douglas as the "virile" leader of a "slave revolt against Rome"; pairing a "psychologically complex" story with plenty of "gory but good" action, it's an "exciting" box-office big-timer that's "matched by few" in the "classic" spectacle sweeps.

Speed

| 18 | 14 | 19 | 20 |

1994 | Directed by Jan de Bont | With Keanu Reeves, Dennis Hopper, Sandra Bullock | 116 minutes | Rated R

"Die Hard on a bus" is the "inanely simple" premise behind this "fast-moving" "high-concept actioner", with "sweetheart" Bullock and "studly SWAT boy" Reeves making a "cute and feisty" twosome as they find themselves "trapped" on a "tense", "nonstop" "thrill ride" aboard a "runaway bus" wired to "go boom"; though it's dismissed as "lightweight bubblegum" with "wooden" line readings from "Mr. Whoa", at least there's "no letup."

Spellbound ◑

| 24 | 25 | 23 | 24 |

1945 | Directed by Alfred Hitchcock | With Gregory Peck, Ingrid Bergman, Leo G. Carroll | 111 minutes | Not Rated

One of the first mainstream movies to tackle psychiatry, this "outstanding" Hitchcock thriller deals with unlocking a "repressed memory", and the "perfect Bergman" and "gorgeous Peck" are a "good match" as doctor and patient; but despite touches like the "ahead-of-its-time dream sequences" designed by Salvador Dali, some analysts dismiss it as "dated Freudian nonsense."

☒ Spellbound

| 28 | - | 27 | 26 |

2003 | Directed by Jeffrey Blitz | Documentary | 97 minutes | Rated G

A "fascinating commentary on American education", this "charming" documentary profiles eight grammar-school contestants bound for the National Spelling Bee in Washington, DC; most surveyors are "a-m-a-z-e-d" that such subject matter can be so much "fun to watch", but the word is this "letter perfect" picture is alternately "poignant", "uplifting" and "completely riveting."

Spider-Man

| 21 | 19 | 20 | 25 |

2002 | Directed by Sam Raimi | With Tobey Maguire, Kirsten Dunst, Willem Dafoe, James Franco | 121 minutes | Rated PG-13

Comic-book mavens marvel at how well this "adaptation captures the spirit of the original" – a literally "loopy tale" of "spider bites boy" (Maguire), who sprouts superpowers and "spins around town on threads", battling "campy, cackling nemesis" Dafoe and kissing "hot" honey Dunst upside down; heroes hail the "CGI effects seamlessly woven" into the "action-packed visuals" but hiss the "wooden acting and predictable plot"; overall, it's caught most folks "in its web."

| | OVERALL | ACTING | STORY | PROD. |

Spider-Man 2
22 | 20 | 21 | 26

2004 | Directed by Sam Raimi | With Tobey Maguire, Kirsten Dunst, Alfred Molina, James Franco | 127 minutes | Rated PG-13

"Spidey tries to hang up his tights" and "live his own life" only to be bugged by "super villain" Doc Ock in this comic-book movie follow-up that's "as good as the original"; expect the usual "jaw-dropping" FX plus a "deeper" exploration of the webslinger's struggles with "guilt, sacrifice" and "love", and get ready for "further sequels" 'cause this franchise has legs.

Spider-Man 3
19 | 17 | 16 | 25

2007 | Directed by Sam Raimi | With Tobey Maguire, Kirsten Dunst, James Franco, Thomas Haden Church | 140 minutes | Rated PG-13

World-saving wallcrawler Spider-Man dabbles with the "dark side" while facing down "three villains for the price of one" in this "shiny" but ultimately "thin" threequel "crammed" with "fancy effects" (i.e. Sandman), "tangled plots" and a "kinda corny" dance interlude featuring an "emo" Peter Parker; at a "lonnng" two-plus hours, not even the "Bruce Campbell cameo" eases fans' "disappointment."

Spirit: Stallion of the Cimarron
21 | - | 21 | 23

2002 | Directed by Kelly Asbury, Lorna Cook | Animated | 83 minutes | Rated G

A "gorgeous" combination of hand-drawn and computer animation "elevates" this "charming tearjerker" about a "spirited wild stallion and man's hapless efforts to tame him"; it's "great for kids and adults who grew up watching old Westerns", with "endearing characters" and a "sad" but "beautiful storyline."

Spirited Away 🅵
27 | - | 25 | 28

2002 | Directed by Hayao Miyazaki | Animated | 125 minutes | Rated PG

"Master storyteller" Miyazaki's "inventive", "visually stunning" Japanese version of *The Wizard of Oz*" meets *Alice in Wonderland*" "transcends the animation genre", bringing viewers to an "enchanted" "spirit world" filled with "bizarre characters", "unexpected sights" and "fantastic artwork"; it's "a tad long" and "has some pretty scary moments in it", so it may be best for "those 10 and up" – "unless you want to spend money on therapy" for the kids later.

Splash
19 | 18 | 19 | 20

1984 | Directed by Ron Howard | With Tom Hanks, Daryl Hannah, John Candy | 111 minutes | Rated PG

More "sweet" than salty yet "not too mushy", this "fish-out-of-water love story" is an "engaging" comedy shored up by Hannah's starmaking splash as a "sexy mermaid" whom Hanks courts and transports to NYC; the fantasy is buoyed by a cast of "charming" characters "you can't help but like", including some "sterling support" from a "scene-stealing" Candy – so dive in and "enjoy."

Splendor in the Grass ✉
25 | 25 | 24 | 22

1961 | Directed by Elia Kazan | With Natalie Wood, Warren Beatty, Zohra Lampert | 124 minutes | Not Rated

There's "heartbreak" in the heartland as "yearning" breeds "teen angst" in this "bittersweet" romance set in pre-Depression Kansas; the very "young" and very "gorgeous" Wood and Beatty supply some "real acting" as a "modern Romeo and Juliet" driven to "wrenching" extremes in this drama of "stolen dreams" and "lost love" that makes some sob sisters "cry just thinking about it."

SpongeBob SquarePants Movie, The
OVERALL	ACTING	STORY	PROD.
16	-	15	18

2004 | Directed by Stephen Hillenburg | Animated | 90 minutes | Rated PG
Cable TV's favorite "little yellow sea creature" soaks up the silver-screen spotlight in this "cheerfully cheesy" cartoon, wherein the hero and a "starfish pal" set out on a "humorous" underwater "road trip"; though guaranteed to make the kiddies "happy as a clam", it fares less swimmingly with adults, despite a "cute cameo" by David Hasselhoff.

Spy Game
19	21	19	19

2001 | Directed by Tony Scott | With Robert Redford, Brad Pitt | 126 minutes | Rated R
With a "creative" but "complicated" plot that flashes "backward, forward and sideways" in its pursuit of "clever cat-and-mouse" action, this "solid" espionage thriller maintains a "hypnotic" grip on you "until the last fulfilling bit"; Redford and Pitt "shine" as a CIA mentor-protégé team – "plus they're easy on the eyes, which never hurts."

Spy Kids
19	17	19	21

2001 | Directed by Robert Rodriguez | With Antonio Banderas, Carla Gugino, Alexa Vega, Daryl Sabara | 88 minutes | Rated PG
Look for "good clean spy fun" in this "appealing" family adventure that's "empowering for kids" in its story of a bungling parental pair of agents "called back into duty", leaving it up to their "cute" tykes to "save the world"; there are plenty of "cool gadgets", so grown-ups might not want to "check their brain" after all.

Spy Kids 2: Island of Lost Dreams
16	15	16	20

2002 | Directed by Robert Rodriguez | With Antonio Banderas, Carla Gugino, Alexa Vega, Daryl Sabara | 100 minutes | Rated PG
An eye-popping parade of "dazzling effects" and "great gizmos" heralds the return of the pint-size secret agent sibs as they "again try to save the world" in this "longer, louder" sci-fi sequel; if the consensus is it's "not nearly as good as the first", it's still a "decent way to keep the kids quiet."

Spy Who Came in from the Cold, The ❶
25	26	25	22

1965 | Directed by Martin Ritt | With Richard Burton, Claire Bloom, Oskar Werner | 112 minutes | Not Rated
"Spying isn't pretty" in this "very cold look at the Cold War" adapted from John Le Carré's "first major success"; Burton's "at his peak" as a "brooding" British secret agent who defects to East Germany, and his "brilliant" work is backed up by "taut direction" and a "stark", "realistic" screenplay – "James Bond, this is not."

Spy Who Loved Me, The
21	17	20	22

1977 | Directed by Lewis Gilbert | With Roger Moore, Barbara Bach, Richard Kiel | 125 minutes | Rated PG
When it comes to "popcorn" action fare, "nobody does it better" than Mr. Bond, and this is "one of Moore's better outings" as 007 pursues a nuclear blackmailer and fights off the "awesome", metal-mouthed nemesis Jaws; if by now the scripts are "superfluous", it's still the leading franchise for "fast cars, fast women" in "clingy clothes" ("oh, James!") and "lots of things that blow up."

	OVERALL	ACTING	STORY	PROD.

Squid and the Whale, The ◐

| 21 | 25 | 20 | 20 |

2005 | Directed by Noah Baumbach | With Jeff Daniels, Laura Linney, Jessie Eisenberg, Owen Kline | 81 minutes | Rated R

"Ultra-real" performances (led by Daniels' "brilliant" turn as a "pompous", has-been writer) propel this "sharply observed" study of a "dysfunctional", "not completely likable" family "riven by divorce"; though "often very funny" in its take on "self-involved parenting" and its "effects on the kids", it's painted with "uncomfortably realistic" strokes – some outright "bizarre" – that "ring so true."

Stagecoach ◑

| 27 | 24 | 26 | 25 |

1939 | Directed by John Ford | With John Wayne, Claire Trevor, John Carradine | 96 minutes | Not Rated

"Wayne's grand entrance" alone immortalizes this "archetypal" Ford Western about a group of stock frontier types "traversing hostile Indian territory" by rickety stage; featuring the young Duke in his "breakthrough role" as a fugitive convict, it rolls along on "great dialogue" and "well-acted" ensemble work interrupted by "viscerally exciting" action scenes, making it a "classic source" of countless tumbleweed "clichés."

Stage Door ◑

| 25 | 26 | 23 | 22 |

1937 | Directed by Gregory La Cava | With Katharine Hepburn, Ginger Rogers, Gail Patrick, Lucille Ball | 92 minutes | Not Rated

A "chick flick for the old guard", this "witty" dramedy is set in a boarding house occupied by "scrappy wannabe actresses" who "live and die for the theatuh"; its "nearly all-female" cast (a "who's who of stars" of the time) is "unusually cohesive", helped along by a "multifaceted screenplay" peppered with plenty of "snappy" patter; most legendary line: Kate's "the calla lilies are in bloom again . . ."

⊠ Stalag 17 ⊠◑

| 27 | 26 | 27 | 24 |

1953 | Directed by Billy Wilder | With William Holden, Don Taylor, Otto Preminger | 120 minutes | Not Rated

Wilder's "wonderful" adaptation of the stage drama supplies the "intrigue" of a "psychological thriller" with some comic relief in this story starring the "properly Oscarized" Holden as a "cynical prisoner" in a WWII POW camp who's "suspected of being a German spy"; thanks to "tremendous acting" and "tense" plotting that "keeps you guessing until the end", this study of military "camaraderie" and "mob judgment" is "not to be missed."

Stand and Deliver

| 20 | 22 | 22 | 17 |

1988 | Directed by Ramon Menendez | With Edward James Olmos, Lou Diamond Phillips | 102 minutes | Rated PG

Giving credit to the "common man", this "inspirational" drama presents Olmos as the real-life Jaime Escalante, a "math teacher who makes a difference" in a tough East LA school by tutoring a class of bad-attitude kids; tough graders say this "good fun flick" also scores as an "underrated" self-esteem booster.

Stand by Me

| 24 | 23 | 25 | 23 |

1986 | Directed by Rob Reiner | With Wil Wheaton, River Phoenix, Corey Feldman | 89 minutes | Rated R

This "wholesome" "coming-of-ager" focuses on preadolescent "best buddies" in '50s Oregon who set out "in search of a missing boy", bonding in the face of various perils and learning about the "real stuff" along the way; a platform for "young talent", it carries a "strong message" about the "struggle to grow up."

Stardust Memories ◑
19 | 20 | 18 | 19

1980 | Directed by Woody Allen | With Woody Allen, Charlotte Rampling, Jessica Harper | 91 minutes | Rated PG

In what could be "his most autobiographical role ever", Allen plays a film director at a weekend retreat badgered by fans "who miss his early, funny pictures" and dismiss his later, more serious work; maybe it's "not his best by a long shot" – antis call it an "explosion of bile aimed at the audience" – although his "tribute to his idols" Bergman and Fellini is "sweet" enough.

Star 80
16 | 16 | 16 | 15

1983 | Directed by Bob Fosse | With Mariel Hemingway, Eric Roberts, Cliff Robertson | 100 minutes | Rated R

Bob Fosse's last film depicts the "tragic true story" of *Playboy* centerfold Dorothy Stratten, an "angelic beauty" bound for "superstardom" whose growing popularity leaves her "boorish husband stewing with resentment"; it's a "gruesome" look at one man's "obsession", but ultimately such an "emotional drain" that many find it too "disturbing" to watch.

Stargate
18 | 17 | 20 | 22

1994 | Directed by Roland Emmerich | With Kurt Russell, James Spader, Jaye Davidson | 121 minutes | Rated PG-13

"Egypt" meets "outer space" in this "interesting" sci-fi flicker about a "portal" discovered in the desert that's an intergalactic wormhole to a "distant world" enslaved by the "powerful" Egyptian god Ra; the ensuing "face-off" is long on "thoughtless action" and "terrific" pyrotechnics but "never delivers" on the "great premise."

Star Is Born, A
25 | 26 | 26 | 26

1954 | Directed by George Cukor | With Judy Garland, James Mason, Jack Carson | 181 minutes | Rated PG

"Forget the other versions": this "heartbreaking" musical drama revisits the Tinseltown parable of fickle celebrity fortunes with the "best Judy ever", showcasing her "true range" as the nobody whose rise to fame is paralleled by her big-name hubby's descent; whether laughing, singing or "turning on the waterworks", Garland gives the "performance of her life", leaving loyalists to lament the Oscar "that got away."

Starman
19 | 20 | 21 | 17

1984 | Directed by John Carpenter | With Jeff Bridges, Karen Allen, Richard Jaeckel | 115 minutes | Rated PG-13

A spacecraft falls to Earth and an "alien and earthling fall for each other" in this "overlooked date movie"; a "first-rate" Bridges plays an "E.T. in human form" who inhabits the bod of Allen's recently deceased husband, leading to "sentimental" getting-to-know-you sessions and a "romantic" road trip that draws to a "sweet" if "predictable" conclusion.

Starship Troopers
15 | 9 | 15 | 21

1997 | Directed by Paul Verhoeven | With Casper Van Dien, Dina Meyer, Denise Richards | 129 minutes | Rated R

"Robert A. Heinlein's classic yarn" about an invasion of "big bad bugs" gets a "campy" rendering in this "full-throttle sci-fi" flick loaded with "amazing" effects; while cynics nix the "appallingly cheesy acting", "trite" plot and "pointless violence", "nonstop action" fans counter that this "critique of militarism" isn't "meant to be taken seriously."

Starsky & Hutch

14 | 15 | 12 | 16

2004 | Directed by Todd Phillips | With Ben Stiller, Owen Wilson, Snoop Dogg | 101 minutes | Rated PG-13

Proving yet again that it can't "leave the original alone", Hollywood un-retires Bay City's "metrosexual" five-o's (and their "fun-to-look-at" Ford Torino) and sends them after a white-collar criminal in this "schlocky" spoof of the '70s TV series; P.S. forget Stiller and Wilson – Snoop Dogg as Huggy Bear is the "best casting" choice.

Starting Over

20 | 20 | 20 | 20

1979 | Directed by Alan J. Pakula | With Burt Reynolds, Jill Clayburgh, Candice Bergen | 105 minutes | Rated R

An "appealing" Reynolds "proves he can act" in this "enjoyable" romantic comedy depicting a middle-aged divorcé's misadventures in born-again bachelorhood ("valium", anyone?); the "good casting" extends to both Clayburgh and Bergen, while the picture's overarching optimism "convinces you there's someone out there for everyone."

Star Trek II: The Wrath of Khan

23 | 19 | 24 | 24

1982 | Directed by Nicholas Meyer | With William Shatner, Leonard Nimoy, DeForest Kelley, Ricardo Montalban | 113 minutes | Rated PG

"Best villain + best story" = "best Trek": so say supporters of this "ripping" sci-fi sequel that hits warp speed when "scenery-chewing" outer-space outlaw Khan hijacks a starship and goes gunning for Admiral Kirk, back for yet one more mission with his familiar Starfleet crew; it offers all the "overblown acting" and "heart of the original", and the windup with Spock on the spot has enough "emotional punch" to "make a Trekkie out of anyone."

Star Trek IV: The Voyage Home

21 | 17 | 21 | 23

1986 | Directed by Leonard Nimoy | With William Shatner, Leonard Nimoy, DeForest Kelley | 119 minutes | Rated PG

The final frontiersmen send us a "message from the future" in this "most accessible" of the sci-fi spin-offs, with Kirk and company "letting their hair down" to indulge in "tongue-in-cheek" interplay as they travel backward through the centuries to join a modern-day "scientific babe" in a mission to "save the whales"; it's a little "lightweight" despite the "timely ecological" theme, but as with the other "even-numbered" entries in the series, the voyaging is "not at all bad."

⊿ Star Wars
(aka Star Wars Episode IV: A New Hope)

28 | 22 | 28 | 29

1977 | Directed by George Lucas | With Mark Hamill, Harrison Ford, Carrie Fisher | 121 minutes | Rated PG

Lucas' "Force is strong" in this "visionary" blockbuster, the "quantum leap" that "redefined sci-fi" and established a "dynasty" by locating the "universal" in a "galaxy far, far away", where "original" "critters" and "futuristic samurais" side with a put-upon princess against an evil Empire; building to a "black hats/white hats" showdown, it's an "entertaining" mix of "modern myth" and "thrill-and-a-half" FX; subsequent space operas "can't touch" it.

| | OVERALL | ACTING | STORY | PROD. |

Star Wars Episode I:
The Phantom Menace   18 | 16 | 18 | 26

1999 | Directed by George Lucas | With Liam Neeson, Ewan McGregor, Natalie Portman | 133 minutes | Rated PG

"After all the hype", here's the "good-looking" sci-fi prequel, which finds an earlier Jedi generation aiding a "planet under blockade" while setting some backstories straight as Obi-Wan and Skywalker *père* are groomed for knighthood; though denounced as a "giant misstep" that makes do with "so-so" storytelling while "pandering to the kiddies" with CGI "overkill" and "irritating" cast members ("why Jar Jar?"), "it's still *Star Wars*", and many "escapists" welcome it as a "worthy addition."

Star Wars Episode II:
Attack of the Clones   17 | 13 | 16 | 24

2002 | Directed by George Lucas | With Hayden Christensen, Ewan McGregor, Natalie Portman | 143 minutes | Rated PG

Unmoved by thunderous legions jeering the "magic is missing", franchise faithfuls stand by this "impressive" second act of the prequel trilogy, lauding its "mesmerizing visuals", "foreboding" moods and "many-questions-answered" plotlines; of course, even diehards don't deny Anakin and Padmé's courtship is a "cardboard"-acted, "dire attempt at romance", yet it's all "worthwhile" for the "showstopping" scene when Yoda fights.

Star Wars Episode III: Revenge of the Sith   23 | 16 | 23 | 28

2005 | Directed by George Lucas | With Hayden Christensen, Ewan McGregor, Ian McDiarmid | 140 minutes | Rated PG-13

"Even though you know" how it wraps up, seeing the "missing pieces of the puzzle" fall into place brings "closure" to a generation of fans who've waited "20-plus years" to learn how Jedi "badass" Anakin Skywalker falls from grace and "becomes Darth Vader" in this "very dark", "epic conclusion" to the beloved space saga; piling on more "dazzling" FX and "campy acting" than ever, it's the "stronger story" this time 'round ("it took Lucas three tries") that explains why it's widely considered "the best of the prequels."

Ⓩ Star Wars Episode V:
The Empire Strikes Back   26 | 21 | 26 | 28

1980 | Directed by Irvin Kershner | With Mark Hamill, Harrison Ford, Carrie Fisher, Billy Dee Williams | 124 minutes | Rated PG

The "darkest of the *Star Wars* series", this "worthy" first sequel features more "depth" in its characterizations and the "best storyline so far", "revealing many important secrets" as the "cosmic struggle continues"; "blissfully free of wooden dialogue", it might be the "most adult" of the "original trilogy", while that open-ended "cliff-hanger" of a finale makes for a suitably "spectacular" windup.

Star Wars Episode VI: Return of the Jedi   24 | 20 | 23 | 28

1983 | Directed by Richard Marquand | With Mark Hamill, Harrison Ford, Carrie Fisher, Billy Dee Williams | 134 minutes | Rated PG

Either a "worthy sequel" or "leftovers", this "wrap-up" episode of the *Star Wars* original trilogy finds the now-classic cast "comfortable in their roles", mugging their way through a "patented good-wins-over-evil storyline" with ample space for "cool special effects" and an "amazing final battle"; loyalists say the force is with it, but skeptics see a "weak entry" overrun with "cute, furry Ewoks", foreshadowing "toy tie-ins" and the "beginnings of Jar Jar."

Station Agent, The

25 | 27 | 23 | 23

2003 | Directed by Thomas McCarthy | With Peter Dinklage, Patricia Clarkson, Bobby Cannavale | 88 minutes | Rated R

"Putting the Q in quirky and the S in subtle", this "quiet little film" also puts the I in indie with its "arty" but "restrained" portrayal of the un-likely friendship between three "eccentrics" in rural New Jersey; while "not much happens" in this "meandering character study", a "great ensemble performance" (especially little person Dinklage's "charisma"-laden turn as a train enthusiast) makes for a "funny", "poi-gnant" flick that "never falls off the track."

Steel Magnolias

24 | 25 | 24 | 23

1989 | Directed by Herbert Ross | With Sally Field, Dolly Parton, Shirley MacLaine, Daryl Hannah | 117 minutes | Rated PG

Break out the "Kleenex" for this "estrogen"-soaked drama, a "major tearjerker" smothered in "Southern-fried flavor", dashed with "laughs" and "memorable one-liners" and played "to the hilt and then some" by a "talented" bunch of "adorable" all-star "belles"; the story of "best girlfriends" in a Looziana beauty parlor bonding through "thick and thin", it's "captivating", "well-made" and "weepy" enough to qualify as the "ultimate chick flick."

St. Elmo's Fire

17 | 17 | 17 | 17

1985 | Directed by Joel Schumacher | With Rob Lowe, Demi Moore, Andrew McCarthy, Judd Nelson | 110 minutes | Rated R

This "nostalgic" '80s "cult classic" starring the "Brat Pack at its finest" addresses "issues faced in life just after college"; sure, there are some "weak spots" and a few moments that are now "unintentionally hilar-ious", but overall, it remains a "favorite" "coming-of-age flick", like "The Big Chill" for Generation X."

Stepford Wives, The

12 | 15 | 12 | 15

2004 | Directed by Frank Oz | With Nicole Kidman, Matthew Broderick, Bette Midler, Glenn Close | 93 minutes | Rated PG-13

Expect "all kitsch and no fright" in this "high-camp" rendition of Ira Levin's "grim" horror/sci-fi novel about an "idyllic" town whose "June Cleaver"-esque housewives are in fact "creepy" robots; no match for the "much better" 1975 version, it's altogether a "waste of a great cast" and, "like the suburbs, bland, bland, bland."

Stepmom

19 | 22 | 19 | 19

1998 | Directed by Chris Columbus | With Julia Roberts, Susan Sarandon, Ed Harris | 124 minutes | Rated PG-13

"Get out the tissues" – "you'll need 'em" – for this "emotional" family drama tackling the "real-life" challenges posed by "divorce, illness and forgiveness"; examining the "complex" relationship be-tween a "Stella Dallas-like mother" and the "pretty young thing" who "snagged her husband", it "jerks those tears" by depicting the "worst fear" for a parent in splitsville: "that someone else will raise the children."

✉ Sting, The ✉
27 | 26 | 27 | 26

1973 | Directed by George Roy Hill | With Paul Newman, Robert Redford, Robert Shaw | 129 minutes | Rated PG

"Deftly" charming its way to Best Picture honors, this "classy" comedy "caper" "succeeds in spades" as a "likable", "fast-paced" vehicle for Newman and Redford, radiating "great rapport" as a pair of grifters playing a gangster for a sucker in Depression-era Chicago; a "funny, intriguing" "period piece" set to "elegant" Joplin rags, it raises the "suspense" stakes with "masterful" plotting and a final "zinger" that saves the sharpest sting for last.

Stir Crazy
20 | 21 | 19 | 18

1980 | Directed by Sidney Poitier | With Gene Wilder, Richard Pryor, JoBeth Williams | 111 minutes | Rated R

The second "outing from the team of Pryor and Wilder" (following *Silver Streak*), this buddy comedy concerns two wrongly imprisoned jokers out to clear their names; though some consider it somewhat downhill from their first matchup, it was popular enough to spawn a TV sitcom.

Stop Making Sense
25 | - | 14 | 24

1984 | Directed by Jonathan Demme | Documentary | With Talking Heads | 88 minutes | Not Rated

"Turn up the sound", because Demme's "alterna-rockumentary" presents a "superior" show from new wave faves the Talking Heads in their "heyday", burning down the house with "energetic music"; the flick proves the "exception to the rule that concerts don't translate" to the big screen and finds bandleader "David Byrne in top form", "swaying" in his trademark "enormous suit."

Story of Adele H., The 🇫
24 | 26 | 24 | 24

1975 | Directed by François Truffaut | With Isabelle Adjani, Bruce Robinson | 96 minutes | Rated PG

"Unrequited love" turns to "single-minded obsession" and then to flat-out "stalking" in this "intense" psychological drama from François Truffaut, the story of a 19th-century woman (based on "Victor Hugo's actual daughter") infatuated with one "cruelly oblivious man"; in the Oscar-nominated turn that made her an international star, Adjani is "near perfect", alternately "radiant, commanding and heartbreaking."

Straight Story, The
24 | 27 | 22 | 21

1999 | Directed by David Lynch | With Richard Farnsworth, Sissy Spacek, Jane Galloway | 111 minutes | Rated G

The "only G-rated" effort from malaise-meister Lynch goes straight for the heart in this "odd" but "compelling" drama of a septuagenarian "who rides his John Deere" power mower cross country to mend fences with his infirm brother; this "interesting" "character study" is polished into an "absolute gem" by "brilliant performances" and a "lovely" meditation on the "ending of the life cycle", but be warned that "travel by tractor" can be a "slow" ride.

Strange Days
17 | 18 | 19 | 19

1995 | Directed by Kathryn Bigelow | With Ralph Fiennes, Angela Bassett, Juliette Lewis | 145 minutes | Rated R

"Virtual reality devices" containing people's "recorded memories and emotions" take "voyeurism" to "intense" extremes in this "original" i "overlooked" sci-fi thriller set in the "frightening future"; led by an "angst-ridden" Fiennes as an ex-cop "trying to solve a murder", it's a "pretty cool" trip that touches upon some "interesting themes", including "drugs, love and loss."

Strangers on a Train ❶

| | 26 | 24 | 27 | 24 |

1951 | Directed by Alfred Hitchcock | With Farley Granger, Robert Walker, Ruth Roman | 101 minutes | Rated PG

Be careful "what you wish for" is the underlying theme of this "fascinating", "forward-thinking" Hitchcock thriller wherein a flippant "promise to exchange murders" spirals out of control into a "dark tale of unwanted bedfellows"; "spine-tingler" aficionados single out Walker's "chilling" turn as a "wacko" mama's boy, and among many "tense moments", the "carousel finale still amazes."

☒ Streetcar Named Desire, A ✉❶

| | 27 | 28 | 26 | 25 |

1951 | Directed by Elia Kazan | With Vivien Leigh, Marlon Brando, Kim Hunter, Karl Malden | 125 minutes | Rated PG

Destined to "hold great forever", this "brilliant interpretation" of Tennessee Williams' "overwrought classic" showcases the "amazing" Brando "exploding onto the scene" ("hey, *Stella!*") in the "legendary" role of a "rugged" slob who engages in "shattering" "psychological warfare" with his delicate sister-in-law (the "wonderful", "so-sad" Leigh); fans say it's worth watching if only for a look at the "virile" Marlon when he was "still acting."

Strictly Ballroom

| | 23 | 21 | 23 | 22 |

1992 | Directed by Baz Luhrmann | With Paul Mercurio, Tara Morice, Bill Hunter | 94 minutes | Rated PG

This "quirky" dose of "flash and flamenco" is a surprise charmer of a romantic comedy pairing a "hot" Aussie hoofer with an "ugly duckling", who proceed to shake up a dance championship with the question "to tango or not to tango?"; a "delightful send-up" of the "viciousness of the competitive ballroom circuit", it amuses with "well-executed" moves, even if onlookers "kinda know" how the strictly by-the-numbers story will turn out.

Stripes

| | 21 | 18 | 18 | 18 |

1981 | Directed by Ivan Reitman | With Bill Murray, Harold Ramis, Warren Oates | 101 minutes | Rated R

"Red-blooded guys" are quick to salute this "service comedy" starring "cynical" Murray as a goldbricking civilian who joins the Army and endures basic training with the idea that it's "all about laughs"; with a "strong comic cast" and gags ranging from the truly "hilarious" to the sublimely "ridiculous", it ranks as "one of the funniest" in its class, though deserters say it "bogs down" midway and caution it's "no *Caddyshack*" – and "that's a fact, Jack."

Stuart Little

| | 19 | 18 | 19 | 21 |

1999 | Directed by Rob Minkoff | With Geena Davis, Hugh Laurie, Jonathan Lipnicki | 84 minutes | Rated PG

Adapted from E.B. White's "sweet" children's classic, this "cute production" craftily combines "amazing animation" and live action to tell the tale of an "adorable" "talking mouse" who's adopted by humans only to be claimed by rodents posing as his "birth parents"; fans applaud its "poignancy", though a few whiskers twitch at the "piffle"-ridden plot that "mangles the original" into a flick "only a little kid could like."

Stuart Little 2
19 | 18 | 18 | 22

2002 | Directed by Rob Minkoff | With Geena Davis, Hugh Laurie, Jonathan Lipnicki | 78 minutes | Rated PG

From the continuing chronicles of mice and men comes this "winner" of a sequel to E.B. White's classic tale, marking a respectable reprise for the "adorable" and "wonderfully animated" titular rodent as he teams up with a feathered friend and "tackles a new adventure"; though it's probably better suited for "grandkids" than grown-ups, keep a hawk's eye peeled for the "adult humor tucked in the dialogue."

Stunt Man, The
22 | 25 | 22 | 21

1980 | Directed by Richard Rush | With Peter O'Toole, Steve Railsback, Barbara Hershey | 131 minutes | Rated R

"Expect the unexpected" in this "entirely original" "Hollywood insider" story about an escaped convict who "strikes a devil's bargain" with a "manipulative" film director to masquerade as a stunt man on a movie shoot; given the "satirical", "red herring"-filled script and an "over-the-top", "eat-the-scenery" turn by O'Toole, many marvel at the picture's "overlooked", "underrated" status.

Suddenly, Last Summer ◑
24 | 26 | 23 | 22

1959 | Directed by Joseph L. Mankiewicz | With Elizabeth Taylor, Katharine Hepburn, Montgomery Clift | 114 minutes | Not Rated

Alright, this "sensational" Tennessee Williams "stunner" about a wealthy woman scheming to have her niece lobotomized in order to "silence her" is "a bit much" – and a little too "murky", "talky" and "icky" for the squeamish; but fans flip for its "baroque excess", Liz's "tight white bathing suit" and, most of all, that truly "shocking ending."

Sugarland Express, The
18 | 20 | 18 | 18

1974 | Directed by Steven Spielberg | With Goldie Hawn, William Atherton, Ben Johnson, Michael Sacks | 110 minutes | Rated PG

"Spielberg's first movie" ("before he went CGI mad") is this "little-seen" true story that "concentrates on characters instead of effects" and even has a "downer ending"; it stars a "young" Goldie, who "runs away with the picture" as a "not-so-nice" gal who springs her hubby from prison in order to "reclaim their baby from foster care."

Sullivan's Travels ◑
27 | 25 | 26 | 25

1941 | Directed by Preston Sturges | With Joel McCrea, Veronica Lake, William Demarest | 90 minutes | Not Rated

A Depression-era movie director suffering from a "mid-career crisis" "develops a conscience" and decides to shoot a truly "serious film" in this "profound comedy" from Preston Sturges; the result is a delightfully "inspirational" flick that not only has "something important to say about America", but also is one of the "best pictures ever made about Hollywood – even though it hardly takes place there."

Summer of '42
21 | 19 | 23 | 19

1971 | Directed by Robert Mulligan | With Jennifer O'Neill, Gary Grimes, Jerry Houser | 103 minutes | Rated R

Sentimental yearning and raging hormones drive this "coming-of-age" romance, which finds a trio of "pubescent boys" spending the first summer after Pearl Harbor goofing off until one of them hooks up with a young soldier's widow; the combination of "humor" and "heartbreak" is also a "moving" remembrance of a "time of war", while the Oscar-winning score alone is "worth the price of admission."

Summertime
23 | 26 | 23 | 24

1955 | Directed by David Lean | With Katharine Hepburn, Rossano Brazzi | 100 minutes | Not Rated

"Venice is the star" of this "bittersweet" love story about an "aging spinster" who "experiences *amore*" while on holiday in "timeless" Italy; there's "not a false note" in Kate's "delicious" performance (though holdouts insist she's "too dynamic" to be an old maid), played against "stunning locales" and a "swooningly romantic score."

Sum of All Fears, The
16 | 15 | 18 | 19

2002 | Directed by Phil Alden Robinson | With Ben Affleck, Morgan Freeman, James Cromwell | 124 minutes | Rated PG-13

"Neo-Nazis" seize a nuclear warhead and restart the Cold War in this "average" suspense thriller that boasts "good production values" but is certainly "not the best of the series" based on the Tom Clancy best-sellers; Affleck's "laughable" as Jack Ryan ("Harrison Ford he ain't"), and the "goodbye-Baltimore" finale "so implausible" that many advise "read the book, it's much better."

Sunday Bloody Sunday
24 | 26 | 24 | 22

1971 | Directed by John Schlesinger | With Peter Finch, Glenda Jackson, Murray Head | 110 minutes | Rated R

"Very adult for its time", this "complex" film about "a man, a woman and their shared male lover" is "still very adult", starting with its "unflinching look at homosexuality"; Oscar nominees Jackson and Finch are "unforgettable" as "lost souls in the modern world" on the opposite sides of this "love triangle", while a "literate" script and "flawless" direction make this "groundbreaking" work "as relevant today as it was then."

☑ Sunset Boulevard ✉◑
28 | 28 | 27 | 27

1950 | Directed by Billy Wilder | With William Holden, Gloria Swanson, Erich Von Stroheim | 110 minutes | Not Rated

"Some of the greatest dialogue ever" (most famously, "I'm ready for my close-up, Mr. DeMille") graces this hybrid of "Gothic" and "film noir", a "scabrous take on Hollywood" from the standpoint of a "struggling screenwriter" trying to "resurrect the career of a silent movie star" who's "not exactly in touch with reality"; given Wilder's "acerbic" direction, an "'in'-joke"-laced script and "pitch-perfect" performances from a "larger-than-life Swanson" and "hunky Holden", "who needs a musical version?"

Sunshine Boys, The
21 | 23 | 19 | 18

1975 | Directed by Herbert Ross | With Walter Matthau, George Burns, Richard Benjamin | 111 minutes | Rated PG

The radiant screen rendition of Neil Simon's Broadway comedy presents Matthau and Burns (who reappears after decades offscreen and snags an Oscar) as a couple of crusty "vaudeville greats who must work together" on a TV reunion show, even though they're given to much bickering; the "funny story" makes for surefire yuks, but razzers report the act as a whole is "not so bright."

| | OVERALL | ACTING | STORY | PROD. |

Sunshine State
18 | 22 | 18 | 18

2002 | Directed by John Sayles | With Edie Falco, Jane Alexander, Ralph Waite, Angela Bassett | 141 minutes | Rated PG-13

A "great ensemble cast" (notably the "terrific" Falco) is the bright ray of sunshine in this "thought provoking" "social drama" set in a moribund Florida community; devotees delight in the "ambitious script" that spins "lots of subplots" and leaves behind "untied loose ends", but detractors yawn "boring" and insist it's "not the best" effort from indie auteur Sayles.

Superman
22 | 19 | 22 | 23

1978 | Directed by Richard Donner | With Christopher Reeve, Margot Kidder, Gene Hackman | 143 minutes | Rated PG

"You'll really believe a man can fly" after a look at this "ahead-of-its-time" superhero fantasy, the "delightful", "campy" saga of a survivor from a doomed planet who grows up to be a "man of steel"; even if the "comic-book sensibility" is "a little silly" and the line readings "stiff", a super "heart shines through" as Reeve turns in the "definitive", "true-blue portrayal" of "all things good" – when he's not "sizing up telephone booths", that is.

Super Size Me
24 | - | 24 | 21

2004 | Directed by Morgan Spurlock | Documentary | 96 minutes | Rated G

Near-"suicide by gluttony" is both "disturbing" and "funny" in this "crowd-pleasing documentary" wherein director/star Spurlock submits himself to an all-McDonald's diet for a full month; although "not the most researched study of fast food" and perhaps "lacking in nutritional substance", this "eye-opening, stomach-churning" "wake-up call" still might send you running for a "piece of fruit."

Suspect
20 | 21 | 22 | 19

1987 | Directed by Peter Yates | With Cher, Dennis Quaid, Liam Neeson | 121 minutes | Rated R

Cher's an ambitious public defender in this "courtroom thriller" about a high-level conspiracy involving a slick lobbyist, a dead Supreme Court justice and a deaf-and-dumb homeless man; though "predictable" and only "relatively involving" to the suspicious, others say it "keeps you wondering" until the "surprise ending."

Suspicion ⊠◑
25 | 26 | 25 | 25

1941 | Directed by Alfred Hitchcock | With Joan Fontaine, Cary Grant, Cedric Hardwicke, Nigel Bruce | 99 minutes | Not Rated

A "poor little rich girl" hooks up with a "potential murderer" in this "top Hitchcock" thriller starring an appropriately "menacing" Grant and a "wimpy" (but Oscar-winning) Fontaine; if some find the picture "a bit tentative" for the master of suspense (who was famously forced to "change the ending"), everyone agrees on its most unforgettable prop, the "scariest looking glass of milk in cinema history."

S.W.A.T.
15 | 15 | 15 | 18

2003 | Directed by Clark Johnson | With Samuel L. Jackson, Colin Farrell, Michelle Rodriguez, LL Cool J | 117 minutes | Rated PG-13

Hollywood's ever-profitable pairing of "guns and testosterone" is the trigger for this "muscle"-bound "peek into the life of a SWAT agent", a "generic" "guy flick" bulging with "badass" coppers and the usual "through-the-roof" action; factor in the plot's "telegraphed twists" and most prefer their "fond memories of the original TV series" over this "tired revival."

Sweet Bird of Youth
24 | 28 | 24 | 23

1962 | Directed by Richard Brooks | With Paul Newman, Geraldine Page, Ed Begley, Shirley Knight | 120 minutes | Not Rated

A "young, gorgeous" Newman and "brilliant" Page ("what a combo!") reprise their stage roles in this cinematic adaptation of Tennessee Williams' play about a wannabe actor/gigolo and a faded, *Sunset Boulevard*-esque movie queen; sure, the story has been somewhat sanitized for the big screen, but most birdies still tweet "how sweet it is . . ."

Sweet Charity
20 | 21 | 19 | 23

1969 | Directed by Bob Fosse | With Shirley MacLaine, John McMartin, Chita Rivera | 149 minutes | Rated G

"Fosse's directorial debut" adapts a boffo Broadway show into an "exciting" musical featuring "MacLaine at her best" as a honey of a dance-hall damsel; look for "over-the-top production numbers" (especially Chita's raucous 'Big Spender') with "memorable staging" and "great tunes", and if the "quirky" story "drifts" when the music stops, charitable types cheer the players for "trying with all their might."

Sweet Hereafter, The
24 | 25 | 23 | 23

1997 | Directed by Atom Egoyan | With Ian Holm, Sarah Polley, Bruce Greenwood | 112 minutes | Rated R

"Haunting" in a "somber" way, this adaptation of Russell Banks' novel is a "beautifully shot", "terribly moving" drama about the "aftermath of a small-town tragedy" and the "dysfunction" it lays bare; the "terrific cast" led by Holm and Polley sees the burg's "delicate balance" upset when a group of children die in a bus crash, and the camera lends a "hypnotic" feel to material that's "smart" but "shrouded in sadness."

Sweet Home Alabama
17 | 18 | 16 | 18

2002 | Directed by Andy Tennant | With Reese Witherspoon, Josh Lucas, Patrick Dempsey | 108 minutes | Rated PG-13

A "country girl turned NYC fashionista" choosing between two suitors "returns to her roots" to make a decision in this "lighthearted", "pass-me-the-popcorn" romantic comedy that's "good for a girls' night out"; while "America's Sweetheart" Reese just "couldn't be cuter", the "no-surprises", "by-the-book" script and "stereotypical", "culture-clash humor" aren't as sweet.

⊠ Sweet Smell of Success, The ◑
27 | 28 | 26 | 26

1957 | Directed by Alexander Mackendrick | With Burt Lancaster, Tony Curtis, Martin Milner | 96 minutes | Not Rated

A "cookie full of arsenic" soaked in "hydrochloric acid", this extra-"tasty" morsel of "moody noir" unearths the "seamy side" of showbiz with its "cynical" "character study" of the "slimy" sorts working the "publicity end": a "superb" Lancaster as a "brutal", Winchell-esque columnist and the "unctuous Curtis" as his publicist toady; brace yourself for "crackling dialogue" and some "beyond beautiful" NYC "nighttime shots" in this "timeless" but never "more timely" picture.

	OVERALL	ACTING	STORY	PROD.

Swept Away 🅵

`24` `24` `24` `24`

1975 | Directed by Lina Wertmüller | With Mariangela Melato, Giancarlo Giannini | 116 minutes | Rated R

Stranding strangers on a "sunbaked isle" long "before the arrival of *Survivor*", Wertmüller's "unforgettable" Italian comedy "steams up the screen" as a snobbish socialite and a coarsely "expressive" boatman develop a "passionate" "love/hate relationship" alone on a Mediterranean cay; the satire "speaks volumes" as a "comment on class" and the "battle of the sexes", though there's a strong undercurrent of "violence" running beneath the beautiful "scenery."

Swimming Pool

`20` `23` `20` `20`

2003 | Directed by François Ozon | With Charlotte Rampling, Ludivine Sagnier, Charles Dance | 103 minutes | Rated R

A burnt-out "older British woman" and a "slutty French girl" share a house in the south of France in this "plenty sexy" psychological thriller that delineates some "wonderfully uncomfortable" "generational differences"; while the "cryptic" climax leaves cynics perplexed – "could someone please explain the ending?" – boobs say it's "worth renting for the nudity" alone.

Swingers

`23` `22` `23` `20`

1996 | Directed by Doug Liman | With Jon Favreau, Vince Vaughn, Heather Graham | 96 minutes | Rated R

"Hooking up in the '90s" gets a "hilarious" but "realistic" spin in this "hip, kinetic" buddy comedy–cum–"cultural phenomenon" about two single guys "finding their mojo" on the "Los Angeles dating scene"; it's "immensely funny", universally "accurate in defining a generation" and "'so money' that it spawned its very own vernacular."

Swing Time ◑

`26` `23` `20` `26`

1936 | Directed by George Stevens | With Fred Astaire, Ginger Rogers, Helen Broderick | 103 minutes | Not Rated

The "easy grace" (and "winged feet") of Astaire and Rogers make for one "magical musical" in this "superb offering" that's voted "the best" of their pairings in this Survey; as usual, "there's not much of a story", but compensations include Fred's "sublime" 'Bojangles of Harlem' number and an "outstanding" Jerome Kern score, highlighted by the Oscar-winning 'The Way You Look Tonight.'

Swiss Family Robinson

`23` `20` `24` `23`

1960 | Directed by Ken Annakin | With John Mills, Dorothy McGuire, James MacArthur | 126 minutes | Rated G

"Action, romance, adventure and comedy" coexist amiably in this "absolute classic" from Walt Disney, a story of castaways shipwrecked on a tropical isle that "bears little resemblance to the novel"; an exercise in "good, clean fun", it's everything a "family movie should be", and that "terrific" treehouse set "still fascinates" smaller fry.

Swordfish

`15` `15` `16` `18`

2001 | Directed by Dominic Sena | With John Travolta, Hugh Jackman, Halle Berry, Don Cheadle | 99 minutes | Rated R

A mother lode of "government secrets and money" tempts "swaggerin'" Travolta and his assembled "team of computer hackers" in this techno-thriller whose "explosive" opening quickly yields to more

| | OVERALL | ACTING | STORY | PROD. |

"lackluster", "predictable" fare; don't bother trying to figure out "who's a white hat or a black hat" and just savor the real "highlight" of this flick: "Halle's topless scene."

Sylvia
`16` `20` `16` `19`

2003 | Directed by Christine Jeffs | With Gwyneth Paltrow, Daniel Craig, Jared Harris, Blythe Danner | 110 minutes | Rated R

"Troubled writer" Sylvia Plath is the subject of this "relentlessly morose" biopic that gets somewhat of a lift from Paltrow's "strong yet fragile" title turn; although it's an "even-handed treatment of an uneven marriage", many find the story too "depressing and pointless", wondering if "her life is interesting enough" to "deserve its own movie."

Syriana
`21` `24` `20` `22`

2005 | Directed by Stephen Gaghan | With Jeffrey Wright, George Clooney, Matt Damon | 126 minutes | Rated R

Holding up a "mirror to current events", this "tough-minded" drama about "the Middle East", "Big Oil" and the "dirty tricks" that bind them together weaves a "complex" (if at times "confusing") tapestry of "intersecting plotlines" loaded with "twists"; Clooney's "fabulous" performance as a "disillusioned CIA agent" is one good reason why this political "wake-up call" rewards "multiple viewings."

Tadpole
`19` `21` `19` `17`

2002 | Directed by Gary Winick | With Aaron Stanford, Sigourney Weaver, Bebe Neuwirth, John Ritter | 78 minutes | Rated PG-13

"Quirky" characters found "only in New York" populate this "witty" indie comedy about a "precocious" prep-schooler who "has a thing for his stepmother"; cynics nix the rather "creepy" premise and the low-budget, "film-school-project" vibe, but agree that Neuwirth's turn as a 40-year-old "guilt-free seductress" is a "most memorable" bonus.

Take the Money and Run
`21` `18` `21` `17`

1969 | Directed by Woody Allen | With Woody Allen, Janet Margolin, Marcel Hillaire | 85 minutes | Rated R

Woody's "first full-fledged feature" wings it with "pure slapstick" and "typical" self-deprecating shtick, depicting the escapades of a "hopeless nerd bank robber" that's "basically a series of blackouts and sketches"; though a bit "threadbare" in between the "patches of brilliance", it packs enough "anarchy and whimsy" to foretell things to come.

Talented Mr. Ripley, The
`18` `21` `19` `21`

1999 | Directed by Anthony Minghella | With Matt Damon, Jude Law, Gwyneth Paltrow | 139 minutes | Rated R

A "lush thriller of mistaken identity" set in '50s Europe, this "unsettling", "underrated" study of a murderous "schmuck-turned-socialite" stars Damon as the "slippery" title character (in a performance that's either "unnervingly good" or totally "botched"); while the "disturbing storyline" played out against "spectacular scenery" enthralls many, critics see little talent in its "lack of warmth" and way-"too-long" running time.

Talk to Her ⊠🎬
`26` `26` `26` `25`

2002 | Directed by Pedro Almodóvar | With Javier Cámara, Darío Grandinetti, Leonor Watling | 112 minutes | Rated R

"Don't think about it too much and it will captivate you": this "brilliant piece of art" by the "risk-taking" Almodóvar, a "haunting", "highly original" "drama, comedy and mystery all in one" is about "two women who have fallen into comas and the men who love them"; a "wonderful cast" tackles a "provocative" "multilayered storyline" that "allows fantasy to play with reality" – "finally, a film for mature audiences!"

Taps
20 | 22 | 21 | 19

1981 | Directed by Harold Becker | With George C. Scott, Timothy Hutton, Ronny Cox, Sean Penn, Tom Cruise | 126 minutes | Rated PG
"*Lord of the Flies* meets *Dead Poets Society*" in this "powerful" Reagan-era feature dubbed the "ultimate military academy drama" for its "plausible" depiction of a soon-to-close school's armed takeover by a platoon of "punchy" cadets; a "who's-who" roster of "before-they-were-famous stars" (like Cruise, Penn and Hutton) fills the ranks of the "sensational young cast", while the more mature Scott lends some "*Patton*"-esque gravitas.

Tarzan
22 | - | 21 | 24

1999 | Directed by Chris Buck, Kevin Lima | Animated | 88 minutes | Rated G
Some of "Disney's best work" "re-creates the magic" of a "classic" in this tale of man and monkey swinging through life via "phenomenally innovative" animation; a "fast-paced adventure" that takes time out for "character" but "keeps things relatively lighthearted", it adds some "thoughtful modern" angles and a "great score", including an Oscar-winning song from Phil Collins.

Tarzan and His Mate ◑
21 | 16 | 19 | 20

1934 | Directed by Cedric Gibbons | With Johnny Weissmuller, Maureen O'Sullivan | 104 minutes | Not Rated
See "what movies were like before the censors" in this rather racy sequel to *Tarzan the Ape Man* flaunting barely there costumes, "nude underwater" frolicking and title characters living together sans holy matrimony; despite some "racist" undertones and acting that "leaves a lot to be desired", some consider it the "best" of the Weissmuller Tarzans.

Tarzan the Ape Man ◑
21 | 16 | 21 | 18

1932 | Directed by W.S. Van Dyke | With Johnny Weissmuller, Maureen O'Sullivan | 99 minutes | Not Rated
An "old-fashioned" fave among the "first real adventure films", this "memorable" intersection of Hollywood and vine finds a Brit lady Jane abducted by the ape-bred hero only to civilize him (and catch a bit of jungle fever herself); Olympic swimmer Weissmuller brings "definitive" bravura to the title character, and thus this "campy" but "trendsetting original" "holds up better" than all the sequels you can shake a banana at.

▣ Taxi Driver
27 | 29 | 25 | 25

1976 | Directed by Martin Scorsese | With Robert De Niro, Jodie Foster, Harvey Keitel, Cybill Shepherd | 113 minutes | Rated R
Confirming "non-NYers' greatest fears" about the "brutal underbelly" of "modern urban life", Scorsese's vividly "cerebral" thriller rolls through "sleazy" streets and "neon" nights charged by De Niro's "monumental performance" as a "creepy", insomniac hack – "you talking to me?" – whose live-wire issues build to "harrowing" magnum force in the "steam-filled" city; overall, its depiction of "urban decay, rage and alienation" is "top-class" but "lurid" and very "intense."

	OVERALL	ACTING	STORY	PROD.

10
17 | 16 | 16 | 17

1979 | Directed by Blake Edwards | With Dudley Moore, Julie Andrews, Bo Derek, Robert Webber | 122 minutes | Rated R

This "midlife crisis movie for men" might be "silly" and "rather dated", but will always be a "time capsule of the American dream, circa 1979" thanks to the iconic image of "Derek in cornrows" bouncing on the beach in "slow motion"; sure, it has about as much depth as the "*Sports Illustrated* swimsuit issue", but it's "still funny" and proves that "short guys can be sexy."

Ten Commandments, The
24 | 21 | 25 | 27

1956 | Directed by Cecil B. DeMille | With Charlton Heston, Yul Brynner, Anne Baxter, Edward G. Robinson | 220 minutes | Rated G

"Let it be written" that DeMille's "over-the-top" biblical blockbuster is the "epic of all epics", a "Cliffs Notes" account of Exodus built on "Heston's finest" role as the "one and only Moses", performer of "monumental" miracles on land and Red Sea; though "fantastic sets" and Brynner's "badass" Egyptian king distract from the "kitschy" script and "overblown" production, it's "entertaining" enough to keep a "cast of thousands" in "constant circulation."

Tender Mercies ✉
24 | 26 | 22 | 22

1983 | Directed by Bruce Beresford | With Robert Duvall, Tess Harper, Betty Buckley, Ellen Barkin | 92 minutes | Rated PG

"Proving that less is more", Duvall delivers a "quiet yet unforgettable" portrait of a "has-been country singer" hiding out in a Texas motel, and transforms a "simple story" into something "truly great"; winner of two Oscars (for Best Actor and Screenplay), it also boasts a "rather good" soundtrack that lends the film its "haunting" air.

Tequila Sunrise
17 | 18 | 17 | 18

1988 | Directed by Robert Towne | With Mel Gibson, Michelle Pfeiffer, Kurt Russell | 115 minutes | Rated R

"Unusually beautiful people" make up a "classic love triangle" – and "what a perfect triangle it is" – in this "decent" drama about a restaurateur involved with a cop and a drug dealer; some say the "usual story line" features too much "froth" and "dead dialogue", but all agree it's worth a look to gaze upon Michelle and Kurt "in their prime" – not to mention Mel "before he found God."

Terminal, The
18 | 22 | 18 | 20

2004 | Directed by Steven Spielberg | With Tom Hanks, Catherine Zeta-Jones, Stanley Tucci | 128 minutes | Rated PG-13

"Every traveler's nightmare" comes true in this story of an "Eastern European stranded for months at JFK" that divides viewers, with fans praising the "spare-no-expense" production and Tom's "gold-standard" performance; but those who say it "just doesn't fly" cite the "strained", "*Castaway*-in-an-airport" story, "unsatisfying" ending and "zero chemistry" between the "not sexy" Hanks and "wasted" Zeta-Jones.

Terminator, The
24 | 18 | 24 | 24

1984 | Directed by James Cameron | With Arnold Schwarzenegger, Michael Biehn, Linda Hamilton | 108 minutes | Rated R

Buckle up for Cameron's "unstoppable breakthrough", this sci-fi/ action "genre-maker" about an "evil cyborg sent from the future" to wreak havoc on the past via Ah-nuld's "seriously scary presence" alone; it "doesn't disappoint" in dispensing "awesome" "violent" mayhem all over '80s LA, and its most famous line – "I'll be back" – was a harbinger of the sequels to come.

Terminator 2: Judgment Day
23 17 22 26

1991 | Directed by James Cameron | With Arnold Schwarzenegger, Linda Hamilton, Edward Furlong | 137 minutes | Rated R

The Terminator's "baaack" as a "kinder, gentler" cyborg in this "outsize thrill ride" that deftly embellishes the initial premise of murderous, "time-traveling" robots; fans say it's a "rare sequel that fulfills the promise of the original", citing the "whiz-bang", "ahead-of-their-time" FX, Hamilton's "buff", "kick-butt" heroine and the one-and-only Arnold, whose "mechanical" performance makes him the "perfect choice to play an android."

Terminator 3: Rise of the Machines
16 13 15 22

2003 | Directed by Jonathan Mostow | With Arnold Schwarzenegger, Nick Stahl, Claire Danes | 109 minutes | Rated R

"Staying true" to its origins, this third entry in the long-unfolding sci-fi series features the usual "bang-up" pyrotechnics and "breezy" plotting, along with a "twist": a fembot Terminatrix villainess; still, foes fret the "franchise has run out of steam", citing "retread special effects", "phoned-in" work from Arnold and that "downer" of an ending; in the final analysis, "they should have stopped at 2."

Terms of Endearment ✉
25 26 24 22

1983 | Directed by James L. Brooks | With Shirley MacLaine, Debra Winger, Jack Nicholson | 132 minutes | Rated PG

A "four-hanky tearjerker" "worth its weight in Kleenex", this "engrossing" "weepie with a spine" starts off comically enough depicting a "tangled mother-daughter relationship" but takes a "serious" turn in the second act when "life-and-death" issues arise; quite the Oscar magnet, it took home Best Picture honors as well as statuettes for the "amazing" MacLaine and Nicholson, who's a "hoot" as the former astronaut who lives next door.

Tess
21 22 21 22

1980 | Directed by Roman Polanski | With Nastassja Kinski, Peter Firth, Leigh Lawson | 172 minutes | Rated PG

"Spectacularly beautiful", this "faithful rendition" of Thomas Hardy's "melancholy" classic *Tess of the D'Urbervilles* stars a "luminous" Kinski as a peasant girl trying to improve her station in life; some say it's "schmaltzy" and "long", but most praise Polanski's "really fine adaptation" and promise you'll "never look at strawberries the same way."

Texas Chainsaw Massacre, The
17 13 17 15

1974 | Directed by Tobe Hooper | With Marilyn Burns, Allen Danziger, Paul A. Partain | 83 minutes | Rated R

Something "like a car wreck", this "alternately repulsive and fascinating" "slashfest" is the "nightmarish" story of innocent folk "falling prey to a cannibalistic family" and is "creepy beyond belief" despite "surprisingly little overt gore"; aficionados call it the "*Casablanca* of horror films" notwithstanding the "low-budget" looks and "bad acting" – but "truly amazing screaming."

	OVERALL	ACTING	STORY	PROD.

Thank You for Smoking
23 | 23 | 23 | 21

2006 | Directed by Jason Reitman | With Aaron Eckhart, Maria Bello, Rob Lowe, Robert Duvall, William H. Macy, Katie Holmes | 92 minutes | Rated R

Eckhart's "killer" portrayal of a "smug" but "lovable" cigarette industry spin doctor has you "rooting for the bad guy" in this "hysterically sarcastic" send-up of "Big Tobacco" and the "art of lobbying"; packed with "intelligent commentary" and featuring a star-studded cast, it "throws some moral curveballs" that leave "plenty to talk about after the credits roll."

That's Entertainment!
25 | – | – | 25

1974 | Directed by Jack Haley Jr | Documentary | With Gene Kelly, Fred Astaire | 127 minutes | Rated G

This "remarkable survey of MGM musicals" lays out a "delicious", "crème-de-la-crème" buffet of glorious "old clips" set up with "narration by some mighty big stars"; showcasing the likes of Kelly and Astaire at their "thrilling" peak, this compilation is "desert-island" viewing and an "entertaining introduction" for young folks to the bygone days of "real talent."

Thelma & Louise ✉
23 | 25 | 23 | 21

1991 | Directed by Ridley Scott | With Susan Sarandon, Geena Davis, Brad Pitt, Harvey Keitel | 129 minutes | Rated R

A "high-powered" "girl-power" flick focusing on a "feminist crime spree", this "groundbreaking" display of "female macho" "rocks" as two everyday gals "finally get back" at the men who've wronged them by becoming "devil-may-care outlaws" on the lam; the "superb storyline" and "stellar performances" keep things "involving" right up to the "heartbreaking", *Butch Cassidy*-esque "bad ending."

There's Something About Mary
21 | 19 | 20 | 19

1998 | Directed by Bobby Farrelly, Peter Farrelly | With Cameron Diaz, Matt Dillon, Ben Stiller | 119 minutes | Rated R

Proceed "at your own risk" as the "ultra-crude" Farrelly brothers "push the limits" of "gross-out comedy" in this "tacky laugh riot" about a "loser with a heart of gold" and the "good-sport" girl he loves that's an "oh-my-gosh" compendium of "high-school humor" and "vulgar" "sight gags" (the "dog", the "zipper", the "hair gel"); but foes moan this movie "made by morons for morons" is "even dumber than *Dumb and Dumber.*"

They Shoot Horses, Don't They?
21 | 24 | 22 | 21

1969 | Directed by Sydney Pollack | With Jane Fonda, Michael Sarrazin, Susannah York | 120 minutes | Rated PG

"Jane Fonda at her world-weariest" provides the glue in this "classic" Depression drama about "desperate" marathon dancers frantically trying to make a buck; though the story's "small" and the sentiments grim, its ensemble cast is "unforgettable" – particularly the "superlative" Gig Young, who copped an Oscar for the role of the slimy emcee.

Thief of Bagdad, The ◗
24 | 22 | 23 | 23

1924 | Directed by Raoul Walsh | With Douglas Fairbanks, Snitz Edwards, Julanne Johnston | 155 minutes | Not Rated

This Arabian Nights fantasy is a "definitive swashbuckler", featuring an "athletic" Fairbanks "at his best" as a charming rogue seeking a princess' hand; one of the most expensive silent movies ever made, it's a "lavish" spectacle with sets by William Cameron Menzies that are "still amazing by today's standards"; in short, it's simply "great."

Thing, The ❶

	OVERALL	ACTING	STORY	PROD.
	23	19	25	19

(aka The Thing from Another World)

1951 | Directed by Christian Nyby | With Kenneth Tobey, Margaret Sheridan | 87 minutes | Not Rated

This "serious" '50s sci-fi suspenser "still holds up" as a "smart" "flying-saucer" shocker about a group of scientists driven to "creepy" extremes in a "claustrophobic, paranoid" encounter with a murderous alien found frozen in the Arctic ice; despite "skimpy" special effects, the "tight script" builds enough "tension" to frighten the "daylights" out of fans, who spurn the "gory remake" – there's nothing like "the real *Thing*."

Thing, The

23 | 19 | 23 | 23

1982 | Directed by John Carpenter | With Kurt Russell, Wilford Brimley, David Clennon | 109 minutes | Rated R

"Chills" abound in Carpenter's "excellent remake of the '51 classic", wherein the Antarctic's most "frigid science outpost" is beset by a "horrible alien" capable of disguising itself in human form; an "imaginative" contribution to the "sci-fi/horror pantheon", it supplies enough "true suspense" to keep the audience "guessing" as the "paranoia" mounts.

Thin Man, The ❶

26 | 25 | 23 | 23

1934 | Directed by W.S. Van Dyke | With William Powell, Myrna Loy, Maureen O'Sullivan | 93 minutes | Not Rated

"Break out the martini glasses": "mystery meets screwball comedy" in this "snazzy" flicker featuring "cool detective" Nick Charles and his "classy wife", Nora, "drinking like fish" and "fluidly" spouting "snappy dialogue" ("double entendre, anyone?") as they investigate a murder; the "suave, sexy fun" is so "cosmopolitan" and "wonderfully evocative of the '30s" that it seems unsporting to point out that the "whodunit" plot is a bit thin.

Thin Red Line, The

19 | 21 | 17 | 22

1998 | Directed by Terrence Malick | With Sean Penn, George Clooney, John Cusack | 170 minutes | Rated R

Malick's "experimental war epic" is made for those who "enjoy thinking about big questions", with Penn exuding "gravity" as a sarge facing the front lines at Guadalcanal with a "star-studded" company of "common soldiers"; "stunning visuals" "attempt to poeticize" the "horror and beauty" of battle and warfare's "emotional effects", though detractors grunt it's "incoherent."

☒ Third Man, The ❶

28 | 28 | 27 | 28

1949 | Directed by Carol Reed | With Joseph Cotten, Alida Valli, Orson Welles, Trevor Howard | 104 minutes | Not Rated

"Oh, that zither!"; this "masterful" piece of "postwar" noir simmers with shadowy "intrigue" as an "alienated" Cotten encounters "romance" and "betrayal" while searching "bombed-out" Vienna for a "mysterious" black marketeer (played by Welles, who makes the most of a "small" role with an "arresting" entrance); graced with "expres-

	OVERALL	ACTING	STORY	PROD.

sionist" lensing, Graham Greene's "clever, dark script" and a "memorable" final fade, it's hailed as "all-around perfect."

Thirteen
21 | 26 | 22 | 19

2003 | Directed by Catherine Hardwicke | With Holly Hunter, Evan Rachel Wood, Nikki Reed | 100 minutes | Rated R

"You won't want to let your kids out of the house" after a gander at this "disturbing" cautionary tale about a pair of "troubled" 13-year-olds who are "harder to control than Mike Tyson"; while critics hiss the "clichéd", "after-school-special" script and "weak ending", far more applaud this "wake-up call" for telling it like it is "without sugar coating."

39 Steps, The ❶
27 | 25 | 27 | 24

1935 | Directed by Alfred Hitchcock | With Robert Donat, Madeleine Carroll | 86 minutes | Not Rated

"You can't go wrong" with this "classic" "British period" Hitchcock nail-biter, a "virtuoso" "thriller diller" wherein an "innocent man wrongly accused" of murder tries to clear his name amid "chase scenes, foreign spy intrigue and romance" (with a woman he winds up "handcuffed" to); sure, the "dated" special effects are on the low-tech side, but this "tense mystery" delivers enough suspense to "keep you on the edge of your seat."

This Boy's Life
21 | 25 | 22 | 21

1993 | Directed by Michael Caton-Jones | With Robert De Niro, Ellen Barkin, Leonardo DiCaprio | 115 minutes | Rated R

Author Tobias Wolff's "autobiographical" sketch of troubled boyhood comes to life via this "poignant" drama starring an "incredible" young DiCaprio, "before he started acting like a movie star"; factor in Barkin's "excellent" portrayal of a struggling mom and a "scary" De Niro (who takes the "evil" stepfather role "to a new low") and there's plenty of "pain and abuse" to digest – a challenge that some find "tough" to handle.

This Is Spinal Tap
26 | 24 | 25 | 22

1984 | Directed by Rob Reiner | With Christopher Guest, Michael McKean, Rob Reiner | 82 minutes | Rated R

"VH1's *Behind the Music*" pales before this "hysterical" "rock mockumentary", an "unbelievably authentic-feeling send-up" of the music industry and superstar "pretensions" that follows an "aging heavy-metal band" taking its act on the road; the "stellar cast" plays an "unforgettable" group of clueless musicians, simulating a "sidesplitting insider's view" that's alarmingly "like the real thing" – except "every single second is funny."

Thomas Crown Affair, The
23 | 23 | 24 | 22

1968 | Directed by Norman Jewison | With Steve McQueen, Faye Dunaway, Paul Burke | 102 minutes | Rated R

This "slick", "grown-up romance" offers a "cat-and-mouse" plot as millionaire McQueen engineers a bank heist for kicks until he encounters Dunaway, a "knockout" insurance sleuth in mad pursuit; their "smoldering", "high-tension" affair is a "stylish" standoff down to the final "checkmate" in that famed chess match, and as for the remake, "do not accept imitations."

Thoroughly Modern Millie
18 | 19 | 16 | 21

1967 | Directed by George Roy Hill | With Julie Andrews, Mary Tyler Moore, Carol Channing | 138 minutes | Rated G

"Roaring '20s" razzle-dazzle makes this musical comedy an "absolute hoot", with "Andrews at her peak" as a big-city rookie trying to land a man; it's played as a "slapstick farce set to song and dance" that alternates new tunes with "flapper-era" standards, and if "silly fluff", all that "jazzy fun" is "entertaining nonetheless."

Thousand Clowns, A ❶
25 | 26 | 24 | 21

1965 | Directed by Fred Coe | With Jason Robards, Barbara Harris, Barry Gordon, Martin Balsam | 118 minutes | Not Rated

A "wonderful" cast including the "brilliant" Robards and Harris (and Oscar-winning Balsam) drives this "touching" but "unusual" comedy about a "nonconformist" whose disdain for the "daily grind" jeopardizes his guardianship of a beloved nephew; based on the Herb Gardner play, it's a "classic" example of the '60s "do-your-own-thing" ethic that nonetheless "has a lot of truth" in it.

Three Coins in the Fountain
21 | 21 | 21 | 22

1954 | Directed by Jean Negulesco | With Clifton Webb, Dorothy McGuire, Jean Peters, Louis Jourdan | 102 minutes | Not Rated

"Rome at its best" is the real "star" of this "good old-fashioned love story" about three husband-hunters making coin-tossing wishes in the Trevi Fountain; it's every 1950s "female's dream" and still "so much emotional fun" that it's easy to ignore the correspondingly overripe 1950s "sentimentality."

Three Days of the Condor
24 | 24 | 25 | 22

1975 | Directed by Sydney Pollack | With Robert Redford, Faye Dunaway, Cliff Robertson | 117 minutes | Rated R

Filmed during the Watergate era, this "paranoid thriller" "still flies" today thanks to Redford's "absorbing" work as an "enigmatic", low-level CIA researcher "caught up in a conspiracy" and dodging an "impersonal assassin"; it's "absorbing", "expertly crafted" stuff, with a "twisty" plot that "puts the intelligence back into, um, intelligence."

Three Faces of Eve, The ✉❶
24 | 27 | 24 | 20

1957 | Directed by Nunnally Johnson | With Joanne Woodward, David Wayne, Lee J. Cobb | 91 minutes | Not Rated

"Incredible" Oscar-winner Woodward delivers a "tour-de-force" turn in this "multiple-personality genre film", an "interesting drama" about a "woman tormented" by triple identities; switching from subdued homemaker to brazen party girl, Woodward does a "stellar" job of "bringing all three characters to life."

300
22 | 20 | 22 | 27

2007 | Directed by Zack Snyder | With Gerard Butler, Lena Headey, Dominic West | 117 minutes | Rated R

"Hunky" Hellenic he-men "wearing next to nothing" duke it out with the Persians at the Battle of Thermopylae in this "cool, stylish" and ultra-"gory" sword 'n' sandal epic adapted from Frank Miller's graphic novel; no question, the "balletic" action sequences and "top-notch" effects are a "treat for the eyes", but a phalanx of fence-sitters fret it's "all bang and no substance."

	OVERALL	ACTING	STORY	PROD.

Three Kings
20 | 21 | 21 | 22

1999 | Directed by David O. Russell | With George Clooney, Mark Wahlberg, Ice Cube | 114 minutes | Rated R

Opening at the close of Desert Storm, this "bold and different" war flick offers a combo of "crackerjack action" and "surprisingly good" acting as "irreverent army guy" Clooney launches a "chase for stolen Kuwaiti gold" that morphs into a "morality tale" midway through; the "insightful" scenario and "creative" visuals make it royally "enjoyable on many levels", though a few are "not impressed" by the "chaotic storyline" and "preachy dialogue."

Three Men and a Baby
16 | 15 | 17 | 16

1987 | Directed by Leonard Nimoy | With Tom Selleck, Steve Guttenberg, Ted Danson | 102 minutes | Rated PG

Like the title implies, "three men care for a baby girl" in this "big-hearted" comedy with a "charming ensemble" cast that makes most viewers "laugh and feel good"; the unamused suggest you "bring insulin" or hold out for the "much better" original French film on which it's based: *Three Men and a Cradle.*

Three Musketeers, The
22 | 22 | 22 | 23

1974 | Directed by Richard Lester | With Oliver Reed, Richard Chamberlain, Michael York | 105 minutes | Rated PG

A "rollicking rendition" of the Dumas classic, this "rousing" "old-fashioned" adventure "stays faithful" to the original tale but spices up the swordplay with "slapstick" and "bawdy" humor as a brave band of swashbucklers defends the queen's honor against that crooked cardinal; the "lavish" 17th-century sets and all-for-one "charm" of the "great cast" ensure its place as the "quintessential" version.

3 Women
25 | 26 | 21 | 23

1977 | Directed by Robert Altman | With Shelley Duvall, Sissy Spacek, Janice Rule | 124 minutes | Rated PG

Altman is "at his trickiest" in this "dreamlike" drama about a downwardly mobile desert-town gal and her "ripe-for-the-picking" roommate who form an "eerie" triangle with a wronged spouse; though the "cryptic narrative" can be "easily dismissed as weird", it's still a "fascinating" exercise in feminine psychology with "super" acting – think "*Single White Female* for the arty set."

Thunderball
22 | 21 | 21 | 23

1965 | Directed by Terence Young | With Sean Connery, Claudine Auger, Adolfo Celi | 130 minutes | Rated PG

Bringing the "basic Bond formula" to the Bahamas, this swimming entry in the superspy series has Connery breaking out his arsenal of "gadgets" and wisecracks against the "very real threat" of stolen nukes held for ransom; the "nonstop action" and "incredible underwater fight sequences" made it a thunderous success in its day, and if now "underappreciated", connoisseurs nevertheless rank it "near the top" of the 007 oeuvre.

Tie Me Up! Tie Me Down! 🄵
20 | 21 | 20 | 20

1990 | Directed by Pedro Almodóvar | With Victoria Abril, Antonio Banderas, Loles Leon | 111 minutes | Rated NC-17

"Madcap" director Almodóvar strikes again in this naughty knotty comedy about a kidnapped, trussed-up B-movie star that's a cross between *"The Collector"* and a soft-core bondage flick; its "sexy", "vivid characters" and "nice" Ennio Morricone soundtrack further spice up a storyline that's already "hysterically funny."

Time After Time
| 23 | 23 | 25 | 21 |

1979 | Directed by Nicholas Meyer | With Malcolm McDowell, Mary Steenburgen, David Warner | 112 minutes | Rated PG
A "clever" bit of "brainy entertainment", this "charming" sci-fi thriller recounts "H.G. Wells chasing Jack the Ripper to modern-day San Francisco" via a "functioning time machine"; a "witty" romp expertly blending "romantic" interludes between McDowell and Steenburgen with "suspenseful" sequencing, it's "well worth seeing" for Warner's "helluva performance" alone.

Time Bandits
| 21 | 19 | 23 | 22 |

1981 | Directed by Terry Gilliam | With John Cleese, Sean Connery, Shelley Duvall | 116 minutes | Rated PG
Gilliam's "warped" "genius" shines in this "bittersweet" time-travel fantasy about the "classic struggle between good and evil", with a sprawling cast that includes a "band of midgets", a "fantastic villain" and some "delightful" cameos; though the FX may be showing their age, there are enough "juicy moments" to justify its "cult-classic" status.

Time Machine, The
| 22 | 17 | 26 | 23 |

1960 | Directed by George Pal | With Rod Taylor, Alan Young, Yvette Mimieux | 103 minutes | Rated G
"Faithful to both the letter and spirit of H.G. Wells' novel", this "grand-daddy of time-travel movies" concerning a 19th-century scientist flabbergasted by the future is "nicely paced" and "fondly remem-bered" for its "thought-provoking storyline" and "good special effects for the era" (which won an Oscar); though the "remake isn't bad", the "much-better" original is the real "gem."

Time to Kill, A
| 18 | 18 | 22 | 19 |

1996 | Directed by Joel Schumacher | With Matthew McConaughey, Sandra Bullock, Samuel L. Jackson | 149 minutes | Rated R
"Very adult" and "suspenseful to the end", this "hard-hitting" Mississippi courtroom drama about racist violence and retribution is a "solid adaptation of the John Grisham novel"; despite the very "Hollywood ending", it's "captivating" thanks to "intelligent" turns from Bullock and McConaughey ("his best role").

Tin Cup
| 18 | 17 | 17 | 18 |

1996 | Directed by Ron Shelton | With Kevin Costner, Rene Russo, Don Johnson, Cheech Marin | 135 minutes | Rated R
Even those with "no interest in golf" admit it's "fun to watch" this "lighthearted" links comedy casting Costner as a "small-time" driving range owner who meets the "glamorous" Russo and signs up for the "PGA tour to win her affections"; foes say *Caddyshack* is better" than this *Bull Durham* wannabe", but praise the "cameos by real-life pros."

Tin Drum, The ✉🅵
| 23 | 23 | 24 | 23 |

1979 | Directed by Volker Schlöndorff | With David Bennett, Mario Adorf, Angela Winkler | 142 minutes | Rated R
A "fine social commentary" about apathy and "life in Nazi Germany", this "disturbing" allegorical drama about a young boy who refuses to

grow old "preserves the spirit of Günter Grass' novel" while charting the rise and fall of the Third Reich; the "well-deserved winner of the Best Foreign Film Oscar", it's a "surreal" work that remains "vivid and haunting" a generation later.

Titanic ✉ | 19 | 16 | 18 | 26 |
1997 | Directed by James Cameron | With Leonardo DiCaprio, Kate Winslet, Billy Zane | 194 minutes | Rated PG-13

Ok, it's "not highbrow stuff", but this "over-the-top spectacular" detailing a "doomed love story" aboard a "doomed ocean liner" thrills with "dazzling" special effects, including a "fantastic" "re-creation of the original ship" and icebergs so real "you can almost touch them"; some torpedo the "shallow" "cardboard characters", "soap opera"-esque script and "weak acting" as "all wet", and whether it's "deserving of its Oscars" – all 11 of them – is still hotly debated.

To Be or Not to Be ◑ | 24 | 24 | 25 | 23 |
1942 | Directed by Ernst Lubitsch | With Carole Lombard, Jack Benny, Robert Stack | 99 minutes | Not Rated

"Life in Nazi-occupied Europe" becomes "exhilarating comedy" in this "funny but poignant" war story, an "oft-overlooked gem" via the ever "clever" Ernst Lubitsch; playing married actors, Benny and Lombard supply "barrels of laughs" – particularly when Jack "does to Shakespeare what the Germans are doing to Poland."

To Catch a Thief | 25 | 25 | 24 | 25 |
1955 | Directed by Alfred Hitchcock | With Grace Kelly, Cary Grant, Jesse Royce Landis | 106 minutes | Not Rated

"Slick, sophisticated and oh-so-cool", this romantic thriller may be "Hitchcock lite", but Grant and Kelly provide plenty of "dazzle" in an amusing trifle about a cat burglar prowling the south of France; maybe the "plot is secondary" to the "enjoyable scenery" and "fab clothes", but there's snappy patter aplenty, notably Grace's classic picnic query "would you prefer a leg or a breast?"

To Die For | 18 | 21 | 19 | 18 |
1995 | Directed by Gus Van Sant | With Nicole Kidman, Matt Dillon, Joaquin Phoenix | 106 minutes | Rated R

A "true tabloid story" becomes "cuttingly observed satire" in this drama about "America's obsession with fame", a "wicked black comedy" due to "Buck Henry's brilliant script" and Van Sant's "incisive" direction; in her "most original role", Kidman "positively shines" as an "ambitious" TV weathergirl "trying to get ahead in her job and out of her marriage" – many say her performance alone is the "reason to see it."

To Have and Have Not ◐ | 26 | 27 | 24 | 24 |
1944 | Directed by Howard Hawks | With Humphrey Bogart, Lauren Bacall, Walter Brennan | 100 minutes | Not Rated

Bacall (in her screen debut) teams with future real-life hubby Bogart to "define star chemistry" in this dramatization of the Hemingway novel about WWII resistance runners; Martinique supplies a sultry backdrop for the two stars to "smolder", especially when Lauren "steams up the screen" with her legendary question "you know how to whistle, don't you?"

	OVERALL	ACTING	STORY	PROD.

☑ To Kill a Mockingbird ✉◐   **29 | 29 | 29 | 26**

1962 | Directed by Robert Mulligan | With Gregory Peck, Mary Badham, Robert Duvall | 129 minutes | Not Rated

"After all these years", this Southern courtroom drama about racism and prejudice "told from the point of view of a young girl" "still packs the same emotional punch"; kudos go to Oscar-winning screenwriter Horton Foote "for not having strayed" from Harper Lee's "original text", and to an "im-peck-able" Peck at his "peak" as the "dad we wish we had"; in short, "Hollywood got this one right."

To Live and Die in L.A.   **20 | 21 | 21 | 20**

1985 | Directed by William Friedkin | With William L. Petersen, Willem Dafoe, John Pankow | 116 minutes | Rated R

With its "bleak" SoCal setting, "morally devoid" characters and atmospheric Wang Chung soundtrack, this "taut", "violent" crime thriller earns a slot in the "quintessential '80s" canon with its "noir"-ish tale of a cop crusading against a counterfeiter; while "no major classic", it's certainly worth fast-forwarding to that "amazing car chase."

Tombstone   **21 | 22 | 21 | 21**

1993 | Directed by George P. Cosmatos | With Kurt Russell, Val Kilmer, Sam Elliott | 130 minutes | Rated R

More than an ok rendition of the "O.K. Corral story", this "slick retelling" brings legends Wyatt Earp and Doc Holliday up to date with good old "modern-day violence"; starring a pistol-packing Russell and "fun-to-watch" Kilmer, it's a "worthy" enough stab at pure "entertainment."

Tom Jones ✉   **25 | 24 | 24 | 25**

1963 | Directed by Tony Richardson | With Albert Finney, Susannah York, Hugh Griffith | 121 minutes | Not Rated

"Richly crafted and craftily acted" – with four Oscars to prove it – this hilariously "bawdy" "period piece par excellence" might be set in 18th-century England but moodwise is more like a "snapshot of the Swinging '60s"; devotees are ever smitten with its "clever script", "lively direction" and Finney's "lusty" title turn, while gourmands eat up that "sexy food-seduction scene."

Tommy   **16 | 14 | 16 | 20**

1975 | Directed by Ken Russell | With Roger Daltrey, Ann-Margret, Oliver Reed, Elton John | 111 minutes | Rated PG

The Who's "seminal rock opera" goes Hollywood in this "over-the-top feast for the senses" that divides voters: ravers revel in the "great score", "Tina Turner as the Acid Queen" and that "scene with Ann-Margret and the baked beans", but bashers bawl it's a "disservice to both musicals and rock 'n' roll."

Tomorrow Never Dies   **20 | 20 | 17 | 21**

1997 | Directed by Roger Spottiswoode | With Pierce Brosnan, Jonathan Pryce, Michelle Yeoh | 119 minutes | Rated PG-13

". . . and neither does James" joke 007 junkies of the juggernaut's 18th entry, wherein "Brosnan fills Connery's" custom-made shoes and "brings back" the secret agent's "cruel streak"; the "thoughtful plot" (something about a mad "media magnate" bent on starting WWIII) is buoyed by "high-tech special effects", though Bond-girl watchers say the picture belongs to the "fabulous" Yeoh.

	OVERALL	ACTING	STORY	PROD.

Tootsie
25 | 27 | 24 | 23

1982 | Directed by Sydney Pollack | With Dustin Hoffman, Jessica Lange, Bill Murray, Teri Garr | 119 minutes | Rated PG

"Cross-dressing doesn't get much better" than this "brilliantly funny" comedy about a long-"struggling actor" who finally achieves success – "as an actress"; though Hoffman might be "one ugly" broad, his "sublime", "think-out-of-the-box" performance mixing "humor with humanity" is beautiful, while a "slick" but "unpredictable script" and an "outstanding" supporting cast make this one a "keeper, not a renter."

☑ Top Gun
22 | 18 | 20 | 24

1986 | Directed by Tony Scott | With Tom Cruise, Kelly McGillis, Val Kilmer | 110 minutes | Rated PG

"Sexy fighter pilots" populate this "absolutely irresistible" "'80s action icon", a roiling mix of "noise", romance and "aerial maneuvers"; Cruise "looks great in uniform" and that "volleyball scene" sure is "hot", but foes dis the "hokey" plot and "intermittent acting" and can't fathom why it's so "inexplicably popular."

☑ Top Hat ◐
27 | 23 | 21 | 26

1935 | Directed by Mark Sandrich | With Fred Astaire, Ginger Rogers, Edward Everett Horton | 101 minutes | Not Rated

"Heaven, I'm in heaven" sigh fans of this "classic '30s musical" spotlighting the big-city charms of a "debonair Astaire" opposite a "feather"-gowned Rogers; sure, there's an "all-hit Irving Berlin score", "amazing production numbers" and a "witty French farce of a script", but in the end, it's "Fred and Ginger dancing cheek-to-cheek" that catapults it to "sublime"-ville.

Topkapi
24 | 22 | 25 | 21

1964 | Directed by Jules Dassin | With Melina Mercouri, Peter Ustinov | 119 minutes | Not Rated

Director "Dassin's '60s caper holds up well", managing to "avoid clichés the same way" its jewel-thief cast "avoid traps" as they engineer a heist in Istanbul; owing to a "clever script" and some "beautifully drawn characters" (like the "sophisticated" Mercouri and "priceless", "Oscar-winning" Ustinov), this "taut" thriller/comedy is reminiscent of an erstwhile *Mission: Impossible.*

Topper ◑
20 | 21 | 21 | 19

1937 | Directed by Norman Z. McLeod | With Roland Young, Constance Bennett, Cary Grant | 97 minutes | Not Rated

Grant and Bennett "never miss a beat" in this "smart" romantic comedy about a pair of martini-swilling, madcap ghosts who must do a good deed to go to heaven; expect lots of laughs when the "delightful" phantoms select uptight banker Cosmo Topper as the beneficiary of their largesse in this "lighthearted" bit of "whimsy."

Topsy-Turvy
23 | 25 | 23 | 26

1999 | Directed by Mike Leigh | With Jim Broadbent, Allan Corduner | 160 minutes | Rated R

This "finely observed story about the stormy partnership of Gilbert and Sullivan" provides a "window into the Victorian age" as well as a "fascinating" glimpse into the "creative process" via a subplot about the first staging of *The Mikado*; "superb" acting (with an especially "grand Broadbent") and a "gorgeous production" make it a "joy to watch" for most, though a few yawn "boring."

Tora! Tora! Tora!
23 | 19 | 25 | 24

1970 | Directed by Richard Fleischer, Kinji Fukasaku, Toshio Masuda | With Martin Balsam, Jason Robards | 144 minutes | Rated G

Surveyors split on this "intricate" war chronicle of the "Japanese attack on Pearl Harbor": defenders say this "ultimate docudrama" is "well done historically", citing its "bilingual plotlines" and over-the-top "stunning" special effects, but curmudgeons counter it's a "comic-book" look at the tragedy.

Torch Song Trilogy
23 | 25 | 25 | 21

1988 | Directed by Paul Bogart | With Harvey Fierstein, Matthew Broderick, Anne Bancroft | 120 minutes | Rated R

A "faithful adaptation" of Fierstein's very "original" stage play, this "moving" account of a gay female impersonator's "need for family" was "very advanced for its time" and "still very entertaining" today; though a few feel it "doesn't translate well to the screen", there are kudos for the "boyish" Broderick and Bancroft's "outstanding" turn as an "archetypical Jewish mother."

Torn Curtain
23 | 24 | 23 | 22

1966 | Directed by Alfred Hitchcock | With Paul Newman, Julie Andrews | 128 minutes | Rated PG

This "compelling" Cold War spy thriller via Alfred Hitchcock concerns an American physicist who defects to East Germany, bent on espionage; while it "isn't the greatest Newman or Andrews" effort, it still "has is moments", notably the 'silent murder' sequence and Lila Kedrova's "compelling" supporting role as a down-and-out countess.

To Sir, With Love
22 | 23 | 24 | 20

1967 | Directed by James Clavell | With Sidney Poitier, Judy Geeson, Christian Roberts | 105 minutes | Not Rated

The "always-excellent" Poitier stars in this "nice little piece of '60s" nostalgia as a "London high school teacher" passing on life lessons to "inner-city punks"; "sweet" and "timeless", it deals with "still-relevant" issues – "race, family conflicts, respect for authority" – in a "genuinely moving" fashion, and Lulu's smashing rendition of the title song "makes the movie."

Total Recall
18 | 14 | 21 | 22

1990 | Directed by Paul Verhoeven | With Arnold Schwarzenegger, Rachel Ticotin, Sharon Stone | 113 minutes | Rated R

"One of Ah-nuld's better" efforts may be this "exciting sci-fi adventure" flick, one of those "is-it-all-a-dream" stories about a secret agent implanted with someone else's memory chip; filmed "just before the age of digital effects" dawned, this "visual tour de force" inspires diverse reactions – "original" vs. "mediocre" – though pacifists are peeved by all that "gratuitous violence."

Touch of Class, A ✉
22 | 24 | 20 | 20

1973 | Directed by Melvin Frank | With George Segal, Glenda Jackson, Paul Sorvino | 106 minutes | Rated PG

The "sublime" Jackson snagged her second Oscar for lending a "touch of magic" to this "funny yet thoughtful" depiction of extramarital bliss between a "sexy" divorcée and a "loosey-goosey" businessman; the "witty" repartee and "classy" treatment of "adult" issues "appeals to both genders", plus the picture also acts as a useful "guide to why you shouldn't cheat on your spouse."

Touch of Evil ◑ | 26 | 24 | 25 | 26 |

1958 | Directed by Orson Welles | With Charlton Heston, Janet Leigh, Orson Welles | 95 minutes | Rated PG-13

"Proof that Welles was more than a one-hit wonder", this "rococo" "pinnacle of film noir" stars the director as a "bloated" Texas border town cop feuding with his south-of-the-border counterpart (Heston in "Mexican blackface"); among its many memorable touches are the "sweeping" opening sequence and the "effortless scene-stealing" by Marlene Dietrich, who has the picture's best line: "lay off the candy bars"; P.S. the "restored version" is "much better" than the original release.

Towering Inferno, The | 18 | 17 | 18 | 22 |

1974 | Directed by John Guillermin, Irwin Allen | With Steve McQueen, Paul Newman, William Holden | 165 minutes | Rated PG

"Make sure you know where all the exits are" before settling into this "big, bad '70s disaster" flick starring a very tall sky-scraper, an out-of-control fire and a "rogues' gallery of great actors"; although the "passable" "special effects were top-drawer for its time", cynical sorts snort it's more of a "made-for-TV movie" by modern standards.

☑ Toy Story | 27 | - | 25 | 28 |

1995 | Directed by John Lasseter | Animated | 81 minutes | Rated G

Ushering in a "new era of animation" with "breakthrough" computer-generated effects, this Pixar-produced "instant classic" is a bona fide "technical wonder"; its "humorous" storyline, "lovable characters" and the "great concept" of walking, talking toys add up to a picture that's not only "equally entertaining for adults and kids" but also "deserving of the franchise it started."

Toy Story 2 | 26 | - | 24 | 28 |

1999 | Directed by John Lasseter, Ash Brannon, Lee Unkrich | Animated | 92 minutes | Rated G

"Not just another wind-up sequel", this "worthy successor" to "one of the best animated films" ever is a "marvel" in its own right, this time following the misadventures of Woody, a toy cowboy who's been "stolen by a greedy collector to be sold to the highest bidder"; Pixar's "wonderfully creative" CGI renderings work their usual magic so well that parents report "you almost don't mind watching it the 8,000 times that your kids request."

Trading Places | 23 | 22 | 23 | 20 |

1983 | Directed by John Landis | With Dan Aykroyd, Eddie Murphy, Jamie Lee Curtis | 118 minutes | Rated R

This "hysterical" treatment of the "classic" "rags-to-riches" "switcheroo" has "pauper" Murphy turned into "prince" Aykroyd and vice-versa; "quickly paced and never boring", it's memorable for "early vintage" Eddie moments, some "funny" business from Dan and the spectacle of Jamie Lee's "exposed breasts."

| | OVERALL | ACTING | STORY | PROD. |

Traffic ✉
23 | 24 | 23 | 25
2000 | Directed by Steven Soderbergh | With Michael Douglas, Benicio Del Toro, Catherine Zeta-Jones | 147 minutes | Rated R

Maybe "more realistic than you want", this "eye-opening portrait of the drug wars" is "poignant, intelligent" and "troubling", using "multiple storylines" to create a "stunning" hybrid of "thriller" and "cautionary tale"; the "amazing use of color", "documentary-like handheld" camerawork and Del Toro's deft, Oscar-winning turn all get the green light, though the highest praise is reserved for its "absolutely brilliant" director.

Training Day ✉
20 | 27 | 19 | 22
2001 | Directed by Antoine Fuqua | With Denzel Washington, Ethan Hawke, Scott Glenn, Tom Berenger | 120 minutes | Rated R

"Denzel shows his scary side" as a "profoundly bad" LA cop with "charisma" in his Oscar-winning role as a detective who has "one day to teach the ropes" to a "rookie" (played by a "holding-his-own" Hawke); the "twisting" plot "grabs you from the very beginning" and takes you on one "wild ride."

Trainspotting
22 | 22 | 20 | 22
1996 | Directed by Danny Boyle | With Ewan McGregor, Ewen Bremner, Robert Carlyle | 94 minutes | Rated R

"Giddy and witty" but also "harrowing and intense", this "graphic" British drama depicting the "daily life of drug addicts" has a "kinetic rawness" about it that "gets right under your skin"; while "not for everyone", its "quirky" cinematography and "outstanding" '80s pop score make for "reality-check" viewing, but bring an "interpreter" – the "Scottish accents are thick."

TransAmerica
24 | 28 | 23 | 22
2005 | Directed by Duncan Tucker | With Felicity Huffman, Kevin Zegers, Fionnula Flanagan | 103 minutes | Rated R

Huffman's "fearless", "dead-on" portrayal of an "uptight" male-to-female transsexual who "learns she has a son" provides this "original" gender-bender dramedy with plenty of "hilarious", "seat-squirming" moments mixed with "compelling", "raw emotion"; ok, it may "drag" in places, but at least its pro-"acceptance" message "pulls no punches."

⚡ Treasure of the Sierra Madre, The ✉◑
27 | 27 | 26 | 24
1948 | Directed by John Huston | With Humphrey Bogart, Walter Huston, Tim Holt | 126 minutes | Not Rated

"Human nature poisoned by greed" is the theme of this "old-fashioned" "treasure hunt", a "wonderful adventure" that won Oscars for the father-and-son Hustons; Bogart exudes "masculine energy" showing "what gold will do to a man" in an "unforgettably powerful" performance that devolves into "paranoia" – and as for the "stunning" black-and-white photography, purists say "we don't need no stinkin' color."

Triplets of Belleville, The ▣
24 | - | 23 | 26
2003 | Directed by Sylvain Chomet | Animated | 80 minutes | Rated PG-13

"Trippy and funny in a way that American animation isn't", this "art house" French cartoon sure "ain't Disney" with its "surreal" plot, "stylized" illustration and "nearly dialogue-free" soundtrack; having something to do with a kidnapped bicyclist rescued by his "grandmère", an "amazing" dog and the "wacky" Triplets of Belleville, it's both "innovative" and "offbeat", and probably more "for adults" than small fry.

Trip to Bountiful, The ✉ | 24 | 26 | 23 | 21

1985 | Directed by Peter Masterson | With Geraldine Page, John Heard, Carlin Glynn, Rebecca De Mornay | 108 minutes | Rated PG

An "elderly lady's wish" to relive her past by visiting her Texas hometown frames this "poignant" stage-to-screen adaptation, a journey through "memory and reality" featuring Page in an "exquisite", Oscar-grabbing turn; the "parable"-esque plot manages to strike "spiritual" chords, but it's the heroine's "suffocating situation" – an "all too common" dilemma for those "in their later years" – that will "haunt" you.

Triumph of the Will ◐🅵 | 27 | - | 17 | 27

1935 | Directed by Leni Riefenstahl | Documentary | 114 minutes | Not Rated

"Perhaps the most powerful (and immoral) documentary" ever made, this "Leni Riefenstahl masterpiece" was commissioned to honor Germany's 1934 National Socialist Party Congress and the metaphorical "enthronement of Hitler"; the "superb" camerawork leads reluctant admirers to admit this "artful" propaganda piece is indeed a "triumph of filmmaking", if not subject matter.

Tron | 18 | 14 | 18 | 22

1982 | Directed by Steven Lisberger | With Jeff Bridges, Bruce Boxleitner, David Warner | 96 minutes | Rated PG

Wired types tout this "underappreciated forerunner to today's special-effects" extravaganzas by dubbing it the "first real geek movie", owing to a storyline that posits what could happen "if you got sucked into your Nintendo"; ok, it could be a tad "dated" now, but it was the "coolest thing since sliced bread when it came out."

Troy | 19 | 19 | 20 | 25

2004 | Directed by Wolfgang Petersen | With Brad Pitt, Orlando Bloom, Eric Bana | 163 minutes | Rated R

Homer's *Iliad* gets the "Hollywood treatment" in this "genuine epic" featuring lots of "oiled", "well-tanned" dudes in "miniskirts" engaged in battles that bear distinct "similarities to WWF wrestling"; wags say Brad's performance is the "only thing more wooden than the Trojan horse" ("too much buff, not enough substance"), but there's applause for the "action-packed" script and "excellent production values."

True Grit ✉ | 22 | 23 | 21 | 22

1969 | Directed by Henry Hathaway | With John Wayne, Glen Campbell, Kim Darby | 128 minutes | Rated G

"Another Western for your library", this "classic" oater is made "especially for Wayne fans" because the Duke took home his first (and only) Oscar here; otherwise, it's standard stuff about a vengeful lawman, though early-in-their-career performances by Dennis Hopper and Robert Duvall keep things lively.

True Lies | 19 | 16 | 20 | 22

1994 | Directed by James Cameron | With Arnold Schwarzenegger, Jamie Lee Curtis | 144 minutes | Rated R

"Arnold is Bond, James Bond" in this "tongue-in-cheek" spy flicker that's a "wonderful combo" of "comedy, action and intrigue"; as his "frumpy wife" turned "drop-dead gorgeous" siren, Jamie Lee is "smoking", while Tom Arnold's a "gas" as the "not-so-super secret-agent sidekick"; throw in "lots of explosions and weapons" and you've got a true "blockbuster" "blastfest."

True Romance
24 | 23 | 24 | 22

1993 | Directed by Tony Scott | With Christian Slater, Patricia Arquette, Dennis Hopper, Christopher Walken | 120 minutes | Rated R
Brace yourself for some "big-time gore" in this "ultraviolent" "true cult classic" about newlyweds on the run, scripted by a "pre–*Pulp Fiction* Quentin Tarantino" and featuring an "all-star" ensemble (including bits by Brad Pitt, Samuel L. Jackson and James Gandolfini "when they were little known"); sticklers note it "steals heartily from *Badlands*", but ultimately, it's "kinetic", "edgy", "weird" and just plain "cool"; best scene: the "showdown between Hopper and Walken."

Truman Show, The
21 | 22 | 23 | 22

1998 | Directed by Peter Weir | With Jim Carrey, Laura Linney, Ed Harris | 103 minutes | Rated PG
This "original", "thought-provoking" fantasy/comedy offers a "departure" for Carrey, who's "unusually restrained" (i.e. "doesn't act like a moron") in the role of an unwitting star of a 24/7 reality TV show set in a "phony world"; though some lookers find "little content" among all the "hype", intellectuals enthuse that this "Big Brother"–ish allegory leaves you "questioning what reality is."

Truth or Dare
15 | - | 14 | 17

1991 | Directed by Alek Keshishian | Documentary | With Madonna | 118 minutes | Rated R
"Ardent Madonna fanatics" say this "behind-the-scenes" documentary of her 1990 tour, a "warts-and-all" portrayal of the superstar "not striking a pose", is "better than it has any right to be"; but knockers claim this "self-absorbed" "vanity project" is just "mugging for the camera", save for the cameo by Warren Beatty, who "looks appropriately embarrassed as her latest boy toy"; most amusing scene: "talking to Daddy on the phone."

Tucker: The Man and His Dream
20 | 21 | 23 | 21

1988 | Directed by Francis Ford Coppola | With Jeff Bridges, Joan Allen, Martin Landau | 110 minutes | Rated PG
For a "revealing look beneath the hood of the American auto industry", this "colorful", "stylish" film features a "terrific" Bridges in the sort of "true-ish story" of a "visionary '40s car maker and his sad defeat" at the hands of competitors and politicians; Coppola-ficionados say this "underrated" film "deserves more notice."

Turning Point, The
23 | 25 | 22 | 23

1977 | Directed by Herbert Ross | With Shirley MacLaine, Anne Bancroft, Mikhail Baryshnikov | 119 minutes | Rated PG
Ascend to "chick-flick heaven" via this "moving" drama that sets the oft-told story of "women choosing between marriage and a career" in a "world-renowned ballet company"; as "longtime friends who took different paths" in life, Bancroft and MacLaine are "brilliant" (especially during that climactic catfight at Lincoln Center), though balletomanes only have eyes for "Baryshnikov's spectacular dance scenes."

☑ 12 Angry Men ◑
28 | 28 | 27 | 23

1957 | Directed by Sidney Lumet | With Henry Fonda, Martin Balsam, Lee J. Cobb, E.G. Marshall | 96 minutes | Not Rated

"Human nature at its best and worst" is on display in this "brilliant courtroom drama" depicting the "hidden agendas" of jurors deciding the fate of a murder defendant; thanks to its "taut" script and an "unforgettable Fonda", this "study of American democracy" is alternately "suspenseful and compelling."

Twelve Monkeys
22 | 23 | 24 | 23

1995 | Directed by Terry Gilliam | With Bruce Willis, Madeleine Stowe, Brad Pitt | 129 minutes | Rated R

Gilliam's "master-of-the-bizarre" status is reinforced by this "complex", "super-ingenious" time-travel tale about the "release of a deadly virus" followed by a "post-apocalyptic" attempt to "save the world"; the sets are "dazzling", Brad 'n' Bruce prove they can "actually act" and if the "*Terminator*-meets-*Brazil*" sci-fi storyline is "confusing", it's "wonderfully" so.

Twelve O'Clock High ◑
26 | 25 | 26 | 23

1949 | Directed by Henry King | With Gregory Peck, Hugh Marlowe, Dean Jagger | 132 minutes | Not Rated

"Peck is marvelous" as a WWII Brigadier General "placing terrible pressure on young American pilots" in this "accurate" depiction of the "burdens of command" and the "human side of war"; a "perfect screenplay" "rooted in historical reality" "manipulates the tension" right up to the compelling climax.

28 Days Later
18 | 17 | 19 | 18

2002 | Directed by Danny Boyle | With Cillian Murphy, Naomie Harris | 113 minutes | Rated R

"Modern-day horror" gets some "low-budget twists" in this "seriously scary" British import that "reinvents the zombie flick for the new millennium" in its story of a "viral disaster" that threatens civilization; while surveyors split on its digital video cinematography ("cool and grainy" versus "looks like it was shot with a bad camcorder"), most agree that the finale "wimps out" – although the DVD includes a number of "alternate endings."

25th Hour
21 | 25 | 20 | 21

2002 | Directed by Spike Lee | With Edward Norton, Philip Seymour Hoffman, Barry Pepper | 135 minutes | Rated R

A drug dealer "with one day left before prison turns to his friends for comfort" in this "captivating film that's even more poignant given its tribute to post-9/11 NYC"; it's "not your typical Spike Lee, but still one of his best" thanks to "superb ensemble acting"; still, some say "it seemed like it was 25 hours long."

21 Grams
22 | 27 | 21 | 21

2003 | Directed by Alejandro González Iñárritu | With Sean Penn, Naomi Watts, Benicio Del Toro | 124 minutes | Rated R

"Not an easy watch", this "disturbing take on love and loss" details the lives of three people who meet as the result of a deadly accident; its "nonlinear storyline" told via "flashbacks and flashforwards" (à la "*Memento*" and "*Pulp Fiction*") might be "intriguing" to some and "confusing" to others, but the "stellar" ensemble supplies enough "brain candy" to make for "compelling" viewing; in sum, be ready for an "emotionally draining downer" that's "moving, intelligent" and guaranteed to "keep you guessing."

20,000 Leagues Under the Sea

OVERALL	ACTING	STORY	PROD.
22	18	25	23

1954 | Directed by Richard Fleischer | With Kirk Douglas, James Mason, Peter Lorre | 127 minutes | Rated G

"Disney's live-action adaptation of the Jules Verne classic" is a "fabulous" undersea adventure starring a "singing", "tight shorts"–wearing Douglas as the heroic 19th-century seafarer who battles both Captain Nemo and a "scary giant squid" who "should have received an Oscar"; even though the special effects look "cheesy" today, overall it's a "real old-fashioned hoot."

Twins

15	15	15	15

1988 | Directed by Ivan Reitman | With Arnold Schwarzenegger, Danny DeVito, Kelly Preston | 105 minutes | Rated PG

For the ultimate "mismatch made in heaven", try this "far-fetched" laughfest about test-tube twins "separated at birth" and later reunited for "wacky" escapades; while the stars are "likable" enough and display relatively "good chemistry", for most this "guilty pleasure" lies somewhere between "ridiculous" and "dopey."

Twister

15	14	14	22

1996 | Directed by Jan de Bont | With Helen Hunt, Bill Paxton, Cary Elwes, Jami Gertz | 114 minutes | Rated PG-13

"Mother nature" runs amok in this "far-fetched disaster movie" about Midwestern meteorologists tracking tornados; though the "fancy computer effects" make the "awesome" twisters "look so real", the "sleepwalking" actors and "easily forgettable" story with "no concern for logic" lead some to snore "major bore."

Two for the Road

24	27	24	24

1967 | Directed by Stanley Donen | With Albert Finney, Audrey Hepburn | 111 minutes | Not Rated

"Love isn't always easy" is the message of this "bittersweet travelogue about the ups and downs of a married couple" that "jumps back and forth in time" as they "find, lose and rekindle" their relationship; Audrey's at her "most charming" and "marvelous together" with Finney amid all that "unmatched European scenery"; meanwhile, the "mesmerizing, melodious" Mancini music "sustains the mood."

☑ 2001: A Space Odyssey

26	19	24	27

1968 | Directed by Stanley Kubrick | With Keir Dullea, Gary Lockwood, William Sylvester | 139 minutes | Rated G

The "*Citizen Kane* of science-fiction films", this "era-defining" Kubrick interpretation of an Arthur C. Clarke story "changed movies forever" with its "haunting view" of a future world of "machine domination"; sure, some modernists find it "slow" and "ponderous", but even those who have "no clue what it all means" say this "coldly magnificent" epic is "undeniably influential" – and add "you'll never hear Strauss' 'Blue Danube Waltz' the same way again"; P.S. "don't bother trying to figure out the ending."

	OVERALL	ACTING	STORY	PROD.

2010

16 | 16 | 17 | 20

1984 | Directed by Peter Hyams | With Roy Scheider, John Lithgow, Helen Mirren, Bob Balaban | 114 minutes | Rated PG

"High-quality special effects" make this sequel to *2001* "relatively worthwhile", not to mention "less confusing", since a "more linear plot" "helps to explain the original storyline"; but foes insist it's "not in the same league at all", merely a "workmanlike" effort with "no transcendence", though admitting it "had an awful lot to live up to."

Two Weeks Notice

16 | 18 | 16 | 17

2002 | Directed by Marc Lawrence | With Sandra Bullock, Hugh Grant | 101 minutes | Rated PG-13

A "playboy" real estate tycoon and a "do-gooder" lawyer meet cute in this "soggy" romantic comedy, a "predictable" "bit of fluff" with an "obvious ending" and "only 10 minutes' worth of laughs"; further faults include a "flimsy script" and "no sense of true chemistry" between the otherwise "likable" leads – "no one in the real world behaves like this."

Two Women ✉️◐🅵

25 | 28 | 25 | 24

1961 | Directed by Vittorio De Sica | With Sophia Loren, Eleanora Brown, Raf Vallone | 99 minutes | Not Rated

The "horror of war" from a "woman's viewpoint" is delineated in this "heartbreaking" Italian drama where a "protective mother and her daughter" bond after being "brutally raped" by a gang of soldiers; best remembered for Sophia's "riveting" performance, it's a "very emotional" film that's "seldom seen these days."

U-571

17 | 17 | 19 | 21

2000 | Directed by Jonathan Mostow | With Matthew McConaughey, Bill Paxton, Harvey Keitel | 116 minutes | Rated PG-13

This "tense" World War II "submarine flick" brings out plenty of "claustrophobia" in its story of a tightly quartered American crew duking it out with a German U-boat under high seas; while it's "no *Das Boot*" (given "so-so acting" and a "could-have-been-better" storyline "full of obvious holes"), it's still a "rousing", bona fide guy movie.

Umbrellas of Cherbourg, The 🅵

24 | 22 | 21 | 26

1964 | Directed by Jacques Demy | With Catherine Deneuve, Nino Castelnuovo | 87 minutes | Not Rated

Ultra-"bright Technicolor" and "captivating" music from Michel Legrand provide the uplift in this "sad story" of love in vain, an diosyncratic French bonbon that's "entirely sung" (a "risky" proposition that ultimately "works"); starring a "fetching young Deneuve", it has the "courage" to turn a potentially "cheesy" premise into "inspiring" filmmaking.

Unbearable Lightness of Being, The

21 | 24 | 21 | 21

1988 | Directed by Philip Kaufman | With Daniel Day-Lewis, Juliette Binoche, Lena Olin | 171 minutes | Rated R

"Romance amid revolution" is the theme of this erudite picture about the "erotic" misadventures of a young Czech surgeon swept up in the '68 Russian invasion of Prague; while the light-headed like the "hottie" cast's "compelling" work, cynics sneer this "yawner" "leaves a lot to be desired" and suggest the title be cut to just plain *Unbearable.*

| | OVERALL | ACTING | STORY | PROD. |

Unbreakable
16 | 19 | 17 | 19

2000 | Directed by M. Night Shyamalan | With Bruce Willis, Samuel L. Jackson, Robin Wright Penn | 107 minutes | Rated PG-13

Ok, it's "hard to live up to *The Sixth Sense*", but this solid follow-up from the Shyamalan/Willis team "keeps you wondering all the time" with its "intriguing" story of a "man struggling with immortality"; though surveyors split on the end result (a "noble failure" vs. "terribly underrated"), holdouts insist it "warrants more than one viewing" to be fully appreciated.

Uncle Buck
17 | 18 | 17 | 17

1989 | Directed by John Hughes | With John Candy, Amy Madigan, Jean Louisa Kelly | 100 minutes | Rated PG

"Among John Candy's best", most "lovable" roles is his heavy-duty turn as a "derelict turned babysitter" in this lightweight comedy; while the "movie itself is just ok", the "funny dialogue" and heroic oafishness of the lead prevail – and an appearance by a pre-*Home Alone* Macaulay Culkin adds to its family appeal.

Under Siege
15 | 11 | 14 | 16

1992 | Directed by Andrew Davis | With Steven Seagal, Tommy Lee Jones, Gary Busey | 102 minutes | Rated R

Think "*Die Hard* on a battleship" to get the gist of this "graphically violent" Seagal vehicle where he "kicks some serious ass" to keep his "reputation afloat"; maybe the plot about lunatic villains thieving nukes is "moronic", but at least the "kill-first-ask-questions-later" sensibility is "entertainingly dumb."

Under the Tuscan Sun
19 | 20 | 18 | 22

2003 | Directed by Audrey Wells | With Diane Lane, Sandra Oh, Raoul Bova | 113 minutes | Rated PG-13

A newly divorced woman buys a house in "picturesque Tuscany" to start her life anew and "find herself" in this "coming-into-bloom" picture, a "feel-good" chick flick worth seeing for Lane's "warm, genuine performance" alone; ok, "it isn't *Enchanted April*" and there's "not much storyline", but it's still "sweet and fun."

Unfaithful
21 | 24 | 20 | 20

2002 | Directed by Adrian Lyne | With Diane Lane, Richard Gere, Olivier Martinez | 124 minutes | Rated R

Diane Lane is "spectacular" and "so convincing" as a modern housewife "torn between guilt and thrills as she embarks on an affair" with a "hot" stranger, and Richard Gere delivers the "most mature, nuanced performance of his career" as the "cuckold" in this "unexpectedly intense film" that's "disturbing in its credibility"; "now if only they'd found a better plot" and a less "lame" ending.

Unfinished Life, An
20 | 22 | 20 | 21

2005 | Directed by Lasse Hallström | With Robert Redford, Jennifer Lopez, Morgan Freeman | 107 minutes | Rated PG-13

"Strong" characters hold together this "moving" story of a rancher and his kin, struggling with "forgiveness" following a series of tragedies; ok, the script may be a bit "thin" and J. Lo's acting rather "stilted", but "great cinematography" and "good jobs" by the "believable" Freeman and "still-hot" Redford "save the movie."

| | OVERALL | ACTING | STORY | PROD. |

Unforgiven ✉   `26` `26` `24` `25`

1992 | Directed by Clint Eastwood | With Clint Eastwood, Gene Hackman, Morgan Freeman | 131 minutes | Rated R

"Clint directs, Clint scores, Clint wins" a Best Picture statuette with this "grim" "anti-Western" that manages to "revise every convention and cliché of the genre" with a "superb script" and cast of "unforgivable", "unforgettable" characters; indeed, it's so "powerful" and "dark", you'll find "no white hats here."

United 93   `25` `23` `25` `25`

2006 | Directed by Paul Greengrass | With Christian Clemenson, Trish Gates, David Alan Basche | 111 minutes | Rated R

A "nightmarish subject" – the 9/11 hijacking of United flight 93 – is "handled with sensitivity" in this tribute to "spontaneous heroism" that's always "riveting" even though "you know the terrible outcome"; admittedly "tough to watch", it's "never overwrought", shot in a "real-time", "documentary" style and enacted by a "largely unknown cast" (along with "people who play themselves"); the end result is by turns "horrifying", "heartbreaking" and "exhausting."

Unmarried Woman, An   `20` `25` `21` `19`

1978 | Directed by Paul Mazursky | With Jill Clayburgh, Alan Bates, Michael Murphy | 130 minutes | Rated R

This "very-much-of-its-time" portrait of a "New Yorkey" divorcée "in transition" offers a "thoughtful", "emotional" examination of a '70s "woman's lib"–style romance; the picture broke "new ground" when originally released, thanks to the "excellent" Clayburgh as the recently "single" gal, though postfeminists posit it may "seem dated now."

Unsinkable Molly Brown, The   `21` `20` `20` `21`

1964 | Directed by Charles Walters | With Debbie Reynolds, Harve Presnell, Ed Begley | 128 minutes | Not Rated

"Think of it as the last big" MGM musical and "you'll be in for a good evening's entertainment" with this "rollicking" bio of a turn-of-the-century "bawdy broad who wants it all and gets it"; warblers adore the "rip-roarin'" Reynolds in the title role, who drowns all doubts about how "she got the name 'unsinkable.'"

Untouchables, The   `22` `22` `22` `22`

1987 | Directed by Brian De Palma | With Kevin Costner, Sean Connery, Robert De Niro | 119 minutes | Rated R

"Sassy" '30s crime drama recounting the epic "good-vs.-evil" struggle between Eliot Ness and Al Capone, as interpreted by Costner and De Niro in "amazing Armani suits"; while this "period piece" has "exciting action" and "style to spare", the most "compelling" work comes from the Oscar-winning Connery as a streetwise copper.

Upside of Anger, The   `22` `26` `21` `22`

2005 | Directed by Mike Binder | With Joan Allen, Kevin Costner, Erika Christensen, Evan Rachel Wood | 118 minutes | Rated R

"Rage and depression" are about to overwhelm an abandoned housewife when a "washed-up baseball player" steps up to the plate to "suffer by her side"; it pairs the "amazing" Allen with a "hang-loose" Costner, but apart from the "great screen chemistry", there's a downside: that "difficult-to-swallow" "surprise" ending.

	OVERALL	ACTING	STORY	PROD.

Uptown Girls

14 | 16 | 15 | 15

2003 | Directed by Boaz Yakin | With Brittany Murphy, Dakota Fanning | 92 minutes | Rated PG-13

"Don't set your expectations too high" before watching this "feel-good" story of a "spoiled rich girl" who goes broke and becomes a nanny for a "poor little trust fund" kid; as "mindless" chick flicks go, it's appropriately "shallow" and "cutesy-pie", though it does attempt to teach a lesson about the "power of friendship" that makes sentimental types "cry like a baby."

Urban Cowboy

18 | 17 | 16 | 17

1980 | Directed by James Bridges | With John Travolta, Debra Winger, Scott Glenn | 132 minutes | Rated PG

Travolta "in tight jeans" plays opposite Winger at her most "adorable" in this "highly watchable" honky-tonk romance about "beer-swigging", "mechanical bull-riding" men and the women who love them; although Debra nearly "steals the show", she's almost bested by an appealing Houston setting.

U.S. Marshals

18 | 20 | 18 | 19

1998 | Directed by Stuart Baird | With Tommy Lee Jones, Wesley Snipes, Robert Downey Jr. | 131 minutes | Rated PG-13

"Same main character, different storyline" sums up the pedigree of this "sequel of sorts" to *The Fugitive*, a "hard-hitting" action flick that brings back Jones' "straight-faced" lawman Sam Gerard for another "edge-of-your-seat" pursuit of an escaped murder suspect; while most find "easy watching" with this "clever" follow-up, critics wonder "where's Harrison Ford?"

☑ Usual Suspects, The ✉

27 | 28 | 28 | 25

1995 | Directed by Bryan Singer | With Gabriel Byrne, Kevin Spacey, Benicio Del Toro, Stephen Baldwin | 106 minutes | Rated R

"Don't blink" or you'll risk missing one of the many "imaginative" twists in this "tricky-as-hell" "instant classic" that may be one of the finest "whodunit" "thrill rides" ever made; fans "watch it at least twice" to absorb the "brilliant" story, admire the "flawless" Spacey and figure out what the heck "Benicio's saying"; as for that "unpredictable finale", you'll "never see it coming."

Van Helsing

15 | 15 | 14 | 21

2004 | Directed by Stephen Sommers | With Hugh Jackman, Kate Beckinsale | 132 minutes | Rated PG-13

"Superficially entertaining", this horror flick-cum-"thrill machine" about a bounty hunter hounding Dracula, Frankenstein and various werewolves should be "pure escapist fun" what with its "nonstop", "over-the-top" special effects, yet many call it a "big mess"; though Jackman "broods elegantly" in the title role, he's up against a "muddled storyline", Beckinsale's "awful accent" and an "overblown" production that seems more about "merchandising" than moviemaking.

Vanity Fair

17 | 19 | 18 | 23

2004 | Directed by Mira Nair | With Reese Witherspoon, James Purefoy, Ramola Garai, Eileen Atkins | 141 minutes | Rated PG-13

A "visually beautiful" interpretation of Thackeray's "bitingly satirical" novel, this "opulent" romance tells the story of a "conniving" social climber trying to "elevate herself into society" in 19th-century Britain; but many say this "less than faithful adaptation" suffers most from a "miscast Reece", who's "more cutesy than cunning" and "never ages" in a story that unwinds over 30 years.

Velvet Goldmine
17 | 22 | 17 | 20

1998 | Directed by Todd Haynes | With Ewan McGregor, Jonathan Rhys Meyers, Christian Bale | 124 minutes | Rated R

This "ode to '70s glam rock", a *Citizen Kane*-like look at a "gender-bending", David Bowie-ish pop star, has "all the elements of a great film": "outstanding performances", a "spellbinding score", "full-frontal nudity", "fab hair and eye makeup"; yet due to an "insipid" script that "dips and drags", some call it "more a collection of wonderful ideas" than a coherent picture.

Vera Drake
24 | 28 | 25 | 23

2004 | Directed by Mike Leigh | With Imelda Staunton | 125 minutes | Rated R

Wherever you stand on Roe vs. Wade, it's "hard not to be moved" by this "devastating portrait" of a "well-meaning abortionist who runs afoul of the law" in '50s London; "delicate" direction by Leigh keeps the "polarizing" material in check, while "flawless" performances by a "magnificent" ensemble (particularly Staunton's "unforgettable" title turn) ensure there's "never a false moment."

Verdict, The
23 | 25 | 23 | 20

1982 | Directed by Sidney Lumet | With Paul Newman, Charlotte Rampling, Jack Warden | 129 minutes | Rated R

A "David-vs.-Goliath" legal struggle is the underpinning of this "underrated" courtroom drama about a "burned-out lawyer trying one last case to keep from going under"; Newman's "intense", "tour-de-force" turn is one of his "greatest" roles (leaving many "stunned" that the Oscar eluded him), while the "mesmerizing" Rampling "excels" as the love interest.

Veronica Guerin
21 | 25 | 22 | 20

2003 | Directed by Joel Schumacher | With Cate Blanchett, Gerard McSorley | 98 minutes | Rated R

"Versatile" Blanchett "shines" as a "determined" Dublin journo "fighting the good fight" against drug lords in this "gripping" thriller based on a true but "tragic" story; if the thick brogues are "hard to follow" and the overall message skews toward "heavy-handedness", most feel it's Guerin-teed to "make you wonder" about some tough issues.

⊿ Vertigo
27 | 26 | 27 | 26

1958 | Directed by Alfred Hitchcock | With James Stewart, Kim Novak | 128 minutes | Rated PG

"Don't look down": this "dizzyingly complex" thriller offers lots of "twists and turns" as it details the "haunting" tale of an "obsessive" man who "tries to mold a woman into a vision of his lost love"; many call it "Hitchcock's crowning achievement" thanks to a Bernard Herrmann score that's "like perfume" as well as "spellbinding" work from a "bewitching Novak" and "Stewart at his darkest"; as for that "fever dream" of a plot, "it's not supposed to make sense."

Very Long Engagement, A 🄵

`22` `24` `22` `25`

2004 | Directed by Jean-Pierre Jeunet | With Audrey Tautou, Gaspard Ulliel | 134 minutes | Rated R

Amélie's "dynamic duo" (director Jeunet and "radiant" actress Tautou) reunite for this "beautifully done" French war saga whose "graphic" depictions of WWI trenches are tempered by a "tearful" story of "lost love"; with "so many characters", the "complex storyline" can be "hard to follow" and "takes time" to develop, leaving some to retitle it *"A Very Long Movie."*

V for Vendetta

`22` `22` `22` `24`

2006 | Directed by James McTeigue | With Natalie Portman, Hugo Weaving, Stephen Rea | 132 minutes | Rated R

"Reminiscent of *1984*" with its "dark" depiction of a "totalitarian" society, this "provocative" futuristic thriller relating the exploits of a "Guy Fawkes–like" rebel is "V for very good" thanks to "spine-tingling" visuals, "swiftly paced" action and "well-acted" characterizations by Portman and Weaving; flirting with the "controversial subject of terrorism", it strikes many as a "not-so-subtle" allusion to "current events."

Victor/Victoria

`23` `24` `23` `23`

1982 | Directed by Blake Edwards | With Julie Andrews, James Garner, Robert Preston | 132 minutes | Rated PG

"What a hoot!" holler fans who "never tire of watching" this musical farce about Parisian nightlife denizens in the '30s; "Andrews lights up the screen" as the titular double-crossed cross-dresser, while Leslie Ann Warren's fabulous floozie is deliciously "over-the-top"; in sum, this "fast-paced", "madcap" tale of "jazz-age gender bending" is "just plain fun."

Videodrome

▽ `17` `17` `20` `19`

1983 | Directed by David Cronenberg | With James Woods, Sonja Smits, Deborah Harry | 87 minutes | Rated R

"Made at the dawn of cable TV and home VCRs", this "seductive psychological thriller" about "how the media controls minds" has earned "cult classic" status thanks to Cronenberg's "weird", "icky-creepy touches" (like the "videotape inserted into Woods' abdomen"); maybe "it played better in 1983", though even then people still couldn't "figure out what it's all about."

View to a Kill, A

`14` `13` `14` `18`

1985 | Directed by John Glen | With Roger Moore, Christopher Walken, Tanya Roberts, Grace Jones | 131 minutes | Rated PG

"Old" Moore caps his 12-year run as 007 – and "not in the best way" – with this "forgettable" installment pitting the secret agent against a psycho industrialist, whose scheme "to corner the world market in microchips" was a silly premise "even in 1985"; granted, it may have "some of the best stunts and title music" of the series and a "scary" Bond girl in Grace Jones, but the final view on this one is "clunker."

Village, The

`16` `19` `17` `19`

2004 | Directed by M. Night Shyamalan | With Bryce Dallas Howard, Joaquin Phoenix, Adrien Brody | 108 minutes | Rated PG-13

Reminiscent of a "long episode of *The Twilight Zone*", this "unusual" thriller visits an isolated "countryside" hamlet where residents sport "period" threads and live under constant fear of "freaky monsters";

there's agreement on the "interesting concept", but director Shyamalan's "signature twist" at the end polarizes voters: buffs bet "you won't see it coming", whereas seen-it-alls sneer "hokey letdown."

Village of the Damned ❶   21 | 19 | 23 | 19

1960 | Directed by Wolf Rilla | With George Sanders, Barbara Shelley, Michael Gwynn | 78 minutes | Not Rated

An "unfortunate town" becomes host to an army of "alien children" with funny eyeballs in this "spooky" British sci-fi flick that "succeeds without a lot of fancy effects"; ever "cool" over 45 years later, it still "creeps out" viewers ("whoever thought kids could be so scary?") who advise "don't bother with the '95 version."

Viva Zapata! ❶   23 | 24 | 22 | 21

1952 | Directed by Elia Kazan | With Marlon Brando, Jean Peters, Anthony Quinn | 113 minutes | Not Rated

Elia Kazan directs a John Steinbeck screenplay in this "passionate" profile of Emiliano Zapata, the revolutionary hero who led a rebellion against Mexican dictator Porfirio Diaz; featuring an "unusual but expert turn" by Brando in the title role (as well as an Oscar-winning turn by Quinn), it's "historical" cinema "at its best" and, given the climate of its 1952 release, an "important political drama."

Volver 🅵   24 | 26 | 23 | 23

2006 | Directed by Pedro Almodóvar | With Penélope Cruz, Carmen Maura, Lola Dueñas | 121 minutes | Rated R

Spanish "master" Almodóvar "just gets better and better", coaxing a "luminously beautiful" performance from "luscious" "muse" Cruz ("no one writes for women the way Pedro does") in this "spellbinding" mother-daughter "family drama"; mixing "tragedy and laughter in the right amounts" with a splash of "Hitchcock", this "sentimental, emotional" concoction "has it all" for fans of cinema *maravillosa.*

Wages of Fear ❶🅵   27 | 26 | 27 | 24

1953 | Directed by Henri-Georges Clouzot | With Yves Montand, Charles Vanel | 148 minutes | Not Rated

"Fasten your seatbelts for a bumpy" ride via this "nerve-racking" "nail-biter" about "down-and-outers" racing a "nitroglycerine-loaded truck" across the mountains of South America; Clouzot's knack for "oh-my-God" suspense and "social commentary" makes it one of the "best art-house action" flicks around.

Wag the Dog   19 | 22 | 22 | 19

1997 | Directed by Barry Levinson | With Dustin Hoffman, Robert De Niro, Anne Heche | 97 minutes | Rated R

Pundits praise this "biting black comedy" that "makes light (and dark) of media-oriented politics" via a "surreal" story about a "nonexistent war created by the government to divert attention" from a presidential scandal; though some wonder if it's a "documentary", others tout this "underrated" political satire for Hoffman and De Niro's "standout" turns.

Waiting for Guffman   25 | 26 | 24 | 23

1996 | Directed by Christopher Guest | With Christopher Guest, Eugene Levy, Fred Willard, Catherine O'Hara | 84 minutes | Rated R

"Anyone who loves the theater and loves to laugh" shouldn't miss this "hilarious" mockumentary about "community theater in the boonies" courtesy of "comic genius" Guest and his "usual incredibly talented ensemble"; it's a "laugh riot from the first frame to the last", with "classic" scenes you'll "quote lines from" – "I'm still searching for *My Dinner with Andre* action figures."

Waitress
24 | 26 | 23 | 23

2007 | Directed by Adrienne Shelly | With Keri Russell, Jeremy Sisto, Nathan Fillion, Andy Griffith | 107 minutes | Rated PG-13

With a "nod to *Alice Doesn't Live Here Anymore*", this "sweet-natured" comic confection about a "small-town" diner waitress "caught in a loveless marriage" has enough ingredients to "steal your heart", including an "outstanding" Russell, the "consummate" Griffith and, of course, those "delicious"-looking pies; indeed, many call this "uplifting" "little jewel" a "rallying cry for women everywhere."

Wait Until Dark
25 | 26 | 27 | 23

1967 | Directed by Terence Young | With Audrey Hepburn, Alan Arkin, Richard Crenna | 107 minutes | Not Rated

This "unforgettable" thriller posits a "simple, nerve-shattering premise": a blind woman, all alone in her apartment, in a "game of cat-and-mouse" with a "brutal psychopath"; gird yourself for an "eerie Henry Mancini soundtrack" and a "twists-and-turns"–laden scenario with "one particularly electrifying moment" that's guaranteed to "have you out of your seat."

⊿ Walk the Line ⊠
25 | 28 | 23 | 25

2005 | Directed by James Mangold | With Joaquin Phoenix, Reese Witherspoon | 136 minutes | Rated PG-13

The "Man in Black" walks again courtesy of this "evocative", "behind-the-music" biopic that pays "touching tribute" to country "legend" Johnny Cash and his "true love", June Carter, the "good woman" who "saved him" from a life of "drugs and temptation"; both Phoenix and Witherspoon are "phenomenal" (yep, "they do their own singing"), and the "foot-stomping" tunes "ain't bad", either; P.S. don't mind the unmistakable "similarity to *Ray*."

Wallace & Gromit in the Curse of the Were-Rabbit
24 | - | 22 | 27

2005 | Directed by Steve Box, Nick Park | Animated | 85 minutes | Rated G

Appearing in their first feature-length flick, "goofy" gadgeteer Wallace and his silently "expressive" pooch Gromit come to the neighborhood's rescue when a "mutated rabbit terrorizes its gardens" in this "jolly good", "for-all-ages" claymation comedy brimming with "Brit wit" and "inventive" visual spectacle; fans beg series creator Nick Park "please sir, may we have some more?"

Wall Street ⊠
22 | 23 | 22 | 21

1987 | Directed by Oliver Stone | With Michael Douglas, Charlie Sheen, Martin Sheen | 125 minutes | Rated R

"Greed is good" in this "quintessential insider's view" of the "go-go '80s" as personified by "ruthless financier" Gordon Gecko, an "ever-so-cool" piece of "Wall Street slime", "brilliantly executed" by the Oscar-winning Douglas; the "world of high finance" in all its "money-making" excess is captured here "like in no other film."

	OVERALL	ACTING	STORY	PROD.

WarGames
`22` `19` `24` `19`

1983 | Directed by John Badham | With Matthew Broderick, Dabney Coleman, John Wood, Ally Sheedy | 114 minutes | Rated PG

A precocious high-school student "hacks into a Defense Department computer" with the potential to "start a nuclear war" in this "way-before-its-time" thriller that wags dub *Fail-Safe* in an '80s mall"; sure, it "seems dated" today, with "primitive technology" and a "preachy ending", but overall the "thoughtful" script remains "urgently relevant."

War of the Roses, The
`17` `20` `17` `18`

1989 | Directed by Danny DeVito | With Michael Douglas, Kathleen Turner, Danny DeVito | 116 minutes | Rated R

"You need a slightly off-color sense of humor" (namely, "black") to enjoy this "daring" comedy about the "disintegration of a marriage" and subsequent "over-the-top divorce shenanigans"; still, the "materialism, ego and folly" are played out with such a "mean-spirited", "venomous edge" that some find it "completely depressing and charmless."

War of the Worlds, The
`23` `16` `24` `23`

1953 | Directed by Byron Haskin | With Gene Barry, Ann Robinson, Les Tremayne | 85 minutes | Rated G

Although the "Orson Welles radio broadcast" is "more famous", this "faithful" filming of the H.G. Wells "sci-fi classic" still clearly telegraphs its "frightening premise" of Martians run amok on Planet Earth; ok, it may be a bit "overstated" and "unintentionally funny today", but boob-tubers tune in "every time it's on television."

War of the Worlds
`15` `14` `16` `22`

2005 | Directed by Steven Spielberg | With Tom Cruise, Dakota Fanning, Justin Chatwin | 116 minutes | Rated PG-13

"Stuff blows up" and "Tom runs away from it" in this "eye-popping", "big-budget" sci-fi remake about a "working-class loser dad" whose kids are threatened by extraterrestrial invaders; since Spielberg gives the plot a contemporary spin with the faintest "undertones of terrorism", many find it "pretty grim for a popcorn flick", capped by that "letdown of an ending"; as for the acting, Fanning's "incessant screaming" and Cruise's "unlikable" character leave some "rooting for the aliens."

Warriors, The
`23` `16` `22` `18`

1979 | Directed by Walter Hill | With Michael Beck, James Remar, David Patrick Kelly | 93 minutes | Rated R

The "seedy cesspool that was NYC in the '70s" serves as the "dystopian" backdrop for this "intriguing" "gangland warfare" flick following a Coney Island crew's perilous trek across rival turf after they're pegged "for a murder they didn't commit"; boasting "great action", "fabulous production design" and even its own "video game", this movie has long enjoyed "cult classic" status – "can you dig it?"

Wayne's World
`17` `14` `15` `15`

1992 | Directed by Penelope Spheeris | With Mike Myers, Dana Carvey, Rob Lowe | 95 minutes | Rated PG-13

"One of the few *Saturday Night Live* skits to soar in a longer format", this parody of local access cable TV shows is an "inventive", "mindless" romp that was one of the biggest box office comedies of the '90s;

it's also the breakout for the pre–*Austin Powers* Myers, who gives an "awesome" rendition of "stupidity at its finest."

Way We Were, The
24 | 25 | 25 | 23

1973 | Directed by Sydney Pollack | With Barbra Streisand, Robert Redford, Bradford Dillman | 118 minutes | Rated PG

"Still a tearjerker after all these years", this "improbable romance" pits a "brainy" Jewish girl opposite a "golden Wasp boy" and "tugs every heartstring available" in its "realistic" depiction of their "ill-fated" affair; Streisand and Redford "at their peak" are "beyond delicious" together, though the most indelible "memories" involve the "famous final scene" at the "Plaza Hotel" with that "sad", Oscar-winning song playing in the background.

We Are Marshall
22 | 21 | 25 | 21

2006 | Directed by McG | With Matthew McConaughey, Matthew Fox, David Strathairn | 124 minutes | Rated PG

This "respectful" treatment of Marshall University's fabled "rise from the ashes" following the 1970 plane crash that claimed the school's entire football team runs the set play of many a sports film – "triumph against adversity" – and "does the story proud"; as for acting, McConaughey's "enthusiasm is contagious" in the role of embattled coach, giving "sentimental saps" more reason to tout this "worthy two-hour investment."

Wedding Banquet, The 🄵
22 | 21 | 25 | 21

1993 | Directed by Ang Lee | With Winston Chao, May Chin, Mitchell Lichtenstein | 106 minutes | Rated R

"Family dynamics" get a "touching" twist in this "gently told" Taiwanese tale about a "marriage of convenience" between a "gay man" hoping to make his parents happy and his green card–seeking bride; this "funny charade" comes to a climax at the titular feast, where "unconditional love" comes "out of the closet" in a "warm-hearted" if "bittersweet finale."

Wedding Crashers
21 | 21 | 20 | 21

2005 | Directed by David Dobkin | With Owen Wilson, Vince Vaughn, Christopher Walken | 119 minutes | Rated R

Fast becoming the "Lemmon and Matthau" of the "overgrown frat boy" set, Wilson and Vaughn play a pair of "opportunistic womanizers" who "prey on weddings" in this "deliciously vulgar" comedy; despite some "mushy" messing around with a "semi-serious love story", overall it delivers enough "flashes of hilarity" to make for "easy viewing."

Wedding Singer, The
17 | 16 | 16 | 16

1998 | Directed by Frank Coraci | With Adam Sandler, Drew Barrymore | 96 minutes | Rated PG-13

Take a "blast to the past" via this romantic comedy set in the "suburban '80s" whose real stars are its retro soundtrack and "tasteless fashion" parade; beyond that, it's a "cute if insipid" chick flick about a down-and-out wedding singer, "dejected love" and its "sweet" redemption.

Weekend at Bernie's
16 | 14 | 16 | 15

1989 | Directed by Ted Kotcheff | With Andrew McCarthy, Jonathan Silverman, Terry Kiser | 97 minutes | Rated PG-13

"So stupid it's funny", this "idiotic" comedy from the "classic '80s" canon serves up "nyuk-nyuks" aplenty when two shlubs "find their boss dead in his beach house but pretend he's alive" to continue "chasing chicks and partying"; it's the kind of picture that "revels in its ridiculousness" – right down to the steadfastly "deadpan" expression on the "actor playing the corpse."

Welcome to the Dollhouse

	OVERALL	ACTING	STORY	PROD.
	22	21	21	19

1995 | Directed by Todd Solondz | With Heather Matarazzo, Matthew Faber, Eric Mabius | 88 minutes | Rated R

A "dead-on look at the horrors" of junior high, this "scathing" study of a "dorky adolescent" "hits close to home" thanks to an "eerily real" performance by Matarazzo as the "picked-on" protagonist; both "cruelly funny" and "disturbingly accurate", it makes some oldsters "worry about young people today."

☒ West Side Story ✉

	OVERALL	ACTING	STORY	PROD.
	27	24	27	27

1961 | Directed by Robert Wise, Jerome Robbins | With Natalie Wood, Richard Beymer, Rita Moreno, George Chakiris | 151 minutes | Not Rated

Starting with that "opening bird's-eye view of Manhattan", this "remarkable musical" that transposes *Romeo and Juliet* to "urban" turf is "sheer perfection" thanks to "fiery acting", Robbins' "superb" streetwise choreography and the "dynamic" Leonard Bernstein/ Stephen Sondheim score; sure, Beymer might be "miscast" and it's "too bad they wouldn't let Natalie sing", but otherwise this Oscar magnet – 10 statuettes including Best Picture – is "forever fabulous."

Westworld

	OVERALL	ACTING	STORY	PROD.
	19	16	21	20

1973 | Directed by Michael Crichton | With Yul Brynner, Richard Benjamin, James Brolin | 88 minutes | Rated PG

You can "see where *Jurassic Park* came from" in this sci-fi thriller whose "irresistible premise" involves a futuristic resort where vacationers live out their Wild West fantasies with robot stand-ins; though sharp-shooters say Brynner is "perfect" as an "android gunslinger" gone haywire, cynics ponder the idea of a "wooden actor playing an automaton."

We Were Soldiers

	OVERALL	ACTING	STORY	PROD.
	21	22	21	23

2002 | Directed by Randall Wallace | With Mel Gibson, Madeleine Stowe, Greg Kinnear, Sam Elliott | 138 minutes | Rated R

The "first ground battle of the Vietnam War" is "authentically replicated", "graphic violence" and all, in this "powerful" profile of the "humanity and courage" of America's soldiers in the thick of "intense action"; with a special salute going to Gibson's portrayal of a "religious man" turned "battlefield leader", some grunt this is "one of the most overlooked" combat pics around.

Whale Rider

	OVERALL	ACTING	STORY	PROD.
	25	26	24	24

2003 | Directed by Niki Caro | With Keisha Castle-Hughes, Rawiri Paratene, Vicki Haughton | 101 minutes | Rated PG-13

Featuring "no stars, no explosions and no CGI effects", this nonetheless "powerful" film tells the "captivating" story of a Maori girl's struggle to help her tribe balance "tradition and the 21st century"; a "refreshing", family-friendly slice of "edutainment" complete with "beautiful" New Zealand vistas and "phenomenal" work by "up-and-comer" Castle-Hughes, this "achingly sad" story will "leave your soul touched."

What About Bob?
18 | **19** | **18** | **17**

1991 | Directed by Frank Oz | With Bill Murray, Richard Dreyfuss, Julie Hagerty | 99 minutes | Rated PG

Proving that "life is indeed baby steps", this "dark" comedy about a "shrink driven nuts" by a "psycho patient" pairs the "screwball" Murray with the "hilarious" Dreyfuss; though the picture might be "as irritating as it is funny", your "sides will hurt" from laughter all the same.

What Dreams May Come
16 | **17** | **15** | **24**

1998 | Directed by Vincent Ward | With Robin Williams, Cuba Gooding Jr., Annabella Sciorra | 113 minutes | Rated PG-13

"Extremely pleasing to the eye", this "beautiful fantasy of the afterlife" "based on the touching Richard Matheson novel" finds Williams desperately trying to rescue his wife's soul from the underworld; but realists report a "sappy", "schmaltzy script" and sum this one up as "visually exquisite, but little else."

Whatever Happened to Baby Jane? ◑
22 | **25** | **23** | **21**

1962 | Directed by Robert Aldrich | With Bette Davis, Joan Crawford, Victor Buono | 134 minutes | Not Rated

"Campy and creepy", this "classic" exercise in Grand Guignol is the last hurrah of Hollywood's "two queen bees" in a "frightening" story of the "hate-hate relationship" between a pair of movie-star sisters; expect an "audacious" Crawford facing off against an "over-the-top" Davis, whose "grotesque" appearance is "too scary to think about" for too long; most memorable scene: Joan's "rat à-la-carte" din-din.

What Lies Beneath
16 | **18** | **16** | **18**

2000 | Directed by Robert Zemeckis | With Harrison Ford, Michelle Pfeiffer, Diana Scarwid | 126 minutes | Rated PG-13

This "chilling" "Hitchcockian" thriller about a "sinister ghost" at loose in the house is a "slick" endeavor, with enough "scary moments" to "make you jump" out of your seat; but foes find the "cable-TV-caliber script" "silly" and "predictable", and wonder what "A-list actors" are doing in this "overwrought", "C-list movie."

What's Eating Gilbert Grape
22 | **25** | **22** | **21**

1993 | Directed by Lasse Hallström | With Johnny Depp, Juliette Lewis, Leonardo DiCaprio, Mary Steenburgen | 118 minutes | Rated PG-13

An "original" study of an ultra-"dysfunctional" family, this "weirdly winning" dramedy features a "quietly intense" Depp opposite a "brilliant" DiCaprio "before he became a celebrity teen idol"; its "loving look at two fringe groups – the obese and the mentally challenged" – turns this "quirky" "coming-of-age" tale into "surprisingly good" moviemaking.

What's Love Got to Do with It
22 | **26** | **22** | **21**

1993 | Directed by Brian Gibson | With Angela Bassett, Laurence Fishburne | 118 minutes | Rated R

That Tina Turner "never did anything nice and easy" is plain to see in this "perfect" biopic depicting how a "gifted" gal "got the strength to move on" from an abusive marriage to super-duper stardom; in a picture that's "all about the acting", Bassett is "outstanding", but be warned that it can be "painful to watch."

	OVERALL	ACTING	STORY	PROD.

What's Up, Doc?

21 | 20 | 21 | 20

1972 | Directed by Peter Bogdanovich | With Barbra Streisand, Ryan O'Neal, Madeline Kahn | 94 minutes | Rated G

"Streisand's like butter" in this "zany" "modern screwball comedy" "reminiscent of *Bringing Up Baby*" wherein some "terrific Ryan-Babs chemistry" is brought to bear on a nutty storyline involving "igneous rocks", identical plaid suitcases and a "fantastic comic car chase through San Francisco"; P.S. "Kahn's a scream" in her film debut.

What Women Want

15 | 17 | 17 | 16

2000 | Directed by Nancy Meyers | With Mel Gibson, Helen Hunt, Marisa Tomei | 126 minutes | Rated PG-13

A misogynist is redeemed after becoming superhumanly "sensitized" to women's inner monologues in this "enjoyably light" chick flick; while it might "miss the mark" due to "predictable" plotting, it's an "original concept" that's "worth it just to see" "Mad Max Mel struggle with pantyhose."

☑ When Harry Met Sally . . .

26 | 25 | 25 | 24

1989 | Directed by Rob Reiner | With Billy Crystal, Meg Ryan, Carrie Fisher, Bruno Kirby | 96 minutes | Rated R

"Can a man and a woman be just friends?"; this romantic comedy – the "king of all date movies" – attempts to answer that question as it details a "terrific take on relationships" that "rings true for many"; written by Nora Ephron as an "ode to Manhattan", it stars an "adorable", "pre-pixie cut" Ryan opposite a "perfect" Crystal, both "forever remembered" for the "infamous orgasm scene" in Katz's Deli that inspired one of the best lines in moviedom: "I'll have what she's having."

Where's Poppa?

23 | 25 | 23 | 21

1970 | Directed by Carl Reiner | With George Segal, Ruth Gordon, Trish Van Devere, Ron Leibman | 82 minutes | Rated R

This "twisted" black comedy from Carl Reiner examines the "sick relationship" between a "senile" mom living with her "dutiful (up-to-a-point)" son; "painfully funny", it's acquired "cult" status over the years for set pieces like the "ape suit scene" and the "tush-biting" sequence; P.S. the jaw-dropping original ending, an extra on the DVD, is truly "insane."

While You Were Sleeping

18 | 19 | 20 | 18

1995 | Directed by Jon Turteltaub | With Sandra Bullock, Bill Pullman, Peter Gallagher | 103 minutes | Rated PG

"Token-booth worker" Bullock "falls in love with two brothers" in this "tender romantic comedy, an "engaging", "Cinderella"-like "fairy tale" trading on "mistaken identity"; sure, it's "feel-good fluff", but the "unique storyline", "sweet" performances and "great chemistry" between the leads add up to an "all-around cute movie."

White Christmas

25 | 21 | 22 | 24

1954 | Directed by Michael Curtiz | With Bing Crosby, Danny Kaye, Rosemary Clooney | 120 minutes | Not Rated

"It wouldn't be Christmas" without a peek at this "sentimental" favorite, a virtual holiday "requirement" with "all the trimmings": "wonderful dance numbers", "essential" Irving Berlin tunes and "Der Bingle" crooning "kringle jingles"; in short, this "classic" is so "charming", it's almost "un-American not to love it"; P.S. sticklers note that Bing originally "made the title song famous in *Holiday Inn*."

White Heat ❶

OVERALL	ACTING	STORY	PROD.
25	28	24	23

1949 | Directed by Raoul Walsh | With James Cagney, Virginia Mayo, Edmond O'Brien | 114 minutes | Not Rated

One part "descent into madness", one part "valentine to mom", this schizophrenic thriller represents the "classic gangster film refined to the nth degree"; as a "homicidal nut job" "mama's boy", Cagney turns in one of his "greatest performances", though the flick's most remembered for the "best last line in movie history": 'made it, ma! top of the world!'

White Oleander

18	23	19	19

2002 | Directed by Peter Kosminsky | With Michelle Pfeiffer, Renée Zellweger, Robin Wright Penn | 109 minutes | Rated PG-13

A "manipulating" mom in prison and a "conflicted teen" shunted from foster home to foster home are the protagonists of this "solid coming-of-age drama" based on the "offbeat", Oprah-endorsed best-seller; maybe it "falls short of being really great" (many say the "book was better"), but at least this "interesting tale of growth and change" is "perfectly cast."

Who Framed Roger Rabbit

24	-	23	27

1988 | Directed by Robert Zemeckis | Animated | With Bob Hoskins, Christopher Lloyd | 103 minutes | Rated PG

This "one-of-a-kind treat" featuring a "glorious mix of live action and animation" boasts an all-star cartoon cast, with appearances by every 'toon from Mickey to Woody (though the "seductive" Jessica Rabbit runs away with the picture); set in the Hollywood of yore, the "classic" noir plot has Hoskins investigating a murder case, with "wonderfully entertaining" results.

Who Killed the Electric Car?

23	-	25	21

2006 | Directed by Chris Paine | Documentary | 92 minutes | Rated PG

Sure to drive "environmentally conscious" sorts "mad" with rage at the "auto and oil industry fat cats" who "control our lives", this "informative" documentary (whose "title speaks for itself") illuminates a "fascinating" but "little-known" episode in eco-history; maybe the presentation veers toward "pedestrian", but overall most see a "great vehicle" for raising awareness and regret it "didn't get more airplay."

Whole Nine Yards, The

17	17	17	17

2000 | Directed by Jonathan Lynn | With Bruce Willis, Matthew Perry, Rosanna Arquette, Amanda Peet | 98 minutes | Rated R

A "fun waste of an hour-and-a-half", this "lightweight" crime comedy tells the story of a "hit man on the lam" in suburbia who moves next door to a "hyper-nervous dentist"; Willis and Perry sit ably atop the "big-budget cast", but it's the "hilarious" Peet who "shows her boobs" and "steals the movie" as a "gangster groupie."

Who's Afraid of Virginia Woolf? ✉❶

25	27	25	23

1966 | Directed by Mike Nichols | With Elizabeth Taylor, Richard Burton, George Segal, Sandy Dennis | 134 minutes | Not Rated

Maybe "Liz made up to look frumpy is a laugh", but otherwise this "scalding adaptation" of Edward Albee's "masterpiece" about an "unraveling marriage" is pretty serious stuff, "brilliantly acted" and "brutally honest"; it's "funny and mean and sad" all at once – "never has a play been converted into a movie" with such "power."

☑ Wild Bunch, The | 27 | 26 | 25 | 27 |

1969 | Directed by Sam Peckinpah | With William Holden, Ernest Borgnine, Robert Ryan | 134 minutes | Rated R

Not for the faint of heart, this "blood-and-guts" Peckinpah "epic" is a "Western to end all Westerns" that "transcends the genre" with an "in-your-face style" that turns "violence into poetry"; starring Holden as the leader of a band of "honorable outlaws", it depicts a "changing world" at the "end of an era" in "unsentimental" terms and manages to be both "noble and perverse at the same time."

Wild One, The ◑ | 22 | 24 | 19 | 20 |

1953 | Directed by László Benedek | With Marlon Brando, Mary Murphy, Lee Marvin | 79 minutes | Not Rated

"Brando on a motorcycle" in "tight black leather" sums up the appeal of this '50s cautionary tale about a gang of bikers that terrorizes a small town; sure, it's "dated" and "mild by today's standards", yet Marlon's "bad-boy attitude" alone keeps it "compelling"; most "unforgettable" exchange: "what are you rebelling against? – whaddya got?"

Wild Strawberries ◑🅵 | 26 | 26 | 24 | 25 |

1959 | Directed by Ingmar Bergman | With Victor Sjöström, Bibi Andersson, Ingrid Thulin | 91 minutes | Not Rated

"Essential Bergman" that's not just for art movie mavens, this "elegiac" "road film about life, death and redemption" "continues to hold up well"; a "bittersweet" story of an "elderly doctor who learns how to love at the last minute of his life", it's ultimately "cathartic and hopeful", even if it displays the director's signature "depressive" streak.

Willow | 20 | 18 | 20 | 22 |

1988 | Directed by Ron Howard | With Val Kilmer, Joanne Whalley, Warwick Davis | 130 minutes | Rated PG

"If you like *Princess Bride*", you'll like this "wonderfully escapist" fantasy featuring "appealing" characters in a sword-and-sorcery story that "seems familiar" to those who dub it a "*Lord of the Rings*" clone; "Kilmer's gorgeous" and there's plenty of "excitement", but some say that it's a "formulaic disappointment."

☑ Willy Wonka and the Chocolate Factory | 26 | 22 | 26 | 26 |

1971 | Directed by Mel Stuart | With Gene Wilder, Jack Albertson, Peter Ostrum | 100 minutes | Rated G

Chocoholics cheer this "delicious family classic" adeptly adapted from the "brilliant Roald Dahl book" about an "underdog" kid who gets a "once-in-a-lifetime" chance to tour a "curious candy factory"; it's such a "blast to watch" (thanks to "psychedelic" sets and "imaginative" vignettes) that it's almost become a "rite of passage" for the stroller set.

Wimbledon | 15 | 16 | 15 | 17 |

2004 | Directed by Richard Loncraine | With Kirsten Dunst, Paul Bettany | 98 minutes | Rated PG-13

"Predictable but pleasant", this tennis-themed romantic comedy woos "teenage girls" with a "cute" court-ship and "sports movie" buffs with "exciting" match play enhanced by "inventive camera tricks"; still, a "far-fetched" premise and "poor" dialogue commit a "double fault" that mars the otherwise "diverting fluff."

Wind and the Lion, The

| 24 | 25 | 24 | 24 |

1975 | Directed by John Milius | With Sean Connery, Candice Bergen, Brian Keith | 119 minutes | Rated PG

This "old-fashioned adventure" about an Arab chieftain's abduction of an American widow is loosely "based on a real incident during Teddy Roosevelt's presidency"; despite the "wonderful desert romance" that blooms between the "charismatic" Connery and "watchable" Bergen, there's "still enough action for the guys" in this "obscure history lesson."

Winged Migration

| 26 | - | 21 | 28 |

2003 | Directed by Jacques Perrin, Jacques Cluzaud, Michel Debats | Documentary | 98 minutes | Rated G

"Soar with the birds" in this "breathtaking" documentary whose "amazing camerawork" puts you shoulder-to-wing with "flocks flying" around the globe on their "moving" migratory journeys; a "masterpiece" that will "awaken your appreciation" of nature's "avian heroes", it "should be required viewing" for budding environmentalists and cinematographers alike; P.S. one welcome feature: there's "no bad acting."

Wings of Desire ❶🅵

| 24 | 24 | 22 | 25 |

1988 | Directed by Wim Wenders | With Bruno Ganz, Solveig Dommartin | 127 minutes | Rated PG-13

A "charming meditation" about the "angels who watch over us", "longing to be human", this "haunting" German film "celebrates the human condition"; "dreamy cinematography" and an "amazing" cast elevate it to "pure poetry" – but don't "judge it by its self-conscious remake", Hollywood's "unfortunate" *City of Angels*.

Witches of Eastwick, The

| 17 | 20 | 18 | 18 |

1987 | Directed by George Miller | With Jack Nicholson, Cher, Susan Sarandon, Michelle Pfeiffer | 118 minutes | Rated R

Three small-town gals take on the devil himself in this "funny but disturbing" comedy, a variation on the "beauty-and-the-beast" theme based on the John Updike novel; no surprise, a "wicked Jack" walks away with the picture, triumphing over the occasionally "weird storyline" and "bizarre" denouement.

Witness ✉

| 23 | 24 | 23 | 22 |

1985 | Directed by Peter Weir | With Harrison Ford, Kelly McGillis, Lukas Haas | 112 minutes | Rated R

"One of Weir's finest", this "quiet" film offers a "sensitive portrayal" of a "small Amish community" that "collides with the violent outside world" in the aftermath of a murder; the actors have "perfect pitch" (particularly the "workmanlike" Ford, who "sizzles" against the "luminous McGillis"), and even if the story's somewhat "improbable", its overall "excellence sneaks up on you."

🅉 Witness for the Prosecution ❶

| 27 | 28 | 28 | 25 |

1957 | Directed by Billy Wilder | With Tyrone Power, Marlene Dietrich, Charles Laughton | 116 minutes | Not Rated

Perhaps the "best murder mystery ever", this "Agatha Christie puzzler" is one of "Wilder's wiliest", featuring "two legends" – an "incredible" Laughton and an "outstanding" Dietrich – along with a courtroom-full of "compelling characterizations"; the dialogue "crackles" and the "plot twists and double twists" right up to the "still shocking ending."

Wiz, The | 16 | 13 | 17 | 19 |
1978 | Directed by Sidney Lumet | With Diana Ross, Michael Jackson, Nipsey Russell, Ted Ross | 134 minutes | Rated G

The "timeless" *Wizard of Oz* is enacted by an all-black cast in this "lively" musical that transposes the action to 1970s NYC (with the "World Trade Center as the Emerald City"); the songs are "catchy" and it costars a "sane" Michael Jackson "before the lunacy", yet most find it "kinda boring" – Ross is "too long in the tooth" to play Dorothy, so it's "no threat to the Judy Garland version."

☑ Wizard of Oz, The | 28 | 26 | 28 | 29 |
1939 | Directed by Victor Fleming | With Judy Garland, Ray Bolger, Jack Haley, Bert Lahr | 101 minutes | Rated G

A "star is born" – the "iconic" "Judy, Judy, Judy" – in this "timeless", "transporting" musical about a Kansas girl "off to see the Wizard" that's been "adored for decades" thanks to its "tremendous" cast, "glorious", "rainbow"-hued score and "inspired" moments involving a pair of "ruby slippers", a pack of "scary flying monkeys" and that "magical", "hello-Technicolor" transition; in Toto, this "landmark in family entertainment" is the ultimate proof that "there's no place like home."

Wolf Man, The ◐ | 20 | 19 | 22 | 19 |
1941 | Directed by George Waggner | With Lon Chaney Jr., Claude Rains, Ralph Bellamy | 70 minutes | Not Rated

This "classic Universal monster" flicker set the "standard for fright" in its day with a hair-raising mix of ominous gypsies, howling werewolves and foreboding full moons; a "superb" Chaney stars as the fuzzy-faced lead, though a few howl about his "hammy" acting chops and "special effects that look damn silly" now.

☑ Woman of the Year ✉◐ | 27 | 28 | 26 | 26 |
1942 | Directed by George Stevens | With Katharine Hepburn, Spencer Tracy, Fay Bainter | 114 minutes | Not Rated

The "war between the sexes was never more fun" than in this first matchup of legendary duo Hepburn and Tracy in what some call the "best" of their eight films together; its Oscar-winning script pits the "right-on" Kate as an "ahead-of-her-time" foreign correspondent against Spence's laid-back sportswriter, but the hands-down winner in this battle of wills is clearly the audience.

Woman Under the Influence, A | 24 | 27 | 22 | 21 |
1974 | Directed by John Cassavetes | With Peter Falk, Gena Rowlands | 155 minutes | Rated R

"Raw, naturalistic performances" lie at the core of this "stunning", "hyper-real" drama about a "housewife's sad decline" into mental illness; a "heartbreaking" Rowlands plays the title role "like a Stradivarius", and even though some "overlong, meandering" scenes can be "difficult to watch", ultimately it's a "tender", "uncompromising" look at the "beautiful mess that is marriage."

	OVERALL	ACTING	STORY	PROD.

Women, The ◑
26 | 26 | 24 | 25

1939 | Directed by George Cukor | With Norma Shearer, Joan Crawford, Rosalind Russell, Paulette Goddard | 133 minutes | Not Rated

"*Meow!*": a "wonderful wallow" in "bitchy backstabbing", this "marvelous" MGM adaptation of Clare Boothe Luce's "snappy" stage play about high-society divorcées boasts an all-star, all-gal cast rattling off "extraordinary fast-paced" dialogue; though the constant "cattiness" can be a turnoff, it's still "required viewing" for "chick flick" and camp followers – "long live Jungle Red!"

Women in Love ✉
23 | 26 | 24 | 23

1969 | Directed by Ken Russell | With Alan Bates, Oliver Reed, Glenda Jackson, Jennie Linden | 131 minutes | Rated R

Ken Russell's "visually amazing", "erotically charged" take on the D.H. Lawrence novel "deals frankly" with two couples' struggle to conform to the marital and sexual conventions of 1920s England; it's a "sensual", "memorable" picture that's most renowned for Jackson's "strong", Oscar-winning turn and that notorious "nude male wrestling scene."

Women on the Verge of a Nervous Breakdown 🄵
24 | 24 | 23 | 22

1988 | Directed by Pedro Almodóvar | With Carmen Maura, Antonio Banderas | 90 minutes | Rated R

Forget the "depressing" title: this "campy", "door-slamming farce" "put director Almodóvar on the map" and is one of the "funniest foreign films" ever made; a "wacky" story of "neurotic characters with different agendas", it also introduced "eye-candy Banderas to the Western world."

Wonder Boys
21 | 24 | 21 | 20

2000 | Directed by Curtis Hanson | With Michael Douglas, Tobey Maguire, Frances McDormand | 111 minutes | Rated R

Douglas shines in this "intelligent" if "overlooked" dramedy as a "humpy-shlumpy" college professor stultified by writer's block compounded by a "midlife crisis"; a "funny, smart and caring" piece of moviemaking, it supplies "many different interwoven storylines" – though calculators say its "parts prove greater than the sum of the whole."

Wonderland
16 | 21 | 17 | 17

2003 | Directed by James Cox | With Val Kilmer, Kate Bosworth, Lisa Kudrow, Josh Lucas | 104 minutes | Rated R

So "raw and violent" that it's "not for all audiences", this "dark", drug-drenched biopic recounts the alleged involvement of "desperate" porn star John Holmes in a notorious multiple murder; the underwhelmed find it alternately "depressing", "pointless" and "heavy-handed", noting that the same general idea was "done much better in *Boogie Nights*."

Woodsman, The
21 | 27 | 21 | 20

2004 | Directed by Nicole Kassell | With Kevin Bacon, Kyra Sedgwick | 87 minutes | Rated R

Venturing far afield from his *Footloose* beginnings, Bacon earns "high marks" for his "daring" turn as a "recovering pedophile" desperately "seeking a second chance" in this "honorably realistic" indie character study; fans warn if you're not in the mood to "feel sorry for" a "fragile" child molester, this one's gonna be "hard to watch."

Woodstock
24 | - | 21 | 23

1970 | Directed by Michael Wadleigh | Documentary | With Jimi Hendrix, The Who | 184 minutes | Rated R

"Drop out, turn on and tune in" to this "seminal pop-culture event", a "groundbreaking" rockumentary about the fabled "peace-and-love" concert that's a "near-perfect snapshot" of the era, "minus the bad acid"; though ticked-off "tie-dyed flower children" sniff the "split-screen stuff gets old" and find "too much mud and not enough Hendrix", peaceniks maintain that this "marathon" movie provides "evidence that the summer of love was no pipe dream."

Wordplay
23 | - | 24 | 21

2006 | Directed by Patrick Creadon | Documentary | 94 minutes | Rated PG

"Word nerds" and even those who've "never completed a crossword in their lives" are "spellbound" by this "excellent" documentary mining "real insights" from the "seemingly boring" world of New York Times "puzzle fanatics", whose "Sunday rituals" are an "American pastime"; celeb solvers like Jon Stewart, Bob Dole and Bill Clinton (in "one of his finer performances") add a "fascinating" layer to the proceedings.

Working Girl
20 | 20 | 21 | 19

1988 | Directed by Mike Nichols | With Melanie Griffith, Harrison Ford, Sigourney Weaver | 109 minutes | Rated R

"Workplace revenge" was never funnier than in this "Cinderella-by-way-of-Wall-Street" "chick flick" that "empowers every woman who's had to put up with a difficult boss"; Griffith's at her "dumb girl/smart girl best", Weaver's "delightfully loathsome" and Ford's "adorable" "not playing an action hero for a change"; favorite line: "I've got a head for business and a bod for sin."

World According to Garp, The
21 | 23 | 22 | 19

1982 | Directed by George Roy Hill | With Robin Williams, Mary Beth Hurt, Glenn Close | 131 minutes | Rated R

An "unforgettable", "modern-day fairy tale" full of "bizarre charac-ters", this adaptation of John Irving's best-seller relates the "weird life" of T.S. Garp, beginning with his conception "when his mother sleeps with a man on his death bed"; though "unusual" is putting it mildly, this "unforgettable" tale is ultimately "affecting."

World Is Not Enough, The
19 | 19 | 18 | 21

1999 | Directed by Michael Apted | With Pierce Brosnan, Denise Richards | 128 minutes | Rated PG-13

Admittedly "pure escapism", 007's 19th trip to the big screen divides voters: fans vow that Pierce is "as good as Sean", but foes growl that "gadgets have replaced characterization and plot" and snicker at the "ludicrous" Richards playing a "short-shorts–wearing nuclear physicist."

Wrong Man, The ❶
22 | 24 | 24 | 21

1956 | Directed by Alfred Hitchcock | With Henry Fonda, Vera Miles, Anthony Quayle | 105 minutes | Not Rated

"Based on a true story" of a musician "falsely accused" of armed rob-bery and the subsequent "pain his family goes through", this "unusual"

Hitchcock drama is "less of a thriller" and more of a psychological study; but despite the "fine cast" and "solid" script, purists label it a "minor" work in the master's oeuvre, saying it "isn't suspenseful" enough.

☒ Wuthering Heights ◐

27 | 27 | 27 | 24

1939 | Directed by William Wyler | With Laurence Olivier, Merle Oberon, David Niven | 103 minutes | Not Rated

This "Gothic romance" is a "charter" member of the "pantheon" of silver screen weepies and the "ultimate" adaptation of the Brontë tale; Olivier's "soulful brooding" as a spurned, lower-caste lover is so "brilliantly intense" that it's inspired generations of maidens to "waste away from heartbreak on the moors" ever after.

X-Files, The

17 | 17 | 16 | 19

1998 | Directed by Rob Bowman | With David Duchovny, Gillian Anderson, Martin Landau | 120 minutes | Rated PG-13

Both "fans and novices appreciate" this blockbuster adaptation of the TV series that's "just like the show" but with some "twists" and an "occasional dirty word" thrown in; it doesn't "answer any questions" and may be "muddled, disappointing" stuff to connoisseurs, but it does "serve as a bridge between seasons" with some "catchy" moments.

X-Men

19 | 18 | 18 | 23

2000 | Directed by Bryan Singer | With Patrick Stewart, Hugh Jackman, Ian McKellen, Halle Berry, James Marsden | 104 minutes | Rated PG-13

Even those "who've never read the comic book" chime in with their "ringing endorsement" of this "true-to-the-source" adaptation of the Marvel sci-fi series; most memorable for Jackman's "starmaking turn", it's such an obvious "setup for a franchise" that many "popcorn" eaters are hungrily "awaiting the sequels."

X-Men: The Last Stand

20 | 19 | 19 | 25

2006 | Directed by Brett Ratner | With Hugh Jackman, Halle Berry, Ian McKellen, Famke Janssen | 104 minutes | Rated PG-13

The "choice to be normal or true to themselves" confronts the mutant superheroes as they battle "discrimination" and each other in this "big bang" finale to the franchise – or is it?; piling on more "spectacular" FX than ever (i.e. the "Golden Gate Bridge ripped from its base"), this "boisterous" juggernaut doesn't let up until the "last scene *after* the credits."

X2: X-Men United

24 | 21 | 22 | 27

2003 | Directed by Bryan Singer | With Patrick Stewart, Hugh Jackman, Ian McKellen, Halle Berry, Brian Cox | 133 minutes | Rated PG-13

"Finally, a sequel to sink your claws into": this "X-cellent" follow-up "tops the mediocre original" "in just about every way" – a "better storyline", "intriguing new characters", a "deservedly bigger role" for the "buff", "brooding" Jackman and "mega-cool special effects" . . . "what a bigger budget will do for a movie"; "can't wait for the next one – and there *will* be a next one."

XXX

15 | 12 | 14 | 20

2002 | Directed by Rob Cohen | With Vin Diesel, Asia Argento, Samuel L. Jackson | 124 minutes | Rated PG-13

"Check your brain at the door" and get snowed under by an avalanche of "terrific stunts" and "blowed-up stuff" in this "steroidal" refashioning of "James Bond" for the "slacker generation"; as for the acting,

Vin's rendition of a "smartass" agent bent on "saving the world" is "kinda stupid", though some Diesel disciples still stand by their man – provided he "zips his flap."

Yankee Doodle Dandy ✉◐

	OVERALL	ACTING	STORY	PROD.
	25	25	23	25

1942 | Directed by Michael Curtiz | With James Cagney, Joan Leslie, Walter Huston | 126 minutes | Not Rated

"Flag-waving", "red-white-and-blue" musical bio of the "all-American" showman George M. Cohan, starring Cagney in full "hoofer" bloom; the story's "whitewashed", but after a few bars of its "patriotic tunes" you'll understand why the "4th of July wouldn't be the same without it."

Year of Living Dangerously, The

24	25	25	24

1983 | Directed by Peter Weir | With Mel Gibson, Sigourney Weaver, Linda Hunt | 117 minutes | Rated PG

An outbreak of "civil war" during the "Sukarno regime" in '60s Indonesia comes alive in this "captivating" "political" drama following a journalist who's covering the conflict; though the "compelling" Gibson and Weaver cast "steamy sparks", Hunt took home an Oscar for her "tour-de-force", "gender-bending role" in this "tense" thriller.

Yellow Submarine

22	-	18	23

1968 | Directed by George Dunning | Animated | 90 minutes | Rated G

"Contagiously fun", this "lighthearted" "hallucination" of a cartoon supplies "eye-popping" "psychedelic" imagery aplenty in recounting a story about the Fab Four's battle to save Pepperland from the Blue Meanies; though the "actual Beatles don't provide" the speaking parts, their performance on the "foot-tapping" soundtrack is "more than enough" – and the music "won't drive parents crazy."

Yentl ∅

18	19	19	20

1983 | Directed by Barbra Streisand | With Barbra Streisand, Mandy Patinkin, Amy Irving | 132 minutes | Rated PG

"La Streisand" does it all – "acts, sings and directs" – in this "under-rated", "impeccably made" musical about a turn-of-the-century Jewish girl masquerading as a "boy in order to study the Talmud"; though foes call it Babs at her "self-indulgent worst", fans counter her "incredible talent" and "amazing attention to detail" make this "emotionally stirring" picture "deserving of more credit."

Yojimbo ◐▣

28	27	26	26

1961 | Directed by Akira Kurosawa | With Toshiro Mifune, Tatsuya Nakadai | 110 minutes | Not Rated

"Kurosawa's classic samurai film" stars Mifune as the "ultimate anti-hero" who "plays both sides" of a village feud between a silk merchant and a sake merchant, and then watches as the depraved "warring factions" destroy each other; the "inspiration" for myriad remakes (*A Fistful of Dollars, Last Man Standing*, etc.), this "far superior" original clearly "shows how great this director really is."

You Can Count on Me

23	26	22	20

2000 | Directed by Kenneth Lonergan | With Laura Linney, Mark Ruffalo, Rory Culkin, Matthew Broderick | 109 minutes | Rated R

Freshman director Lonergan "doesn't take a false step" in this "compelling", "character-driven" indie film about the "family bonds" between a "messed-up brother and sister" and the divergent paths their lives have taken; you can count on lots of "terrific acting" (with a "breakout performance from Linney") and a "lifelike lack of final resolution" that makes this a "sleeper with a heart."

☑ Young Frankenstein ◖ — 27 | 26 | 25 | 25

1974 | Directed by Mel Brooks | With Gene Wilder, Peter Boyle, Marty Feldman, Madeline Kahn, Cloris Leachman | 108 minutes | Rated PG

"Frankenstein Sr. would be proud" of this "insanely hysterical" "spoof of the Mary Shelley" horror classic that's Mel Brooks' "high-water mark" ("who else would have the monster" perform 'Puttin' on the Ritz' wearing a tuxedo?); Wilder is "pure genius" in the title role backed up by an "endlessly amusing" cast of characters spouting some of the "most quoted" dialogue in movie history; best line: a toss-up between "walk this way", "what knockers" and "hump? what hump?"; best song: Kahn's rendition of 'Ah! Sweet Mystery of Life', no contest.

Young Guns — 15 | 12 | 15 | 17

1988 | Directed by Christopher Cain | With Emilio Estevez, Kiefer Sutherland, Lou Diamond Phillips, Charlie Sheen | 107 minutes | Rated R

This "good Wild West romp 'n' stomp flick" featuring the "Brat Pack" in all their glory chronicles the beginnings of Billy the Kid's felonious career with his band of misfits, the Regulators; though "hardly the best movie ever", it works when you're in the mood for "interesting escapist fun."

You Only Live Twice — 22 | 21 | 20 | 22

1967 | Directed by Lewis Gilbert | With Sean Connery, Mie Hama, Donald Pleasence | 117 minutes | Rated PG

"Despite the absurdity of a six-foot-plus Scotsman as a spy in Japan", diehards declare this espionage flicker one of the "better Connery Bonds", given its amusing "'60s Tokyo" settings and that "great Nancy Sinatra" theme song; ok, it might be "cheesy" and "doesn't age well", but camp followers claim that's what makes it "all the more fun now."

You've Got Mail — 18 | 20 | 18 | 18

1998 | Directed by Nora Ephron | With Tom Hanks, Meg Ryan, Parker Posey, Greg Kinnear, Jean Stapleton | 119 minutes | Rated PG

Manhattan's "Upper West Side looks like Paris" in this "feel-good" romantic comedy, a "remake of The Shop Around the Corner" updated to "today's techie, e-mail-ish world"; though a tad too "cutesy pie" and "predictable" for cynics, "chick flick" fans find it "enchanting" thanks to that "great chemistry between Hanks and Ryan."

Y Tu Mamá También 🄵 — 24 | 24 | 23 | 21

2002 | Directed by Alfonso Cuarón | With Maribel Verdu, Gael García Bernal, Diego Luna, Diana Bracho | 105 minutes | Rated R

Two "upper-middle-class Mexican boys" "learn the facts of life" and then some from a "sexy older woman" during a road trip "that takes some unexpected turns" in this muy caliente "coming-of-age" character study; some say "everything takes a back seat (no pun intended)" to the "very explicit sex scenes" – whew! – but more cerebral types see it more as a "passionate film about life, youth and love" that's "far greater than the sum of its parts."

	OVERALL	ACTING	STORY	PROD.

Z ✉🅵
26 | **25** | **26** | **24**

1969 | Directed by Costa-Gavras | With Yves Montand, Irene Papas, Jean-Louis Trintignant, Jacques Perrin | 127 minutes | Rated PG
Unfortunately all "too true", this fact-based account of the assassination of a left-leaning scientist in a right-wing country is a crackerjack "political thriller" that's "deeply affecting" and "not easy to watch"; Montand is "nothing less than superb" in the title role, while director Costa-Gavras makes this "documentary-like" "exposé" of corruption "captivating from the first scene."

Zelig ◑
20 | **20** | **21** | **21**

1983 | Directed by Woody Allen | With Woody Allen, Mia Farrow | 79 minutes | Rated PG
What could be "Forrest Gump's ancestor" is the much "more charming (and neurotic) Zelig", a human chameleon who somehow manages to play a prominent role in 20th-century world events with "dryly comedic" results; it's an unusual, "technically complex" outing for the usually straightforward Allen that "warps history" by "digitally" inserting our hero into vintage "newsreel footage", but cynics say this "curiosity piece" has only "one clever idea" and "should have been funnier."

Ziegfeld Follies
24 | **21** | **-** | **26**

1946 | Directed by Vincente Minnelli et al | With Fred Astaire, Gene Kelly, Lena Horne, Judy Garland, Lucille Ball | 110 minutes | Not Rated
"Nearly every great star at MGM" is showcased in this "episodic" musical revue featuring "memorable" song-and-dance routines (like Fred Astaire and Gene Kelly in their only appearance together) interspersed with "dated comedy skits"; overall, it may be a "mixed bag", but aficionados swoon over the "lavishly ridiculous" highlights: a "breathtaking" Judy Garland number, "rare footage of Fanny Brice" and "Lucille Ball as a glamour girl with a whip."

Zodiac
21 | **24** | **22** | **22**

2007 | Directed by David Fincher | With Jake Gyllenhaal, Mark Ruffalo, Anthony Edwards, Robert Downey Jr. | 158 minutes | Rated R
The "stars align" for this "chilling" thriller about San Francisco's "never-solved" Zodiac killings of the '60s and '70s, with "special kudos" to Fincher's "artful reconstruction of the era" and to Gyllenhaal, Ruffalo and Downey Jr. for conveying the "frustration of a stalled murder investigation"; but the "fanatical" adherence to "realism" fires up foes, who fault the resulting "slow" pace and "lack of resolution."

Zoolander
16 | **16** | **15** | **16**

2001 | Directed by Ben Stiller | With Ben Stiller, Owen Wilson, Will Ferrell | 89 minutes | Rated PG-13
Think "*Spinal Tap* for models" to get the gist of this "silly takeoff on the fashion industry" wherein a "cheek-sucking" male supermodel is brainwashed into being an assassin; sourpusses say its gleeful depiction of "narcissistic ninnies" reflects the general "dumbing down of America", though a few argue that this future "cult classic" redeems itself with "snarky cameos" and "physical shtick", i.e. Ben and Owen's infamous "walk-off."

Zorba the Greek ◑

25 | 27 | 25 | 23

1964 | Directed by Michael Cacoyannis | With Anthony Quinn, Alan Bates, Irene Papas, Lila Kedrova | 142 minutes | Not Rated

There's ex-zorba-tant praise for this "still-fresh" drama about an Englishman visiting Crete on an existential quest, only to fall under the spell of a "person full of passion", the "flamboyant" Zorba; Quinn's "breakout" performance, plus some "memorable" theme music and dancing, keep this "feel-good" "affirmation of life" so "exciting and entertaining" that repeaters faithfully "see it every year."

Zulu

24 | 24 | 25 | 24

1964 | Directed by Cy Endfield | With Stanley Baker, Jack Hawkins, Michael Caine | 138 minutes | Not Rated

The "true story of valor in the face of incredible odds", this "epic treatment of a 19th-century British military disaster" is played out against the "broad canvas of Africa" and features an "unknown Caine" in his "first big film"; "visually stunning", it's "historically accurate without sacrificing dramatic appeal", and the "tension's unrelenting."

INDEXES

Decades

Listings include Overall ratings. ☑ indicates movies with the highest ratings, popularity and importance.

1910s/1920s

Birth of a Nation	25
Cabinet of Dr. Caligari	26
Cocoanuts, The	24
General, The	28
Gold Rush	28
Greed	28
Intolerance	27
Metropolis	27
Napoléon	29
Nosferatu	26
Potemkin	27
Thief of Bagdad	24

1930s

Adventures of Robin Hood	25
Alexander Nevsky	26
☑ All Quiet on Western Front	28
Angels with Dirty Faces	24
Animal Crackers	26
Anna Christie	26
Anna Karenina	26
Awful Truth	25
Beau Geste	25
Blue Angel	25
Bride of Frankenstein	25
Bringing Up Baby	27
Camille	26
Captain Blood	23
Captains Courageous	25
City Lights	28
Dark Victory	25
David Copperfield	27
Day at the Races	24
Destry Rides Again	25
Dinner at Eight	27
Dracula	24
☑ Duck Soup	27
Flying Down to Rio	23
Footlight Parade	23
42nd Street	24
Frankenstein	25
Freaks	23
Front Page	24
Fury	25
Gay Divorcee	25
Gold Diggers of 1933	25
☑ Gone with the Wind	28
Goodbye, Mr. Chips	25
Grand Hotel	25
Grand Illusion	28

Gunga Din	25
Hell's Angels	24
Holiday	27
Horse Feathers	24
Hound of the Baskervilles	22
Hunchback/Notre Dame	26
I'm No Angel	23
Invisible Man	22
☑ It Happened One Night	28
Jezebel	25
King Kong	25
Lady Vanishes	25
Little Caesar	24
Lost Horizon	25
M	26
Modern Times	28
Monkey Business	26
Mr. Deeds Goes to Town	25
Mr. Smith Goes to Washington	26
Mummy, The	24
Mutiny on the Bounty	25
My Man Godfrey	25
Night at the Opera	26
Ninotchka	25
Nothing Sacred	23
Of Mice and Men	26
Only Angels Have Wings	21
Public Enemy	25
Rules of the Game	27
Scarlet Empress	24
Shall We Dance	25
She Done Him Wrong	22
☑ Snow White	27
Stagecoach	27
Stage Door	25
Swing Time	26
Tarzan and His Mate	21
Tarzan the Ape Man	21
Thin Man	26
39 Steps	27
☑ Top Hat	27
Topper	20
Triumph of the Will	27
☑ Wizard of Oz	28
Women, The	26
☑ Wuthering Heights	27

1940s

Adam's Rib	26
All the King's Men	25
Arsenic and Old Lace	26

DECADES

Wolf Man	20
✓ Woman of the Year	27
Yankee Doodle Dandy	25
Ziegfeld Follies	24

1950s

✓ Affair to Remember	26
✓ African Queen	28
Alice in Wonderland	24
✓ All About Eve	28
American in Paris	26
Anastasia	23
Anatomy of a Murder	26
Around the World in 80 Days	22
Asphalt Jungle	24
Auntie Mame	25
Baby Doll	20
Bad and the Beautiful	24
Bad Day at Black Rock	24
Bad Seed	22
Band Wagon	26
Barefoot Contessa	24
Bell, Book and Candle	22
Ben-Hur	26
Big Heat	25
Blackboard Jungle	23
Black Orpheus	26
Born Yesterday	26
✓ Bridge on the River Kwai	28
Brigadoon	24
Bus Stop	21
Caine Mutiny	27
Carmen Jones	23
Carousel	24
Cat on a Hot Tin Roof	25
Cheaper By the Dozen	22
✓ Christmas Carol	27
Cinderella	26
Damn Yankees	24
Day the Earth Stood Still	25
Desk Set	25
Diabolique	26
Dial M for Murder	25
Diary of Anne Frank	23
D.O.A.	22
East of Eden	24
Father of the Bride	23
5,000 Fingers of Dr. T.	20
Fly, The	20
Forbidden Planet	25
400 Blows	27
Friendly Persuasion	24
From Here to Eternity	26
Funny Face	24
Gentlemen Prefer Blondes	23

Giant	24
Gigi	24
Godzilla	16
Gunfight at O.K. Corral	20
Guys and Dolls	24
Harvey	26
✓ High Noon	28
High Society	23
House of Wax	21
How to Marry a Millionaire	22
Imitation of Life	21
Invasion/Body Snatchers	24
I Want to Live!	24
Jailhouse Rock	18
Johnny Guitar	19
Journey to Center of Earth	19
Killing, The	25
King and I	27
King Solomon's Mines	20
Kiss Me Deadly	24
Kiss Me Kate	24
Lady and the Tramp	26
Ladykillers, The	21
La Strada	27
Lavender Hill Mob	25
Lili	24
Limelight	24
Love in the Afternoon	24
Love Is Many-Splendored...	22
Lust for Life	23
Magnificent Obsession	22
Man Who Knew Too Much	24
Man with the Golden Arm	24
Marty	25
Member of the Wedding	25
Mister Roberts	27
Mon Oncle	26
Moulin Rouge	21
Mouse That Roared	23
Mr. Hulot's Holiday	25
Niagara	21
✓ Night of the Hunter	27
Nights of Cabiria	27
✓ North by Northwest	28
No TIme for Sergeants	23
Oklahoma!	24
Old Yeller	24
Oliver Twist	25
On the Beach	26
✓ On the Waterfront	28
Operation Petticoat	19
✓ Paths of Glory	28
Peter Pan	25
Peyton Place	20
Pickup on South Street	23

Picnic	24
Pillow Talk	20
⊠ Place in the Sun	27
⊠ Quiet Man	27
⊠ Rashomon	29
⊠ Rear Window	28
Rebel Without a Cause	24
Rififi	26
Rio Bravo	24
Robe, The	22
⊠ Roman Holiday	27
Room at the Top	24
Sabrina	25
⊠ Searchers, The	27
Seven Brides/Seven Brothers	24
⊠ Seven Samurai	29
Seventh Seal	27
7th Voyage of Sinbad	20
Seven Year Itch	23
Shane	26
Show Boat	23
⊠ Singin' in the Rain	28
Sleeping Beauty	25
Smiles of a Summer Night	26
⊠ Some Like It Hot	28
South Pacific	24
⊠ Stalag 17	27
Star Is Born	25
Strangers on a Train	26
⊠ Streetcar Named Desire	27
Suddenly, Last Summer	24
Summertime	23
⊠ Sunset Boulevard	28
⊠ Sweet Smell of Success	27
Ten Commandments	24
Thing, The	23
Three Coins in the Fountain	21
Three Faces of Eve	24
To Catch a Thief	25
Touch of Evil	26
⊠ 12 Angry Men	28
20,000 Leagues Under Sea	22
⊠ Vertigo	27
Viva Zapata!	23
Wages of Fear	27
War of the Worlds	23
White Christmas	25
Wild One	22
Wild Strawberries	26
⊠ Witness for the Prosecution	27
Wrong Man	22

1960s

Absent-Minded Professor	19
Advise & Consent	27

Agony and the Ecstasy	23
Alamo, The	18
Alfie	22
Americanization of Emily	24
Anne of the Thousand Days	26
Apartment, The	25
Barbarella	13
Barefoot in the Park	23
Battle of Algiers	28
Becket	26
Bedazzled	20
Belle de Jour	24
Bells Are Ringing	24
Billy Liar	22
Birdman of Alcatraz	22
Birds, The	24
Blowup	26
Bob & Carol & Ted & Alice	17
Bonnie and Clyde	25
Born Free	24
⊠ Breakfast at Tiffany's	26
Breathless	25
Bride Wore Black	25
Bullitt	22
Butch Cassidy	26
Butterfield 8	23
Bye Bye Birdie	19
Cactus Flower	21
Camelot	21
Cape Fear	25
Cat Ballou	21
Charade	26
Charly	21
Children's Hour	24
Cincinnati Kid	24
Cleopatra	19
Collector, The	23
Contempt	25
Cool Hand Luke	26
Counterfeit Traitor	25
Damned, The	23
Darling	22
⊠ Days of Wine and Roses	27
Detective, The	20
Dirty Dozen	21
Divorce Italian Style	24
⊠ Doctor Zhivago	27
Don't Look Back	25
Dr. No	23
⊠ Dr. Strangelove	28
Easy Rider	23
8½	26
El Cid	19
Elmer Gantry	25
Elvira Madigan	20

Endless Summer	24
Exodus	23
Experiment in Terror	25
Faces	22
Fahrenheit 451	21
Fail-Safe	24
Fantastic Voyage	19
Finian's Rainbow	21
Fistful of Dollars	19
Flight of the Phoenix	25
For a Few Dollars More	23
Fortune Cookie	23
From Russia With Love	23
Funny Girl	26
Funny Thing Happened...	22
Georgy Girl	23
☒ Goldfinger	26
Goodbye, Columbus	19
Good, the Bad and the Ugly	24
☒ Graduate, The	27
☒ Great Escape	27
Great Race	20
Guess Who's Coming...	25
Guns of Navarone	23
Gypsy	20
Hard Day's Night	24
Hatari!	21
Heart Is a Lonely Hunter	25
Hello, Dolly!	20
Help!	19
Hiroshima, Mon Amour	25
How the West Was Won	23
Hud	26
Hush... Hush, Sweet Charlotte	24
Hustler, The	25
In Cold Blood	25
Inherit the Wind	26
In the Heat of the Night	24
Ipcress File	25
Irma La Douce	21
It's a Mad Mad Mad World	24
Judgment at Nuremberg	26
Jules and Jim	24
Juliet of the Spirits	25
Jungle Book	23
King of Hearts	26
Knife in the Water	24
La Dolce Vita	25
L'Avventura	24
☒ Lawrence of Arabia	29
Leopard, The	25
Lilies of the Field	25
☒ Lion in Winter	28
Lolita	24
Longest Day	24

Lord of the Flies	23
Love Bug	18
Magnificent Seven	26
Man and a Woman	24
☒ Manchurian Candidate	27
☒ Man for All Seasons	28
Man Who Shot Liberty Valance	25
Marnie	21
☒ Mary Poppins	27
Midnight Cowboy	26
Miracle Worker	25
Misfits, The	21
Music Man	25
Mutiny on the Bounty	22
☒ My Fair Lady	27
Never on Sunday	24
Night of the Iguana	23
Night of the Living Dead	22
Nutty Professor	21
Ocean's Eleven	16
Odd Couple	25
Oliver!	24
Once Upon a Time/West	25
101 Dalmatians	24
One, Two, Three	23
On Her Majesty's/Service	19
Our Man Flint	19
Paint Your Wagon	18
Parent Trap	23
Pawnbroker, The	26
Persona	27
Pink Panther	24
Pit and the Pendulum	22
Planet of the Apes	23
Point Blank	20
Prime of Miss Jean Brodie	25
☒ Producers, The	26
☒ Psycho	28
Raisin in the Sun	26
Repulsion	25
Requiem for a Heavyweight	26
Romeo and Juliet	26
Rosemary's Baby	24
Russians Are Coming...	21
Sand Pebbles	24
Satyricon	20
Servant, The	25
Seven Days in May	26
Ship of Fools	23
Shoot the Piano Player	25
Shot in the Dark	23
☒ Sound of Music	28
Spartacus	26
Splendor in the Grass	25
Spy Who Came in from Cold	25

Getaway, The	22	Midnight Express	24
Gimme Shelter	25	Missouri Breaks	16
☒ Godfather, The	29	Monty Python/Holy Grail	26
☒ Godfather Part II	29	Moonraker	16
Goodbye Girl	21	Muppet Movie	24
☒ Grease	23	Murder by Death	21
Great Gatsby	22	Murder on the Orient Express	23
Great Santini	22	My Brilliant Career	25
Great White Hope	25	My Night at Maud's	26
Grey Gardens	25	Nashville	23
Hair	20	Network	24
Halloween	22	New York, New York	19
Harder They Come	25	1900	22
Harold and Maude	25	Norma Rae	24
Heartbreak Kid	20	North Dallas Forty	19
Heaven Can Wait	21	Nosferatu the Vampyre	22
High Anxiety	21	Oh, God!	17
High Plains Drifter	18	Omen, The	21
I Never Sang for My Father	27	On a Clear Day You Can See...	20
In-Laws, The	24	☒ One Flew Over Cuckoo's...	27
Interiors	23	Outlaw Josey Wales	25
Invasion/Body Snatchers	19	Out-of-Towners	20
☒ Jaws	26	Owl and the Pussycat	17
Jeremiah Johnson	23	Paper Chase	23
Jerk, The	22	Paper Moon	22
Jesus Christ Superstar	21	Papillon	26
Julia	25	Parallax View	24
Klute	20	☒ Patton	27
Kramer vs. Kramer	23	Pete's Dragon	20
La Cage aux Folles	24	Picnic at Hanging Rock	24
Lady Sings the Blues	22	Pink Flamingos	18
Last Detail	22	Play It Again, Sam	22
Last Picture Show	23	Play Misty for Me	22
Last Tango in Paris	17	Poseidon Adventure	19
Last Waltz	26	Pretty Baby	17
Lenny	24	Prisoner of Second Avenue	22
Life of Brian	23	Pumping Iron	17
Little Big Man	24	Rescuers, The	23
Live and Let Die	19	Robin and Marian	20
Longest Yard	17	Rocky	25
Looking for Mr. Goodbar	18	Rocky Horror Picture Show	21
Lord of Rings	15	Rose, The	19
Love Story	19	Ruling Class	23
MacArthur	21	Ryan's Daughter	22
Man Called Horse	22	Same Time, Next Year	22
Manhattan	26	Saturday Night Fever	22
Man Who Fell to Earth	18	Save the Tiger	22
Man Who Would Be King	25	Scenes from a Marriage	25
Man with the Golden Gun	18	Seduction of Joe Tynan	22
Marathon Man	24	Serpico	23
Marriage of Maria Braun	25	Seven Beauties	26
MASH	26	1776	22
McCabe & Mrs. Miller	23	Shaft	17
Mean Streets	24	Shampoo	16
Meatballs	18	Silent Movie	20

DECADES

Color Purple	26	Four Seasons	21
Colors	20	Fox and the Hound	18
Coming to America	18	Frances	23
Conan the Barbarian	16	French Lieutenant's Woman	22
Crimes and Misdemeanors	26	Friday the 13th	16
Crocodile Dundee	17	Full Metal Jacket	24
Crossing Delancey	23	F/X	21
Dangerous Liaisons	24	Gallipoli	25
Dark Crystal	24	⁊ Gandhi	27
Das Boot	28	Ghostbusters	21
Dead Calm	20	Gloria	22
Dead Men Don't Wear Plaid	20	Glory	25
⁊ Dead Poets Society	24	Gods Must Be Crazy	22
Dead Ringers	18	Good Morning, Vietnam	22
Dead Zone	21	Goonies, The	23
Deathtrap	22	Gorillas in the Mist	19
Desperately Seeking Susan	15	Gremlins	19
Die Hard	23	Greystoke	15
Diner	25	Gung Ho	17
Dirty Dancing	21	Hairspray	19
Dirty Rotten Scoundrels	22	Hannah and Her Sisters	24
Diva	24	Heartburn	19
Do the Right Thing	23	Heathers	21
Down and Out/Beverly Hills	17	Heaven's Gate	14
Down by Law	24	Heavy Metal	20
Dressed to Kill	20	Henry V	26
Driving Miss Daisy	24	Highlander	19
Drugstore Cowboy	19	History of the World: Pt. I	22
Dune	14	Honey, I Shrunk the Kids	16
Eating Raoul	18	Hoosiers	23
Educating Rita	18	Hope and Glory	26
Eight Men Out	24	House of Games	24
Elephant Man	24	Hunger, The	20
Empire of the Sun	25	Indiana Jones/Last Crusade	24
Escape from New York	15	Indiana Jones/Temple of Doom	22
⁊ E.T.	26	Innerspace	15
Evil Dead	22	Jagged Edge	22
Excalibur	22	Jean de Florette	27
Eyewitness	23	Jewel of the Nile	19
Fabulous Baker Boys	20	Karate Kid	19
Fame	21	Killing Fields	26
Fanny and Alexander	26	King of Comedy	23
Fast Times/Ridgemont High	22	Kiss of the Spider Woman	22
Fatal Attraction	22	La Bamba	20
Ferris Bueller's Day Off	23	Labyrinth	22
Field of Dreams	22	Last Emperor	26
First Blood: Rambo	18	Last Metro	24
Fish Called Wanda	23	Last Temptation of Christ	22
⁊ Fitzcarraldo	27	Legend	18
Flashdance	16	Lethal Weapon	21
Fletch	19	License to Kill	14
Fly, The	16	Little Mermaid	24
Footloose	17	Little Shop of Horrors	19
48 HRS.	19	Living Daylights	14
For Your Eyes Only	18	Local Hero	26

Lost in America	20	Polyester	19
Mad Max	20	Postman Always Rings...	20
Mad Max/Thunderdome	17	Pretty in Pink	19
Manhunter	21	⧇ Princess Bride	27
Married to the Mob	17	Private Benjamin	17
Mask	21	Prizzi's Honor	21
Meaning of Life	24	Purple Rain	14
Melvin and Howard	22	Purple Rose of Cairo	21
Midnight Run	23	Quest for Fire	17
Midsummer Night's Sex	18	Radio Days	23
Missing	24	Raging Bull	26
Mission, The	24	Ragtime	21
Mississippi Burning	23	⧇ Raiders of the Lost Ark	28
Mommie Dearest	17	Rain Man	25
Money Pit	16	Raising Arizona	23
⧇ Moonstruck	24	Ran	27
Moscow on the Hudson	19	Reds	21
Mosquito Coast	16	Repo Man	17
Mr. Mom	18	Right Stuff	26
My Beautiful Laundrette	23	Risky Business	20
My Bodyguard	18	Road Warrior	22
My Dinner with Andre	21	RoboCop	16
My Favorite Year	22	Roger & Me	24
My Left Foot	25	Romancing the Stone	20
My Life As a Dog	25	Room with a View	26
Mystic Pizza	17	Roxanne	21
Naked Gun	20	Runaway Train	21
Name of the Rose	22	Running Man	17
National Lampoon's Vacation	22	Ruthless People	20
Natural, The	23	Salvador	21
Never Say Never Again	18	Say Anything	23
Nightmare on Elm Street	19	Scarface	22
Night Shift	19	Scrooged	19
9½ Weeks	15	Sea of Love	20
9 to 5	18	Secret of NIMH	24
No Way Out	20	Sex, Lies and Videotape	19
Octopussy	17	She's Gotta Have It	21
Officer and a Gentleman	22	Shining, The	25
Once Upon a Time/America	24	Shirley Valentine	24
On Golden Pond	24	⧇ Shoah	28
Ordinary People	25	Sid & Nancy	18
⧇ Out of Africa	25	Silkwood	22
Outrageous Fortune	15	Silverado	24
Outsiders, The	22	Sixteen Candles	22
Parenthood	22	Soldier's Story	26
Paris, Texas	22	Something Wild	20
Passage to India	25	Sophie's Choice	26
Pee-wee's Big Adventure	19	Spaceballs	18
Peggy Sue Got Married	19	Splash	19
Pennies from Heaven	17	Stand and Deliver	20
Personal Best	15	Stand by Me	24
Pink Floyd The Wall	23	Stardust Memories	19
Places in the Heart	20	Star 80	16
Platoon	25	Starman	19
Poltergeist	22	Star Trek II	23

Star Trek IV	21
☒ Star Wars V/Empire Strikes	26
Star Wars VI/Return of Jedi	24
Steel Magnolias	24
St. Elmo's Fire	17
Stir Crazy	20
Stop Making Sense	25
Stripes	21
Stunt Man	22
Suspect	20
Taps	20
Tender Mercies	24
Tequila Sunrise	17
Terminator, The	24
Terms of Endearment	25
Tess	21
Thing, The	23
This Is Spinal Tap	26
Three Men and a Baby	16
Time Bandits	21
To Live and Die in L.A.	20
Tootsie	25
☒ Top Gun	22
Torch Song Trilogy	23
Trading Places	23
Trip to Bountiful	24
Tron	18
Tucker	20
Twins	15
2010	16
Unbearable Lightness of Being	21
Uncle Buck	17
Untouchables, The	22
Urban Cowboy	18
Verdict, The	23
Victor/Victoria	23
Videodrome	17
View to a Kill	14
Wall Street	22
WarGames	22
War of the Roses	17
Weekend at Bernie's	16
☒ When Harry Met Sally...	26
Who Framed Roger Rabbit	24
Willow	20
Wings of Desire	24
Witches of Eastwick	17
Witness	23
Women on the Verge	24
Working Girl	20
World According to Garp	21
Year of Living Dangerously	24
Yentl	18
Young Guns	15
Zelig	20

1990s

Ace Ventura	15
Addams Family	17
Adventures of Priscilla	23
Affliction	20
Age of Innocence	22
Air Force One	18
Aladdin	24
Alice	20
All About My Mother	25
☒ American Beauty	24
American History X	25
American Pie	19
American President	21
Amistad	21
Analyze This	18
Anastasia	20
Anna and the King	19
Antonia's Line	25
Antz	20
Apollo 13	24
Armageddon	15
☒ As Good As It Gets	22
Austin Powers	19
Avalon	24
Awakenings	22
Babe	25
Backdraft	18
Barton Fink	20
Basic Instinct	19
Basquiat	17
Batman Returns	16
Beauty/Beast	26
Beethoven	16
Before Sunrise	23
Being John Malkovich	22
Benny & Joon	21
Big Daddy	17
Big Lebowski	20
Big Night	24
Birdcage, The	22
Blade	18
Bodyguard, The	14
Boogie Nights	19
Bottle Rocket	22
Boys Don't Cry	23
Boys on the Side	15
Boyz N the Hood	23
☒ Braveheart	26
Breaking the Waves	23
Bridges of Madison Co.	19
Brothers McMullen	19
Buena Vista Social Club	25
Bug's Life	24
Bugsy	18

Independence Day	19	Mummy, The	19
Indochine	23	My Best Friend's Wedding	19
Insider, The	25	My Cousin Vinny	22
Interview with the Vampire	19	My Girl	20
In the Company of Men	20	My Own Private Idaho	19
In the Line of Fire	20	Naked Lunch	17
In the Name of the Father	23	Natural Born Killers	14
Iron Giant	24	Nightmare Before Christmas	24
Jacob's Ladder	19	Notting Hill	19
James and the Giant Peach	20	Nutty Professor	15
Jerry Maguire	21	101 Dalmatians	18
JFK	19	Opposite of Sex	19
Joy Luck Club	25	Outbreak	16
Jumanji	18	Out of Sight	21
Jurassic Park	22	Paris is Burning	24
☒ L.A. Confidential	26	Patch Adams	16
La Femme Nikita	23	Patriot Games	21
Last of the Mohicans	22	Pelican Brief	16
L.A. Story	20	People vs. Larry Flynt	18
Last Seduction	22	Phenomenon	18
League of Their Own	20	Philadelphia	24
Leaving Las Vegas	20	Piano, The	21
Legends of the Fall	20	Player, The	23
Liar Liar	16	Pleasantville	20
Life Is Beautiful	27	Pocahontas	17
Like Water for Chocolate	25	Portrait of a Lady	16
Lion King	25	Postcards from the Edge	18
Little Princess	24	Prelude to a Kiss	16
Little Women	21	Presumed Innocent	20
Lock, Stock and Two...	23	☒ Pretty Woman	23
Lone Star	25	Primal Fear	22
Longtime Companion	23	Primary Colors	16
Lost Highway	16	Prince of Egypt	19
Love! Valour! Compassion!	21	Prince of Tides	19
Madness of King George	22	Professional, The	25
Magnolia	20	Psycho	14
Malcolm X	23	☒ Pulp Fiction	26
Mallrats	18	Quiz Show	21
Mambo Kings	20	Rainmaker, The	21
Man on the Moon	16	Ransom	16
Mask, The	17	Reality Bites	19
Mask of Zorro	18	Red Violin	24
☒ Matrix, The	25	Remains of the Day	24
Maverick	18	Replacement Killers	16
Mediterraneo	21	Reservoir Dogs	24
Men in Black	21	Reversal of Fortune	23
Metropolitan	20	River Runs Through It	22
Mighty Aphrodite	18	Robin Hood: Prince of Thieves	16
Miller's Crossing	22	Rock, The	20
Misery	21	Romeo + Juliet	19
Mission: Impossible	16	Romy & Michele's/Reunion	14
Mr. Holland's Opus	21	Ronin	20
Mrs. Brown	22	Rudy	23
Mrs. Doubtfire	20	Run Lola Run	23
Mulan	23	Rush Hour	19

DECADES

DECADES

DECADES

Genres/Special Features

Listings include Overall ratings. ☑ indicates movies with the highest ratings, popularity and importance.

ACTION/ADVENTURE

Adventures of Robin Hood	25
Aguirre: The Wrath of God	25
Around the World in 80 Days	22
Backdraft	18
Batman	20
Batman Begins	23
Batman Returns	16
Benji	19
Beverly Hills Cop	20
Black Stallion	24
Blade	18
Blood Diamond	25
Bourne Identity	20
Bourne Supremacy	21
Cannonball Run	17
Captain Blood	23
Captains Courageous	25
Cast Away	20
Catch Me If You Can	23
Charlie's Angels	13
Chronicles of Narnia	23
Clash of the Titans	18
Cliffhanger	15
Con Air	14
Conan the Barbarian	16
Contact	20
Count of Monte Cristo	19
Crimson Tide	21
Crocodile Dundee	17
Crouching Tiger	24
Daredevil	14
Day After Tomorrow	16
Deep, The	17
Deep Impact	15
Deliverance	25
Die Hard	23
Easy Rider	23
Eight Below	22
Enter the Dragon	23
Evil Dead	22
Excalibur	22
Face/Off	18
Fantastic Four	14
Fantastic Voyage	19
Fifth Element	19
First Blood: Rambo	18
☑ Fitzcarraldo	27
Flight of the Phoenix	25
Fly Away Home	22

From Dusk Till Dawn	18
Gauntlet, The	17
Getaway, The	22
☑ Gladiator	23
Gods Must Be Crazy	22
Goonies, The	23
☑ Great Escape	27
Great Race	20
Greystoke	15
Grindhouse	21
Hatari!	21
Hell's Angels	24
Hero	25
Hidalgo	20
Highlander	19
House of Flying Daggers	24
Independence Day	19
Indiana Jones/Last Crusade	24
Indiana Jones/Temple of Doom	22
I, Robot	18
Jewel of the Nile	19
Journey to Center of Earth	19
Jumanji	18
Jurassic Park	22
Kill Bill Vol. 1	23
Kill Bill Vol. 2	25
King Kong (1933)	25
King Kong (2005)	20
King Solomon's Mines	20
Knight's Tale	18
Kung Fu Hustle	23
Ladder 49	19
Lara Croft: Tomb Raider	13
Last Samurai	23
☑ Lawrence of Arabia	29
Legend	18
Lethal Weapon	21
Longest Yard (1974)	17
☑ Lord of Rings/Fellowship	27
☑ Lord of Rings/Return	28
☑ Lord of Rings/Two Towers	27
Mad Max	20
Mad Max/Thunderdome	17
Magnificent Seven	26
Man Who Would Be King	25
Mark of Zorro	22
Mask of Zorro	18
Master and Commander	23
☑ Matrix, The	25
Matrix Reloaded	21

GENRE/FEATURES

ADDITIONS

(Movies added since the last edition of the book)

GENRE/FEATURES

Our Man Flint	19	Shopgirl	18
Owl and the Pussycat	17	Short Cuts	22
Painted Veil	23	Shrek the Third	20
☒ Pan's Labyrinth	27	Silent Movie	20
Parallax View	24	16 Blocks	17
Paris is Burning	24	Slaughterhouse-Five	22
Passage to India	25	Sleepers	22
Pennies from Heaven	17	Sliding Doors	21
Personal Best	15	Soldier's Story	26
Picnic at Hanging Rock	24	Sounder	26
Pink Floyd The Wall	23	Spider-Man 3	19
Pirates Caribbean/World's End	21	SpongeBob SquarePants	16
Pirates Caribbean/Dead Man	20	Spy Game	19
Pitch Black	19	Stage Door	25
Point Blank	20	Stardust Memories	19
Polyester	19	Star 80	16
Portrait of a Lady	16	Starting Over	20
Possession	17	Stepford Wives	12
Prelude to a Kiss	16	Stepmom	19
Prestige, The	22	Strange Days	17
Prime	17	Stunt Man	22
Prize Winner of Defiance, OH	22	Summertime	23
Producers, The	18	Sweet Bird of Youth	24
Professional, The	25	Swing Time	26
Proof	18	Swordfish	15
Psycho	14	Tadpole	19
Purple Rain	14	Taps	20
Pursuit of Happyness	23	Tender Mercies	24
☒ Queen, The	26	Tequila Sunrise	17
Quest for Fire	17	This Boy's Life	21
Ragtime	21	Thousand Clowns	25
Rainmaker, The	21	Three Days of the Condor	24
Replacement Killers	16	300	22
Rififi	26	3 Women	25
Romy & Michele's/Reunion	14	Tin Cup	18
Ronin	20	To Live and Die in L.A.	20
Rudy	23	Torch Song Trilogy	23
Running Man	17	Torn Curtain	23
Rush Hour 2	17	Touch of Class	22
Saboteur	23	Toy Story 2	26
Salvador	21	Trip to Bountiful	24
Save the Tiger	22	Turning Point	23
Saw II	19	Twins	15
Say Anything	23	Unfinished Life	20
Scarlet Street	25	United 93	25
Score, The	17	U.S. Marshals	18
Scrooged	19	Velvet Goldmine	17
Sea of Love	20	Videodrome	17
Seduction of Joe Tynan	22	Village, The	16
Shaft	17	Viva Zapata!	23
Shall We Dance	25	Volver	24
Shall We Dance?	17	Waitress	24
She Done Him Wrong	22	WarGames	22
She's Gotta Have It	21	War of the Worlds (2005)	15
Shop Around the Corner	24	Warriors, The	23

AMERICANA

ANIMATED

(* Not for children)

GENRE/FEATURES

101 Dalmatians (1961)	24
Over the Hedge	23
Peter Pan (1953)	25
Pete's Dragon	20
Pinocchio	26
Pocahontas	17
Polar Express	21
Prince of Egypt	19
Rescuers, The	23
Robots	20
Secret of NIMH	24
Shark Tale	19
☑ Shrek	26
Shrek 2	26
Shrek the Third	20
Sleeping Beauty	25
☑ Snow White	27
Song of the South	23
South Park*	20
Space Jam	16
Spirit: Stallion of Cimarron	21
Spirited Away	27
SpongeBob SquarePants	16
Tarzan	22
☑ Toy Story	27
Toy Story 2	26
Triplets of Belleville*	24
Wallace & Gromit	24
Who Framed Roger Rabbit	24
Yellow Submarine	22

BIOGRAPHIES

Agony and the Ecstasy	23
Alexander Nevsky	26
☑ Amadeus	26
American Splendor	23
Anastasia (1956)	23
Anne of the Thousand Days	26
Antwone Fisher	23
Auto Focus	16
Aviator, The	23
Basquiat	17
Becket	26
Before Night Falls	22
Beyond the Sea	19
Birdman of Alcatraz	22
Bonnie and Clyde	25
Born Free	24
Buddy Holly Story	21
Bugsy	18
☑ Capote	26
☑ Cinderella Man	25
Cleopatra	19
Coal Miner's Daughter	24
Confessions/Dangerous Mind	19

De-Lovely	20
Diary of Anne Frank	23
Don't Look Back	25
Ed Wood	20
Elephant Man	24
Elizabeth	24
Evita	19
Finding Neverland	25
Frances	23
Frida	25
Funny Girl	26
Funny Lady	15
☑ Gandhi	27
Gods and Monsters	23
Gorillas in the Mist	19
Great White Hope	25
Gypsy	20
Henry & June	20
Hoffa	19
Hurricane, The	21
Iris	24
Julia	25
Kid Stays in the Picture	21
Kinsey	22
La Bamba	20
Lady Sings the Blues	22
Last Emperor	26
Last King of Scotland	25
☑ Lawrence of Arabia	29
Lenny	24
Lust for Life	23
MacArthur	21
Madness of King George	22
Malcolm X	23
☑ Man for All Seasons	28
Man on the Moon	16
Miracle Worker	25
Mommie Dearest	17
Mrs. Brown	22
Napoléon	29
☑ Patton	27
People vs. Larry Flynt	18
Pocahontas	17
Pollock	22
Pride of the Yankees	22
☑ Queen, The	26
Raging Bull	26
Ray	26
Reds	21
Scarlet Empress	24
Sergeant York	25
Sid & Nancy	18
Song of Bernadette	22
Star 80	16
Sylvia	16

Tucker	20
Unsinkable Molly Brown	21
Viva Zapata!	23
☒ Walk the Line	25
What's Love Got to Do with It	22
Yankee Doodle Dandy	25
Young Guns	15

BLACK COMEDIES

After Hours	21
American Psycho	19
Arsenic and Old Lace	26
Bad Santa	18
Beetlejuice	20
Being John Malkovich	22
Being There	26
Brazil	24
Clerks	23
Discreet Charm	24
Divorce Italian Style	24
☒ Dr. Strangelove	28
Eating Raoul	18
Ed Wood	20
Election	22
Fear and Loathing/Las Vegas	15
Fortune Cookie	23
Front, The	23
Gremlins	19
Groundhog Day	22
Happiness	23
Harold and Maude	25
Heathers	21
Kind Hearts and Coronets	26
King of Comedy	23
Ladykillers, The (1956)	21
Ladykillers, The (2004)	15
Life of Brian	23
Lolita	24
MASH	26
Meaning of Life	24
Monsieur Verdoux	25
Monty Python/Holy Grail	26
Night Shift	19
Nurse Betty	15
Pink Flamingos	18
Polyester	19
Prizzi's Honor	21
☒ Producers, The	26
Producers, The	18
Royal Tenenbaums	20
Ruling Class	23
Russians Are Coming...	21
Ruthless People	20
Secretary	21
Slaughterhouse-Five	22

Something Wild	20
Stepford Wives	12
Stunt Man	22
Time Bandits	21
To Die For	18
Wag the Dog	19
War of the Roses	17
Weekend at Bernie's	16
Welcome to the Dollhouse	22
What About Bob?	18
Where's Poppa?	23

BLOCKBUSTERS

(Annual highest grossing movies with year of release)

Aladdin	1992	24
Armageddon	1998	15
Back to the Future	1985	23
Bambi	1942	26
Batman	1989	20
Bells of St. Mary's	1945	24
Ben-Hur	1959	26
☒ Best Years of Our Lives	1946	28
Birth of a Nation	1915	25
☒ Blazing Saddles	1974	25
☒ Bridge on the River Kwai	1957	28
Butch Cassidy	1969	26
Cleopatra	1963	19
☒ E.T.	1982	26
Exorcist, The	1973	25
☒ Forrest Gump	1994	24
French Connection	1971	25
Funny Girl	1968	26
Ghostbusters	1984	21
☒ Godfather, The	1972	29
Going My Way	1944	24
☒ Gone with the Wind	1939	28
☒ Graduate, The	1967	27
☒ Grease	1978	23
☒ Harry Potter/Sorcerer's	2001	24
Home Alone	1990	19
Honey, I Shrunk the Kids	1989	16
How Grinch Stole Xmas	2000	17
Independence Day	1996	19
☒ Jaws	1975	26
Jurassic Park	1993	22
King Kong (1933)	1933	25
King Solomon's Mines	1950	20
Kramer vs. Kramer	1979	23
☒ Lawrence of Arabia	1962	29
☒ Lord of Rings/Return	2003	28
Love Story	1970	19
☒ Mary Poppins	1964	27
Mister Roberts	1955	27
Mrs. Miniver	1942	25
Night at the Opera	1935	26

GENRE/FEATURES

Peyton Place	1957	20
Pirates Caribbean/Dead Man	2006	20
🅩 Raiders of the Lost Ark	1981	28
Rain Man	1988	25
Red River	1948	26
Robe, The	1953	22
Robin Hood: Prince	1991	16
Rocky	1976	25
🅩 Saving Private Ryan	1998	26
Sergeant York	1941	25
Shrek 2	2004	26
🅩 Snow White	1937	27
🅩 Sound of Music	1965	28
South Pacific	1958	24
Spartacus	1960	26
Spider-Man	2002	21
🅩 Star Wars	1977	28
Star Wars I/Phantom Menace	1999	18
Star Wars III/Revenge of Sith	2005	23
🅩 Star Wars V/Empire Strikes	1980	26
Star Wars VI/Return of Jedi	1983	24
Ten Commandments	1956	24
Terminator 2: Judgment Day	1991	23
Thin Man	1934	26
Three Men and a Baby	1987	16
Titanic	1997	19
🅩 Top Gun	1986	22
🅩 Toy Story	1995	27
Twister	1996	15
Under Siege	1992	15
🅩 West Side Story	1961	27
White Christmas	1954	25

BUDDY FILMS

About a Boy	21
Analyze That	14
Analyze This	18
Auto Focus	16
Blues Brothers	22
Breaking Away	24
Brokeback Mountain	24
Butch Cassidy	26
City Slickers	20
Down by Law	24
Easy Rider	23
48 HRS.	19
F/X	21
Ghost World	23
Gloria	22
Gunga Din	25
Harold & Kumar/White Castle	19

Lethal Weapon	21
Man Who Would Be King	25
Mean Streets	24
Men in Black	21
Men in Black II	14
Midnight Cowboy	26
Midnight Run	23
Motorcycle Diaries	23
Night Shift	19
North Dallas Forty	19
Odd Couple	25
Outrageous Fortune	15
Roger Dodger	18
Rush Hour	19
Rush Hour 2	17
Sahara	17
Starsky & Hutch	14
Stir Crazy	20
Swingers	23
Thelma & Louise	23
Wedding Crashers	21

CAMP CLASSICS

Adventures of Priscilla	23
Auntie Mame	25
Barbarella	13
Birdcage, The	22
Bride of Frankenstein	25
Conan the Barbarian	16
Duel in the Sun	23
Eating Raoul	18
Evil Dead	22
Fly, The (1958)	20
Gentlemen Prefer Blondes	23
Godzilla	16
🅩 Grease	23
Hairspray	19
How to Marry a Millionaire	22
Hush... Hush, Sweet Charlotte	24
Imitation of Life	21
I'm No Angel	23
I Want to Live!	24
Johnny Guitar	19
La Cage aux Folles	24
Little Shop of Horrors	19
Mildred Pierce	26
Mommie Dearest	17
9½ Weeks	15
Pee-wee's Big Adventure	19
Peyton Place	20
Pillow Talk	20
Pink Flamingos	18
Poseidon Adventure	19
Rocky Horror Picture Show	21
Shaun of the Dead	22

GENRE/FEATURES

Wedding Singer	17
What Women Want	15
☑ When Harry Met Sally...	26
White Oleander	18
Women, The	26
Working Girl	20
You've Got Mail	18

CHILDREN/FAMILY

(See also Animated)

Annie	19
Babe	25
Bad News Bears	18
Beethoven	16
Bells of St. Mary's	24
Big	23
Black Stallion	24
Born Free	24
Bridge to Terabithia	22
Casper	15
Charlie/Choc. Factory	18
Charlotte's Web	23
Cheaper By the Dozen (2003)	17
☑ Christmas Carol	27
Christmas Story	26
Cool Runnings	18
Dark Crystal	24
David Copperfield	27
Dr. Dolittle	16
Eight Below	22
Elf	21
☑ E.T.	26
Father of the Bride (1950)	23
Father of the Bride (1991)	20
Fly Away Home	22
Freaky Friday (1976)	18
Freaky Friday (2003)	21
Free Willy	17
George of the Jungle	17
Goonies, The	23
Great Race	20
Harry Potter/Chamber	24
Harry Potter/Goblet of Fire	24
Harry Potter/Prisoner	24
☑ Harry Potter/Sorcerer's	24
Hidalgo	20
Holes	23
Honey, I Shrunk the Kids	16
Hook	17
How the Grinch Stole Xmas	17
☑ It's a Wonderful Life	27
Journey to Center of Earth	19
Jungle Book (1942)	24
Labyrinth	22
Lemony Snicket	18

Lili	24
Little Princess	24
Love Bug	18
☑ Mary Poppins	27
Mrs. Doubtfire	20
Nanny McPhee	21
National Velvet	24
Old Yeller	24
Oliver!	24
101 Dalmatians (1996)	18
Parent Trap	23
Pee-wee's Big Adventure	19
Peter Pan (2003)	20
☑ Princess Bride	27
Princess Diaries	18
Remember the Titans	20
Rookie, The	22
Santa Clause	19
Sounder	26
☑ Sound of Music	28
Spy Kids	19
Spy Kids 2	16
Stuart Little	19
Stuart Little 2	19
Swiss Family Robinson	23
Three Men and a Baby	16
Tron	18
20,000 Leagues Under Sea	22
Whale Rider	25
Willow	20
☑ Willy Wonka	26
Wiz, The	16
☑ Wizard of Oz	28

CITY SETTINGS

L A

☑ Adaptation	22
American Gigolo	19
Bad and the Beautiful	24
Barfly	18
Barton Fink	20
Beverly Hills Cop	20
☑ Big Sleep	27
Bodyguard, The	14
Boyz N the Hood	23
☑ Chinatown	27
Clueless	21
Crash	26
Day of the Locust	20
D.O.A.	22
Down and Out/Beverly Hills	17
Ed Wood	20
Gods and Monsters	23
Grand Canyon	18
Kiss Kiss Bang Bang	20

GENRE/FEATURES

Klute	20
Madagascar	21
Maid in Manhattan	14
Manhattan	26
Marathon Man	24
Marty	25
Mean Streets	24
Melinda and Melinda	17
Metropolitan	20
Midnight Cowboy	26
Mighty Aphrodite	18
Miracle on 34th Street	25
☑ Moonstruck	24
Moscow on the Hudson	19
My Favorite Year	22
Network	24
New York, New York	19
Odd Couple	25
Once Upon a Time/America	24
On the Town	23
☑ On the Waterfront	28
Out-of-Towners	20
Owl and the Pussycat	17
Pawnbroker, The	26
Pieces of April	21
Pollock	22
Prizzi's Honor	21
Quiz Show	21
Radio Days	23
Ransom	16
☑ Rear Window	28
Rent	19
Rosemary's Baby	24
Saturday Night Fever	22
Serpico	23
Six Degrees of Separation	21
Spider-Man	21
Spider-Man 2	22
Spider-Man 3	19
Sunshine Boys	21
☑ Sweet Smell of Success	27
☑ Taxi Driver	27
Tootsie	25
25th Hour	21
Unfaithful	21
Unmarried Woman	20
Wall Street	22
Warriors, The	23
☑ West Side Story	27
☑ When Harry Met Sally...	26
Working Girl	20
You've Got Mail	18

PARIS

Amélie	26
American in Paris	26
Before Sunset	21
Belle de Jour	24
Bourne Identity	20
Breathless	25
Charade	26
☑ Children of Paradise	28
Da Vinci Code	19
Diva	24
Dreamers, The	17
400 Blows	27
Funny Face	24
Gigi	24
Henry & June	20
Hunchback/Notre Dame (1939)	26
Irma La Douce	21
Last Tango in Paris	17
Love in the Afternoon	24
Moulin Rouge	21
Moulin Rouge!	23
Rififi	26
Shoot the Piano Player	25
Victor/Victoria	23

ROME

Ben-Hur	26
Bicycle Thief	27
Cleopatra	19
Funny Thing Happened...	22
☑ Gladiator	23
La Dolce Vita	25
Open City	28
☑ Roman Holiday	27
Satyricon	20
Spartacus	26
Talented Mr. Ripley	18
Three Coins in the Fountain	21

SAN FRANCISCO

Basic Instinct	19
Birdman of Alcatraz	22
Birds, The	24
Bullitt	22
Conversation, The	25
Dead Man Walking	23
Dirty Harry	21
Experiment in Terror	25
48 HRS.	19
Foul Play	21
Game, The	22
Invasion/Body Snatchers (1978)	19
Jagged Edge	22
Love Bug	18
Pursuit of Happyness	23
Rock, The	20
Time After Time	23
Towering Inferno	18

Z Vertigo 27
What's Up, Doc? 21
Zodiac 21

COMEDIES

(See also Black Comedies,
Dramedies, Screwball Comedies)
Absent-Minded Professor 19
Ace Ventura 15
Adam's Rib 26
Addams Family 17
Adventures of Priscilla 23
Z Airplane! 24
Amarcord 26
American Pie 19
American Werewolf/London 20
Analyze That 14
Analyze This 18
Anger Management 13
Z Animal House 24
Z Annie Hall 27
Apprenticeship/Duddy Kravitz 22
Arthur 20
Auntie Mame 25
Austin Powers 19
Baby Boom 19
Bad News Bears 18
Bananas 23
Barbershop 20
Barefoot in the Park 23
Bedazzled 20
Beethoven 16
Bell, Book and Candle 22
Best in Show 24
Beverly Hills Cop 20
Big 23
Big Business 19
Big Daddy 17
Big Lebowski 20
Bill & Ted's 15
Birdcage, The 22
Bishop's Wife 24
Z Blazing Saddles 25
Breakfast Club 22
Bridget Jones's Diary 21
Brighton Beach Memoirs 22
Bringing Down the House 19
Bring It On 17
Broadway Danny Rose 22
Brother from Another Planet 23
Bruce Almighty 18
Bullets Over Broadway 21
Cactus Flower 21
Z Caddyshack 24
Cat Ballou 21

Charlie's Angels 13
Chasing Amy 20
Cheaper By the Dozen (1950) 22
Cheaper By the Dozen (2003) 17
City Slickers 20
Clueless 21
Coming to America 18
Cool Runnings 18
Crocodile Dundee 17
Crossing Delancey 23
Cry-Baby 17
Dave 21
Dead Men Don't Wear Plaid 20
Deconstructing Harry 16
Desk Set 25
Desperately Seeking Susan 15
Dirty Rotten Scoundrels 22
Dodgeball 16
Down and Out/Beverly Hills 17
Down with Love 18
Dr. Dolittle 16
Dumb and Dumber 15
Eat Drink Man Woman 25
Elf 21
Emma 22
Failure to Launch 15
Family Man 16
Fast Times/Ridgemont High 22
Father of the Bride (1950) 23
Father of the Bride (1991) 20
Ferris Bueller's Day Off 23
Fever Pitch 20
50 First Dates 18
First Wives Club 17
Fish Called Wanda 23
Fletch 19
40 Year Old Virgin 19
Foul Play 21
Four Weddings and a Funeral 21
Freaky Friday (1976) 18
Freaky Friday (2003) 21
Freshman, The 21
Full Monty 22
General, The 28
George of the Jungle 17
Get Shorty 20
Ghostbusters 21
Gods Must Be Crazy 22
Gold Rush 28
Goodbye, Columbus 19
Goodbye Girl 21
Z Graduate, The 27
Great Dictator 26
Great Race 20
Gremlins 19

GENRE/FEATURES

Grosse Pointe Blank	22
Grumpy Old Men	21
Gung Ho	17
Hairspray	19
Harold & Kumar/White Castle	19
Harvey	26
Hatari!	21
Heartbreak Kid	20
Heaven Can Wait (1943)	24
High Anxiety	21
History of the World: Pt. I	22
Hitch	21
Hollywood Ending	15
Home Alone	19
Honey, I Shrunk the Kids	16
Hot Fuzz	24
How to Lose a Guy...	19
How to Marry a Millionaire	22
Hudsucker Proxy	22
I'm No Angel	23
Importance of Being Earnest	21
In & Out	17
Innerspace	15
It's a Mad Mad Mad World	24
I Was a Male War Bride	21
Jackass: The Movie	13
Jerk, The	22
Jungle Book (1967)	23
Just Like Heaven	19
Kissing Jessica Stein	21
Knight's Tale	18
Kung Fu Hustle	23
La Cage aux Folles	24
L.A. Story	20
Lavender Hill Mob	25
Legally Blonde	19
Liar Liar	16
Little Big Man	24
Local Hero	26
Lost in America	20
Love Actually	22
Love Bug	18
Maid in Manhattan	14
Mallrats	18
Manhattan	26
Man Who Came to Dinner	26
Married to the Mob	17
Mask, The	17
Matchstick Men	20
Maverick	18
Mean Girls	20
Meatballs	18
Mediterraneo	21
Meet the Fockers	18
Meet the Parents	19

Midnight Run	23
Midsummer Night's Sex	18
Mighty Aphrodite	18
Mighty Wind	23
Miss Congeniality	15
Mister Roberts	27
Modern Times	28
Money Pit	16
Monkey Business	26
Mon Oncle	26
Monster-in-Law	15
Mouse That Roared	23
Mr. Blandings	23
Mr. Deeds Goes to Town	25
Mr. Hulot's Holiday	25
Mr. Mom	18
Mrs. Doubtfire	20
Muppet Movie	24
Murder by Death	21
Must Love Dogs	16
My Best Friend's Wedding	19
My Big Fat Greek Wedding	23
My Cousin Vinny	22
My Favorite Year	22
My Little Chickadee	23
Naked Gun	20
Napoleon Dynamite	19
National Lampoon's Vacation	22
9 to 5	18
No Time for Sergeants	23
Notting Hill	19
Nutty Professor (1963)	21
Nutty Professor (1996)	15
O Brother, Where Art Thou?	22
Odd Couple	25
Oh, God!	17
Old School	20
One, Two, Three	23
Operation Petticoat	19
Out-of-Towners	20
Outrageous Fortune	15
Owl and the Pussycat	17
Parent Trap	23
Pee-wee's Big Adventure	19
Peggy Sue Got Married	19
Pillow Talk	20
Pink Panther	24
Play It Again, Sam	22
Postcards from the Edge	18
Pretty in Pink	19
☑ Pretty Woman	23
Princess Diaries	18
Private Benjamin	17
Purple Rose of Cairo	21
Radio Days	23

Repo Man	17
Risky Business	20
Romy & Michele's/Reunion	14
Roxanne	21
Rush Hour	19
Rush Hour 2	17
Santa Clause	19
School of Rock	20
Seven Year Itch	23
Shall We Dance?	17
Shampoo	16
Shaun of the Dead	22
She Done Him Wrong	22
She's Gotta Have It	21
Shirley Valentine	24
Shot in the Dark	23
Silent Movie	20
Silver Streak	19
Sister Act	18
Sixteen Candles	22
Slap Shot	22
Sleeper	23
Sleepless in Seattle	21
Smiles of a Summer Night	26
Smokey and the Bandit	16
Z Some Like It Hot	28
Something's Gotta Give	23
South Park	20
Spaceballs	18
Starsky & Hutch	14
Starting Over	20
Stir Crazy	20
Strictly Ballroom	23
Stripes	21
Sunshine Boys	21
Swingers	23
Tadpole	19
Take the Money and Run	21
10	17
Thank You for Smoking	23
There's Something About Mary	21
This Is Spinal Tap	26
Thousand Clowns	25
Three Men and a Baby	16
Tie Me Up! Tie Me Down!	20
Tin Cup	18
Tom Jones	25
Tootsie	25
Topkapi	24
Topper	20
Touch of Class	22
Trading Places	23
Twins	15
Two for the Road	24

Two Weeks Notice	16
Uncle Buck	17
Unmarried Woman	20
Waiting for Guffman	25
Waitress	24
Wayne's World	17
Wedding Banquet	22
Wedding Crashers	21
Wedding Singer	17
What Women Want	15
Z When Harry Met Sally...	26
While You Were Sleeping	18
Whole Nine Yards	17
Wimbledon	15
Witches of Eastwick	17
Z Woman of the Year	27
Working Girl	20
Z Young Frankenstein	27
You've Got Mail	18
Zelig	20
Ziegfeld Follies	24
Zoolander	16

COMIC BOOK ADAPTATIONS

Addams Family	17
Akira	23
American Splendor	23
Annie	19
Barbarella	13
Batman	20
Batman Begins	23
Batman Returns	16
Blade	18
Casper	15
Daredevil	14
Dick Tracy	13
Fantastic Four	14
Fritz the Cat	16
Ghost World	23
Heavy Metal	20
History of Violence	22
Men in Black	21
Men in Black II	14
Road to Perdition	23
Sin City	22
Spider-Man	21
Spider-Man 2	22
Spider-Man 3	19
Superman	22
300	22
V for Vendetta	22
X-Men	19
X-Men: The Last Stand	20
X2: X-Men United	24

GENRE/FEATURES

COMING OF AGE

CRIME

(See also Film Noir)

Lock, Stock and Two...	23
Lucky Number Slevin	21
M	26
Manhunter	21
Married to the Mob	17
Matchstick Men	20
Mean Streets	24
Miller's Crossing	22
Monsieur Verdoux	25
Monster	24
Mystic River	26
Natural Born Killers	14
Nurse Betty	15
Ocean's Eleven (1960)	16
Ocean's Eleven (2001)	19
Ocean's Twelve	14
Once Upon a Time/America	24
☒ On the Waterfront	28
Out of Sight	21
Panic Room	18
Prizzi's Honor	21
Public Enemy	25
☒ Pulp Fiction	26
☒ Rear Window	28
Red Dragon	19
Reservoir Dogs	24
Road to Perdition	23
Scarface	22
Score, The	17
Serpico	23
Shoot the Piano Player	25
Sleepers	22
Snatch	21
☒ Sting, The	27
Sugarland Express	18
To Catch a Thief	25
To Live and Die in L.A.	20
Traffic	23
Training Day	20
True Romance	24
25th Hour	21
Untouchables, The	22
☒ Usual Suspects	27
Whole Nine Yards	17
Wonderland	16

CULT FILMS

Adventures of Priscilla	23
After Hours	21
Akira	23
☒ All About Eve	28
American Splendor	23
Barbarella	13
Barfly	18
Being John Malkovich	22

Big Lebowski	20
Bill & Ted's	15
☒ Blade Runner	26
Blue Velvet	22
Brazil	24
☒ Breakfast at Tiffany's	26
Breakfast Club	22
Brother from Another Planet	23
☒ Casablanca	29
☒ Children of Paradise	28
Clerks	23
Clockwork Orange	25
Crying Game	22
Dawn of the Dead	19
Dirty Dancing	21
Donnie Darko	22
Down by Law	24
☒ Dr. Strangelove	28
Dune	14
Eating Raoul	18
8½	26
Enter the Dragon	23
Eraserhead	21
Eternal Sunshine	23
Evil Dead	22
☒ Fantasia	28
Fear and Loathing/Las Vegas	15
Ferris Bueller's Day Off	23
Fight Club	23
5,000 Fingers of Dr. T.	20
Fletch	19
Forbidden Planet	25
Freaks	23
Friday the 13th	16
From Dusk Till Dawn	18
Gods Must Be Crazy	22
☒ Grease	23
Grey Gardens	25
Grindhouse	21
☒ Gun Crazy	27
Harold and Maude	25
Heathers	21
Heavy Metal	20
Highlander	19
☒ It's a Wonderful Life	27
Kill Bill Vol. 1	23
Kill Bill Vol. 2	25
King of Hearts	26
Life of Brian	23
Little Shop of Horrors	19
Mad Max	20
☒ Manchurian Candidate (1962)	27
Meaning of Life	24
Melvin and Howard	22
Monty Python/Holy Grail	26

Mulholland Dr.	20
My Dinner with Andre	21
Napoleon Dynamite	19
Night of the Living Dead	22
Pee-wee's Big Adventure	19
Pink Flamingos	18
Pink Floyd The Wall	23
Polyester	19
☑ Princess Bride	27
Raising Arizona	23
Red Shoes	26
Repo Man	17
Repulsion	25
Road Warrior	22
Rocky Horror Picture Show	21
Royal Tenenbaums	20
Ruling Class	23
Rushmore	23
Serenity	23
7th Voyage of Sinbad	20
☑ Shawshank Redemption	28
Showgirls	5
Sin City	22
☑ Sound of Music	28
☑ Star Wars	28
St. Elmo's Fire	17
Stunt Man	22
Texas Chainsaw Massacre	17
Time Bandits	21
True Romance	24
28 Days Later	18
Videodrome	17
Village of the Damned	21
Waiting for Guffman	25
Warriors, The	23
Welcome to the Dollhouse	22
Where's Poppa?	23
☑ Willy Wonka	26
☑ Wizard of Oz	28

DATE MOVIES

Amélie	26
☑ Annie Hall	27
Barefoot in the Park	23
Before Sunrise	23
Before Sunset	21
Big Chill	23
Bodyguard, The	14
Bull Durham	22
Butterflies Are Free	21
☑ Casablanca	29
Chocolat	22
Dirty Dancing	21
Eternal Sunshine	23

Fabulous Baker Boys	20
Failure to Launch	15
Fever Pitch	20
Four Weddings and a Funeral	21
Frankie & Johnny	20
Georgy Girl	23
Ghost	21
High Fidelity	21
How to Lose a Guy...	19
Jerry Maguire	21
Just Like Heaven	19
Love Actually	22
Love Story	19
Man and a Woman	24
Mediterraneo	21
☑ Moonstruck	24
My Big Fat Greek Wedding	23
Notting Hill	19
Officer and a Gentleman	22
Prelude to a Kiss	16
☑ Pretty Woman	23
Prince of Tides	19
Romancing the Stone	20
☑ Roman Holiday	27
Romeo and Juliet	26
Saturday Night Fever	22
Say Anything	23
☑ Shakespeare in Love	24
Shopgirl	18
Sideways	23
Sleepless in Seattle	21
Sliding Doors	21
Something's Gotta Give	23
Starman	19
Strictly Ballroom	23
Summer of '42	21
Titanic	19
Way We Were	24
Wedding Singer	17
What Women Want	15
☑ When Harry Met Sally...	26
Wimbledon	15
You've Got Mail	18

DISASTER FLICKS

(See also End of the World)

☑ Airplane!	24
Airport	17
Backdraft	18
China Syndrome	22
Perfect Storm	16
Poseidon Adventure	19
Titanic	19
Towering Inferno	18
Twister	15

DOCUMENTARIES

Bowling for Columbine	22
Buena Vista Social Club	25
Celluloid Closet	25
Don't Look Back	25
Endless Summer	24
Enron/Smartest Guys	25
Fahrenheit 9/11	21
Fog of War	26
Gimme Shelter	25
Grey Gardens	25
Hoop Dreams	26
Inconvenient Truth	24
Kid Stays in the Picture	21
Last Waltz	26
☒ March of the Penguins	26
Murderball	25
Paris is Burning	24
Pumping Iron	17
Roger & Me	24
☒ Shoah	28
☒ Sorrow and the Pity	29
☒ Spellbound (2003)	28
Stop Making Sense	25
Super Size Me	24
That's Entertainment!	25
Triumph of the Will	27
Truth or Dare	15
Who Killed the Electric Car?	23
Winged Migration	26
Woodstock	24
Wordplay	23

DRAMAS

(See also Crime, Dramedies, Film Noir)

Absence of Malice	21
Accidental Tourist	20
Advise & Consent	27
Affliction	20
Age of Innocence	22
Agnes of God	21
Akeelah and the Bee	26
Alfie	22
Alice Doesn't Live Here	24
All That Jazz	24
All the King's Men	25
All the President's Men	25
All the Right Moves	16
American Gigolo	19
American History X	25
Amistad	21
Anna Christie	26
Anna Karenina	26
Antonia's Line	25
Atlantic City	24

Au Revoir Les Enfants	27
Avalon	24
Aviator, The	23
Awakenings	22
Babel	22
Babette's Feast	26
Baby Doll	20
Bad and the Beautiful	24
Bad Education	23
Bang the Drum Slowly	23
Barefoot Contessa	24
Barfly	18
Barry Lyndon	20
☒ Beautiful Mind	26
Belle de Jour	24
☒ Best Years of Our Lives	28
Bicycle Thief	27
Billy Elliot	25
Birdy	23
Blackboard Jungle	23
Black Orpheus	26
Blowup	26
Blue Angel	25
Blue Velvet	22
Boogie Nights	19
☒ Breaker Morant	27
Breaking Away	24
Breaking the Waves	23
Breathless	25
Butterfield 8	23
Caine Mutiny	27
Candidate, The	20
Carnal Knowledge	22
Cat on a Hot Tin Roof	25
Changing Lanes	16
Chariots of Fire	26
Charly	21
Children of a Lesser God	23
Children's Hour	24
Cider House Rules	22
Cincinnati Kid	24
Cinderella Liberty	19
Cinema Paradiso	26
☒ Citizen Kane	28
Closer	19
Coach Carter	21
Cold Mountain	22
Color of Money	16
Color Purple	26
Coming Home	23
Conformist, The	26
Contempt	25
Contender, The	19
Conversation, The	25
Crash	26

GENRE/FEATURES

subscribe to zagat.com

GENRE/FEATURES

Witness	23
☑ Witness for the Prosecution	27
Woman Under the Influence	24
Women in Love	23
Woodsman, The	21
Wrong Man	22
☑ Wuthering Heights	27
Year of Living Dangerously	24
Yentl	18
Yojimbo	28
You Can Count on Me	23
Zorba the Greek	25

DRAMEDIES

(Part comedy, part drama)

About a Boy	21
About Last Night. . .	17
About Schmidt	21
☑ Adaptation	22
☑ African Queen	28
Alice	20
☑ All About Eve	28
All About My Mother	25
Almost Famous	23
☑ American Beauty	24
American Graffiti	24
Americanization of Emily	24
American Splendor	23
Anniversary Party	18
Apartment, The	25
☑ As Good As It Gets	22
Barton Fink	20
Beaches	22
Being Julia	23
Bend It Like Beckham	26
Benny & Joon	21
Big Chill	23
Big Fish	22
Big Night	24
Billy Liar	22
Biloxi Blues	21
Bob & Carol & Ted & Alice	17
Boys on the Side	15
☑ Breakfast at Tiffany's	26
Breakfast on Pluto	19
Broadcast News	23
Broken Flowers	16
Brothers McMullen	19
Bull Durham	22
Bus Stop	21
Butterflies Are Free	21
Calendar Girls	23
Charade	26
City Lights	28
Coffee and Cigarettes	18

Confessions/Dangerous Mind	19
Cooler, The	22
Cool Hand Luke	26
Cousin, Cousine	21
Crimes and Misdemeanors	26
Dazed and Confused	22
Devil Wears Prada	22
Diary of a Mad Housewife	20
Diner	25
Dinner at Eight	27
Divine Secrets/Ya-Ya	16
Do the Right Thing	23
Down by Law	24
Family Stone	16
☑ Fargo	25
Fight Club	23
Fisher King	21
Five Easy Pieces	24
☑ Forrest Gump	24
Four Seasons	21
Fried Green Tomatoes	23
Friends with Money	16
Front Page	24
Garden State	22
Georgy Girl	23
Ghost World	23
Going My Way	24
Good Girl	18
Good Morning, Vietnam	22
☑ Good Will Hunting	24
Gosford Park	23
Guess Who's Coming...	25
Hannah and Her Sisters	24
Heartburn	19
Heaven Can Wait (1978)	21
High Fidelity	21
Husbands and Wives	22
Igby Goes Down	20
In Her Shoes	18
Irma La Douce	21
☑ It's a Wonderful Life	27
Jerry Maguire	21
Juliet of the Spirits	25
Junebug	21
King of Comedy	23
King of Hearts	26
Kinky Boots	23
Lady Vanishes	25
League of Their Own	20
Letter to Three Wives	24
Life Aquatic/Steve Zissou	16
Life Is Beautiful	27
Limelight	24
Little Miss Sunshine	24
Longest Yard (1974)	17

GENRE/FEATURES

GENRE/FEATURES

FILM NOIR

Pickup on South Street	23
Point Blank	20
Postman Always Rings... (1946)	25
Postman Always Rings... (1981)	20
Rififi	26
Scarlet Street	25
Seven	23
Sin City	22
Sorry, Wrong Number	25
Strangers on a Train	26
⊠ Sunset Boulevard	28
⊠ Sweet Smell of Success	27
⊠ Third Man	28
Touch of Evil	26
White Heat	25
Who Framed Roger Rabbit	24

FOOD-THEMED

Babette's Feast	26
Big Night	24
Chocolat	22
Diner	25
Dinner at Eight	27
Dinner Rush	23
Discreet Charm	24
Eat Drink Man Woman	25
Fried Green Tomatoes	23
Like Water for Chocolate	25
My Big Fat Greek Wedding	23
Mystic Pizza	17
9½ Weeks	15
Spanglish	19
Super Size Me	24
Tom Jones	25
Waitress	24
Wedding Banquet	22

FOREIGN FILMS

AUSTRALIAN

Adventures of Priscilla	23
Babe	25
⊠ Breaker Morant	27
Crocodile Dundee	17
Gallipoli	25
Mad Max	20
Mad Max/Thunderdome	17
My Brilliant Career	25
Piano, The	21
Picnic at Hanging Rock	24
Rabbit-Proof Fence	26
Road Warrior	22
Shine	22
Strictly Ballroom	23
Year of Living Dangerously	24

BRAZILIAN

City of God	26
Motorcycle Diaries	23

BRITISH

About a Boy	21
Alfie	22
Anne of the Thousand Days	26
Barry Lyndon	20
Becket	26
Bedazzled	20
Bend It Like Beckham	26
Billy Elliot	25
Billy Liar	22
Blowup	26
Born Free	24
Brazil	24
⊠ Bridge on the River Kwai	28
Bridget Jones's Diary	21
⊠ Brief Encounter	27
Calendar Girls	23
Chariots of Fire	26
⊠ Christmas Carol	27
Clockwork Orange	25
Constant Gardener	23
Crying Game	22
Darling	22
Day of the Jackal	25
Death on the Nile	19
Diamonds Are Forever	20
Die Another Day	19
Dirty Pretty Things	23
Don't Look Now	24
Dreamers, The	17
Dr. No	23
Educating Rita	18
Elizabeth	24
Enchanted April	24
English Patient	22
Fahrenheit 451	21
For Your Eyes Only	18
Four Weddings and a Funeral	21
French Lieutenant's Woman	22
From Russia With Love	23
Full Monty	22
⊠ Gandhi	27
Georgy Girl	23
Girl with a Pearl Earring	21
GoldenEye	19
Goodbye, Mr. Chips	25
⊠ Great Expectations	27
Greystoke	15
Hamlet (1948)	27
Hamlet (1996)	24
Hard Day's Night	24
Help!	19

GENRE/FEATURES

FRENCH

Amélie	26
Au Revoir Les Enfants	27
Barbarella	13
Beauty/Beast (1947)	28
Belle de Jour	24
Black Orpheus	26
Breathless	25
Bride Wore Black	25
☑ Children of Paradise	28
Claire's Knee	23
Contempt	25
Cousin, Cousine	21
Day for Night	27
Diabolique	26
Discreet Charm	24
Diva	24
Emmanuelle	16
400 Blows	27
Grand Illusion	28
Hiroshima, Mon Amour	25
Indochine	23
Jean de Florette	27
Jules and Jim	24
King of Hearts	26
La Cage aux Folles	24
La Femme Nikita	23
Last Metro	24
Man and a Woman	24
☑ March of the Penguins	26
Mon Oncle	26
Mr. Hulot's Holiday	25
My Night at Maud's	26
Name of the Rose	22
Napoléon	29
Oliver Twist (2005)	20
Paris, Texas	22
☑ Pianist, The	28
Professional, The	25
Quest for Fire	17
Rififi	26
Rules of the Game	27
☑ Shoah	28
Shoot the Piano Player	25
☑ Sorrow and the Pity	29
Story of Adele H.	24
Swimming Pool	20
Tess	21
Triplets of Belleville	24
Umbrellas of Cherbourg	24
Very Long Engagement	22
Wages of Fear	27
Winged Migration	26
Z	26

GERMAN

Aguirre: The Wrath of God	25
Blue Angel	25
Cabinet of Dr. Caligari	26
Das Boot	28
☑ Fitzcarraldo	27
☑ Lives of Others	28
M	26
Marriage of Maria Braun	25
Metropolis	27
Nosferatu	26
Nosferatu the Vampyre	22
Run Lola Run	23
Tin Drum	23
Triumph of the Will	27
Wings of Desire	24

GREEK

Never on Sunday	24
Zorba the Greek	25

INDIAN

Monsoon Wedding	24

IRISH

Breakfast on Pluto	19
In America	26
In the Name of the Father	23
Magdalene Sisters	25
My Left Foot	25

ITALIAN

Amarcord	26
Battle of Algiers	28
Bicycle Thief	27
Cinema Paradiso	26
Conformist, The	26
Damned, The	23
Death in Venice	24
Divorce Italian Style	24
8½	26
Fistful of Dollars	19
For a Few Dollars More	23
Garden of the Finzi-Continis	25
Good, the Bad and the Ugly	24
Il Postino	24
Juliet of the Spirits	25
La Dolce Vita	25
La Strada	27
Last Tango in Paris	17
L'Avventura	24
Leopard, The	25
Life Is Beautiful	27
Mediterraneo	21
Nights of Cabiria	27
1900	22
Once Upon a Time/West	25

GENRE/FEATURES

GENRE/FEATURES

Dangerous Lives/Altar Boys	19	Possession	17
Deconstructing Harry	16	Prime	17
Dinner Rush	23	Real Women Have Curves	21
Donnie Darko	22	Requiem for a Dream	25
Door in the Floor	19	Reservoir Dogs	24
Down by Law	24	Roger Dodger	18
Dying Gaul	17	Room with a View	26
Eating Raoul	18	Salvador	21
Eraserhead	21	Saw	18
Evil Dead	22	Saw II	19
Faces	22	Secretary	21
Far From Heaven	24	Sex, Lies and Videotape	19
Frida	25	Shattered Glass	21
Friends with Money	16	She's Gotta Have It	21
Fritz the Cat	16	Short Cuts	22
Garden State	22	Sideways	23
Girl with a Pearl Earring	21	Squid and the Whale	21
Gods and Monsters	23	Station Agent	25
Gods Must Be Crazy	22	Sunshine State	18
☑ Good Night, and Good Luck	25	Swingers	23
Happiness	23	Tadpole	19
Harder They Come	25	Texas Chainsaw Massacre	17
Henry V	26	This Is Spinal Tap	26
Home at the End of World	18	Torch Song Trilogy	23
Hustle & Flow	23	Touch of Class	22
Illusionist, The	23	TransAmerica	24
In the Company of Men	20	Trip to Bountiful	24
Junebug	21	21 Grams	22
Kissing Jessica Stein	21	Upside of Anger	22
Laurel Canyon	18	Velvet Goldmine	17
Little Miss Sunshine	24	Waitress	24
Longtime Companion	23	Welcome to the Dollhouse	22
Lost Highway	16	Whale Rider	25
Lost in Translation	21	Woman Under the Influence	24
Love Song for Bobby Long	19	Wonderland	16
Love! Valour! Compassion!	21	Woodsman, The	21
Lucky Number Slevin	21	You Can Count on Me	23
Man from Elysian Fields	21		
Metropolitan	20	JAMES BOND	
Monster	24	Casino Royale	23
Monster's Ball	22	Diamonds Are Forever	20
Monty Python/Holy Grail	26	Die Another Day	19
My Beautiful Laundrette	23	Dr. No	23
My Big Fat Greek Wedding	23	For Your Eyes Only	18
My Dinner with Andre	21	From Russia With Love	23
Night of the Living Dead	22	GoldenEye	19
One Hour Photo	18	☑ Goldfinger	26
Opposite of Sex	19	License to Kill	14
Painted Veil	23	Live and Let Die	19
Passion of the Christ	22	Living Daylights	14
Pieces of April	21	Man with the Golden Gun	18
Pink Flamingos	18	Moonraker	16
Pollock	22	Never Say Never Again	18
Polyester	19	Octopussy	17
Portrait of a Lady	16	On Her Majesty's/Service	19

subscribe to zagat.com

GENRE/FEATURES

Sense and Sensibility	26
Serpico	23
Seven Days in May	26
Sheltering Sky	16
Shining, The	25
Shipping News	18
Shopgirl	18
Short Cuts	22
☑ Silence of the Lambs	27
Sisterhood/Traveling Pants	19
Slaughterhouse-Five	22
Sophie's Choice	26
Sounder	26
Spy Who Came in from Cold	25
Spy Who Loved Me	21
Stepford Wives	12
Sum of All Fears	16
Swiss Family Robinson	23
Talented Mr. Ripley	18
Tarzan	22
Tarzan and His Mate	21
Tarzan the Ape Man	21
Terms of Endearment	25
Tess	21
They Shoot Horses...	21
Thin Man	26
Thin Red Line	19
Three Musketeers	22
Thunderball	22
Time Machine	22
Time to Kill	18
Tin Drum	23
To Have and Have Not	26
☑ To Kill a Mockingbird	29
Tom Jones	25
Topper	20
☑ Treasure of the Sierra Madre	27
20,000 Leagues Under Sea	22
☑ 2001: A Space Odyssey	26
2010	16
Unbearable Lightness of Being	21
Vanity Fair	17
War of the Roses	17
War of the Worlds (1953)	23
War of the Worlds (2005)	15
☑ Willy Wonka	26
☑ Wizard of Oz	28
Women in Love	23
World According to Garp	21
☑ Wuthering Heights	27
You Only Live Twice	22

MARTIAL ARTS

Crouching Tiger	24
Enter the Dragon	23
Hero	25
House of Flying Daggers	24
Karate Kid	19
Kill Bill Vol. 1	23
Kill Bill Vol. 2	25
Kung Fu Hustle	23
Last Samurai	23
Magnificent Seven	26
☑ Matrix, The	25
Matrix Reloaded	21
Matrix Revolutions	15
Ran	27
Rush Hour	19
Rush Hour 2	17
☑ Seven Samurai	29
Yojimbo	28

MOVIES ABOUT MOVIES

☑ Adaptation	22
Anniversary Party	18
Aviator, The	23
Bad and the Beautiful	24
Bad Education	23
Barefoot Contessa	24
Barton Fink	20
Boogie Nights	19
Cinema Paradiso	26
Contempt	25
Day for Night	27
Day of the Locust	20
Dreamers, The	17
Dying Gaul	17
Ed Wood	20
8½	26
Frances	23
Kid Stays in the Picture	21
Mommie Dearest	17
Mulholland Dr.	20
Notting Hill	19
Player, The	23
Postcards from the Edge	18
Purple Rose of Cairo	21
Shadow of the Vampire	20
☑ Singin' in the Rain	28
Stardust Memories	19
Star Is Born	25
Stunt Man	22
Sullivan's Travels	27
☑ Sunset Boulevard	28

MUSICALS

All That Jazz	24
American in Paris	26
Annie	19
Band Wagon	26

GENRE/FEATURES

Bells Are Ringing	24
Beyond the Sea	19
Blues Brothers	22
Brigadoon	24
Buck Privates	22
Buddy Holly Story	21
Bye Bye Birdie	19
Cabaret	26
Cabin in the Sky	24
Camelot	21
Carmen Jones	23
Carousel	24
Z Chicago	27
Damn Yankees	24
Dancer in the Dark	22
De-Lovely	20
Dreamgirls	23
Easter Parade	22
Evita	19
Fame	21
Fiddler on the Roof	26
Finian's Rainbow	21
5,000 Fingers of Dr. T.	20
Footlight Parade	23
42nd Street	24
Funny Face	24
Funny Girl	26
Funny Lady	15
Funny Thing Happened...	22
Gay Divorcee	25
Gentlemen Prefer Blondes	23
Gigi	24
Gold Diggers of 1933	25
Z Grease	23
Guys and Dolls	24
Gypsy	20
Hair	20
Hard Day's Night	24
Hedwig and the Angry Inch	21
Hello, Dolly!	20
Help!	19
High Society	23
Holiday Inn	23
Jailhouse Rock	18
Jesus Christ Superstar	21
King and I	27
Kiss Me Kate	24
La Bamba	20
Little Shop of Horrors	19
Mambo Kings	20
Z Mary Poppins	27
Meet Me in St. Louis	26
Moulin Rouge!	23
Music Man	25
Z My Fair Lady	27

New York, New York	19
Oklahoma!	24
Oliver!	24
On a Clear Day You Can See...	20
On the Town	23
Paint Your Wagon	18
Pennies from Heaven	17
Phantom of the Opera	21
Pink Floyd The Wall	23
Producers, The	18
Purple Rain	14
Rent	19
Rocky Horror Picture Show	21
Seven Brides/Seven Brothers	24
1776	22
Shall We Dance	25
Show Boat	23
Z Singin' in the Rain	28
Z Sound of Music	28
South Pacific	24
Sweet Charity	20
Swing Time	26
That's Entertainment!	25
Thoroughly Modern Millie	18
Tommy	16
Z Top Hat	27
Umbrellas of Cherbourg	24
Unsinkable Molly Brown	21
Velvet Goldmine	17
Victor/Victoria	23
Z West Side Story	27
White Christmas	25
Wiz, The	16
Z Wizard of Oz	28
Yankee Doodle Dandy	25
Yentl	18
Ziegfeld Follies	24

OCCUPATIONS

DOCTORS

Awakenings	22
Charly	21
Dark Victory	25
Dead Ringers	18
Dr. Dolittle	16
Elephant Man	24
Girl, Interrupted	18
Greed	28
Last King of Scotland	25
Marathon Man	24
MASH	26
Nurse Betty	15
Z One Flew Over Cuckoo's...	27
Outbreak	16

GENRE/FEATURES

PROSTITUTES

SPIES
(See also James Bond)

TEACHERS

GENRE/FEATURES

BEST ACTOR

subscribe to zagat.com

GENRE/FEATURES

Olivia de Havilland
Heiress, The 27

Gwyneth Paltrow
🎬 Shakespeare in Love 24

Patricia Neal
Hud 26

Julia Roberts
Erin Brockovich 21

Susan Sarandon
Dead Man Walking 23

Simone Signoret
Room at the Top 24

Sissy Spacek
Coal Miner's Daughter 24

Meryl Streep
Sophie's Choice 26

Barbra Streisand
Funny Girl 26

Susan Hayward
I Want to Live! 24

Hilary Swank
Boys Don't Cry 23
🎬 Million Dollar Baby 27

Jessica Tandy
Driving Miss Daisy 24

Charlize Theron
Monster 24

Emma Thompson
Howards End 22

Reese Witherspoon
🎬 Walk the Line 25

Joanne Woodward
Three Faces of Eve 24

BEST DIRECTOR

🎬 All About Eve 28
🎬 All Quiet on Western Front 28
🎬 Amadeus 26
🎬 American Beauty 24
🎬 Annie Hall 27
Apartment, The 25
Awful Truth 25
🎬 Beautiful Mind 26
Ben-Hur 26
🎬 Best Years of Our Lives 28
Born on the 4th of July 20
🎬 Braveheart 26
🎬 Bridge on the River Kwai 28
Brokeback Mountain 24
Cabaret 26
🎬 Casablanca 29
Dances with Wolves 23
Deer Hunter 26
🎬 Departed, The 26
English Patient 22
🎬 Forrest Gump 24

French Connection 25
From Here to Eternity 26
🎬 Gandhi 27
Gentleman's Agreement 26
Giant 24
Gigi 24
🎬 Godfather Part II 29
Going My Way 24
🎬 Gone with the Wind 28
🎬 Graduate, The 27
🎬 Grapes of Wrath 28
🎬 How Green Was My Valley 27
🎬 It Happened One Night 28
Kramer vs. Kramer 23
Last Emperor 26
🎬 Lawrence of Arabia 29
Letter to Three Wives 24
🎬 Lord of Rings/Return 28
Lost Weekend 25
🎬 Man for All Seasons 28
Marty 25
Midnight Cowboy 26
🎬 Million Dollar Baby 27
Mr. Deeds Goes to Town 25
Mrs. Miniver 25
🎬 My Fair Lady 27
Oliver! 24
🎬 One Flew Over Cuckoo's... 27
🎬 On the Waterfront 28
Ordinary People 25
🎬 Out of Africa 25
🎬 Patton 27
🎬 Pianist, The 28
🎬 Place in the Sun 27
Platoon 25
🎬 Quiet Man 27
Rain Man 25
Reds 21
Rocky 25
🎬 Saving Private Ryan 26
🎬 Schindler's List 29
🎬 Silence of the Lambs 27
🎬 Sound of Music 28
🎬 Sting, The 27
Terms of Endearment 25
Titanic 19
Tom Jones 25
Traffic 23
🎬 Treasure of the Sierra Madre 27
Unforgiven 26
🎬 West Side Story 27

BEST FOREIGN LANGUAGE FILM

All About My Mother 25
Amarcord 26

GENRE/FEATURES

Piano, The	21
Pillow Talk	20
⊠ Place in the Sun	27
Places in the Heart	20
⊠ Producers, The	26
⊠ Pulp Fiction	26
Rain Man	25
⊠ Roman Holiday	27
Room at the Top	24
Room with a View	26
⊠ Schindler's List	29
Sense and Sensibility	26
⊠ Shakespeare in Love	24
⊠ Silence of the Lambs	27
Sling Blade	25
Splendor in the Grass	25
⊠ Sting, The	27
⊠ Sunset Boulevard	28
Talk to Her	26
Tender Mercies	24
Terms of Endearment	25
Thelma & Louise	23
⊠ To Kill a Mockingbird	29
Tom Jones	25
Traffic	23
⊠ Treasure of the Sierra Madre	27
⊠ Usual Suspects	27
Witness	23
⊠ Woman of the Year	27

RELIGION

Agnes of God	21
Agony and the Ecstasy	23
Bells of St. Mary's	24
Ben-Hur	26
Bruce Almighty	18
Dangerous Lives/Altar Boys	19
Da Vinci Code	19
Elmer Gantry	25
Exorcist, The	25
Going My Way	24
Hunchback/Notre Dame (1939)	26
Intolerance	27
Jesus Christ Superstar	21
Last Temptation of Christ	22
Life of Brian	23
Magdalene Sisters	25
Name of the Rose	22
Oh, God!	17
Passion of the Christ	22
Prince of Egypt	19
Robe, The	22
Song of Bernadette	22
Ten Commandments	24
Yentl	18

ROAD MOVIES

Adventures of Priscilla	23
Boys on the Side	15
Broken Flowers	16
Cannonball Run	17
Easy Rider	23
Gauntlet, The	17
Little Miss Sunshine	24
Lost in America	20
Midnight Run	23
Motorcycle Diaries	23
National Lampoon's Vacation	22
Paris, Texas	22
Smokey and the Bandit	16
Something Wild	20
Straight Story	24
Sugarland Express	18
Thelma & Louise	23
TransAmerica	24
Y Tu Mamá También	24

ROCK 'N' ROLL

Almost Famous	23
Blackboard Jungle	23
Blues Brothers	22
Buddy Holly Story	21
Bye Bye Birdie	19
Don't Look Back	25
Fame	21
Footloose	17
Gimme Shelter	25
⊠ Grease	23
Hair	20
Hard Day's Night	24
Hedwig and the Angry Inch	21
Help!	19
High Fidelity	21
Jailhouse Rock	18
Jesus Christ Superstar	21
La Bamba	20
Last Waltz	26
Little Shop of Horrors	19
Pink Floyd The Wall	23
Purple Rain	14
Rocky Horror Picture Show	21
Rose, The	19
Saturday Night Fever	22
School of Rock	20
Sid & Nancy	18
Stop Making Sense	25
This Is Spinal Tap	26
Tommy	16
Truth or Dare	15
Velvet Goldmine	17
Wayne's World	17

subscribe to zagat.com

Jane Eyre	25	☑ Rebecca	27
Jerry Maguire	21	Reds	21
Jezebel	25	Red Shoes	26
Jules and Jim	24	Remains of the Day	24
Just Like Heaven	19	Rent	19
Kiss Me Kate	24	Robin and Marian	20
Lady and the Tramp	26	Romancing the Stone	20
☑ Lady Eve	28	Romeo and Juliet	26
L.A. Story	20	Romeo + Juliet	19
Last Tango in Paris	17	Room with a View	26
Laura	27	Roxanne	21
Like Water for Chocolate	25	Ryan's Daughter	22
Lili	24	Sabrina	25
Little Children	24	Same Time, Next Year	22
Lost Horizon	25	Saturday Night Fever	22
Love in the Afternoon	24	Save the Last Dance	17
Magnificent Obsession	22	Say Anything	23
Man and a Woman	24	Shall We Dance	25
Manhattan	26	Shall We Dance?	17
Marty	25	Shine	22
Match Point	22	Shop Around the Corner	24
Memoirs of a Geisha	21	Shopgirl	18
Misfits, The	21	Sid & Nancy	18
Monster's Ball	22	Sliding Doors	21
☑ Moonstruck	24	Smiles of a Summer Night	26
Moulin Rouge	21	South Pacific	24
Moulin Rouge!	23	Spanglish	19
Mrs. Brown	22	Spellbound (1945)	24
Must Love Dogs	16	Splash	19
My Big Fat Greek Wedding	23	Starman	19
My Brilliant Career	25	Starting Over	20
☑ My Fair Lady	27	St. Elmo's Fire	17
My Girl	20	Story of Adele H.	24
9½ Weeks	15	Strictly Ballroom	23
Ninotchka	25	Summer of '42	21
Nothing Sacred	23	Summertime	23
☑ Notorious	27	Swing Time	26
Out of Sight	21	Talk to Her	26
Painted Veil	23	10	17
Pearl Harbor	14	Tess	21
Personal Best	15	Thomas Crown Affair	23
☑ Philadelphia Story	27	Three Coins in the Fountain	21
Piano, The	21	Titanic	19
Picnic	24	To Catch a Thief	25
Pillow Talk	20	To Have and Have Not	26
☑ Place in the Sun	27	Tootsie	25
Play It Again, Sam	22	☑ Top Hat	27
Possession	17	Topper	20
Prelude to a Kiss	16	Two for the Road	24
Pretty in Pink	19	Umbrellas of Cherbourg	24
Pride & Prejudice (2005)	23	Unbearable Lightness of Being	21
Prince of Tides	19	Upside of Anger	22
Punch-Drunk Love	17	Urban Cowboy	18
☑ Quiet Man	27	Vanity Fair	17
Reality Bites	19	☑ Vertigo	27

GENRE/FEATURES

SCREWBALL COMEDIES

Animal Crackers	26
Awful Truth	25
Ball of Fire	26
Born Yesterday	26
Bringing Up Baby	27
Cocoanuts, The	24
Day at the Races	24
☒ Duck Soup	27
His Girl Friday	26
Horse Feathers	24
In-Laws, The	24
Intolerable Cruelty	15
☒ It Happened One Night	28
☒ Lady Eve	28
Miracle of Morgan's Creek	23
My Man Godfrey	25
Night at the Opera	26
Nothing Sacred	23
Palm Beach Story	25
☒ Philadelphia Story	27
Raising Arizona	23
Thin Man	26
What's Up, Doc?	21
Women on the Verge	24

SILENT

Birth of a Nation	25
Cabinet of Dr. Caligari	26
City Lights	28
General, The	28
Gold Rush	28
Greed	28
Intolerance	27
Metropolis	27
Modern Times	28
Napoléon	29
Nosferatu	26
Potemkin	27
Thief of Bagdad	24

SOUNDTRACKS

(See also Musicals; * Best Score Oscar winner)

Adventures of Robin Hood*	25
Aladdin*	24
Alexander Nevsky	26
Alfie	22
All That Jazz*	24
Almost Famous	23
☒ Amadeus	26
Amarcord	26
☒ American Beauty	24
American Gigolo	19
American Graffiti	24

American in Paris*	26
Anatomy of a Murder	26
Around the World in 80 Days*	22
Barry Lyndon*	20
Basquiat	17
Beauty/Beast (1991)*	26
Bells Are Ringing	24
Ben-Hur*	26
Beyond the Sea	19
Big Chill	23
Blackboard Jungle	23
Black Orpheus	26
Blue Velvet	22
Bodyguard, The	14
Born Free*	24
☒ Braveheart	26
☒ Breakfast at Tiffany's*	26
☒ Bridge on the River Kwai*	28
☒ Brief Encounter	27
Brokeback Mountain*	24
Buddy Holly Story*	21
Buena Vista Social Club	25
Butch Cassidy*	26
Cabaret*	26
Camelot*	21
Cat Ballou	21
Cat People (1982)	16
Charade	26
Chariots of Fire*	26
☒ Chinatown	27
Cinema Paradiso	26
Clockwork Orange	25
Cold Mountain	22
Crouching Tiger*	24
Damn Yankees	24
Dances with Wolves*	23
Days of Heaven	23
☒ Days of Wine and Roses*	27
Dazed and Confused	22
Death in Venice	24
De-Lovely	20
Desperately Seeking Susan	15
Diner	25
Dinosaur	19
Dirty Dancing	21
Diva	24
☒ Doctor Zhivago*	27
Donnie Darko	22
Don't Look Back	25
Down by Law	24
Dracula (1931)	24
Dreamgirls	23
Dumbo*	24
Easter Parade*	22
Easy Rider	23

8½	26
8 Mile	19
El Cid	19
Elvira Madigan	20
Emma*	22
Empire of the Sun	25
English Patient*	22
⧖ E.T.*	26
Exodus*	23
Fame*	21
⧖ Fantasia	28
Fantasia 2000	24
Far From Heaven	24
Fear and Loathing/Las Vegas	15
Fiddler on the Roof*	26
Fight Club	23
First Blood: Rambo	18
Flashdance	16
Footloose	17
Forbidden Planet	25
⧖ Forrest Gump	24
Frida*	25
Full Monty*	22
Funny Thing Happened...*	22
Garden State	22
Gigi*	24
Gimme Shelter	25
⧖ Gladiator	23
⧖ Godfather, The	29
⧖ Godfather Part II*	29
Gold Diggers of 1933	25
⧖ Goldfinger	26
⧖ Gone with the Wind	28
Good, the Bad and the Ugly	24
⧖ Graduate, The	27
⧖ Great Escape	27
Great Gatsby	22
Hard Day's Night	24
Harder They Come	25
Harold and Maude	25
⧖ Harry Potter/Sorcerer's	24
Hatari!	21
Heavy Metal	20
Hedwig and the Angry Inch	21
Hello, Dolly!*	20
High Fidelity	21
⧖ High Noon*	28
Hunger, The	20
Hustle & Flow	23
I Am Sam	21
Il Postino*	24
In Cold Blood	25
Irma La Douce*	21
I Want to Live!	24
Jailhouse Rock	18

⧖ Jaws*	26
Journey to Center of Earth	19
Jungle Book (1967)	23
King and I*	27
La Bamba	20
Lady Sings the Blues	22
Last Emperor*	26
Last of the Mohicans	22
La Strada	27
Last Tango in Paris	17
Last Waltz	26
⧖ Lawrence of Arabia*	29
Life Is Beautiful*	27
Lili*	24
Limelight*	24
⧖ Lion in Winter*	28
Lion King*	25
Little Mermaid*	24
Local Hero	26
Lock, Stock and Two...	23
⧖ Lord of Rings/Fellowship*	27
⧖ Lord of Rings/Return*	28
⧖ Lord of Rings/Two Towers	27
Lost Highway	16
Love Is Many-Splendored...*	22
Love Story*	19
Magnificent Seven	26
Magnolia	20
Mambo Kings	20
Man and a Woman	24
Man Who Knew Too Much	24
Man with the Golden Arm	24
Mark of Zorro	22
⧖ Mary Poppins*	27
Mean Streets	24
Mediterraneo	21
Midnight Cowboy	26
Midnight Express*	24
Mighty Wind	23
Mission, The	24
Music Man*	25
⧖ My Fair Lady*	27
Nashville	23
Natural, The	23
Nightmare Before Christmas	24
⧖ Night of the Hunter	27
1900	22
⧖ North by Northwest	28
⧖ Now, Voyager*	27
O Brother, Where Art Thou?	22
Oklahoma!*	24
Oliver!*	24
Omen, The*	21
Once Upon a Time/West	25
On the Town*	23

Out of Africa*	25	Stop Making Sense	25
Phantom of the Opera	21	Strictly Ballroom	23
Piano, The	21	Summer of '42*	21
Pink Floyd The Wall	23	Sunset Boulevard*	28
Pink Panther	24	Superman	22
Place in the Sun*	27	Sweet Smell of Success	27
Pleasantville	20	Talk to Her	26
Pocahontas	17	Tarzan	22
Pretty in Pink	19	Taxi Driver	27
Princess Bride	27	Third Man	28
Psycho	28	This Is Spinal Tap	26
Pulp Fiction	26	Thoroughly Modern Millie*	18
Purple Rain*	14	Thunderball	22
Raiders of the Lost Ark	28	Tie Me Up! Tie Me Down!	20
Ray	26	Titanic	19
Red Shoes*	26	To Kill a Mockingbird	29
Red Violin*	24	Tom Jones*	25
Repo Man	17	Tommy	16
Repulsion	25	Top Gun	22
Rescuers, The	23	To Sir, With Love	22
Right Stuff*	26	Touch of Evil	26
Rocky	25	Trainspotting	22
Romeo and Juliet	26	Truth or Dare	15
Romy & Michele's/Reunion	14	Two for the Road	24
Room with a View	26	2001: A Space Odyssey	26
Rose, The	19	Urban Cowboy	18
Run Lola Run	23	Vertigo	27
Rushmore	23	Victor/Victoria*	23
Saturday Night Fever	22	Wait Until Dark	25
Say Anything	23	Walk the Line	25
Schindler's List*	29	Way We Were*	24
School of Rock	20	Wedding Singer	17
Seven Brides/Seven Brothers*	24	West Side Story*	27
7th Voyage of Sinbad	20	What's Love Got to Do with It	22
Shaft	17	When Harry Met Sally...	26
Shakespeare in Love*	24	Wild Bunch	27
Shall We Dance	25	Willy Wonka	26
Shine	22	Wind and the Lion	24
Shrek	26	Wizard of Oz*	28
Sisters	22	Woodstock	24
Sleepless in Seattle	21	Yankee Doodle Dandy*	25
Snow White	27	Yellow Submarine	22
Song of Bernadette	22	Young Frankenstein	27
Sound of Music*	28	Zorba the Greek	25
South Park	20	Zulu	24
Spartacus	26		
Spellbound (1945)*	24	SPORTS	
Stagecoach*	27		
Stand by Me	24	BASEBALL	
Star Trek II	23	Bad News Bears	18
Star Wars*	28	Bang the Drum Slowly	23
Star Wars V/Empire Strikes	26	Bull Durham	22
Star Wars VI/Return of Jedi	24	Damn Yankees	24
St. Elmo's Fire	17	Eight Men Out	24
Sting, The*	27	Fever Pitch	20
		League of Their Own	20

Hair	20
Hamlet (1948)	27
Hamlet (1996)	24
Harvey	26
Heaven Can Wait (1943)	24
Hedwig and the Angry Inch	21
Heiress, The	27
Hello, Dolly!	20
Henry V	26
High Society	23
His Girl Friday	26
History Boys	22
Holiday	27
I Never Sang for My Father	27
Inherit the Wind	26
Irma La Douce	21
Jesus Christ Superstar	21
Jezebel	25
Key Largo	26
King and I	27
Kiss Me Kate	24
La Cage aux Folles	24
Letter, The	25
☑ Lion in Winter	28
Little Foxes	26
Little Shop of Horrors	19
Love! Valour! Compassion!	21
Madness of King George	22
☑ Man for All Seasons	28
Man Who Came to Dinner	26
Member of the Wedding	25
Miracle Worker	25
Mister Roberts	27
Music Man	25
☑ My Fair Lady	27
Night of the Iguana	23
Odd Couple	25
Oklahoma!	24
Oliver!	24
On a Clear Day You Can See...	20
One, Two, Three	23
On Golden Pond	24
On the Town	23
Owl and the Pussycat	17
Paint Your Wagon	18
Peter Pan (1953)	25
Peter Pan (2003)	20
Phantom of the Opera	21
☑ Philadelphia Story	27
Picnic	24
Play It Again, Sam	22
Prelude to a Kiss	16
Prisoner of Second Avenue	22
Producers, The	18
Proof	18

Raisin in the Sun	26
Real Women Have Curves	21
Rent	19
Rocky Horror Picture Show	21
Romeo and Juliet	26
Romy & Michele's/Reunion	14
Rope	22
Roxanne	21
Ruling Class	23
Same Time, Next Year	22
1776	22
Seven Year Itch	23
She Done Him Wrong	22
Shirley Valentine	24
Shop Around the Corner	24
Show Boat	23
Six Degrees of Separation	21
Sleuth	25
Soldier's Story	26
☑ Sound of Music	28
South Pacific	24
Stage Door	25
☑ Stalag 17	27
Steel Magnolias	24
☑ Streetcar Named Desire	27
Suddenly, Last Summer	24
Summertime	23
Sunshine Boys	21
Sweet Bird of Youth	24
Sweet Charity	20
Thousand Clowns	25
Torch Song Trilogy	23
Trip to Bountiful	24
Unsinkable Molly Brown	21
Wait Until Dark	25
☑ West Side Story	27
Who's Afraid of V. Woolf?	25
☑ Witness for the Prosecution	27
Wiz, The	16
Women, The	26

SWASHBUCKLERS

Adventures of Robin Hood	25
Captain Blood	23
Count of Monte Cristo	19
Mark of Zorro	22
Mask of Zorro	18
Master and Commander	23
Mutiny on the Bounty (1935)	25
Mutiny on the Bounty (1962)	22
Pirates Caribbean/World's End	21
Pirates Caribbean/Dead Man	20
Pirates Caribbean/The Curse	24
Robin and Marian	20
Robin Hood: Prince of Thieves	16

GENRE/FEATURES

GENRE/FEATURES

Cat Ballou	21	Misfits, The	21
City Slickers	20	Missing, The	18
Dances with Wolves	23	Missouri Breaks	16
Destry Rides Again	25	My Darling Clementine	25
Duel in the Sun	23	My Little Chickadee	23
Fistful of Dollars	19	Oklahoma!	24
For a Few Dollars More	23	Once Upon a Time/West	25
Fort Apache	23	Outlaw Josey Wales	25
Good, the Bad and the Ugly	24	Ox-Bow Incident	27
Gunfight at O.K. Corral	20	Paint Your Wagon	18
Heaven's Gate	14	Red River	26
⚡ High Noon	28	Rio Bravo	24
High Plains Drifter	18	⚡ Searchers, The	27
How the West Was Won	23	Shane	26
Hud	26	She Wore a Yellow Ribbon	24
Jeremiah Johnson	23	Silverado	24
Johnny Guitar	19	Spirit: Stallion of Cimarron	21
Legends of the Fall	20	Stagecoach	27
Little Big Man	24	Tombstone	21
Magnificent Seven	26	True Grit	22
Man Called Horse	22	Unforgiven	26
Man Who Shot Liberty Valance	25	Viva Zapata!	23
Maverick	18	⚡ Wild Bunch	27
McCabe & Mrs. Miller	23	Young Guns	15